FERGUSON

CAREER RESOURCE GUIDE TO

GRANTS, SCHOLARSHIPS, AND OTHER FINANCIAL RESOURCES

VOLUME 2

Ferguson

An imprint of Infobase Publishing

Ferguson Career Resource Guide to Grants, Scholarships, and Other Financial Resources

Ferguson
An imprint of Infobase Publishing
132 West 31st Street
New York, NY 10001

ISBN-10: 0-8160-6491-1
ISBN-13: 978-0-8160-6491-5

Library of Congress Cataloging-in-Publication Data

Ferguson career resource guide to grants, scholarships, and other financial resources.
   p. cm.
 Includes bibliographical references and index.
 ISBN 0-8160-6491-1 (alk. paper)
 1. Student aid—United States. 2. Scholarships—United States. 3. Grants-in-aid—United States. I. J.G. Ferguson Publishing Company.
  LB2337.4.F47 2007
  378.3—dc22   2006017904

Ferguson books are available at special discounts when purchased in bulk quantities for businesses, associations, institutions, or sales promotions. Please call our Special Sales Department in New York at (212) 967-8800 or (800) 322-8755.

You can find Ferguson on the World Wide Web at http://www.fergpubco.com

Text design by David Strelecky
Cover design by Salvatore Luongo

Printed in the United States of America

VB MSRF 10 9 8 7 6 5 4 3 2 1

This book is printed on acid-free paper.

CONTENTS

VOLUME 2

STUDENT PROFILE–BASED AID

MINORITIES

The following section details scholarships, fellowships, grants, and awards for minorities at the undergraduate and graduate levels.

Alpha Kappa Alpha Educational Advancement Foundation Inc.
Attn: Scholarship Application Enclosed
5656 Stony Island Avenue
Chicago, IL 60637
773-947-0026
akaeaf@aol.com
http://www.akaeaf.org
Scholarship Name: This African-American service sorority offers a variety of merit-based and need-based scholarships. *Academic Area: Open. *Age Group: Undergraduate students, graduate students. *Eligibility: Requirements vary, depending upon the scholarship. Applicants need not be members of Alpha Kappa Alpha to apply. The sorority supports students without regard to sex, race, creed, color, ethnicity, religion, sexual orientation, or disability. *Application Process: Undergraduate applicants should submit a completed application (available for download each November), a personal statement, three letters of recommendation, and official transcripts. Graduate students should also include a current resume and documentation of project and/or research plans. All applications should have the applicant's Social Security number on each page. Visit the sorority's Web site to download an application. *Amount: $750 to $1,500. *Deadline: January 15.

Ameen Rihani Organization
Ameen Rihani Scholarship Program
1010 Wayne Avenue, Suite 420
Silver Spring, MD 20910
http://www.ameenrihani.org
Scholarship Name: Ameen Rihani Scholarship. *Academic Area: Open. *Age Group: Undergraduate students. *Eligibility: Applicants must be U.S. citizens (or permanent residents) of Lebanese or other Arab descent who will be entering college or university in the fall of the year in which they apply for the scholarship. They also must be full-time, degree-seeking students who have demonstrated academic excellence in high school by attaining at least a 3.25 GPA. Applicants must be active participants in extracurricular activities as well as community activities and should be able to demonstrate leadership abilities. Preference is given to students with an interest in studying literature, philosophy, or political science. *Application Process: Applicants must be nominated by a teacher, counselor, or principal. They must submit an application along with official transcripts, college or university acceptance letter, a two-inch by three-inch color photo, additional recommendation forms, and a short personal essay (detailed on the application). Visit the organization's Web site to download an application, nomination form, and recommendation form. *Amount: $1,500, plus select Ameen Rihani works. *Deadline: May 31.

American Academy of Child and Adolescent Psychiatry (AACAP)
Attn: Earl Magee
3615 Wisconsin Avenue, NW
Washington, DC 20016-3007
202-966-7300, ext. 115
emagee@aacap.org
http://www.aacap.org/awards/index.htm
Fellowship Name: Jeanne Spurlock Minority Medical Student Clinical Fellowship in Child and Adolescent Psychiatry. *Academic Area: Medicine (psychiatry). *Age Group: Medical students. *Eligibility: Applicants must be medical students with an interest or specialty in child and adolescent psychiatry. They also must be African American, Asian American, Native American, Alaskan Native, Mexican American, Hispanic, or Pacific Islander students who are currently enrolled in accredited medical schools in the United States. Applicants must desire the opportunity for a 12-week summer fellowship experience with a mentor, as well as be able to attend the annual conference, where they will be required to present their clinical experience at a New Research Poster Session. *Application Process: Applicants should submit a completed application along with a two-page personal statement, a resume, a letter verifying good standing in medical school, and a letter of support from the mentor detailing the proposed mentorship. Six copies of the application packet must be submitted. Applicants should visit the academy's Web site to download an application. *Amount: $3,000 for 12 weeks of work/fellowship experience, plus an all-expense paid trip to the AACAP annual meeting.

*Deadline: March 15.

American Academy of Child and Adolescent Psychiatry (AACAP)

Attn: Earl Magee
3615 Wisconsin Avenue, NW
Washington, DC 20016-3007
202-966-7300, ext. 115
emagee@aacap.org
http://www.aacap.org/awards/index.htm

Fellowship Name: Jeanne Spurlock Research Fellowship in Drug Abuse and Addiction for Minority Medical Students. *Academic Area: Medicine (psychiatry). *Age Group: Medical students. *Eligibility: Applicants must be medical students with an interest or specialty in child and adolescent psychiatry. They also must be African American, Asian American, Native American, Alaskan Native, Mexican American, Hispanic, or Pacific Islander students who are currently enrolled in accredited medical schools in the United States Applicants must desire the opportunity for a 12-week summer research experience. *Application Process: Applicants should submit a completed application along with a two-page personal statement, a resume, a letter verifying good standing in medical school, and a letter of support from the mentor detailing the proposed mentorship. Six copies of the application packet should be submitted. Applicants should visit the academy's Web site to download an application. *Amount: $3,000, plus an all-expense paid trip to the AACAP annual meeting. *Deadline: March 15.

American Academy of Physician Assistants (AAPA)- African Heritage Caucus (AHC)

Attn: Cydney Powers, AAPA-AHC Scholarship Chair
950 North Washington Street
Alexandria, VA 22314
702-243-1797
cydneyb@gmail.com
http://www.aapa.org/caucus/scholar.html

Scholarship Name: AAPA_AHC Scholarship. *Academic Area: Medicine (physician assisting). *Age Group: Undergraduate students. *Eligibility: Applicants must be of African, Latino, Asian, American Indian, or Pacific Islander descent. Applicants must be members of the African Heritage Caucus, be attending an accredited physician-assisting program, be in good academic standing, and demonstrate financial need. *Application Process: Applicants must submit one completed application with two copies, a passport photo (preferably 4"

x 6"), transcripts and school budget, and a letter of verification of financial aid assistance. Visit the academy's Web site to download an application. *Amount: Varies. *Deadline: March 1.

American Architectural Foundation (AAF)

Attn: Mary Felber
1799 New York Avenue, NW
Washington, DC 20006
202-626-7511
mfelber@archfoundation.org
http://www.archfoundation.org/aaf/aaf/Programs. Scholarships.htm

Scholarship Name: American Institute of Architects (AIA)/AAF Minority/Disadvantaged Scholarship. *Academic Area: Architecture. *Age Group: Undergraduate students. *Eligibility: Applicants must be high school seniors or college freshmen accepted into or enrolled in a National Architectural Accrediting Board-accredited program who are nominated by someone who is familiar with the student's interest and ability to succeed in architecture. Such individuals would be high school guidance counselors, architects, or members of the AIA. Applicants must be nominated in order to receive an application packet. Applicants must belong to a minority group and should be able to demonstrate financial need. *Application Process: Once applicants are nominated (nomination forms are available for download from the foundation's Web site), an application packet will be mailed to the applicant. Applicants should submit a completed application along with supporting documents. *Amount: $500 to $2,500, renewable for two additional years. *Deadline: Nominations due December 7; Applications due mid-January.

American Association of Blacks in Energy (AABE)

927 15th Street, NW, Suite 200
Washington, DC 20005
202-371-9530
aabe@aabe.org
http://www.aabe.org

Scholarship Name: AABE Scholarships. *Academic Area: Engineering (open), mathematics, physical sciences. *Age Group: Undergraduate students. *Eligibility: Applicants must be African American, Hispanic American, or Native American high school seniors who have applied to one or more accredited colleges/universities, plan to major in engineering, mathematics, or the physical sciences, and have a minimum of a B average, both overall and in math and science courses. *Application Process: Applicants should submit a completed application form, high school transcripts, two letters of recommendation (one academic and one nonacademic), and a copy of their parent's or guardian's signed tax return for the previous year (or a verified FAFSA form). Applications should be submitted to the regional AABE office nearest the applicant. Do not submit applications to the national office. Visit the organization's Web site to download an application and to locate your regional office. *Amount: $1,500 to $3,000. *Deadline: March 4.

American Association of Critical-Care Nurses (AACN)
101 Columbia
Aliso Viejo, CA 92656-4109
800-899-2226
info@aacn.org
http://www.aacn.org
Scholarship Name: BSN Educational Advancement Scholarship. *Academic Area: Nursing (critical care). Age Group: Undergraduate students. *Eligibility: Applicant must be an AACN member in good standing, have an active RN license, maintain a cumulative GPA of at least 3.0, and also must be currently working in critical care or have worked in critical care for at least one year in the last three years. Also must currently be enrolled in an accredited nursing program and have junior or upper division status. Twenty percent of scholarship funds will be awarded to ethnic minorities. *Application Process: Applicants must submit a completed application by mail, followed by final grade reports. Letters of verification from your place of employment and school also must be sent. Visit the association's Web site to download an application. *Amount: $1,500. Deadline: April 1.

American Association of Critical-Care Nurses (AACN)
101 Columbia
Aliso Viejo, CA 92656-4109
800-899-2226
info@aacn.org
http://www.aacn.org
Scholarship Name: Graduate Educational Advancement Scholarship. *Academic Area: Nursing (critical care). Age Group: Graduate students. *Eligibility: Applicant must be an AACN member in good standing, have an active RN license, maintain a cumulative GPA of at least 3.0, and also must be currently working in critical care or have worked in critical care for at least one year in the last three years. Also must be a graduate of a baccalaureate

degree program and be currently enrolled in a graduate program leading to a master's or doctorate in nursing. Alternately, may also be enrolled in a faculty supervisor's clinical practicum leading to eligibility for the CCNS exam. Twenty percent of total scholarship funds are awarded to ethnic minorities. *Application Process: Applicants must submit a completed application by mail, followed by final grade reports. Letters of verification from your place of employment and schools also must be sent. *Amount: $1,500. Deadline: April 1.

American Association of Law Libraries
Attn: Chair, Scholarships Committee
53 West Jackson, Suite 940
Chicago, IL 60604
312-939-4764
membership@aall.org
http://www.aallnet.org/services/sch_strait.asp
Scholarship Name: George A. Strait Minority Scholarship Endowment. *Academic Area: Library sciences. *Age Group: Graduate students. *Eligibility: Minority college students who plan to pursue a career in law librarianship and are degree candidates in an ALA-accredited library school or an ABA-accredited law school (with at least one quarter/semester remaining after scholarship is awarded) are eligible to apply. Applicants must demonstrate financial need. *Application Process: Application packets should include an official transcript, verification of acceptance or attendance at a postsecondary program, three letters of recommendation, and a personal statement describing the applicant's reasons for applying for the scholarship and his or her interest in law librarianship. *Amount: Varies. *Deadline: April 1.

American Association of University Women (AAUW)
AAUW Educational Foundation
Career Development Grants
301 ACT Drive, Dept. 60
Iowa City, IA 52243-4030
319-337-1716, ext. 60
aauw@act.org
http://www.aauw.org/fga/fellowships_grants/career_development.cfm
Grant Name: AAUW Career Development Grant. *Academic Area: Open. *Age Group: Graduate students. *Eligibility: Applicants must be women who hold a bachelor's degree and are preparing to advance their careers, change careers, or reenter the work force. Special consideration is given to AAUW

members, women of color, and women pursuing their first advanced degree or credentials in nontraditional fields. Course work must be taken at an accredited two- or four-year college or university, or at a technical school that is fully licensed or accredited by an agency recognized by the U.S. Department of Education. Applicants pursuing doctoral-level work are not eligible. *Application Process: Applicants should submit a completed application along with a proposal narrative, budget, recommendation form, and filing fee. Visit the organization's Web site to download an application. *Amount: $2,000 to $8,000. *Deadline: December 15.

American Bar Association (ABA)
ABA Legal Opportunity Scholarship Fund-Application
321 North Clark Street
Chicago, IL 60610-4714
312-988-5415, 800-285-2221
mastronardi@staff.abanet.org
http://www.abanet.org/fje/allenbroussard.html
Scholarship Name: Allen E. Broussard Scholarship.
*Academic Area: Law. *Age Group: Law students.
*Eligibility: Minority college students who plan to attend California Bay-area law schools are eligible to apply. Applicants must have achieved a cumulative GPA of 2.5, be U.S. citizens (or permanent residents of the U.S.) who are entering their first year of law school, and demonstrate financial need. *Application Process: Applicants may complete the ABA Legal Opportunity Scholarship Fund (another scholarship offered by the ABA) application. Application packets should include an official transcript, verification of acceptance by a law program, two letters of recommendation (with at least one from a professor), and a personal statement (no longer than 1,000 words) describing the applicant's interest in studying law, potential financial need, and personal activities, such as community service. *Amount: $5,000 (renewable for two more years). *Deadline: March 1.

American Bar Association (ABA)
ABA Legal Opportunity Scholarship Fund-Application
321 North Clark Street
Chicago, IL 60610-4714
312-988-5415, 800-285-2221
mastronardi@staff.abanet.org
http://www.abanet.org/fje/losfpage.html
Scholarship Name: The Legal Opportunity Scholarship Fund provides financial assistance to encourage

minorities to pursue careers in law. *Academic Area: Law. *Age Group: Law students. *Eligibility: Minority college students who are citizens or permanent residents of the United States and who are entering students at an American Bar Association-accredited law school are eligible to apply. Applicants must also have a cumulative GPA of 2.5 on a 4.0 scale. *Application Process: Application packets should include an official transcript, verification of acceptance by a law program, two letters of recommendation (with at least one from a professor), and a personal statement (no longer than 1,000 words) describing the applicant's interest in studying law, potential financial need, and personal activities, such as community service. *Amount: $5,000 (renewable for two more years). *Deadline: March 1.

American Chemical Society (ACS)
Attn: Robert J. Hughes, Manager
ACS Scholars Program
1155 16th Street, NW
Washington, DC 20036
202-872-6250, 800-227-5558, ext. 6250
r_hughes@acs.org
http://www.chemistry.org/portal/a/c/s/1/acsdisplay.
    html?DOC=minorityaffairs\scholars.html
Scholarship Name: ACS Scholars Program. *Academic Area: Biochemistry, chemistry, engineering (chemical). *Age Group: Undergraduate students. *Eligibility: Applicants should be high school seniors or college freshmen, sophomores, or juniors; U.S. citizens or permanent residents of the United States; and of African American, Hispanic/Latino, or American Indian descent. They should also be full-time students, high academic achievers in chemistry or science (minimum GPA 3.0), and able to demonstrate financial need. *Application Process: Applicants should submit a completed application along with their FAFSA report, ACT or SAT scores, official transcripts, and two letters of recommendation. Visit the society's Web site to download an application. *Amount: Up to $3,000. *Deadline: March 1.

American Correctional Association (ACA)
Attn: Dr. Martin Luther King Jr. Scholarship Award
    Committee
4380 Forbes Boulevard
Lanham, MD 20706-4322
301-918-1800

debbis@aca.org

http://www.aca.org/pastpresentfuture/awards.asp

Scholarship Name: Dr. Martin Luther King Jr. Scholarship Award. *Academic Area: Criminal justice. *Age Group: Undergraduate students, graduate students. *Eligibility: Applicants should be members of a minority group who are pursuing a college education at a four-year institution in criminal justice. They must also demonstrate financial need, academic achievement, and a commitment to the ideals and philosophy of Dr. Martin Luther King Jr. Applicants do not have to be members of the ACA, but they do have to be nominated by a member. *Application Process: Applicants should submit a completed application along with a 250-word reflection on Dr. Martin Luther King's ideals and philosophy. Visit the association's Web site to download an application. *Amount: Contact the association for information. *Deadline: June 1.

American Dental Association Foundation

211 East Chicago Avenue

Chicago, IL 60611

312-440-2547

adaf@ada.org

http://www.ada.org/ada/prod/adaf/prog_scholarship_prog.asp

Scholarship Name: Minority Dental Student Scholarship. *Academic Area: Medicine (dentistry). *Age Group: Dental students. *Eligibility: African American, Hispanic American, and Native American students who are entering their second year of dental education may apply. Applicants must have a GPA of at least 3.0. *Application Process: Applicants should obtain an application from their dental schools and allied dental health programs. *Amount: Up to $2,500. *Deadline: July 31.

American Dental Hygienists' Association (ADHA)

ADHA Institute for Oral Health

Scholarship Award Program

444 North Michigan Avenue, Suite 3400

Chicago, IL 60611-3980

800-735-4916

institute@adha.net

http://www.adha.org/institute/Scholarship/application.htm

Scholarship Name: American Dental Hygienists' Association Institute Minority Scholarship. *Academic Area: Medicine (dental hygiene). *Age Group: Undergraduate students, graduate students.

*Eligibility: Applicants must be college sophomores, juniors, or seniors or graduate students; belong to any minority group that is currently underrepresented in dental hygiene programs (African Americans, Hispanics, Asians, Native Americans, males); and have completed at least one year in an accredited dental hygiene program in the United States, with a minimum GPA of 3.0 on a 4.0 scale. Applicants should also be active members of the Student ADHA or the ADHA. Graduate students should hold an active dental hygiene license. Documented financial need of at least $1,500 is required. *Application Process: Applicants should submit a completed application along with all required supporting materials. Visit the organization's Web site after January 1 of each year for updated submission requirements. A downloadable application is also available via the organization's Web site. *Amount: $1,000 to $2,000. *Deadline: June 30.

American Geological Institute (AGI)

Attn: Minority Geoscience Student Scholarship Coordinator

4220 King Street

Alexandria, VA 22302-1502

703-379-2480

http://www.agiweb.org/education/mpp.html

Scholarship Name: American Geological Institute Minority Geoscience Student Scholarships. *Academic Area: Geosciences. *Age Group: Undergraduate students, graduate students. *Eligibility: Applicants must be U.S. citizens and verifiable members of a minority group. They must also demonstrate financial need and be enrolled full time in an academic program leading to a degree in one of the geosciences. Applicable majors include the following: geology, geophysics, geochemistry, hydrology, meteorology, physical oceanography, planetary geology, or earth-science education. *Application Process: Applicants should submit a completed application along with a 250-word personal statement, official transcripts and ACT/SAT/GRE scores, and three letters of recommendation. Visit the association's Web site to download an application. *Amount: $500 to $3,000. *Deadline: March 1.

American Health and Beauty Aids Institute (AHBAI)

Fred Luster Sr. Education Foundation

PO Box 19510

Chicago, Illinois 60619-0510

708-333-8740

ahbai1@sbcglobal.net
http://www.ahbai.org
Scholarship Name: AHBAI Fred Luster Sr. Education Foundation-College-Bound Student Scholarships. *Academic Area: Business, chemistry, engineering (open). *Age Group: Undergraduate students. *Eligibility: Candidates must be college-bound high school seniors enrolled at a four-year college with a minimum 3.0 grade point average. Applicants must demonstrate scholastic achievement, financial need, and participation in extracurricular activities. *Application Process: Applicants must submit a completed application form, two letters of recommendation, official high school transcript, proof of income (W2), and a black-and-white photograph (for publicity purposes). Visit the organization's Web site to download an application. *Amount: $250 to $500. *Deadline: April 15.

American Health and Beauty Aids Institute (AHBAI)
Fred Luster Sr. Education Foundation
PO Box 19510
Chicago, Illinois 60619-0510
708-333-8740
ahbai1@sbcglobal.net
http://www.ahbai.org
Scholarship Name: AHBAI Fred Luster Sr. Education Foundation-Scholarship for Basic Cosmetology Students. *Academic Area: Cosmetology. *Age Group: Open. *Eligibility: Applicants must be currently enrolled in or have been accepted by a state-approved cosmetic art training facility prior to applying for scholarship. Applicants must also have completed an initial 300 hours before funds are approved or disbursed to the facility, and they must have maintained a minimum of 85 percent passing grade and 85 percent attendance. Applications will be rated based on scholastic record, attendance record, participation in extracurricular activities, and awards and honors received. *Application Process: Applicants must submit a completed application form, copy of high school diploma or GED equivalent, official transcript from cosmetology training facility, two letters of recommendation, and a black-and-white photograph (for publicity purposes). Visit the organization's Web site to download an application. *Amount: $250 to $500. *Deadline: November 8.

American Hotel and Lodging Foundation
Attn: Crystal Hammond
1201 New York Avenue, NW, Suite 600

Washington, DC 20005-3931
202-289-3188
ahlef@ahlef.org
http://www.ahlef.org/scholarships_hyatt_hotel.asp
Scholarship Name: Hyatt Hotels Fund for Minority Lodging Management Students. *Academic Area: Business, hospitality, management. *Age Group: Undergraduate students. *Eligibility: The applicant's university must be a member of the Council on Hotel, Restaurant, and Institutional Education. Applicants must be minority students pursuing a degree in hotel management. Applicants should inquire in their dean's office for additional eligibility requirements. *Application Process: Each university nominates one student most qualified according to the criteria to compete in the competition. Students should express their interest in the scholarship to their dean's office in order to be considered for nomination. *Amount: $2,000. *Deadline: April 1.

American Hotel and Lodging Foundation
Attn: Crystal Hammond
1201 New York Avenue, NW, Suite 600
Washington, DC 20005-3931
202-289-3188
ahlef@ahlef.org
http://www.ahlef.org/scholarships_rama.asp
Scholarship Name: Rama Scholarship for the American Dream. *Academic Area: Business, hospitality, management. *Age Group: Undergraduate students. *Eligibility: Applicants must be attending one of 14 participating schools: Bethune-Cookman College, California State Polytechnic University, Cornell University, Florida International University, Georgia State University, Greenville Technical College, Howard University, Johnson & Wales University, Michigan State University, New York University, University of Central Florida, University of Houston, University of South Carolina, and Virginia Polytechnic Institute and State University. Preference is given to students of Asian-Indian descent and other minority groups and to JHM Hotels employees. *Application Process: Students should express their interest in the scholarship to their dean's office in order to be considered for nomination. *Amount: Awards vary. *Deadline: Contact the foundation for deadline information.

American Indian College Fund
Citigroup Scholarship and Career Exploration Program
8333 Greenwood Boulevard
Denver, CO 80221

800-776-3863, 303-426-8900
kjewett@collegefund.org
http://www.collegefund.org
Scholarship Name: Citigroup Scholarship and Career Exploration Program. *Academic Area: Open. *Age Group: Undergraduate students. *Eligibility: Applicants must be attending one of four tribal colleges in South Dakota and must be attending school full time. They must have attained and will maintain a 3.0 cumulative grade point average (students who have not yet completed a year of college will be required to achieve a 3.0 in the first year of the scholarship program); commit to organizing and participating in the Citigroup Career Exploration Day; have demonstrated leadership, service and commitment to the American Indian community; and be of American Indian or Alaskan Native decent. Scholarships are need based and students majoring in business, information technology, and computer science are highly encouraged to apply. *Application Process: Applicants should submit a completed application form and packet including a signed authorization form for release of information, official college transcripts, completed FAFSA, a 500-word personal statement, two letters of recommendation, tribal enrollment information or proof of descendancy, and a small color photograph. Visit the association's Web site to download an application. *Amount: $2,500. *Deadline: May 1.

American Indian College Fund
Ford Motor Company/American Indian College Fund Corporate Scholars Program
8333 Greenwood Boulevard
Denver, CO 80221
800-776-3863, 303-426-8900
kjewett@collegefund.org
http://www.collegefund.org
Scholarship Name: Ford/American Indian College Fund Corporate Scholars Program. *Academic Area: Business, education, engineering (open), mathematics, science. *Age Group: Undergraduate students. *Eligibility: Applicants must have achieved sophomore status; declared a major in one of the aforementioned fields; have at least a 3.0 grade point average; demonstrate leadership and commitment to the American Indian community; be American Indian, Alaska Native, or Hawaii Native; have submitted a Federal Application for Federal Student Aid; and attend one of the 34 tribal colleges. *Application Process: Applicants should submit a completed application form, a one-page personal

essay, a leadership evaluation form, a financial need analysis, proof of tribal enrollment or descendancy, a recommendation letter from a faculty member, and a small color photograph. Visit the association's Web site to download an application. *Amount: $2,000. *Deadline: May 1.

American Indian College Fund
General Mills Tribal College Scholarship Program
8333 Greenwood Boulevard
Denver, CO 80221
800-776-3863, 303-426-8900
kjewett@collegefund.org
http://www.collegefund.org
Scholarship Name: General Mills Tribal College Scholarship Program. *Academic Area: Open. *Age Group: Undergraduate students. *Eligibility: Applicants must be enrolled in a tribal college or university in the states of California, Minnesota, or New Mexico. Applicants must be full-time students in either an associate or bachelor's degree program, have demonstrated exceptional academic achievement and financial need, and demonstrated leadership, service and commitment to the American Indian community. Applicants must be of American Indian or Alaskan Native decent. *Application Process: Applicants should submit a completed application form and packet including a completed FAFSA. Visit the association's Web site to download an application. *Amount: $2,000. *Deadline: May 1.

American Indian College Fund
Lockheed Martin/American Indian College Fund Scholars Program
8333 Greenwood Boulevard
Denver, CO 80221
800-776-3863, 303-426-8900
kjewett@collegefund.org
http://www.collegefund.org
Scholarship Name: Lockheed Martin/American Indian College Fund Scholarship. *Academic Area: Engineering (open). *Age Group: Undergraduate students. *Eligibility: Applicants must have achieved sophomore status and have declared a major in pre-engineering at a tribal college, with plans to graduate or transfer to an Accreditation Board for Engineering and Technology (ABET)-accredited institution, have at least a 3.0 grade point average, plan to complete a bachelor's degree in engineering at an ABET-accredited university or college, demonstrate leadership and commitment to the American Indian

community, and be American Indian or Alaska Native with proof of descendancy. *Application Process: Applicants should submit a completed application form and packet including a signed authorization form for release of information, letter of acceptance from ABET-accredited institution if transferring, official college transcripts, a 500-word personal statement, two letters of recommendation, tribal enrollment information or proof of descendancy, a small color photograph, and a copy of their resume. Visit the association's Web site to download an application. *Amount: $5,000. *Deadline: August 1.

American Indian College Fund
Morgan Stanley/American Indian College Fund Scholarship and Career Development Program
8333 Greenwood Boulevard
Denver, CO 80221
800-776-3863, 303-426-8900
kjewett@collegefund.org
http://www.collegefund.org
Scholarship Name: Morgan Stanley Tribal College Scholars Program. *Academic Area: Business, finance. *Age Group: Undergraduate students. *Eligibility: Applicants must be enrolled full time in an associate or bachelor's degree program at an accredited tribal college or university, have at least a 3.0 grade point average, demonstrate leadership and commitment to the American Indian community, and be an American Indian or Alaska Native. *Application Process: Applicants should submit a completed application form and packet, including proof of tribal enrollment or descendancy. Visit the association's Web site to download an application. *Amount: $2,500. *Deadline: May 1.

American Indian College Fund
Nissan North America Inc.
Tribal College Transfer Program
8333 Greenwood Boulevard
Denver, CO 80221
800-776-3863, 303-426-8900
kjewett@collegefund.org
http://www.collegefund.org
Scholarship Name: Nissan North America Scholars Program *Academic Area: Open. *Age Group: Undergraduate students. *Eligibility: Applicants must be college sophomores by the fall semester and enrolled full time in an associate degree program at a tribal college or university. Applicants should

have demonstrated general academic achievement and plan to transfer to a bachelor's degree program at a tribal college or at a mainstream institution. Applicants must also have demonstrated leadership, service, and commitment to the American Indian community and be American Indian or Alaska Native with proof of descendancy. *Application Process: Applicants should submit a completed application form and packet including a signed authorization form for release of information, official college transcripts, 500-word personal statement, two letters of recommendation, tribal enrollment information or proof of descendancy, and a small color photograph. Visit the association's Web site to download an application. *Amount: $2,000. *Deadline: May 1.

American Indian Education Foundation
10029 SW Nimbus Avenue, Suite 200
Beaverton, OR 97008
866-866-8642
bcantor@nrc1.org
http://www.aiefprograms.org
Scholarship Name: Freshman Scholarship. *Academic Area: Open. *Age Group: Undergraduate students. *Eligibility: Native American high school seniors are eligible to apply. Applicants must have an ACT score of at least 14 and attend school full time. *Application Process: Applicants should submit academic transcripts, a copy of their SAT or ACT scores, verification of acceptance into a university, a completed application, and an essay that details their personal, academic, and career interests, financial need, and service to the community (including the Native American community). They must also submit documentation verifying tribal affiliation and a photo. Visit the foundation's Web site to download an application. *Amount: $3,000. *Deadline: May 4.

American Indian Education Foundation
10029 SW Nimbus Avenue, Suite 200
Beaverton, OR 97008
866-866-8642
bcantor@nrc1.org
http://www.aiefprograms.org
Scholarship Name: Paul Francis and Josephine Nipper Memorial Scholarship. *Academic Area: Open. *Age Group: Undergraduate students. *Eligibility: Native American high school seniors and college students who plan to or who are currently attending an accredited two- or four-year postsecondary institution

may apply. Applicants must have an ACT score of at least 14, attend school full time, and show a strong commitment to improving their community. *Application Process: Applicants should submit academic transcripts, a copy of their SAT or ACT scores, verification of acceptance into a university, a completed application, and an essay that details their personal, academic, and career interests, financial need, and service to the community (including the Native American community). Visit the foundation's Web site to download an application. *Amount: Awards vary. *Deadline: May 4.

American Indian Education Foundation

10029 SW Nimbus Avenue, Suite 200
Beaverton, OR 97008
866-866-8642
bcantor@nrc1.org
http://www.aiefprograms.org
Scholarship Name: Undergraduate Scholarship. *Academic Area: Open. *Age Group: Undergraduate students. *Eligibility: Native American students who plan to return or who are currently attending an accredited two- or four-year postsecondary institution may apply. Applicants must have an ACT score of at least 14 and attend school full time. *Application Process: Applicants should submit academic transcripts, a copy of their SAT or ACT scores, verification of acceptance into a university, a completed application, and an essay that details their personal, academic, and career interests; financial need; and service to the community (including the Native American community). Visit the foundation's Web site to download an application. *Amount: $1,500. *Deadline: May 4.

American Indian Graduate Center

4520 Montgomery Boulevard, NE, Suite 1B
Albuquerque, NM 87109
505-881-4584, 800-628-1920
http://www.aigc.com
Scholarship Name: The center, in cooperation with the United Negro College Fund and the Bill and Melinda Gates Foundation, offers the Gates Millennium Scholarship. *Academic Area: Open. *Age Group: Undergraduate students. *Eligibility: Minority high school seniors (including Native Americans) planning to enroll full time in a postsecondary institution are eligible to apply. Applicants must also have a GPA of at least 3.3 on a 4.0 scale, demonstrate leadership abilities, show financial need, and be citizens or legal permanent residents or nationals of the United States. *Application Process: Visit the center's Web site for information on application requirements. *Amount: Varies. *Deadline: January 13.

American Indian Graduate Center

Attn: Marveline Vallo
4520 Montgomery Boulevard, NE, Suite 1B
Albuquerque, NM 87109
505-881-4584, 800-628-1920
marveline@aigc.com
http://www.aigc.com
Fellowship Name: Graduate Fellowship. *Academic Area: Open. *Age Group: Graduate students. Eligibility: Applicants must be pursuing a post-baccalaureate graduate or professional degree as a full-time student at an accredited institution in the United States, able to demonstrate financial need, and an enrolled member of a federally recognized American Indian tribe or Alaska Native group, or provide documentation of descendancy (possess one-fourth degree federally recognized Indian blood). *Application Process: Applicants should submit a completed application along with a financial need form, a tribal eligibility certificate form, and three self-addressed, stamped postcards. Visit the organization's Web site to request an application. *Amount: Awards vary. *Deadline: Contact the organization for deadlines.

American Indian Library Association

Attn: Associate Dean Joan S. Howland, Treasurer
Law Library/Law School
229 19th Avenue South
Minneapolis, MN 55455
http://www.nativeculturelinks.com/aila.html
Scholarship Name: American Indian Library Association Library School Scholarship. *Academic Area: Library sciences. *Age Group: Graduate students. *Eligibility: Applicants must be American Indian or Alaskan Native students who are enrolled in or accepted into an American Library Association-accredited master's program in library science. Applicants must also take at least six hours of classes per semester and demonstrate financial need as well as sustained involvement in the American Indian community. *Application Process: Applicants should submit a completed application along with proof of tribal enrollment, two letters of recommendation, a 250-word or less personal statement, and a resume. Visit the

association's Web site to download an application form. *Amount: $500. *Deadline: April 1.

American Indian Science and Engineering Society (AISES)
Attn: Scholarship Coordinator
PO Box 9828
Albuquerque, NM 87119-9828
505-765-1052
info@aises.org
http://www.aises.org
Scholarship Name: A.T. Anderson Memorial Scholarship. *Academic Area: Engineering (open), mathematics, medicine (open), natural resources, physical sciences, science. *Age Group: Undergraduate students, graduate students. *Eligibility: Applicants must be enrolled as full-time students at an accredited four-year college or university or a two-year college or university. Applicants also must be current AISES members with a minimum GPA of 2.0. Proof of membership in an American Indian tribe is required (or proof of one-quarter American Indian or Alaskan native blood). High school seniors are also eligible to apply for this scholarship. *Application Process: Applicants should submit a completed application form, a 500-word personal statement, two letters of recommendation, official transcripts, a resume, and proof of tribal enrollment. Visit the association's Web site for membership information and to download an application. *Amount: $1,000 for undergraduate students; $2,000 for graduate students. *Deadline: June 15.

American Indian Science and Engineering Society (AISES)
Attn: Scholarship Coordinator
PO Box 9828
Albuquerque, NM 87119-9828
505-765-1052
info@aises.org
http://www.aises.org
Scholarship Name: Burlington Northern Santa Fe Foundation Scholarship. *Academic Area: Business, engineering (open), mathematics, medicine (open), science, technology. *Age Group: Undergraduate students. *Eligibility: Applicants must be American Indian high school seniors residing in one of the following states serviced by the Burlington Northern and Santa Fe Pacific Corporation and its affiliated companies: Arizona, California, Colorado, Kansas,

Minnesota, Montana, New Mexico, North Dakota, Oklahoma, Oregon, South Dakota, and Washington. Applicants also must be current AISES members with a minimum 2.0 GPA. Proof of membership in an American Indian tribe is required (or proof of one-quarter American Indian or Alaskan native blood). *Application Process: Applicants should submit a completed application form, a 500-word personal statement, two letters of recommendation, official transcripts, a resume, and proof of tribal enrollment. Visit the association's Web site for membership information and to download an application. *Amount: $2,500. *Deadline: April 15.

American Indian Science and Engineering Society (AISES)
Attn: Scholarship Coordinator
PO Box 9828
Albuquerque, NM 87119-9828
505-765-1052
info@aises.org
http://www.aises.org
Scholarship Name: EPA Tribal Lands Environmental Science Scholarship. *Academic Area: Engineering (environmental), science. *Age Group: Undergraduate students, graduate students. *Eligibility: Applicant must be a full-time junior or senior or a full-time graduate student at an accredited four-year college or university or graduate college or university. Applicants also must be current AISES members with a minimum 2.7 GPA. Applicants also must be U.S. citizens or permanent U.S. residents. *Application Process: Applicants should submit a completed application form, a 500-word personal statement, two letters of recommendation, official transcripts, a resume, and proof of tribal enrollment. Visit the association's Web site for membership information and to download an application. *Amount: $4,000. *Deadline: June 15.

American Indian Science and Engineering Society (AISES)
Attn: Scholarship Coordinator
PO Box 9828
Albuquerque, NM 87119-9828
505-765-1052
info@aises.org
http://www.aises.org
Scholarship Name: General Motors Engineering Scholarship. *Academic Area: Engineering (open). *Age Group: Undergraduate students, graduate

students. *Eligibility: Applicants must be enrolled as full-time students at an accredited college or university and must be current AISES members. Applicants must have a minimum cumulative GPA of 3.0. General Motors gives preference to electrical, industrial, or mechanical engineering majors. Applicants must provide proof of at least 1/4 American Indian blood or at least 1/4 Alaskan Native blood. High school seniors are also eligible to apply for this scholarship. *Application Process: Applicants should submit a completed application form, a 500-word personal statement, two letters of recommendation, official transcripts, a resume, and proof of tribal enrollment. Visit the association's Web site for membership information and to download an application. *Amount: $3,000. *Deadline: June 15.

American Indian Science and Engineering Society (AISES)

Attn: Scholarship Coordinator
PO Box 9828
Albuquerque, NM 87119-9828
505-765-1052
info@aises.org
http://www.aises.org

Scholarship Name: Henry Rodriguez Reclamation College Scholarship and Internship. *Academic Area: Engineering (open), science. *Age Group: Undergraduate students. *Eligibility: Applicants must be enrolled as full-time students at an accredited college or university, current AISES members, and U.S. citizens or permanent residents. Applicants must have a minimum cumulative GPA of 2.5 and must be enrolled members of a federally recognized Indian tribe. They must also agree to serve an eight- to 10-week paid internship with the Bureau of Reclamation prior to graduation in Washington, D.C. or Denver, Colorado. High school seniors are also eligible to apply for this scholarship. *Application Process: Applicants should submit a completed application form, a 500-word personal statement, two letters of recommendation, official transcripts, a resume, and proof of tribal enrollment. Visit the association's Web site for membership information and to download an application. *Amount: $5,000. *Deadline: June 15.

American Institute for Foreign Study (AIFS)

AIFS College Division
River Plaza
9 West Broad Street
Stamford, CT 06902-3788
800-727-2437
http://www.aifsabroad.com/ays/scholarships.htm

Scholarship Name: AIFS Diversity/Minority Scholarship. *Academic Area: Open. *Age Group: Undergraduate students. *Eligibility: Applicants must be African American, Asian American, Hispanic American, Native American, or Pacific Islanders. They must also meet the minimum requirements for the program to which they are applying, have at least a 3.0 minimum cumulative GPA, show leadership potential and be involved in extracurricular activities centered on multicultural or international issues. *Application Process: Applicants should submit a completed application along with a $95 application fee, one letter of reference, and an essay of up to 1,000 words on "How studying abroad will change my life." Visit the institute's Web site to download an application. *Amount: Full program fees, plus round trip airfare for the winner; three runners up receive $2,000 each. *Deadline: April 15, October 15.

American Institute of Certified Public Accountants (AICPA)

Minority Doctoral Fellowships Program
1211 Avenue of the Americas
New York, NY 10036-8775
212-596-6200
http://www.aicpa.org/nolimits/become/ships/AICPA.htm

Fellowship Name: AICPA Fellowship for Minority Doctoral Students. *Academic Area: Accounting. *Age Group: Graduate students. Eligibility: Applicants must have applied to and/or been accepted into an accredited doctoral program with a concentration in accounting, have earned a master's degree and/or completed a minimum of three years full-time experience in the practice of accounting, attend or plan to attend school on a full-time basis and, agree not to work full time in a paid position or accept responsibility for teaching more than one course per semester as a teaching assistant or, dedicate more than one quarter of their time as a research assistant. Applicants must be U.S. citizens who are African American, Native American/Alaskan Native, or of Pacific Island races, or of Hispanic ethnic origin. *Application Process: Applicants should submit a completed application along with official transcripts, and two letters of recommendation. Visit the institute's Web site to download an application. *Amount: Up to $12,000. *Deadline: April 1.

American Institute of Certified Public Accountants (AICPA)
Attn: AICPA Minority Initiatives Committee
1211 Avenue of the Americas
New York, NY 10036-8775
212-596-6200
http://www.aicpa.org/members/div/career/mini/smas.htm
Scholarship Name: AICPA Scholarship for Minority Accounting Students. *Academic Area: Accounting. *Age Group: Undergraduate students, graduate students. *Eligibility: Undergraduate minority students at regionally accredited institutions who have completed at least 30 semester hours of study (including six hours of accounting work) are eligible to apply. Applicants must also have a GPA of at least 3.3, be attending school full time, and be U.S. citizens. The scholarship is also available to graduate students who meet certain educational criteria. Contact the institute for more information. *Application Process: Application packets should include a letter of recommendation from either a faculty member or a certified public accountant, an official transcript, and a completed financial aid worksheet (included with the application form). Visit the institute's Web site to download an application. *Amount: $5,000. *Deadline: June 1.

American Institute of Chemical Engineers (AIChE)
3 Park Avenue
New York, NY 10016-5991
212-591-7107, 800-242-4363
awards@aiche.org
http://students.aiche.org/pdfs/MAC college 05.pdf
Scholarship Name: Minority Scholarship Award for College Students. *Academic Area: Engineering (chemical). *Age Group: Undergraduate students. *Eligibility: Applicants must be AIChE national student members at the time of application, undergraduates in chemical engineering, and members of a minority group (i.e., African American, Hispanic, Native American, or Alaskan Native) that is underrepresented in chemical engineering. Applicants are judged based on academic record (minimum 3.0 GPA), participation in AIChE student and professional activities, a personal statement, and financial need. *Application Process: Applicants must submit a completed application, a personal statement, official transcripts, a letter of financial need from financial aid officer, and a letter of recommendation from AIChE student chapter advisor, department chair, or chemical engineering faculty member. *Amount: $1,000. *Deadline: May 15.

American Institute of Chemical Engineers (AIChE)
3 Park Avenue
New York, NY 10016-5991
212-591-7107, 800-242-4363
awards@aiche.org
http://students.aiche.org/pdfs/MAC incoming 05.pdf
Scholarship Name: Minority Scholarship Award for Incoming College Freshmen. *Academic Area: Engineering (chemical). *Age Group: Undergraduate students. *Eligibility: Applicants must be high school seniors who are members of a minority group (i.e., African American, Hispanic, Native American, or Alaskan Native) that is underrepresented in chemical engineering. Applicants must be planning to enroll in a four-year university offering a science/engineering degree. Applicants are encouraged to choose classes leading to a degree in science or engineering, and they are judged based on academic record (minimum 3.0 GPA), participation in school and work activities, a personal statement, and financial need. *Application Process: Applicants must submit a completed application, a personal statement, official transcripts, a letter verifying financial need from parent/guardian, and a letter of recommendation from a high school counselor or math/science teacher. Visit the institute's Web site to download an application. *Amount: $1,000. *Deadline: May 15.

American Library Association (ALA)
Attn: Scholarship Committee
50 East Huron Street
Chicago, IL 60611
800-545-2433, ext. 4277
scholarships@ala.org
http://www.ala.org/hrdr/scholarship
Scholarship Name: LITA/LSSI Minority Scholarship. *Academic Area: Library sciences. *Age Group: Graduate students. *Eligibility: Applicants must be U.S. or Canadian citizens currently enrolled in an ALA-accredited master's program who are qualified members of a principal minority group (American Indian or Alaskan native, Asian or Pacific Islander, African American, or Hispanic). Candidates must not have earned more than 12 hours toward a Master of Library Science degree. Economic need is considered when all other criteria are equal. This scholarship is awarded annually by the Library and Information

Technology Association (LITA), a division of the American Library Association, and Library Systems and Services, Inc. *Application Process: An online application must be submitted, which includes a personal statement and three references. Official transcripts from your undergraduate university must be submitted by mail. Visit the association's Web site to submit an application. *Amount: $2,500. *Deadline: March 1.

American Library Association (ALA)
Attn: Scholarship Committee
50 East Huron Street
Chicago, IL 60611
800-545-2433, ext. 4277
scholarships@ala.org
http://www.ala.org/hrdr/scholarship
Scholarship Name: LITA/OCLC Minority Scholarship. *Academic Area: Library sciences. *Age Group: Graduate students. *Eligibility: Applicants must be U.S. or Canadian citizens currently enrolled in an ALA accredited master's program who are qualified members of a principal minority group (American Indian or Alaskan native, Asian or Pacific Islander, African American, or Hispanic). Candidates must not have earned more than 12 hours toward a Master of Library Science degree. Economic need is considered when all other criteria are equal. The scholarship, awarded jointly and annually by OCLC Inc. and the Library and Information Technology Association (LITA), is designed to encourage the entry of qualified persons into the library and automation field who have a strong commitment to the use of automated systems in libraries. *Application Process: An online application must be submitted, which includes a personal statement and three references. Official transcripts from your undergraduate university must be submitted by mail. Visit the association's Web site to submit an application. *Amount: $3,000. *Deadline: March 1.

American Library Association (ALA)
Attn: Wendy Prellwitz, Program Officer
ALA Office for Diversity and Spectrum
50 East Huron Street
Chicago, IL 60611
800-545-2433, ext. 5048
spectrum@ala.org
http://www.ala.org/hrdr/scholarship
Scholarship Name: Spectrum Scholarship. *Academic Area: Library sciences. *Age Group: Graduate students. *Eligibility: Applicants must be U.S. or Canadian citizens currently enrolled in an ALA-accredited program who are members of one of the following ethnic minorities: American Indian/Alaska Native, Asian, Black/African American, Hispanic/Latino, or Native Hawaiian/Other Pacific Islander. Applicant shall have completed no more than a third of the credit requirements toward her or his Master's of Library Information Science or school library media degree. *Application Process: An online application must be submitted, which includes a personal statement and three references. Official transcripts from your undergraduate university must be submitted by mail. Visit the association's Web site to submit an application. *Amount: $5,000. *Deadline: March 1.

American Medical Association (AMA) Foundation
Attn: Dina Lindenberg, Program Officer
515 North State Street
Chicago, IL 60610
312-464-4193
dina.lindenberg@ama-assn.org
http://www.ama-assn.org/ama/pub/category/14772.html
Scholarship Name: AMA Foundation Minority Scholars Award. *Academic Area: Medicine. *Age Group: Medical students. *Eligibility: Applicants must be rising second or third year students of minority background, including African American/Black, Native American, Native Hawaiian, Alaska Native, or Hispanic/Latino. *Application Process: Medical schools are invited to submit up to two nominees. Contact the AMA Foundation program officer for further application details. *Amount: $10,000. *Deadline: Nominations are due April 15.

American Meteorological Society (AMS)
Attn: Donna Fernandez, Development Program Coordinator
Minority Scholarship
45 Beacon Street
Boston, MA 02108
617-227-2426 ext. 246
dfernand@ametsoc.org
http://www.ametsoc.org/amsstudentinfo/scholfeldocs
Scholarship Name: AMS/Industry Minority Scholarships. *Academic Area: Meteorology. *Age Group:

Undergraduate students. *Eligibility: Applicants must be entering their freshman year of college in the fall and belong to a traditionally underrepresented minority group in the sciences—Hispanic, Native American, or Black/African American. Applicants must plan to pursue careers in the atmospheric or related oceanic and hydrologic sciences. *Application Process: Applicants should submit a completed application along with an official high school transcript, a copy of SAT or ACT scores, a 500-word essay, and a letter of recommendation from a high school teacher or guidance counselor. All originals must be mailed to the closest AMS local chapter listed at the bottom of the application. Photocopies should be mailed to the AMS main office in Boston. Visit the association's Web site to download an application. *Amount: $3,000. *Deadline: February 10.

American Nurses Association (ANA)

Substance Abuse and Mental Health Services
    Administration Minority Fellowship Program
Attn: Janet Jackson, Program Manager
8515 Georgia Avenue, Suite 400
Silver Spring, MD 20910-3492
301-628-5247
jjackson@ana.org
http://nursingworld.org/emfp
Fellowship Name: Clinical Research Pre-Doctoral
    Fellowship. *Academic Area: Nursing (substance
    abuse and mental health). *Age Group: Graduate
    students. *Eligibility: Applicants must be master's-
    prepared nurses who are members of a minority
    group and committed to pursuing doctoral study on
    minority psychiatric-mental health and substance
    abuse issues. They also must be U.S. citizens and
    members of the association. *Application Process:
    Applicants must complete and electronically submit
    an application form, a scientifically based essay,
    and curriculum vitae. Additionally, four letters of
    recommendation, transcripts, a copy the applicant's
    active RN license, published articles or scholarly
    writing, proof of admittance to a Ph.D. program, and
    a copy of current ANA membership card must all be
    sent via mail. Visit the association's Web site for more
    information and to submit an application.*Amount:
    Fellowship awards vary. *Deadline: March 1.

American Philosophical Society

Phillips Fund Grant for Native American Research
Attn: Linda Musumeci

104 South Fifth Street
Philadelphia, PA 19106-3386
215-440-3400
Lmusumeci@amphilsoc.org
http://www.amphilsoc.org/grants/phillips.htm
Grant Name: Phillips Fund Grant for Native America
    Research. *Academic Area: History, linguistics. *Age
    Group: Graduate students, recent Ph.D.'s. *Eligibility:
    Applicants must plan to conduct research in the
    area of Native American linguistics, ethnohistory,
    or the history of studies of Native Americans in the
    continental United States and Canada. *Application
    Process: Applicants should submit a completed
    application via e-mail. Applications are available for
    download from the society's Web site. *Amount: Up to
    $3,000. *Deadline: March 1.

American Physical Society (APS)

Attn: APS Minority Scholarship
One Physics Ellipse
College Park, MD 20740-3844
301-209-3232
http://www.aps.org/educ/com/scholars/index.cfm
Scholarship Name: APS Minority Scholarship for
    Undergraduate Physics Majors. *Academic Area:
    Physics. *Age Group: Undergraduate students.
    *Eligibility: Applicants must be an African American,
    Hispanic American, or Native American U.S. citizen or
    permanent resident who is majoring in or planning
    to major in physics. High school seniors and college
    freshmen and sophomores are eligible to apply for
    this scholarship. *Application Process: Applicants
    must submit a completed application along with a
    personal statement, official transcripts, two letters of
    reference, and ACT/SAT scores. Legal residents must
    also submit a copy of their Alien Registration Card
    (green card). *Amount: $2,000 for the first year, $3,000
    for renewal years. *Deadline: February 3.

American Physiological Society (APS)

APS Education Office
Explorations in Biomedicine UGSRF Program
9650 Rockville Pike
Bethesda, MD 20814-3991
301-634-7132
education@the-aps.org
http://www.the-aps.org/awards/student.htm
Fellowship Name: Explorations in Biomedicine
    Undergraduate Summer Research Fellowship for
    Native Americans. *Academic Area: Physiology.

*Age Group: Undergraduate students. *Eligibility: Applicants must be Native American undergraduate students with little or no research experience in the life sciences, but who are interested in learning more about biomedical research. *Application Process: Applicants should submit a completed application form along with transcripts, a personal statement, and two letters of recommendation. Visit the society's Web site to download an application. *Amount: $3,500 to $4,000 (work and living expenses); up to $1,000 (travel expenses for Experimental Biology annual conference). *Deadline: February 3.

American Physiological Society (APS)
APS Minority Travel Fellowship Awards Program
9650 Rockville Pike
Bethesda, MD 20814-3991
301-634-7226
education@the-aps.org
http://www.the-aps.org/awards/student.htm
Fellowship Name: Minority Travel Fellowship
Award. *Academic Area: Physiology. *Age Group: Undergraduate students, graduate students, post-doctoral scholars. *Eligibility: Applicants must demonstrate financial need and be members of one of the following underrepresented minority groups: African Americans, Native Americans, Native Alaskans, Hispanic Americans, or Pacific Islanders. *Application Process: Applicants should submit a completed application along with a current curriculum vitae, letter of recommendation from their advisor, and a summary of estimated expenses. Visit the association's Web site to download an application. *Amount: Awards vary. *Deadline: November 9.

American Physiological Society (APS)
APS Education Office
Porter Physiology Fellowship
9650 Rockville Pike
Bethesda, MD 20814-3991
301-634-7132
education@the-aps.org
http://www.the-aps.org/awards/student.htm
Fellowship Name: Porter Physiology Fellowship for Minorities. *Academic Area: Physiology. *Age Group: Graduate students. *Eligibility: Applicants must be African American, Hispanic American, Native American, Native Alaskan, or Native Pacific Islander; U.S. citizens or permanent residents; and accepted into or currently enrolled in a graduate program in

physiology. *Application Process: Applicants should submit a completed application form along with supporting materials. Visit the society's Web site to download an application. *Amount: $20,772. *Deadline: January 15.

American Planning Association (APA)
Attn: Kriss Blank, Leadership Affairs Associate
APA Judith McManus Scholarship
122 South Michigan Avenue, Suite 1600
Chicago, IL 60603-6107
312-431-9100
kblank@planning.org
http://www.planning.org/institutions/scholarship.htm
Scholarship Name: Judith McManus Scholarship.
*Academic Area: Planning. *Age Group: Undergraduate students, graduate students. *Eligibility: Applicants must be women, U.S. citizens, and members of one of the following minority groups: African American, Hispanic American, or Native American. Applicants must be enrolled in or officially accepted into an approved Planning Accreditation Board (PAB) planning program, demonstrate a commitment to planning, strong academic achievement and/or improvement, professional presentation, and financial need. High school seniors are also eligible to apply for this scholarship. *Application Process: Applicants must submit a completed application along with a two- to five-page personal background statement describing career goals, two letters of recommendation, official transcripts of college work completed, written verification from the student's school of the average cost per academic year, a resume (optional), a copy of acceptance letter (incoming students only), and a notarized statement of financial independence signed by parent(s), also optional. Visit the APA's Web site to download an application. *Amount: $2,000 to $4,000. *Deadline: April 30.

American Planning Association (APA)
Attn: Kriss Blank, Leadership Affairs Associate
APA Planning Fellowship Orgram
122 South Michigan Avenue, Suite 1600
Chicago, IL 60603
312-431-9100
kblank@planning.org
http://www.planning.org/institutions/scholarship.htm
Fellowship Name: APA Planning Fellowship Program.
*Academic Area: Planning. *Age Group: Graduate

students. *Eligibility: Applicants must be African American, Hispanic American, or Native American first- or second-year graduate students who are citizens of the United States and enrolled in an approved Planning Accreditation Board (PAB) graduate planning program. Applicants must also demonstrate financial need. *Application Process: Applicants should submit a completed application along with a personal statement, two letters of recommendation, transcripts, a resume (optional), copy of acceptance from a PAB-accredited graduate planning school (incoming students only), and a notarized statement of financial independence. Visit the association's Web site to download an application. *Amount: $1,000 to $5,000. *Deadline: April 30.

American Political Science Association (APSA)
1527 New Hampshire Avenue, NW
Washington, DC 20036-1206
202-483-2512
apsa@apsanet.org
http://www.apsanet.org/section_427.cfm
Fellowship Name: APSA Minority Fellows Program. *Academic Area: Political science. *Age Group: Graduate students. *Eligibility: Applicants must members of one of the following racial/ethnic minority groups: African Americans, Latinos/as, or Native Americans (federal- and state-recognized tribes). They must demonstrate an interest in teaching and potential for research in political science, be U.S. citizens at time of award, demonstrate financial need, and be entering a doctoral program for the first time. *Application Process: Applicants should submit a completed application along with a personal statement (maximum 500 words), official transcripts, three letters of recommendation, and GRE scores. Visit the association's Web site to download an application. *Amount: $4,000. *Deadline: October 31.

American Psychological Association
HIV/AIDS Application
750 First Street, NE
Washington, DC 20002-4242
202-336-6127
mfp@apa.org
http://www.apa.org/mfp
Fellowship Name: HIV/AIDS Research Fellowship. *Academic Area: Psychology. *Age Group: Graduate students. *Eligibility: Applicants must be American citizens or permanent resident aliens, demonstrate a

strong commitment to a career in HIV/AIDS research related to ethnic minorities, enrolled full time in a doctoral program, and be members of one of the following ethnic minorities: African American, Alaskan Native, American Indian, Asian American, Hispanic/Latino, Native Hawaiian, or Pacific Islander. *Application Process: Applicants should submit a completed application along with a cover letter, two essays, curriculum vita, three recommendations, transcripts, and GRE scores. Visit the association's Web site to download an application. *Amount: Awards vary. *Deadline: January 15.

American Psychological Association
MHSAS Application
750 First Street, NE
Washington, DC 20002-4242
202-336-6127
mfp@apa.org
http://www.apa.org/mfp
Fellowship Name: Mental Health and Substance Abuse Services (MHSAS) Fellowship. *Academic Area: Psychology. *Age Group: Graduate students. *Eligibility: Applicants must be American citizens or permanent resident aliens, demonstrate a strong commitment to a career in ethnic minority mental health and substance abuse services, be enrolled full time in an APA-accredited doctoral program, and be members of one of the following ethnic minority groups: African American, Alaskan Native, American Indian, Asian American, Hispanic/Latino, Native Hawaiian, or Pacific Islander. *Application Process: Applicants should submit a completed application along with a cover letter, two essays, a curriculum vita, three recommendations, transcripts, and GRE scores. Visit the association's Web site to download an application. *Amount: Awards vary. *Deadline: January 15.

American Psychological Association
MHR Application
750 First Street, NE
Washington, DC 20002-4242
202-336-6127
mfp@apa.org
http://www.apa.org/mfp
Fellowship Name: Mental Health Research (MHR) Fellowship. *Academic Area: Psychology. *Age Group: Graduate students. *Eligibility: Applicants must be American citizens or permanent resident aliens, demonstrate a strong commitment to a career in

mental health research related to ethnic minorities, be enrolled full time in a doctoral program, and be members of one of the following ethnic minority groups: African American, Alaskan Native, American Indian, Asian American, Hispanic/Latino, Native Hawaiian, or Pacific Islander. *Application Process: Applicants should submit a completed application along with a cover letter, two essays, a curriculum vita, three recommendations, transcripts, and GRE scores. Visit the association's Web site to download an application. *Amount: Awards vary. *Deadline: January 15.

American Society for Microbiology
Education Board
1752 N Street, NW
Washington, DC 20036
202-942-9283
fellowships-careerinformation@asmusa.org
http://www.asm.org/Awards/index.asp?bid=14956
Fellowship Name: Microbiology Undergraduate Research Fellowship (MURF). *Academic Area: Microbiology. *Age Group: Undergraduate students. *Eligibility: Applicants must be U.S. citizens or permanent U.S. residents, enrolled as full-time matriculating undergraduate students during the 2006-2007 academic year at an accredited U.S. institution, be a member of an underrepresented group in microbiology, have taken introductory courses in biology, chemistry, and, preferably, microbiology prior to submission of the application, have a strong interest in obtaining a Ph.D., or M.D./Ph.D. in the microbiological sciences, and have lab research experience. *Application Process: Applicants should submit a completed application along with supporting materials. Applications are available to download from the society's Web site in September of each year. *Amount: Up to $3,500, plus travel and lodging expenses. *Deadline: February 1.

American Society for Microbiology
Education Board
1752 N Street, NW
Washington, DC 20036
202-942-9283
fellowships-careerinformation@asmusa.org
http://www.asm.org/Awards/index.asp?bid=14956
Fellowship Name: Robert D. Watkins Graduate Research Fellowship. *Academic Area: Microbiology. *Age Group: Graduate students. *Eligibility: Applicants

must be formally admitted to a doctoral program in the microbiological sciences at an accredited U.S. institution, have successfully completed the first year of the graduate program, be student members of the society, mentored by a society member, U.S. citizens or a permanent residents, members of an underrepresented group in microbiology, and not have funding OR have funding that will expire by the start date of the fellowship. *Application Process: Applicants must apply online via the society's Web site. Three letters of recommendation and official transcripts also must be submitted. *Amount: $57,000 (over three years). *Deadline: May 1.

American Society of Criminology (ASC)
Attn: Todd R. Clear, Chair, Minority Scholar/Mentor Committee
John Jay College of Criminal Justice
899 10th Avenue
New York, NY 10019
212-237-8470
tclear@jjay.cuny.edu
http://www.asc41.com
Grant Name: ASC Undergraduate Student Minority Scholar/Mentor Research Grant. *Academic Area: Criminal justice. *Age Group: Undergraduate students. *Eligibility: Applicants must be undergraduate students from underrepresented minority groups, and near the end of their sophomore year of study. *Application Process: Mentors must submit a written recommendation, student transcripts, a description of the proposed collaborative research project, and a description of additional proposed mentoring activities. Student applicants must submit a personal statement and statement on how the Mentoring Grant will better enable the applicant to pursue his or her academic goals. Contact the society for further application details. *Amount: $10,000 and travel allowance. *Deadline: Nominations due May 1.

American Society of Mechanical Engineers (ASME)
Attn: Mary James Legatski, Manager of Leadership & Diversity
103 South Newport Way
Dagsboro, DE 19939-9219
legatskim@asme.org
http://www.asme.org/Communities/Diversity/Diversity_Action_Grant.cfm?IMAGE.X=8\&IMAGE.Y=11
Grant Name: Diversity Action Grant. *Academic Area: Engineering (mechanical). *Age Group: Undergraduate

students. *Eligibility: Applicants must be interested in promoting diversity and inclusion within their own ASME Student Section, within the society membership, and within the engineering community at large. *Application Process: Applicants should submit a detailed budget plan, including the amount of money requested; information on groups with which their section will be partnering or collaborating; and the project objectives, methodology, and evaluation plan. *Amount: $500 to $1,500. *Deadline: November 1.

American Society of Mechanical Engineers (ASME)
Attn: Maisha Phillips
Three Park Avenue
New York, NY 10016
212-591-8131
Phillipsm@asme.org
http://www.asme.org/Education/FinancialAid/
    Fellowships/Graduate_Teaching_Fellowships.cfm
Fellowship Name: ASME Graduate Teaching Fellowship.
    *Academic Area: Engineering (mechanical). *Age
    Group: Graduate students. *Eligibility: Applicant must
    be a Ph.D. student in mechanical engineering, with
    a demonstrated interest in a teaching career and
    must be a U.S. citizen or permanent resident, have an
    undergraduate degree from an Accreditation Board
    for Engineering and Technology-accredited program,
    and be a student member of ASME. Preference
    is given to women and minority applicants.
    *Application Process: Applicants should submit a
    completed application along with undergraduate
    GPA, GRE scores, a current resume or curriculum vita,
    two letters of recommendation from faculty or M.S.
    committee, transcripts of all academic work, and a
    statement about their interest in a faculty career. Visit
    the society's Web site to download an application.
    *Amount: $5,000. *Deadline: October 21.

**American Society of Radiologic Technologists
    Education and Research Foundation**
Scholarship Program
15000 Central Avenue, SE
Albuquerque, NM 87123-3917
800-444-2778, ext. 2541
foundation@asrt.org
http://www.asrt.org/content/ASRTFoundation/
    AwardsandScholarships/Awards_Scholarships.aspx
Scholarship Name: Royce Osborn Minority Student
    Scholarship. *Academic Area: Medicine (radiologic
    sciences). *Age Group: Undergraduate students.
    *Eligibility: Applicants must be academically

outstanding, minority (African American, Native American, Native Alaskan, Hispanic American, Asian American, or Pacific Islander) students attending an entry-level radiologic sciences program. They also must be U.S. citizens, nationals, or permanent residents, have maintained a 3.0 GPA, and demonstrate financial need. *Application Process: Applicants must submit a completed application, official transcripts, an evaluation form, and an essay. Visit the society's Web site to download an application and evaluation form. *Amount: Up to $4,000. *Deadline: February 1.

American Sociological Association (ASA)
ASA Minority Affairs Program
1307 New York Avenue, NW, Suite 700
Washington, DC 20005-4701
202-383-9005
minority.affairs@asanet.org
http://www.asanet.org/page.ww?section=Funding&nam
    e=Minority+Fellowship+Program
Fellowship Name: ASA Minority Fellowship Program.
    *Academic Area: Sociology. *Age Group: Graduate
    students. *Eligibility: Applicants must be minority
    students who are currently enrolled in Ph.D.
    programs and demonstrate commitment to a
    research career focusing on National Institute of
    Mental Health (NIMH)- and National Institute of Drug
    Abuse (NIDA)-relevant research. Applicants must be
    enrolled in a Ph.D. program in sociology departments,
    which have NIMH- and NIDA-relevant research
    programs and/or those with faculty who are currently
    researching areas relevant to the NIMH and NIDA.
    Applicants must be Black/African American, Latino,
    American Indian or Alaskan Native, Asian, or Pacific
    Islander. Applicants also must be citizens, noncitizen
    nationals of the United States, or have been lawfully
    admitted into the United States. and possess an Alien
    Registration Card. *Application Process: Applicants
    must submit a completed application, an essay, three
    letters of recommendation, transcripts, a curriculum
    vitae (optional), published research papers (optional),
    and GRE scores (optional). Visit the association's Web
    site to download an application. *Deadline: January
    31. *Amount: $15,000 to $20,772.

American Speech-Language-Hearing Association
Attn: Emily Diaz, Project Assistant
10801 Rockville Pike
Rockville, MD 20852
301-897-5700, ext. 4314

ediaz@asha.org
http://www.ashfoundation.org/foundation/grants
Scholarship Name: International Student Scholarship.
*Academic Area: Medicine (open). *Age Group:
Graduate students. *Eligibility: Applicants must be
full-time international/minority students studying
communication sciences and disorders who
demonstrate outstanding academic achievement.
*Application Process: Interested candidates should
write to the association for more information.
Applications are available for download from the
association's Web site. *Amount: $2,000 to $4,000.
*Deadline: Contact the association for information.

American Speech-Language-Hearing Association
Attn: Emily Diaz, Project Assistant
10801 Rockville Pike
Rockville, MD 20853
301-897-5700, ext. 4314
ediaz@asha.org
http://www.ashfoundation.org/foundation/grants
Scholarship Name: Minority Student Scholarship.
*Academic Area: Medicine (open). *Age Group:
Graduate students. *Eligibility: Applicants must be
racial/ethnic minority students who are U.S. citizens
and who have been accepted into a graduate
program for audiology or speech-language pathology.
*Application Process: Interested candidates should
write to the association for more information.
Applications are available for download from the
association's Web site. *Amount: $2,000 to $4,000.
*Deadline: Contact the association for information.

American Water Works Association (AWWA)
Attn: Scholarship Coordinator
6666 West Quincy Avenue
Denver, CO 80235
303-347-6206
swheeler@awwa.org
http://www.awwa.org/About/scholarships.cfm
Scholarship Name: Holly A. Cornell Scholarship.
*Academic Area: Engineering (water supply and
treatment). *Age Group: Graduate students. *Eligibility:
Applicants must be female and/or minority master's
degree students in pursuit of advanced training
in the field of water supply and treatment. They
must demonstrate a quality academic record and
have potential to provide leadership in the field of
water supply and treatment. *Application Process:
Applicants must submit a completed application,
official transcripts of all university education, official

copies of GRE scores (required), three letters of
recommendation, a proposed curriculum of study, and
a one- to two-page statement describing their career
objectives. Visit the association's Web site to download
an official application. *Amount: $5,000. *Deadline:
January 15.

Appraisal Institute
Attn: Wendy Woodburn
550 West Van Buren Street, Suite 1000
Chicago, IL 60607
312-335-4100
wwoodburn@appraisalinstitute.org
http://www.appraisalinstitute.org/membership/sub_
    min_wom_sch_fund.asp
Scholarship Name: Minorities and Women Educational
Scholarship Program. *Academic Area: Real estate.
*Age Group: Undergraduate students. *Eligibility:
Applicants must be from a racial, ethnic, or gender
group underrepresented in the real estate appraisal
profession. Such groups include women, American
Indians or Alaska Natives, Asians, Black or African
Americans, Hispanics or Latinos, and Native
Hawaiians or other Pacific Islanders. Applicants must
be full- or part-time students enrolled in real estate
courses with a degree-granting two- or four-year
college or university. They must also maintain a
cumulative GPA of 2.5 and be able to demonstrate
financial need. *Application Process: Applicants
should submit a completed application along
with two letters of recommendation, transcripts, a
500-word essay, and a photograph (optional). One
original application packet and two copies should be
mailed. Visit the institute's Web site to download an
application. *Amount: $1,000 (minimum). *Deadline:
April 15.

Arkansas Department of Higher Education
114 East Capitol Avenue
Little Rock, AR 72201
501-371-2013
finaid@adhe.arknet.edu
http://www.arkansashighered.com/minoritygrant.html
Grant Name: Freshman/Sophomore Minority Grant
Program. *Academic Area: Education. *Age Group:
Undergraduate students. *Eligibility: African American,
Hispanic American, and Asian American college
freshmen and sophomores majoring in education
at select Arkansas schools may apply. Applicants
also must be residents of Arkansas, planning to or
currently attending select postsecondary institutions

in Arkansas, demonstrate financial need, and sign a statement of interest that establishes their interest in teaching. *Application Process: Applicants should contact the department for information on application requirements. *Amount: $1,000. *Deadline: Applications are accepted throughout the year.

Armed Forces Communications and Electronics Association Educational Foundation

Attn: Norma Corrales
4400 Fair Lakes Court
Fairfax, VA 22033-3899
703-631-6149, 800-336-4583, ext. 6149
scholarship@afcea.org
http://www.afcea.org/education/scholarships/graduate/grad2.asp

Scholarship Name: Ralph W. Shrader Diversity Scholarship. *Academic Area: Computer science, electrical energy, engineering (chemical), engineering (communications), engineering (electrical), mathematics, physics. *Age Group: Graduate students. *Eligibility: Applicants must belong to an ethnic or racial minority group, or be female, to apply for this scholarship. Applicants must be U.S. citizens who are pursuing a master's degree full time at an accredited university in the United States and who also can demonstrate financial need. *Application Process: Applicants should submit a completed application along with transcripts, a dissertation abstract or description of planned internship, a list of publications (if available), two letters of recommendation, and a copy of certificate of military service or discharge papers (if applicable). Visit the association's Web site to download an application. *Amount: $3,000. *Deadline: February 1.

Asian American Journalists Association (AAJA)

Attn: Brandon Sugiyama, Student Programs Coordinator
1182 Market Street, Suite 320
San Francisco, CA 94102
415-346-2051, ext. 102
brandons@aaja.org
http://www.aaja.org/programs/for_students/scholarships

Scholarship Name: AAJA/Cox Foundation Scholarship. *Academic Area: Broadcasting, journalism, photojournalism. *Age Group: Undergraduate students, graduate students. *Eligibility: Applicants must be full-time students with a commitment to the field of journalism, possess sensitivity to Asian American and Pacific Islander issues as demonstrated

by community involvement, have journalistic ability, and demonstrate financial need. High school seniors are also eligible to apply for this scholarship. *Application Process: Applicants should submit a completed application, resume, official transcripts (two copies), a 500-word personal essay, and work samples (which will not be returned). Three copies of the completed packet are required. Visit the association's Web site to download an application. *Amount: Up to $2,500. *Deadline: March 10.

Asian American Journalists Association (AAJA)

Attn: Brandon Sugiyama, Student Programs Coordinator
1182 Market Street, Suite 320
San Francisco, CA 94102
415-346-2051, ext. 102
brandons@aaja.org
http://www.aaja.org/programs/for_students/scholarships/

Scholarship Name: AAJA/S.I. Newhouse Foundation Scholarships. *Academic Area: Journalism. *Age Group: Undergraduate students, graduate students. *Eligibility: Applicants must be full-time students with a commitment to the field of journalism, possess sensitivity to Asian American and Pacific Islander issues as demonstrated by community involvement, have journalistic ability, and demonstrate financial need. While the scholarship is open to all students, the AAJA especially encourages applicants from historically underrepresented Asian Pacific American groups, including Vietnamese, Cambodians, Hmong, and other Southeast Asians, South Asians, and Pacific Islanders. S.I. Newhouse scholarship winners will be eligible for summer internships with a Newhouse publication. High school seniors are also eligible to apply for this scholarship. *Application Process: Applicants should submit a completed application, resume, official transcripts (and two copies), a 500-word personal essay, and work samples (which will not be returned). Three copies of the completed packet are required. Visit the association's Web site to download an application. *Amount: Up to $5,000. *Deadline: March 10.

Asian American Journalists Association (AAJA)

Attn: Brandon Sugiyama, Student Programs Coordinator
1182 Market Street, Suite 320
San Francisco, CA 94102
415-346-2051, ext. 102
brandons@aaja.org
http://www.aaja.org/programs/for_students/scholarships/

Scholarship Name: Mary Moy Quan Ing Memorial Scholarship. *Academic Area: Journalism. *Age Group: Undergraduate students. *Eligibility: Applicants must be high school seniors who plan on being full-time students, have a commitment to the field of journalism, possess sensitivity to Asian American and Pacific Islander issues as demonstrated by community involvement, have journalistic ability, and demonstrate financial need. *Application Process: Applicants should submit a completed application, resume, official transcripts (two copies), a 500-word personal essay, and work samples (which will not be returned). Three copies of the completed packet are required. Visit the association's Web site to download an application. *Amount: $2,000. *Deadline: March 10.

Asian American Journalists Association (AAJA)
Attn: Brandon Sugiyama, Student Programs Coordinator
1182 Market Street, Suite 320
San Francisco, CA 94102
415-346-2051, ext. 102
brandons@aaja.org
http://www.aaja.org/programs/for_students/scholarships
Scholarship Name: Minoru Yasui Memorial Scholarship. *Academic Area: Broadcasting, journalism. *Age Group: Undergraduate students, graduate students. *Eligibility: Applicants must be full-time male students with a commitment to the field of journalism, possess sensitivity to Asian American and Pacific Islander issues as demonstrated by community involvement, have journalistic ability, and demonstrate financial need. This scholarship is awarded to a promising male Asian American broadcaster. High school seniors are also eligible to apply. *Application Process: Applicants should submit a completed application, resume, official transcripts (two copies), a 500-word personal essay, and work samples (which will not be returned). Three copies of the completed packet are required. Visit the association's Web site to download an application. *Amount: $2,000. *Deadline: March 10.

Asian American Writers' Workshop
16 West 32nd Street, Suite 10A
New York, NY 10001
212-494-0061
desk@aaww.org
http://www.aaww.org/aaww_awards.html
Award Name: Asian American Literary Award. *Academic Area: English/literature, writing. *Age Group: Open. *Eligibility: Applicants must demonstrate expertise in a literary genre and/or experience in academic environments relevant to Asian American literature. Applicants must be of Asian descent living in the United States. The work must have been published originally in English during the calendar year preceding the award year. Note: Self-published works will not be considered. *Application Process: Applicants should submit a completed application along with four copies of the work and a $100 entry fee. Visit the workshop's Web site to download an application. *Amount: Awards vary. *Deadline: April 22.

Asian Cultural Council (ACC)
437 Madison Avenue, 37th Floor
New York, NY 10022-7001
212-812-4300
acc@accny.org
http://www.asianculturalcouncil.org/programs.html
Fellowship Name: ACC Fellowships. *Academic Area: Performing arts (open), visual arts (open). *Age Group: Open. *Eligibility: Applicants must be Asian, wishing to pursue research, training, and a creative program in the United States. *Application Process: Applicants should send a brief description of the activity for which assistance is being sought to the council. If the proposed activity falls within the ACC's guidelines, application materials requesting more detailed information will be provided by the ACC, and applicants will be informed as to when their proposals can be presented to the trustees of the council for formal review. Visit the council's Web site for further information. *Amount: Awards vary. *Deadline: February 1.

Asian Cultural Council (ACC)
437 Madison Avenue, 37th Floor
New York, NY 10022-7001
212-812-4300
acc@accny.org
http://www.asianculturalcouncil.org/programs.html
Grant Name: Japan-United States Arts Program. *Academic Area: Performing arts (open), visual arts (open). *Age Group: Open. *Eligibility: Applicants must have the desire to study and understand Japanese art and culture. Japanese artists, scholars, and specialists travel to the United States for research, observation, and creative work, and

their American counterparts visit Japan for similar purposes. *Application Process: Interested candidates should contact the council for further application information. *Amount: Awards vary. *Deadline: Contact the council for deadline information.

Asian Cultural Council (ACC)

437 Madison Avenue, 37th Floor
New York, NY 10022-7001
212-812-4300
acc@accny.org
http://www.asianculturalcouncil.org/programs.html
Award Name: John D. Rockefeller 3rd Award of the Asian Cultural Council. *Academic Area: Performing arts (open), visual arts (open). *Age Group: Open. *Eligibility: Candidates, from Asia or the United States, must have made significant contributions to the international understanding, practice, or study of the visual or performing arts of Asia. *Application Process: Candidates must be nominated by artists, scholars, and others professionally involved in Asian art and culture. Contact the council for further information about nominating a candidate. *Amount: $30,000. *Deadline: Contact the council for deadline information.

Aspen Institute

Attn: John Russell, Program Coordinator
One Dupont Circle, Suite 700
Washington, DC 20036
202-736-5800
hearstinfo@aspeninstitute.org
http://www.nonprofitresearch.org/newsletter1530/
   newsletter.htm
Fellowship Name: William Randolph Hearst Endowed Fellowship for Minority Students. *Academic Area: Open. *Age Group: Undergraduate students, graduate students. *Eligibility: Applicants must be U.S. citizens who are members of a traditionally underrepresented minority group. They should also demonstrate academic achievement, excellent communication skills, and financial need. Applicants with a background in the social sciences or humanities are preferred. Applicants must want to participate in an internship that will introduce them to all aspects of working for a nonprofit organization. *Application Process: Applicants should submit a letter of interest (with dates of availability), a resume, transcript, a financial aid letter stating financial need, and two letters of reference. Visit the organization's Web site to learn more about the internship experience. *Amount:

$2,500 to $5,000. *Deadline: March 15, July 15, and December 15.

Association for Women Geoscientists (AWG)

Attn: Kim Begay-Jackson
Minority Scholarship
PO Box 30645
Lincoln, NE 68503-0645
651-426-3316
minorityscholarship@awg.org
http://www.awg.org/eas/scholarships.html
Scholarship Name: AWG Minority Scholarship. *Academic Area: Geosciences. *Age Group: Undergraduate students. *Eligibility: Applicants must be African American, Hispanic American, or Native American women pursuing or planning to pursue a degree in geology, geophysics, geochemistry, hydrology, meteorology, physical oceanography, planetary geology, or earth science education at an accredited college or university. High school seniors are also eligible to apply for this scholarship. *Application Process: Applicants must submit a completed application, a statement of their academic and career goals, two letters of recommendation, high school and college transcripts, and SAT or ACT scores. Visit the association's Web site to download an application as well as to find information about additional scholarships in geosciences available in select regional areas. *Amount: $5,000. *Deadline: May 15.

Association of American Geographers (AAG)

AAG Dissertation Research Grants
Attn: Ehsan M. Khater, Office Coordinator
1710 16th Street, NW
Washington, DC 20009-3198
202-234-1450
ekhater@aag.org
http://www.aag.org/grantsawards/dissertationresearch.
   html
Grant Name: Paul Vouras Fund. *Academic Area: Geography. *Age Group: Graduate students. *Eligibility: Applicants should demonstrate high standards of scholarship and propose relevant doctoral dissertation research in geography. Preference is given to applicants who are minorities. Applicants must also be AAG members for at least one year at the time of application. *Application Process: Applicants should submit a completed application along with a proposal describing the problem they hope to solve, outlining the methods

and data they intend to use, and summarizing the results they expect. Budget items should be included within the body of the proposal. Visit the association's Web site to download an application. *Amount: $500. *Deadline: December 31.

Association of Black Cardiologists Inc.
Attn: Ms. Meredith Carter, PR and Special Events Manager
6849-B2 Peachtree Dunwoody Road, NE
Atlanta, GA 30328
678-302-4222, 800-753-9222
mcarter@abcardio.org
http://www.abcardio.org/awards.htm
Scholarship Name: Dr. Richard Allen Williams Scholarship. *Academic Area: Medicine (physicians). *Age Group: Medical Students. *Eligibility: Applicants must be African American or other racial minority who are enrolled in a cardiology program and who exhibit exceptional leadership skills. Applicants must also demonstrate a commitment to cardiology research and promotion of health in African American communities. *Application Process: Applicants should submit a letter of interest along with official medical school transcripts, two letters of recommendation from professors, a curriculum vitae, and a photograph. Visit the association's Web site to download a brochure about Dr. Richard Allen Williams and additional scholarship details. *Amount: Contact the association for details. *Deadline: May 13.

Association of Black Cardiologists Inc.
6849-B2 Peachtree Dunwoody Road, NE
Atlanta, GA 30328
678-302-4222, 800-753-9222
abcardio@abcardio.org
http://www.abcardio.org/awards.htm
Fellowship Name: Fourth Year Cardiology Subspecialty Fellowship Award. *Academic Area: Medicine (physicians). *Age Group: Medical Students. *Eligibility: Applicants must be African American or other racial minorities who are enrolled in a cardiology program with a electrophysiology or interventional subspecialty emphasis. They also must be nearing their fourth year of study, as this award pays for the fourth year of study in such a program. *Application Process: Applicants should contact the association to receive an official application and additional information. Visit the association's Web site for further updates. *Amount: Fully funded fourth

year of study. *Deadline: Contact the association for deadline information.

Association of Black Women Historians
Attn: Wanda A. Hendricks, Ph.D., National Director
c/o University of South Carolina
204 Flinn Hall
Columbia, SC 29208
803-777-4007
nationaldirector@abwh.org
http://www.abwh.org
Scholarship Name: Drusilla Dunjee Houston Memorial Scholarship Award. *Academic Area: History. *Age Group: Graduate students. *Eligibility: Candidates must be African-American female graduate students in history. *Application Process: Candidates must be nominated for the award. *Amount: $300. *Deadline: August 1.

Association of Black Women Historians
Attn: Wanda A. Hendricks, Ph.D., National Director
c/o University of South Carolina
204 Flinn Hall
Columbia, SC 29208
803-777-4007
nationaldirector@abwh.org
http://www.abwh.org
Award Name: The Lillie M. Newton Hornsby Memorial Award is given for exemplary historical research. *Academic Area: History. *Age Group: Undergraduate students. *Eligibility: African-American females with accomplishments in historical research may be nominated. Applicants must be either at the end of their junior year or beginning their senior year. *Application Process: Candidates must be nominated for the award. Contact the association for more information. *Amount: $250. *Deadline: September 1.

Association of Latino Professionals in Finance and Accounting (ALPFA)
c/o Hispanic Scholarship Fund
510 West Sixth Street, Suite 400
Los Angeles, CA 90014
800-644-4223
HCF-Info@hispanicfund.org
http://www.alpfa.org/index.cfm?fuseaction=Page.viewPage&pageId=354
Scholarship Name: The association, in conjunction with the Hispanic College Fund, offers the ALPFA Scholarship Program. *Academic Area: Accounting,

finance, information technology. *Age Group: Undergraduate students, graduate students. *Eligibility: Hispanic students who plan to enroll as full-time undergraduate or graduate students in an accounting, finance, information technology, or a related field are eligible to apply. Applicants must be also be U.S. citizens and have a minimum cumulative 3.0 GPA on a 4.0 scale. *Application Process: Visit the Hispanic Scholarship Fund's Web site to download an application. *Amount: Awards range from $1,000 to $5,000. *Deadline: March 31.

Association of Latino Professionals in Finance and Accounting (ALPFA)

510 West Sixth Street, Suite 400
Los Angeles, CA 90014
213-243-0004
scholarships@national.alpha.org
http://www.alpfa.org/index.cfm?fuseaction=Page. viewPage&pageId=354
Fellowship Name: ALPFA/Babson Fellowship. *Academic Area: Business. *Age Group: Graduate students. *Eligibility: Applicants must be ALPFA members who are pursuing or planning to pursue a full-time MBA at Babson College in Massachusetts. Candidates in both one- and two-year programs of study are eligible. *Application Process: Applicants should request current application information from the ALPFA or visit Babson College's scholarship Web page (http://www3.babson.edu/MBA/finaid/Scholarships-and-fellowships.cfm) for information about application procedures. *Amount: $15,000 to full tuition. *Deadline: April 15.

Association of Latino Professionals in Finance and Accounting (ALPFA)/Bentley McCallum Graduate School of Business

Bentley McCallum Graduate School of Business
Office of Financial Assistance
175 Forest Street
Waltham, MA 02452
781-891-3168
gradaid@bentley.edu
http://www.bentley.edu/financial-aid/graduate_students.cfm
Scholarship Name: Bentley Graduate Merit Scholarship. *Academic Area: Business. *Age Group: Graduate students. *Eligibility: Applicants must be active ALPFA members who are accepted into the Bentley McCallum Graduate School of Business's MBA or MS program.

Applicants also must be pursuing full-time graduate study. *Application Process: Applicants should first apply and be accepted into one of these programs. For further information about applying for the scholarship, contact the scholarship coordinator at Bentley College directly. *Amount: Contact the college for scholarship amounts. *Deadline: Contact the college for details.

Association of Latino Professionals in Finance and Accounting (ALPFA)/Goldman Sachs MBA Fellowship

Attn: Martin Rodriguez
Goldman Sachs
Human Capital Management
Diversity Recruiting
180 Maiden Lane, 23rd Floor
New York, NY 10038
212-855-6184
martin.rodriguez@gs.com
http://www.alpfa.org/index.cfm?fuseaction=Page. viewPage&pageId=354
Fellowship Name: Goldman Sachs MBA Fellowship. *Academic Area: Business. *Age Group: Graduate students. *Eligibility: Applicants must be ALPFA members who are accepted into one of 10 graduate schools of business (visit the ALPFA's Web site for a list of participating schools). They also must be African American, Hispanic American, or Native American and agree to become full-time employees at Goldman Sachs after graduation. *Application Process: Applicants should visit the ALPFA's Web site for further information about applying for admission and for scholarship application forms and procedures. *Amount: Full-paid tuition, plus stipend. *Deadline: April 16.

Association on American Indian Affairs (AAIA)

Attn: Lisa Wyzlic, Director of Scholarship Programs
966 Hungerford Drive, Suite 12-B
Rockville, MD 20850
240-314-7155
lw.aaia@verizon.net
http://www.indian-affairs.org
Scholarship Name: This association offers a variety of scholarships for Native Americans. *Academic Area: Open. *Age Group: Undergraduate students, graduate students. *Eligibility: Applicants must be from the continental United States or Alaska, and must show proof of being at least one-quarter American Indian and proof of tribal enrollment. Applicants also must be full-time students, show financial

need, and demonstrate academic achievement. *Application Process: Applicants should submit a completed application form and packet including a financial need analysis form with signature from their financial aid office, a certificate of Indian blood and proof of tribal enrollment, an essay addressing their educational goals and life experiences (not to exceed three pages), two letters of recommendation, most recent transcripts, and current financial aid award letter. Visit the association's Web site at the end of March for further information and to download an application. *Amount: Awards vary. *Deadline: August 1. Do not mail applications prior to May 1.

Association on American Indian Affairs (AAIA)
Attn: Lisa Wyzlic, Director of Scholarship Programs
966 Hungerford Drive, Suite 12-B
Rockville, MD 20850
240-314-7155
lw.aaia@verizon.net
http://www.indian-affairs.org
Fellowship Name: Florence Young Memorial Fellowship. *Academic Area: Performing arts (open), visual arts (open). *Age Group: Graduate students. *Eligibility: Applicants should have certification proving at least one-quarter Indian blood and demonstrate financial need and academic merit. *Application Process: Applicants should submit an application along with a copy of transcripts, a current financial aid award letter, two recommendations, an essay detailing their educational goals, a certificate proving Native American heritage, and a financial needs analysis. Visit the association's Web site to download an application. *Amount: $5,000. *Deadline: August 1.

Association on American Indian Affairs (AAIA)
Attn: Lisa Wyzlic, Director of Scholarship Programs
966 Hungerford Drive, Suite 12-B
Rockville, MD 20850
240-314-7155
lw.aaia@verizon.net
http://www.indian-affairs.org
Fellowship Name: Sequoyah Graduate Fellowship. *Academic Area: Open. *Age Group: Graduate students. *Eligibility: Applicants should have certification proving at least one-quarter Indian blood and demonstrate financial need and academic merit. *Application Process: Applicants should submit an application along with a copy of transcripts, a current financial aid award letter, two recommendations, an

essay detailing their educational goals, a certificate proving Native American heritage, and a financial needs analysis. Visit the association's Web site to download an application. *Amount: $1,500. *Deadline: August 1.

Bell Labs
c/o Lucent Technologies Foundation
600 Mountain Avenue, Room 6F4
Murray Hill, NJ 07974
908-582-7906
foundation@lucent.com
http://www.lucent.com/news/foundation/blgrfp
Fellowship Name: The Bell Labs Graduate Research Fellowship Program seeks to increase the number of women and minorities pursuing Ph.D.'s in science, math, engineering, and technology. Fellows will be exposed to a variety of research environments by participating in ongoing research activities at Bell Laboratories. *Academic Area: Communications science, computer science, engineering (computer), engineering (electrical), engineering (open), engineering (mechanical), information science, mathematics, physics, statistics. *Age Group: Graduate students. *Eligibility: Women and/or minorities (U.S. citizens or permanent residents) pursuing full-time doctoral studies in chemical engineering, chemistry, communications science, computer science, computer engineering, electrical engineering, information science, materials science, mathematics, mechanical engineering, operations research, physics, or statistics are eligible to apply. Candidates are selected based on their academic achievement and their potential as research scientists. The fellowship is geared toward graduating college seniors, but is also open to first-year graduate students. *Application Procedure: Contact the foundation for guidelines. *Amount: An annual stipend of $17,000, a $250 book allotment per semester, and $1,000 annually for travel expenses to conferences. (Renewable for up to four years.) *Deadline: Contact the foundation for more information.

Biophysical Society
Attn: Yvonne Cissel, Committee & Meeting Manager
9650 Rockville Pike
Bethesda, MD 20814
301-634-7114
ycissel@biophysics.org
http://www.biophysics.org/NSBPApplication2005Info.pdf
Scholarship Name: Herman R. Branson Summer Mini

Course in Biophysics Scholarship. *Academic Area: Biophysics. *Age Group: Undergraduate students. *Eligibility: Applicants must belong to an ethnic/racial minority and must have completed two semesters of calculus-based introductory general physics. *Application Process: Applicants must submit a completed application, a copy of their college transcripts, one letter of recommendation from a faculty member, and a 750-word essay detailing their career aspirations. Visit the association's Web site to download an application. *Amount: Full tuition, room and board, and a grant toward travel and living expenses for the five-week course. *Deadline: March 7

Black Caucus of the American Library Association Inc.
Attn: Michael Walker
Attn: E. J. Josey Scholarship Committee
PO Box 1738, Hampton, VA 23669
mcwalker@vsu.edu
http://www.bcala.org/awards/josey.htm
Scholarship Name: E. J. Josey Scholarship Award. *Academic Area: Library sciences. *Age Group: Graduate students. *Eligibility: Applicants must be African American students enrolled in, or accepted to, ALA-accredited programs. Applicants also must be citizens of the United States or Canada. *Application Process: Applicants must submit, via e-mail, a cover letter providing their name, address, phone number, and graduate program; the name of their school; and their anticipated date of graduation. Applicants must also submit an essay of 1,000 to 1,200 words discussing the current theme chosen for each year. Essays will be judged on the basis of good argument development and critical analysis, clear language, conciseness, and creativity. Visit the organization's Web site for information about current essay topics. *Amount: $2,000. *Deadline: January 13.

Black Women Lawyers Association (BWLA) of Greater Chicago Inc.
Attn: BWLA Scholarship Committee
321 South Plymouth Court, Suite 600
Chicago, IL 60604
312-554-2088
scholarship@bwla.org
http://www.bwla.org
Scholarship Name: Black Women Lawyers Association of Greater Chicago Scholarship. *Academic Area: Law. *Age Group: Law students. *Eligibility: Applicants must be enrolled in an accredited law school in Illinois

and be in good academic standing. *Application Process: Applicants must submit one official law school transcript, one letter of recommendation from a law school professor or staff member, a resume detailing their contact information and community service involvement, and a 1,000-word essay on a specific topic. Visit the association's Web site for further information on current essay questions. *Amount: Awards vary. *Deadline: February 17.

Black Women Lawyers Association of Los Angeles
Attn: Karen E. Pointer
Attn: Scholarship Selection Committee
PO Box 8179
Los Angeles, CA 90008
213-538-0137
kpointer@lpclawyers.com
http://www.blackwomenlawyersla.org
Scholarship Name: Black Women Lawyers Association of Los Angeles Scholarship. *Academic Area: Law. *Age Group: Law students. *Eligibility: Applicants must be second- or third-year full-time law students, fourth-year night-program law students in attendance at an accredited law school, or have passed the California first year student's examination. They must demonstrate financial need, be involved in community service projects, and exhibit strong academic achievement as well as legal writing ability. *Application Process: Applicants must submit a completed application along with required documents. Visit the association's Web site to request an application and instructions. *Amount: Awards vary. *Deadline: April 9.

Black Women Lawyers Association of New Jersey
PO Box 22524
Trenton, NJ 08607
abwlnj@yahoo.com
http://www.abwlnj.org
Scholarship Name: Black Women Lawyers Association of New Jersey Scholarship. *Academic Area: Law. *Age Group: Law students. *Eligibility: Contact the association for eligibility requirements. *Application Process: Contact the association for information on current scholarship opportunities. *Amount: Awards vary. *Deadline: Deadlines vary.

Brown Foundation for Educational Equity, Excellence and Research
Scholarship Program
PO Box 4862

Topeka, KS 66604
785-235-3939
BrownFound@juno.com
http://brownvboard.org/foundation/scholarships/
brownscholar
Scholarship Name: Brown Foundation Academic
Scholarship. *Academic Area: Education. *Age
Group: Undergraduate students. *Eligibility:
Applicants must be entering their junior year of
college and enrolled in an accredited teacher
education program at least half time. They must
also demonstrate academic excellence (minimum
GPA of 3.0), commitment to community, and
career goals that are in sync with the Brown
Foundation's mission. *Application Process:
Applicants should submit a completed
application along with essays and two completed
recommendation forms. Visit the foundation's
Web site to download an application and
recommendation forms. *Amount: $1,000 per year
for two years. *Deadline: March 30.

**Brown Foundation for Educational Equity, Excellence
and Research**
Scholarship Program
PO Box 4862
Topeka, KS 66604
785-235-3939
BrownFound@juno.com
http://brownvboard.org/foundation/scholarships/
toddbook
Award Name: Lucinda Todd Book Awards. *Academic
Area: Education. *Age Group: Undergraduate
students. *Eligibility: Applicants must be entering
their freshman year of college, demonstrate a
commitment to teacher education, be accepted
into a college or university with an accredited
teacher education program, and have maintained
at least a 3.0 GPA during high school. *Application
Process: Applicants should submit a completed
application along with essays and two completed
recommendation forms. Visit the foundation's
Web site to download an application and
recommendation forms. *Amount: $300 to be
applied to the purchase of books. *Deadline:
March 30.

**California Adolescent Nutrition and Fitness Program
(CANFit)**
CANfit Program Scholarships

2140 Shattuck Avenue, Suite 610
Berkeley, CA 94704
510-644-1533
info@confit.org
http://www.canfit.org/scholarships.html
Scholarship Name: CANFit Graduate Scholarship.
*Academic Area: Culinary arts, education, public
health, wellness. *Age Group: Graduate students.
*Eligibility: Applicants must be of African American,
American Indian/Alaska Native, Asian American,
Pacific Islander or Latino/Hispanic descent and
enrolled in a graduate degree program (master's
or doctoral) in California, in the field of culinary
arts, nutrition, physical education, or public health
nutrition. Students in American Dietetic Association-
approved preprofessional practice programs in
California are also eligible. Applicants must have
completed at least 12 college credit hours with at
least a 3.0 GPA. *Application Process: Applicants
should submit a completed application along with
supporting materials. Applications are available for
download from the organization's Web site after
January 1. *Amount: Awards vary. *Deadline:
March 31.

**California Adolescent Nutrition and Fitness Program
(CANFit)**
CANfit Program Scholarships
2140 Shattuck Avenue, Suite 610
Berkeley, CA 94704
510-644-1533
info@confit.org
http://www.canfit.org/scholarships.html
Scholarship Name: CANFit Undergraduate
Scholarship. *Academic Area: Culinary arts,
education, public health, wellness. *Age Group:
Undergraduate students. *Eligibility: Applicants
must be of African American, American Indian/
Alaska Native, Asian American, Pacific Islander
or Latino/Hispanic descent and enrolled in a
bachelor's degree program in California in the field
of culinary arts, nutrition, or physical education.
Applicants must have completed at least 50
college credit hours with at least a 2.5 GPA (except
for culinary arts students). *Application Process:
Applicants should submit a completed application
along with supporting materials. Applications are
available for download from the organization's
Web site after January 1. *Amount: Awards vary.
*Deadline: March 31.

California Chicano News Media Association (CCNMA)

CCNMA Inland Chapter Scholarships
PO Box 20562
Riverside, CA 92516-0562
951-688-6391
ccnmainland@hotmail.com
http://www.ccnma.org
Scholarship Name: CCNMA Inland Chapter Scholarship. *Academic Area: Journalism. *Age Group: Undergraduate students. *Eligibility: Applicants must be students of Latino heritage living in Riverside or San Bernardino counties in California who are interested in journalism or communications careers. They also must be high school seniors or college students who will be attending college in the fall. *Application Process: Applicants must submit a completed application form, an essay, two letters of recommendation, official transcripts, five to seven journalistic writing samples, and proof of enrollment. Visit the CCNMA Web site to download an application. *Amount: $250 to $2,000. *Deadline: February 17.

California Librarians Black Caucus (CLBC)

Scholarship Award
Northern Chapter
3226 Hood Street
Oakland, CA 94605
scholarship@clbc.org
http://www.clbc.org/scholar.html
Scholarship Name: Eunice J. H. Parker Scholarship Award. *Academic Area: Library sciences. *Age Group: Graduate students. *Eligibility: Applicants must be African American students pursuing graduate or post-graduate degrees in library and information studies. They also must be members of the CLBC. *Application Process: Applicants must submit a completed application, proof of enrollment, and an essay. Visit the CLBC Web site for application details. *Amount: Varies. *Deadline: May 31.

California Librarians Black Caucus (CLBC)

Attn: Stephanie Brasley
University of California-Los Angeles
College Library, Box 951450
Los Angeles, CA 90095-1450
scholarship@clbc.org
http://www.clbc.org/scholar.html
Scholarship Name: Louise Jane Moses-Agnes Davis Memorial Scholarship. *Academic Area: Library sciences. *Age Group: Graduate students. *Eligibility:

Applicants must be African American students pursuing a graduate degree in library information science at an accredited college/university in California. They also must be California residents. *Application Process: Applicants must submit a completed application and personal statement. Visit the CLBC Web site to download an application. *Amount: Varies. *Deadline: October 21.

California Library Association (CLA)

717 20th Street, Suite 200
Sacramento, CA 95814
916-447-8541
info@cla-net.org
http://www.cla-net.org/awards/ednayelland.php
Scholarship Name: CLA Scholarship for Minority Students in Memory of Edna Yelland. *Academic Area: Library sciences. *Age Group: Graduate students. *Eligibility: Applicants must belong to an underrepresented minority group, be U.S. citizens or permanent residents as well as residents of the state of California at the time of application, and be enrolled or accepted into an accredited graduate American Library Association-accredited program in the state of California. They also must be able to demonstrate financial need. *Application Process: Applicants should submit a completed application along with two references, a one-page essay, a list of alternate scholarships and/or aid sources received, and a statement of financial circumstances. Visit the association's Web site to download an application. *Amount: $2,500. *Deadline: May 31.

California School Library Association

Attn: Leadership for Diversity Committee
1001 26th Street
Sacramento, CA 95816
916-447-2684
csla@pacbell.net
http://schoollibrary.org/awa/scholarships.htm
Scholarship Name: Leadership for Diversity Scholarship. *Academic Area: Library sciences. *Age Group: Undergraduate students, graduate students. *Eligibility: Applicants must be minority students enrolled in a college or university library media teacher credential program that has been accredited by the Commission on Teacher Credentialing. Applicants must also intend to work for at least three years as a library media teacher in California upon completion of the program. Financial need will

be taken into consideration. *Application Process: Applicants must submit a completed application, a personal statement, two letters of recommendation, and transcripts. Visit the association's Web site to download an application. *Amount: Contact the association for details.. *Deadline: June 30.

California Teachers Association (CTA)
Attn: CTA Scholarship Committee
Attn: Human Rights Department
PO Box 921
Burlingame, CA 94011
650-697-1400
http://www.cta.org/InsideCTA/ScholarshipsWorkshops/ScholarshipsWorkshops.htm
Scholarship Name: Martin Luther King Jr. Memorial Scholarship. *Academic Area: Education. *Age Group: Undergraduate students. *Eligibility: Applicants must be ethnic minorities pursuing degrees in public education. Applicants must be active members of the CTA, dependent children of an active, retired, or deceased CTA member, or a Student CTA member. *Application Process: Applicants must submit a completed application and proof of registration in an accredited institution of higher learning. Application will be made available on the association's Web site in January of each year. *Amount: Varies. *Deadline: Contact the association for more information.

Catching the Dream Inc.
Attn: Scholarship Affairs Office
8200 Mountain Road, NE, Suite 203
Albuquerque, NM 87110
505-262-2351, ext. 116
NScholarsh@aol.com
http://www.catchingthedream.org/wst_page4.html
Scholarship Name: MESBEC Scholarship Program. *Academic Area: Business, computer science, education, engineering (open), mathematics, and science. *Age Group: Undergraduate students, graduate students. *Eligibility: Applicants must be one-quarter Native American, enrolled in a federally recognized, state-recognized, or terminated tribe, and plan to attend or be currently attending school full time. They should also have high ACT or SAT scores, excellent grades, work experience, leadership skills, and a commitment to their Native American community. High school seniors are also eligible to apply for this scholarship. *Application Process: Applicants must submit proof of high school completion, college admission, and tribal

enrollment; an essay detailing their career plans; and a completed application, which is available for download at the organization's Web site. *Amount: $500 to $5,000. *Deadline: Varies.

Catching the Dream Inc.
Attn: Scholarship Affairs Office
8200 Mountain Road, NE, Suite 203
Albuquerque, NM 87110
505-262-2351, ext. 116
NScholarsh@aol.com
http://www.catchingthedream.org/wst_page4.html
Scholarship Name: The Native American Leadership Education Scholarship Program is open to Native Americans who are paraprofessionals in Indian schools. *Academic Area: Counseling, education. *Age Group: Undergraduate students, graduate students. *Eligibility: Applicants must be one-quarter Native American, enrolled in a federally recognized, state-recognized, or terminated tribe, and plan to attend or be currently attending school full time. They should also have high ACT or SAT scores, excellent grades, work experience, leadership skills, and a commitment to their Native American community. High school seniors are also eligible to apply for this scholarship. *Application Process: Applicants must submit proof of high school completion, college admission, and tribal enrollment; an essay detailing their career plans; and a completed application, which is available for download at the organization's Web site. *Amount: $500 to $5,000. *Deadline: Varies.

Catching the Dream Inc.
Attn: Scholarship Affairs Office
8200 Mountain Road, NE, Suite 203
Albuquerque, NM 87110
505-262-2351, ext. 116
NScholarsh@aol.com
http://www.catchingthedream.org/wst_page4.html
Scholarship Name: Tribal Business Management Scholarship. *Academic Area: Banking, business, economics, finance, management. *Age Group: Undergraduate students, graduate students. *Eligibility: Applicants must be one-quarter Native American, enrolled in a federally recognized, state-recognized, or terminated tribe, and plan to attend or be currently attending school full time. They should also have high ACT or SAT scores, excellent grades, work experience, leadership skills, and plan to work in economic development for tribes. High school

seniors are also eligible to apply for this scholarship. *Application Process: Applicants must submit proof of high school completion, college admission, and tribal enrollment; an essay detailing their career plans; and a completed application, which is available for download at the organization's Web site. *Amount: $500 to $5,000. *Deadline: Varies.

Center for the Advancement of Hispanics in Science and Engineering Education
8100 Corporate Drive, Suite 401
Landover, MD 20785
301-918-1014
yep@cahsee.org
http://www.cahsee.org/programs/yep.php
Fellowship Name: Young Educators Program Fellowship. *Academic Area: Engineering (open), mathematics, science, technology. *Age Group: Undergraduate students, graduate students. *Eligibility: Applicants must be college seniors or graduate students majoring in a program focused on science, technology, math, or engineering. Applicants should be willing and able to dedicate an entire summer to the fellowship in Washington, D.C., as well as demonstrate a desire to gain teaching experience. Two weeks will be spent in intense seminar training, five weeks in the classroom teaching Hispanic high school students, and one week developing a writing project summarizing the experience. *Application Process: Applicants should submit a completed application along with a resume. Visit the center's Web site for further information about the program and to download an application. *Amount: $2,750 to $3,000, plus housing and air-travel expenses paid. *Deadline: Contact the center for deadline information.

Chi Eta Phi Sorority Inc.
3029 13th Street, NW
Washington, DC 20009
202-232-3858
chietaphi@erols.com
http://www.chietaphi.com/scholar.html#ewel
Scholarship Name: Aliene Carrington Ewell Scholarship. *Academic Area: Nursing (open). *Age Group: Undergraduate students. *Eligibility: Applicants must currently be pursuing a nursing degree and demonstrate scholastic ability, financial need, and leadership potential. Although a large number of sorority members are African American, this scholarship is open to students of all races.

*Application Process: Contact the sorority via e-mail for information on application availability. *Amount: Awards vary. *Deadline: Deadlines vary.

Chi Eta Phi Sorority Inc.
3029 13th Street, NW
Washington, DC 20009
202-232-3858
chietaphi@erols.com
http://www.chietaphi.com
Scholarship Name: Mabel Keaton Staupers National Scholarship Award. *Academic Area: Nursing (open). *Age Group: Undergraduate students, graduate students. *Eligibility: Applicants must be pursuing a baccalaureate, master's, or doctoral degree in nursing. Applicants should have contributed to the recruitment and retention of minorities into nursing, the advancement of minority nurses in education and nursing, and have demonstrated leadership skills. Applicants also must be members of both Chi Eta Phi and the American Nurses Association. *Application Process: Contact the sorority via e-mail for information on application availability. *Amount: Awards vary. *Deadline: Deadlines vary.

Chinese American Medical Society (CAMS)
Attn: David Y. Wang, M.D.
Attn: Chairman, CAMS Scholarship Committee
170 East 87th Street, Apartment E9A
New York, NY 10128
212-722-4228
dwang007@yahoo.com
http://www.camsociety.org
Scholarship Name: CAMS Scholarships. *Academic Area: Medicine (dentistry), medicine (open), science. *Age Group: Undergraduate students, graduate students. *Eligibility: Applicants must demonstrate either academic excellence and/or financial need. *Application Process: Applicants should submit a completed application form along with a letter from the dean of students verifying good standing, two letters of recommendation, transcripts, a personal statement, and current curriculum vitae. Since some scholarships are allotted for merit and others financial hardship, those with financial hardship should also submit a personal letter stating these hardships as well as a letter from the dean or a teacher corroborating this statement. Visit the organization's Web site to download an application. *Amount: Inquire by e-mail for information about the awards. *Deadline: March 31.

Colorado Commission on Higher Education

1380 Lawrence Street, Suite 1200
Denver, CO 80204
303-866-2723
CCHE@state.co.us
http://www.state.co.us/sfa.html
Grant Name: Colorado Diversity Grant. *Academic Area: Open. *Age Group: Undergraduate students. *Eligibility: Applicants must be from an underrepresented minority group, residents of Colorado, planning to attend or currently attending select postsecondary institutions in Colorado, and demonstrate financial need. *Application Process: Contact the commission for information on application requirements. *Amount: Varies. *Deadline: Varies.

Colorado Society of CPAs Educational Foundation

Attn: Gena Mantz, Scholarship Coordinator
7979 East Tufts Avenue, Suite 1000
Denver, CO 80237-2845
303-773-2877, 800-523-9082
gmantz@cocpa.org
http://www.cocpa.org/student_faculty/scholarships.asp
Scholarship Name: Ethnic Diversity College Scholarship. *Academic Area: Accounting. *Age Group: Undergraduate students, graduate students. *Eligibility: Applicants must be declared accounting majors who are attending a Colorado college or university and who have completed at least eight semester hours of accounting courses (with at least one at an intermediate level). They must also demonstrate academic achievement by maintaining at least a 3.0 GPA and be of African American, Hispanic, Asian American, Native American, or Pacific Islander descent. *Application Process: Applicants should submit a completed application along with transcripts. Visit the society's Web site to download an application. *Amount: $1,000. *Deadline: June 30.

Colorado Society of CPAs Educational Foundation

Attn: Gena Mantz, Scholarship Coordinator
7979 East Tufts Avenue, Suite 1000
Denver, CO 80237-2845
303-773-2877
gmantz@cocpa.org
http://www.cocpa.org/student_faculty/scholarships.asp
Scholarship Name: Ethnic Diversity High School Scholarship. *Academic Area: Accounting. *Age Group: Undergraduate students. *Eligibility: Applicants must be Colorado high school seniors who

are enrolled in the upcoming summer or fall semester at a Colorado community college or Colorado college or university that offers a program (or transferable credit) in accounting. They also must be of African American, Hispanic, Asian American, Native American, or Pacific Islander descent, and must demonstrate academic achievement with a GPA of at least 3.0. Students also must be enrolled in at least six semester or quarter hours. *Application Process: Applicants should submit a completed application along with transcripts and ACT or SAT scores. Visit the society's Web site to download an application. *Amount: $1,000. *Deadline: March 1.

Columbia College

Attn: Chuck Smith, Contest Facilitator
Theater Department
72 East 11th Street
Chicago, IL 60605
312-344-6136
theatre@colum.edu
http://www.colum.edu/undergraduate/theater/calendar.php?action=full&id=66
Award Name: Theodore Ward Prize for African-American Playwriting. *Academic Area: English/literature, performing arts (open), writing. *Age Group: Open. *Eligibility: Applicants should be African Americans who are addressing the African-American experience in their work, and who wish to have the opportunity to gain exposure to Chicago's professional theater community through staged readings and/or fully mounted productions. *Application Process: Interested candidates should contact the contest facilitator for submission instructions. *Amount: Awards vary. *Deadline: Contact the contest facilitator for deadline information.

Committee on Institutional Cooperation (CIC)

Attn: Chris Cosat, Secretary
1819 South Neil Street, Suite D
Champaign, IL 61820
217-265-8005
cosat@uiuc.edu
http://www.cic.uiuc.edu/programs/FreeApp/archive/RequestForm/GraduateRecruitment.shtml
Award Name: CIC FreeApp Award. *Academic Area: Open. *Age Group: Graduate students. *Eligibility: Applicants must be underrepresented minority students seeking admission to graduate school. A bachelor's degree must be completed by the August

preceding enrollment in the graduate program. Applicants must be applying for admission to a Ph.D. program or master of fine arts program, be a U.S. citizen or permanent resident, have a minimum GPA of 3.0, and intend to pursue an academic and/or research career. *Application Process: Applicants should visit the committee's Web site to download an application. *Amount: Awards vary. *Deadline: Deadlines vary.

Community Foundation for Palm Beach and Martin Counties

Attn: Carolyn Jenco, Grants Manager/Scholarship Coordinator
700 South Dixie Highway, Suite 200
West Palm Beach, FL 33401
561-659-6800
cjenco@cfpbmc.org
http://www.yourcommunityfoundation.org/scholarship/program.asp?program

Scholarship Name: Community Foundation Scholarship Program. *Academic Area: Open. *Age Group: Undergraduate students. *Eligibility: Applicants must be graduating high school seniors who reside in Palm Beach or Martin County, Florida, and plan to pursue a degree full time at an accredited two- or four-year college, university, or vocational school. Applicants must also demonstrate financial need and academic achievement. The Scholarship Program designates a variety of scholarships for minority students. *Application Process: Applicants must submit a completed application, an essay, official transcripts, proof of Florida residency, student/parent IRS Form 1040, and a writing sample (if specified by specific scholarship requirements). Visit the foundation's Web site to download an application. *Amount: $750 to $2,500. *Deadline: February 1.

Conference of Minority Public Administrators (COMPA)

Attn: Chris Snead, COMPA Awards Committee
22 Lincoln Street
Hampton, VA 23669
757-727-6377
csndad@hampton.gov
http://www.natcompa.org

Scholarship Name: Ronald H. Brown Memorial Scholarship. *Academic Area: Open. *Age Group: Undergraduate students. *Eligibility: Minority high school seniors who attend a public high school in the city where COMPA holds its annual conference (which varies by year) may apply. Applicants must also have a minimum GPA of 3.25 on a 4.0 scale and a minimum ACT/SAT score of 22 or 1000. *Application Process: Applicants should submit an application along with an acceptance letter to a four-year institution of higher learning, official high school transcripts and ACT/SAT scores, and a two-page essay describing how the student's future goals align with Ronald H. Brown's philosophy of fighting to create opportunities for people of every race, social class, and nationality. Visit the association's Web site to find the applicable city for each given year as well as to download an application form. *Amount: $1,000. *Deadline: Contact the organization for further information.

Conference of Minority Public Administrators (COMPA)

Attn: Chris Snead, Chair
COMPA Awards Committee
22 Lincoln Street
Hampton, VA 23669
757-727-6377
csnead@hampton.gov
http://www.natcompa.org

Grant Name: The COMPA Travel Grant provides funding for students to travel to COMPA's annual conference. *Academic Area: Government. *Age Group: Undergraduate students, graduate students. *Eligibility: Applicants must be students who are not employed full time and aspire to attend the conference for the purpose of networking, presenting theses or dissertations, and/or participating as panelists for various student/practitioner/academia tracks. *Application Process: Applicants should visit the conference's Web site to download an application form. *Amount: $400. *Deadline: January 7.

Conference of Minority Transportation Officials (COMTO)

Attn: Paralee Shivers, National Scholarship Chairperson
COMTO National Scholarship Program
818 18th Street, NW, Suite 850
Washington, DC 20006
202-530-0551
pcheatham@comto.org
http://www.comto.org/start.htm

Scholarship Name: This organization offers numerous scholarships to minorities. *Academic Area:

Transportation. *Age Group: Undergraduate students, graduate students. *Eligibility: Applicants should visit the organization's Web site in early February for specific eligibility requirements for individual awards. High school seniors and college students are eligible to apply for this scholarship. *Application Process: Applicants should submit a completed application along with two letters of recommendation, an acceptance letter from their university/college (where applicable), official transcripts, a resume, a 500-word cover letter with introduction and career goals, and a headshot (3"x 5") photo. Winners must agree to attend an award luncheon or send a videotape of their acceptance of the award. *Amount: $1,500 to $10,000. *Deadline: March 31.

Congressional Black Caucus Foundation (CBCF)
1720 Massachusetts Avenue, NW
Washington, DC 20036
202-263-2800
http://www.cbcfinc.org
Scholarship Name: Congressional Black Caucus Spouses Education Scholarship. *Academic Area: Education. *Age Group: Undergraduate students, graduate students. *Eligibility: Applicants must be academically talented and highly motivated students who intend to pursue full-time undergraduate, graduate, or doctoral degrees. Applicants must have a minimum 2.5 GPA, demonstrate academic achievement, exhibit leadership ability, and participate in community service activities. All applicants must reside or attend school in a congressional district represented by a Congressional Black Caucus member. High school seniors are also eligible to apply for this scholarship. *Application Process: Applicants should submit a completed application form and packet including a resume, high school or college transcripts, two letters of recommendation, a 500-word personal essay, and a recent photo. Visit the foundation's Web site to download an application. Applications should be mailed to the applicant's local CBCF office; visit the foundation's Web site to determine the address of your local office. *Amount: Awards vary. *Deadline: May 1.

Congressional Black Caucus Foundation (CBCF)
1720 Massachusetts Avenue, NW
Washington, DC 20036
202-263-2800
http://www.cbcfinc.org

Scholarship Name: Congressional Black Caucus Spouses Performing Arts Scholarship. *Academic Area: Performing arts (open). *Age Group: Undergraduate students, graduate students. *Eligibility: Applicants must be academically talented and highly motivated students who intend to pursue full-time undergraduate, graduate, or doctoral degrees. Applicants must have a minimum 2.5 GPA, demonstrate academic achievement, exhibit leadership ability, and participate in community service activities. All applicants must reside or attend school in a congressional district represented by a Congressional Black Caucus member. High school seniors are also eligible to apply for this scholarship. *Application Process: Applicants should submit a completed application form and packet including a resume, high school or college transcripts, two letters of recommendation, a 500-word personal essay, and a recent photo. Applicants must also submit a video recording of their most recent performance. Applications and videos must be submitted to the Local Scholarship Selection Committee for review. Visit the foundation's Web site to download an application and to determine the address of your local office. *Amount: $3,000 *Deadline: May 1.

Congressional Black Caucus Foundation (CBCF)
1720 Massachusetts Avenue, NW
Washington, DC 20036
202-263-2800
http://www.cbcfinc.org
Scholarship Name: Congressional Black Caucus Spouses Cheerios Brand Health Initiative Scholarship. *Academic Area: Medicine (open). *Age Group: Undergraduate students, graduate students. *Eligibility: Applicants must be academically talented and highly motivated students who intend to pursue full-time undergraduate, graduate, or doctoral degrees in a health-related profession. Applicants must have a minimum 2.5 GPA, demonstrate academic achievement, exhibit leadership ability, and participate in community service activities. All applicants must reside or attend school in a congressional district represented by a Congressional Black Caucus member. High school seniors are also eligible to apply for this scholarship. *Application Process: Applicants should submit a completed application form and packet including a resume, high school or college transcripts, two letters of recommendation, a 500-word personal essay, and

a recent photo. Visit the foundation's Web site to download an application. Applications should be mailed to the applicant's local CBCF office; visit the foundation's Web site to determine the address of your local office. *Amount: Awards vary. *Deadline: May 1.

Congressional Black Caucus Foundation (CBCF)
1720 Massachusetts Avenue, NW
Washington, DC 20036
202-263-2800
http://www.cbcfinc.org
Scholarship Name: Congressional Black Caucus Foundation Vivien Thomas Scholarship for Medical Science and Research. *Academic Area: Medicine (open), science. *Age Group: Undergraduate students. *Eligibility: Applicants must intend to focus on improving human health, exemplify high academic standards, and demonstrate need of financial assistance to realize their dreams of earning a college degree. High school seniors are also eligible to apply for this scholarship. *Application Process: Applicants should submit a completed application form and packet including a resume, high school or college transcripts, two letters of recommendation, a 500-word personal essay, and a recent photo. Visit the foundation's Web site to download an application. Applications should be mailed to the applicant's local CBCF office; visit the foundation's Web site to determine the address of your local office. This award is sponsored by GlaxoSmithKline. *Amount: Awards vary. *Deadline: May 1.

Congressional Hispanic Caucus Institute (CHCI)
CHCI Public Policy Fellowship
911 Second Street, NE
Washington, DC 20002
202-543-1771, 800-392-3532
chci@chci.org
http://www.chci.org/chciyouth/fellowship/fellowship.htm
Fellowship Name: CHCI Public Policy Fellowship. *Academic Area: Public policy. *Age Group: Graduate students. *Eligibility: Applicants must be recent college graduates or current graduate students who demonstrate high academic achievement, remarkable participation in public service oriented activities, leadership skills and potential for growth, and superior analytical and communication skills. Applicants also must be of Hispanic descent and U.S.

citizens or legal permanent residents. *Application Process: Applicants should submit a completed application along with supporting materials. Visit the organization's Web site to download an application. *Amount: $2,061 monthly stipend. *Deadline: March 1.

Congressional Hispanic Caucus Institute (CHCI)
Attn: Reynaldo Casas, Scholarship and Educational Services Manager
911 Second Street, NE
Washington, DC 20002
202-543-1771, 800-392-3532
rcasas@chci.org
http://www.chci.org
Scholarship Name: CHCI Scholarship Award. *Academic Area: Open. *Age Group: Undergraduate students, graduate students. *Eligibility: Applicants should be U.S. citizens or legal permanent residents with a history of consistent, active participation in public service-oriented activities. Applicants should be accepted into an accredited community college, four-year university, or a graduate/professional program and must be enrolled as full-time students. Applicants should also demonstrate financial need and have good writing skills. High school seniors are also eligible to apply for this scholarship. *Application Process: Applicants should submit a completed application along with two letters of recommendation in sealed and signed envelopes, a resume outlining all extracurricular activities, responses to two essay questions, a copy of their Student Aid Report, and a self-addressed stamped postcard. Visit the organization's Web site to download an application. *Amount: $5,000 (to attend graduate school), $2,500 (to attend a four-year university); $1,000 (to attend a two-year community college). *Deadline: March 1.

Connecticut Department of Higher Education (CTDHE)
Minority Teacher Incentive Grant Program
61 Woodland Street
Hartford, CT 06105-2326
860-447-1855
mtip@ctdhe.org
http://www.ctdhe.org/SFA/pdfs/MTIP%20Brochure%20and%20Form.pdf
Grant Name: Minority Teacher Incentive Grant. *Academic Area: Education. *Age Group: Undergraduate students. *Eligibility: Applicants must

be minorities, college juniors or seniors, residents of Connecticut, and currently pursuing an education-related major full time at a select postsecondary institution in Connecticut. College graduates who plan to attend the Department of Higher Education's Alternate Route to Certification may also apply. *Application Process: Applicants must be nominated by the dean of education at their school. *Amount: Up to $5,000 a year (for two years), plus up to $2,500 a year (for up to four years) to repay college loans. *Deadline: Nominations are due October 1.

Consortium for Graduate Study in Management (CGSM)

5585 Pershing, Suite 240
St. Louis, MO 63112-4621
314-877-5500, 888-658-6814
frontdesk@cgsm.org
http://www.cgsm.org
Fellowship Name: CGSM Fellowship. *Academic Area: Business. *Age Group: Graduate students. *Eligibility: Applicants must be African Americans, Hispanic Americans, or Native Americans who are U.S. citizens or permanent residents and who can demonstrate a commitment to the consortium's mission to enhance diversity in business by reducing the underrepresentation of minorities in graduate business schools. They should also be full-time students who are seeking a graduate degree from one of the consortium's member schools and who already have earned a bachelor's degree (in any discipline). *Application Process: Applicants must apply online and will also be required to participate in an interview. They should also submit transcripts, two references, a resume, answers to essay questions, and GMAT scores. An application fee is also required. The number of schools to which the applicants are applying for the fellowship determines the amount. Visit the consortium's Web site for a complete explanation of the application process, as well as a list of member schools and application fees. *Amount: Awards vary. *Deadline: January 15.

Cuban American National Foundation

Mas Family Scholarships
PO Box 440069
Miami, FL 33144-9926
305-592-7768
http://www.canf.org/2005/principal-ingles.htm
Scholarship Name: Mas Family Scholarship. *Academic Area: Business, communications science, economics,

engineering (open), international relations, journalism. *Age Group: Undergraduate students, graduate students. *Eligibility: Applicants must demonstrate financial need, and place in the top 10 percent of their high school class. They also must be Cuban American students who are direct descendants of those that left Cuba (at least one parent or two grandparents) or were born in Cuba themselves. Applicants must also demonstrate strong leadership qualities and commitment to the advancement of a free society. High school seniors and college students may apply for this scholarship. *Application Process: Applicants must submit a completed application and two essays. Contact the Foundation to obtain an application and for further application details. *Amount: Up to $10,000 per year (for four years). *Deadline: March 31.

Dallas-Fort Worth Association of Black Communicators (DFW/ABC)

Attn: Ira J. Hadnot, Scholarship Chair
Attn: DFW/ABC Scholarship Committee
A. H. Belo Building
Communications Center, Lock Box 11
Dallas, TX 75265
469-330-9696
scholarship@dfwabc.org
http://www.dfwabc.org/scholarships.htm
Scholarship Name: DFW/ABC Future Journalists Scholarship. *Academic Area: Advertising, communications science, graphic design, journalism, public relations, writing. *Age Group: Undergraduate students. *Eligibility: Applicants must be minority high school seniors or undergraduate students who can demonstrate a commitment to a career in communication, either written or visual. Applicants must be permanent residents of one of the following counties in Texas: Collin, Dallas, Denton, Ellis, Hunt, or Tarrant. Applicants must also agree to attend the award ceremony. *Application Process: Applicants should submit a completed application along with a 250-word typewritten autobiography and samples of their work. Scholarships will be awarded in two categories: written and visual communication. Students applying in the "written" category should submit two writing samples. Students applying in the "visual" category should submit five samples of work. For a complete, detailed description on the types of materials to submit and submission procedures, visit the association's Web site. Applications are available

for download from the association's Web site as well.
*Amount: $500 to $2,000, eligible to reapply yearly.
*Deadline: March 15.

Daughters of the American Revolution (DAR)

Attn: Scholarships
1776 D Street, NW
Washington, DC 20006-5303
202-628-1776
http://www.dar.org/natsociety/edout_scholar.cfm
Scholarship Name: American Indian Scholarship.
*Academic Area: Open *Age Group: Undergraduate
students, graduate students. *Eligibility: Applicants
must be Native Americans, and proof of American
Indian blood is required by letter or proof papers.
Applicants must demonstrate financial need, academic
achievement, and have a 2.75 GPA or higher. They must
be enrolled in a two- or four-year college or university
or technical school. Graduate students are eligible,
but undergraduate students are given preference.
*Application Process: All applicants must obtain a letter
of sponsorship from their local DAR chapter. Applicants
should send a stamped, self-addressed business size
envelope to obtain the name and address of their
state scholarship chairman and an application. Visit
the organization's Web site for the mailing address.
*Amount: $500. *Deadline: April 1, October 1.

Daughters of the American Revolution (DAR)

Attn: Scholarships
1776 D Street, NW
Washington, DC 20006-5303
202-628-1776
http://www.dar.org/natsociety/edout_scholar.cfm
Scholarship Name: Frances Crawford Marvin American
Indian Scholarship. *Academic Area: Open. *Age
Group: Undergraduate students. *Eligibility:
Applicants must be Native Americans, and proof of
American Indian blood is required by letter or proof
papers. They must also demonstrate financial need,
academic achievement, and have a 3.0 GPA or higher.
Applicants must be enrolled full-time at a two- or
four-year college or university. *Application Process:
All applicants must obtain a letter of sponsorship
from their local DAR chapter. Applicants should send
a stamped, self-addressed business size envelope to
obtain the name and address of their state scholarship
chairman and an application. Visit the organization's
Web site for the mailing address. *Amount: Awards
vary. *Deadline: February 1.

Disciples Home Missions of the (Christian Church [Disciples of Christ])

PO Box 1986
Indianapolis, IN 46206-1986
888-346-2631
mail@dhm.disciples.org
http://www.homelandministries.org/Scholarships/
guidelines.htm
Scholarship Name: David Tamotsu Kagiwada Memorial
Scholarship. *Academic Area: Religion. *Age Group:
Undergraduate students, seminary students.
*Eligibility: Applicants must be Asian American
Christian Church (Disciples of Christ) members
who intend to become ordained ministers of the
church. Applicants should maintain at least a C+ GPA,
demonstrate financial need, be enrolled full time,
and be under care of a regional Commission on the
Ministry (or in the process). *Application Process:
Applicants should submit an online application and
send all supporting materials via mail. Supporting
materials include five letters of reference and
transcripts. Visit the church's Web site to apply online.
*Amount: Awards vary. *Deadline: March 15.

Disciples Home Missions of the [Christian Church (Disciples of Christ)]

PO Box 1986
Indianapolis, IN 46206-1986
888-346-2631
mail@dhm.disciples.org
http://www.homelandministries.org/Scholarships/
guidelines.htm
Scholarship Name: Star Supporter Scholarship/
Loan. *Academic Area: Religion. *Age Group:
Undergraduate students, seminary students.
*Eligibility: Applicants must be African American
Christian Church (Disciples of Christ) members
who intend to become ordained ministers of the
church. Applicants should maintain at least a C+ GPA,
demonstrate financial need, be enrolled full time,
and be under care of a regional Commission on the
Ministry (or in the process). Applicants who fulfill
a three-year commitment of full-time professional
ministry do not have to repay the loan. Applicants
who do not fulfill this commitment must repay
the amount awarded (with interest) on a monthly
installment basis. *Application Process: Applicants
should submit an online application and send all
supporting materials via mail. Supporting materials
include five letters of reference and transcripts. Visit

the church's Web site to apply online. *Amount: Awards vary. *Deadline: March 15.

Eddie Robinson Foundation
3391 Peachtree Road, NE, Suite 105
Atlanta, GA 30326
404-475-8408 ext. 205
info@eddierobinson.com
http://www.eddierobinson.com
Scholarship Name: Eddie Robinson Eighth Grade and High School Senior Scholarship. *Academic Area: Open. *Age Group: Eighth grade students, high school seniors. *Eligibility: Applicants must have distinguished themselves as leaders among their peers in the school and community, excel in the athletic arena while maintaining excellence in the classroom, and display a can-do attitude despite obstacles. *Application Process: Applicants should submit a typed list of scholastic achievements, athletic accomplishments, community involvement activities, and extracurricular activities, a 500-word typed essay about how they will mirror the values of Eddie Robinson, official transcripts, ACT or SAT scores (high school students), and two letters of recommendation. Awards are distributed once a student can prove enrollment in an institution of higher education. *Amount: Awards vary. *Deadline: Contact the foundation for deadlines.

Entomological Society of America
10001 Derekwood Lane, Suite 100
Lanham, MD 20706-4876
301-731-4535
esa@entsoc.org
http://www.entsoc.org/awards/student/beck.htm
Fellowship Name: Stan Beck Fellowship. *Academic Area: Entomology. *Age Group: Undergraduate students, graduate students. *Eligibility: Applicants must be accepted into or enrolled in a degree program in entomology in a college or university in the United States, Mexico, or Canada. Applicants should also be able to demonstrate financial need based on some kind of environmental condition, minority status, or physical limitation. *Application Process: Applicants should visit the foundation's Web site for a detailed description of the application process. Applications must be submitted online and are subject to a detailed list of standards. Applicants should submit an application along with a curriculum vitae, a letter of nomination, a description of their academic studies

and plans, official transcripts, a personal statement, and three additional letters of support. *Amount: Awards vary. *Deadline: July 1.

Florida Department of Education
Office of Student Financial Assistance
1940 North Monroe Street, Suite 70
Tallahassee, FL 32303-4759
888-827-2004
osfa@fldoe.org
http://www.firn.edu/doe/bin00065/jmfactsheet.htm
Grant Name: José Martí Scholarship Challenge Grant Fund. *Academic Area: Open. *Age Group: Undergraduate students, graduate students. *Eligibility: Applicants must be Hispanic American, residents of Florida, planning to attend or currently attending select postsecondary institutions in Florida, have a GPA of at least 3.0, and demonstrate financial need. Priority will be given to applicants who are high school seniors. *Application Process: Contact the department for information on application requirements. *Amount: $2,000. *Deadline: Varies.

Florida Institute of CPAs Educational Foundation
Attn: Betsy Wilson, Scholarship Coordinator
325 West College Avenue
Tallahassee, FL 32301
850-224-2727, ext. 200
wilsonb@ficpa.org
http://www1.ficpa.org/ficpa/Visitors/Careers/EdFoundation/Scholarships/Available
Scholarship Name: 1040K Race Scholarship. *Academic Area: Accounting. *Age Group: Undergraduate students, graduate students. *Eligibility: Applicants must be African American residents of Dade County, Florida, who are enrolled full time in their fourth or fifth year of accounting at Barry University, Florida Atlantic University, Florida International University, Florida Memorial College, Nova Southeastern University, St. Thomas University, or the University of Miami. *Application Process: Candidates should contact their accounting scholarship chairperson at their school in January to receive an application. If you do not know who to contact, contact the foundation's scholarship coordinator for further information. Applications and transcripts should be submitted to the school accounting scholarship chairperson. *Amount: Awards vary. *Deadline: March 15.

Foley & Lardner LLP
Attn: Robert Meek
One Independent Drive
Jacksonville, FL 32202-5017
904-359-8709, 904-359-2000
rmeek@foley.com
http://apps.foley.com/students/opportunities/
minorityscholarships
Scholarship Name: Foley and Lardner LLP Minority
Scholarship Program. *Academic Area: Law. *Age
Group: Law students. *Eligibility: Applicants must be
minority students in their first year of law school at
Duke University, the University of Florida, Georgetown
University, the University of Michigan, Northwestern
University, Stanford University, the University of
California-Los Angeles, or the University of Wisconsin.
Applicants must demonstrate community and/or
university involvement and academic achievement.
*Application Process: Contact Foley and Lardner LLP
for application details. *Amount: $5,000. *Deadline:
Contact Foley and Lardner LLP for more information.

Foundation for Digestive Health and Nutrition
Attn: Director of Foundation Operations
4930 Del Ray Avenue
Bethesda, MD 20814
301-222-4005
awards@fdhn.org
http://www.fdhn.org/html/awards/elect_app.html
Scholarship Name: Student Research Fellowship Award.
*Academic Area: Medicine (gastroenterology and
nutrition). *Age Group: Undergraduate students,
graduate students, and medical students. *Eligibility:
Applicants must be high school, undergraduate,
graduate, or medical students performing digestive
disease or nutrition research. University student
applicants must not receive salary support from other
agencies. Women and minorities are encouraged
to apply. Several fellowship awards are reserved
each year for underrepresented minority applicants.
*Application Process: Applicants must submit
a completed application, a scientific abstract, a
biographical sketch, and a research summary. Visit
the foundation's Web site to download an application
and to obtain further application details. *Amount:
$2,000 to $3,000. *Deadline: March 5.

**Frederick Douglass Institute for African and African-
American Studies**
Attn: Director for Research Fellowships
University of Rochester

RC Box 270440
302 Morey Hall
Rochester, NY 14627-0440
585-275-7235
fdi@troi.cc.rochester.edu
http://www.rochester.edu/College/AAS/fellowships.php
Fellowship Name: Postdoctoral Fellowship. *Academic
Area: African American studies. *Age Group:
Postgraduate students. *Eligibility: Applicants must
have a Ph.D. before the start date of the fellowship,
and must desire to complete a one-year research
project while teaching one course per semester.
*Application Process: Applicants should submit a
completed application form along with a three- to
five-page description of the project, writing samples, a
curriculum vitae, and three letters of recommendation
relating to the proposed research project. Visit the
institute's Web site to download an application.
*Amount: $35,000. *Deadline: January 31.

**Frederick Douglass Institute for African and African-
American Studies**
Attn: Director for Research Fellowships
University of Rochester
RC Box 270440
302 Morey Hall
Rochester, NY 14627-0440
585-275-7235
fdi@troi.cc.rochester.edu
http://www.rochester.edu/College/AAS/fellowships.php
Fellowship Name: Predoctoral Fellowship. *Academic
Area: African American studies. *Age Group:
Graduate students. *Eligibility: Applicants must
have completed all of the required courses and
qualifying exams necessary for the completion
of their degree program. They also must have
written at least one chapter of their dissertation.
This fellowship's purpose is to allow the applicant
time to work on his or dissertation. *Application
Process: Applicants should submit a completed
application form along with a sample chapter of
the dissertation and a dissertation prospectus, a
curriculum vitae, an official transcript, and three
letters of recommendation. Visit the institute's Web
site to download an application. *Amount: $18,000.
*Deadline: January 31.

Fredrikson & Byron Foundation, P.A.
Attn: Greta Larson
200 South Sixth Street, Suite 4000
Minneapolis, MN 55402-1425

glarson@fredlaw.com
http://www.fredlaw.com/firm/scholarship.htm
Scholarship Name: Fredrikson & Byron Foundation Minority Scholarship. *Academic Area: Law. *Age Group: Law students. *Eligibility: Applicants must be minority law students interested in the private practice of law in larger corporate law firms in the upper Midwest. *Application Process: Applicants must submit a completed application, two letters of recommendation, a writing sample, current and undergraduate transcripts, and a resume. Visit the foundation's Web site to download an application. *Amount: Varies. *Deadline: March 31.

Fund for Theological Education (FTE)

Attn: Nikol Reed, Fellowships Administrator
825 Houston Mill Road, Suite 250
Atlanta, GA 30329
404-727-1451
http://www.thefund.org/programs
Fellowship Name: FTE Dissertation Fellowship. *Academic Area: Religion. *Age Group: Graduate students. *Eligibility: African-American students who are pursuing religion or theology graduate studies and who are in the final writing stage of their dissertations may apply. Their dissertation committee must have approved the dissertation research proposal and writing plan and given permission to proceed before the applicant submits the application for the Dissertation Fellows Program. Applicants must be able to write full time during the fellowship year. *Application Process: Applicants should submit a completed application along with a curriculum vitae, dissertation prospectus and one-page abstract, transcripts, list of dissertation advisor and committee members, two letters of recommendation, budget statement form, and documentation from their school showing financial aid received. Visit the fund's Web site to download an application. *Amount: Up to $15,000 stipend, plus full tuition scholarship. *Deadline: February 1.

Fund for Theological Education (FTE)

Attn: Nikol Reed, Fellowships Administrator
825 Houston Mill Road, Suite 250
Atlanta, GA 30329
404-727-1451
http://www.thefund.org/programs
Fellowship Name: FTE Doctoral Fellowship. *Academic Area: Religion. *Age Group: Graduate students. *Eligibility: Applicants must be African-American students preparing to enter their first year of an accredited Ph.D. or Th.D. program in religion or theology. They must be committed to becoming a leader within theological education, and be giving strong consideration to teaching or conducting research in a theological school. Applicants also must be U.S. citizens. *Application Process: Applicants should submit a completed application along with a curriculum vitae, two-page essay, transcripts, GRE scores (copies acceptable), two letters of recommendation, budget statement form, and documentation from school showing financial aid received. Visit the fund's Web site to download an application. *Amount: Up to $15,000 stipend, plus full tuition scholarship (renewable for a second year). *Deadline: March 1.

Gates Millennium Scholars Program

PO Box 1434
Fairfax, VA 22313
877-690-4677
https://www.gmsp.org/gmsp_app/pdfforms.aspx
Scholarship Name: Gates Millennium Scholars Program. *Academic Area: Open. *Age Group: Undergraduate students. *Eligibility: Applicants must be African American, American Indian/Alaska Native, Asian Pacific Islander American, or Hispanic American and be citizens/legal permanent residents or nationals of the United States. They must also have attained a cumulative GPA of 3.3 on a 4.0 scale (unweighted) at the time of nomination, be entering a U.S. accredited college or university as full-time degree seeking freshmen, and have demonstrated leadership abilities through participation in community service, extracurricular, or other activities. Applicants must also meet all Federal Pell Grant eligibility criteria. *Application Process: Applicants must submit a nominee form, a nomination form, and a recommendation form. Visit the Scholars Program Web site for further application details and to download required forms. *Amount: Varies. *Deadline: January 13.

Golf Course Superintendents Association of America (GCSAA)

Attn: Amanda Howard, Employment Administrator
1421 Research Park Drive
Lawrence, KS 66049-3859
800-472-7878, ext. 4424
ahoward@gcsaa.org
http://www.gcsaa.org/students/scholarships/default.asp
Scholarship Name: Scotts Company Scholars Program Scholarship. *Academic Area: Golf course management. *Age Group: Undergraduate students. *Eligibility:

Applicants must be college freshmen, sophomores, or juniors or graduating high school seniors accepted to accredited universities, colleges, or junior colleges for the next academic year. The primary goal of the program is to seek out promising students from diverse ethnic, cultural, and socioeconomic backgrounds. This would include females, minorities, and individuals with disabilities who wish to pursue careers in the green industry. *Application Process: Contact Amanda Howard for application materials. *Amount: $500 (finalists) and $2,500 (winners). *Deadline: March 1.

Government Finance Officers Association
Attn: Scholarship Committee
203 North LaSalle Street, Suite 2700
Chicago, IL 60601-1210
312-977-9700
http://www.gfoa.org/services/scholarships.shtml
Scholarship Name: Minorities in Government Finance Scholarship. *Academic Area: Accounting, business, economics, finance, government, political science, public policy. *Age Group: Undergraduate students, graduate students. *Eligibility: Applicants must be college juniors or seniors or graduate students majoring in one of the following fields (with a focus on government): accounting, business administration, economics, finance, or political science. They also must be U.S. citizens or permanent residents who belong to one of the following minority groups: African American, American Indian or Alaskan native, Asian native, Hawaiian or Pacific Islander, Hispanic, or Latino. Applicants should demonstrate academic achievement and a commitment to a career in the governmental sector. *Application Process: Applicants should submit an application along with a personal statement regarding their career plans, transcripts, a resume, and letters of recommendation (optional). Visit the association's Web site to download an application. *Amount: $5,000. *Deadline: February 3.

Health Resources and Services Administration (HRSA)
U.S. Department of Health and Human Services
Attn: Tobey Manns
Parklawn Building
5600 Fishers Lane
Rockville, MD 20857
301-443-2100
http://bhpr.hrsa.gov/diversity/hcop/default.htm
Grant Name: Health Careers Opportunity Program Grant. *Academic Area: Medicine (open). *Age

Group: Undergraduate students, graduate students. *Eligibility: Applicants must come from a disadvantaged background, which is defined as an environment that has inhibited the individual from obtaining the knowledge, skills, and abilities to succeed in a health professions school or program and/or a student from a family with an annual income below a level based on low-income thresholds. Applicants must be U.S. citizens or possess a visa permitting permanent U.S. residence. High school seniors and college students may apply. *Application Process: Applicants should contact the administration for information about application procedures. *Amount: Awards vary. *Deadline: Contact the administration for deadline information.

Health Resources and Services Administration (HRSA)
U.S. Department of Health and Human Services
5600 Fishers Lane
Rockville, MD 20857
http://bhpr.hrsa.gov/dsa/lds.htm
Loan Name: Loan for Disadvantaged Students. *Academic Area: Medicine (dentistry), medicine (open), medicine (physicians), pharmaceutical sciences. *Age Group: Open. *Eligibility: Disadvantaged students, including minorities, who are interested in pursuing careers in the health sciences may apply. Applicants must be citizens, nationals, or lawful permanent residents of the United States or the District of Columbia, the Commonwealths of Puerto Rico or the Marianas Islands, the Virgin Islands, Guam, the American Samoa, the Trust Territory of the Pacific Islands, the Republic of Palau, the Republic of the Marshall Islands, or the Federated State of Micronesia. *Application Process: Students should contact the financial aid office of their school to see if the loan program is available. *Amount: Not to exceed the cost of attendance (tuition, reasonable educational expenses, and reasonable living expenses). *Loan Repayment Deadline: Varies. *Application Deadline: Varies.

Health Resources and Services Administration (HRSA)
U.S. Department of Health and Human Services
Attn: Daniel Reed
Parklawn Building
5600 Fishers Lane
Rockville, MD 20857
301-443-2982
DReed1@hrsa.gov
http://bhpr.hrsa.gov/diversity/mffp/default.htm

Fellowship Name: Minority Faculty Fellowship Program. *Academic Area: Medicine (open). *Age Group: Open. *Eligibility: Applicants must be racial and ethnic minorities underrepresented in the health professions who are interested in teaching, administration, or research positions at a health professions institution. *Application Process: Applicants should contact the organization for further information on the application process. *Amount: Awards vary. *Deadline: Contact the organization for deadline information.

Health Resources and Services Administration (HRSA)
U.S. Department of Health and Human Services
200 Independence Avenue, SW
Washington, DC 20201
202-619-0257, 877-696-6775
http://bhpr.hrsa.gov/dsa/sds.htm
Scholarship Name: Scholarship for Disadvantaged Students. *Academic Area: Medicine (open), nursing (open). *Age Group: Undergraduate students, graduate students. *Eligibility: Disadvantaged students, including minority students, who are enrolled full time in health professions and nursing programs are eligible to apply. Applicants must demonstrate financial need and be citizens, nationals, or lawful permanent residents of the United States. High school seniors are also eligible to apply for this scholarship. *Application Process: Applicants should apply for this scholarship at the student financial aid office of the school they plan to attend. *Amount: Varies. *Deadline: Varies.

Hispanic Association of Colleges and Universities (HACU)
HACU Scholarship Program
One Dupont Circle, NW, Suite 605
Washington, DC 20036
202-833-8361
hnip@hacu.net
http://www.hacu.net/hacu/Student_Resources1_ EN.asp?SnID=1721883662
Scholarship Name: HACU Scholarships. *Academic Area: Open. *Age Group: Undergraduate, graduate students. *Eligibility: Applicants should be attending a HACU member or partner college or university and meet all additional criteria for the scholarship for which they are applying. Scholarship requirements vary. Visit the association's Web site for a complete listing of scholarships and their eligibility requirements. High school seniors are also

eligible to apply for selected scholarships offered by the association. *Application Process: Scholarship materials are to be sent to the financial aid office at HACU-member and -partner colleges and universities. Applications are available for download during the early months of each year. Visit the organization's Web site for more information or send inquiries via e-mail. Amount: $500 to $2,000. *Deadline: May 27.

Hispanic Association of Colleges and Universities (HACU)/National Education Loan Network
8415 Datapoint Drive, Suite 400
San Antonio, TX 78229
866-866-7372
http://www.nelnet.net/hacu
Loan Name: HACU, in cooperation with the National Education Loan Network, offers loans to parents of Hispanic students via its Educational Loan Program. *Academic Area: Open. *Age Group: Open. *Eligibility: Parents of Hispanic students who are attending HACU-member colleges and universities may apply. *Application Process: Contact either organization for details. *Amount: Varies. *Loan Repayment Deadline: Varies. *Application Deadline: Contact either organization for details.

Hispanic College Fund (HCF)
Attn: HCF Scholarship Selection Committee
1717 Pennsylvania Avenue, NW, Suite 460
Washington, DC 20006
800-644-4223
hcf-info@hispanicfund.org
http://www.hispanicfund.org
Scholarship Name: El Nuevo Constructor Scholarship. *Academic Area: Construction. *Age Group: Undergraduate students. *Eligibility: Hispanic students who are planning to or currently pursuing a bachelor's or associate degree in a construction-related field may apply. Applicants must also have a GPA of at least 3.0; be U.S. citizens; and attend school full time. High school seniors are also eligible to apply for this scholarship. *Application Process: Visit the HCF's Web site to apply online. *Amount: Awards range from $500 to $5,000. *Deadline: April 15.

Hispanic College Fund (HCF)
Attn: HCF Scholarship Selection Committee
1717 Pennsylvania Avenue, NW, Suite 460
Washington, DC 20006
800-644-4223

hcf-info@hispanicfund.org
http://www.hispanicfund.org
Scholarship Name: Lockheed Martin Scholarship.
*Academic Area: Computer science, engineering
(open). *Age Group: Undergraduate students.
*Eligibility: Hispanic students who are planning to or
currently pursuing a bachelor's degree in computer
science, engineering, or a related major may apply.
Applicants must have a GPA of at least 3.0, be U.S.
citizens, and attend school full time. High school
seniors are also eligible to apply for this scholarship.
*Application Process: Visit the HCF's Web site to apply
online. *Amount: Awards range from $500 to $5,000.
*Deadline: April 15.

Hispanic College Fund (HCF)
Attn: HCF Scholarship Selection Committee
1717 Pennsylvania Avenue, NW, Suite 460
Washington, DC 20006
800-644-4223
hcf-info@hispanicfund.org
http://www.hispanicfund.org
Scholarship Name: M&T Bank Scholarship. *Academic
Area: Business, computer science, engineering
(open). *Age Group: Undergraduate students.
*Eligibility: Hispanic students residing in Maryland,
Virginia, Pennsylvania, or New York are eligible to
apply. Applicants must have a GPA of at least 3.0; be
planning to or currently pursuing a bachelor's degree
in business, computer science, engineering, or a
business-related major; be U.S. citizens; and attend
school full time. High school seniors are also eligible
to apply for this scholarship. *Application Process: Visit
the HCF's Web site to apply online. *Amount: Awards
range from $500 to $5,000. *Deadline: April 15.

Hispanic College Fund (HCF)
Attn: HCF Scholarship Selection Committee
1717 Pennsylvania Avenue, NW, Suite 460
Washington, DC 20006
800-644-4223
hcf-info@hispanicfund.org
http://www.hispanicfund.org
Scholarship Name: Sallie Mae Fund First in My Family
Scholarship. *Academic Area: Open. *Age Group:
Undergraduate students. *Eligibility: Hispanic
students who are the first person in their families to
attend college may apply. Applicants must have a GPA
of at least 3.0, be U.S. citizens, and plan to attend or
be currently attending school full time. High school

seniors are also eligible to apply for this scholarship.
*Application Process: Visit the HCF's Web site to apply
online. *Amount: Awards range from $500 to $5,000.
*Deadline: April 15.

Hispanic Dental Association (HDA) Foundation
1224 Centre West, Suite 400B
Springfield, IL 62704
800-852-7921
HispanicDental@hdassoc.org
http://www.hdassoc.org/site/epage/8351_351.htm
Scholarship Name: Colgate-Palmolive / HDA Foundation
Scholarship. *Academic Area: Medicine (dentistry),
public health. *Age Group: Graduate students.
*Eligibility: Applicants must be accepted into or
currently enrolled in a Master's in Public Health or a
Dental Public Health program, be of Hispanic origin (at
least one parent of Hispanic descent), be a permanent
resident of the United States, have credentials in a
dental profession either in the United States or abroad,
and show evidence of commitment and dedication to
serve the Hispanic community. *Application Process:
Applicants should submit a completed application
along with a curriculum vitae, an advanced education
verification form, and two letters of recommendation.
Visit the association's Web site to download an
application. *Amount: $10,000. *Deadline: August 1.

Hispanic Dental Association (HDA)
1224 Centre West, Suite 400B
Springfield, IL 62704
800-852-7921
HispanicDental@hdassoc.org
http://www.hdassoc.org/site/epage/8351_351.htm
Scholarship Name: Dr. Genaro Romo Jr. & HDA
Foundation Scholarship. *Academic Area: Medicine
(dentistry) *Age Group: Undergraduate students.
*Eligibility: Applicants must be accepted into or
currently enrolled at the University of Illinois Chicago
School of Dentistry, Dental and Dental Hygiene.
*Application Process: Applicants should submit
a completed application along with supporting
documents. Contact the association for further
information about the application process. *Amount:
$500 to $1,000. *Deadline: Varies.

Hispanic Dental Association (HDA)
1224 Centre West, Suite 400B
Springfield, IL 62704
800-852-7921

HispanicDental@hdassoc.org

http://www.hdassoc.org/site/epage/8351_351.htm

Scholarship Name: Dr. Juan D. Villarreal & HDA Foundation Scholarship. *Academic Area: Medicine (dental hygiene), medicine (dentistry). *Age Group: Undergraduate dental students. *Eligibility: Applicants must be accepted into or currently enrolled in an accredited dental school in the state of Texas. Applicants must demonstrate scholastic achievement, a commitment to community service, leadership skill, and a commitment to improving health in the Hispanic community. *Application Process: Applicants should submit a completed application along with supporting documents. Contact the association for further information about the application process. *Amount: $500 to $1,000. *Deadline: Contact the association for deadline information.

Hispanic Dental Association (HDA)

1224 Centre West, Suite 400B

Springfield, IL 62704

800-852-7921

HispanicDental@hdassoc.org

http://www.hdassoc.org/site/epage/8351_351.htm

Scholarship Name: Procter & Gamble Oral Care & HDA Foundation Scholarship. *Academic Area: Medicine (dental hygiene), medicine (dentistry). *Age Group: Undergraduate students, dental students. *Eligibility: Applicants must be accepted into or currently enrolled in an accredited dental, dental hygiene, dental assisting, or dental technician program. They must demonstrate scholastic achievement, a commitment to community service, leadership skill, and a commitment to improving health in the Hispanic community. *Application Process: Applicants should submit a completed application along with supporting documents. Contact the association for further information about the application process. *Amount: $500 to $1,000. *Deadline: Varies.

Hispanic Heritage Foundation

2600 Virginia Avenue, NW, Suite 406

Washington, DC 20037

202-861-9797, 866-665-2112

contact@hispanicheritageawards.org

http://www.hispanicheritageawards.org

Award Name: Hispanic Heritage Youth Award. *Academic Area: Open. *Age Group: Undergraduate students. *Eligibility: Applicants must be high school seniors who demonstrate leadership in their communities as well as academic achievement in the classroom. (The average GPA is 3.5.) The award's purpose is to identify and promote the next generation of Hispanic role models. *Application Process: Interested candidates should visit the foundation's Web site for further information. Contact the foundation with questions about the application procedure. *Amount: $3,000 to $5,000 (plus travel expenses and prizes for national award winners). *Deadline: Contact the foundation for deadline information.

Hispanic Link Journalism Foundation

1420 N Street, NW

Washington, DC 20005

202-234-0280

http://www.hispaniclink.org/foundation/fellowshipinternship.htm

Fellowship Name: Hispanic Link Journalism Foundation Fellowship. *Academic Area: Journalism, writing. *Age Group: Open. *Eligibility: Applicants should be of Hispanic descent, demonstrate potential to become skilled journalists, express themselves exceptionally well through writing, possess outstanding analytical skills, and have a desire to live and work in Washington, D.C., for the one-year length of the fellowship. Educational background and journalism experience are not prerequisites. Candidates must be able to persuade the fellowship committee of their desire and ability to become leaders in the field of journalism. *Application Process: Contact the foundation for application procedures. *Amount: $20,800, plus benefits. *Deadline: Contact the foundation for deadline information.

Hispanic National Bar Association Foundation

Attn: Duard Bradshaw, President

815 Connecticut Avenue, NW, Suite 500

Washington, DC 20006

330-434-3000

dbradshaw@rodericklinton.com

http://www.hnba.com

Scholarship Name: This foundation offers various scholarships for law students administered through the Hispanic Scholarship Fund. *Academic Area: Law. *Age Group: Law students. *Eligibility: Students interested in being considered for this program must be graduate students accepted into an accredited law school in the United States. Students must have a 3.0 GPA or higher and be enrolled as full-time students. Applicants should visit the

Hispanic Scholarship Fund's Web site at http://www.hsf.net for further information about specific eligibility requirements for individual scholarships. *Application Process: Applications are available beginning August 1 through October 15. Visit the Hispanic Scholarship Fund's Web site to download applications. *Amount: Awards vary. *Deadline: October 15.

Hispanic Public Relations Association (HPRA)

Attn: Susie Gonzalez, College Outreach Committee Director
660 S. Figueroa Street, Suite 1140
Los Angeles, CA 90017
sgonzalez_hpra@yahoo.com
http://www.hprala.org
Scholarship Name: HPRA Scholarship. *Academic Area: Public relations. *Age Group: Undergraduate students. *Eligibility: Applicants must be deserving Hispanic college juniors or seniors attending four-year colleges and universities in Southern California. Applicants must have at least a 2.7 cumulative GPA and a 3.0 GPA in their major. Preference is given to students majoring in public relations. *Application Process: Applicants should submit a completed application form, one letter of recommendation from an academic professor, a letter of recommendation from an employer or internship supervisor (if available), official university transcripts, a one- to two-page personal statement explaining the applicant's career and educational aspirations as well as his or her involvement in the Hispanic community, a one-page resume, and a writing sample (press kits, newspaper clips, short stories, research papers). Contact Susie Gonzalez via e-mail with questions. *Amount: Awards vary. *Deadline: July 15.

Hispanic Scholarship Fund

55 Second Street, Suite 1500
San Francisco, CA 94105
877-473-4636
scholar1@hsf.net
http://www.hsf.net
Scholarship Name: The fund offers a variety of scholarships to Hispanic students. Since 1975, it has awarded more than 68,000 scholarships in excess of $144 million. *Academic Area: Open. *Age Group: Undergraduate students, graduate students. *Eligibility: Applicants must be U.S. citizens or permanent residents, be of Hispanic

heritage, apply for federal financial aid using the FAFSA, be completing their first undergraduate or graduate degree, and attend school full time. High school seniors are also eligible to apply for this scholarship. *Application Process: Applicants must submit a completed application (including essays), transcript, an enrollment verification form, and recommendations. *Amount: Varies by scholarship. *Deadline: Varies.

Hispanic-Serving Health Professions Schools (HSHPS)

1120 Connecticut Avenue, NW, Suite 260
Washington, DC 20036
202-293-2701
hshps@hshps.org
http://www.hshps.com/fellowship.html
Fellowship Name: HSHPS/Office of Minority Health Fellowship Program. *Academic Area: Biology, medicine (physicians), public health. *Age Group: Graduate students, medical students. *Eligibility: Applicants must have completed all of the courses for a doctoral degree, received a nomination from the president or dean of their institution, have a demonstrated interest in Hispanic health, and be U.S. citizens or permanent residents with work eligibility. *Application Process: Applicants must submit a completed application along with two letters of recommendation, current curriculum vitae, letter of support, personal statement, proof of citizenship or eligibility to work in the United States, and a development training prospectus. Visit the association's Web site to download an application. *Amount: Awards vary. *Deadline: Deadlines vary.

Hispanic-Serving Health Professions Schools (HSHPS)

1120 Connecticut Avenue, NW, Suite 260
Washington, DC 20036
202-293-2701
hshps@hshps.org
http://www.hshps.com
Scholarship Name: HSHPS is the only national organization representing Hispanic-serving health professions schools. It provides information on scholarships offered by corporations, federal agencies, and other nonprofit organizations *Academic Area: Medicine (open). *Age Group: Varies by scholarship. *Eligibility: Varies by scholarship. *Application Process: Varies by scholarship. *Amount: Varies by scholarship. *Deadline: Varies by scholarship.

Hispanic Theological Initiative

12 Library Place
Princeton, NJ 08540
609-252-1721, 800-575-5522
hti@ptsem.edu
http://www.htiprogram.org/scholarships/doctoral.htm
Grant Name: Hispanic Theological Initiative Doctoral
Grant. *Academic Area: Religion. *Age Group: Graduate
students. *Eligibility: Applicant must be full-time
Latino/a doctoral student. The student's institution
must partner with the initiative in providing the student
with a tuition scholarship, as well. Applicants also
must be U.S. or Canadian citizens, or legal immigrants.
*Application Process: Applicants should submit a
completed application along with transcripts, other
supporting documentation, and recommendations
by professors and Latino/a community members. Visit
the initiative's Web site for further information and to
download an application. *Amount: $15,000, renewable
for a second year. *Deadline: December 7.

Indianapolis Association of Black Journalists (IABJ)

Attn: Courtenay Edelhart, IABJ Scholarship Committee
Chair
PO Box 441795
Indianapolis, IN 46244-1795
317-388-8163
courtenay.edelhart@indystar.com
http://www.iabj.net/applications.htm
Scholarship Name: Lynn Dean Ford/Indianapolis
Association of Black Journalists Scholarship. *Academic
Area: Communications science, journalism, writing.
*Age Group: Undergraduate students. *Eligibility:
Applicants must be Indiana high school graduates
who plan to enroll as communications or journalism
majors in an accredited college or university,
or current college students attending four-year
Indiana colleges or universities and majoring in
communications or journalism. Applicants must be
African American. *Application Process: Applicants
must submit a completed application, two letters of
recommendation, writing samples, and an essay. Visit
the association's Web site to download an application.
*Amount: $1,000. *Deadline: Contact the association
for more information.

Indian American Scholarship Fund

Attn: Dr. Anuj Manocha, Coordinator
719 Vinings Estates Drive
Mableton, GA 30126
770-944-0506
manochaa@bellsouth.net
http://www.iasf.org/index.htm
Scholarship Name: Indian American Scholarship.
*Academic Area: Open. *Age Group: Undergraduate
students. *Eligibility: Applicants must be high school
seniors graduating from a school in the state of
Georgia who have been admitted to a full-time, four-
year college or university. Applicants must have one
or both parents or grandparents who originated in
present day India (Pakistan and Bangladesh are not
included). They should also be able to demonstrate
financial need or outstanding academic achievement.
*Application Process: Applicants should submit
a completed application along with transcripts, a
resume, SAT scores, a copy of a letter that details
the student's financial aid package, and a 1040 tax
return from the previous year. Students applying for a
scholarship based primarily on financial need should
also include a brief statement outlining their family's
financial resources. Visit the association's Web site to
download an application. *Amount: $500 to $2,500.
*Deadline: April 17 (for those applying based on merit);
May 8 (for those applying based on financial need).

Indiana State Teachers Association (ISTA)

ISTA Scholarships
150 West Market Street, Suite 900
Indianapolis, IN 46204-2875
317-263-3400, 800-382-4037
http://www.ista-in.org/sam.cfm?xnode=1467
Scholarship Name: Damon P. Moore Scholarship.
*Academic Area: Education. *Age Group:
Undergraduate students. *Eligibility: Applicants must
be ethnic minority students in Indiana, graduating
high school seniors, and planning to attend a college
or university to pursue a teaching certificate. They
also must demonstrate academic achievement,
community involvement, and leadership ability.
*Application Process: Applicants should submit a
completed application along with current official high
school transcripts, two letters of recommendation,
and a typed essay (topic outlined on the application).
Visit the association's Web site to download an
application. *Amount: $1,000, renewable for three
additional years. *Deadline: March 3.

Indiana State Teachers Association (ISTA)

ISTA Scholarships
150 West Market Street, Suite 900

Indianapolis, IN 46204-2875
317-263-3400, 800-382-4037
http://www.ista-in.org/sam.cfm?xnode=1467
Scholarship Name: Louis B Russell Scholarship. *Academic Area: Industrial technology. *Age Group: Undergraduate students. *Eligibility: Applicants must be ethnic minority students in Indiana, graduating high school seniors, and planning to attend an accredited postsecondary educational institution. They also must demonstrate academic achievement, community involvement, and leadership ability. *Application Process: Applicants should submit a completed application along with current official high school transcripts, two letters of recommendation, and a typed essay (topic outlined on the application). Visit the association's Web site to download an application. *Amount: $1,000, renewable for a second year. *Deadline: March 3.

Indian Health Service

Scholarship Program
801 Thompson Avenue, Suite 120
Rockville, MD 20852
301-443-6197
http://www.ihs.gov/JobsCareerDevelop/DHPS/
   Scholarships/Scholarship_index.asp
Scholarship Name: Health Professions Pregraduate Scholarship. *Academic Area: Medicine (dentistry), medicine (open), medicine (podiatry). *Age Group: Undergraduate students. *Eligibility: Applicants must be American Indian or Alaska Native, enrolled into or planning to enroll in a bachelor degree program, and planning to serve Native American people at the completion of their training. High school seniors are also eligible to apply for this scholarship. *Application Process: The applicant should submit two faculty/employer recommendations, a completed application, an official transcript, and documentation of Native American heritage. An application is available at the service's Web site. *Amount: Full tuition and related fees, plus a stipend for daily living needs. *Deadline: Varies. Contact the organization for details.

Indian Health Service

Scholarship Program
801 Thompson Avenue, Suite 120
Rockville, MD 20852
301-443-6197
http://www.ihs.gov/JobsCareerDevelop/DHPS/
   Scholarships/Scholarship_index.asp
Scholarship Name: Health Professions Preparatory Scholarship. *Academic Area: Medicine (open), nursing (open). *Age Group: Undergraduate students. *Eligibility: Applicants must be American Indian or Alaska Native, be enrolled or plan to enroll in a preprofessional postsecondary education program, and plan to serve Native American people at the completion of their training. High school seniors are also eligible to apply for this scholarship. *Application Process: The applicant should submit two faculty/employer recommendations, a completed application, an official transcript, and documentation of Native American heritage. An application is available at the service's Web site. *Amount: Full tuition and related fees, plus a stipend for daily living needs. *Deadline: Varies. Contact the organization for details.

Indian Health Service

Scholarship Program
801 Thompson Avenue, Suite 120
Rockville, MD 20852
301-443-6197
http://www.ihs.gov/JobsCareerDevelop/DHPS/
   Scholarships/Scholarship_index.asp
Scholarship Name: Health Professions Scholarship. *Academic Area: Medicine (dental hygiene), medicine (dentistry), medicine (open), medicine (sonography), nursing (open), psychology, social work. *Age Group: Undergraduate students, graduate students. *Eligibility: Applicants must be American Indian or Alaska Native college juniors and seniors, be enrolled or plan to enroll in an undergraduate or graduate program, and plan to serve Native American people at the completion of their training. Applicants also must be willing to work for the Indian Health Service one year for every year of financial aid that they receive *Application Process: The applicant should submit two faculty/employer recommendations, a completed application, an official transcript, and documentation of Native American heritage. An application is available at the service's Web site. *Amount: Full tuition and related fees, plus a stipend for daily living needs. *Deadline: Varies. Contact the organization for details.

Institute of Food Technologists (IFT)

Attn: Elizabeth Plummer
IFT Scholarship Department
525 West Van Buren, Suite 1000
Chicago, IL 60607

312-782-8424
ejplummer@ift.org
http://www.ift.org
Scholarship Name: Institute of Food Technologists/
MasterFoods USA Undergraduate Mentored
Scholarship. *Academic Area: Food sciences.
*Age Group: Undergraduate students. *Eligibility:
Applicants must be enrolled or planning to enroll
in an accredited college/university with an IFT-
sanctioned food science department, be minorities
(African American, Native Indian, Hispanic American,
or Asian American), and maintain a minimum 3.0 GPA.
*Application Process: Applicants must apply through
their food science departments to IFT. They must
submit a completed application, official transcripts, a
letter of recommendation, and a mentoring statement
(signed by the department head). Visit the IFT Web
site to download an application. *Amount: $4,000 per
year (two-year scholarship). *Deadline: February 1.

Institute of Industrial Engineers
Attn: Bonnie Cameron, Headquarters Operations
Administrator
3577 Parkway Lane, Suite 200
Norcross, GA 30092
770-449-0461, ext. 105, 800-494-0460
bcameron@iienet.org
http://www.iienet.org/public/articles/index.cfm?Cat=525
Scholarship Name: United Parcel Service Scholarship
for Minority Students. *Academic Area: Engineering
(industrial). *Age Group: Undergraduate students.
*Eligibility: Applicants should be full-time students
in the United States or its territories , Canada and
Mexico, who belong to an underrepresented minority
group. They must also be active institute members,
have a GPA of at least 3.4, and demonstrate financial
need. *Application Process: Applicants must be
nominated by institute department heads before
they can apply. Once nominated, applicants will
receive an application packet by mail. Visit the
institute's Web site for further information about
the nomination and application process. *Amount:
$4,000. *Deadline: Nominations must be received by
November 15.

**Institute of Real Estate Management (IREM)
Foundation**
IREM Foundation Administrator
Attn: Brooker Scholarship
430 North Michigan Avenue

Chicago, IL 60611
312-329-6008
custserv@irem.org
http://www.irem.org
Scholarship Name: George M. Brooker Collegiate
Scholarship for Minorities. *Academic Area: Business,
management. *Age Group: Undergraduate students,
graduate students. *Eligibility: Applicants must be
minority college students who plan to enter real
estate management and make it their career. They
also must be U.S. citizens, members of a minority
(non-white) group, have declared a major in real
estate or a related field, and have maintained at
least a 3.0 GPA on a 4.0 scale. Applicants must also
have completed at least two courses in real estate.
*Application Process: Applicants must submit a
completed application, official transcripts, three
letters of recommendation, a personal statement,
and an additional letter of recommendation
from IREM chapter president or officer. Visit the
foundation's Web site to download an application.
*Amount: $1,000 to $2,500. *Deadline: March 31.

INTEL Corporation
Corporate US Headquarters
2200 Mission College Boulevard
Santa Clara, CA 95052
408-765-8080
http://www.intel.com/community
Scholarship Name: This company offers scholarships
to women, including minorities. *Academic
Area: Computer science, engineering (electrical),
engineering (computer), information technology.
*Age Group: Undergraduate students. *Eligibility:
Intel awards renewable scholarships for women and
underrepresented minority high school seniors who
plan to attend one of a number of collaborating
universities at Intel sites in the United States.
These scholarship programs are administered at
the relevant Intel sites and are available only for
study at the designated collaborating universities.
Visit the company's Web site for more information.
*Application Process: Applicants must apply for
scholarships through the collaborating universities.
Applications should be requested from these
organizations. Visit Intel's Web site for a complete list
of participating institutions in the United States and
abroad. *Amount: Awards vary. Traditionally, awards
are $2,500 per year and include an Intel Mentor.
*Deadline: Deadlines vary.

Intertribal Timber Council
Attn: Education Committee
1112 NE 21st Avenue
Portland, OR 97232
503-282-4296
itc1@teleport.com
http://www.itcnet.org/picard.html
Scholarship Name: Truman D. Picard Scholarship.
*Academic Area: Natural resources. *Age Group:
Undergraduate students. *Eligibility: Applicants
should be planning to pursue or pursuing a career
in natural resources and demonstrate financial
need as well as academic achievement. High school
seniors are also eligible to apply for this scholarship.
*Application Process: Applicants should submit
a letter, not to exceed two pages, demonstrating
their interest in natural resources, commitment to
education, community and culture, academic merit,
and financial need. Applicants should also submit
a resume, three letters of reference, and validated
enrollment in a federally recognized tribe or Native
Alaska Corporation as established by the U.S.
government. High school seniors should provide
documented proof of application to an institution to
study in the area of natural resources as well as high
school transcripts. College students should provide
documented proof of study in the area of natural
resources along with college transcripts. *Amount:
$1,200 for high school students; $1,800 for students
already attending college. *Deadline: March 31.

Investigative Reporters and Editors Inc.
Attn: John Green, Membership Coordinator
University of Missouri School of Journalism
138 Neff Annex
Columbia, MO 65211
573-882-2042
jgreen@ire.org
http://www.ire.org/training/fellowships.html
Fellowship Name: Minority Fellowship. *Academic Area:
Journalism. *Age Group: Open. *Eligibility: Applicants
must identify themselves with one of the following
minority groups: Black/African American, American
Indian/Alaskan, Native American, Asian American,
Native Hawaiian/Pacific Islander, or Hispanic/Latino.
Applicants should contact the organization by e-mail
or phone for additional eligibility requirements.
*Application Process: Applicants can obtain
applications by contacting the organization. *Amount:
Awards vary, covering the costs of conference

attendance. *Deadline: Contact the organization for
deadline information.

**Jacki Tuckfield Memorial Graduate Business
   Scholarship Fund**
Attn: Scholarship Committee
1160 Northwest 87 Street
Miami, FL 33150-2544
305-371-2711
http://www.jackituckfield.org/requirements.htm
Scholarship Name: Jacki Tuckfield Memorial Graduate
Business Scholarship. *Academic Area: Business. *Age
Group: Graduate students. *Eligibility: Applicants
should be African American full-time students who
are residents of South Florida and who intend to
pursue their professional careers in South Florida.
*Application Process: Applicants should submit a
completed application along with official transcripts,
a letter of recommendation, a current resume, and
a color passport photo. Visit the organization's Web
site to download an application, or contact the
organization by phone to have an application mailed
to you. *Amount: $1,000. *Deadline: May 11.

**Japanese American Bar Association (JABA)
   Educational Foundation**
Attn: Scholarship Selection Committee
Attn: James Toma
PO Box 86063
Los Angeles, CA 90086
310-785-6881
jtoma@ggfirm.com
http://www.jabaonline.org
Scholarship Name: JABA Educational Foundation
Scholarship. *Academic Area: Law. *Age Group:
Law students. *Eligibility: Applicants must be law
students who participate in the Asian Pacific American
community, have financial need, demonstrate academic
achievement, and plan to practice law in Southern
California. *Application Process: Applicants must
submit a completed application along with a personal
statement (not to exceed 500 words), a resume, and law
school transcripts (unofficial copies are acceptable). Visit
the foundation's Web site to download an application.
*Amount: $1,500. *Deadline: February 3.

Japanese American Citizens League (JACL)
1765 Sutter Street
San Francisco, CA 94115
415-921-5225

jacl@jacl.org
http://www.jacl.org
Scholarship Name: Japanese American Citizens
League Scholarship. *Academic Area: Open. *Age
Group: Undergraduate students, graduate students.
*Eligibility: Applicants must be active National JACL
members at either the individual or student/youth
level. For membership applications, visit the league's
Web site. Also visit the JACL's Web site for eligibility
requirements for specific scholarships. High school
seniors and college students are eligible to apply for
this scholarship. *Application Process: Applicants
should submit a personal statement, letter of
recommendation, official transcripts including SAT
and/or ACT test scores, and documentation of work
experience and community involvement. Visit the
league's Web site to download an application or
request one by sending a self-addressed, stamped,
size #10 envelope to the organization. *Amount:
Awards vary. *Deadline: March 1 (entering freshmen);
April 1 (all other students, except entering freshmen).

Japanese American Citizens League (JACL)
1765 Sutter Street
San Francisco, CA 94115
415-921-5225
jacl@jacl.org
http://www.jacl.org/scholarships.html
Award Name: Ruby Yoshino Schaar Biennium Playwright
Award. *Academic Area: Writing. *Age Group: Open.
*Eligibility: Applicants must be interested in telling the
story of the Japanese American or Japanese Canadian
experience in North America. *Application Process:
Applicants should contact the Japanese American
Citizens League for application procedures. *Amount:
Awards vary. *Deadline: Contact the organization for
deadline information.

Kappa Phi Iota Sorority
kappa_phi_iota@hotmail.com
http://www.angelfire.com/nj/kappaphiiota
Scholarship Name: This historically black sorority with
a strong literary focus offers scholarships to women.
*Academic Area: English/literature, writing. *Age
Group: Students (of all ages). *Eligibility: Applicants
must be members of Kappa Phi Iota and exhibit
excellence and potential in writing. *Application
Process: Applicants should contact their local chapters
for more information about scholarship funds
available. Or, contact the national office by e-mail

for application information. *Amount: Awards vary.
*Deadline: Deadlines vary.

Kennedy Center American College Theater Festival
2700 F Street, NW
Washington, DC 20566
202-416-8000, 800-444-1325
http://www.kennedy-center.org/education/actf
Award Name: Paula Vogel Award in Playwriting.
*Academic Area: English/literature, Performing
arts (open), writing. *Age Group: Undergraduate
students, graduate students. *Eligibility: Applicants
must be full-time degree seeking students who
have written a play that celebrates diversity and
encourages tolerance while exploring issues of
disempowered voices not traditionally considered
mainstream. *Application Process: All scripts should
be typed following the standard play manuscript
format (e.g., Samuel French style sheet). Clear
photocopies or letter-quality computer printouts are
acceptable. All manuscripts must be firmly bound
in a cover. Visit the organization's Web site for a
more detailed description of submission guidelines.
*Amount: $2,500 (first place), and the playwright
will be awarded a fellowship to attend at New Play
Development Laboratory; $1,000 (second place), and
a grant of $250 to the producing department of the
play for its support of the work. *Deadline: Contact
the organization for deadline information.

Knight Ridder
50 West San Fernando Street
San Jose, CA 95113
408-938-7700
http://www.kri.com/career/internships.html
Scholarship Name: Historically Black Colleges/
Universities Scholarship. *Academic Area: Advertising,
business, journalism. *Age Group: Undergraduate
students. *Eligibility: Applicants must be minority
students entering their junior year at either Howard
University in Washington, D.C., or Florida A&M
University in Tallahassee, Florida. *Application
Process: Interested candidates who attend these
two historically black colleges should visit their
college placement office for information about the
application process. *Amount: $2,500, plus a summer
internship. Students who maintain a 3.0 GPA during
their junior year receive an additional $2,500 for
their senior year. *Deadline: Contact your college
placement office for deadline information.

Knight Ridder
50 West San Fernando Street
San Jose, CA 95113
408-938-7700
http://www.kri.com/career/internships.html
Scholarship Name: The Knight Ridder Minority Scholars Program. *Academic Area: Business, journalism. *Age Group: Undergraduate students. *Eligibility: Applicants must be minority graduating high school seniors who live in communities where a Knight Ridder publication is published. Applicants must demonstrate exceptional academic achievement. *Application Process: Applicants should visit the company's Web site to find the contact office in their area. Interested candidates should contact their local office for further information about applying in their specific region. Some regional areas have applications for download at the company's Web site. *Amount: Awards vary. *Deadline: Deadlines vary, but are typically between mid December and early January.

Korean-American Scientists and Engineers Association (KSEA)
1952 Gallows Road, Suite 300
Vienna, VA 22182
703-748-1221
sejong@ksea.org
http://www.ksea.org/index.asp
Scholarship Name: This association offers numerous scholarships for students of Korean heritage. *Academic Area: Engineering (open), science. *Age Group: Varies by scholarship. *Eligibility: Applicants must be undergraduate or graduate students in the United States; of Korean heritage, majoring in science, engineering, or a related field; and members of the KSEA. Students may apply for KSEA membership at the time of scholarship application. *Application Process: Applicants should submit a completed application form, a curriculum vitae that includes work experience and extracurricular activities, official transcripts, test scores (relevant SAT or GRE scores), a 500-word essay on either their career goals and their contributions to society or the meaning of Korean heritage in their life, and three letters of recommendation. Visit the association's Web site to download an application. *Amount: $1,000. *Deadline: February 15.

KPMG Foundation
Attn: Anita C. English, Scholarship Administrator
Three Chestnut Ridge Road

Montvale, NJ 07645
http://www.kpmgfoundation.org/index.asp
Scholarship Name: Minority Accounting Doctoral Scholarship. *Academic Area: Accounting. *Age Group: Graduate students. *Eligibility: African American, Hispanic American, or Native American students who have been accepted into a full-time doctoral program are eligible to apply. Applicants must be citizens of the United States or permanent residents and be enrolled full time. *Application Process: Applicants should submit the following materials: a cover letter detailing their reasons for pursuing a Ph.D. in accounting, a copy of their most current resume, copies of their undergraduate and graduate transcripts, and a completed application. *Amount: Up to $10,000. *Deadline: May 1.

La Unidad Latina Foundation
359 Prospect Avenue
Brooklyn, NY 11215
foundation@launidadlatina.org
http://foundation.launidadlatina.org
Scholarship Name: La Unidad Latina Foundation Scholarship. *Academic Area: Open. *Age Group: Undergraduate students, graduate students. *Eligibility: Contact the foundation for information about eligibility requirements. *Application Process: Contact the foundation for information about application procedures. *Amount: $250 to $1,000. *Deadline: Varies.

Lambda Alpha Upsilon Fraternity Inc.
Attn: Orlando Ortiz, National Director of Programming
29 John Street, PMB 181
New York, NY 10038
programming@lambdas.com
http://www.lambdas.com/events/josechiu
Scholarship Name: Jose Chiu Scholarship. *Academic Area: Open. *Age Group: Undergraduate students. *Eligibility: Applicant should be a member of Lambda Alpha Upsilon. The award's purpose is to cover the cost of books for a deserving, qualified brother pursuing undergraduate studies. *Application Process: Applicants should contact Orlando Ortiz via e-mail for an application and for further information. *Amount: Awards vary. *Deadline: Contact the organization for deadlines.

Lambda Alpha Upsilon Fraternity Inc.
Attn: Orlando Ortiz, National Director of Programming
29 John Street, PMB 181

New York, NY 10038
programming@lambdas.com
http://www.lambdas.com
Scholarship Name: Lambda Way Scholarship
Fund. *Academic Area: Education. *Age Group:
Undergraduate students, graduate students.
*Eligibility: Applicant should not have a previous
affiliation with Lambda Alpha Upsilon, and should
have achieved a GPA of 3.0 or better. *Application
Process: Applicants should contact Orlando Ortiz via
e-mail for an application and for further information.
*Amount: Awards vary. *Deadline: Contact the
organization for deadlines.

Lambda Theta Nu Sorority
1220 Rosecrans, #543
San Diego, CA 92106
http://www.lambdathetanu.org
Scholarship Name: Lambda Scholarships are available
at the local chapter level. *Academic Area: Open.
*Age Group: Undergraduate students. *Eligibility:
Applicants must be female high school seniors of
Latino heritage with a dedication to community
service and empowerment of the Latino community.
Applicants also must be planning to attend an
accredited community college, university, or
technical or vocational school. *Application Process:
Applicants must submit a completed application
to the appropriate local chapter (which can be
found on the sorority's Web site). A personal
statement addressing family background, scholastic
achievements, educational and career goals,
commitment to Latina/o community, and financial
need should also be enclosed, along with one letter
of recommendation from a high school administrator,
teacher, or community leader and official high school
transcripts. Visit the sorority's Web site to download an
application. *Amount: Awards vary. *Deadline: May 1.

Latin American Educational Foundation (LAEF)
Attn: Scholarship Selection Committee
924 West Colfax Avenue, Suite 103
Denver, CO 80204
303-446-0541
jcontreras@laef.org
http://www.laef.org
Scholarship Name: LAEF Scholarship. *Academic
Area: Open. *Age Group: Undergraduate students.
*Eligibility: Applicants must be residents of the state
of Colorado; of Hispanic heritage and/or actively

involved in the Hispanic community; accepted
to an accredited college, university, or vocational
school; maintain a minimum 3.0 cumulative
grade point average; and fulfill at least 10 hours
of community service during the year of funding.
Applicants must also demonstrate financial need.
*Application Process: Applicants should submit a
completed application, most recent federal income
tax returns (or parents' return if under age 24),
a one-page personal essay, a list of community
service and extracurricular activities, two letters of
recommendation, relevant high school or college
transcripts, and verification of SAT and/or ACT
scores. Visit the organization's Web site to download
the application. *Amount: Awards vary. *Deadline:
February 15. Applications should not be mailed
before September 1.

Latin American Professional Women's Association
Attn: Ms. Magdalena Duran
3514 North Broadway, PO Box 31532
Los Angeles, CA 90031
213-227-9060
Scholarship Name: Latin American Professional Women's
Association Scholarship. *Academic Area: Open. *Age
Group: Age 23 and up. *Eligibility: Applicant must be a
female of Hispanic decent who is returning to school.
*Application Process: Applicants should contact the
association by mail for an application. *Amount: $500.
*Deadline: April 1.

Latino Medical Student Association
2550 Corporate Place, Suite C202
Monterey Park, CA 91754
lmsaregional@lmsa.net
http://www.lmsa.net/scholarships.htm
Scholarship Name: Janine Gonzalez MCAT Scholarship.
*Academic Area: Medicine (open). *Age Group: Pre-
medical students. *Eligibility: Applicants must have
completed at least two years at a four-year institution
and be able to demonstrate financial need, academic
and extracurricular achievement. They must also
be committed to pursuing a professional career
in medicine and dedication to serving the Latino
community. *Application Process: Applications are
available for download from the association's Web
site in September. Visit the association's Web site to
fill out a membership registration form to be updated
regarding current and new scholarship opportunities.
*Amount: Awards vary. *Deadline: December 1.

Latino Professional Network

PO Box 6019
Boston, MA 02209
617-247-1818
info@lpn.org
http://www.lpn.org

Scholarship Name: This organization offers scholarship opportunities for Hispanic Americans. *Academic Area: Open. *Age Group: Varies by scholarship. *Eligibility: Candidates should contact the network for eligibility requirements and information. Scholarships offered are in partnership with Harvard University and Bentley College. *Application Process: Contact the network regarding the availability of scholarships and the application process. *Amount: Awards vary. *Deadline: Varies.

League of United Latin American Citizens (LULAC)

National Education Service Centers
2000 L Street, NW, Suite 610
Washington, DC 20036
202-835-9646
scholarship@lnesc.org
http://www.lulac.org

Scholarship Name: General Electric /LULAC Scholarship. *Academic Area: Business, engineering. *Age Group: Undergraduate students. *Eligibility: Applicants must be full-time college sophomores through seniors pursuing a bachelor's degree at an accredited college or university in the United States, have a college grade point average of at least 3.25 on a 4.0 scale, and must be U.S. citizens or legal residents. *Application Process: Applicants should submit a completed and signed application, college transcript, letters of reference from three adults, and a typed personal statement of not more than 300 words describing their professional and career goals. Visit the league's Web site to download an application. *Amount: $5,000. *Deadline: July 15.

League of United Latin American Citizens (LULAC)

2000 L Street, NW, Suite 610
Washington, DC 20036
202-835-9646
scholarship@lnesc.org
http://www.lulac.org

Scholarship Name: General Motors/League of United Latin American Citizens Scholarship. *Academic Area: Engineering (open). *Age Group: Undergraduate students. *Eligibility: Applicants must be full-time students planning to or currently pursuing a bachelor's degree at an accredited college or university in the United States. High school seniors are also eligible to apply for this scholarship. *Application Process: Applicants should submit a completed application packet. Visit the league's Web site to download an application. *Amount: $2,000. *Deadline: Contact the league for deadline information.

Lee and Low Books

Attn: New Voices Award
95 Madison Avenue
New York, NY 10016
212-779-4400
general@leeandlow.com
http://www.leeandlow.com/editorial/voices.html

Award Name: Lee and Low Books, a publisher of multicultural children's literature, offers the Lee and Low New Voices Award for a picture book story by a writer of color. *Academic Area: English/literature, writing. *Age Group: Open. *Eligibility: Writers of color who are U.S. residents and who have not published a children's picture book may apply. *Application Process: Applicants should include a cover letter (which features their contact information, a short biographical note, and relevant cultural and ethnic information) and a self-addressed, stamped envelope for return of the manuscript. Submissions through agents will not be accepted. Manuscripts may be fiction or nonfiction, but must focus on the interests of children of color ages 2 to 10. They also must be no longer than 1,500 words. *Amount: New Voices Award: $1,000, plus a standard publication contract with the publishing company; Honor Award: $500. *Deadline: October 31.

Los Angeles Council of Black Professional Engineers

Attn: AL-BEN Scholarship Committee
PO Box 881029
Los Angeles, CA 90009
310-635-7734
corettak@earthlink.net
http://www.lablackengineers.org

Scholarship Name: The AL-BEN Scholarship Awards and Incentives Program. *Academic Area: Computer science, engineering (open), mathematics, science. *Age Group: Undergraduate students. *Eligibility: Applicants should demonstrate academic achievement and a commitment to community service. While there are no restrictions on where applicants are from, preference is given to Southern California residents. High school seniors and undergraduate students are eligible to apply for this scholarship. *Application Process: Applicants should submit a completed application, two letters of recommendation, a two-page essay, and official transcripts. Visit the association's Web site to download an application. *Amount: $500 to $1,000. *Deadline: March 5.

Magic Johnson Foundation
Scholarship Department
9100 Wilshire Boulevard, Suite 700, East Tower
Beverly Hills, CA 90212
310-256-4400
scholars@magicjohnson.org
http://www.magicjohnson.org/tm_index.php
Scholarship Name: Taylor Michaels Scholarship. *Academic Area: Open. *Age Group: Undergraduate students. *Eligibility: Applicants must be high school seniors planning to attend a four-year college or university, have a GPA of at least 2.5, and be a resident of Atlanta, Cleveland, Houston, Los Angeles, or New York City. Applicants should also be involved in extracurricular activities or community service activities. Recipients will be required to participate in Life and Practical Skills classes conducted by the Magic Johnson Foundation and must attend the annual week-long Leadership Conference. Graduating scholars are required to become peer mentors to incoming scholarship recipients as well as to volunteer for the organization. *Application Process: Applicants must submit a completed application along with a one-page essay, high school transcripts, two letters of recommendation, a copy of parent's or guardian's W-2 forms, and a current photo. Visit the foundation's Web site to download an application. *Amount: $1,000 to full scholarships. *Deadline: February 3.

Massachusetts Black Librarians Network
PO Box 240825
Boston, MA 02124-0014
massblibnetwork@gmail.com
http://web.simmons.edu/~mbln/awards.html
Scholarship Name: June Mullins Scholarship. *Academic Area: Library sciences. *Age Group: Graduate students. *Eligibility: Applicants must be African American U.S. citizens who are planning to enroll in a master's

program in library and information science accredited by the American Library Association. *Application Process: Applicants must submit a completed application, official transcripts, and two letters of recommendation. Visit the network's Web site to download an application. *Amount: Varies. *Deadline: January 31.

Media Action Network for Asian Americans (MANAA)
MANAA Scholarship
PO Box 11105
Burbank, CA 91510
manaaletters@yahoo.com
http://www.manaa.org
Scholarship Name: Media Action Network for Asian Americans Media Scholarship. *Academic Area: Film/video, writing. *Age Group: Undergraduate students, graduate students. *Eligibility: Applicants must desire to advance a positive and enlightened understanding of the Asian Pacific American experience in the mainstream media. Applicants must exhibit strong academic achievement and personal merit. Financial need is also considered. *Application Process: Applicants should submit a copy of all official transcripts, completed financial aid documents, two letters of recommendation, and a double-spaced essay of not more than 1,000 words. A work sample consisting of a short film or screenplay is highly recommended. *Amount: $1,000. *Deadline: June 1.

Medical Library Association
Professional Development Department
Attn: Lisa C. Fried
65 East Wacker Place, Suite 1900
Chicago, IL 60601-7246
312-419-9094, ext. 28
mlapd2@mlahq.org
http://www.mlanet.org/awards/grants
Scholarship Name: Medical Library Association Scholarship for Minority Students. *Academic Area: Library sciences. *Age Group: Undergraduate students, graduate students. *Eligibility: Applicants must be members of a minority group, defined as African-American, Hispanic, Asian, Native American, or Pacific Islander, wishing to study health sciences librarianship. They also must be college seniors entering an American Library Association-accredited graduate library school or must have completed no more than half of their graduate program at the time the award is made in February. Applicants must be

citizens or permanent residents of the United States or Canada. *Application Process: Applicants must submit nine copies of a completed application form and personal statement. They must also submit a single copy of two to three letters of recommendation and official transcripts. Visit the association's Web site to download an application. *Amount: Up to $5,000. *Deadline: December 1.

Mexican American Legal Defense and Educational Fund (MALDEF)

MALDEF Law School Scholarship Program
634 South Spring Street, 11th Floor
Los Angeles, CA 90014
213-629-2512
http://www.maldef.org
Scholarship Name: MALDEF Law School Scholarship. *Academic Area: Law. *Age Group: Law students. *Eligibility: Applicants can be entering their first, second, or third year of law school, but must be attending full time for the upcoming school year to qualify. Applicants must demonstrate involvement in and commitment to service in the Latino community through the legal profession, academic and professional achievement, and financial need. *Application Process: Applicants should submit a completed and signed MALDEF application, a current resume, a typed 750-word personal statement, an official undergraduate transcript (or photocopy), official law school transcripts (if the applicant has already completed some law school), a letter of recommendation describing involvement in the Latino community, a letter of recommendation from a professor, a completed financial need statement, and a copy of the LSDAS Report with LSAT scores. Visit the fund's Web site to download an application. *Amount: $3,000 to $7,000. *Deadline: October 1.

Minami, Lew & Tamaki LLP

Attn: Dale Minami
360 Post Street, 8th Floor
San Francisco, CA 94108
http://www.takasugifellowship.com
Fellowship Name: Robert M. Takasugi Public Interest Fellowship. *Academic Area: Law. *Age Group: Law students, professionals. *Eligibility: All fellows must work at a public interest "sponsoring" organization in either the San Francisco Bay area or the Greater Los Angeles Metropolitan area, subject to approval by the fellowship. Applicants should be members

of an underrepresented minority group, including women, and may be law students or graduates. *Application Process: Applicants should submit a cover letter, resume, three references (without letters), and answers to several questions listed on the organization's Web site. Visit the organization's Web site for further information. *Amount: Up to $5,000. *Deadline: March 18.

Minority Nurse Magazine Scholarship

Attn: Pam Chwedyk
Career Recruitment Media
211 West Wacker Drive, Suite 900
Chicago, IL 60606
312-525-3095
pchwedyk@alloymarketing.com
http://www.minoritynurse.com/features/financial/01-13-05a.html
Scholarship Name: Minority Nurse Magazine Scholarship Program. *Academic Area: Nursing (open). *Age Group: Undergraduate students, graduate students. *Eligibility: Applicants must be U.S. citizens or permanent residents who are members of a racial or ethnic minority group, enrolled in their third or fourth year of an accredited bachelor of science in nursing program in the U.S. or an accelerated master's entry program, demonstrate financial need, and maintain at least a 3.0 GPA. *Application Process: Applicants should submit a completed application along with transcripts, two letters of recommendation, a letter from a financial aid officer stating the applicant's unmet need, and a 250-word personal statement. Visit the organization's Web site to download an application. *Amount: $500 and $1,000. *Deadline: June 15.

Mystic Seaport Museum

The Munson Institute of American Maritime Studies
75 Greenmanville Avenue, PO Box 6000
Mystic, CT 06355-0990
860-572-5359
munson@mysticseaport.org
http://www.mysticseaport.org/index.cfm?fuseaction=home.viewpage&page_id=BA0F6A5D-D0B2-1CEA-5778CABEA131F76E
Fellowship Name: The Paul Cuffe Memorial Fellowship is offered to encourage research that considers the participation of Native and African Americans in the maritime activities of New England, primarily its southeastern shores. Fellowships support research

and writing, a portion of which should normally be carried out in the Mystic area. *Academic Area: Maritime studies. *Age Group: Open. *Eligibility: Applicants should have a proposed research project and be members of an ethnic or racial minority. *Application Process: Applicants should send a curriculum vitae or resume, a full description of the proposed project, a preliminary bibliography, brief project budget, and contact information for three references. Visit the museum's Web site for further information. *Amount: Up to $2,400. *Deadline: March 30.

National Academy of Sciences
Fellowships Office, GR 346A
500 Fifth Street, NW
Washington, DC 20001
202-334-2872
infofell@nas.edu
http://www.nationalacademies.org/grantprograms.html
Fellowship Name: The Ford Foundation Diversity Fellowships-Dissertation Awards provide one year of financial support for students working to complete a dissertation leading to a Doctor of Philosophy or Doctor of Science degree. *Academic Area: Anthropology, archaeology, art history, astronomy, chemistry, communications science, computer science, earth science, economics, engineering (open), English/literature, ethnomusicology, foreign languages, geography, history, linguistics, mathematics, philosophy, physics, planning, political science, psychology, religion, sociology, visual arts (history). *Age Group: Graduate students. *Eligibility: Applicants must be U.S. citizens, have excellent academic achievement, and be committed to a career in teaching and research. The Fellowship is available to people of all races, although special consideration will be given to Alaska Natives (Eskimo or Aleut), Black/African Americans, Mexican Americans/Chicanas/Chicanos, Native American Indians, Native Pacific Islanders (Polynesian/Micronesian), and Puerto Ricans. *Application Process: Applicants should submit academic transcripts, a statement detailing their previous research, an annotated bibliography, an essay that explains their plan and timeline for completing the dissertation, a personal statement, letters of recommendation, a completed application (available at the organization's Web site), and other documentation. *Amount: $21,000. *Deadline: December 1.

National Academy of Sciences
Fellowships Office, GR 346A
500 Fifth Street, NW
Washington, DC 20001
202-334-2872
infofell@nas.edu
http://www.nationalacademies.org/grantprograms.html
Fellowship Name: The Ford Foundation Diversity Fellowships-Predoctoral Awards provide three years of financial support for students pursuing graduate study leading to a Doctor of Philosophy or Doctor of Science degree. The fellowship is available to people of all races, although special consideration will be given to Alaska Natives (Eskimo or Aleut), Black/African Americans, Mexican Americans/Chicanas/Chicanos, Native American Indians, Native Pacific Islanders (Polynesian/Micronesian), and Puerto Ricans. *Academic Area: Anthropology, archaeology, astronomy, chemistry, communications science, computer science, earth science, economics, engineering (open), English/literature, foreign languages, geography, history, international relations, linguistics, mathematics, performance study, philosophy, physics, planning, political science, psychology, religion, sociology, urban planning, visual arts (history). *Age Group: Graduate students. *Eligibility: Applicants must be U.S. citizens, have excellent academic achievement, and be committed to a career in teaching and research. Applicants may be college seniors, students who have completed undergraduate study, students who have completed some graduate study, and those already enrolled in a Ph.D. or Sc.D. program that can prove that they will benefit from a three-year fellowship. *Application Process: Applicants should submit academic transcripts, a maximum four-page essay that describes their proposed plan of graduate study and research, a personal statement, letters of recommendation, a completed application (available at the organization's Web site), and other documentation. *Amount: $21,000 per year. *Deadline: November 17.

National Action Council for Minorities in Engineering (NACME)
440 Hamilton Avenue, Suite 302
White Plains, NY 10601-1813
914-539-4010, 800-888-9929, ext. 222
scholarships@nacme.org
http://www.nacme.org

Scholarship Name: This association offers scholarship funding for minority students. *Academic Area: Engineering (open). *Age Group: Varies by scholarship. *Eligibility: Applicants must be African American, American Indian, or Latino Americans. *Application Process: This association has partnered with 32 universities to create the NACME Scholars (Block Grant) Program. Applicants should visit the association's Web site to view the participating colleges and universities and to discover the application process for each one. Contact NACME for additional information. *Amount: Awards vary. *Deadline: Deadlines vary.

National Alaska Native American Indian Nurses Association (NANAINA)
3700 Reservoir Road, NW
Washington, DC 20057
888-566-8773
http://www.nanaina.com/scholarship/main.html
Award Name: National Alaska Native American Indian Nurses Association Merit Award. *Academic Area: Nursing. *Age Group: Undergraduate students, graduate students. *Eligibility: Applicants must be NANAINA members, enrolled in a U.S. federally or state recognized tribe, and enrolled full time in undergraduate or graduate nursing programs at accredited or state-approved schools of nursing. *Application Process: Applicants must submit a completed application, proof of enrollment in a federally/state recognized tribe, a letter of recommendation, and transcripts. Visit the NANAINA Web site to download an application. *Amount: $750. *Deadline: Varies.

National Alliance of Black School Educators (NABSE) Foundation
Attn: Executive Director
310 Pennsylvania Avenue, SE
Washington, DC 20003
202-608-6310, 800-221-2654
Eguidugli@nabse.org
http://www.nabse.org/foundation.htm
Grant Name: Research Grant. *Academic Area: Education. *Age Group: Graduate students. *Eligibility: Applicants must be African-American students pursuing careers in education. Contact the organization for further eligibility requirements. *Application Process: Applicants should contact the foundation for information on application procedures. *Amount:

Awards vary. *Deadline: Contact the foundation for deadline information.

National Alliance of Black School Educators (NABSE)
310 Pennsylvania Avenue, SE
Washington, DC 20003
202-608-6310, 800-221-2654
http://www.nabse.org
Scholarship Name: This association offers scholarships to minorities. *Academic Area: Education. *Age Group: Varies by scholarship. *Eligibility: Contact the foundation of the NABSE for further information. *Application Process: Contact the foundation of the NABSE for information on the availability of funds and the process for applying. This association also lists links to more than 30 other sources of scholarship aid for minority students in a variety of disciplines. *Amount: Awards vary. *Deadline: Varies.

National Asian Pacific American Bar Association (NAPABA) Foundation
Attn: Parkin Lee, Esq.
New York Life Investment Management, LLC
51 Madison Avenue, Room 1104
New York, NY 10010
foundation@napaba.org
http://www.napaba.org
Scholarship Name: Anheuser-Busch NAPABA Law Foundation Presidential Scholarship. *Academic Area: Law. *Age Group: Law students. *Eligibility: Applicants must be enrolled at last half time as a law degree candidate at an accredited law school in the United States. *Application Process: Applicants should submit a completed application form along with an official copy of their most recent law school transcript (or for first-year law students, a statement from their law school certifying that they are law degree candidates enrolled at least half-time), a resume, and two letters of recommendation from persons not related to them. Applicants who wish to demonstrate financial need may also submit a copy of their law school application for financial assistance. Visit the foundation's Web site to download an application. *Amount: $5,000. *Deadline: September 13.

National Asian Pacific American Bar Association (NAPABA) Foundation
Attn: Parkin Lee, Esq.
New York Life Investment Management, LLC
51 Madison Avenue, Room 1104

New York, NY 10010
foundation@napaba.org
http://www.napaba.org
Scholarship Name: NAPABA Law Foundation Scholarship. *Academic Area: Law. *Age Group: Law students. *Eligibility: Applicants must be enrolled as a law degree candidate at an accredited law school in the United States at least half-time. *Application Process: Applicant should submit a completed application form along with an official copy of the applicant's most recent law school transcript (or for first-year law students, a statement from their law school certifying that they are law degree candidates enrolled at least half-time), a resume, and two letters of recommendation from persons not related to the applicant. Applicants who wish to demonstrate financial need may also submit a copy of their law school application for financial assistance. Visit the foundation's Web site to download an application. *Amount: $2,500. *Deadline: September 13.

National Asian Pacific American Bar Association (NAPABA) Foundation

Attn: Parkin Lee, Esq.
New York Life Investment Management, LLC
51 Madison Avenue, Room 1104
New York, NY 10010
foundation@napaba.org
http://www.napaba.org/napaba/showpage.asp?code=scholarships
Fellowship Name: Law Partners Community Law Fellowship. *Academic Area: Law. *Age Group: Law students. *Eligibility: Applicants must be Asian American law students who are committed to serving and contributing to the Asian Pacific American community. *Application Process: Contact the foundation for information on the application process. *Amount: Varies. *Deadline: Varies.

National Association for Black Geologists and Geophysicists

Attn: Scholarship Committee
4212 San Felipe, Suite 420
Houston, TX 77027-2902
nabgg_us@hotmail.com
http://www.nabgg.com
Scholarship Name: National Association for Black Geologists and Geophysicists Scholarship. *Academic Area: Geosciences. *Age Group: Undergraduate students, graduate students. *Eligibility: Applicants

must be members of a minority group and U.S. citizens (or possess a valid student visa). GPA requirements vary from 2.5 to 3.9, depending upon the scholarship. *Application Process: Applicants should submit a completed application along with a personal statement, official transcripts, and two letters of recommendation. Visit the association's Web site to download an application. *Amount: Awards vary. *Deadline: April 30.

National Association for Equal Opportunity in Higher Education (NAFEO)

NAFEO Member Services and Program Office
8701 Georgia Avenue, Suite 200
Silver Spring, MD 20910
301-650-2240
http://www.nafeo.org
Scholarship Name: This organization offers scholarships to minorities. *Academic Area: Mathematics. *Age Group: Undergraduate students. *Eligibility: Varies by scholarship. *Application Process: Visit the association's Web site for links to specific programs at select universities. *Amount: Awards vary. *Deadline: Deadlines vary.

National Association of Black Accountants (NABA) Inc.

Attn: National Scholarship Program
7249-A Hanover Parkway
Greenbelt, MD 20770
301-474-6222
http://www.nabainc.org
Scholarship Name: NABA Scholarship Fund. *Academic Area: Accounting, business, finance. *Age Group: Undergraduate students, graduate students. *Eligibility: Applicants must be members of an ethnic minority who are currently enrolled full time as undergraduate freshmen, sophomores, juniors, or first-year seniors or as graduate students enrolled or accepted into a Master's of Accountancy program. Applicants must be active NABA members in good standing. Dues can be submitted with a scholarship application. GPA requirement will vary, depending upon the scholarship. *Application Process: Applicants must submit a completed application form along with official transcripts, financial aid transcripts, a resume, and a 500-word personal biography discussing the applicant's career objectives, leadership abilities, and community involvement. Applicants may also include information about how they have overcome

a personal, family, or financial hardship. Applications are available by contacting the national office directly. *Amount: $1,000 to $6,000. *Deadline: January 31. (Note: NABA membership dues must be received by December 31.)

National Association of Black Accountants (NABA) Inc.
7249-A Hanover Parkway
Greenbelt, MD 20770
301-474-6222
http://www.nabainc.org/pages/Student_
  CaseCompetition.jsp
Award Name: The National Association of Black Accountants offers the Student Case Competition for student members of the association. *Academic Area: Accounting. *Age Group: Undergraduate students, graduate students. *Eligibility: Student members of the NABA may apply. *Application Process: Teams of four to six students are asked to solve an accounting-related issue at the association's annual convention. A panel of judges from public accounting firms, corporate accounting firms, and academia choose the winners. *Amount: A monetary award is provided to winning teams. *Deadline: Contact the NABA for details.

National Association of Black Journalists (NABJ)
8701-A Adelphi Road
Adelphi, MD 20783-1716
301-445-7100
http://www.nabj.org/media_institute/fellowships/index.
  html
Fellowship Name: The NABJ/United Nations Fellowship allows African-American journalists the opportunity to cover international summits in Africa. *Academic Area: Journalism. *Age Group: Undergraduate students, graduate students, professionals. *Eligibility: African-American journalists who are members of the NABJ may apply. Past applicants have been between the ages of 18 and 30. *Application Process: Contact the NABJ for information on the application process. *Amount: Varies. *Deadline: Varies.

National Association of Black Journalists (NABJ)
8701-A Adelphi Road
Adelphi, MD 20783-1716
301-445-7100 ext. 108
http://www.nabj.org/programs/scholarships/index.html
Scholarship Name: This association offers numerous

scholarships to minorities. *Academic Area: Journalism. *Age Group: Undergraduate students, graduate students. *Eligibility: Applicants must be NABJ members attending an accredited four-year institution in the United States or be candidates for graduate school. Applicants should contact the association for further eligibility requirements for specific scholarships. *Application Process: Applicants should submit four copies of a completed application, two letters of recommendation, samples of work, resume, transcripts, and a 500- to 800-word essay. Applicants can apply for up to two separate scholarship awards and should contact the association for further information on individual scholarships. *Amount: Up to $5,000. *Deadline: April 1.

National Association of Black Scuba Divers
PO Box 91630
Washington, DC 20090-1630
800-521-6227
secy@nabsdivers.org
http://www.nabsdivers.org
Scholarship Name: This organization offers scholarship funds to minority students. *Academic Area: Science. *Age Group: Open. *Eligibility: Applicants should contact the organization about the specific eligibility requirements and availability of scholarship funds. *Application Process: Applicants should contact the association to receive information about application procedures and scholarship funds available. *Amount: Varies. *Deadline: Varies.

National Association of Black Telecommunications Professionals
Attn: Cynthia Newman
2020 Pennsylvania Avenue, NW
PO Box 735
Washington, DC 20006
800-946-6228
http://www.nabtp.org/about/scholarships.shtml
Scholarship Name: The NABTP Collegian. *Academic Area: Business, communications science, computer science, engineering (open). *Age Group: Undergraduate students, graduate students. *Eligibility: Applicants must be majoring in a telecommunications-related field (computer science, business, engineering, mass communication), and show notable achievements through academics, extracurricular, and community activities. *Application Process: Applicants should contact the organization

for updated application procedures and scholarship availability. *Amount: $2,000. Deadline: Contact the organization for deadlines.

National Association of Collegiate Directors of Athletics (NACDA)

Attn: Becky Parke or Brian Horning
24651 Detroit Road
Westlake, OH 44145
440-892-4000
bparke@nacda.com, bhorning@nacda.com
http://nacda.collegesports.com/foundation/nacda-foundation-mclendon.html

Scholarship Name: John McLendon Memorial Minority Postgraduate Scholarship. *Academic Area: Athletics administration. *Age Group: Graduate students. *Eligibility: Applicants must be nominated by an NACDA-member institution and be full-time college seniors or individuals who have graduated with an undergraduate degree who seek to obtain either a graduate degree in athletics administration or an MBA in a sports specialization program. Applicants must also meet the federal guidelines (Title VII of the Civil Rights Act of 1964) for definition as a minority. Applicants must have maintained a 3.0 GPA on a 4.0 scale and have demonstrated leadership qualities on a college/university or community level. *Application Process: Applicant must submit a completed application signed by both the student's academic advisor and the student. Visit the association's Web site to download an application. *Amount: $10,000. *Deadline: June 17.

National Association of Health Services Executives (NAHSE)

NAHSE Educational Assistance Program
8630 Fenton Street, Suite 126
Silver Spring, MD 20910
202-628-3953
nahsehq@nahse.org
http://www.nahse.org

Scholarship Name: This organization offers several scholarships to minorities. *Academic Area: Medicine (open). *Age Group: Undergraduate students, graduate students. *Eligibility: Applicants must be enrolled or planning to enroll in an accredited college or university, pursuing a bachelor's or master's degree. They must be able to demonstrate financial need and must have a minimum GPA of 2.5 (for undergraduates) and 3.0 (for graduate students). Applicants also must be NAHSE members. High school seniors are also

eligible to apply for this scholarship. *Application Process: Applicants should submit a completed application along with as essay as described in the application materials, resume, transcripts (all that are applicable), three reference letters, two pictures (3" x 5"), and a NAHSE student membership application (if dues have not already been paid). Visit the association's Web site to download an application. *Amount: Awards vary. *Deadline: July 1.

National Association of Health Services Executives (NAHSE)

8630 Fenton Street, Suite 126
Silver Spring, MD 20910
202-628-3953
nahsehq@nahse.org
http://www.nahse.org/eweb/DynamicPage.aspx?Site=NAHSE&WebKey=15d71c6b-6843-43d5-b539-c95d2c1a37f6

Award Name: Everett V. Fox Student Case Competition. *Academic Area: Medicine (open). *Age Group: Graduate students. *Eligibility: Applicants must be minority graduate students in health administration programs or a related field who are interested in applying their creativity, knowledge, and experience to analyze the real and diverse issues facing a health care organization. *Application Process: Applicants must apply as teams of one to three students. Three weeks prior to the competition each team receives the case study to analyze and form recommendations. During the competition, each team has 20 minutes to present their analysis and recommendations, which is followed by a 10-minute question and answer period. Presentations are made before a panel of judges representing leaders in the health care field, corporate sponsors, and academia. Visit the association's Web site to download a registration form. A $150 registration fee, per team, is required. *Amount: $1,000 to $3,000. *Deadline: September 2.

National Association of Hispanic Journalists (NAHJ)

1000 National Press Building
529 14th Street, NW
Washington, DC 20045-2001
202-662-7145, 888-346-NAHJ
nahj@nahj.org
http://www.nahj.org

Scholarship Name: This organization offers numerous scholarships to students of Hispanic descent. *Academic Area: Broadcasting, journalism. *Age

Group: Undergraduate students, graduate students. *Eligibility: Applicants should visit the organization's Web site to view a complete listing of individual scholarship in their respective categories since each scholarship has different requirements for eligibility. High school seniors are also eligible to apply for some scholarships offered by the association. *Application Process: Applicants should submit a completed (typed) application along with most recent W-2 forms (parents'/guardians' or applicants' if they are independent), a one-page resume, work samples (limit four), two letters of recommendation, official transcripts (in sealed envelopes), and a typed autobiographical essay written in the third person as a news story. Visit the organization's Web site to download an application as well as to review any additional application items necessary for specific scholarships. *Amount: $1,000 to $10,000. *Deadline: January 28.

National Association of Hispanic Nurses (NAHN)
Attn: Maria Castro, NAHN Awards and Scholarship
  Committee Chair
1501 16th Street, NW
Washington, DC 20036
202-387-2477
info@thehispanicnurses.org
http://www.thehispanicnurses.org
Scholarship Name: AETNA/National Coalition of Ethnic Minority Nurse Associations Scholars Program. *Academic Area: Nursing (open). *Age Group: Undergraduate students, graduate students. *Eligibility: Hispanic nursing students who are currently enrolled in four-year or master's degree nursing programs may apply. Applicants must also have a GPA of at least 3.0 and be NAHN members. *Application Process: Applicants should submit two letters of recommendation that support their ability to perform research to help eliminate disparities in health care, an official sealed transcript, a completed application, a three- to four-page statement that details their qualifications and their leadership in the Hispanic community, and a copy of their current NAHN membership card. *Amount: $2,000. *Deadline: April 15.

National Association of Hispanic Nurses (NAHN)
Attn: Maria Castro, NAHN Awards and Scholarship
  Committee Chair
1501 16th Street, NW
Washington, DC 20036
202-387-2477

info@thehispanicnurses.org
http://www.thehispanicnurses.org
Scholarship Name: Juanita Robles-Lopez/Pampers Parenting Institute and Proctor and Gamble Scholarship. *Academic Area: Nursing (midwifery), nursing (neonatal). *Age Group: Undergraduate students. *Eligibility: Hispanic nursing students who are currently enrolled in a graduate maternal-child nursing program may apply. Applicants must also have a GPA of at least 3.0 and be NAHN members. *Application Process: Applicants should submit two letters of recommendation, an official sealed transcript, a completed application, a three- to four-page statement detailing the maternal child needs affecting the Hispanic community and their potential leadership in this area, and a copy of their current NAHN membership card. *Amount: $2,000. *Deadline: April 15.

National Association of Hispanic Nurses (NAHN)
Attn: Maria Castro, NAHN Awards and Scholarship
  Committee Chair
1501 16th Street, NW
Washington, DC 20036
202-387-2477
info@thehispanicnurses.org
http://www.thehispanicnurses.org
Scholarship Name: National Scholarship. *Academic Area: Nursing (open). *Age Group: Undergraduate students. *Eligibility: Hispanic nursing students who are currently enrolled in an accredited school of nursing and who are U.S. citizens or legal residents of the United States may apply. Applicants must also have a GPA of at least 3.0, show potential for leadership in nursing, demonstrate financial need, and be NAHN members. *Application Process: Applicants should submit one letter of recommendation, an official sealed transcript, a completed application, and other documentation. *Amount: Varies. *Deadline: April 15.

National Association of Multicultural Engineering Program Advocates (NAMEPA) Inc.
1133 West Morse Boulevard, Suite 201
Winter Park, FL 32789
407-647-8839
namepa@namepa.org
http://www.namepa.org/pages/services.htm
Scholarship Name: NAMEPA Multicultural Scholarship. *Academic Area: Engineering (open), mathematics, science. *Age Group: Visit the organization's Web

site for updated specific information regarding age categories. *Eligibility: Applicants must be advocates of the organization's mission of providing diversity in the engineering, math, and science fields by promoting these disciplines to traditionally under-represented minority groups. *Application Process: This organization's scholarship program is currently being revised. Check its Web site for updates or contact the organization for further information about the availability of scholarship funds. *Amount: Awards vary. *Deadline: Contact the organization for deadline information.

National Association of Negro Business and Professional Women's Clubs (NANBPWC) Inc.
1806 New Hampshire Avenue, NW
Washington, DC 20009-3298
202-483-4206
nanbpwc@aol.com
http://www.nanbpwc.org
Scholarship Name: Dr. Julianne Malveaux Scholarship. *Academic Area: Economics, journalism. *Age Group: Undergraduate students. *Eligibility: Applicants must be African-American women who are United States citizens and have a 3.0 GPA. They also must be college sophomores or juniors enrolled in accredited colleges or universities and majoring in economics, journalism, or a related field. *Application Process: Applicants should submit a completed application, two letters of recommendation, official transcripts, and an essay (topic found on association's Web site) . Visit the association's Web site to download an application, or request application information by e-mail. *Amount: $1,000. *Deadline: April 30.

National Association of Negro Business and Professional Women's Clubs (NANBPWC) Inc.
1806 New Hampshire Avenue, NW
Washington, DC 20009-3298
202-483-4206
nanbpwc@aol.com
http://www.nanbpwc.org
Scholarship Name: NANBPWC Scholarship. *Academic Area: Business. *Age Group: Undergraduate students. *Eligibility: Applicants must be high school seniors who aspire to business or professional education at the college or university level. Applicants should have a 3.0 GPA and must be referred by a NANBPWC club member. *Application Process: Applicants should submit a completed application, an official transcript

of first-semester grades of senior year, two letters of recommendation, and a 300-word (minimum) essay addressing the topic, "Why is education important to me?" Visit the association's Web site to download an application, or request application information by e-mail. *Amount: $1,000. *Deadline: March 1.

National Association of School Psychologists (NASP)
Attn: Katie Britton
NASP-ERT Minority Scholarship Program
4340 East West Highway, Suite 402
Bethesda, MD 20814
301-657-0270, ext. 234
kbritton@naspweb.org
http://www.nasponline.org/about_nasp/minority.html
Scholarship Name: NASP-ERT Minority Scholarship Program for Graduate Training in School Psychology. *Academic Area: Psychology. *Age Group: Graduate students. *Eligibility: Applicants must be full- or part-time minority students in good academic standing who have been enrolled or accepted for enrollment in a NASP-approved and/or regionally accredited school psychology program in the United States, with the aim of becoming a practicing school psychologist. They also must be NASP members and U.S. citizens, and maintain at least a 3.0 GPA. Doctoral students are not eligible to apply. *Application Process: Applicants must submit a completed application, a resume, a personal statement, two letters of recommendation, financial information (including Student Aid Report, most recent W-2s, and school financial statement), and official transcripts. Visit the association's Web site to download an application. *Amount: $5,000 per year. *Deadline: January 23.

National Black Association for Speech-Language and Hearing (NBASLH)
800 Perry Highway, Suite 3
Pittsburgh, PA 15229
412-366-1177
NBASLH@nbaslh.org
http://www.nbaslh.org
Scholarship Name: This association offers scholarships for minorities. *Academic Area: Medicine (open). *Age Group: Varies by scholarship. *Eligibility: Candidates should visit the association's Web site for updated scholarship information. *Application Process: Candidates should contact the organization by e-mail for application information and visit the Web site. *Amount: Awards vary. *Deadline: Varies.

National Black Law Student Association (NBLSA)
1225 11th Street, NW
Washington, DC 20001-4217
http://www.nblsa.org
Scholarship Name: This organization offers three essay-based scholarships for minorities. *Academic Area: Law. *Age Group: Varies by scholarship. *Eligibility: Applicants must be members of the NBLSA. *Application Process: The directions, criteria, and essays for the scholarships are posted on the NBLSA Web site each September 1. *Amount: $500 to $1,000. *Deadline: November 1.

National Black MBA Association (NBMBAA) Inc.
Attn: Lori Johnson
180 North Michigan Avenue, Suite 1400
Chicago, IL 60601
312-236-2622, ext. 8086
scholarship@nbmbaa.org
http://www.nbmbaa.org/scholarship.cfm#06mba
Scholarship Name: NBMBAA MBA Scholarship. *Academic Area: Business. *Age Group: Graduate students. *Eligibility: Applicants must be attending an AACSB (Association to Advance Collegiate Schools of Business)-accredited graduate school full time (at time of award) in the United States and must be members of a minority group. *Application Process: Applicants should submit a two-page, typed essay that addresses one of the topics listed on the association's Web site. Essays should have a cover page with essay title and author's name. To accommodate blind review, ONLY the cover page should contain the author's name. Applicants should also submit a resume, and sealed transcripts of all college course work. In addition to the scholarship award, recipients are required to attend the Association's Annual Conference and Exposition, which is paid for (registration, housing, and travel) by the organization. *Amount: Up to $15,000. *Deadline: April 17.

National Black MBA Association (NBMBAA) Inc.
Attn: Ph.D. Fellowship Program
180 North Michigan Avenue, Suite 1400
Chicago, IL 60601
312-236-2622, ext. 8086
scholarship@nbmbaa.org
http://www.nbmbaa.org/scholarship.cfm
Fellowship Name: NBMBAA Ph.D. Fellowship Program. *Academic Area: Business, management. *Age Group: Graduate students. *Eligibility: African-American students who are enrolled in a full-time doctoral business or management program or related major may apply. The program must be accredited by the AACSB. *Application Process: Applicants must submit official transcripts, a completed application, a current curriculum vita or a resume, a 5" X 7" black-and-white photograph for use in public relations, and a competitive research paper that answers the following questions: What is one of the major questions in your field that needs to be addressed? And what unique perspective can black scholars provide to this discussion? They must also agree to become lifetime members of the association. *Amount: $13,000 for those who have successfully completed their comprehensive exams; $7,000 for all other applicants. *Deadline: May 16.

National Black MBA Association (NBMBAA) Inc.
Attn: Lori Johnson
180 North Michigan Avenue
Chicago, IL 60601
312-236-2622, ext. 8086
scholarship@nbmbaa.org
http://www.nbmbaa.org
Scholarship Name: NBMBAA Undergraduate Scholarship. *Academic Area: Business. *Age Group: Undergraduate students. *Eligibility: Applicants must be minority students. *Application Process: This scholarship is implemented at the local chapter level only. Applicants should visit the organization's Web site for a listing of local chapters, and contact their local chapter directly. *Amount: $1,000. *Deadline: Deadlines vary by chapter.

National Black MBA Association (NBMBAA) Inc.- Atlanta Chapter
PO Box 54656
Atlanta, GA 30308-0656
404-572-8001
http://www.atlbmba.org/index.php?option=com_content&task=blogsection&id=40&Itemid=102
Scholarship Name: National Black MBA Association Scholarships. *Academic Area: Business. *Age Group: Undergraduate students, graduate students. *Eligibility: Applicants should contact the association for specific eligibility requirements for individual scholarships. As a general rule, applicants must be minority students in the Richmond, Georgia area who are pursuing a degree relating to business. *Application Process: Contact the association for

detailed information about scholarship availability as well as application procedures. *Amount: Awards vary. *Deadline: Contact the association for deadline information.

National Black MBA Association (NBMBAA) Inc.- Chicago Chapter
PO Box 8513
Chicago, IL 60680
312-459-9161
education@ccnbmbaa.org
http://www.ccnbmbaa.org/default.asp?id=22
Scholarship Name: National Black MBA Association Scholarships. *Academic Area: Business. *Age Group: Undergraduate students, graduate students. *Eligibility: Applicants should contact the association for specific eligibility requirements for individual scholarships. As a general rule, applicants must be minority students in the Chicago, Illinois area who are pursuing a degree relating to business. Applicants may be high school students, undergraduate students, or graduate students. *Application Process: Contact the association for detailed information about scholarship availability as well as application procedures. Applicants will be required to write an essay and undergo an interview process. *Amount: Awards vary. *Deadline: Contact the association for deadline information.

National Black MBA Association (NBMBAA) Inc.- Cleveland Chapter
PO Box 22839
Beachwood, OH 44122
clevelandblackmbas@yahoo.com
http://www.clevelandblackmbas.org/education/scholarship_programs.htm
Scholarship Name: National Black MBA Association Scholarship. *Academic Area: Business, management. *Age Group: Graduate students. *Eligibility: Applicants must be minority students enrolled in a graduate program in business or management at a college or university in the United States. Applicants must be able to attend the Cleveland Chapter's corporate reception and to participate on the student relations committee of the Cleveland Chapter. *Application Process: Applicants should submit a completed application along with a resume, transcripts, a photograph, and three copies of a two-page, typed essay addressing a topic listed on the association's Web site. Visit the association's Web site to download

an application and to review the essay topic. *Amount: $1,000. *Deadline: October 31.

National Black MBA Association (NBMBAA) Inc.- Richmond Metropolitan Chapter
Attn: Faye Brown, Committee Chair
PO Box 15492
Richmond, VA 23227
804-222-2005
scholarship@ricbmbaa.org
http://www.ricbmbaa.org/organization.htm
Scholarship Name: National Black MBA Association Scholarships. *Academic Area: Business. *Age Group: Undergraduate students, graduate students. *Eligibility: Applicants should contact the association for specific eligibility requirements for individual scholarships. As a general rule, applicants must be minority students in the Richmond, Virginia area who are pursuing a degree relating to business. *Application Process: Contact the association for detailed information about scholarship availability as well as application procedures. *Amount: Awards vary. *Deadline: Contact the association for deadline information.

National Black MBA Association (NBMBAA) Inc.-San Francisco Chapter
Attn: Eric Frandson, Scholarship Coordinator
PO Box 193683
San Francisco, CA 94119-3683
510-386-2622
ericfrandson@mba.berkeley.edu
http://www.sfnbmbaa.org/programs.html
Scholarship Name: National Black MBA Association Scholarship. *Academic Area: Business. *Age Group: Undergraduate students, graduate students. *Eligibility: Applicants should be African American residents of the San Francisco Bay Area or enrolled in a college in the area who are pursuing, or intend to pursue, a degree in business. *Application Process: Applicants should submit a completed application along with official transcripts, proof of enrollment or admittance to a business program, two letters of recommendation, a resume, a statement describing projected college expenses, and a three-page typed essay on a topic relating to business. There are three different scholarship applications—one for high school seniors, one for undergraduate students, and one for graduate students. Visit the association's Web site to learn more about the essay topic and to

download the appropriate application. *Amount: $1,500 (high school seniors); $2,000 (undergraduate students); $2,500 (graduate students).

National Black MBA Association (NBMBAA) Inc.-South Florida Chapter

Attn: Patricia Williams, Chairperson
piw8620@aol.com
http://www.sfmba.com/programs.html
Scholarship Name: National Black MBA Association Scholarship. *Academic Area: Business. *Age Group: Undergraduate students, graduate students. *Eligibility: Applicants must be minority students who are permanent residents of the state of Florida and who are pursuing or planning to pursue a degree in business administration. Applicants must demonstrate academic excellence and participation in extracurricular activities. *Application Process: Applicants should submit a completed application along with transcripts and an essay. Visit the association's Web site in late January for updated application information. *Amount: $1,000 (undergraduate students); $1,500 (graduate students). *Deadline: April. Contact the organization for a specific date.

National Black MBA Association (NBMBAA) Inc.-St. Louis Chapter

PO Box 5296
St. Louis, MO 63115-0296
636-230-2404
http://www.stlbmbaa.org/drupal/?q=node/42
Scholarship Name: National Black MBA Association Scholarship. *Academic Area: Business. *Age Group: Undergraduate students. *Eligibility: Applicants must be minority graduating high school seniors or undergraduate students who are enrolled in or accepted into a college or university business program. *Application Process: Applicants must submit a completed application along with a two-page, typewritten essay on a specific topic. Official transcripts are also required. Visit the association's Web site to download an application and to view the essay questions. *Amount: $4,500 (first place); $3,000 (second place); $1,500 (third place). *Deadline: June 30.

National Black MBA Association (NBMBAA) Inc.-Twin Cities Chapter

PO Box 2709
Minneapolis, MN 55402

651-223-7373
scholar@nbmbaatc.org
http://www.nbmbaatc.org/scholarships.html
Scholarship Name: National Black MBA Association-Twin Cities Chapter Scholarship Program. *Academic Area: Business. *Age Group: Undergraduate students, graduate students. *Eligibility: Applicants must be African American students pursuing either an undergraduate or graduate degree in business. Applicants must be residents of the Twin Cities region. *Application Process: Visit the association's Web site to obtain application details and to download an application. *Amount: Varies. *Deadline: April 29.

National Black MBA Association (NBMBAA) Inc.-Washington, D.C. Chapter

PO Box 14042
Washington, DC 20044
202-628-0138
info@dcbmbaa.org
http://www.dcbmbaa.org/orgovrview/programs.htm
Scholarship Name: National Black MBA Association Scholarship. *Academic Area: Business. *Age Group: Undergraduate students, graduate students. *Eligibility: Applicants should contact the association for specific eligibility requirements for individual scholarships. As a general rule, applicants must be minority students in the Washington, D.C. area who are pursuing a degree relating to business. *Application Process: Contact the association for detailed information about scholarship availability as well as application procedures. *Amount: Awards vary. *Deadline: Contact the association for deadline information.

National Black Nurses' Association (NBNA) Inc.

Attn: Scholarship Committee
8630 Fenton Street, Suite 330
Silver Springs, MD 20910-3803
800-575-6298
NBNA@erols.com
http://www.nbna.org
Scholarship Name: This organization offers scholarships for minorities. *Academic Area: Nursing (open). *Age Group: Undergraduate students. *Eligibility: Applicant must be currently enrolled in a nursing program (BSN, AD, diploma, LPN, or LVN) and in good scholastic standing. Applicant also must be a member of the NBNA, including a local-chapter member, and must have at least one full year of school remaining.

*Application Process: Applicants should submit a completed application form, official transcripts from an accredited school of nursing, a two-page essay, and two letters of recommendation—one from the applicant's school of nursing and one from the applicant's local chapter. Applicants may also choose to send supporting materials that document participation in student nurse activities and involvement in the African-American community. Visit the association's Web site to download an application. *Amount: $500 to 2,000. *Deadline: April 15.

National Black Police Association (NBPA)
NBPA Scholarship Award
3251 Mt. Pleasant Street, NW, 2nd Floor
Washington, DC 20010-2103
202-986-2070
nbpanatofc@worldnet.att.net
http://www.blackpolice.org/Scholarship.html
Scholarship Name: Alphonso Deal Scholarship Award.
*Academic Area: Criminal justice. *Age Group: Undergraduate students. *Eligibility: Applicants must be high school seniors, United States citizens, of good character, and be accepted by a college or university (two-year colleges are acceptable). *Application Process: Applicant should submit a completed application, high school transcript, and a recommendation from his or her principal, counselor, or teacher. Visit the association's Web site to download an application. *Amount: Awards vary. *Deadline: June 1.

National Center for American Indian Enterprise Development (NCAIED)
Attn: Tracey Jennings
Attn: NCAIED Scholarship Committee
953 East Juanita Avenue
Mesa, AZ 85204
800-462-2433, ext. 234
events@ncaied.org
http://www.ncaied.org/fundraising/scholar.html
Scholarship Name: American Indian Fellowship in Business Scholarship. *Academic Area: Business. *Age Group: Undergraduate students, graduate students. *Eligibility: Native Americans who are studying business full time at the postsecondary level are eligible to apply. College juniors and seniors and graduate students may apply. *Application Process: Applicants must submit academic transcripts, documentation of tribal enrollment, a completed

application (available for download at the center's Web site), a statement that details their reasons for pursuing higher education and post-college career plans, and separate essays (250 words each) that specifically address their community involvement, personal challenges, and business experience (paid or volunteer). *Amount: Varies. *Deadline: August 4.

National Consortium for Graduate Degrees for Minorities in Engineering and Science (GEM) Inc.
PO Box 537
Notre Dame, IN 46556
574-631-7771
https://was.nd.edu/gem/gemwebapp/public/gem_04_100.htm
Fellowship Name: GEM Fellowship. *Academic Area: Engineering (open), physical sciences, science. *Age Group: Graduate students. *Eligibility: Applicants must be U.S. citizens who are members of an underrepresented minority group (Native American, African American, Latino, Puerto Rican, or other Hispanic American). They also must be accepted into or enrolled in a graduate program leading to a master's degree or a Ph.D. Applicants in master's programs must maintain a 2.8 GPA, while Ph.D. candidates must maintain a 3.0 GPA. All applicants must be willing to intern for a GEM company. *Application Process: Applicants must apply online. Visit the consortium's Web site for a detailed explanation of the application registration and online process. Supporting materials may be submitted by mail. Supporting materials include official transcripts, three letters or recommendation, and GRE scores (recommended). *Amount: Awards vary. *Deadline: November 1.

National Consortium for Graduate Degrees for Minorities in Engineering and Science (GEM) Inc.
PO Box 537
Notre Dame, IN 46556
574-631-7771
http://was.nd.edu/gem/gemwebapp/public/gem_01_100.htm
Fellowship Name: MS Engineering Fellowship Program.
*Academic Area: Biochemistry, chemistry, computer science, engineering (open), environmental science, information technology, mathematics, pharmaceutical sciences, physics. *Age Group: Graduate students. *Eligibility: Minority college juniors and seniors, as well as graduate students, with an interest in engineering

and science may apply. *Application Process: Contact GEM for information on application guidelines. *Amount: $10,000 stipend, plus full tuition and fees at a GEM member university. *Deadline: Varies.

National Consortium for Graduate Degrees for Minorities in Engineering and Science (GEM) Inc.
PO Box 537
Notre Dame, IN 46556
574-631-7771
http://was.nd.edu/gem/gemwebapp/public/gem_01_100.htm
Fellowship Name: Ph.D. Engineering Fellowship Program. *Academic Area: Engineering (open). *Age Group: Graduate students. *Eligibility: Underrepresented minority students who have completed or are currently enrolled in a master's program in engineering or a related field may apply. *Application Process: Contact GEM for information on application guidelines. *Amount: $14,000 stipend, plus full tuition and fees at a GEM member university. *Deadline: Varies.

National Consortium for Graduate Degrees for Minorities in Engineering and Science (GEM) Inc.
PO Box 537
Notre Dame, IN 46556
574-631-7771
http://was.nd.edu/gem/gemwebapp/public/gem_01_100.htm
Fellowship Name: Ph.D. Science Fellowship Program. *Academic Area: Biology, chemistry, computer science, earth science, mathematics, physics. *Age Group: Graduate students. *Eligibility: Minority college juniors and seniors and graduate students who plan to or who are currently pursuing doctoral degrees in the natural sciences may apply. *Application Process: Contact GEM for information on application guidelines. *Amount: $14,000 stipend, plus full tuition and fees at a GEM member university. *Deadline: Varies.

National Dental Association Foundation
3517 16th Street, NW
Washington, DC 20010
202-588-1697
admin@ndaonline.org
http://www.ndaonline.org/ndafoundation.asp
Scholarship Name: Colgate-Palmolive Dental Hygiene and Dental Assistant Scholarship. *Academic Area: Medicine (dental assisting), medicine (dental

hygiene). *Age Group: Undergraduate students. *Eligibility: Applicants must be U.S. citizens or permanent residents who are members of an underrepresented minority group. They also must exhibit academic achievement and be able to demonstrate financial need and a commitment to community service. Applicants should also be able to show proof of student membership in the National Dental Hygienists Association or the National Dental Assistants Association. *Application Process: Applicants should submit a completed online form and application along with a letter or request for consideration, a Student Aid Report, two letters of recommendation, and transcripts. Visit the association's Web site to fill out and print the online application. *Amount: $500 (dental hygiene students), $250 (dental assistant students). *Deadline: May 15.

National Dental Association Foundation
3517 16th Street, NW
Washington, DC 20010
202-588-1697
admin@ndaonline.org
http://www.ndaonline.org/ndafoundation.asp
Scholarship Name: Colgate-Palmolive Freshman-Only Scholarship. *Academic Area: Medicine (dentistry). *Age Group: Dental students. *Eligibility: Applicants must be U.S. citizens or permanent residents who are members of an underrepresented minority group. They also must be freshmen who exhibit academic achievement and are able to demonstrate financial need and a commitment to community service. Applicants must intend to be full-time students. *Application Process: Applicants should submit a completed online form and application along with a letter or request for consideration, Student Aid Report, two letters of recommendation, and a letter from the dean or office of administration of the dental school stating that the applicant will be attending the school. Visit the association's Web site to fill out and print the online application. *Amount: $2,000, renewable for three additional years. *Deadline: May 15.

National Dental Association Foundation
3517 16th Street, NW
Washington, DC 20010
202-588-1697
admin@ndaonline.org
http://www.ndaonline.org/ndafoundation.asp

Scholarship Name: Colgate-Palmolive 2nd, 3rd, and 4th year Post-Doctoral Scholarship. *Academic Area: Medicine (dental assisting), medicine (dentistry). *Age Group: Undergraduate students, dental students. *Eligibility: Applicants must be U.S. citizens or permanent residents who are members of an underrepresented minority group. They also must have completed the first year of their dental program and be able to demonstrate financial need and a commitment to community service. *Application Process: Applicants should submit a completed online form and application along with a letter or request for consideration, Student Aid Report, two letters of recommendation (one from the dean), and proof of member ship in the Students National Dental Association. Postdoctoral students should also send a curriculum vitae, a description of their program, and a nomination letter from their program director. Visit the association's Web site to fill out and print the online application. *Amount: $1,000 (undergraduate students); $10,000 (dental students). *Deadline: May 15.

National Education Loan Network (Nelnet)
888-486-4722
http://www.nelnet.net
Loan Name: Nelnet, one of the leading education finance companies in the nation, provides loans to students, including minorities. *Academic Area: Open. *Age Group: Open. *Eligibility: College students at all levels may apply. *Application Process: Contact Nelnet for information on specific loan programs. *Amount: Varies. *Loan Repayment Deadline: Varies by loan. *Application Deadline: Applications are accepted throughout the year.

National Foundation for Infectious Diseases
Attn: Grants Manager
4733 Bethesda Avenue, Suite 750
Bethesda, MD 20814-5278
301-656-0003
info@nfid.org
http://www.nfid.org/fellow/tropical.pdf
Scholarship Name: Colin L. Powell Minority Postdoctoral Fellowship in Tropical Disease Research. *Academic Area: Medicine (biomedical science). *Age Group: Post-doctoral scholars. *Eligibility: Applicants must be minority researchers who aim to specialize in the area of tropical disease research. They also must be underrepresented minorities with expertise in the biomedical sciences. Applicants must be permanent

residents or U.S. citizens. *Application Process: Applicants must submit one original and four copies of a completed application, a letter from the lab director or departmental chairman overseeing the research, a curriculum vitae, a research proposal, and a statement of recognition that acknowledgement of support must be cited. *Amount: $30,000. *Deadline: January 4.

National Society of Hispanic MBAs
Attn: Julie Aretz, Scholarship America
One Scholarship Way, PO Box 297
Saint Peter, MN 56082
507-931-1682
scholarships@nshmba.org
http://www.nshmba.org/scholarships.asp
Scholarship Name: The Association provides scholarships to Hispanics pursuing a master's in business administration. *Academic Area: Business. *Age Group: Graduate students. *Eligibility: Hispanic students who are studying business at the graduate level are eligible to apply. Applicants must have at least one parent who is Hispanic or both parents who are at least half Hispanic, be U.S. citizens, have a GPA of at least 3.0, and be members of the association. *Application Process: Applicants must submit their undergraduate and graduate transcripts, two letters of recommendation, a completed application, and a copy of their Student Aid Report. *Amount: $2,500 to $5,000 (full-time students); $1,500 (part-time students). *Deadline: Varies.

National Institutes of Health (NIH)
Office of Loan Repayment and Scholarship
2 Center Drive, Room 2E24 (MSC 0230)
Bethesda, MD 20892
888-352-3001
ugsp@nih.gov
http://ugsp.info.nih.gov/default.htm
Scholarship Name: National Institutes of Health Undergraduate Scholarship Program. *Academic Area: Medicine (open). *Age Group: Undergraduate students. *Eligibility: Applicants must be high school seniors or undergraduate students; U.S. citizens, nationals, or qualified noncitizens; and enrolled, or accepted for enrollment, at an accredited four-year undergraduate institution. They must also maintain a minimum 3.5 GPA or be in the top 5 percent of their class; be committed to pursuing careers in biomedical, behavioral, and social science health-related

research; and from disadvantaged backgrounds. *Application Process: Applicants must submit a completed application, an application checklist, an applicant information form, an undergraduate institution certification form, and three applicant recommendation forms. Visit the NIH Web site to download an application. *Amount: Up to $20,000 per year. *Deadline: February 28.

National Medical Fellowships (NMF) Inc.
Five Hanover Square, 15th Floor
New York, NY 10004
212-483-8880
info@nmfonline.org
http://www.nmf-online.org/Programs/MeritAwards/
   meritawards.htm
Award Name: Aura E. Severinghaus Award. *Academic Area: Medicine (physicians). *Age Group: Medical students. *Eligibility: Applicants must belong to one of the following underrepresented, minority groups: African Americans, mainland Puerto Ricans, Mexican Americans, Native Hawaiians, Alaska Natives, or American Indians. Applicants also must be seniors attending the College of Physicians and Surgeons of Columbia University who demonstrate outstanding academic achievement, leadership, and service to the community. *Application Process: There is no application for this award. A committee of faculty and administrators at the College of Physicians and Surgeons of Columbia University selects the student most deserving of this award and presents the candidate's dossier to NMF for final approval. *Amount: $2,000. *Deadline: Deadlines vary.

National Medical Fellowships (NMF) Inc.
Five Hanover Square, 15th Floor
New York, NY 10004
212-483-8880
info@nmfonline.org
http://www.nmf-online.org/Programs/MeritAwards/
   meritawards.htm
Award Name: Franklin C. McLean Award. *Academic Area: Medicine (physicians). *Age Group: Medical students. *Eligibility: Applicants must be students in their senior year of medical school who have exhibited outstanding academic achievement, leadership, and service to their communities. Applicants also must be African Americans, mainland Puerto Ricans, Mexican Americans, Native Hawaiians, Alaska Natives, or American Indians who are U.S. citizens attending

medical degree-granting institutions accredited by the Liaison Committee on Medical Education of the Association of American Medical Colleges, or in D.O. degree-granting colleges of osteopathic medicine accredited by the Bureau of Professional Education of the American Osteopathic Association. *Application Process: Candidates must be nominated by their medical school deans. Schools are required to submit letters of recommendation and official academic transcripts for each candidate. *Amount: $3,000. *Deadline: July 21.

National Medical Fellowships (NMF) Inc.
Gerber Fellowship in Pediatric Nutrition
Five Hanover Square, 15th Floor
New York, NY 10004
http://www.nmf-online.org/Programs/Fellowships/
   fellowships.htm
Fellowship Name: Gerber Foundation Fellowship in Pediatric Nutrition. *Academic Area: Medicine (physicians). *Age Group: Medical students. *Eligibility: African American, mainland Puerto Rican, Mexican American, Native Hawaiian, Alaska Native, and American Indian medical students or residents who are conducting research in pediatric nutrition may apply. Applicants must be U.S. citizens and demonstrate strong academic achievement and an interest in pursuing careers in pediatric nutrition research. *Application Process: Applicants must submit a letter of recommendation from their medical school dean or director of graduate education, a letter of commitment from their mentor or principal investigator detailing the research project they will conduct, an official academic transcript, a curriculum vitae, a statement of their career goals and how the fellowship will help them achieve these goals, a two-page description of the research project (written by the applicant), and a completed application (available for download online at the organization's Web site). *Amount: $3,000. *Deadline: Typically in October.

National Medical Fellowships (NMF) Inc.
Five Hanover Square, 15th Floor
New York, NY 10004
212-483-8880
info@nmfonline.org
http://www.nmf-online.org/Programs/MeritAwards/
   meritawards.htm
Award Name: Henry G. Halladay Award. *Academic Area: Medicine (physicians). *Age Group: Medical students.

*Eligibility: Applicants must be African-American men enrolled in the first year of medical school who have overcome significant obstacles to obtain a medical education. Applicants must be U.S. citizens by the application deadline. Applicants born outside of the United States, or whose parents were born outside the United States, must submit proof of citizenship. *Application Process: There is no special application for these awards. NMF staff members review first-year, need-based scholarship applications and select five students who, on the basis of recommendations, personal statements, and financial need, are most deserving of these awards. For more information on need-based scholarships visit the association's Web site. *Amount: $760. *Deadline: Deadlines vary.

National Medical Fellowships (NMF) Inc.
Five Hanover Square, 15th Floor
New York, NY 10004
212-483-8880
info@nmfonline.org
http://www.nmf-online.org/Programs/MeritAwards/
  meritawards.htm
Award Name: Metropolitan Life Foundation Award for Academic Excellence in Medicine. *Academic Area: Medicine (physicians). *Age Group: Medical students. *Eligibility: Applicants must be second-through fourth-year underrepresented medical students who demonstrate outstanding academic achievement and leadership. Applicants must also demonstrate financial need and must also attend medical school or have legal residence in a select group of cities. Visit the association's Web site to view a list of eligible cities. *Application Process: Applicants should submit a completed application along with a letter of recommendation, transcripts, a 500-word essay, documented proof of financial need, proof of residency, and a curriculum vitae. Contact the association for an official application. *Amount: $4,000. *Deadline: February 25.

National Medical Fellowships (NMF) Inc.
Five Hanover Square, 15th Floor
New York, NY 10004
212-483-8880
info@nmfonline.org
http://www.nmf-online.org/Programs/MeritAwards/
  meritawards.htm
Award Name: National Medical Association Special Awards Program. *Academic Area: Medicine

(physicians). *Age Group: Medical students. *Eligibility: Applicants must be African-American medical students who demonstrate extraordinary accomplishments, academic excellence, leadership and potential for outstanding contributions to medicine. Applicants should also be active participants in their communities. *Application Process: Applicants should submit an application along with a letter of recommendation, a 500-word essay, and academic transcripts. There are several awards offered in this category. Visit the association's Web site to view additional requirements for specific awards. Visit the association's Web site to download an application. *Amount: $2,250 to $5,000. *Deadline: May 7.

National Medical Fellowships (NMF) Inc.
Need-Based Scholarship Program
Five Hanover Square, 15th Floor
New York, NY 10004
212-483-8880
http://www.nmf-online.org/Programs/Scholarships/
  scholarships.htm
Scholarship Name: Need-Based Scholarship Program. *Academic Area: Medicine (physicians). *Age Group: Medical students. *Eligibility: Students from ethnic groups that are underrepresented in the medical profession (specifically, African Americans, Mexican Americans, Native Americans, Alaska Natives, Native Hawaiians, and mainland Puerto Ricans) may apply. Applicants must be U.S. citizens who have been accepted to an accredited U.S. medical school and are first- or second-year medical students. *Application Process: The application packet should include a completed application, a signed personal statement, financial aid transcripts, a letter of recommendation, and copies of federal tax forms. Visit the organization's Web site to download an application. *Amount: Awards range from $500 to $10,000. *Deadline: June 30.

National Medical Fellowships (NMF) Inc.
Five Hanover Square, 15th Floor
New York, NY 10004
212-483-8880
info@nmfonline.org
http://www.nmf-online.org/Programs/MeritAwards/
  meritawards.htm
Award Name: Ralph W. Ellison Memorial Prize. *Academic Area: Medicine (physicians). *Age Group: Medical students. *Eligibility: Applicants must in their senior year of medical school and must be African

Americans, mainland Puerto Ricans, Mexican Americans, Native Hawaiians, Alaska Natives, or American Indians who are U.S. citizens attending medical doctor degree-granting institutions accredited by the Liaison Committee on Medical Education of the Association of American Medical Colleges, or in D.O. degree-granting colleges of osteopathic medicine accredited by the Bureau of Professional Education of the American Osteopathic Association. *Application Process: Applicants must submit a letter of recommendation from their dean, a statement of 500 words or more that details their interest in medicine and career plans, a curriculum vitae, an academic transcript, and a completed application (available at the organization's Web site). *Amount: $500. *Deadline: March 18.

National Medical Fellowships (NMF) Inc.
Five Hanover Square, 15th Floor
New York, NY 10004
212-483-8880
info@nmfonline.org
http://www.nmf-online.org/Programs/MeritAwards/
meritawards.htm
Award Name: William and Charlotte Cadbury Award. *Academic Area: Medicine (physicians). *Age Group: Medical students. *Eligibility: Applicants must in their senior year of medical school and must be African Americans, mainland Puerto Ricans, Mexican Americans, Native Hawaiians, Alaska Natives, or American Indians who are U.S. citizens attending medical doctor degree-granting institutions accredited by the Liaison Committee on Medical Education of the Association of American Medical Colleges, or in D.O. degree-granting colleges of osteopathic medicine accredited by the Bureau of Professional Education of the American Osteopathic Association. *Application Process: There is no open application for this program. Candidates must be nominated by their medical school deans. Schools are required to submit letters of recommendation and official academic transcripts for each candidate. Those wishing to be nominated for the award should contact their medical school dean. *Amount: $2,000. *Deadline: July 21.

National Medical Fellowships (NMF) Inc.
W.K. Kellogg Foundation in Health Research
1627 K Street, NW, Suite 1200
Washington, DC 20006-1702
202-296-4431

http://www.nmf-online.org/Programs/Fellowships/
fellowships.htm
Fellowship Name: W.K. Kellogg Foundation Doctoral Fellowship in Health Policy. *Academic Area: Medicine (open). *Age Group: Graduate students. *Eligibility: African Americans, Asian Americans, Hispanic Americans, and Native Americans enrolled in graduate programs in public health, health policy, or social policy may apply. Applicants must be accepted for admission into one of the following academic institutions: Heller Graduate School of Brandeis University, Mailman School of Public Health at Columbia University, Harvard School of Public Health, Johns Hopkins School of Hygiene and Public Health, RAND Graduate School, University of California-Los Angeles School of Public Health, University of Michigan School of Public Health, or University of Pennsylvania. They also must be U.S. citizens and committed to working with underserved populations upon completion of their doctorate. *Application Process: Applicants must submit official academic transcripts; a resume or curriculum vitae; a 500- to 1,000-word essay detailing their qualifications, their interest in one of the fellowship focus areas, and how the fellowship will help support their career goals; copies of published articles or abstracts; and a completed application (available for download online at the organization's Web site). *Amount: Tuition, fees, and a partial living stipend for up to five years. *Deadline: Typically in June.

National Minority Junior Golf Scholarship Association (NMJGSA)
Attn: Scholarship Committee
4950 East Thomas Road
Phoenix, AZ 85018
602-258-7851
sdean@nmjgsa.org
http://www.nmjgsa.org/scholarships.html
Scholarship Name: NMJGSA Scholarship. *Academic Area: Open. *Age Group: Undergraduate students. *Eligibility: Applicants must be minority high school seniors or college undergraduates who exhibit golfing ability combined with academic achievement, commitment to community service, and financial need. *Application Process: Applicants should visit the association's Web site to register in the association's database before submitting a completed application along with high school transcripts, a one-page essay, a headshot photo, and two references. Being in the association's database means students will

be updated as additional funds become available for future awards. Visit the association's Web site to download application and reference forms. *Amount: $1,000 to $6,000. *Deadline: May15.

National Newspaper Publishers Association
3200 13th Street, NW
Washington, DC 20010
202-588-8764
http://www.nnpa.org
Scholarship Name: This organization has scholarship funds for minorities. *Academic Area: Journalism. *Age Group: Undergraduate students, graduate students. *Eligibility: For eligibility requirements, contact the association by e-mail. *Application Process: Applicants should contact the organization by e-mail for information about available scholarship and the application process. *Amount: Awards vary. *Deadline: Varies.

National Physical Science Consortium (NPSC)
Attn: Program Administrator
3716 South Hope, Suite 348
Los Angeles, CA 90007-4344
800-854-NPSC
npschq@npsc.org
http://npsc.org
Fellowship Name: National Physical Science Consortium Fellowship. *Academic Area: Astronomy, biochemistry, computer science, engineering (open), geology, mathematics, physical sciences, physics, science. *Age Group: Graduate students, professionals. *Eligibility: Students and professionals, especially women and underrepresented minorities, who are interested in earning a Ph.D. are eligible to apply. Applicants must be U.S. citizens who plan to or who are currently pursuing graduate work at an NPSC member institution. *Application Procedure: Applicants should apply online at the consortium's Web site. Required documents include academic transcripts and three to five letters of recommendation from professors and employers. *Amount: $16,000. *Deadline: November 5. Contact the consortium for details.

National Restaurant Association Educational Foundation/MultiCultural Foodservice & Hospitality Alliance
175 West Jackson Boulevard, Suite 1500
Chicago, IL 60604-2814
312-715-1010, ext. 733
scholars@foodtrain.org
http://www.nraef.org/scholarships/mfha
Scholarship Name: National Restaurant Association Educational Foundation/MultiCultural Foodservice and Hospitality Alliance Undergraduate Diversity Scholarship. *Academic Area: Business, management. *Age Group: Undergraduate students. *Eligibility: Applicants must be African American, Asian American, and/or Native American full-time or substantial part-time undergraduate students pursuing course work in the restaurant and foodservice industry. They also must be citizens of the United States, its territories (American Samoa, District of Columbia, Guam, Puerto Rico and U.S. Virgin Islands) or permanent resident aliens that have already completed one grading term; have a minimum 2.75 GPA on a 4.0 scale; have a minimum of 750 hours of work experience in the restaurant and food service industry. *Application Process: Applicants must submit a completed application, a copy of their college curriculum, official transcripts, paycheck stubs or letter from employer, and one to three letters of recommendation from current or previous employers. Contact the association for further application details. *Amount: $2,000. *Deadline: August 26.

National Society of Black Engineers
1454 Duke Street
Alexandria, VA 22314
703-549-2207, ext. 305
scholarships@nsbe.org
http://www.nsbe.org
http://www.nsbe.org/precollege/scholarships/index.html
Scholarship Name: This organization offers many corporate scholarships for minorities. *Academic Area: Engineering (open). *Age Group: Varies by scholarship. *Eligibility: All scholarships require academic excellence. However, some do not require as high of a GPA as others. Visit the society's Web site after September 15 for complete eligibility requirements for individual scholarships. *Application Process: Applicants can download applications and instructions from the society's Web site. *Amount: $500 to $7,500. *Deadline: Deadlines vary.

National Society of Black Physicists
Attn: Scholarship Committee Chair
6704G Lee Highway
Arlington, VA 22205
703-536-4207

scholarship@nsbp.org
http://www.nsbp.org
Scholarship Name: Robert A. Ellis Scholarship in Physics. *Academic Area: Physics. *Age Group: Undergraduate students. *Eligibility: Contact the society by e-mail for specific eligibility requirements. *Application Process: Applicants should visit the society's Web site to download an application. *Amount: Varies. *Deadline: December 1.

National Society of Black Physicists
Attn: Scholarship Committee Chair
6704G Lee Highway
Arlington, VA 22205
703-536-4207
scholarship@nsbp.org
http://www.nsbp.org
Scholarship Name: Elmer S. Imes Scholarship in Physics. *Academic Area: Physics. *Age Group: Undergraduate students. *Eligibility: Contact the society by e-mail for specific eligibility requirements. *Application Process: Applicants should visit the society's Web site to download an application. *Amount: Varies. *Deadline: December 1.

National Society of Black Physicists (NSBP)
NSBP Scholarship
6704G Lee Highway
Arlington, VA 22205
703-536-4207
scholarship@nsbp.org
http://www.nsbp.org
Scholarship Name: National Society of Black Physicists/ American Astronomical Society Commemorative Scholarships. *Academic Area: Physics. *Age Group: Undergraduate students, graduate students. *Eligibility: Applicants should be physics majors with an emphasis in astronomy, astrophysics, or space science. Several scholarships are offered, so contact the organization by e-mail for specific eligibility requirements. *Application Process: Applicants should visit the organization's Web site to download an application. *Amount: $1,000. *Deadline: January 6.

National Society of Black Physicists (NSBP)
NSBP Scholarship
6704G Lee Highway
Arlington, VA 22205
703-536-4207

scholarship@nsbp.org
http://www.nsbp.org
Scholarship Name: National Society of Black Physicists/ Black Enterprise Magazine Commemorative Scholarships. *Academic Area: Physics. *Age Group: Undergraduate students. *Eligibility: Applicants must be declared physics majors approaching their junior or senior year of college. Several scholarships are offered, so contact the organization for specific eligibility requirements. *Application Process: Applicants should visit the society's Web site to download an application. *Amount: $1,000. *Deadline: January 6.

National Society of Black Physicists (NSBP)
NSBP Scholarship
6704G Lee Highway
Arlington, VA 22205
703-536-4207
scholarship@nsbp.org
http://www.nsbp.org
Scholarship Name: National Society of Black Physicists and Lawrence Livermore National Laboratory Undergraduate Scholarship. *Academic Area: Physics. *Age Group: Undergraduate students. *Eligibility: Applicants must be U.S. citizens. The recipient will be required to participate in a summer internship at Lawrence Livermore National Laboratory for at least one summer during his or her undergraduate education. The scholarship winner also receives full travel support to attend the Annual Conference of the National Society of Black Physicists and Black Physics Students and receive the award. Recipients must maintain a B average for the scholarship to be renewable. High school seniors are also eligible to apply for this scholarship. *Application Process: Visit the society's Web site to download an application. *Amount: $5,000. *Deadline: January 6.

National Society of Hispanic MBAs (NSHMBA)
Attn: Julie Aretz, Scholarship America
One Scholarship Way, PO Box 297
Saint Peter, MN 56082
507-931-1682
scholarships@nshmba.org
http://www.nshmba.org
Scholarship Name: NSHMBA Scholarship. *Academic Area: Business. *Age Group: Graduate students. *Eligibility: Applicants must be enrolled in an MBA program at an accredited college or university for

the fall semester. Applicants must be members of the NSHMBA (registration available on the Web site for nonmembers), be U.S. citizens or legal permanent residents, have at least a 3.0 GPA, and come from a Hispanic background where at least one parent is Hispanic or both parents are half Hispanic. *Application Process: Applicants must submit all undergraduate and graduate transcripts, two letters of recommendation, a Student Aid Report, and a copy of the first page of the previous year's IRS form 1040 on which the student is claimed as an exemption. Applicants must also complete an application, which is either available after April 5 to be downloaded from the organization's Web site or can be requested by e-mail. *Amount: $2,500 to $5,000 for full-time students; $1,500 for part-time students. *Deadline: Varies.

National Society of Professional Engineers
Educational Foundation
1420 King Street
Alexandria, VA 22314-2794
703-684-2800
ed@nspe.org
http://www.nspe.org
Scholarship Name: Maureen L. & Howard N. Blitman, P.E. Scholarship to Promote Diversity in Engineering. *Academic Area: Engineering (open). *Age Group: Undergraduate students. *Eligibility: Applicants must be high school seniors, members of an ethnic minority underrepresented in the field of engineering (African American, Hispanic American, or Native American), and U.S. citizens who plan to enroll in a program that is accredited by the Engineering Accreditation Commission of the Accreditation Board for Engineering and Technology. Applicants are judged on their grade point averages, internship experience or community involvement, faculty recommendations, honors and awards received, and their answers to four questions on the application. *Application Process: Applicant must submit a completed application, high school transcripts, two teacher recommendations, and a copy of either the SAT or ACT scores. Visit the society's Web site to download an application. *Amount: $5,000. *Deadline: March 1.

National Strength and Conditioning Association (NSCA) Foundation
1885 Bob Johnson Drive
Colorado Springs, CO 80906

800-815-6826
nsca@nsca-lift.org
http://www.nsca-lift.org/Foundation
Scholarship Name: Minority Scholarship. *Academic Area: Wellness. *Age Group: Graduate students. *Eligibility: Applicants must be minorities, at least 17 years old, planning to enter into the field of strength and conditioning. Minority is defined as "ethnic minority," as determined by the U.S. Census Bureau. Applicants must be one of four ethnic qualifications: Black, Hispanic, Asian American, or Native American. They must also demonstrate they have been accepted into an accredited institution working toward a graduate degree in the strength and conditioning field, and be NSCA members for at least one year prior to the application deadline date. College seniors may apply. *Application Process: Applicants must submit a cover letter of application, an application form, a resume, original transcripts, three letters of recommendation, and a personal statement. Visit the foundation's Web site for further details. *Amount: $1,000. *Deadline: March 15.

National Technical Association
26100 Brush Avenue, Suite 315
Cleveland, OH 44132
216-289-4682
http://www.ntaonline.org
Scholarship Name: The National Technical Association is dedicated to encouraging minority youth and women to choose careers in science and technology, and recognizing, honoring, and preserving the legacy of minority pioneers in technological fields. It offers scholarships to minorities when funds are available. *Academic Area: Science, technology. *Age Group: Varies by scholarship. *Eligibility: Applicants must be members of the organization, demonstrate financial need, and excel academically. *Application Process: Most scholarships require essays, letters of recommendation, and transcripts to be submitted. Contact the association for scholarship availability and application procedures. An online information request form is available. *Amount: Varies by scholarship. *Deadline: Contact the association for specific deadlines.

National Trust for Historic Preservation
Attn: Mildred Colodny Scholarship Committee
1785 Massachusetts Avenue, NW
Washington, DC 20036-2117

800-944-6847
david_field@nthp.org
http://www.nationaltrust.org/help/colodny.html
Scholarship Name: The Mildred Colodny Scholarship
for the Study of Historic Preservation was created
to increase diversity and multiculturalism in the
field of preservation. *Academic Area: History. *Age
Group: Undergraduate students, graduate students.
*Eligibility: Minority students interested in the field of
historic preservation are eligible to apply. Applicants
must be students in their final year of undergraduate
study or graduate students. *Application Process:
The application packet should include a completed
application (available for download at the trust's
Web site), a resume (detailing work, internship, or
volunteer experience), academic transcripts, and
two letters of recommendation. *Amount: Varies.
*Deadline: January 31.

National Urban Fellows Inc.
102 West 38th Street, Suite 700
New York, NY 10018
212-730-1700
http://www.nuf.org
Fellowship Name: The National Urban Fellows Program
is a full-time graduate program comprised of two
semesters of academic course work and a nine-
month mentorship, leading to a Master of Public
Administration degree from Bernard M. Baruch
College, School of Public Affairs, City University
of New York. *Academic Area: Open. *Age Group:
Graduate students, early career professionals.
*Eligibility: Applicants must be U.S. citizens from
diverse backgrounds, have a bachelor's degree, have
three to five years of experience in a management
capacity, demonstrate leadership abilities and
high personal standards, meet the admission
requirements of Baruch College, and be committed
to helping solve urban and rural problems through
public service. *Application Process: Applicants
should submit a completed application (available
for download at the organization's Web site), an
autobiographical statement, a statement of career
goals, a resume, academic transcripts, and three
letters of recommendation. A $50 nonrefundable
application fee is also required. *Amount: A
$25,000 stipend, full tuition, a relocation allowance,
reimbursement for travel associated with the
program, and a book allowance. *Deadline: Last
Friday in February.

National Urban League
120 Wall Street
New York, NY 10005
212-558-5300
info@nul.org
http://www.nul.org
Scholarship Name: This organization offers more than
50 scholarships for minorities. *Academic Area: Varies
by scholarship. *Age Group: Varies by scholarship.
*Eligibility: Visit the league's Web site for links to more
than 50 scholarships available to African American
and minority students. *Application Process:
Applicants should visit the league's Web site for more
information on application procedures or request
further information from the organization by e-mail.
*Amount: Awards vary. *Deadline: January 31.

National Weather Association
1697 Capri Way
Charlottesville, VA 22911
434-296-9966
NatWeaAsoc@aol.com
http://www.nwas.org/award.html
Scholarship Name: National Weather Association
David Sankey Minority Scholarship in Meteorology.
*Academic Area: Meteorology. *Age Group:
Undergraduate students, graduate students.
*Eligibility: Applicants must be minority
undergraduate or graduate students pursuing
a degree and career in meteorology. They also
must be at least in their sophomore year of study.
Applicants classified as seniors must have one more
fall (September-December) semester to complete
after the scholarship is awarded or document that
they have been accepted into graduate school.
*Application Process: Applicants must submit a
completed application, official transcripts, two letters
of recommendation, and a personal statement. Visit
the association's Web site to download an application.
*Amount: $1,000. *Deadline: April 15.

National Women's Studies Association (NWSA)
Attn: Dr. Pat Washington
4537 Alamo Drive
San Diego, CA 92115
619-582-5383
TheMorganGirl@aol.com
http://www.nwsa.org
Scholarship Name: NWSA Women of Color Caucus
Student Essay Awards. *Academic Area: Women's

studies. *Age Group: Undergraduate students, graduate students. *Eligibility: Applicants must be women of African American, Latina/Latino, Asian/Asian American/Pacific Islander, or Native American/American Indian/Alaskan Native descent. Candidates should visit the association's Web site for specific eligibility requirements for individual awards (there are several awards in this category). *Application Process: Applicants must submit an original and unpublished essay, between 15 and 25 pages (excluding bibliography), on white, letter-quality paper, with clearly legible text (do not submit work on onion skin paper). Essays must be in 12-point font, double-spaced, with one-inch margins on all sizes, and page numbers centered at the bottom of each page. Include in the upper right corner of the title page only the writer's name, address, phone number, e-mail address, college or university affiliation, and student status. *Amount: $400. *Deadline: February 15.

Native American Journalists Association (NAJA)
Al Neuharth Media Center
555 Dakota Street
Vermillion, SD 57069
605-677-5282
info@naja.com
http://www.naja.com
Scholarship Name: NAJA Scholarship. *Academic Area: Broadcasting, education, journalism. *Age Group: Undergraduate students, graduate students. *Eligibility: Applicants must be Native American students who are current paid members of the organization ($10 for high school students, $20 for college students). Applicants must demonstrate financial need, academic achievement, and a desire to work in journalism. *Application Process: Applicants must submit a completed application; a cover letter stating financial need, area of interest (print, broadcast, photojournalism, new media, journalism education), and reasons for pursuing a career in journalism; a brief description of any college courses taken; a copy of their FAFSA application or report; one copy of school transcripts; three letters of recommendation; work samples (if available); and a financial profile. Proof of enrollment in a federal- or state-recognized tribe may be requested. Visit the organization's Web site to download an application. *Amount: $500 to $5,000. *Deadline: April 14.

Native American Women's Health Education Resource Center
PO Box 572
Lake Andes, SD 57356-0572
605-487-7072
http://www.nativeshop.org/nawherc.html
Scholarship Name: This organization offers scholarships to minorities. *Academic Area: Open. *Age Group: Varies by scholarship. *Eligibility: Applicants must be female Native Americans. *Application Process: Applicants should contact the organization to inquire about current, available scholarship funds. *Amount: Awards vary. *Deadline: Contact the center for more information about deadlines.

The Newberry Library
60 West Walton Street
Chicago, IL 60610-7324
312-255-3666
research@newberry.org
http://www.newberry.org/research/L3rfellowships.html
Fellowship Name: Frances C. Allen Fund (a one-month to one-year fellowship that encourages Native American women to pursue advanced study). *Academic Area: Open (special emphasis on the humanities and social sciences). *Age Group: Graduate students. *Eligibility: Women of Native American heritage are eligible to apply. Allen Fellows are expected to spend a large part of their tenure at the Newberry's D'Arcy McNickle Center for American Indian History. *Application Procedure: Applicants should submit a cover sheet, a project description, a curriculum vitae, and letters of reference. Visit the Newberry's Web site for more information. *Amount: Up to $8,000 (may include travel expenses). *Deadline: March 1.

The Newberry Library
60 West Walton Street
Chicago, IL 60610-7324
312-255-3666
research@newberry.org
http://www.newberry.org/research/L3rfellowships.html
Fellowship Name: The Susan Kelly Power and Helen Hornbeck Tanner Fellowship is provided for two months of residential research at the Newberry Library. *Academic Area: Humanities. *Age Group: Graduate students, post-doctoral scholars. *Eligibility: Native American Ph.D. candidates and post-doctoral scholars may apply. *Application Process: Applicants should submit a project description of 1,500 words, a

curriculum vitae, three letters of reference, and a cover sheet (available at the Newberry's Web site), which details their personal and professional background. *Amount: $2,400. *Deadline: March 1.

Nisei Student Relocation Commemorative Fund Inc.
19 Scenic Drive
Portland, CT 06480
info@nsrcfund.org
http://www.nsrcfund.org/donations/namedscholarships.html
Scholarship Name: Named Scholarships. *Academic Area: Open. *Age Group: Undergraduate students, graduate students. *Eligibility: Candidates must be of Japanese American descent and exhibit academic excellence. For further information about eligibility, contact the association. *Application Process: These scholarships are awarded by a committee, which selects scholars based on academic accomplishments. Contact the association for further information about how to be considered for these scholarships. *Amount: $1,000. *Deadline: Contact the association for deadline information.

Northwest Journalists of Color (NJC)
The Seattle Times
Attn: Michael Ko
1120 John Street
Seattle, WA 98109
mko@aajaseattle.org
http://www.aajaseattle.org/7a.htm
Scholarship Name: Northwest Journalist of Color Scholarship. *Academic Area: Journalism. *Age Group: Undergraduate students. *Eligibility: Applicants must be high school seniors residing in the state of Washington or undergraduate students at accredited U.S. universities who are pursuing degrees and careers in journalism. The NJC is comprised of the Seattle chapters of the Asian American Journalists Association, the National Association of Black Journalists, the Native American Journalists Association, and the Latino Media Association. Applicants must be Asian American, African American, Native American, or Latino. *Application Process: Applicants must submit a completed application, transcripts, and an essay. Visit the NJC Web site to download an application. *Amount: Varies. *Deadline: May 6.

Office of Naval Research (ONR)
North Carolina A&T State University
College of Engineering

ONR-HBCU Future Engineering Faculty Fellowship Program
Attn: Program Director
551 McNair Hall
Greensboro, NC 27411
910-334-7760
jck@ncat.edu
http://www.onr.navy.mil/sci%5Ftech/industrial/363/hbec.asp
Fellowship Name: Historically Black Colleges and Universities (HBCUs) Future Engineering Faculty Fellowship Program. *Academic Area: Engineering (aerospace), Engineering (chemical), engineering (civil), engineering (electrical), engineering (mechanical), engineering (ocean). *Age Group: Graduate students. *Eligibility: Applicants must intend to pursue a Ph.D. in engineering and must also want to teach engineering at one of the historically black colleges or universities (HBCU). They also must be U.S. citizens or nationals of the United States who have demonstrated academic achievement and who have been nominated by one of the participating HBCUs. *Application Process: Applicants should contact the program director for information on the nomination and application process. Visit the organization's Web site for additional detailed information about the fellowship. *Amount: Full tuition for three years, plus a stipend. *Deadline: Contact the program director for deadline information.

Ohio Newspapers Foundation
Attn: Kathy Pouliot, Secretary
1335 Dublin Road, Suite 216B
Columbus, OH 43215
614-486-6677
kpouliot@ohionews.org
http://www.ohionews.org/scholarships.html
Scholarship Name: Minority Scholarship. *Academic Area: Journalism. *Age Group: Undergraduate students. *Eligibility: Applicants must be college-bound high school seniors who have a minimum GPA of 2.5 and are of African American, Hispanic, Asian American, or American Indian descent. Applicants should have a commitment to a future career in print journalism. *Application Process: Applicants should submit a completed application along with high school transcripts, a 750 to 1,000-word autobiography, and two letters of recommendation. Students may also submit up to two published articles. Visit the

foundation's Web site to download an application. *Amount: $1,500. *Deadline: March 31.

Omega Delta Phi Fraternity
Attn: Daniel Hyliard, National Director of Scholastics
2413 Maple Drive
Jackson, MI 49203
dan.hyliard@omegadeltaphi.com
http://www.omegadeltaphi.com
Scholarship Name: Brother of the Year "Untouchable" Undergraduate Scholarship. *Academic Area: Open. *Age Group: Undergraduate students. *Eligibility: Members of this Hispanic fraternity who have provided an exceptional number of service hours to their organization may apply. Applicants should demonstrate a high level of academic achievement as well as hard work and dedication to Omega Delta Phi. *Application Process: Applicants should submit a completed application form, including the signatures of chapter/colony president and committee chair verifying hours served, two letters of recommendation, transcripts, and personal statement. Visit the fraternity's Web site to download an application. *Amount: $1,000. *Deadline: June 20.

Omega Delta Phi Fraternity
Attn: Daniel Hyliard, National Director of Scholastics
2413 Maple Drive
Jackson, MI 49203
dan.hyliard@omegadeltaphi.com
http://www.omegadeltaphi.com
Scholarship Name: "Carlos Contreras" Brother of the Year Graduate Scholarship. *Academic Area: Open. *Age Group: Graduate students. *Eligibility: Members of this Hispanic fraternity who have demonstrated significant leadership contributions to their organization may apply. Applicants should also demonstrate a high level of academic achievement as well as a commitment to community service. *Application Process: Applicants should submit a completed application form, two letters of recommendation, transcripts, and personal statement. Visit the fraternity's Web site to download an application. *Amount: $1,000. *Deadline: June 20.

Omega Phi Beta Sorority Inc.
Attn: Director of Reach for the Gold Book Scholarship
Grand Central Station, PO Box 3352
New York, NY 10163
reachforgold@omegaphibeta.org
http://www.omegaphibeta.org

Scholarship Name: Reach for the Gold Book Scholarship (Academic). *Academic Area: Open. *Age Group: Undergraduate students. *Eligibility: Applicants must be female high school seniors of color graduating from high school in May/June and accepted to a full-time college or university program for the fall semester. Applicants also must be U.S. citizens or legal residents with a high school academic average of 3.7/4.0 and a minimum ACT score of 23 or SAT score of 900. *Application Process: Applicants must submit an official high school transcript; a copy of their ACT or SAT scores; one letter of recommendation from a teacher, guidance counselor, or school official; a 500-word personal essay; and a business size, self-addressed stamped envelope. *Amount: $500, to cover the cost of books. *Deadline: Must be postmarked between April 1 and May 15.

Omega Phi Beta Sorority Inc.
Attn: Director of Reach for the Gold Book Scholarship
Grand Central Station, PO Box 3352
New York, NY 10163
reachforgold@omegaphibeta.org
http://www.omegaphibeta.org
Scholarship Name: Reach for the Gold Book Scholarship ("Benevolence," Community Service). *Academic Area: Open. *Age Group: Undergraduate students. *Eligibility: Applicants must be female high school seniors of color graduating from high school in May/June and accepted to a full-time college or university program for the fall semester. They also must be U.S. citizens or legal residents with a high school academic average of 2.7/4.0 and a demonstrated involvement in community service projects. *Application Process: Applicants must submit an official high school transcript; one letter of recommendation from a teacher, guidance counselor, or school official; one letter of recommendation from a community service agency verifying involvement; a 500-word personal essay; and a business size, self-addressed stamped envelope. *Amount: $500, to cover the cost of books. *Deadline: Must be postmarked between April 1 and May 15.

Omega Psi Phi Fraternity Inc.
Attn: Charles R. Drew Scholarship Commission
International Headquarters
3951 Snapfinger Parkway
Decatur, GA 30035

404-284-5533

http://www.oppf.org/

Scholarship Name: Founders' Memorial Scholarship and District and National Scholar of the Year Award. *Academic Area: Open. *Age Group: Varies by scholarship. *Eligibility: Members of Omega Psi Phi Fraternity (an African-American service organization) may apply. Applicants must maintain at least a B average, participate in extra curricular activities, and demonstrate community or campus involvement. *Application Process: These scholarships all begin the process by requiring nomination at the chapter and then district levels. Each chapter can submit one nomination to the district scholarship committee. Fraternity members should contact their local chapter president for additional information on being nominated. *Amount: Varies by scholarship. *Deadline: Varies by district.

Omega Psi Phi Fraternity Inc.

Attn: Charles R. Drew Scholarship Commission
International Headquarters
3951 Snapfinger Parkway
Decatur, GA 30035
404-284-5533
http://www.omegapsiphifraternity.org

Scholarship Name: George E. Meares Memorial Scholarship. *Academic Area: Criminal justice, social sciences, social work. *Age Group: Graduate students. *Eligibility: Applicants must be U.S. citizens and members of Omega Psi Phi Fraternity (an African-American service organization). *Application Process: Applicants should request an application from the Charles R. Drew Scholarship Commission of the Fraternity or from the George E. Meares Scholarship Fund. Completed applications should be sent directly to the George E. Meares Scholarship Fund. Contact the fraternity for further information. *Amount: Up to $1,000. *Deadline: April 1.

Omega Psi Phi Fraternity Inc.

Attn: Charles R. Drew Scholarship Commission
International Headquarters
3951 Snapfinger Parkway
Decatur, GA 30035
404-284-5533
http://www.omegapsiphifraternity.org

Scholarship Name: Herman S. Dreer Scholarship/ Leadership Award. *Academic Area: Open. *Age Group: Undergraduate students. *Eligibility: Members of Omega Psi Phi Fraternity (an African-American service organization) may apply. Applicants must have completed their first year at a four-year college; exemplify the cardinal principles of manhood, scholarship perseverance, and uplift; and maintain a 2.7 or higher GPA. *Application Process: Applicants should submit their credentials to their district representatives for consideration to the International Scholarship Commission. Only one applicant per district can be nominated. *Amount: Awards vary. *Deadline: 30 days following the close of the annual district meeting.

Omega Psi Phi Fraternity Inc.

Attn: Charles R. Drew Scholarship Commission
International Headquarters
3951 Snapfinger Parkway
Decatur, GA 30035
404-284-5533
http://www.omegapsiphifraternity.org

Scholarship Name: Ronald E. McNair Scientific Achievement Award. *Academic Area: Biology, chemistry, mathematics, physics. *Age Group: Undergraduate students. *Eligibility: Applicants must be college juniors or seniors maintain at least a 3.5 GPA, and be members of Omega Psi Phi Fraternity (an African-American service organization) in good financial standing. *Application Process: Applicants should inquire at the chapter level regarding application procedures. Contact the national office with additional questions about obtaining an application. *Amount: $500. *Deadline: June 30.

Organization of American Historians (OAH)

112 North Bryan Avenue, PO Box 5457
Bloomington, IN 47408-5457
812-855-7311
http://www.oah.org/activities/awards/hugginsquarles/ index.html

Award Name: OAH Huggins-Quarles Award. *Academic Area: History. *Age Group: Graduate students. *Eligibility: Applicants must be graduate students of color at the dissertation research stage of their Ph.D. program. *Application Process: Applicants should submit a five-page dissertation proposal (which should include a definition of the project, an explanation of the project's significance and contribution to the field, and a description of its most important primary sources), along with a one-page itemized budget explaining travel and research plans. The application should be accompanied by a letter from the dissertation advisor. A complete copy of the application should be mailed to each committee member. Visit the OAH's Web site for a complete listing of committee members and their addresses. *Amount: $1,000 to $2,000. *Deadline: December 1.

Organization of Black Airline Pilots (OBAP)

Attn: William Davis
OBAP/Delta Scholarship
8630 Fenton Street, Suite 126
Silver Spring, MD 20910
800-538-6227
nationaloffice@obap.org
http://www.obap.org/Programs/programs-scholarship.asp

Scholarship Name: Delta Air Lines Boeing B737-800 Type Rating Certificate Scholarship. *Academic Area: Aviation. *Age Group: Undergraduate students, early career professionals. *Eligibility: Applicants must be pursuing or hold a baccalaureate degree, have a minimum GPA of 2.5 (on a 4.0 scale), possess leadership potential, and be a current OBAP member in good standing (dues paid). Applicants must hold commercial, instrument and multiengine land certificates, have a minimum of 500 hours total time, and a current first class FAA medical certificate. Application Process: Applicants should submit resumes that include all certifications/ratings, total flying time, all schools attended, academic honors, scholarships, awards, special achievements, and any military history (if applicable). Applicant should include in the application package a copy of his or her driver's license, driving record for the past seven years (including dates and locations of any moving violations) as well as any convictions of any type of violations of the law (moving or not), with dates and locations. Applicants should also submit a copy of his or her current passport. *Amount: *$35,000 (value of six-week program and paid expenses). *Deadline: June 15.

Organization of Black Airline Pilots (OBAP)

8630 Fenton Street, Suite 126
Silver Spring, MD 20910
800-538-6227
nationaloffice@obap.org
http://www.obap.org/Programs/programs-scholarship.asp

Scholarship Name: OBAP Professional Pilot Development Scholarship. *Academic Area: Aviation. *Age Group: Open. *Eligibility: Some scholarships may require OBAP membership, while others will not. *Application Process: There is no reliable schedule that identifies when scholarship offers will be available. Notice of available scholarships will be provided to OBAP members through its Web site, newsletter, and the NewsFlash@obap.org e-mail list. *Amount: Awards vary. *Deadline: Deadlines vary by scholarship.

Organization of Chinese Americans (OCA)

OCA-Avon Scholarship
1001 Connecticut Avenue, NW, Suite 601
Washington, DC 20036
oca@ocanatl.org
http://www.ocanatl.org/bin/htmlos/02210.2.3266155583300024868

Scholarship Name: OCA-Avon Scholarship. *Academic Area: Open. *Age Group: Undergraduate students. *Eligibility: Applicants must be Asian Pacific American women who are entering their first year of college in the fall semester, able to demonstrate financial need, and permanent residents or U.S. citizens. They must also have maintained a GPA of 3.0. *Application Process: Applicants should submit a completed application along with supporting materials. Information is available on the organization's Web site in March of each year. You may also contact the organization by mail or e-mail for application instructions. *Amount: $2,000. *Deadline: Contact the organization for deadline information.

Organization of Chinese Americans (OCA)

OCA-KFC Essay Contest
1001 Connecticut Avenue, NW, Suite 601
Washington, DC 20036
oca@ocanatl.org
http://www.ocanatl.org/bin/htmlos/0216.2.2892990508700009630

Contest Name: OCA-KFC Essay Contest. *Academic Area: Open. *Age Group: High school students. *Eligibility: Applicants must be Asian Pacific Americans in grades nine through 12. *Application Process: Applicants should submit a completed application along with five copies of an 800- to 1,000-word essay, in response to a topic posted on the organization's Web site in February of each year. Check the organization's Web site in February of each year for the essay topic and to download an application. You may also contact the organization by mail or e-mail for further instructions. *Amount: $1,000 (first place); $500 (second place); $300 (third place). *Deadline: Contact the organization for deadline information.

Organization of Chinese Americans (OCA)
OCA-UPS Gold Mountain Scholarship
1001 Connecticut Avenue, NW, Suite 601
Washington, DC 20036
oca@ocanatl.org
http://www.ocanatl.org/bin/
    htmlos/0216.2.3946744895700009630
Scholarship Name: OCA-UPS Gold Mountain Scholarship. *Academic Area: Open. *Age Group: Undergraduate students. *Eligibility: Applicants must be Asian Pacific American, the first in their immediate families to be attending college, entering their first year of college in the fall semester, able to demonstrate financial need, and permanent residents or U.S. citizens. Applicants must also have maintained a GPA of 3.0. *Application Process: Applicants should submit a completed application along with supporting materials. Further information is available on the organization's Web site in March of each year. You may also contact the organization by mail or e-mail for application instructions. *Amount: $2,000. *Deadline: Contact the organization for deadline information.

Organization of Chinese Americans (OCA)
OCA-Verizon Scholarship
1001 Connecticut Avenue, NW, Suite 601
Washington, DC 20036
oca@ocanatl.org
http://www.ocanatl.org/bin/
    htmlos/0216.2.4094275948300009630
Scholarship Name: OCA-Verizon Scholarship. *Academic Area: Open. *Age Group: Undergraduate students. *Eligibility: Applicants must be Asian Pacific American, entering their first year of college in the fall semester, able to demonstrate financial need, and permanent residents or U.S. citizens. Applicants must also have maintained a GPA of 3.0. *Application Process: Applicants should submit a completed application along with supporting materials. Further information is available on the organization's Web site in March of each year. You may also contact the organization by mail or e-mail for application instructions. *Amount: $2,000. *Deadline: Contact the organization for deadline information.

Pacific Islanders in Communications
Attn: Gus Cobb-Adams
Scholarship Committee
1221 Kapi'olani Boulevard, Suite 6A-4
Honolulu, HI 96814-3513
808-591-0059
gcobb-adams@piccom.org
http://www.piccom.org
Scholarship Name: Pacific Islanders in Communications Scholarship Fund. *Academic Area: Broadcasting, communications science. *Age Group: Undergraduate students, graduate students. *Eligibility: Applicants must be at least 18 years of age; be pursuing a degree, certificate, and/or other certification in media and/or communications at the undergraduate, graduate, and unclassified levels of study; demonstrate academic proficiency and/or have demonstrated experience in media and/or communications or a related field; demonstrate commitment to the Pacific Islander community; and demonstrate a need for financial assistance. High school seniors are also eligible to apply for this scholarship. *Application Process: Applicants should submit a completed application form, a 500-word essay, a copy of the U.S. Department of Education's Free Application for Federal Student Aid, three letters of recommendation from non-family members, and current transcripts. Visit the organization's Web site to download an application. *Amount: Up to $5,000. *Deadline: March 3.

Page Education Foundation
PO Box 581254
Minneapolis, MN 55458-1254
612-332-0406
info@page-ed.org
http://www.page-ed.org/mechanics.html
Grant Name: Page Educational Foundation Grant. *Academic Area: Open. *Age Group: Undergraduate students. *Eligibility: Applicants must be graduating high school seniors or undergraduate students of color who are attending or intend to attend a college or university in Minnesota. Applicants must also demonstrate financial need, a positive attitude toward education, and a commitment to community service. *Application Process: Candidates should visit the foundation's Web site for information about the program. E-mail the organization to receive an application. Applicants should submit the application along with a 400- to 500-word essay, three letters of recommendation, transcripts, and copy of the

Free Application for Federal Student Aid or their parents' federal tax return. *Amount: $900 to $2,500; renewable based on performance. *Deadline: May 1.

Paul and Daisy Soros Fellowships for New Americans
400 West 59th Street
New York, NY 10019
212-547-6926
pdsoros_fellows@sorosny.org
http://www.pdsoros.org
Fellowship Name: The Paul and Daisy Soros Fellowship for New Americans provides graduate education opportunities for new immigrants. *Academic Area: Open. *Age Group: Graduate students. *Eligibility: Resident aliens who are 30 years of age or younger as of November 1 of the year of application may apply. *Application Process: Applicants should submit two essays on specified topics, three recommendation letters, a one- to two-page resume, and a completed application (available at the organization's Web site). *Amount: A maintenance grant of $20,000 and a tuition grant of one-half the tuition cost of the fellow's U.S. graduate program (up to a maximum of $16,000 per academic year) are provided. *Deadline: November 1.

PEN American Center
Attn: Stacy Leigh
588 Broadway, Suite 303
New York, NY 10012
212-334-1660, ext. 109
stacyleigh@pen.org
http://www.pen.org/page.php/prmID/280
Award Name: The PEN American Center offers the PEN/Beyond Margins Award for book-length works by authors of color. *Academic Area: English/literature, writing. *Age Group: Open. *Eligibility: African, Arab, Asian, Caribbean, Latino, and Native American writers who have published a book in the United States during the current calendar year may apply. Preference is given to works of fiction, literary nonfiction, biography/memoir, and other works of literary character. *Application Process: Only publishers and agents may submit books (including official letters of recommendation). Books that have been self-published are not eligible. *Amount: $1,000. *Deadline: December 30.

Phi Beta Sigma Fraternity Inc.
Attn: Brother Michael W. Hines, International Director of Education

Two Belmonte Circle
Atlanta, GA 30311
404-752-1210
mhines@pbseducation1914.org
http://www.pbseducation1914.org
Scholarship Name: Phi Beta Sigma Scholarships. *Academic Area: Open. *Age Group: Undergraduate students, graduate students. *Eligibility: Applicants must be active members of Phi Beta Sigma (an African-American service organization) in good standing and maintain at least a 3.0 GPA. *Application Process: Applicants should submit a completed application along with official transcripts, three letters of recommendation, a resume, list of involvement with national programs and special events, a list of any previously received scholarships (and duration), an essay outlining career ambitions and goals, and a picture (headshot). Visit the fraternity's Web site to download an application. *Amount: Awards vary. *Deadline: April 1.

Phi Delta Psi Fraternity Inc.
Memorial Scholarship Program
8200 East Jefferson, Suite 907
Detroit, MI 48214
pdpsi@phideltapsifraternity.org
http://www.phideltapsifraternity.org/service.htm
Scholarship Name: This fraternity offers scholarship funding through its Memorial Scholarship Fund. *Academic Area: Open. *Age Group: Undergraduate students, graduate students. *Eligibility: Applicants must be members of Phi Delta Psi Fraternity (an African-American service organization). *Application Process: Applicants should contact the fraternity for further information about the availability of scholarship funds and the application process. Members should contact their chapter president for further information or contact the national office by e-mail. *Amount: Awards vary. *Deadline: Varies.

Philadelphia Association of Black Journalists
Attn: Nia Ngina Meeks
PO Box 8232
Philadelphia, PA 19101
215-492-2980
nmeeks@pasenate.com
http://www.pabj.org/pabjscholarship.htm
Scholarship Name: Philadelphia Association of Black Journalists Scholarship. *Academic Area: Journalism. *Age Group: Undergraduate students. *Eligibility:

Applicants must be African American high school seniors attending a public or private high school in the city of Philadelphia. Applicants must plan to pursue a degree from a four-year college or university. They must also maintain at least a 2.5 GPA and demonstrate an interest in pursuing a career in journalism. *Application Process: Applicants must submit a completed application, transcripts, a two-page personal profile, a writing sample, and two letters of recommendation. Visit the association's Web site to download an application. *Amount: $1,000. *Deadline: May 16.

Philadelphia Association of Black Journalists
Attn: Nia Ngina Meeks
PO Box 8232
Philadelphia, PA 19101
215-492-2980
nmeeks@pasenate.com
http://www.pabj.org/tribunescholarship.htm
Scholarship Name: Philadelphia Tribune Scholarship. *Academic Area: Journalism. *Age Group: Undergraduate students. *Eligibility: Applicants must be residents of Philadelphia who are either high school seniors planning to attend a historically black college or university or college students already attending a historically black college or university (HBCU). Applicants must maintain at least a 2.5 GPA, be majoring in or planning to major in journalism, and interested in pursuing a career in print journalism. *Application Process: Applicants must submit a completed application, transcripts, an essay, a writing sample, a critique of The Tribune or other local paper (college students only), proof of acceptance at a HBCU (high school students only), and two letters of recommendation. *Amount: $1,000. *Deadline: May 16.

Philippine Nurses Association of America (PNAA) Inc.
Attn: Josie Villanueva
24556 Mando Drive
Laguna Niguel, CA 92677-4079
949-831-4247
josie.villanueva@med.va.gov
http://www.pnaa03.org/04_7_Awards_Scholarship.html
Scholarship Name: PNAA Nursing Scholarship. *Academic Area: Nursing (open). *Age Group: Graduate students. *Eligibility: Applicants must be enrolled in an accredited master's or doctoral nursing program, current members of the PNAA, and demonstrate academic achievement by maintaining

at least a 3.0 GPA. *Application Process: Applicants should submit a completed application along with a letter of acceptance to an accredited program, transcripts, two letters of recommendation, a resume, and a 150-word essay. Visit the association's Web site to download an application. *Amount: $1,000. *Deadline: Two months prior to the national convention. Visit the association's Web site for dates.

Pi Delta Psi Fraternity Inc.
Church Street Station
PO Box 2920
New York, NY 10008-2920
917-421-3900
president@pideltapsi.com
http://www.pideltapsi.com/index_actual.html
Scholarship Name: Pi Delta Psi Academic Award. *Academic Area: Open. *Age Group: Undergraduate students. *Eligibility: Applicants must be members of Pi Delta Psi Fraternity (an Asian American service organization) who have achieved the highest academic excellence. Candidates must be full-time students. *Application Process: Applicants must be nominated by the president of his school's chapter, who must submit a letter of intent for his nominee at the end of each year. Each school must include documentation and an explanation as to why each of these individuals should be considered. The applicant must also supply an original copy of his current semester transcript. Applicants should request further information from their local chapter president. *Amount: $250. *Deadline: Contact the fraternity for deadline information.

Pi Delta Psi Fraternity Inc.
Church Street Station
PO Box 2920
New York, NY 10008-2920
917-421-3900
president@pideltapsi.com
http://www.pideltapsi.com/index_actual.html
Scholarship Name: Pi Delta Psi Award (aka The Odie Award). *Academic Area: Open. *Age Group: Undergraduate students. *Eligibility: Applicants must be members of Pi Delta Psi Fraternity (an Asian American service organization) who have shown exceptional dedication to the fraternity as well as outstanding contribution to the community. Applicants will have shown exemplary conduct as

honorable men and the poise of great role models. *Application Process: The president must state why this nominee should be considered a candidate, due to his leadership skills or his dedications and contributions to the fraternity and the community. Applicants should request further information from their local chapter president. *Amount: $250. *Deadline: Contact the fraternity for deadline information.

The Playwrights' Center

Many Voices Residency
2301 Franklin Avenue East
Minneapolis, MN 55406-1099
612-332-7481, ext. 10
info@pwcenter.org
http://www.pwcenter.org/fellowships_MV.asp
Grant Name: Many Voices Residency. *Academic Area: Performing arts (theatre), writing. *Age Group: Open. *Eligibility: Applicants should be artists of color pursuing the opportunity to develop new work in the field of playwriting. Many Voices is designed to increase cultural diversity in the contemporary theater, both locally and nationally. Applicants must be U.S. citizens or permanent residents and recipients must maintain residency in Minnesota or within 100 miles of the Twin Cities during the grant year. *Application Process: Applicants should submit a completed application form along with a one-page personal statement and/or resume, a writing sample of any length, and a one-page description of goals for the residency. Application packets should be submitted in four collated, bound packets. Visit the center's Web site to download an application. *Amount: Awards vary. *Deadline: July 30.

Presbyterian Church USA

Attn: Laura Bryan
100 Witherspoon Street
Louisville, KY 40202-1396
888-728-7228
http://www.pcusa.org/financialaid/graduate.htm
Grant Name: Native American Supplemental Grant. *Academic Area: Religion. *Age Group: Graduate students. *Eligibility: Applicants must be Native Americans preparing to serve in a Presbyterian Church USA congregation. Applicants must be members of the Presbyterian Church, U.S. citizens or permanent residents, demonstrate financial need, and be pursuing a first professional degree in preparation for

a church occupation. *Application Process: Applicants should submit a completed application along with supporting documents. Visit the organization's Web site to download an application. *Amount: $500 to $1,500. *Deadline: June 1.

Presbyterian Church USA

Attn: Laura Bryan
100 Witherspoon Street
Louisville, KY 40202-1396
888-728-7228
http://www.pcusa.org/financialaid/graduate.htm
Grant Name: Racial Ethnic Supplemental Grant. *Academic Area: Religion. *Age Group: Graduate students. *Eligibility: Applicants must be African American, Alaska Native, Asian American, Hispanic American, or Native American students who have been awarded the Presbyterian Study Grant (a grant that is available to all ethnic groups) and have remaining need. Applicants must be preparing to serve in a Presbyterian Church USA congregation, and must currently be members of the Presbyterian Church USA, U.S. citizens or permanent residents, demonstrate financial need, and be pursuing a first professional degree in preparation for a church occupation. *Application Process: Applicants should submit a completed application along with supporting documents. Visit the organization's Web site to download an application. *Amount: $500 to $1,000. *Deadline: October 15.

Presbyterian Church USA

Attn: Kathy Smith
Financial Aid for Studies
100 Witherspoon Street
Louisville, KY 40202-1396
888-728-7228
http://www.pcusa.org/financialaid/undergraduate.htm
Scholarship Name: Student Opportunity Scholarship. *Academic Area: Open. *Age Group: Undergraduate students. *Eligibility: Students who are members of the Presbyterian Church USA, U.S. citizens or permanent residents of the United States, who have completed their second year of college and maintained at least a 2.5 GPA are eligible to apply. Preference will be given to racial ethnic students. Applicants must also demonstrate financial need and attend college full time. *Application Process: Contact the Presbyterian Church USA for information. *Amount: Scholarships range from $200 to $2,000. *Deadline: May 22.

Professional Hispanics in Energy
20505 Yorba Linda Boulevard, Suite 324
Yorba Linda, CA 92886-7109
714-777-7729
http://www.phie.org
Scholarship Name: This organization offers scholarships
for Hispanic students. *Academic Area: Geosciences.
*Age Group: Varies by scholarship. *Eligibility:
Applicants must be deserving students of Hispanic
descent who are pursuing careers related to energy
and the environment. *Application Process: Contact
the organization by phone or e-mail (visit the Web
site to submit a question) for further information
about the scholarship application process. *Amount:
Awards vary. *Deadline: Contact the organization for
deadline information.

Professional Women of Color (PWC)
Dream Grant
PO Box 5196
New York, NY 10185
212-714-7190
TLawr64783@aol.com
http://www.pwcnetwork.org/dreamgrant.html
Grant Name: The Professional Women of Color Dream
Grant helps minority women start a business, attend
an educational program, finish a research project,
or introduce a new product. *Academic Area: Open.
*Age Group: Undergraduate students, graduate
students, professionals. *Eligibility: Current members
of PWC are eligible to apply. *Application Procedure:
Applicants should submit a 300- to 1,000-word essay
that details their project/venture, a resume, a one-
page bio, and a 3 ½" x 5" black-and-white headshot.
An application fee of $50 is required. *Amount:
Grants range from $3,000 to $5,000. *Deadline: Varies.
Contact PWC for more information.

Public Relations Society of America Foundation
33 Maiden Lane, 11th Floor
New York, NY 10038-5150
212-460-1424
foundation@prsa.org
http://www.prsa.org/_About/prsafoundation/
scholarships.asp?ident=prsa8.5
Scholarship Name: Multicultural Affairs Scholarship.
*Academic Area: Public relations. *Age Group:
Undergraduate students, graduate students.
*Eligibility: Applicants must be minority college
students who demonstrate outstanding academic
achievement and commitment to the practice of

public relations. *Application Process: Applicants must
submit an essay on a designated topic. Contact the
society for essay guidelines and application details.
*Amount: $1,500. *Deadline: Varies.

Radio-Television News Directors Foundation (RTNDF)
Attn: Irving Washington
1600 K Street, NW, Suite 700
Washington, DC 20006-2838
202-467-5218
irvingw@rtndf.org
http://www.rtnda.org/asfi/scholarships/minority.shtml
Scholarship Name: Carole Simpson Scholarship.
*Academic Area: Broadcasting, journalism. *Age
Group: Undergraduate students. *Eligibility: Minority
students whose career objective is electronic
journalism (radio or television) and who have at
least one full year of college remaining are eligible to
apply. Applicants must also attend college full time.
Note: Freshmen cannot apply. *Application Process:
Contact the foundation for details. *Amount: $2,000.
*Deadline: Varies.

Radio-Television News Directors Foundation (RTNDF)
Attn: Irving Washington
1600 K Street, NW, Suite 700
Washington, DC 20006-2838
202-467-5218
irvingw@rtndf.org
http://www.rtnda.org/asfi/scholarships/minority.shtml
Scholarship Name: Ed Bradley Scholarship. *Academic
Area: Broadcasting, journalism. *Age Group:
Undergraduate students. *Eligibility: Minority students
whose career objective is electronic journalism (radio
or television) and who have at least one full year of
college remaining are eligible to apply. Applicants
must also attend college full time. Note: Freshmen
cannot apply. *Application Process: Contact the RTNDF
for details. *Amount: $10,000. *Deadline: Varies.

Radio-Television News Directors Foundation (RTNDF)
Attn: Irving Washington
1600 K Street, NW, Suite 700
Washington, DC 20006-2838
202-467-5218
irvingw@rtndf.org
http://www.rtnda.org/asfi/scholarships/minority.shtml
Scholarship Name: Ken Kashiwahara Scholarship.
*Academic Area: Broadcasting, journalism. *Age Group:
Undergraduate students. *Eligibility: Minority students
whose career objective is electronic journalism (radio or

television) and who have at least one full year of college remaining are eligible to apply. Applicants must also attend college full time. Note: Freshmen cannot apply. *Application Process: Contact the foundation for details. *Amount: $2,500. *Deadline: Varies.

Reforma

Attn: Barbara Scotto, Chair, Pura Belpré Award Committee
c/o ALSC
50 East Huron
Chicago, IL 60611-2795
barbara_scotto@brookline.mec.edu
http://www.reforma.org/belpreawardGeneric.html
Award Name: Pura Belpré Award. *Academic Area: Visual arts (open), writing. *Age Group: Open. *Eligibility: Applicants must be Latino/Latina writers and illustrators whose work best portrays, affirms, and celebrates the Latino cultural experience in an outstanding work of literature for children and youth. Books for children up to age 14 are considered. The books must be published in the United States or Puerto Rico, and the author(s) or illustrator(s) must be residents or citizens of the United States or Puerto Rico. *Application Process: Applicants should contact the association by e-mail for further information about how to apply. *Amount: Awards vary. *Deadline: December 31.

Reforma

Attn: Reforma Scholarship Committee
PO Box 7453
Tucson, AZ 85725
480-471-7452
http://www.reforma.org/scholarship.htm
Scholarship Name: REFORMA Scholarship. *Academic Area: Library sciences. *Age Group: Graduate students. *Eligibility: Applicants must qualify for graduate study in library science and be citizens or permanent residents of the United States. *Application Process: Applicants should submit a completed application, two recommendations, transcripts, a personal statement, and a current resume. Visit the association's Web site to download an application form. *Amount: $1,500. *Deadline: March 15.

Robert a Toigo Foundation

Attn: Fellowship Program Administrator
1230 Preservation Park Way
Oakland, CA 94612
510-763-5771
info@toigofoundation.org
http://www.toigofoundation.org/toigofoundation/ Content/FellowShip/FellowshipHome.htm
Fellowship Name: Robert Toigo Fellowship. *Academic Area: Business, finance. *Age Group: Graduate students. *Eligibility: Minority students who have been accepted into an MBA program may apply. Applicants must be U.S. citizens or permanent residents and planning to pursue a career in finance (including, but not limited to investment management, investment banking, corporate finance [noninvestment banking], real estate, private equity, venture capital, sales and trading, research, or financial services consulting). *Application Process: An application is available at the foundation's Web site. *Amount: $5,000 toward two years of graduate school tuition. *Deadline: Varies.

Robert Wood Johnson Foundation

Attn: Nina Ardery, Deputy Director
Amos Medical Faculty Development Program
8701 Georgia Avenue, Suite 411
Silver Spring, MD 20910
301-565-4080
amfdp@starpower.net
http://www.amfdp.org
Fellowship Name: The Foundation's Amos Medical Faculty Development Program seeks to "increase the number of faculty from historically disadvantaged backgrounds who can achieve senior rank in academic medicine." The program provides four-year postdoctoral research awards to physicians. *Academic Area: Medicine (physicians). *Age Group: Medical students, professionals. *Eligibility: Applicants must be historically disadvantaged physicians, U.S. citizens or permanent residents of the United States, currently completing or have completed their formal clinical training, and planning to pursue academic careers. They also must be willing to conduct four consecutive years of formal research, work to improve health care for the underserved, and serve as role models for faculty and students and faculty from disadvantaged backgrounds. Physicians who have recently completed their formal clinical training will receive priority in the selection process. *Application Process: Applicants should submit a completed proposal and application, which includes information on their academic background, research experiences and interests, and career objectives, as well as professional references and a plan for working with a mentor during the program. Semifinalists will be picked from the initial group of applicants

and participate in an interview with a selection committee. Finalists will be chosen from this group. *Amount: $75,000 a year, plus a $26,350 annual grant toward support of research activities. *Deadline: Typically in March.

Ron Brown Scholar Program
1160 Pepsi Place, Suite 206
Charlottesville, VA 22901
434-964-1588
http://www.ronbrown.org/p-elig.htm
Scholarship Name: Ron Brown Scholar Program. *Academic Area: Open. *Age Group: Undergraduate students. *Eligibility: African-American high school seniors who plan to attend college full time may apply. Applicants must be U.S. citizens or permanent residents. Current college students may not apply. *Application Process: Visit the program's Web site for information. *Amount: Varies. *Deadline: November 15 (for various program scholarships); January 9 (for the Ron Brown Scholarship only).

Sallie Mae
PO Box 4600
Wilkes-Barre, PA 18773-4600
888-272-5543
http://www.salliemae.com
Loan Name: Sallie Mae, which calls itself "the nation's No. 1 paying-for-college company," provides federally guaranteed student loans to students, including minorities. *Academic Area: Open. *Age Group: Undergraduate students, graduate students. *Eligibility: High school seniors and college students at all levels may apply. *Application Process: Contact Sallie Mae for information on specific loan programs. *Amount: Varies. *Loan Repayment Deadline: Varies by loan. *Application Deadline: Applications are accepted throughout the year.

Salvadoran American Leadership and Educational Fund
Attn: Mayra Soriano, Educational Youth Programs Manager
1625 West Olympic Boulevard, Suite 718
Los Angeles, CA 90015
213-480-1052
msoriano@salef.org
http://www.salef.org/Scholarships.html
Scholarship Name: Fulfilling Our Dreams Scholarship. *Academic Area: Open. *Age Group: Undergraduate students, graduate students. *Eligibility: Applicants must be of Central American, Salvadoran, or other Latino background, and must demonstrate academic achievement by maintaining at least a 2.5 GPA. Applicants must reside and study in California, be graduating high school seniors or current college students, and able to demonstrate financial need and a commitment to community service. They must agree to participate in a mentorship program for high school students (or other community service) if they receive an award. *Application Process: Applicants should submit a completed application along with two letters of recommendation, an 800-word personal essay, a resume, official transcripts, parents' federal tax return (previous year), a copy of their financial aid award letter, and a color photo. Visit the fund's Web site to download an application. *Amount: $500 to $2,500. *Deadline: June 30.

School of American Research
PO Box 2188
Santa Fe, NM 87504-2188
505-954-7200
scholar@sarsf.org
http://www.sarweb.org/home/nativeprograms.htm
Fellowship Name: The Katrin H. Lamon Resident Scholar Fellowship Program provides Native American scholars the opportunity to complete a book-length manuscript or doctoral dissertation during a nine-month residential tenure. *Academic Area: Humanities, science. *Age Group: Graduate students, professionals. *Eligibility: Native American scholars may apply. *Application Process: Contact the school for information on the application process. *Amount: Fellows receive an apartment, office, stipend of up to $40,000, and other benefits. *Deadline: November 15.

School of American Research
PO Box 2188
Santa Fe, NM 87504-2188
505-954-7200
info@sarsf.org
http://www.sarweb.org/home/nativeprograms.htm
Fellowship Name: The School of American Research offers several Artist Fellowships for Native American artists. *Academic Area: Visual arts (open). *Age Group: Open. *Eligibility: Native American artists may apply. *Application Process: Contact the school for information on the application process. *Amount: Varies by fellowship. *Deadline: Varies.

Small Business Administration (SBA)

740 15th Street, NW, 3rd Floor
Washington, DC 20005-3544
800-827-5722, 202-272-0345
http://www.sba.gov/starting_business/special/
minorities.html

Loan Name: The Small Business Administration (SBA) provides several loan programs, including the 8(a) Minority Program, to entrepreneurs. *Academic Area: Open. *Age Group: Open. *Eligibility: Minority entrepreneurs with a viable business plan are eligible to apply. *Application Process: Contact the SBA for details. *Amount: Varies. *Loan Repayment Deadline: Varies. *Application Deadline: Contact the SBA for details.

Smithsonian Institution

Office of Fellowships
MRC 902, PO Box 37012, Victor Building, Suite 9300
Washington, DC 20013-7012
202-275-0655
siofg@si.edu
http://www.si.edu/ofg/Applications/SIFELL/SIFELLapp.
htm

Fellowship Name: The Smithsonian Institution offers a variety of fellowships to minority students. *Academic Area: Open. *Age Group: Graduate students, post-doctoral scholars. *Eligibility: Minority students may apply. Contact the Smithsonian for eligibility guidelines for specific fellowships. *Application Process: Application requirements vary by fellowships, but all applicants will be required to submit a research proposal, a curriculum vitae, academic transcripts, and letters of reference. *Amount: Fellowships range from $4,500 to $40,000. *Deadline: January 15.

Society for Advancement of Chicanos and Native Americans in Science (SACNAS)

Attn: Pixan Serna, Genome Scholars Program
PO Box 8526
Santa Cruz, CA 95061-8526
831-459-0170, ext. 238
pixan@sacnas.org
http://www.sacnas.org

Scholarship Name: SACNAS Genome Scholars Program. *Academic Area: Bioinformatics, genomics. *Age Group: Undergraduate students, graduate students. *Eligibility: Applicants should be graduating college seniors who are accepted into a graduate program or students who are already enrolled in a graduate

program in genomics or bioinformatics. Applicants must be current SACNAS members who are U.S. citizens or permanent residents. *Application Process: Applicants should submit a completed application along with GRE test scores, a letter of reference, a personal statement, a faculty mentor personal profile, a faculty mentor personal statement, a supporting essay, and official transcripts. Visit the society's Web site to download an application. *Amount: $25,000. *Deadline: February 28.

Society for Advancement of Chicanos and Native Americans in Science (SACNAS)

Attn: Pixan Serna, Student/Mentor Fellowship
PO Box 8526
Santa Cruz, CA 95061-8526
831-459-0170, ext. 238
pixan@sacnas.org
http://www.sacnas.org/genomicopportunity.html

Fellowship Name: The Student/Mentor Summer Workshop Fellowship allows fellows to attend the SACNAS National Conference and other genomics/bioinformatics conferences and workshops with their faculty mentor. *Academic Area: Bioinformatics, genomics. *Age Group: Graduate students. *Eligibility: Applicants, as well as their faculty mentors, must be members of the society. They also must be enrolled in a graduate program in bioinformatics or genomics. *Application Process: Applicants should submit an essay detailing why they deserve the fellowship, information on their educational background and experiences, information on their mentor, and a completed application (available at the society's Web site). *Amount: Payment for travel and lodging costs for the SACNAS National Conference and other related opportunities. *Deadline: February 28.

Society for American Archaeology

Scholarship Applications
900 Second Street, NE, Suite 12
Washington, DC 20002-3557
202-789-8200
info@saa.org
https://ecommerce.saa.org/saa/staticcontent/
staticpages/adminDir/awardDisplay.cfm?award=A-
ACPNSFS

Scholarship Name: Arthur C. Parker and National Science Foundation Scholarship. *Academic Area: Archaeology. *Age Group: Undergraduate students, graduate students. *Eligibility: Applicants must be attending an accredited college or university in the U.S. and must be from one of the following ethnic groups: Native Americans, Pacific Islanders from the United States, or Indigenous peoples from Canada. High school seniors and college students may apply. *Application Process: Applicants should submit a completed application along with a one-page personal statement, a brief description of a specific archeological methods training program, an itemized budget, and documentation of native identity. Visit the society's Web site to download an application. *Amount: Awards vary. *Deadline: December 15.

Society of Actuaries/Casualty Actuarial Society
Attn: Summer Cole
475 North Martingale Road, Suite 600
Schaumburg, IL 60173-2226
847-706-3509
scole@soa.org
http://www.beanactuary.org/minority/scholarship.cfm
Scholarship Name: Actuarial Scholarship for Minority Students. *Academic Area: Actuarial science. *Age Group: Undergraduate students, graduate students. *Eligibility: Applicants must be African American, Hispanic American, or Native American undergraduate or graduate students pursuing a degree leading to a career in actuary science. Applicants must have a GPA of at least 3.0 and an SAT score of at least 600 and ACT score of at least 30. They also usually major in mathematics, actuarial science, or business and have attempted or already passed an actuarial exam. *Application Process: Applicants must submit a completed application, two nomination forms, a financial statement, a Student Aid Report, an estimate of tuition, fees, and other expenses, official transcripts, and official educational exam (SAT/ACT/etc.) scores. Visit http://www.beanactuary.org to download the application. *Amount: Varies. *Deadline: April 14.

Society of Hispanic Professional Engineers (SHPE)
Attn: Rafaela Schwan, SHPE/AHETEMS Programs Director
AHETEMS Scholarship Program
University of Texas at Arlington
College of Engineering, Box 19019
Arlington, TX 76019-0019
817-272-1116
rschwan@shpe.org
http://www.shpe.org
Scholarship Name: SHPE/AHETEMS Scholarship. *Academic Area: Engineering (open), mathematics,

science, technology. *Age Group: Undergraduate students, graduate students. *Eligibility: Applicants must be U.S. citizens or legal residents who have graduated from an accredited U.S. high school, are accepted into or attending an accredited two-year or four-year college or university in the United States or Puerto Rico, enrolled full time, maintain a minimum GPA of 2.5 on a 4.0 (for high school seniors and undergraduates) and 3.25 on a 4.0 scale (for graduate students), and are society members in good standing. Scholarships are both merit- and need- based. *Application Process: Applicants should submit a completed application, personal statement, transcripts, and a recommendation letter. Visit the society's Web site to download an application. *Amount: $1,000 to $3,000. *Deadline: April 1.

Society of Manufacturing Engineers Education Foundation
Attn: Scholarship Review Committee
One SME Drive, PO Box 930
Dearborn, MI 48121
313-425-3300
foundation@sme.org
http://www.sme.org/cgi-bin/smeefhtml.pl?/foundation/scholarships/schl_briefly.html&&&SEF&
Scholarship Name: Edward S. Roth Manufacturing Engineering Scholarship. *Academic Area: Engineering (manufacturing). *Age Group: Undergraduate students, graduate students. *Eligibility: Minority students planning to enroll or currently enrolled full time in a degree program in manufacturing engineering in the United States or Canada are eligible to apply. Applicants must have a GPA of at least 3.0 on a 4.0 scale, be U.S. citizens, and plan to attend one of the following schools: Boston University, Bradley University, Brigham Young University, California Polytechnic State University, Central State University, University of Massachusetts, University of Miami, Miami University, St. Cloud State University, University of Texas-Pan American, Utah State University, and Worcester Polytechnic Institute. Preference will be given to students demonstrating financial need. High school seniors are also eligible to apply for this scholarship. *Application Process: Applicants must submit a maximum 300-word statement detailing their career objectives, a student resume, an official transcript, two recommendation letters, and a completed application (available at the foundation's Web site). *Amount: Varies. *Deadline: February 1.

Society of Manufacturing Engineers Education Foundation

Attn: Scholarship Review Committee
One SME Drive, PO Box 930
Dearborn, MI 48121
313-425-3300
foundation@sme.org
http://www.sme.org/cgi-bin/smeefhtml.pl?/foundation/scholarships/schl_briefly.html&&&SEF&

Scholarship Name: Caterpillar Scholars Award. *Academic Area: Engineering (manufacturing). *Age Group: Undergraduate students. *Eligibility: Minority students planning to enroll or currently enrolled full time in a degree program in manufacturing engineering in the United States or Canada are eligible to apply. Applicants must have a GPA of at least 3.0 on a 4.0 scale. High school seniors are also eligible to apply for this scholarship. *Application Process: Applicants must submit a maximum 300-word statement detailing their career objectives, a student resume, an official transcript, two recommendation letters, and a completed application (available at the foundation's Web site). *Amount: $2,000. *Deadline: February 1.

Society of Mexican American Engineers and Scientists Inc.

Attn: Scholarship Committee
711 West Bay Area Boulevard, Suite 206
Webster, TX 77598-4051
281-557-3677
execdir@maes-natl.org
http://www.maes-natl.org

*Scholarship Name: This association offers five types of scholarships—Padrino, Founders, Presidential, Graduate Student, and General Scholarships—for Hispanic students. *Academic Area: Engineering (open), science. *Age Group: Undergraduate students, graduate students. *Eligibility: All applicants must be current society student members who are enrolled as full-time students in an accredited college or university in the United States prior to submission of the application. Community college applicants must be enrolled in transferable majors to a four-year institution offering a baccalaureate degree. Applicants will be evaluated for all scholarship awards including the top awards of Padrino, Founders, and Presidential Scholarships. Selection is based on financial need, academic achievement, personal qualities, strengths, and leadership abilities. *Application Process: Applicants should submit a completed application

and an additional three copies of the scholarship application packet to the national office. At least one recommendation form and school transcripts are also required. Recommendation letters should be in a sealed envelope and do not need to be copied. Visit the society's Web site to download an application. *Amount: $1,000 to $3,000. *Deadline: October 6.

Society of Professional Journalists-Greater Los Angeles Chapter

Attn: Scholarship Committee
California State University-Long Beach
Department of Journalism
1250 Bellflower
Long Beach, CA 90840
http://www.spj.org/losangeles/2005_application.pdf

Scholarship Name: Ken Inouye Scholarship. *Academic Area: Journalism. *Age Group: Undergraduate students, graduate students. *Eligibility: Applicants must be members of ethnic minorities who either reside in Los Angeles, Ventura, or Orange counties in California or attend a four-year college/university in one of those counties. They also must be journalism majors who have completed at least their sophomore year and have at least one semester remaining in either an undergraduate or graduate degree program. *Application Process: Applicants must submit a completed application, a resume, work samples, and an essay. Visit the society's Web site to download an application. *Amount: $500 to $1,000. *Deadline: April 15.

Society of Professional Journalists-Mid-Florida Pro Chapter

Attn: Dr. Bonnie Jefferis, Coordinator of Mass Communications
St. Petersburg College
2465 Drew Street
Clearwater, FL 33756
JefferisB@spcollege.edu
http://www.spj.org/midflorida/tylerinfo.htm

Scholarship Name: Tyler Ward Minority Journalism Scholarship. *Academic Area: Journalism. *Age Group: Undergraduate students. *Eligibility: Applicants must be minority college students majoring in journalism who are either from the mid-Florida region or are attending a mid-Florida college or university. *Application Process: Applicants must submit an essay, a letter of recommendation, and work samples. Visit the society's Web site for further details. *Amount: $1,000. *Deadline: November 1.

Special Libraries Association
331 South Patrick Street
Alexandria, VA 22314-3501
703-647-4900
sla@sla.org
http://www.sla.org/content/learn/scholarship/sch-index/
    index.cfm
Scholarship Name: Affirmative Action Scholarship.
    *Academic Area: Library science. *Age Group:
    Graduate students. *Eligibility: Applicants must be
    citizens of the United States of America either by birth
    or naturalization or permanent resident aliens and a
    member of a minority group defined as Black (African
    American), Hispanic, Asian or Pacific Islander, American
    Indian, Aleutian (Alaskan) native, or native Hawaiian.
    Special consideration will be given to members of the
    Special Libraries Association and to persons who have
    worked in and for special libraries. Preference will also
    be given to those who display an aptitude for and
    interest in special library work. College seniors may
    apply. *Application Process: Applicants must submit
    five copies of a completed application, a personal
    statement, official transcripts, a letter of provisional
    acceptance or evidence of enrollment, three letters of
    recommendation, and evidence of financial need. Visit
    the association's Web site to download an application.
    *Amount: $6,000. *Deadline: October 31.

Studio Museum in Harlem
AIR Program
144 West 125th Street
New York, NY 10027
212-864-4500
http://www.studiomuseum.org/air_overview.html
Grant Name: Artists-In-Residence Program. *Academic
    Area: Visual arts (open). *Age Group: Open. *Eligibility:
    Applicants must be African-American artists or
    artists of African descent, able to demonstrate at
    least three years of professional commitment, and
    currently engaged in studio work. Applicants may not
    attend school during the residency or produce art
    as a hobby. *Application Process: Applicants should
    submit a completed application along with a resume,
    an artist statement, 10 slides or one video, a slide
    list, supplementary materials (reviews, catalogues,
    brochures), a self-addressed stamped postcard and
    envelope, and two letters of recommendation. Visit
    the museum's Web site to download an application.
    *Amount: $15,000, plus $1,000 for materials.
    *Deadline: April 1.

Tennessee Education Association (TEA)
Attn: Jeanette DeMain
Sahli-Woodall Scholarship Fund
801 Second Avenue North
Nashville, TN 37201-1099
615-242-8392, 800-342-8367
stea@tea.nea.org
http://www.teateachers.org/about_tea/
    Constituent%20Groups/stea.htm
Scholarship Name: Don Sahli-Kathy Woodall
    Scholarship Fund. *Academic Area: Education. *Age
    Group: Undergraduate students, graduate students.
    *Eligibility: Applicants must be pursuing or planning
    to pursue a degree and career in education.
    Applicants must be TEA or Student TEA members
    or the child of a TEA member depending on the
    scholarship for which the applicant applies. The
    Scholarship Fund offers one scholarship specifically
    for high school seniors who are minorities planning
    to major in education. Visit the association's Web site
    for specific scholarship details. *Application Process:
    Applicants must submit a completed application, an
    essay, and two letters of recommendation. Visit the
    association's Web site to download an application.
    *Amount: $500 to $1,000. *Deadline: March 1.

Texas Library Association (TLA)
Attn: Catherine W. Lee, Director of Administration
3355 Bee Cave Road, Suite 401
Austin, TX 78746
512-328-1518
catherine@txla.org
http://www.txla.org/html/awards/scholar/century.html
Scholarship Name: Century Scholarship. *Academic Area:
    Library sciences. *Age Group: Graduate students.
    *Eligibility: Applicants must be American Library
    Association (ALA) Century Scholars enrolled in an ALA-
    recognized master's degree program in library and
    information studies at a Texas university. They must
    also agree to work at least two years in a Texas library
    following the completion of the master's degree
    program and be TLA members. *Application Process:
    Applicants must submit a completed application and
    verification of enrollment. Visit the association's Web
    site to download an application. *Amount: $2,000.
    *Deadline: January 31.

Texas Library Association (TLA)
Attn: Catherine W. Lee, Director of Administration
3355 Bee Cave Road, Suite 401

Austin, TX 78746
512-328-1518
catherinel@txla.org
http://www.txla.org/html/awards/scholar/spectapp.html
Scholarship Name: Texas Library Association Spectrum
Scholarship. *Academic Area: Library sciences. *Age
Group: Graduate students. *Eligibility: Applicants
must be American Library Association (ALA) Spectrum
Scholars enrolled in an ALA-recognized master's
degree program in library and information studies
at a Texas university. Applicants must agree to work
at least two years in a Texas library following the
completion of their master's degree program and
be TLA members. *Application Process: Applicants
must submit a completed application and verification
of enrollment. Visit the association's Web site
to download an application. *Amount: $2,000.
*Deadline: January 31.

Thurgood Marshall Scholarship Fund (TMSF)
Attn: Paul Allen
90 William Street, Suite 1203
New York, NY 10038
212-573-8888
pallen@tmsf.org
http://www.thurgoodmarshallfund.org
Scholarship Name: Sidney B. Williams Jr. Intellectual
Property Law School Scholarship. *Academic
Area: Law. *Age Group: Law students, early career
professionals. *Eligibility: Sponsored by the American
Intellectual Property Law Education Foundation,
this scholarship is awarded to minority students
developing a career in intellectual property law
or holding a past or present, full- or part-time
position in an area related to intellectual property
law. Applicants must also have a demonstrated
financial need and outstanding academic
performance in the undergraduate level and law
school level (if applicable). All applicants must
be U.S. citizens. *Application Process: Applicants
should submit a completed application form, a
FAFSA report, all academic transcripts, and two
letters of recommendation. Visit the fund's Web site
to download an application. *Amount: $10,000 per
school year, renewable upon reapplication, for up to
three academic years. *Deadline: February 24.

Thurgood Marshall Scholarship Fund (TMSF)
Attn: Paul Allen
90 William Street, Suite 1203

New York, NY 10038
212-573-8888
pallen@tmsf.org
http://www.thurgoodmarshallfund.org
Scholarship Name: Thurgood Marshall Scholarship
Fund. *Academic Area: Open. *Age Group: Varies
by scholarship. *Eligibility: Applicants must be
enrolled, accepted, or planning to enroll full time
in one of the 47 Thurgood Marshall Scholarship
Fund member schools. They must be U.S. citizens
who have demonstrated commitment to academic
excellence and community service, and have financial
need. *Application Process: Applicants must contact
their campus TMSF scholarship coordinator for
an application. Application packages consist of a
general information form, enrollment/certification
of academic standing, acceptance form, financial aid
information, high school transcripts (for incoming
freshmen), undergraduate transcripts (for graduate
and law school), resume or personal information form,
recommendation letters, an essay, and a personal
photograph/headshot. These materials are submitted
to the scholarship coordinator on campus. Applicants
should consult their schools concerning the selection
process. *Amount: $2,200 per semester (average).
*Deadline: Deadlines vary.

United Methodist Communications
Attn: Perryman Scholarship Committee
Communications Resourcing Team-UMCom
PO Box 320
Nashville, TN 37202-0320
888-278-4862
scholarships@umcom.org
http://umcom.org/pages/news.asp?class=6&ID=305&typ
e=2&product_id=0
Scholarship Name: Leonard M. Perryman
Communications Scholarship for Ethnic Minority
Students. *Academic Area: Communications science,
journalism, religion. *Age Group: Undergraduate
students. *Eligibility: Applicants must be United
Methodist ethnic minorities who have demonstrated
exceptional academic achievement, journalistic
talent, involvement in the church, career goals, and
potential as religious communicators. They also
must be enrolled juniors or seniors at an accredited
college or university in the United States. *Application
Process: Applicants should submit a completed
application along with evidence of junior or senior
enrollment status, official transcripts, three letters

of recommendation, a photo, three samples of journalistic work, and a personal statement. Visit the organization's Web site to download an application. *Amount: $2,500. *Deadline: March 15.

United Methodist Communications
Attn: REM Fellowship Committee
CRT/United Methodist Communicators
PO Box 320
Nashville, TN 37202-0320
888-278-4862
http://archives.umc.org/interior.asp?ptid=1&mid=6891
Fellowship Name: Judy Weidman Racial Ethnic Minority Fellowship. *Academic Area: Communications science, religion. *Age Group: Recent college graduates. *Eligibility: Applicants must be recent seminary or college graduates who have majored or specialized in communications and who are interested in pursuing a career with the United Methodist Church in a communications capacity. Applicants must be members of the United Methodist church and be of racial ethnic minority heritage. They also must be willing and able to relocate for one year. *Application Process: Applicants should submit a completed application along with a 400- to 500-word personal statement, three communications samples, three letters of recommendation, a photo, and official transcripts. Visit the organization's Web site for detailed information about the application process and the year-long experience. *Amount: $30,000, plus benefits and paid moving expenses. *Deadline: March 15.

United States Bureau of Indian Affairs
Attn: Edward Parisian, Director
Office of Indian Education Programs
1849 C Street, NW
MS-3512 MIB
Washington, DC 20240-0001
202-208-6123
http://www.oiep.bia.edu
Grant Name: Higher ED Grant. *Academic Area: Open. *Age Group: Undergraduate students. *Eligibility: Applicants must be at least one-quarter degree Indian blood, accepted for admission to a nationally accredited institution of higher education that provides a course of study conferring the associate of arts or bachelor's degree, and demonstrate financial need. High school seniors and undergraduate students may apply. *Application Process: Applicants should contact their tribe for application information.

The grant application is available from the education office of the tribe they are affiliated with or possess membership. Visit the bureau's Web site for more information. *Amount: Awards vary. *Deadline: Deadlines vary.

United States Department of Agriculture
Cooperative State Research, Education, and Extension Service
Attn: Audrey Trotman, National Program Leader
1400 Independence Avenue, SW, Stop 2201
Washington, DC 20250-2201
202-720-1973
http://www.csrees.usda.gov/fo/fundview.cfm?fonum=1110
Grant Name: Higher Education Multicultural Scholars Program. *Academic Area: Agriculture, food sciences. *Age Group: Undergraduate students, graduate students. *Eligibility: These grants are awarded to U.S. public or private nonprofit colleges/universities that offer baccalaureate degree or first professional degree programs in at least one discipline of food and agricultural sciences; land-grant colleges/universities, including those in insular areas; colleges/universities with significant minority enrollment and a demonstrable capacity to teach food and agricultural sciences; and other colleges/universities with a demonstrable capacity to teach food and agricultural sciences. The grants are then awarded to minority students at the institutions. *Application Process: Institutions interested in applying should visit the service's Web site to download an application. *Amount: $40,000 to $100,000. *Deadline: June 1.

United States Department of Education
400 Maryland Avenue, SW
Washington, DC 20202
800-433-3243
http://studentaid.ed.gov/PORTALSWebApp/students/english/index.jsp
Loan Name: The U.S. Department of Education's Federal Student Aid Program provides students (including minorities) with $74 billion a year in loans, grants, and work-study assistance. *Academic Area: Open. *Age Group: Undergraduate students, graduate students. *Eligibility: College students at all levels may apply. *Application Process: Contact the U.S. Department of Education for information on specific programs. *Amount: Varies. *Loan Repayment Deadline: Varies by loan. *Application Deadline: Varies.

Urban Financial Services Coalition

Attn: Herbert W. Whiteman, Jr. Scholarship
2121 K Street, NW, Suite 800
Washington, DC 20037
202-261-3569
ufscf@ufscfoundation.org
http://www.ufscfoundation.org
Scholarship Name: Herbert W. Whiteman Jr. Scholarship.
*Academic Area: Business, finance. *Age Group:
Undergraduate students, graduate students.
*Eligibility: Applicants must exhibit academic
excellence (maintain at least a 3.0 GPA) and
demonstrate leadership ability. *Application Process:
Applicants should submit a completed application, a
letter of reference, a current resume, an acceptance
letter from a college or a registration invoice, and a
400- to 500-word essay on "Excellence in Leadership-
How Do You Personally Exemplify the Quality?" Visit
the coalition's Web site to download an application.
*Amount: Awards vary. *Deadline: Contact the
coalition for details.

Virginia Society of Certified Public Accountants (VSCPA)

Attn: Molly Wash, Scholarship Coordinator
VSCPA Educational Foundation
PO Box 4620
Glen Allen, VA 23058-4620
800-733-8272
vscpa@vscpa.com
http://www.vscpa.com/CPAStudent_Zone/Awards_
and_Scholarships/VSCPA_Minority_Undergrad_
Scholarship.aspx
Scholarship Name: Minority Undergraduate Scholarship.
*Academic Area: Accounting. *Age Group:
Undergraduate students. *Eligibility: Applicants must
be members of a minority group, U.S. citizens, and
enrolled in an accredited Virginia college or university
with the intent to pursue a bachelor's degree in
accounting. They also should have completed at
least three hours of accounting course work and be
registered for at least three more hours. Applicants
should also be maintaining at least a 3.0 GPA.
*Application Process: Applicants should submit a
completed application along with an essay, a letter of
recommendation from a faculty member, a resume,
transcripts, and any additional documentation proving
enrollment in additional accounting credit hours. Visit
the society's Web site to download an application.
*Amount: Awards vary. *Deadline: April 17.

Wells Fargo Education Financial Services

Student Loans
PO Box 5185
Sioux Falls, SD 57117-5185
800-658-3567
http://www.wellsfargo.com/student/loans/undergrad/
index.jhtml
Loan Name: Wells Fargo, a financial services company,
provides a variety of loans to students, including
minorities. *Academic Area: Open. *Age Group:
Undergraduate students, graduate students, medical
students. *Eligibility: College students at all levels
may apply. *Application Process: Contact Wells Fargo
for information on specific loan programs. *Amount:
Varies. *Loan Repayment Deadline: Varies by loan.
*Application Deadline: Applications are accepted
throughout the year.

Wisconsin Higher Educational Aids Board

Attn: Sandy Thomas
PO Box 7885
Madison, WI 53707-7885
608-266-0888
sandy.thomas@heab.state.wi.us
http://www.heab.state.wi.us
Grant Name: Indian Student Assistance Grant. *Academic
Area: Open. *Age Group: Undergraduate students,
graduate students. *Eligibility: Applicants must be
at least 25 percent Native American, demonstrate
financial need, be legal residents of Wisconsin,
and plan to enroll or be currently enrolled at
select Wisconsin colleges. *Application Process:
An application is available at the board's Web site.
*Amount: $250 to $1,100. *Deadline: Varies.

Wisconsin Higher Educational Aids Board

Attn: Mary Lou Kuzdas
PO Box 7885
Madison, WI 53707-7885
608-267-2212
mary.kuzdas@heab.state.wi.us
http://www.heab.state.wi.us
Grant Name: Minority Undergraduate Retention Grant.
*Academic Area: Open. *Age Group: Undergraduate
students. *Eligibility: Applicants must be African
American, American Indian, Hispanic American, or
Southeast Asian from Laos, Cambodia, or Vietnam;
demonstrate financial need, be legal residents of
Wisconsin, and be college sophomores, juniors, or
seniors at select Wisconsin colleges. *Application

Process: Contact the board for information on application requirements. *Amount: $250 to $2,500. *Deadline: Varies.

Worldstudio Foundation
AIGA Scholarships
164 Fifth Avenue
New York, NY 10010
212-807-1990
http://www.worldstudio.org/schol/eligibility.html
Scholarship Name: Worldstudio AIGA Scholarship.
*Academic Area: Architecture, graphic design, visual arts (open). *Age Group: Undergraduate students, graduate students. *Eligibility: Applicants must be full-time students pursuing an undergraduate or graduate degree in the arts, including fine arts, commercial arts, design, or architecture. They also must demonstrate financial need, maintain at least a 2.0 GPA, and have a commitment to community service. Members of ethnic or racial minorities are given preference over nonminority applicants. *Application Process: Applicants must submit an online and written application. The online application includes a personal statement, a 10-piece portfolio, and a self-portrait. Official college transcripts and two letters of recommendation must accompany the written application. Visit the foundation's Web site to view the online application guidelines and download the written application. *Amount: $1,000 to $5,000. *Deadline: April 14.

Xerox Technical Minority Scholarship Program
150 State Street, 4th Floor
Rochester, NY 14614
http://www.xerox.com/downloads/usa/en/s/scholar.doc
Scholarship Name: Xerox Technical Minority Scholarship. *Academic Area: Engineering (open), science, technology. *Age Group: Undergraduate students, graduate students. *Eligibility: Applicants must be U.S. citizens or permanent residents enrolled in an undergraduate or graduate technical science or engineering program at a four-year institution. They also must be full-time students maintaining a minimum B average and African American, Asian, Pacific Islander, Native American, Alaskan, or Hispanic. *Application Process: Applicants must submit a completed application and resume. Visit Xerox's Web site to download an application. *Amount: $1,000 to $10,000. *Deadline: September 15.

Zeta Phi Beta Sorority Inc.
National Educational Foundation
1734 New Hampshire Avenue, NW
Washington, DC 20009
202-387-3103
IHQ@zphib1920.org
http://www.zphib1920.org/nef/schapp.pdf
Fellowship Name: Deborah Partridge Wolfe International Fellowship. *Academic Area: Open. *Age Group: Undergraduate students, graduate students. *Eligibility: African-American students who are pursuing undergraduate or graduate education in any discipline may apply. This fellowship is available to U.S. students studying abroad and foreign students studying in the United States. Applicants do not need to be members of Zeta Phi Beta Sorority to be eligible for this fellowship. *Application Process: Applicants should submit three letters of recommendation, academic transcripts, a brief overview of their academic plans, a completed application (available at the sorority's Web site), and a 150-word (or more) essay that details their academic goals and why they should receive the award. *Amount: $500 to $1,000. *Deadline: February 1.

Zeta Phi Beta Sorority Inc.
National Educational Foundation
1734 New Hampshire Avenue, NW
Washington, DC 20009
202-387-3103
IHQ@zphib1920.org
http://www.zpbnef1975.org/schapp.pdf
Scholarship Name: Isabel M. Herson Scholarship in Education. *Academic Area: Education. *Age Group: Undergraduate students, graduate students. *Eligibility: This African-American sorority's scholarship does not require sorority membership. Applicants must be female, full-time students pursuing a degree in elementary or secondary education. *Application Process: Applicants must submit a completed application, a 150-word personal essay describing their educational goals and professional aspirations, and three letters of recommendation. Visit the foundation's Web site to download an application. *Amount: $500 to $1,000. *Deadline: February 1.

Zeta Phi Beta Sorority Inc.
National Educational Foundation
1734 New Hampshire Avenue, NW

Washington, DC 20009

202-387-3103

IHQ@zphib1920.org

http://www.zpbnef1975.org/schapp.pdf

Scholarship Name: Lullelia W. Harrison Scholarship in Counseling. *Academic Area: Counseling. *Age Group: Undergraduate students, graduate students. *Eligibility: This African-American sorority's scholarship does not require sorority membership. Applicants must be female full-time students. *Application Process: Applicants must submit a completed application, a 150-word personal essay describing their educational goals and professional aspirations, and three letters of recommendation. Visit the foundation's Web site to download an application. *Amount: $500 to $1,000. *Deadline: February 1.

Zeta Phi Beta Sorority Inc.

National Educational Foundation

1734 New Hampshire Avenue, NW

Washington, DC 20009

202-387-3103

IHQ@zphib1920.org

http://www.zphib1920.org/nef/schapp.pdf

Fellowship Name: Mildred Cater Bradham Social Work Fellowship. *Academic Area: Social work. *Age Group: Graduate students. *Eligibility: Members of Zeta Phi Beta Sorority (an African-American service organization) who are pursuing a graduate or professional degree in social work at an accredited college or university may apply. Students must plan to study full time. *Application Process: Applicants should submit three letters of recommendation, academic transcripts, a completed application (available at the sorority's Web site), and a 150-word (or more) essay that details their academic goals and why they should receive the award. *Amount: $500 to $1,000. *Deadline: February 1.

Zeta Phi Beta Sorority Inc.

National Educational Foundation

1734 New Hampshire Avenue, NW

Washington, DC 20009

202-387-3103

IHQ@zphib1920.org

http://www.zphib1920.org/nef/schapp.pdf

Fellowship Name: Nancy B. Woolridge McGee Graduate Fellowship. *Academic Area: Open. *Age Group: Graduate students. *Eligibility: Members of Zeta

Phi Beta Sorority (an African-American service organization) who are pursuing a graduate or professional degree at an accredited college or university may apply. Students must plan to study full time. *Application Process: Applicants should submit three letters of recommendation, academic transcripts, proof of enrollment, a completed application (available at the sorority's Web site), and a 150-word+ essay that details their academic goals and why they should receive the award. *Amount: $500 to $1,000. *Deadline: February 1.

Zeta Phi Beta Sorority Inc.

National Educational Foundation

1734 New Hampshire Avenue, NW

Washington, DC 20009

202-387-3103

IHQ@zphib1920.org

http://www.zpbnef1975.org/schapp.pdf

Scholarship Name: S. Evelyn Lewis Memorial Scholarship in Medical Health Sciences. *Academic Area: Medicine (open). *Age Group: Undergraduate students, graduate students. *Eligibility: This African-American sorority's scholarship does not require sorority membership. Applicants must be female, full-time students pursuing a degree in medicine or health sciences. *Application Process: Applicants must submit a completed application, a 150-word personal essay describing their educational goals and professional aspirations, and three letters of recommendation. Visit the foundation's Web site to download an application. *Amount: $500 to $1,000. *Deadline: February 1.

Zeta Phi Beta Sorority Inc.

National Educational Foundation

1734 New Hampshire Avenue, NW

Washington, DC 20009

202-387-3103

IHQ@zphib1920.org

http://www.zpbnef1975.org/schapp.pdf

Scholarship Name: Zeta Phi Beta General Graduate Scholarship. *Academic Area: Open. *Age Group: Graduate students. *Eligibility: This African-American sorority's scholarship does not require sorority membership. Applicants must be female, full-time students pursuing a master's, doctoral, or post-doctoral degree. *Application Process: Applicants must submit a completed application, a 150-word personal essay describing their educational goals and professional aspirations, and three letters of recommendation. Visit the foundation's Web site to download an application. *Amount: Up to $2,500. *Deadline: February 1.

Zeta Phi Beta Sorority Inc.
National Educational Foundation
1734 New Hampshire Avenue, NW
Washington, DC 20009
202-387-3103
IHQ@zphib1920.org
http://www.zpbnef1975.org/schapp.pdf
Scholarship Name: Zeta Phi Beta General Undergraduate Scholarship. *Academic Area: Open. *Age Group: Undergraduate students. *Eligibility: This African-American sorority's scholarship does not require sorority membership. Applicants must be full-time students or enrolled as full-time students for the upcoming fall semester. High school seniors are also eligible to apply for this scholarship. *Application Process: Applicants must submit a completed application, a 150-word personal essay describing their educational goals and professional aspirations, proof of enrollment

or university acceptance, and three letters of recommendation. Visit the foundation's Web site to download an application. *Amount: $500 to $1,000. *Deadline: February 1.

Zeta Phi Beta Sorority Inc.
National Educational Foundation
1734 New Hampshire Avenue, NW
Washington, DC 20009
202-387-3103
http://www.zpbnef1975.org/schapp.pdf
Scholarship Name: Zora Neale Hurston Scholarship. *Academic Area: Anthropology. *Age Group: Graduate students. *Eligibility: This African-American sorority's scholarship does not require sorority membership. Applicants must be female, full-time students pursuing a degree in anthropology or a related field. *Application Process: Applicants must submit a completed application, a 150-word personal essay describing their educational goals and professional aspirations, and three letters of recommendation. Visit the foundation's Web site to download an application. *Amount: $500 to $1,000. *Deadline: February 1.

PEOPLE WITH DISABILITIES

RELATED SECTIONS: *The following financial aid resources are available to students with disabilities. Aid for undergraduate and graduate study is listed.*

Alaska-Fairbanks, University of
Office of Financial Aid
101 Eielson Building
PO Box 756360
Fairbanks, AK 99775
888-474-7256
financialaid@uaf.edu
http://www.uaf.edu/finaid
Scholarship Name: Eugene and Loretta Rafson Scholarship for Students with Disabilities. *Academic Area: Open. *Age Group: Undergraduate students. *Eligibility: Physically disabled college students who need financial assistance are eligible to apply. *Application Process: Contact the University of Alaska-Fairbanks Foundation for application details. *Amount: $750. *Deadline: Write or call for details.

Alexander Graham Bell Association for the Deaf and Hard of Hearing
Attn: Manager, Financial Aid and Scholarship Programs
3417 Volta Place, NW
Washington, DC 20007
202-337-5220
info@agbell.org
http://www.agbell.org/DesktopDefault.aspx?p=College_Scholarship_Awards
Scholarship Name: Allie Raney Hunt Scholarship. *Academic Area: Open. *Age Group: Undergraduate students, graduate students. *Eligibility: Applicants must be full-time students accepted into or enrolled in a college or university, and who have had a moderate to profound hearing loss prior to spoken language acquisition. Applicants must be oral deaf. *Application Process: Applicants should submit a completed application along with three letters of recommendation, a waiver of access form, all applicable official transcripts, and a current unaided and aided audiogram (hearing aid users) or recent mapping report (cochlear implant users). Visit the association's Web site to download an application and a waiver of access form. *Amount: $2,000. *Deadline: April 15.

Alexander Graham Bell Association for the Deaf and Hard of Hearing
Attn: Manager, Financial Aid and Scholarship Programs
3417 Volta Place, NW
Washington, DC 20007
202-337-5220
info@agbell.org
http://www.agbell.org/DesktopDefault.aspx?p=College_Scholarship_Awards
Scholarship Name: Bennion Family Scholarship. *Academic Area: Open. *Age Group: Undergraduate students. *Eligibility: Applicants must be full-time students accepted into or enrolled in a college or university, and who have had a moderate to profound hearing loss prior to spoken language acquisition. Applicants must use spoken communication as their primary form of communication. *Application Process: Applicants should submit a completed application along with three letters of recommendation, a waiver of access form, all applicable official transcripts, and a current unaided and aided audiogram (hearing aid users) or recent mapping report (cochlear implant users). Visit the association's Web site to download an application and a waiver of access form. *Amount: $2,000. *Deadline: April 15.

Alexander Graham Bell Association for the Deaf and Hard of Hearing
Attn: Manager, Financial Aid and Scholarship Programs
3417 Volta Place, NW
Washington, DC 20007
202-337-5220
info@agbell.org
http://www.agbell.org/DesktopDefault.aspx?p=College_Scholarship_Awards
Scholarship Name: Deaf and Hard of Hearing Section (DHHS) Scholarship Fund. *Academic Area: Open. *Age Group: Undergraduate students, graduate students. *Eligibility: Applicants must be full-time students accepted into or enrolled in a college or university, and who have had a moderate to profound hearing loss prior to spoken language acquisition. Applicants must use spoken communication as their primary form of communication and must be members of Alexander Graham Bell Association for the Deaf and Hard of Hearing and the DHHS. *Application Process: Applicants should submit a completed application along with three letters of recommendation, a waiver of access form, all applicable official transcripts, and

a current unaided and aided audiogram (hearing aid users) or recent mapping report (cochlear implant users). Visit the association's Web site to download an application and a waiver of access form. *Amount: $1,000. *Deadline: April 15.

Alexander Graham Bell Association for the Deaf and Hard of Hearing

Attn: Manager, Financial Aid and Scholarship Programs
3417 Volta Place, NW
Washington, DC 20007
202-337-5220
info@agbell.org
http://www.agbell.org/DesktopDefault.aspx?p=College_ Scholarship_Awards

Scholarship Name: Elsie M. Bell Grosvenor Scholarship. *Academic Area: Open. *Age Group: Undergraduate students, graduate students. *Eligibility: Applicants must be full-time students accepted into a mainstream college in the Washington, DC, area, who have had a moderate to profound hearing loss prior to spoken language acquisition, and who use spoken communication as their primary form of communication. *Application Process: Applicants should submit a completed application along with three letters of recommendation, a waiver of access form, all applicable official transcripts, and a current unaided and aided audiogram (hearing aid users) or recent mapping report (cochlear implant users). Visit the association's Web site to download an application and a waiver of access form. *Amount: $2,000. *Deadline: April 15.

Alexander Graham Bell Association for the Deaf and Hard of Hearing

Attn: Manager, Financial Aid and Scholarship Programs
3417 Volta Place, NW
Washington, DC 20007
202-337-5220
info@agbell.org
http://www.agbell.org/DesktopDefault.aspx?p=College_ Scholarship_Awards

Scholarship Name: Federation of Jewish Women's Organization Scholarship. *Academic Area: Open. *Age Group: Undergraduate students, graduate students. *Eligibility: Applicants must be full-time students accepted into or enrolled in a college or university, and who have had a moderate to profound hearing loss prior to spoken language acquisition. Applicants must use spoken communication as their primary form of communication. Preference is given to female Jewish

applicants. *Application Process: Applicants should submit a completed application along with three letters of recommendation, a waiver of access form, all applicable official transcripts, and a current unaided and aided audiogram (hearing aid users) or recent mapping report (cochlear implant users). Visit the association's Web site to download an application and a waiver of access form. *Amount: $2,000. *Deadline: April 15.

Alexander Graham Bell Association for the Deaf and Hard of Hearing

Attn: Manager, Financial Aid and Scholarship Programs
3417 Volta Place, NW
Washington, DC 20007
202-337-5220
info@agbell.org
http://www.agbell.org/DesktopDefault.aspx?p=College_ Scholarship_Awards

Scholarship Name: George H. Nofer Scholarship. *Academic Area: Law, public policy. *Age Group: Graduate students, law students. *Eligibility: Applicants must be full-time students accepted into an accredited law school or graduate program in public policy, and who have had a moderate to profound hearing loss prior to spoken language acquisition. Applicants must use spoken communication as their primary form of communication. They should also have a minimum undergraduate GPA of 3.0. *Application Process: Applicants should submit a completed application along with three letters of recommendation, a waiver of access form, all applicable official transcripts, and a current unaided and aided audiogram (hearing aid users) or recent mapping report (cochlear implant users). Visit the association's Web site to download an application and a waiver of access form. *Amount: $5,000 (renewable for two additional years with a 3.0 GPA). *Deadline: April 15.

Alexander Graham Bell Association for the Deaf and Hard of Hearing

Attn: Manager, Financial Aid and Scholarship Programs
3417 Volta Place, NW
Washington, DC 20007
202-337-5220
info@agbell.org
http://www.agbell.org/DesktopDefault.aspx?p=College_ Scholarship_Awards

Scholarship Name: Herbert P. Feibelman Jr. Scholarship. *Academic Area: Open. *Age Group: Undergraduate students, graduate students. *Eligibility: Applicants must be full-time students accepted into or enrolled in a college or university, who have had a moderate to profound hearing loss prior to spoken language acquisition, and who use spoken communication as their primary form of communication. They must be members (or the children of members) in good standing of the Alexander Graham Bell Association for the Deaf and Hard of Hearing. *Application Process: Applicants should submit a completed application along with three letters of recommendation, a waiver of access form, all applicable official transcripts, and a current unaided and aided audiogram (hearing aid users) or recent mapping report (cochlear implant users). Visit the association's Web site to download an application and a waiver of access form. *Amount: $2,500. *Deadline: April 15.

Alexander Graham Bell Association for the Deaf and Hard of Hearing
Attn: Manager, Financial Aid and Scholarship Programs
3417 Volta Place, NW
Washington, DC 20007
202-337-5220
info@agbell.org
http://www.agbell.org/DesktopDefault.aspx?p=College_Scholarship_Awards
Scholarship Name: Ladies' Auxiliary National Rural Letter Carriers Scholarship. *Academic Area: Open. *Age Group: Undergraduate students, graduate students. *Eligibility: Applicants must be full-time students accepted into or enrolled in a college or university, and who have had a moderate to profound hearing loss prior to spoken language acquisition. Applicants must use spoken communication as their primary form of communication. Contact the association for further eligibility requirements. *Application Process: Applicants should submit a completed application along with three letters of recommendation, a waiver of access form, all applicable official transcripts, and a current unaided and aided audiogram (hearing aid users) or recent mapping report (cochlear implant users). Visit the association's Web site to download an application and a waiver of access form. *Amount: $2,000. *Deadline: April 15.

Alexander Graham Bell Association for the Deaf and Hard of Hearing
Attn: Manager, Financial Aid and Scholarship Programs
3417 Volta Place, NW
Washington, DC 20007

202-337-5220
info@agbell.org
http://www.agbell.org/DesktopDefault.aspx?p=College_Scholarship_Awards
Scholarship Name: Louis DiCarlo Scholarship. *Academic Area: Open. *Age Group: Graduate students. *Eligibility: Applicants must be full-time students accepted into or enrolled in a graduate program, and who have had a moderate to profound hearing loss prior to spoken language acquisition. Applicants must use spoken communication as their primary form of communication. *Application Process: Applicants should submit a completed application along with three letters of recommendation, a waiver of access form, all applicable official transcripts, and a current unaided and aided audiogram (hearing aid users) or recent mapping report (cochlear implant users). Visit the association's Web site to download an application and a waiver of access form.. *Amount: $2,000. *Deadline: April 15.

Alexander Graham Bell Association for the Deaf and Hard of Hearing
Attn: Manager, Financial Aid and Scholarship Programs
3417 Volta Place, NW
Washington, DC 20007
202-337-5220
info@agbell.org
http://www.agbell.org/DesktopDefault.aspx?p=College_Scholarship_Awards
Scholarship Name: Lucille B. Abt Scholarship. *Academic Area: Open. *Age Group: Undergraduate students, graduate students. *Eligibility: Applicants must be full-time students accepted into or enrolled in a college or university, and who have had a moderate to profound hearing loss prior to spoken language acquisition. Applicants must use spoken communication and lip reading as their primary form of communication. *Application Process: Applicants should submit a completed application along with three letters of recommendation, a waiver of access form, all applicable official transcripts, and a current unaided and aided audiogram (hearing aid users) or recent mapping report (cochlear implant users). Visit the association's Web site to download an application and a waiver of access form. *Amount: $5,000. *Deadline: April 15.

Alexander Graham Bell Association for the Deaf and Hard of Hearing
Attn: Manager, Financial Aid and Scholarship Programs
3417 Volta Place, NW

Washington, DC 20007
202-337-5220
info@agbell.org
http://www.agbell.org/DesktopDefault.aspx?p=College_
   Scholarship_Awards
Scholarship Name: Robert H. Weitbrecht Scholarship.
   *Academic Area: Engineering (general), science.
   *Age Group: Undergraduate students, graduate
   students. *Eligibility: Applicants must be full-
   time students accepted into or enrolled in
   a college or university, and who have had a
   moderate to profound hearing loss prior to
   spoken language acquisition. They must also use
   spoken communication as their primary form
   of communication and demonstrate leadership
   potential. *Application Process: Applicants should
   submit a completed application along with three
   letters of recommendation, a waiver of access form,
   all applicable official transcripts, and a current
   unaided and aided audiogram (hearing aid users)
   or recent mapping report (cochlear implant users).
   Visit the association's Web site to download an
   application and a waiver of access form. *Amount:
   $2,500. *Deadline: April 15.

**Alexander Graham Bell Association for the Deaf and
   Hard of Hearing**
Attn: Manager, Financial Aid and Scholarship Programs
3417 Volta Place, NW
Washington, DC 20007
202-337-5220
info@agbell.org
http://www.agbell.org/DesktopDefault.aspx?p=College_
   Scholarship_Awards
Scholarship Name: Samuel M. and Gertrude G. Levy
   Scholarship. *Academic Area: Open. *Age Group:
   Undergraduate students. *Eligibility: Applicants
   must be full-time students accepted into or enrolled
   in a college or university, and who have had a
   moderate to profound hearing loss prior to spoken
   language acquisition. Applicants must be oral deaf.
   *Application Process: Applicants should submit
   a completed application along with three letters
   of recommendation, a waiver of access form, all
   applicable official transcripts, and a current unaided
   and aided audiogram (hearing aid users) or recent
   mapping report (cochlear implant users). Visit the
   association's Web site to download an application
   and a waiver of access form. *Amount: $2,000.
   *Deadline: April 15.

**Alexander Graham Bell Association for the Deaf and
   Hard of Hearing**
Attn: Manager, Financial Aid and Scholarship Programs
3417 Volta Place, NW
Washington, DC 20007
202-337-5220
info@agbell.org
http://www.agbell.org/DesktopDefault.aspx?p=College_
   Scholarship_Awards
Scholarship Name: Volta Scholarship Fund. *Academic
   Area: Open. *Age Group: Undergraduate students,
   graduate students. *Eligibility: Applicants must be full-
   time students accepted into or enrolled in a college or
   university, and who have had a moderate to profound
   hearing loss prior to spoken language acquisition.
   Applicants must be oral deaf. *Application Process:
   Applicants should submit a completed application
   along with three letters of recommendation, a waiver
   of access form, all applicable official transcripts, and
   a current unaided and aided audiogram (hearing aid
   users) or recent mapping report (cochlear implant
   users). Visit the association's Web site to download an
   application and a waiver of access form. *Amount:
   $2,000. *Deadline: April 15.

**Alexander Graham Bell Association for the Deaf and
   Hard of Hearing**
Attn: Manager, Financial Aid and Scholarship Programs
3417 Volta Place, NW
Washington, DC 20007
202-337-5220
info@agbell.org
http://www.agbell.org/DesktopDefault.aspx?p=College_
   Scholarship_Awards
Scholarship Name: Walter W. and Thelma C. Hissey
   College Scholarship Fund. *Academic Area: Open. *Age
   Group: Undergraduate students, graduate students.
   *Eligibility: Applicants must be full-time students
   accepted into or enrolled in a college or university,
   and who have had a moderate to profound hearing
   loss prior to spoken language acquisition. Applicants
   must use spoken communication as their primary form
   of communication. *Application Process: Applicants
   should submit a completed application along with three
   letters of recommendation, a waiver of access form, all
   applicable official transcripts, and a current unaided and
   aided audiogram (hearing aid users) or recent mapping
   report (cochlear implant users). Visit the association's
   Web site to download an application and a waiver of
   access form. *Amount: $5,000. *Deadline: April 15.

American Academy of Allergy, Asthma and Immunology
555 East Wells Street, Suite 1100
Milwaukee, WI 53202-3823
414-272-6071
info@aaaai.org
http://www.aaaai.org
Scholarship Name: Award of Excellence Asthma Scholarship. *Academic Area: Open. *Age Group: Graduating high school students. *Eligibility: Applicants must be high school seniors with asthma who need financial assistance to attend college. They also must be U.S. or Canadian citizens. *Application Process: For the second portion of the application process, applicants must submit documentation via mail from their physician (to confirm diagnosis of asthma) and high school counselor or principal. Contact the academy for more information. *Amount: $1,000. *Deadline: Contact the academy for details.

American Academy of Allergy, Asthma and Immunology
555 East Wells Street, Suite 1100
Milwaukee, WI 53202-3823
414-272-6071
info@aaaai.org
http://www.aaaai.org
Scholarship Name: Tanner McQuiston Memorial Scholarship. *Academic Area: Open. *Age Group: Graduating high school students. *Eligibility: Applicants must be high school seniors with asthma who need financial assistance to attend college. They also must be U.S. or Canadian citizens. *Application Process: For the second portion of the application process, applicants must submit documentation via mail from their physician (to confirm diagnosis of asthma) and high school counselor or principal. Contact the academy for more information. *Amount: $1,000. *Deadline: Contact the academy for details.

American Academy of Allergy, Asthma and Immunology
555 East Wells Street, Suite 1100
Milwaukee, WI 53202-3823
414-272-6071
info@aaaai.org
http://www.aaaai.org
Award Name: Merit Award. *Academic Area: Open. *Age Group: Undergraduate students. *Eligibility: Applicants must be high school seniors with asthma who need financial assistance to attend college. They also must be U.S. or Canadian citizens. *Application Process: An initial application must be completed at the academy's Web site. For the second portion of the application process, applicants must submit documentation via mail from their physician (to confirm diagnosis of asthma) and high school counselor or principal. Contact the academy for more information. *Amount: $100. *Deadline: Contact the academy for details.

American Cancer Society-Florida Division
1001 South MacDill Avenue
Tampa, FL 33629
800-444-1410, ext. 405
mwestley@cancer.org
http://www.cancer.org
Scholarship Name: R.O.C.K. College Scholarship. *Academic Area: Open. *Age Group: Undergraduate students, graduate students. *Eligibility: Applicants must be high school seniors or college students who have had cancer before age 21 and wish to attend an accredited Florida university, community college, or vocational technical school. They must also be residents of Florida and U.S. citizens. *Application Process: Applicants must submit a completed application along with three letters of recommendation, financial aid form, recent 1040 IRS form, personal essay, academic transcript, and SAT or ACT scores. *Amount: Up to $2,000, plus $300 for textbooks. *Deadline: April 10.

American Council of the Blind
Scholarship Program
Attn: Terry Pacheco
1155 15th Street, NW, Suite 1004
Washington, DC 20005
800-424-8666
http://www.acb.org
Scholarship Name: Various General Scholarships. *Academic Area: Open. *Age Group: Undergraduate students, graduate students. *Eligibility: Students who are legally blind and admitted to an academic, vocational, technical, or professional training program are eligible to apply. Applicants must have a GPA of at least 3.3 for most scholarships. High school seniors are eligible to apply, as are part-time students who are working full time. *Application Process: Applicants must submit a completed application (available online), an autobiographical sketch,

certification of legal blindness, certified transcripts, a letter of recommendation, and proof of acceptance from a postsecondary school. *Amount: Awards vary. *Deadline: March 1.

American Council of the Blind of Minnesota
Attn: Michael Malver
PO Box 7341
Minneapolis, MN 55407
612-673-0664
mmalver@visi.com
http://www.acb.org/minnesota/Scholarship.html
Scholarship Name: American Council of the Blind of Minnesota Scholarship. *Academic Area: Open. *Age Group: Undergraduate students, graduate students. *Eligibility: Applicants must be legally blind high school seniors or college students who are residents of Minnesota. *Application Process: Applicants should email the council to request an application. *Amount: $750. *Deadline: Typically late May.

American Council of the Blind of Ohio (ACBO)
Attn: ACBO Scholarship Committee
3114 Manning Avenue
Cincinnati, OH 45211
800-835-2226
kmorlock@gcfn.org
http://www.acbohio.org
Scholarship Name: American Council of the Blind of Ohio Scholarships. *Academic Area: Open (study areas vary by scholarship). *Age Group: Undergraduate students, graduate students. *Eligibility: Applicants must be legally blind high school seniors or college students who are residents of Ohio (or who attend a college in Ohio) and have a GPA of at least 3.0. Note: One scholarship is offered to both blind and sighted students. *Application Process: Applicants must submit three reference forms, an official copy of transcripts, a certificate of legal blindness, and a 250- to 500-word essay. . *Amount: Varies. *Deadline: August 1.

American Council of the Blind of South Carolina
PO Box 481
Columbia, SC 29202
803-735-1052
http://www.acb.org/southcarolina
Scholarship Name: Educational Scholarship. *Academic Area: Open. *Age Group: Undergraduate students, graduate students. *Eligibility: Blind full-time college students who reside in South Carolina are eligible to

apply. Scholarships are awarded based on academic achievement, community service, and financial need. *Application Process: Contact the council for details. *Amount: $1,000. *Deadline: Typically in September.

American Council of the Blind of Texas
Attn: Nolan Dyer, Scholarship Committee Chairperson
374 County Road 2206
Texarkana, TX 75501
903-832-5038
http://www.acbtexas.org/scholarshipinfo.html
Scholarship Name: Educational Scholarship. *Academic Area: Open. *Age Group: Undergraduate students, graduate students. *Eligibility: Applicants must be legally blind high school seniors or college students, residents of Texas, and have a GPA of at least 2.75. *Application Process: Applications must submit a completed scholarship application, documentation of legal or total blindness, proof of Texas residency, high school transcripts, two to three letters of recommendation, and a one- to two-page typewritten autobiography. *Amount: $1,000. *Deadline: Contact the council for the deadline date.

American Foundation for the Blind
Attn: Scholarship Committee
11 Penn Plaza, Suite 300
New York, NY 10001
212-502-7600
afbinfo@afb.net
http://www.afb.org
Contest Name: Gladys C. Anderson Memorial Scholarship. *Academic Area: Performing arts (music-classical), performing arts (music-religious). *Age Group: Undergraduate students, graduate students. *Eligibility: Applicants must be visually impaired undergraduate or graduate women studying classical or religious music. *Application Process: Applicants must submit a completed application, an essay, official transcripts, a letter of acceptance, three letters of recommendation, proof of legal blindness and citizenship, and a performance tape (not to exceed 30 minutes). Visit the Foundation's Web site to complete an online application. *Amount: $1,000. *Deadline: April 30.

American Foundation for the Blind
Attn: Scholarship Committee
11 Penn Plaza, Suite 300
New York, NY 10001
212-502-7600

afbinfo@afb.net
http://www.afb.org
Scholarship Name: Rudolph Dillman Memorial
Scholarship. *Academic Area: Rehabilitation. *Age
Group: Undergraduate students, graduate students.
*Eligibility: Applicants must be visually impaired
undergraduate and graduate students studying
rehabilitation and/or education of persons who
are blind or visually impaired *Application Process:
Applicants must submit a completed application,
an essay, official transcripts, a letter of acceptance,
three letters of recommendation, and proof of
legal blindness, citizenship, and financial need. Visit
the foundation's Web site to complete an online
application. *Amount: $2,500. *Deadline: April 30.

American Foundation for the Blind
Attn: Scholarship Committee
11 Penn Plaza, Suite 300
New York, NY 10001
212-502-7600
afbinfo@afb.net
http://www.afb.org
Scholarship Name: Paul and Ellen Ruckes Scholarship.
*Academic Area: Computer science, engineering
(general), life sciences, physical sciences. *Age Group:
Undergraduate students, graduate students. *Eligibility:
Applicants must be visually impaired undergraduate or
graduate students studying engineering or computer,
life sciences, or physical sciences. *Application Process:
Applicants must submit a completed application,
an essay, official transcripts, a letter of acceptance,
three letters of recommendation, and proof of legal
blindness and citizenship. Visit the foundation's Web site
to complete an online application. *Amount: $1,000.
*Deadline: April 30.

American Legion Auxiliary
777 North Meridian Street, Third Floor
Indianapolis, IN 46204-1420
317-955-3845
alahq@legion-aux.org
http://www.legion-aux.org
Scholarship Name: Non-Traditional Student
Scholarship. *Academic Area: Open. *Age Group:
Undergraduate students. *Eligibility: Students who
plan to return to the classroom after an extended
period of time, who have completed at least one
year of college, and are in need of financial aid
to continue their education are eligible for this
scholarship. Applicants must also have been dues-

paying members of The American Legion, Auxiliary,
or Sons of The American Legion for at least the
two years prior. They should also demonstrate
leadership abilities and academic excellence.
*Application Process: Applicants should submit a
completed application along with high school and
college transcripts and their work history. Visit the
auxiliary's Web site to download an application.
*Amount: $1,000. *Deadline: March 1.

American Nuclear Society
Outreach Department
555 North Kensington Avenue
La Grange Park, IL 60526
708-352-6611
http://www.ans.org
Scholarship Name: Robert A. Dannels Scholarship.
*Academic Area: Engineering (nuclear), nuclear
science. *Age Group: Graduate students. *Eligibility:
Full-time graduate students enrolled in nuclear
science, nuclear engineering, or other nuclear-related
major are eligible to apply. The scholarship is open to
all graduate students, but students with disabilities
are especially encouraged to apply. *Application
Process: Contact the Outreach Department for
details. *Amount: $3,500. *Deadline: *Deadline:
February 1.

Arizona Kidney Foundation
Scholarship Fund
4203 East Indian School Road, Suite 140
Phoenix, AZ 85018
602-840-1644
http://www.azkidney.org/patient.htm
Scholarship Name: Bidstrup Scholarship. *Academic
Area: Open. *Age Group: Undergraduate students,
graduate students. *Eligibility: Applicants must be
high school seniors or college students who are
undergoing dialysis treatment or who have had a
kidney transplant. They must also be residents of
Arizona. *Application Process: Contact the foundation
for application details. *Amount: Varies. *Deadline:
Varies.

Arizona State University (ASU)
Disability Resource Center (DRC)
Attn: Jim Hermauer, Supervisor, Disability Access
PO Box 873202
Tempe, AZ 85287-3202
480-965-1234, 480-965-9000 (TDD)
Disability-Q@asu.edu

http://www.asu.edu/studentaffairs/ed/drc/scholarships.
htm

Scholarship Name: Andrew M. Brown Scholarships.
*Academic Area: Open. *Age Group: Undergraduate
students, graduate students. *Eligibility: Applicants
must be high school seniors or college students,
maintain a minimum 2.5 GPA, demonstrate financial
need, be planning to pursue or currently pursuing a
full-time degree program at ASU, and be registered
with the DRC as a qualified student with a disability.
*Application Process: Applicants must submit
a completed application, a two-page personal
statement, and a letter of recommendation. Visit the
DRC Web site to download an application. *Amount:
$200 to $2,156 per year. *Deadline: June 1.

Arizona State University (ASU)
Disability Resource Center (DRC)
Attn: Jim Hermauer, Supervisor, Disability Access
PO Box 873202
Tempe, AZ 85287-3202
480-965-1234, 480-965-9000 (TDD)
Disability-Q@asu.edu
http://www.asu.edu/studentaffairs/ed/drc/scholarships.
htm

Scholarship Name: Donald & Dorothy Colee
Scholarship. *Academic Area: Open. *Age Group:
Undergraduate students, graduate students.
*Eligibility: Applicants must be high school seniors or
college students, have a physical disability, maintain
at least a 3.0 GPA, and be residents of Arizona. They
must also demonstrate financial need, be planning
to or currently pursuing a full-time degree program,
and be registered with the Disability Resource Center
as a qualified student with a disability. *Application
Process: Applicants must submit a completed
application, a two-page personal statement, and a
letter of recommendation. Visit the DRC Web site to
download an application. *Amount: $200 to $2,156
per year. *Deadline: June 1.

Arizona State University (ASU)
Disability Resource Center (DRC)
Attn: Jim Hermauer, Supervisor, Disability Access
PO Box 873202
Tempe, AZ 85287-3202
480-965-1234, 480-965-9000 (TDD)
Disability-Q@asu.edu
http://www.asu.edu/studentaffairs/ed/drc/scholarships.
htm

Scholarship Name: DRC Regents' Scholarship.
*Academic Area: Open. *Age Group: Undergraduate
students. *Eligibility: Applicants must be
undergraduate students with disabilities who
are Arizona residents, and maintain at least a 3.0
GPA. They must also demonstrate financial need,
be pursuing a full-time degree program, and be
registered with the DRC as a qualified student with
a disability. *Application Process: Applicants must
submit a completed application, a two-page personal
statement, and a letter of recommendation. Visit the
DRC Web site to download an application. *Amount:
$200 to $2,156 per year. *Deadline: June 1.

Arizona State University (ASU)
Disability Resource Center (DRC)
Attn: Jim Hermauer, Supervisor, Disability Access
PO Box 873202
Tempe, AZ 85287-3202
480-965-1234, 480-965-9000 (TDD)
Disability-Q@asu.edu
http://www.asu.edu/studentaffairs/ed/drc/scholarships.
htm

Scholarship Name: Ethelmae S. Merriam Scholarship.
*Academic Area: Open. *Age Group: Undergraduate
students, graduate students. *Eligibility: Applicants
must be high school seniors or college students,
maintain a minimum 2.5 GPA, demonstrate financial
need, be pursuing a full-time degree program, and be
registered with the DRC as a qualified student with
a disability. *Application Process: Applicants must
submit a completed application, a two-page personal
statement, and a letter of recommendation. Visit the
DRC Web site to download an application. *Amount:
$200 to $2,156 per year. *Deadline: June 1.

Arizona State University (ASU)
Disability Resource Center (DRC)
Attn: Jim Hermauer, Supervisor, Disability Access
PO Box 873202
Tempe, AZ 85287-3202
480-965-1234, 480-965-9000 (TDD)
Disability-Q@asu.edu
http://www.asu.edu/studentaffairs/ed/drc/scholarships.
htm

Scholarship Name: Steven & Mary Rosenfield
Scholarship. *Academic Area: Open. *Age Group:
Undergraduate students. *Eligibility: Applicants must
have a documented specific learning disability and/or
attention deficit hyperactivity disorder. Applicants must

be high school seniors beginning their first semester in college. Preference is given to Northern California residents. Applicants must maintain a minimum 2.5 GPA, demonstrate financial need, be pursuing a full-time degree program, and be registered with the DRC as a qualified student with a disability. *Application Process: Applicants must submit a completed application, a two-page personal statement, and a letter of recommendation. Visit the DRC Web site to download an application. *Amount: $200 to $2,156 per year. *Deadline: June 1.

Arizona State University (ASU)
Disability Resource Center (DRC)
Attn: Jim Hermauer, Supervisor, Disability Access
PO Box 873202
Tempe, AZ 85287-3202
480-965-1234, 480-965-9000 (TDD)
Disability-Q@asu.edu
http://www.asu.edu/studentaffairs/ed/drc/scholarships.htm
Scholarship Name: Julie Sargent Memorial Scholarship. *Academic Area: Open. *Age Group: Undergraduate students. *Eligibility: Applicants must have juvenile arthritis and be undergraduate students who are residents of Arizona. They must also maintain a minimum 2.5 GPA, demonstrate financial need, be pursuing a full-time degree program, and be registered with the DRC as a qualified student with a disability. *Application Process: Applicants must submit a completed application, a two-page personal statement, and a letter of recommendation. Visit the DRC Web site to download an application. *Amount: $200 to $2,156 per year. *Deadline: June 1.

Arizona State University (ASU)
Office of Financial Aid
PO Box 870412
Tempe, AZ 85287-0412
480-965-3355
http://www.asu.edu
Scholarship Name: Sertoma Communicative Disorders Scholarship. *Academic Area: Audiology, speech pathology. *Age Group: Graduate students. *Eligibility: Applicants must be full-time, graduate-level students at ASU studying speech language pathology or audiology. *Application Process: Contact the Office of Financial Aid for application details. *Amount: $2,500 to $5,000. *Deadline: Applications are available from December through April 1.

Arizona, University of
Disability Resource Center (DRC)
1224 East Lowell Street
Tucson, AZ 85721
520-621-3268 (Voice/TTY)
uadrc@email.arizona.edu
http://drc.arizona.edu/drc/scholarship.shtml
Scholarship Name: Various scholarships for disabled students. *Academic Area: Open. *Age Group: Undergraduate students, graduate students. *Eligibility: Students who demonstrate financial need and have a minimum 2.5 cumulative GPA are eligible to apply.*Application Process: Applications are available through a student's disability specialist. *Amount: $1,500 to $2,000. *Deadline: *Deadline: Mid-April.

Association for Glycogen Storage Disease
PO Box 896
Durant, IA 52747
563-785-6038
maryc@agsdus.org
http://www.agsdus.org
Scholarship Name: The association offers scholarships to students with glycogen storage disease. *Academic Area: Open. *Age Group: Undergraduate students, graduate students. *Eligibility: Students who have a confirmed diagnosis of glycogen storage disease and who are paid members of the Association (or whose parents are members) may apply.*Application Process: Contact the association for details. *Amount: Varies. *Deadline: *Deadline: Varies.

Association for Education and Rehabilitation of the Blind and Visually Impaired
1703 North Beauregard Street, Suite 440
Alexandria, VA 22311
703-671-4500, ext. 201
bsherr@aerbvi.org
http://www.aerbvi.org
Scholarship Name: William and Dorothy Ferrell Scholarship. *Academic Area: Disability services. *Age Group: Undergraduate students, graduate students. *Eligibility: Applicants must be legally blind individuals studying for a career in the field of services to persons who are blind or visually impaired. *Application Process: Visit the association's Web site to download an application. *Amount: Varies. *Deadline: March 15.

Association for the Education and Rehabilitation of the Blind and Visually Impaired of Ohio (AERO)
1568 Lafayette Drive
Columbus, OH 43220
ward.5@osu.edu
http://www.aerohio.org/schgrts/schol-grant.htm
Scholarship Name: AERO Personnel Preparation Scholarship. *Academic Area: Rehabilitation. *Age Group: Undergraduate or graduate students. *Eligibility: Applicants must be at least juniors in an accredited college or university, majoring in rehabilitation counseling, rehabilitation teaching, orientation and mobility, or education of students with visual disabilities. Applicants must have a 3.0 GPA and be residents of Ohio. *Application Process: Applicants must submit a completed application, three letters of recommendation, proof of acceptance to educational institution, a short description of volunteer or work history, and a personal essay. Visit the association's Web site to download an application. *Amount: $1,000. *Deadline: May 1.

Association of Blind Citizens
PO Box 246
Holbrook, MA 02343
781-961-1023
scholarship@assocofblindcitizens.org
http://www.assocofblindcitizens.org
Scholarship Name: Reggie Johnson Memorial Scholarship. *Academic Area: Open. *Age Group: Undergraduate students, graduate students. *Eligibility: Applicants must be legally blind high school seniors or college students who are U.S. legal residents. *Application Process: Applicants must submit a completed application, transcripts, a certificate of legal blindness, two letters of recommendation, and a biographical sketch (on disk). Visit the association's Web site to download an application. *Amount: $1,000 to $3,000. *Deadline: April 15.

Association of Universities and Colleges of Canada
350 Albert Street, Suite 600
Ottawa, ON K1R 1B1
Canada
613-563-1236
awards@aucc.ca
*http://*www.aucc.ca/scholarships/open/mattinson_ e.html
Scholarship Name: Mattinson Endowment Fund Scholarship for Disabled Students. *Academic Area:

Open. *Age Group: Undergraduate students. *Eligibility: Applicants must be Canadian citizens or legal residents with disabilities who are attending a Canadian degree-granting institution, college, or university. *Application Process: Contact the association for application details. *Amount: $2,500. *Deadline: Varies.

Autism Society of America
7910 Woodmont Avenue, Suite 300
Bethesda, MD 20814-3067
301-657-0881, 800-328-8476
http://www.autism-society.org/site/PageServer?pagena me=ASAFoundation
Scholarship Name: Eden Services Charles H. Hoens Jr. Scholars Program. *Academic Area: Open. *Age Group: Undergraduate students, graduate students. *Eligibility: Applicants must be individuals with autism who have successfully met all the requirements for admission into an accredited postsecondary program of study. The program is open to high school seniors and current college students. *Application Process: Contact the foundation for application details. *Amount: $1,000. *Deadline: February 28.

Beacon College
105 East Main Street
Leesburg, FL 34748
352-787-7660
admissions@beaconcollege.edu
http://www.beaconcollege.edu/Admissions/finaid.htm
Beacon College is one of only two post-secondary institutions in the United States established exclusively to serve students with learning disabilities. It offers a variety of scholarships and grants to students. *Academic Area: Open. *Age Group: Undergraduate students. *Eligibility: High school seniors and college students who have learning disabilities and who are planning to or are currently attending the college may apply. *Application Process: Contact the college for details. *Amount: Varies. *Deadline: Contact the college for details.

Blanche Fischer Foundation
1511 Southwest Sunset Boulevard, Suite 1-B
Portland, OR 97239
503-819-8205
bff@bff.org
http://www.bff.org
Scholarship Name: Blanche Fischer Foundation Grant. *Academic Area: Open. *Age Group: Adults. *Eligibility:

Applicants must be physically disabled, reside in Oregon, and demonstrate financial need. Applicants may apply for grants to help cover the cost of a variety of expenses, including non-tuition educational expenses and skills training equipment. *Application Process: Applicants must submit a completed application, verification of disability (from a health care professional), and a quote of expected expenses. Visit the foundation's Web site to download an application. *Amount: Varies. *Deadline: Varies.

Blind Information Technology Specialists
c/o American Council of the Blind
1155 15th Street, NW, Suite 1004
Washington, DC 20005
800-424-8666
info@acb.org
http://www.acb.org/bits
Scholarship Name: Kellie Cannon Scholarship. *Academic Area: Computer science. *Age Group: Undergraduate students, graduate students. *Eligibility: Applicants must have a visual impairment and wish to prepare for a career in the computer science field. *Application Process: Contact the American Council for the Blind for application details. *Amount: Varies. *Deadline: Varies.

Boomer Esiason Foundation
Attn: Jerry Cahill
417 Fifth Avenue, Second Floor
New York, NY 10016
646-344-3765
jcahill@esiason.org
http://www.cfambassador.com
Scholarship Name: Boomer Esiason Foundation Scholarship. *Academic Area: Open. *Age Group: Undergraduate students, graduate students. *Eligibility: Applicants must be undergraduate or graduate students with cystic fibrosis. Applicants must demonstrate academic achievement, community service, and financial need. *Application Process: Applicants must submit a completed application, a recent photograph, a letter of diagnosis (from physician), a letter confirming financial need (from a social worker), recent W2 forms for both parents, an essay, a letter of acceptance from academic institution, a detailed breakdown of tuition expenses, and transcripts. Visit the foundation's Web site to download an application. *Amount: $500 to $2,000. *Deadline: Varies.

Brigham Young University
University Accessibility Center
1520 WSC
Provo, UT 84602
801-422-2767, 801-422-0436 (TTY)
scholarships@byu.edu
http://saas.byu.edu/depts/finaid
Scholarship Name: Brigham Young University Scholarships for Students with Disabilities. *Academic Area: Open. *Age Group: Undergraduate students, graduate students. *Eligibility: Applicants must be disabled students who demonstrate financial need. *Application Process: Contact the Brigham Young University Accessibility Center for application details. *Amount: Varies. *Deadline: Varies.

California Association for Postsecondary Education and Disability (CAPED)
Attn: Janet Shapiro, Disabled Students Programs and Services
Santa Barbara City College
721 Cliff Drive
Santa Barbara, CA 93109
805-965-0581, ext. 2365
shapiro@sbcc.net
http://www.caped.net/scholarship.html
Scholarship Name: CAPED General Excellence Scholarship. *Academic Area: Open. *Age Group: Undergraduate students, graduate students. *Eligibility: Applicants must be college students with disabilities who demonstrate high academic achievement and are involved in their community as well as campus life. Undergraduate applicants must have a minimum GPA of 2.5; graduate-level applicants must have a GPA of at least 3.0. *Application Process: Applicants must submit a completed application, a cover letter, a letter of recommendation, verification of disability, transcripts, and proof of enrollment. Visit the association's Web site to download an application. *Amount: $1,500. *Deadline: September 1.

California Association for Postsecondary Education and Disability (CAPED)
Attn: Janet Shapiro, Disabled Students Programs and Services
Santa Barbara City College
721 Cliff Drive
Santa Barbara, CA 93109
805-965-0581, ext. 2365

shapiro@sbcc.net
http://www.caped.net/scholarship.html
Scholarship Name: Cindy Kolb Memorial Scholarship.
*Academic Area: Open. *Age Group: Undergraduate
students, graduate students. *Eligibility: Applicants
must be students with disabilities attending
a four-year college or university in California.
Undergraduate applicants must have a minimum
GPA of 2.5; graduate-level applicants must have a
GPA of at least 3.0. *Application Process: Applicants
must submit a completed application, a cover letter,
a letter of recommendation, verification of disability,
transcripts, and proof of enrollment. Visit the
association's Web site to download an application.
*Amount: $1,000. *Deadline: September 1.

**California Association for Postsecondary Education
and Disability (CAPED)**
Attn: Janet Shapiro, Disabled Students Programs and
Services
Santa Barbara City College
721 Cliff Drive
Santa Barbara, CA 93109
805-965-0581, ext. 2365
shapiro@sbcc.net
http://www.caped.net/scholarship.html
Scholarship Name: Lynn M. Smith Memorial
Scholarship. *Academic Area: Open. *Age Group:
Undergraduate students, graduate students.
*Eligibility: Applicants must be community college
students with disabilities who are pursuing a
vocational career goal at a California postsecondary
institution. They must also have a minimum GPA of
2.5. *Application Process: Applicants must submit
a completed application, a cover letter, a letter of
recommendation, verification of disability, transcripts,
and proof of enrollment. Visit the association's Web
site to download an application. *Amount: $1,000.
*Deadline: September 1.

**California Association for Postsecondary Education
and Disability (CAPED)**
Attn: Janet Shapiro, Disabled Students Programs and
Services
Santa Barbara City College
721 Cliff Drive
Santa Barbara, CA 93109
805-965-0581, ext. 2365
shapiro@sbcc.net
http://www.caped.net/scholarship.html

Scholarship Name: Steve Fasteau Past Presidents'
Scholarship. *Academic Area: Open. *Age Group:
Undergraduate students, graduate students.
*Eligibility: Applicants must be college students with
disabilities at California postsecondary institutions.
Undergraduate applicants must have a minimum GPA
of 2.5; graduate-level applicants must have a GPA of at
least 3.0. *Application Process: Applicants must submit
a completed application, a cover letter, a letter of
recommendation, verification of disability, transcripts,
and proof of enrollment. Visit the association's Web
site to download an application. *Amount: $1,000.
*Deadline: September 1.

**California Association for Postsecondary Education
and Disability (CAPED)**
Attn: Janet Shapiro, Disabled Students Programs and
Services
Santa Barbara City College
721 Cliff Drive
Santa Barbara, CA 93109
805-965-0581, ext. 2365
shapiro@sbcc.net
http://www.caped.net/scholarship.html
Scholarship Name: Susan Bunch Memorial Scholarship.
*Academic Area: Open. *Age Group: Undergraduate
students, graduate students. *Eligibility: Applicants
must be students with disabilities who are pursuing a
college degree at a California postsecondary institution.
Undergraduate applicants must have a minimum GPA
of 2.5; graduate-level applicants must have a GPA of at
least 3.0. *Application Process: Applicants must submit
a completed application, a cover letter, a letter of
recommendation, verification of disability, transcripts,
and proof of enrollment. Visit the association's Web
site to download an application. *Amount: $1,000.
*Deadline: September 1.

**California Association for Postsecondary Education
and Disability (CAPED)**
Attn: Janet Shapiro, Disabled Students Programs and
Services
Santa Barbara City College
721 Cliff Drive
Santa Barbara, CA 93109
805-965-0581, ext. 2365
shapiro@sbcc.net
http://www.caped.net/scholarship.html
Scholarship Name: Walter Young Memorial Scholarship.
*Academic Area: Open. *Age Group: Undergraduate

students, graduate students. *Eligibility: Applicants must be college students at a California postsecondary institution who are blind or visually impaired. Undergraduate applicants must have a minimum GPA of 2.5; graduate-level applicants must have a GPA of at least 3.0. *Application Process: Applicants must submit a completed application, a cover letter, a letter of recommendation, verification of disability, transcripts, and proof of enrollment. Visit the association's Web site to download an application. *Amount: $1,000. *Deadline: September 1.

California Association for Postsecondary Education and Disability (CAPED)
Attn: Janet Shapiro, Disabled Students Programs and Services
Santa Barbara City College
721 Cliff Drive
Santa Barbara, CA 93109
805-965-0581, ext. 2365
shapiro@sbcc.net
http://www.caped.net/scholarship.html
Scholarship Name: William May Memorial Scholarship. *Academic Area: Open. *Age Group: Undergraduate students, graduate students. *Eligibility: Applicants must be college students with disabilities at a California postsecondary institution. Undergraduate applicants must have a minimum GPA of 2.5; graduate-level applicants must have a GPA of at least 3.0. *Application Process: Applicants must submit a completed application, a cover letter, a letter of recommendation, verification of disability, transcripts, and proof of enrollment. Visit the association's Web site to download an application. *Amount: $1,000. *Deadline: September 1.

California Council of the Blind
578 B Street
Hayward, CA 94541
510-537-7877
http://www.ccbnet.org
Scholarship Name: California Council of the Blind Scholarship. *Academic Area: Open. *Age Group: Undergraduate students, graduate students. *Eligibility: Applicants must be residents of California who are legally blind, planning to (high school seniors) or currently enrolled as full-time students in accredited colleges/universities or vocational schools, and demonstrate financial need. *Application Process: Applicants must submit a completed

application, a personal statement, transcripts, and a letter of recommendation. Visit the council's Web site to download an application. *Amount: Varies. *Deadline: Varies.

California Governor's Committee on Employment of People with Disabilities
800 Capitol Mall, MIC 41
Sacramento, CA 95814
800-695-0350, 916-654-9820 (TTY)
http://www.disabilityemployment.org/youth.htm
Scholarship Name: Hal Connolly Scholarship. *Academic Area: Open. *Age Group: Undergraduate students *Eligibility: Applicants must be high school seniors at California public or private schools who have participated in varsity sports despite a disability. They need not plan to take part in sports while in college. Applicants must be disabled, have a GPA of at least 2.8, and be age 19 or under on January 1 of the same calendar year in which they apply. *Application Process: Visit the California Governor's Committee Web site to download an application. *Amount: $1,000. *Deadline: Varies.

California-Hawaii Elks Association
5450 East Lamona Avenue
Fresno, CA 93727-2224
599-255-4531
http://www.chea-elks.org/vocationalgrant.html
Grant Name: California-Hawaii Elks Association Vocational Grant. *Academic Area: Open. *Age Group: Undergraduate students, adults. *Eligibility: Applicants must be California or Hawaii residents who plan to pursue an eligible vocational/technical course, which culminates in an associate degree, diploma, or certificate. Applicants with disabilities are encouraged to apply. Applicants may be high school seniors or other prospective students who require training or retraining to compete in the workplace. Note: Individuals planning to transfer to a four-year school to pursue a bachelor's degree may not apply. *Application Process: Applicants must submit a completed application, a personal statement, four letters of recommendation (two from educators), transcripts or work record (from the previous two years), a letter of acceptance to vocational program, a copy of official documentation of residency status (if a naturalized U.S. citizen), and a vocational course pamphlet. Visit the association's Web site to download an application. *Amount: $1,000. *Deadline: Varies.

California-Hawaii Elks Association
California-Hawaii Elks Major Project Inc.
5450 East Lamona Avenue
Fresno, CA 93727-2224
599-255-4531
http://www.chea-elks.org/uspsd.html
Scholarship Name: Undergraduate Scholarship Program for Students with Disabilities. *Academic Area: Open. *Age Group: Undergraduate students. *Eligibility: Applicants must be California or Hawaii residents with physical impairments, neurological impairments, visual impairments, hearing impairments, and/or speech-language disorders who are pursuing their goals in higher education. Applicants must be sponsored by an Elks member from California or Hawaii. High school seniors are also eligible to apply. *Application Process: Applicants must submit a completed application, an essay, a financial statement, official transcripts, and two letter of recommendation. Visit the association's Web site to download an application. *Amount: $1,000 to $2,000. *Deadline: March 15.

California State University (CSU)
Office of the Chancellor
401 Golden Shore, Fourth Floor
Long Beach, CA 90802-4210
562-985-2692
http://www.calstate.edu/hr/flp
Loan Name: Chancellor's Doctoral Incentive/Forgivable Loan Program. *Academic Area: Open. *Age Group: Graduate students. *Eligibility: Individuals preparing for academic teaching careers are eligible to apply, particularly those interested in applying and competing for CSU instructional faculty positions. *Application Process: Contact the program administrator for additional information. *Amount: Loans of $10,000 per year to a total of $30,000 over a five-year period are available. Twenty percent of the amount borrowed is forgiven for each year of teaching at CSU. *Deadline: Typically in February. Contact the program administrator for additional information.

California State University-Bakersfield
Office of Financial Aid and Scholarships
Building SA 114
9001 Stockdale Highway 48SA
Bakersfield, CA 93311
661-654-3016
financialaid@csub.edu
http://www.csub.edu/FinAid

Scholarship Name: California State University-Bakersfield Scholarships for Students with Disabilities. *Academic Area: Open. *Age Group: Undergraduate students, graduate students. *Eligibility: Applicants must be student with disabilities who demonstrate financial need. *Application Process: Contact the California State University-Bakersfield Office of Financial Aid and Scholarships for application details. *Amount: Varies. *Deadline: Varies.

California State University-Fresno
Scholarship Office
5150 North Maple Avenue, JA64
Fresno, CA 93740
559-278-6572
http://studentaffairs.csufresno.edu/scholarships/default.htm
Scholarship Name: Becky Honda Memorial Scholarship. *Academic Area: Open. *Age Group: Undergraduate students, graduate students. *Eligibility: Applicants must be students with disabilities who demonstrate financial need. *Application Process: Contact the CSU-Fresno Financial Aid Office for application details. *Amount: Varies. *Deadline: Varies.

Cancer Survivor's Fund
PO Box 792
Missouri City, TX 77459
281-437-7142
info@cancersurvivorsfund.org
http://www.cancersurvivorsfund.org
Scholarship Name: Cancer Survivors' Fund Scholarship. *Academic Area: Open. *Age Group: Undergraduate students, graduate students. *Eligibility: Applicants must be cancer survivors or currently diagnosed with cancer. Applicants must reside in Texas and be enrolled in or accepted for enrollment in an undergraduate or graduate school. Upon receipt of a scholarship, applicants must agree to do volunteer work to use their cancer experience to help other young cancer patients and survivors coping with a life threatening or life-altering events. *Application Process: Applicants must submit a completed application, a letter of acceptance (to a postsecondary institution), two letters of recommendation, verification of medical history and current status (from physician), an essay, and a release form. Visit the fund's Web site to download an application and release form. *Amount: Varies. *Deadline: January 31.

Canyons, College of the

Office of Admissions
26455 Rockwell Canyon Road
Santa Clarita, CA 91355
661-259-7800
http://www.canyons.edu

Scholarship Name: College of the Canyons Scholarship for Students with Disabilities. *Academic Area: Open. *Age Group: Undergraduate students. *Eligibility: Applicants must be disabled high school seniors or college students who demonstrate financial need. *Application Process: Contact the College of the Canyons Office of Admissions for application details. *Amount: Varies. *Deadline: Varies.

Central Intelligence Agency (CIA)

PO Box 12727
Arlington, VA 22209-8727
800-368-3886
http://www.cia.gov/employment/student.html#usp

Scholarship Name: CIA Undergraduate Scholarship. *Academic Area: Open. *Age Group: Undergraduate students, graduate students. *Eligibility: Applicants must be at least 18 years of age by April 1 of their high school senior year, score 1000 or higher on the SAT or 21 or higher on the ACT, have a 3.0 GPA, and demonstrate financial need. High school seniors and college sophomores with disabilities are eligible to apply. *Application Process: Contact the CIA for application details. *Amount: Up to $18,000 per year. *Deadline: November 1.

Cerritos College

Financial Aid Office
11110 Alondra Boulevard
Norwalk, CA 90650
562-860-2451
finaid-staff-list@cerritos.edu
http://www.cerritos.edu/finaid

Scholarship Name: Ron Fornier Scholarship. *Academic Area: Open. *Age Group: Undergraduate students. *Eligibility: Applicants must be enrolled in Cerritos College's Disabled Students Program, have a minimum 2.0 GPA, and demonstrate financial need. *Application Process: Contact the Cerritos College Financial Aid Office for application details. *Amount: Varies. *Deadline: Varies.

ChairScholars Foundation Inc.

16101 Carancia Lane
Odessa, FL 33556-3278
813-920-2737
info@chairscholars.org
http://www.chairscholars.org

Scholarship Name: ChairScholars Foundation Inc. Scholarship. *Academic Area: Open. *Age Group: Undergraduate students. *Eligibility: Applicants must be high school seniors or college freshmen who are physically challenged (although they do not have to use a wheelchair) and have serious financial need. Applicants must also have a minimum B+ average, be under 21, and demonstrate some form of major community service or social contribution in the past. *Application Process: Applicants must submit contact/personal details, an essay, a parent or guardian's most recent federal income tax return, standardized test scores, a photo, three letters of recommendation, transcripts, and a list of honors and achievements. Visit the foundation's Web site for further application details. *Amount: $3,000 to $5,000. *Deadline: March 1.

The Chicago Lighthouse

Mary Kathryn and Michael Panitch Scholarship Program
Attn: Scholarship Program Coordinator
1850 West Roosevelt Road
Chicago, IL 60608-1298
312-666-1331
scholarships@chicagolighthouse.org
http://www.thechicagolighthouse.org/_content/Downloads/ScholarshipInfo.pdf

Scholarship Name: Cara Dunne Yates Scholarship. *Academic Area: Open. *Age Group: Graduate students. *Eligibility: Applicants must be blind or visually impaired students who are pursuing a graduate degree. Special consideration is given to those applicants who are pursuing law degrees. *Application Process: Applicants must submit a completed application, a one-page essay, and a letter of recommendation (optional). Visit The Chicago Lighthouse Web site to download an application. *Amount: Varies. *Deadline: May 1.

The Chicago Lighthouse

Mary Kathryn and Michael Panitch Scholarship Program
Attn: Scholarship Program Coordinator
1850 West Roosevelt Road
Chicago, IL 60608-1298
312-666-1331
scholarships@chicagolighthouse.org
http://www.thechicagolighthouse.org/_content/Downloads/ScholarshipInfo.pdf

Scholarship Name: Carl J. Konrath Scholarship. *Academic Area: Open. *Age Group: Undergraduate students, graduate students. *Eligibility: Applicants must be blind or visually impaired students who have made a distinguished personal achievement. This scholarship is open to high school seniors and college students. *Application Process: Applicants must submit a completed application, a one-page essay, and a letter of recommendation (optional). Visit The Chicago Lighthouse Web site to download an application. *Amount: Varies. *Deadline: May 1.

The Chicago Lighthouse
Mary Kathryn and Michael Panitch Scholarship Program
Attn: Scholarship Program Coordinator
1850 West Roosevelt Road
Chicago, IL 60608-1298
312-666-1331
scholarships@chicagolighthouse.org
http://www.thechicagolighthouse.org/_content/
    Downloads/ScholarshipInfo.pdf
Scholarship Name: Daniel G. Lee Scholarship. *Academic Area: Open. *Age Group: Undergraduate students, graduate students. *Eligibility: Applicants must be blind or visually impaired students who are pursuing vocational training. *Application Process: Applicants must submit a completed application, a one-page essay, and a letter of recommendation (optional). Visit The Chicago Lighthouse Web site to download an application. *Amount: Varies. *Deadline: May 1.

The Chicago Lighthouse
Mary Kathryn and Michael Panitch Scholarship Program
Attn: Scholarship Program Coordinator
1850 West Roosevelt Road
Chicago, IL 60608-1298
312-666-1331
scholarships@chicagolighthouse.org
http://www.thechicagolighthouse.org/_content/
    Downloads/ScholarshipInfo.pdf
Scholarship Name: Gene Cilio Scholarship. *Academic Area: Open. *Age Group: Undergraduate students. *Eligibility: Applicants must be blind or visually impaired high school seniors who will be entering their first semester of college/university. *Application Process: Applicants must submit a completed application, a one-page essay, and a letter of recommendation (optional). Visit The Chicago Lighthouse Web site to download an application. *Amount: Varies. *Deadline: May 1.

The Chicago Lighthouse
Mary Kathryn and Michael Panitch Scholarship Program
Attn: Scholarship Program Coordinator
1850 West Roosevelt Road
Chicago, IL 60608-1298
312-666-1331
scholarships@chicagolighthouse.org
http://www.thechicagolighthouse.org/_content/
    Downloads/ScholarshipInfo.pdf
Scholarship Name: Mary Zabelski Scholarship. *Academic Area: Open. *Age Group: Undergraduate students. *Eligibility: Applicants must be blind or visually impaired students who are on their way to earning an undergraduate degree. *Application Process: Applicants must submit a completed application, a one-page essay, and a letter of recommendation (optional). Visit The Chicago Lighthouse Web site to download an application. *Amount: Varies. *Deadline: May 1.

The Chicago Lighthouse
Mary Kathryn and Michael Panitch Scholarship Program
Attn: Scholarship Program Coordinator
1850 West Roosevelt Road
Chicago, IL 60608-1298
312-666-1331
scholarships@chicagolighthouse.org
http://www.thechicagolighthouse.org/_content/
    Downloads/ScholarshipInfo.pdf
Scholarship Name: Medical Scholarship. *Academic Area: Medicine (general): *Age Group: Undergraduate students, graduate students. *Eligibility: Applicants must be blind or visually impaired students who are pursuing a degree in the field of medicine. *Application Process: Applicants must submit a completed application, a one-page essay, and a letter of recommendation (optional). Visit The Chicago Lighthouse Web site to download an application. *Amount: Varies. *Deadline: May 1.

Christian Record Services Inc.
4444 South 52nd Street
Lincoln, NE 68516-1302
402-488-0981
info@christianrecord.org
http://www.christianrecord.org
Scholarship Name: Christian Record Services Inc. Scholarship. *Academic Area: Open. *Age Group: Undergraduate students. *Eligibility: Applicants must be legally blind high school seniors planning to pursue a bachelor's degree full time. They must also demonstrate

financial need. *Application Process: Applicants must submit a completed application, a personal statement, a financial budget, a photograph, and three scholarship evaluation forms. Visit the Christian Record Services Inc. Web site to download an application and evaluation form. *Amount: $500. *Deadline: April 1.

Council of Citizens with Low Vision International
1155 15 Street, NW, Suite 1004
Washington, DC 20005
800-733-2258
http://www.cclvi.org/scholarship.html
Scholarship Name: Fred Scheigert Scholarship. *Academic Area: Open. *Age Group: Undergraduate students. *Eligibility: Applicants must be high school seniors who have been accepted into college and current undergraduates with low vision. They must also maintain at least a 3.0 GPA and attend college full time. *Application Process: Applicants must submit a completed application, an essay, transcripts, two letters of recommendation, a letter from an ophthalmologist verifying specific vision acuity, and a letter of acceptance (if applicable). Visit the council's Web site to download an application. *Amount: Varies. *Deadline: April 15.

Crohn's and Colitis Foundation of America
386 Park Avenue South, 17th Floor
New York, NY 10016
800-932-2423
http://www.greatcomebacks.com
Scholarship Name: Ina Brudnick Scholarship. *Academic Area: Open. *Age Group: Undergraduate students. *Eligibility: Applicants must be undergraduate college students with Crohn's disease, ulcerative colitis, or have undergone ostomy surgery. They must also be under 24 years of age, and priority is given to an individual who can demonstrate how he or she has overcome major obstacles in life. *Application Process: Contact the foundation for application details. *Amount; $2,500. *Deadline: Typically in January.

Curry College
Student Financial Services
1071 Blue Hill Avenue
Milton, MA 02186
800-333-2146
Fin-Aid@curry.edu
http://www.curry.edu/Admissions/Financial+Aid
Grant Name: Jennifer Ann Phillips Scholarship. *Academic Area: Education. *Age Group: Undergraduate students.

*Eligibility: Applicants must be sophomores, juniors, or seniors who are learning disabled or students who are interested in teaching the learning disabled. Preference will be given to applicants with both qualifications. Recipients are under moral obligation to repay the grant (interest free) as soon as possible. *Application Process: Contact Curry College's Student Financial Services for application details. *Amount: Up to $3,500. *Deadline: Varies.

Cystic Fibrosis Scholarship Foundation
2814 Grant Street
Evanston, IL 60201
847-328-0127
mkbcfsf@aol.com
http://www.cfscholarship.org
Loan Name: General Scholarship. *Academic Area: Open. *Age Group: Undergraduate students. *Eligibility: High school seniors and college students with cystic fibrosis who need financial assistance are eligible to apply.*Application Process: Applicants must submit an application (available online), tax return, doctor's note, academic transcripts, and an essay (question varies). *Amount: $1,000 to $2,000. *Deadline: *Deadline: March 17.

Daughters of the American Revolution (DAR)
Committee Services Office
Attn: Scholarships
1776 D Street, NW
Washington, DC 20006-5303
202-879-3293
http://www.dar.org
Scholarship Name: Margaret Howard Hamilton Scholarship. *Academic Area: Open. *Age Group: Undergraduate students. *Eligibility: Applicants must be high school students with learning disabilities who have been accepted into the Harvey and Bernice Jones Learning Center at the University of the Ozarks-Clarksville, Arkansas. Candidates must be sponsored by a local DAR chapter. *Application Process: Applications must be requested directly through the Learning Center upon acceptance into this program. *Amount: $1,000 per year. *Deadline: April 15.

Delta Gamma Foundation
3250 Riverside Drive, PO Box 21397
Columbus, OH 43221
614-481-8169
http://www.deltagamma.org/scholarships_fellowships_and_loans_2.shtml

Scholarship Name: Wilma H. Wright Memorial Scholarship. *Academic Area: Open. *Age Group: Undergraduate students, graduate students. *Eligibility: Applicants must be members of Delta Gamma who are visually impaired or who wish to prepare to work with the visually impaired. They must also have a 3.0 GPA and should be participants in chapter, campus, and community activities. *Application Process: Contact the foundation for application details. *Amount: $1,000. *Deadline: February 1.

The Ear Foundation
Minnie Pearl Scholarship Program
1817 Patterson Street
Nashville, TN 37203
800-545-HEAR (Voice/TDD)
info@earfoundation.org
http://www.earfoundation.org/education.
    asp?content=minnie_pearl_scholarship
Scholarship Name: Minnie Pearl Scholarship. *Academic Area: Open. *Age Group: Undergraduate students. *Eligibility: Applicants must be high school seniors who have a significant bilateral hearing loss and a minimum 3.0 GPA. Applicants must be accepted, but not yet in attendance at a junior college, university, or technical school. They must be mainstreamed hearing-impaired students, U.S. citizens, and planning on attending college/university full time. *Application Process: Applicants must submit a completed application, an audiology report for both ears from the past 12 months, transcripts, three letters of recommendation, and a photograph. Visit the foundation's Web site to download an application. *Amount: $2,500 per year, plus a $500 bonus award for recipients who maintain at least a 3.5 cumulative GPA. *Deadline: February 16.

Eastern Amputee Golf Association (EAGA)
2015 Amherst Drive
Bethlehem, PA 18015-5606
888-868-0992
info@eaga.org
http://www.eaga.org
Scholarship Name: EAGA College Scholarships. *Academic Area: Open. *Age Group: Undergraduate students. *Eligibility: Applicant must be an EAGA amputee member and/or members of his or her family who needs financial assistance. Award recipients must maintain a 2.0 GPA to continue receiving the scholarship over its four-year duration. Undergraduate college students and high school seniors may apply. *Application Process: Contact the association for details. *Amount: $1,000. *Deadline: June 30.

Edinboro University of Pennsylvania
Financial Aid Office
Hamilton Hall
Edinboro, PA 16444
888-611-2680
finaid@edinboro.edu
http://www.edinboro.edu/cwis/admin/development/
    disabledscholarships.html
Grant Name: Charlotte W. Newcombe Foundation Grant. *Academic Area: Open. *Age Group: Undergraduate students, graduate students. *Eligibility: Applicants must be physically disabled students who are enrolled at least half time, having completed at least one semester of course work toward a degree or certification program. Applicants should be able to demonstrate financial need along with special needs relating to their handicaps that are not being met by another other agency or alternative form of financial aid. *Application Process: Applicants should contact the Financial Aid Office to receive an application along with application procedures. *Amount: $300 to $750. *Deadline: Contact the Financial Aid Office for deadline information.

Edinboro University of Pennsylvania
Financial Aid Office
Hamilton Hall
Edinboro, PA 16444
888-611-2680
finaid@edinboro.edu
http://www.edinboro.edu/cwis/admin/development/
    disabledscholarships.html
Scholarship Name: Charlotte W. Newcombe Scholarship. *Academic Area: Open. *Age Group: Undergraduate students, graduate students. *Eligibility: Applicants must have a physical disability and have registered with the Office for Students with Disabilities. Applicants must have completed at least one semester of full-time work towards a degree or certification program, maintaining at least a 2.0 GPA. *Application Process: Applicants should contact the Office for Students with Disabilities as well as the Financial Aid Office regarding scholarship application procedures. *Amount: Awards vary. *Deadline: Contact the Financial Aid Office for deadline information.

Edinboro University of Pennsylvania
Financial Aid Office
Hamilton Hall

Edinboro, PA 16444
888-611-2680
finaid@edinboro.edu
http://www.edinboro.edu/cwis/admin/development/
   disabledscholarships.html
Scholarship Name: Mabel Hamlett Scholarship. *Academic
   Area: Open. *Age Group: Undergraduate students,
   graduate students. *Eligibility: Applicants must be
   full-time students with a physical disability who have
   completed at least one semester of course work,
   maintaining at least a 2.0 GPA. Applicants must also
   have financial need. *Application Process: Contact the
   Financial Aid Office to receive an application along
   with application procedures. *Amount: Awards vary.
   *Deadline: Contact the Financial Aid Office for deadline
   information.

Edinboro University of Pennsylvania
Financial Aid Office
Hamilton Hall
Edinboro, PA 16444
888-611-2680
finaid@edinboro.edu
http://www.edinboro.edu/cwis/admin/development/
   disabledscholarships.html
Scholarship Name: SGA Scholarship for Students
   with Disabilities. *Academic Area: Open. *Age
   Group: Undergraduate students, graduate students.
   *Eligibility: Applicants must be full-time students who
   have completed at least one semester of full-time
   work towards a degree or certificate program while
   maintaining at least a 2.0 GPA. Applicants must have
   a learning or physical disability. *Application Process:
   Applicants should contact the Financial Aid Office
   for details about the application process. *Amount:
   Awards vary. *Deadline: Contact the Financial Aid
   Office for deadline information.

Eli Lilly and Company
c/o Lilly Secretariat
PMB 327, 310 Busse Highway
Park Ridge, IL 60068-3251
800-809-8202
lillyscholarships@reintegration.com
http://www.reintegration.com/resources/scholarships
Scholarship Name: Lilly Reintegration Scholarship.
   *Academic Area: Open. *Age Group: Undergraduate
   students, graduate students. *Eligibility:
   Applicants must be diagnosed with schizophrenia,
   schizophreniform, schizoaffective disorder, or bipolar
   disorder and be currently receiving medical treatment

for the disease. *Application Process: Contact Eli Lilly
   and Company for application details. *Amount: Varies.
   *Deadline: Varies.

Elizabeth City State University
Office of Financial Aid
227 Marion D. Thorpe Administration Bldg.
Campus Box 914
Elizabeth City, NC 27909
252-335-3283
http://www.ecsu.edu/prospective/financialaid.cfm
Scholarship Name: The university offers financial
   aid and vocational rehabilitation scholarships for
   students with disabilities. *Academic Area: Open.
   *Age Group: Undergraduate students. *Eligibility:
   Students with disabilities who demonstrate financial
   need are eligible. *Application Process: Contact the
   Office of Financial Aid for details. *Amount: Varies.
   *Deadline: *Deadline: Contact the Office of Financial
   Aid for details.

Elks National Foundation
Attn: Scholarship Department
2750 North Lakeview Avenue
Chicago, IL 60614-1889
773-755-4732
scholarship@elks.org
http://www.elks.org/enf/scholars/mvs.cfm
Scholarship Name: Most Valuable Student Scholarship
   Competition. *Academic Area: Open. *Age Group:
   Undergraduate students. *Eligibility: Applicants must
   be U.S. citizens who are high school seniors planning
   to pursue a four-year degree on a full-time basis. They
   must also demonstrate financial need, leadership, and
   academic excellence. Applicants with disabilities are
   encouraged to apply. *Application Process: Visit the
   foundation's Web site to download an application.
   Applications must be submitted to the applicant's
   local Elks Lodge. *Amount: $1,000 to $15,000 per year.
   *Deadline: January 13.

Ethel Louise Armstrong (ELA) Foundation Inc.
Attn: Deborah Lewis, Executive Director
2460 North Lake Avenue, PMB #128
Altadena, CA 91001
626-398-8840
executivedirector@ela.org
http://www.ela.org/scholarships/scholarships.html
Scholarship Name: Ethel Louise Armstrong Foundation
   Scholarship. *Academic Area: Open. *Age Group:
   Graduate students. *Eligibility: Applicants must be

female graduate students with physical disabilities who are enrolled in a college/university in the United States. Applicants must be active in a local, state, or national disability organization. *Application Process: Applicants must submit a completed application, an ELA Verification of Disability form, an essay, two letters of recommendation, and transcripts. Visit the Foundation's Web site to download an application. *Amount: $500 to $2,000. *Deadline: June 1.

Exceptional Nurse Inc.
Attn: Scholarship Committee
13019 Coastal Circle
Palm Beach Gardens, FL 33410
561-627-9872
ExceptionalNurse@aol.com
http://www.exceptionalnurse.com/scholarship.html
Scholarship Name: Anna May Rolando Scholarship Award. *Academic Area: Nursing (open). *Age Group: Undergraduate students, graduate students. *Eligibility: Applicants must have applied to or been admitted to a college nursing program, be attending or planning to attend school full time, and be able to provide documentation of a disability. Preference is given to graduate students who have a proven history of working with individuals with disabilities. *Application Process: Applicants should submit a completed application along with official transcripts, an essay, three letters of recommendation focusing on academic achievements and personal character, and official documentation of a disability. Visit the organization's Web site to download an official application. *Amount: $500. *Deadline: June 1.

Exceptional Nurse Inc.
Attn: Scholarship Committee
13019 Coastal Circle
Palm Beach Gardens, FL 33410
561-627-9872
ExceptionalNurse@aol.com
http://www.exceptionalnurse.com/scholarship.html
Scholarship Name: Caroline Simpson Maheady Scholarship Award. *Academic Area: Nursing (open). *Age Group: Undergraduate students, graduate students. *Eligibility: Applicants must have applied to or been admitted to a college nursing program, be attending or planning to attend school full time, and be able to provide documentation of a disability. Undergraduate applicants of Scottish descent, with a history of working with individuals

with disabilities, are given preference. *Application Process: Applicants should submit a completed application along with official transcripts, an essay, three letters of recommendation focusing on academic achievements and personal character, and official documentation of a disability. Visit the organization's Web site to download an official application. *Amount: $250. *Deadline: June 1.

Exceptional Nurse Inc.
Attn: Scholarship Committee
13019 Coastal Circle
Palm Beach Gardens, FL 33410
561-627-9872
ExceptionalNurse@aol.com
http://www.exceptionalnurse.com/scholarship.html
Scholarship Name: ExceptionalNurse.com Scholarship. *Academic Area: Nursing (open). *Age Group: Undergraduate students, graduate students. *Eligibility: Applicants must have applied to or been admitted to a college nursing program, be attending or planning to attend school full time, and be able to provide documentation of a disability. Undergraduate applicants are given preference. *Application Process: Applicants should submit a completed application along with official transcripts, an essay, three letters of recommendation focusing on academic achievements and personal character, and official documentation of a disability. Visit the organization's Web site to download an official application. *Amount: $250. *Deadline: June 1.

Exceptional Nurse Inc.
Attn: Scholarship Committee
13019 Coastal Circle
Palm Beach Gardens, FL 33410
561-627-9872
ExceptionalNurse@aol.com
http://www.exceptionalnurse.com/scholarship.html
Scholarship Name: Genevieve Julia Scholarship Award. *Academic Area: Nursing (open). *Age Group: Undergraduate students, graduate students. *Eligibility: Applicants must have applied to or been admitted to a college nursing program, be attending or planning to attend school full time, and be able to provide documentation of a disability. *Application Process: Applicants should submit a completed application along with official transcripts, an essay, three letters of recommendation focusing on academic achievements and personal character, and official

documentation of a disability. Visit the organization's Web site to download an official application. *Amount: $500. *Deadline: June 1.

Exceptional Nurse Inc.
Attn: Scholarship Committee
13019 Coastal Circle
Palm Beach Gardens, FL 33410
561-627-9872
ExceptionalNurse@aol.com
http://www.exceptionalnurse.com/scholarship.html
Scholarship Name: Jill Laura Creedon Scholarship. *Academic Area: Nursing (open). *Age Group: Undergraduate students, graduate students. *Eligibility: Applicants must have applied to or been admitted to a college nursing program, be attending or planning to attend school full time, and be able to provide documentation of a disability or medical condition. Undergraduate applicants are given preference. *Application Process: Applicants should submit a completed application along with official transcripts, an essay, three letters of recommendation focusing on academic achievements and personal character, and official documentation of a disability or medical condition. The Johnson & Johnson Campaign for Nursing's Future sponsors this scholarship honoring Jill Laura Creedon. Visit the organization's Web site to read a sample essay written by Jill Laura Creedon and to download an application. *Amount: $500. *Deadline: June 1.

Exceptional Nurse Inc.
Attn: Scholarship Committee
13019 Coastal Circle
Palm Beach Gardens, FL 33410
561-627-9872
ExceptionalNurse@aol.com
http://www.exceptionalnurse.com/scholarship.html
Scholarship Name: Mary Serra Gili Scholarship Award. *Academic Area: Nursing (open). *Age Group: Undergraduate students, graduate students. *Eligibility: Applicants must have applied to or been admitted to a college nursing program, be attending or planning to attend school full time, and be able to provide documentation of a disability. *Application Process: Applicants should submit a completed application along with official transcripts, an essay, three letters of recommendation focusing on academic achievements and personal character, and official documentation of a disability. Visit the organization's

Web site to download an official application. *Amount: $250. *Deadline: June 1.

Florida Council of the Blind
2915 Circle Ridge Drive
Orange Park, FL 32065
904-272-8405
http://www.fcb.org/FCBSchApInfo.htm
Scholarship Name: The council offers scholarships for academic achievement and upward mobility, and a scholarship for a part-time student. *Academic Area: Open. *Age Group: Undergraduate students, graduate students. *Eligibility: Florida residents who are legally blind are eligible (although they do not need to attend college in Florida to be eligible). Candidates must have a good prior academic record. *Application Process: Contact the council for details. *Amount: Awards range from $500 to $1,500. *Deadline: *Deadline: Contact the council for details.

Fordham University School of Law
33 West 60th Street, 2nd Floor
New York, NY 10023
212-636-6815
financialaid@law.fordham.edu
http://law.fordham.edu/financialaid.htm
Scholarship Name: Amy Reiss Scholarship. *Academic Area: Law. *Age Group: Graduate students. *Eligibility: Applicants must be disabled (vision, hearing, mobility impaired, etc.) students who demonstrate financial need. Preference is given to blind or partially blind students. *Application Process: Contact the Fordham University School of Law for application details. *Amount: Varies (partial tuition is paid for three years). *Deadline: Varies.

Forward Face
Attn: Scholarship Committee
317 East 34th Street, Suite 901A
New York, NY 10016
212-684-5860
Camille@forwardface.org
http://www.forwardface.org/fr_contact.html
Scholarship Name: Forward Face Scholarship. *Academic Area: Open. *Age Group: 13 years of age and older. *Eligibility: Applicants must have a craniofacial condition. *Application Process: Applicants should submit a completed application along with an essay on how the applicant hopes to make a difference in the world and two letters

of recommendation. Visit the organization's Web site to download an application. *Amount: $1,000. *Deadline: February 1.

Foundation for Science and Disability

Attn: Dr. E. C. Keller Jr.
West Virginia University
Morgantown WV 26506 - 6057
http://www.as.wvu.edu/~scidis/organizations/fsd_main.html
Award Name: Student Award Program. *Academic Area: Engineering (general), mathematics, medicine, science, technology. *Age Group: Graduate students. *Eligibility: Applicants must be fourth-year undergraduate students who have been admitted to graduate school or graduate students already pursuing a graduate education. Applicants must have a disability. *Application Process: Applicants should contact the foundation to receive specific application instructions. *Amount: $1,000. *Deadline: Contact the foundation for deadline information.

Foundation Northwest

Old City Hall
North 221 Wall Street, Suite 624
Spokane, WA 99201-0826
888-267-5606
admin@foundationnw.org
http://foundationnw.org
Scholarship Name: Ren H. Rice Scholarship. *Academic Area: Open. *Age Group: Undergraduate students. *Eligibility: Applicants must be Spokane-area residents who are 21 years or younger. Applicants must be legally free in foster care, guardianship, or group homes, emancipated minors, non-legally free minors living the majority of their lives in foster care, or physically disabled. Applicants must attend or plan to attend a Washington state college/university. *Application Process: Contact the foundation for application details. *Amount: Varies (covers tuition, fees, and books). *Deadline: Varies.

Frostburg State University

Disability Support Services(DSS)
150 Pullen Hall
Frostburg, MD 21532
301-687-4483 (Voice/TTY)
lpullen@frostburg.edu
http://www.frostburg.edu/ungrad/faid/scholar/instit.htm

Scholarship Name: Delta Chi Disabled Student Scholarship. *Academic Area: Open. *Age Group: Undergraduate students. *Eligibility: Applicants must be enrolled as full-time students, demonstrate academic ability, and have documented disabilities. *Application Process: Contact DSS for application details. *Amount: $300. *Deadline: March 1.

Gallaudet University

Financial Aid Office
800 Florida Avenue, NE
Washington, DC 20002
202-651-5290 (Voice/TTY), 800-995-0990 (Voice/TTY)
Financial.Aid@gallaudet.edu
http://financialaid.gallaudet.edu
Gallaudet is one of only a few postsecondary institutions in the United States established exclusively to serve the deaf. It offers financial aid to needy students. *Academic Area: Open. *Age Group: Undergraduate students. *Eligibility: Deaf high school seniors or college students in need of financial assistance are eligible to apply. *Application Process: Contact the university for details. *Amount: Varies. *Deadline: Contact the university for details.

Gallaudet University Alumni Association

Peikoff Alumni House
800 Florida Avenue, NE
Washington, DC 20002
202-651-5060
alumni.relations@gallaudet.edu
http://alumni.gallaudet.edu
The alumni association offers scholarships to help deaf and hard of hearing students finance graduate training. *Academic Area: Open. *Age Group: Graduate students. *Eligibility: Graduates of Gallaudet University and others who are deaf and are pursuing doctoral studies are eligible. *Application Process: Contact the association for details. *Amount: Varies. *Deadline: *Deadline: Varies.

Galveston College

Financial Aid Office
4015 Avenue Q
Galveston, TX 77550
409-944-4242
http://www.gc.edu/gc/Scholarships.asp?SnID=2117619514
Scholarship Name: Houston Metropolitan Area Diagnosticians Scholarship. *Academic Area: Open.

*Age Group: Undergraduate students. *Eligibility: Disabled students who need financial assistance are eligible to apply. *Application Process: Contact the college's financial aid office for details. *Amount: $750. *Deadline: April 18.

Georgia Council of the Blind
Attn: Scholarship Committee Chair
850 Dogwood Road, Suite A-400-604
Lawrenceville, GA 30044-7218
877-667-6815
marshafarrow@alltel.net
http://www.georgiacounciloftheblind.org/scholarship.aspx
Scholarship Name: Georgia Council of the Blind Scholarship. *Academic Area: Open. *Age Group: Undergraduate students, graduate students. *Eligibility: Applicants must be students who are legally blind or sighted students who are financially dependent on legally blind parent(s). They must also be accepted into vocational/technical school, junior or four-year college, or master's or doctoral program at an accredited university. Applicants must be legal residents of the state of Georgia. *Application Process: Applicants must submit a completed application, transcripts, certification of legal blindness, two letters of recommendation, a financial statement, a list of extracurricular activities, a personal statement, and an audio cassette of the applicant reading a personal statement. Visit the council's Web site to download an application. *Amount: Up to $1,000. *Deadline: June 15.

Georgia Institute of Technology
Office of Student Financial Planning and Services
225 North Avenue
Atlanta, GA 30332-0460
404-894-4160
finaid@gatech.edu
http://www.finaid.gatech.edu/scholarships/found_end.php#feagin
Scholarship Name: Roy and Zou Feagin Scholarship. *Academic Area: Open. *Age Group: Undergraduate students. *Eligibility: Applicants must be students with mobility impairments, hearing impairments, visual impairments, learning disabilities, psychological disabilities, and other disabilities. Applicants must maintain at least a 2.0 GPA, show leadership qualities, and demonstrate financial need. *Application Process: Contact the institute's Office of Student Financial

Planning and Services for application details. *Amount: Varies. *Deadline: Varies.

Georgia, University of
Scholarship Review Committee
Disability Resource Center
114 Clark Howell Hall
Athens, GA 30602-3338
706-542-8719, 706-542-8778 (TTY)
http://www.drc.uga.edu/applications.html
Scholarship Name: Gregory Charles Johnson Scholarship. *Academic Area: Open. *Age Group: Undergraduate students, graduate students. *Eligibility: College students who have a disability due to a trauma who are currently attending the university may apply. They must also be registered with the Disability Resource Center, be a Georgia resident, have a GPA of at least 2.5, and have completed 30 hours of course work. *Application Process: Applicants must submit a completed application (available at the Disability Resource Center's Web site), a letter of recommendation, a transcript, and an essay that details how the applicant will use the scholarship. *Amount: One year of tuition. *Deadline: July 29.

Georgia, University of
Attn: Scholarship Review Committee
Disability Resource Center
114 Clark Howell Hall
Athens, GA 30602-3338
706-542-8719, 706-542-8778 (TTY)
http://www.drc.uga.edu/applications.html
Scholarship Name: Joe Coile Scholarship. *Academic Area: Open. *Age Group: Undergraduate students, graduate students. *Eligibility: College students with disabilities who are currently attending the university may apply. Applicants must show leadership qualities in on- or off-campus organizations. They must also be registered with the Disability Resource Center, be a Georgia resident, have a GPA of at least 2.0, and have completed 30 hours of course work. *Application Process: Applicants must submit a completed application (available at the Disability Resource Center's Web site), a letter of recommendation, a transcript, and an essay. *Amount: $500. *Deadline: July 29.

Georgia, University of
Attn: Scholarship Review Committee
Disability Resource Center

114 Clark Howell Hall
Athens, GA 30602-3338
706-542-8719, 706-542-8778 (TTY)
http://www.drc.uga.edu/applications.html
Scholarship Name: Margaret Ann Towson Scholarship.
*Academic Area: Open. *Age Group: Undergraduate
students, graduate students. *Eligibility: College
students with documented visual impairments who
are currently attending the university may apply.
They must also be registered with the Disability
Resource Center, be a Georgia resident, have a
GPA of at least 2.5, and have completed 30 hours
of course work. *Application Process: Applicants
must submit a completed application (available at
the Disability Resource Center's Web site), a letter
of recommendation, a transcript, and an essay that
details how the applicant will use the scholarship.
*Amount: $600. *Deadline: July 29.

Georgia, University of
Attn: Scholarship Review Committee
Disability Resource Center
114 Clark Howell Hall
Athens, GA 30602-3338
706-542-8719, 706-542-8778 (TTY)
http://www.drc.uga.edu/applications.html
Award Name: Matthew Peddicord Award. *Academic
Area: Open. *Age Group: Undergraduate students,
graduate students. *Eligibility: College students
with a disability due to a chronic illness who are
currently attending the university may apply.
They must also be registered with the Disability
Resource Center, be a Georgia resident, have a
GPA of at least 2.0, and have completed 30 hours
of course work. *Application Process: Applicants
must submit a completed application (available at
the Disability Resource Center's Web site), a letter
of recommendation, a transcript, and an essay that
details how the applicant will use the scholarship.
*Amount: $500. *Deadline: July 29.

Gore Family Memorial Foundation
4747 Ocean Drive, #204
Ft Lauderdale, FL 33308
Scholarship Name: Gore Family Memorial Foundation
Scholarship. *Academic Area: Open. *Age Group:
Undergraduate students, graduate students.
*Eligibility: Students with severe disabilities are
eligible to apply. Financial need is taken into
consideration. *Application Process: Contact the

foundation for details.*Amount: $1,000 to $2,000.
*Deadline: *Deadline: Varies.

Grand Valley State University
Disability Support Services
1 Campus Drive, 200 STU
Allendale, MI 49401-9403
616-331-2490
http://www.gvsu.edu/financialaid/index.
cfm?id=000BBD1A-4FAA-1EC5-ABC380E715660177
Scholarship Name: Berkowitz Scholarship for
Handicapped Students. *Academic Area: Open.
*Age Group: Undergraduate students, graduate
students. *Eligibility: Applicants must be full-time
students with disabilities attending Grand Valley
State University. *Application Process: Contact the
university's Disability Support Services department
for application details. *Amount: $500 (amount
may be higher depending on available funding).
*Deadline: March 15.

Harper College
Scholarships and Financial Assistance
Building C, 1200 West Algonquin Road, Room C102
Palatine, IL 60067-7398
847-925-6248, 847-397-7600 (TTY)
finaid@harpercollege.edu
http://64.118.66.193/page.cfm?p=1423
Scholarship Name: ADS Alumni Scholarship. *Academic
Area: Open. *Age Group: Undergraduate students.
*Eligibility: Applicants must be attending or planning
to attend Harper College. They must have a disability
and be registered with the Access and Disabilities
Services office. Community and school activity
participation and GPA are taken into consideration.
*Application Process: Applicants should submit
a completed application along with a personal
statement. Visit the school's Web site to download
an application or to fill out an online application.
*Amount: Awards vary. *Deadline: April 28.

Harper College
Scholarships and Financial Assistance
Building C, 1200 West Algonquin Road, Room C102
Palatine, IL 60067-7398
847-925-6248, 847-397-7600 (TTY)
finaid@harpercollege.edu
http://64.118.66.193/page.cfm?p=1423
Scholarship Name: Donald and Patricia Torisky
Endowment Fund. *Academic Area: Open. *Age Group:

Undergraduate students. *Eligibility: Applicants must be attending or planning to attend Harper College. They must possess a disability and be registered with the Access and Disabilities Services office. Community and school activity participation and GPA are taken into consideration. Contact the school's Access and Disability Services office for any additional criteria. *Application Process: Applicants should submit a completed application along with a personal statement. Visit the school's Web site to download an application or to fill out an online application. *Amount: Awards vary. *Deadline: April 28.

Harper College
Scholarships and Financial Assistance
Building C, 1200 West Algonquin Road, Room C102
Palatine, IL 60067-7398
847-925-6248, 847-397-7600 (TTY)
finaid@harpercollege.edu
http://64.118.66.193/page.cfm?p=1423
Scholarship Name: Glenda F. Nuccio Memorial Scholarship. *Academic Area: Open. *Age Group: Undergraduate students. *Eligibility: Applicants must be attending or planning to attend Harper College. They must possess a disability and be registered with the Access and Disabilities Services office. Community and school activity participation and GPA are taken into consideration. Contact the school's Access and Disability Services office for additional criteria. *Application Process: Applicants should submit a completed application along with a personal statement. Visit the school's Web site to download an application or to fill out an online application. *Amount: Awards vary. *Deadline: April 28.

Harper College
Scholarships and Financial Assistance
Building C, 1200 West Algonquin Road, Room C102
Palatine, IL 60067-7398
847-925-6248, 847-397-7600 (TTY)
finaid@harpercollege.edu
http://64.118.66.193/page.cfm?p=1423
Scholarship Name: Midge C. Smith Memorial Scholarship. *Academic Area: Open. *Age Group: Undergraduate students. *Eligibility: Applicants must be attending or planning to attend Harper College. They must possess a disability and be registered with the Access and Disabilities Services office. Community and school activity participation and GPA are taken into consideration. Contact the school's Access and

Disability Services office for any additional criteria. *Application Process: Applicants should submit a completed application along with a personal statement. Visit the school's Web site to download an application or to fill out an online application. *Amount: Awards vary. *Deadline: April 28.

Hawkeye Community College
Financial Aid Office
Hawkeye Center - Main Campus
1501 East Orange Road
Waterloo, IA 50704
800-670-4769, ext. 4020
finaid@hawkeyecollege.edu
http://www.hawkeyecollege.edu/currentstudents/financialaid.asp
Scholarship Name: Civitan Club Scholarship. *Academic Area: Open. *Age Group: Undergraduate students. *Eligibility: Applicants must be currently enrolled Hawkeye Community College students with disabilities who demonstrate financial need. *Application Process: Contact the college's Financial Aid Office for application details. *Amount: $250. *Deadline: April 1.

Hawkeye Community College
Financial Aid Office
Hawkeye Center - Main Campus
1501 East Orange Road
Waterloo, IA 50704
800-670-4769, ext. 4020
finaid@hawkeyecollege.edu
http://www.hawkeyecollege.edu/currentstudents/financialaid.asp
Scholarship Name: Jimmie Robinson Scholarship. *Academic Area: Open. *Age Group: Undergraduate students. *Eligibility: Applicants must be high school seniors or currently enrolled Hawkeye Community College students with physical disabilities who demonstrate financial need. *Application Process: Contact the college's Financial Aid Office for application details. *Amount: $350. *Deadline: April 1 and November 1.

Hemophilia Federation of America
1405 West Pinhook Road, Suite 101
Lafayette, LA 70503
800-230-9797
info@hemophiliafed.org
http://www.hemophiliafed.org/scholarships.php

Grant Name: Artistic Encouragement Grant. *Academic Area: Performing arts (general), visual arts (general). *Age Group: Open. *Eligibility: Applicants must be individuals with blood clotting disorders who are interested in pursuing some kind of artistic expression for which they require funds to complete. *Application Process: Applicants should submit a completed application along with an essay on the importance of the blood clotting community in their life, two letters of reference, a brief project summary, a portfolio or sample of work, a timeline for completion of the project, and a statement of financial need, such as the most recent tax return. Visit the federation's Web site to download an application. *Amount: $1,500. *Deadline: April 1.

Hemophilia Federation of America
1405 West Pinhook Road, Suite 101
Lafayette, LA 70503
800-230-9797
info@hemophiliafed.org
http://www.hemophiliafed.org/scholarships.php
Scholarship Name: Educational Scholarship. *Academic Area: Open. *Age Group: Undergraduate students, graduate students. *Eligibility: Applicants must be individuals with blood clotting disorders who are seeking postsecondary education from a college, university, or trade school. *Application Process: Applicants should submit a completed application along with an essay on the importance of the blood clotting community in their life, two letters of reference, a brief project summary, a portfolio or sample of work, a timeline for completion of the project, and a statement of financial need, such as the most recent tax return. If postsecondary training has not already been completed, the applicant must provide proof of acceptance into or enrollment in an educational institution. Visit the federation's Web site to download an application. *Amount: $1,500. *Deadline: April 1.

Hemophilia Foundation of Southern California
33 South Catalina Avenue, Suite 102
Pasadena, CA 91106
800-371-4123
hfsc@hemosocal.org
http://www.hemosocal.org
Scholarship Name: Christopher Pitkin Memorial Scholarship. *Academic Area: Open. *Age Group: Undergraduate students, graduate students.

*Eligibility: Applicants must be students with blood clotting disorders (as well as members of their family/spouses) who plan to or are currently pursuing postsecondary education. *Application Process: Contact the Hemophilia Foundation of Southern California for application details. *Amount: $500 to $1,000. *Deadline: August 25.

Hemophilia Health Services (HHS)
Attn: Scholarship Program Administrators
PO Box 23737
Nashville, TN 37202-3737
615-320-3149
scholarship@hemophiliahealth.com
http://www.hemophiliahealth.com/consumers/products_services/scholarship.htm
Scholarship Name: HHS Memorial Scholarship. *Academic Area: Open. *Age Group: Undergraduate students, graduate students. *Eligibility: College students with hemophilia and related bleeding disorders are eligible to apply. Applicants must be U.S. citizens. High school seniors may also apply. *Application Process: Applicants must submit a completed application, which is available on HHS's Web site. *Amount: $1,500. *Deadline: May 1.

Hemophilia Health Services (HHS)
Attn: Scholarship Program Administrators
PO Box 23737
Nashville, TN 37202-3737
615-320-3149
scholarship@hemophiliahealth.com
http://www.hemophiliahealth.com/consumers/products_services/scholarship.htm
Scholarship Name: Scott Tarbell Memorial Scholarship. *Academic Area: Computer science, mathematics. *Age Group: Undergraduate students. *Eligibility: College students with hemophilia and related bleeding disorders who plan to, or who are currently pursuing, a degree or certification in computer science and/or mathematics are eligible to apply. Applicants must be U.S. citizens. High school seniors may also apply. *Application Process: Applicants must submit a completed application, which is available on HHS's Web site.*Amount: $1,500. *Deadline: May 1.

Illinois at Urbana-Champaign, University of
Office of Student Financial Aid
620 East John Street, MC-303
Champaign, IL 61820-5712

217-333-0100
http://www.osfa.uiuc.edu
Scholarship Name: Joseph and Elizabeth Davey
Scholarship. *Academic Area: Open. *Age Group:
Undergraduate students, graduate students.
*Eligibility: Applicant must be physically disabled
students who demonstrate financial need.
*Application Process: Contact the University's Office
of Student Financial Aid for application details.
*Amount: Varies. *Deadline: Varies.

Illinois at Urbana-Champaign, University of
Division Of Rehabilitation-Education Services (DRES)
Attn: Scholarship Committee
1207 South Oak Street
Champaign, IL 61820
217-333-4603 (Voice/TTY)
disability@uiuc.edu
http://www.disability.uiuc.edu/services/scholarship
*The DRES provides scholarships to disabled students to
help finance college study. *Academic Area:* Open.
*Age Group: Undergraduate students, graduate
students. *Eligibility: Students with disabilities who
are attending the university are eligible to apply.
*Application Process: Applicants must submit a
completed application, which is available at the
division's Web site.*Amount: Varies. *Deadline: May 1.

Immune Deficiency Foundation
Attn: Scholarship/Medical Programs
40 West Chesapeake Avenue, Suite 308
Towson, MD 21204
800-296-4433
idf@primaryimmune.org
http://www.primaryimmune.org/services/scholarship.
htm
Scholarship Name: Immune Deficiency Foundation
Scholarship. *Academic Area: Open. *Age Group:
Undergraduate students. *Eligibility: Students with a
diagnosed primary immune deficiency disease who
are planning to attend, or are currently attending,
a college or a technical training school are eligible
to apply. Selection is based on financial need.
*Application Process: Contact the foundation for
details. *Amount: $750 to $2,000. *Deadline: March 31.

**Indiana University - Purdue University Fort Wayne
(IPFW)**
Financial Aid Services
Kettler Hall

2101 East Coliseum Boulevard
Fort Wayne, IN 46805-1499
260-481-6820
http://www.ipfw.edu/financial/finaid/process
Scholarship Name: Sidney and Viola Hutner Scholarship.
*Academic Area: Open. *Age Group: Undergraduate
students. *Eligibility: Applicants must be incoming
IPFW freshmen with superior academic records. They
must also demonstrate financial need and maintain
at least a 3.0 GPA. Applicants with disabilities will
be given first consideration for this scholarship.
*Application Process: Applicants must be nominated
by their high school guidance counselors. Applicants
should contact their guidance counselors or the IPFW
Financial Aid Services office for application details.
*Amount: Varies. *Deadline: March 31.

International Alumnae of Delta Epsilon
Attn: Fellowship Award Committee
2453 Bear Den Road
Frederick, MD 21701
fellowship@iades.org
http://www.iades.org/FAF/default.htm
Fellowship Name: Betty G. Miller Fellowship Award.
*Academic Area: Open. *Age Group: Graduate
students. *Eligibility: Deaf women enrolled in
doctoral programs are eligible to apply. Candidates
must have a GPA of at least 3.0. *Application Process:
Applicants must submit a completed application,
academic transcripts, two letters of recommendation,
and a recent audiogram or a letter from a certified
audiologist, doctor or other appropriate professional
verifying hearing loss. *Amount: $1,200. *Deadline:
Typically in August.

Iowa, University of
Student Disability Services
3100 Burge Hall
Iowa City, IA 52242-1214
319-335-1462, 319-335-1498 (TTY)
http://www.uiowa.edu/~sds
Scholarship Name: David Braverman Scholarship.
*Academic Area: Open. *Age Group: Graduate
students. *Eligibility: Applicants must be students
with disabilities at the University of Iowa. They must
also possess strong academic records and intend
to serve their community. *Application Process:
Contact the university's Student Disability Services
department for application details. *Amount: $1,500.
*Deadline: Varies.

Italian Catholic Federation

675 Hegenberger Road, Suite 230
Oakland, CA 94621
888-ICF-1924
info@icf.org
http://www.icf.org/applications.html
Scholarship Name: Gifts of Love Scholarship. *Academic Area: Open. *Age Group: Undergraduate students, graduate students. *Eligibility: Applicants must be individuals with disabilities who desire formal instruction or training to obtain further academic, athletic, vocational, or creative arts skills. *Application Process: Visit the federation's Web site to download an application. *Amount: Varies. *Deadline: Varies.

Kappa Kappa Gamma Foundation

Attn: Foundation Administrator
530 East Town Street, PO Box 38
Columbus, OH 43216-0038
866-KKG-1870
http://www.kappa.org
Scholarship Name: Rose McGill Fund. *Academic Area: Open. *Age Group: Undergraduate students. *Eligibility: Applicants must be Kappa Kappa Gamma members who demonstrate financial need and have faced a sudden illness or misfortune. *Application Process: Contact the foundation for application details. *Amount: Varies. *Deadline: Varies.

Kent State University

Student Disability Services
Michael Schwartz Center, Room 181
Kent, OH 44242-0001
330-672-3391 (Voice/TTY)
finaid@kent.edu
http://www.registrars.kent.edu/disability
Scholarship Name: Cunningham Award. *Academic Area: Open. *Age Group: Undergraduate students, graduate students. *Eligibility: Applicants must be Kent State University students with spinal cord injuries who demonstrate financial need. *Application Process: Contact Student Disability Services for application details. *Amount: $500. *Deadline: February 15.

Kentucky, University of

Disability Resource Center
2 Alumni Gym
Lexington, KY 40506-0029
859-257-2754
msfogg0@uky.edu
http://www.uky.edu/TLC/grants/uk_ed/services/drc.html
Scholarship Name: Carol Adelstein Award. *Academic Area: Open. *Age Group: Undergraduate students, graduate students. *Eligibility: Applicants must be University of Kentucky students with disabilities who have inspired the university community through academic achievement, leadership, extracurricular activities, or social and personal qualities. *Application Process: Contact the Disability Resource Center for application details. *Amount: Up to $2,000. *Deadline: Varies.

Kentucky, University of

Disability Resource Center
2 Alumni Gym
Lexington, KY 40506-0029
859-257-2754
msfogg0@uky.edu
http://www.uky.edu/TLC/grants/uk_ed/services/drc.html
Scholarship Name: Varney Scholarship. *Academic Area: Open. *Age Group: Undergraduate students, graduate students. *Eligibility: Applicants must be students at the University of Kentucky with cystic fibrosis. *Application Process: Contact the Disability Resource Center for application details. *Amount: $700. *Deadline: Varies.

Landmark College

River Road South
Putney, VT 05346
802-387-6736
cmullins@landmark.edu
http://www.landmarkcollege.org/admissions/financial_aid_tuition.html#scholarships
Scholarship Name: Landmark Endowment Scholarship. *Academic Area: Open. *Age Group: Undergraduate students. *Eligibility: Students attending the college who demonstrate financial need may apply. *Application Process: Contact the college for information. *Amount: $1,000. *Deadline: Contact the college for details.

Landmark College

River Road South
Putney, VT 05346
802-387-6736
cmullins@landmark.edu
http://www.landmarkcollege.org/admissions/financial_aid_tuition.html#scholarships

Scholarship Name: Landmark College Recognition Scholarship. *Academic Area: Open. *Age Group: Undergraduate students. *Eligibility: Students attending the college who have individual and distinct talents are eligible to apply. *Application Process: Contact the college for information. *Amount: $5,000 to $20,000. *Deadline: Contact the college for details.

Landmark College
River Road South
Putney, VT 05346
802-387-6736
cmullins@landmark.edu
http://www.landmarkcollege.org/admissions/financial_aid_tuition.html#scholarships
Scholarship Name: Landmark College Scholarship. *Academic Area: Open. *Age Group: Undergraduate students. *Eligibility: Students attending the college who demonstrate financial need are eligible. *Application Process: Contact the college for information. *Amount: $5,000 to $25,000. *Deadline: Contact the college for details.

Lighthouse International
Scholarship Awards Program
Attn: Kelly Boyle, Scholarship Coordinator
111 East 59th Street
New York, NY 10022-1202
212-821-9200
kboyle@lighthouse.org
http://www.lighthouse.org/events/scholarship_awards.htm
Award Name: College-Bound Award. *Academic Area: Open. *Age Group: Undergraduate students. *Eligibility: Applicants must be blind or partially sighted high school seniors or recent graduates who are enrolled or planning to enroll in college. *Application Process: Applicants must submit an application, personal essay, documentation verifying vision impairment, recent transcripts, letter of acceptance, and two letters of recommendation. . *Amount: $5,000. *Deadline: March 1.

Lighthouse International
Scholarship Awards Program
Attn: Kelly Boyle, Scholarship Coordinator
111 East 59th Street
New York, NY 10022-1202
212-821-9200

kboyle@lighthouse.org
http://www.lighthouse.org/events/scholarship_awards.htm
Award Name: Graduate Award. *Academic Area: Open. *Age Group: Graduate students. *Eligibility: Applicants must be blind or partially sighted individuals who have either graduated from college or are currently college seniors who plan to pursue a graduate degree. *Application Process: Applicants must submit an application, personal essay, documentation verifying vision impairment, recent transcripts, letter of acceptance, and two letters of recommendation. . *Amount: $5,000. *Deadline: March 1.

Lighthouse International
Scholarship Awards Program
Attn: Kelly Boyle, Scholarship Coordinator
111 East 59th Street
New York, NY 10022-1202
212-821-9200
kboyle@lighthouse.org
http://www.lighthouse.org/events/scholarship_awards.htm
Award Name: Undergraduate Award I. *Academic Area: Open. *Age Group: Undergraduate students. *Eligibility: Applicants must be blind or partially sighted individuals who have already completed some course work towards an undergraduate degree. *Application Process: Applicants must submit an application, personal essay, documentation verifying vision impairment, recent transcripts, letter of acceptance, and two letters of recommendation. . *Amount: $5,000. *Deadline: March 1.

Lighthouse International
Scholarship Awards Program
Attn: Kelly Boyle, Scholarship Coordinator
111 East 59th Street
New York, NY 10022-1202
212-821-9200
kboyle@lighthouse.org
http://www.lighthouse.org/events/scholarship_awards.htm
Award Name: Undergraduate Award II. *Academic Area: Open. *Age Group: Undergraduate students. *Eligibility: Applicants must be blind or partially sighted individuals who are actively pursing an undergraduate degree after an absence of at least 10 years from high school. *Application Process:

Applicants must submit an application, personal essay, documentation verifying vision impairment, recent transcripts, letter of acceptance, and two letters of recommendation. . *Amount: $5,000. *Deadline: March 1.

Lions Club International
300 West 22nd Street
Oak Brook, IL 60523-8842
630-571-5466
lcif@lionsclub.org
http://www.lionsclubs.org
Local Lions Clubs often sponsor scholarships or other forms of assistance to aid blind or visually impaired persons in their area of academic interest. *Academic Area: Open. *Age Group: Undergraduate students, graduate students. *Eligibility: Requirements vary from chapter to chapter. *Application Process: Varies. Contact your local Lions Club for details. *Amount: Varies. *Deadline: Varies. For details on programs in your area, contact your local Lions Club.

Maharishi University of Management
Office of Admissions and Financial Aid
1000 North Fourth Street
Fairfield, IA 52557
641-472-1156
finaid@mum.edu
http://www.mum.edu/financial_aid/welcome.html
Scholarship Name: Shelley Hoffman Scholarship. *Academic Area: Open. *Age Group: Undergraduate students. *Eligibility: Applicants must be students at Maharishi University of Management with cerebral palsy and/or outstanding creative writing skills. Applicants must maintain at least a 2.0 GPA. *Application Process: Contact the Maharishi University of Management Office of Admissions and Financial Aid for application details. *Amount: $200 to $1,500. *Deadline: May 15.

Marin, College of
College of Marin Foundation
PO Box 446
Kentfield, CA 94914
415-485-9382
comf@marin.cc.ca.us
http://www.comf.org/scholarships.html
Scholarship Name: Burke Sisters Memorial Scholarship. *Academic Area: Open. *Age Group: Undergraduate students. *Eligibility: Applicants must be College of

Marin students with disabilities who have completed at least 15 units. Applicants must maintain at least a 2.75 GPA and be enrolled in at least six units at the time of application. *Application Process: Applicants must submit a completed application, a letter of recommendation, and a personal statement. Visit the foundation's Web site to download an application. *Amount: Varies. *Deadline: March 4.

Marin, College of
College of Marin Foundation
PO Box 446
Kentfield, CA 94914
415-485-9382
comf@marin.cc.ca.us
http://www.comf.org/scholarships.html
Scholarship Name: San Rafael Indoor Sports Club Scholarship. *Academic Area: Open. *Age Group: Undergraduate students. *Eligibility: Applicants must be College of Marin students with physical disabilities who have completed at least 15 units. Applicants must maintain at least a 2.75 GPA and be enrolled in at least six units at the time of application. *Application Process: Applicants must submit a completed application, a letter of recommendation, and a personal statement. Visit the foundation's Web site to download an application. *Amount: Varies. *Deadline: March 4.

Marquette University
Office of Disability Services
PO Box 1881
Milwaukee, WI 53201-1881
414-288-3270
http://www.marquette.edu/oses/disabilityservices
This private four-year university offers financial aid and scholarships to its students with disabilities via its Office of Disability Services. *Academic Area: Open. *Age Group: Undergraduate students, graduate students. *Eligibility: Financially needy students with disabilities are eligible to apply. *Application Process: Contact the Office of Disability Services for details. *Amount: Awards vary according to need. *Deadline: Contact the Office of Disability Services for details.

Marshalltown Community College
Financial Aid Office
3700 South Center Street
Marshalltown, IA 50158
641-752-7106, ext. 210

Nancy.Ellis@iavalley.edu
http://www.iavalley.cc.ia.us/mcc/FinancialAid
Scholarship Name: Legion of Guardsmen Auxiliary Scholarship. *Academic Area: Open. *Age Group: Undergraduate students. *Eligibility: Applicants must be female students who are residents of Marshall County and who demonstrate financial need. Disabled students are encouraged to apply. Application Process: Contact the Financial Aid Office for application details. *Amount: Varies. *Deadline: Varies.

Marshalltown Community College
Financial Aid Office
3700 South Center Street
Marshalltown, IA 50158
641-752-7106, ext. 210
Nancy.Ellis@iavalley.edu
http://www.iavalley.cc.ia.us/mcc/FinancialAid
Scholarship Name: Patti Bacino Memorial Scholarship. *Academic Area: Open. *Age Group: Undergraduate students. *Eligibility: Applicants must be sophomores who are returning adult students. Applicants with English as a second language, single parents, and students with disabilities are encouraged to apply. *Application Process: Contact the Financial Aid Office for application details. *Amount: Varies. *Deadline: Varies.

Mays Mission for the Handicapped
604 Colonial Drive
Heber Springs, AR 52145
501-362-7526
info@maysmission.org
http://www.maysmission.org/schol.html
This organization offers scholarships to individuals with physical and/or mental disabilities. *Academic Area: Open. *Age Group: Undergraduate students. *Eligibility: Applicants must be able to document a significant disability, have a score of 18 or better on the ACT or 870 on the SAT, and be enrolled full time in a four-year undergraduate program. Recipients must maintain a GPA of at least 2.3. *Application Process: Prospective applicants may request an application by phone or email. *Amount: Varies. *Deadline: June 30 and November 1.

McLennan Community College
Office of Financial Aid
1400 College Drive

Waco, TX 76708
254-299-8698
http://www.mclennan.edu/departments/foundation/specific.htm
Scholarship Name: Herb Barsh Hot Lions Scholarship. *Academic Area: Open. *Age Group: Undergraduate students. *Eligibility: Applicants must be physically challenged high school seniors or college students who demonstrate financial need. Applicants must have a minimum high school "B" average, a GED score of 50, or a college GPA of 2.5. *Application Process: Contact the Office of Financial Aid for application details. *Amount: $500. *Deadline: February 10.

Michigan Association for Deaf, Hearing, and Speech Services
2929 Covington Court, Suite 200
Lansing, MI 48912-4939
800-YOUR-EAR
http://www.madhs.org
Scholarship Name: Brian McCartney Memorial Scholarship. *Academic Area: Open. *Age Group: Undergraduate students. *Eligibility: Applicants must be Michigan high school seniors with hearing or speech impairments. They must also maintain a minimum 2.5 GPA and be U.S. citizens. *Application Process: Contact the association for application details. *Amount: Varies. *Deadline: Typically at the end of March.

Michigan Commission for the Blind
Victor Building
201 North Washington, 2nd Floor
PO Box 30652
Lansing, MI 48909
517-373-2062, 800-292-4200
Scholarship Name: Roy Johnson Scholarship. *Academic Area: Open. *Age Group: Graduate students. *Eligibility: Applicants must be blind students who hold a bachelor's degree from any college in the country who plan to pursue graduate study at a college or university in Michigan. *Application Process: Contact the commission for application details. *Amount: $250 to $1,000. *Deadline: May.

Michigan, University of
Office of Financial Aid
2011 Student Activities Building, 515 East Jefferson Street

Ann Arbor, MI 48109-1316
734-763-6600
financial.aid@umich.edu
http://www.finaid.umich.edu
Scholarship Name: Thomas Komar Scholarship.
*Academic Area: Open. *Age Group: Undergraduate
students. *Eligibility: Applicants must be disabled
entering freshmen at the University of Michigan
who demonstrate financial need. Applicants must be
registered with the University of Michigan Office of
Services for Students with Disabilities. *Application
Process: Contact the Office of Financial Aid for
application details. *Amount: $1,000 to $6,000.
*Deadline: Varies.

Missouri-Columbia, University of
Office of Disability Services
A038 Brady Commons
Columbia, MO 65211
573-882-4696, 573-882-8054 (TTY)
disabilityservices@missouri.edu
http://disabilityservices.missouri.edu/scholarships.html
Scholarship Name: Frank Hodges Jr. Physical Disability
Scholarship. *Academic Area: Open. *Age Group:
Undergraduate students, graduate students.
*Eligibility: Applicants must be students at the
University of Missouri-Columbia with physical
disabilities (mobility, vision, hearing, or health
related). They must also be registered with the
Office of Disability Services, be receiving academic
accommodations, and maintain a minimum 2.0 GPA.
*Application Process: Contact the Office of Disability
Services for application details. Academic transcripts
must be submitted with applications. *Amount:
Varies. *Deadline: April 22.

Ms. Wheelchair America Program Inc.
Attn: Denise DiNoto, Executive Director
8610 Glenfield Way
Louisville, KY 40241
518-461-2527
director@mswheelchairamerica.org
http://www.mswheelchairamerica.org
Contest Name: Ms. Wheelchair America Program.
*Academic Area: Open. *Age Group: Ages 21
through 60. *Eligibility: Women who use wheelchairs
on a regular basis may compete for the title of
Ms. Wheelchair America. Applicants must be U.S.
citizens. *Application Process: Contestants are
judged on their accomplishments, self-perception,
and communication and projection skills. Women

compete first at the state level; winners of state
competitions then advance to compete at the
national level. *Amount: Winners at the state level
receive approximately $100, and the national winner
receives $250. *Deadline: Contact the organization
for additional details.

**National Aeronautics and Space Administration
(NASA)**
Attn: Lloyd Evans
NASA Langley Research Center
100 NASA Road
Hampton, VA 23681-2199
757-864-5209
l.b.evans@larc.nasa.gov
http://edu.larc.nasa.gov
Grant Name: NASA Graduate Student Researchers
Program. *Academic Area: Engineering (general),
mathematics, science. *Age Group: Graduate
students. *Eligibility: Graduate students with
disabilities who are attending accredited U.S.
universities on a full-time basis may apply.
*Application Process: Contact NASA for details.
*Amount: The maximum yearly award is $24,000.
*Deadline: February 1.

National Amputee Golf Association (NAGA)
Scholarship Grant Program
11 Walnut Hill Road
Amherst, NH 03031
info@nagagolf.org
http://www.nagagolf.org/scholarship1.shtml
Scholarship Name: NAGA Educational Scholarship Grant.
*Academic Area: Open. *Age Group: Undergraduate
students. *Eligibility: Applicants must be NAGA
members who have lost a limb, or dependents of
NAGA members. Applicants must be planning to or
currently pursuing an undergraduate or two-year
vocational/technical degree at an accredited college,
vocational/technical school, or institution. They
must also be at least part-time students, maintain a
minimum 2.0 GPA, and demonstrate financial need.
*Application Process: Applicants must submit a
resume, a letter of acceptance, Student Aid Report,
and a cover letter. Visit the NAGA's Web site for
further application details. *Amount: $2,000 per year.
*Deadline: August 1.

National Association of the Deaf
Miss Deaf America Pageant
814 Thayer Avenue

Silver Spring, MD 20910-4500
mda@nad.org
http://www.nad.org/site/pp.asp?c=foINKQMBF&b=103
756
Contest Name: Miss Deaf America Pageant. *Academic
Area: Open. *Age Group: Ages 18 through 28.
*Eligibility: Deaf women between the ages of 18 and
28 are eligible to compete for the title of Miss Deaf
America. *Application Process: Women compete first
at the state level; winners of state competitions then
advance to compete at the national competition.
*Amount: Winners receive transportation to
the national competition and small cash grants.
*Deadline: Contact the National Association of the
Deaf for information. The competition is held every
two years.

National Center for Learning Disabilities Inc.

Anne Ford Scholarship
381 Park Avenue South, Suite 1401
New York, NY 10016-8806
212-545-7510
AFScholarship@ncld.org
http://www.ncld.org/awards/afscholarinfo.cfm
Scholarship Name: Anne Ford Scholarship. *Academic
Area: Open. *Age Group: Undergraduate students.
*Eligibility: Applicants must be high school seniors
with identified learning disabilities who intend
on pursuing undergraduate degrees. They must
also maintain at least a 3.0 GPA, be U.S. citizens,
and demonstrate financial need. *Application
Process: Applicants must submit a completed
application, a personal statement, transcripts, three
letters of recommendation, a financial statement
(if applicable), standardized test scores, and
documentation of learning disability. Visit the center's
Web site to download an application. *Amount:
$10,000. *Deadline: December 31.

National Federation of Music Clubs

Attn: Norma Bibb
3211 "A" Clarendon Drive
Springfield, IL 62704-5511
http://www.nfmc-music.org/Competitions/
Annual%20Student/Annual%20Student.html
Scholarship Name: Hinda Honigman Award for the
Blind. *Academic Area: Performing arts (music). *Age
Group: Ages 16 through 25. *Eligibility: High school
students and college students who are pursuing
advanced musical studies may apply. Applicants must
be blind vocal or instrumental musicians who are

between the ages of 16 and 25. *Application Process:
Contact the federation for audition/application
details. *Amount: $650 (winner) and $350 (runner-
up). *Deadline: February 1.

National Federation of Music Clubs

Attn: Sharon Booker, Chair
325 North Via Del Ciruelo
Green Valley, AZ 85614
http://www.nfmc-music.org
Scholarship Name: Music for the Blind Award.
*Academic Area: Performing arts (music). *Age
Group: Ages 19 through 30. *Eligibility: Applicants
must be blind composers, between the ages of 19
and 30, who are seeking postsecondary training.
*Application Process: Applicants must submit a
manuscript and $3 application fee. Contact the
Federation for further application details. *Amount:
$200. *Deadline: March 1.

National Federation of Music Clubs

1336 North Delaware Street
Indianapolis, IN 46202-2481
317-638-4003
info@nfmc-music.org
http://www.nfmc-music.org
*Regional scholarships are offered to blind musicians
in each area in which the National Federation has
affiliates. *Academic Area:* Performing arts (general).
*Age Group: Varies. *Eligibility: Student musicians
who are blind may apply. *Application Process:
Applicants must submit a recommendation from a
teacher, as well as an audiotape presenting at least
three different selections performed by the musician.
*Amount: Varies. *Deadline: Contact the federation
for details.

National Federation of the Blind

Attn: Peggy Elliott, Chairman, Scholarship Committee
805 Fifth Avenue
Grinnell, IA 50112
641-236-3366
http://www.nfb.org/sch_intro.htm
This organization offers approximately 30 scholarships
for full-time, postsecondary education. *Academic
Area: Open. *Age Group: Undergraduate students,
graduate students. *Eligibility: Legally blind students
pursuing or planning to pursue postsecondary
education full time are eligible to apply. Other
restrictions may apply; contact the federation for
further information. Scholarships are awarded on

the basis of scholastic excellence, financial need, and community service. *Application Process: Applicants must submit a personal statement, two letters of recommendation, current academic transcripts, standardized test scores (high school students only), a letter of recommendation from a federation state president or designee, and a completed application (available for download at the federation's Web site). *Amount: Scholarships ranging from $3,000 to $12,000 are available. *Deadline: March 31.

National Federation of the Blind of Alabama
Attn: Scholarship Committee
1177 Dogwood Lane
Birmingham, AL 35215
334-501-2001
http://www.nfbofalabama.org/scholar.html
Scholarship Name: National Federation of the Blind of Alabama Scholarship. *Academic Area: Open. *Age Group: Undergraduate students, graduate students. *Eligibility: Applicants must be blind or visually impaired graduating high school seniors who intend to pursue postsecondary education or college students. They must also be residents of Alabama and demonstrate academic excellence, community service, and financial need. *Application Process: Applicants must submit a complete application, up to three letters of recommendation, and transcripts. Visit the Federation's Web site to download an application. *Amount: $500. *Deadline: January 31.

National Federation of the Blind of Arizona
Attn: Vicki Hodges, Scholarship Committee
4630 East Thomas Road, E-11
Phoenix, AZ 85018
602-956-0230
vjazz@extremezone.com
http://www.nfbarizona.com
Scholarship Name: James R. Carlock Scholarship. *Academic Area: Open. *Age Group: Undergraduate students, graduate students. *Eligibility: Applicants must be legally blind or visually impaired college students or graduating high school seniors who intend to pursue postsecondary education. They must also be Arizona residents and attending school in Arizona full time. *Application Process: Applicants must submit a completed application, a personal statement, a state officer's letter, two letters of recommendation, and official transcripts. *Amount: $1,000. *Deadline: March 31.

National Federation of the Blind of California
175 East Olive Avenue, Suite 308
Burbank, CA 91502
818-558-6524
nfbcal@sbcglobal.net
http://www.nfbcal.org/nfbc/scholarships.html
The federation awards national and state scholarships to legally blind high school seniors and current college students. *Academic Area: Open. *Age Group: Undergraduate students, graduate students. *Eligibility: Visually impaired high school seniors and college students who are California residents may apply. *Application Process: Visit the federation's Web site for details. *Amount: Varies. *Deadline: Typically in May.

National Federation of the Blind of Colorado
2233 West Shepperd Avenue
Littleton, CO 80120
800-401-4NFB
http://www.nfbco.org/scholarships.htm
The federation awards national and state scholarships to legally blind high school seniors and current college students. *Academic Area: Open. *Age Group: Undergraduate students, graduate students. *Eligibility: Visually impaired students from Colorado are eligible to apply. Selection is based on academic record, need, and community involvement. *Application Process: Applicants must submit a personal letter of introduction, two letters of recommendation, a current academic transcript, a letter from a state officer of the National Federation of the Blind of Colorado or chapter president stating that that he or she has discussed the scholarship with the applicant, and a completed application. Visit the federation's Web site to download an application. *Amount: $3,000 to $12,000. *Deadline: Typically in September.

National Federation of the Blind of Connecticut
580 Burnside Avenue, Suite 1
East Hartford, CT 06108
860-289-1971
info@nfbct.org
http://www.nfbct.org/html/schform.htm
The federation awards national and state scholarships to legally blind high school seniors and current college students. *Academic Area: Open. *Age Group: Undergraduate students, graduate students. *Eligibility: Graduating high school seniors and college students who are blind or visually impaired

and residents of Connecticut (or attending school in Connecticut) may apply. Scholarships are awarded based on academic excellence, community service, and financial need. *Application Process: Applicants must submit a personal letter of introduction, two letters of recommendation, official academic transcripts, a letter from an officer of the National Federation of the Blind of Connecticut stating that that he or she has discussed the scholarship with the applicant, and a completed application. Visit the federation's Web site for an application. *Amount: $2,000 to $5,000. *Deadline: Typically in September.

National Federation of the Blind of Florida
Attn: Kathy Davis, President
121 Deer Lake Circle
Ormond Beach, FL 32174
888-282-5972
president@nfbflorida.org
http://www.nfbflorida.org
Scholarship Name: Educational Scholarship. *Academic Area: Open. *Age Group: Undergraduate students, graduate students. *Eligibility: Blind college students who reside in Florida and have a GPA of at least 2.70 are eligible to apply. High school seniors may also apply. *Application Process: Contact the federation for details. *Amount: $1,000. *Deadline: Contact the federation for details.

National Federation of the Blind of Idaho
Attn: Dana Ard, President
301 Bruce Avenue
Boise, ID 83712
208-345-3906
Danaard@myexcel.com
http://www.nfbidaho.org/education/scholorship.htm
The federation awards national and state scholarships to legally blind high school seniors and current college students. *Academic Area: Open. *Age Group: Undergraduate students, graduate students. *Eligibility: Blind college students in Idaho are eligible to apply. Scholarships are awarded based on academic excellence, community service, and financial need. *Application Process: Contact the federation for details. *Amount: Varies. *Deadline: Contact the federation for details.

National Federation of the Blind of Illinois (NFBI)
Attn: Chairperson, NFBI Scholarship Committee
5817 North Nina

Chicago, IL 60631
773-631-1093
dkent5817@worldnet.att.net
http://www.nfbofillinois.org
Scholarship Name: Kenneth Jernigan Scholarship. *Academic Area: Open. *Age Group: Undergraduate students, graduate students. *Eligibility: Applicants must be legally blind residents of, or students in, Illinois, who are enrolled full-time in a regular accredited two-year, four-year, or graduate college or university program. Applicants must demonstrate academic excellence, community service, and financial need. *Application Process: Applicants must submit a completed application, a personal essay, two letters of recommendation, and transcripts. Visit the federation's Web site to download an application. *Amount: $1,000. *Deadline: March 31.

National Federation of the Blind of Illinois (NFBI)
Attn: Deborah Kent Stein, Chairman, NFBI Scholarship Committee
5817 North Nina
Chicago, IL 60631
773-631-1093
dkent5817@worldnet.att.net
http://www.nfbofillinois.org
Scholarship Name: Peter Grunwald Scholarship. *Academic Area: Open. *Age Group: Undergraduate students, graduate students. *Eligibility: Applicants must be legally blind residents of, or students in, Illinois, who are enrolled full time in a regular accredited two-year, four-year, or graduate college or university program. Applicants must demonstrate academic excellence, community service, and financial need. *Application Process: Applicants must submit a completed application, personal essay, two letters of recommendation, and transcripts. Visit the federation's Web site to download an application. *Amount: $1,500. *Deadline: March 31.

National Federation of the Blind of Kansas
Attn: Carol C. Clark, Recording Secretary
11905 Mohawk Lane
Leawood, KS 66209-1038
913-339-9341
circa1944@aol.com
http://www.nfbks.org/state/nfb-sklr.shtml
Scholarship Name: Kenneth Tiede Memorial Scholarship. *Academic Area: Open. *Age Group: Undergraduate students, graduate students. *Eligibility: Applicants

must be graduating high school seniors or college students who are blind or visually impaired and are legal residents of the state of Kansas. They must plan to study either at a technical school or at a college or university. *Application Process: Applicants must submit a completed application and a letter of recommendation from a federation officer or board member. Contact the federation for further application details. *Amount: Varies. *Deadline: Varies.

National Federation of the Blind of Massachusetts
Scholarship Program
140 Wood Street
Somerset, MA 02726-5225
508-679-8543
nfbmass@earthlink.net
http://www.nfbmass.org
Scholarship Name: National Federation of the Blind of Massachusetts Scholarship. *Academic Area: Open. *Age Group: Undergraduate students, graduate students. *Eligibility: Applicants must be legally blind residents of Massachusetts who have been accepted by or are attending postsecondary institutions of higher education on a full-time basis. They must also demonstrate academic excellence, community service, and financial need. *Application Process: Applicants must submit a completed application, a personal letter, two letters of recommendation, and transcripts. Visit the federation's Web site to download an application. *Amount: At least $500. *Deadline: February 6.

National Federation of the Blind of Missouri
3910 Tropical Lane
Columbia, MO 65202
573-874-1774
info@nfbmo.org
http://www.nfbmo.org
The federation offers educational scholarships to blind students. *Academic Area: Open. *Age Group: Undergraduate students, graduate students. *Eligibility: Blind high school seniors and college students who are residents of Missouri are eligible to apply. *Application Process: Contact the federation for details. *Amount: Varies. *Deadline: Contact the federation for details.

National Federation of the Blind of New York State
PO Box 09-0363
Brooklyn, NY 11209
718-567-7821
office@nfbny.org
http://www.nfbny.org
The federation provides a small number of scholarships to help defer postsecondary education expenses. *Academic Area: Open. *Age Group: Undergraduate students, graduate students. *Eligibility: Blind high school seniors and college students who are residents of New York are eligible to apply. *Application Process: Contact the federation for details. *Amount: Varies. *Deadline: Contact the federation for details.

National Federation of the Blind of Ohio
Attn: Dr. J. Webster Smith, Chair, Scholarship Committee
2 Canterbury Street
Athens, Ohio 45701740-593-4838
jsmith1@ohiou.edu
http://www.nfbohio.org/scholarship.html
The federation offers educational scholarships to blind students. *Academic Area: Open. *Age Group: Undergraduate students, graduate students. *Eligibility: Blind high school seniors and college students who are residents of Ohio are eligible to apply. Scholarships are awarded based on academic excellence, community service, and financial need. *Application Process: Applicants should submit a letter of introduction, two letters of recommendation, academic transcripts, a letter from an officer of the National Federation of the Blind of Ohio stating that that he or she has discussed the scholarship with the applicant, and a completed application. Visit the federation's Web site for an application. *Amount: One $1,500 and one $1,000 scholarship. *Deadline: Typically in June.

National Federation of the Blind of Oregon (NFBO)
Attn: NFBO Scholarship Committee
2005 Main Street
Springfield, OR 97478
541-726-6924
nfb_or@msn.com
http://www.nfb-or.org/scholarships.htm
The federation awards national and state scholarships to legally blind students. *Academic Area: Open. *Age Group: Undergraduate students, graduate students. *Eligibility: Blind high school seniors and college students who are residents of Oregon are eligible to apply. Scholarships are awarded based on academic excellence, professional promise, and leadership potential. *Application Process: Applicants must submit

a letter of introduction, two letters of recommendation, academic transcripts, and a completed application (available at the federation's Web site). Applicants must also participate in an interview with the NFBO of Oregon president or the president's designee. *Amount: One for at least $1,500, two for at least $1,000. *Deadline: Typically in March and June.

National Federation of the Blind of South Dakota
Attn: Bob Brown, President
901 South Chicago Street
Hot Springs, SD 57747
605-745-5599
b2228@gwtc.net
http://www.nfb.org/states/sd.htm
Scholarship Name: Anna Marklund Scholarship. *Academic Area: Open. *Age Group: Undergraduate students, graduate students. *Eligibility: Applicants must be blind students from South Dakota who are enrolled or planning to enroll in postsecondary education. *Application Process: Contact the Federation for application details. *Amount: $1,000. *Deadline: Varies.

National Federation of the Blind of Texas
Attn: Elizabeth Campbell, Scholarship Committee Chairman
6909 Rufus Drive
Austin, TX 78752-3123
512-323-5444
scholarship@nfb-texas.org
http://www.nfb-texas.org
The federation offers several educational scholarships to blind students. *Academic Area: Open. *Age Group: Undergraduate students, graduate students. *Eligibility: Blind full-time college students who are residents of Texas are eligible to apply. Scholarships are awarded based on academic excellence, community service, and financial need. High school seniors may also apply. *Application Process: Applicants must submit a letter detailing why they believe they should receive the scholarship, two letters of recommendation, an academic transcript, a letter of acceptance to a postsecondary institution, and a doctor's statement with proof of legal blindness. *Amount: $1,000 to $2,000. *Deadline: Typically in June.

National Federation of the Blind of Utah
Attn: Ron Gardner, President
132 Penman Lane
Bountiful, UT 84010-7634
president@nfbutah.org
http://www.nfbutah.org
The federation awards national and a small number of state scholarships to students. *Academic Area: Open. *Age Group: Undergraduate students, graduate students. *Eligibility: Blind high school seniors and college students from Utah are eligible to apply. *Application Process: Contact the federation for details. *Amount: Varies. *Deadline: Contact the federation for details.

National Federation of the Blind of Vermont
PO Box 1354
Montpelier, VT 05601
http://www.nfbvt.org
The federation provides scholarships to help defer postsecondary education expenses. *Academic Area: Open. *Age Group: Undergraduate students, graduate students. *Eligibility: Blind students who are permanent residents of Vermont are eligible to apply. *Application Process: Contact the federation for details. *Amount: $300 to $600. *Deadline: Applications are typically due in the summer.

National Federation of the Blind of Washington
Attn: Rita Szantay, State Scholarship Chairperson
1420 Fifth Avenue, Suite 2200
Seattle, WA 98101
206-224-7242
info@nfbw.org
http://www.nfbw.org
The federation provides scholarships to help defer postsecondary education expenses. *Academic Area: Open. *Age Group: Undergraduate students, graduate students. *Eligibility: Blind high school seniors and college students who are residents of Washington are eligible to apply. Applicants must plan to pursue or be currently pursuing full-time study. *Application Process: Applicants must submit a personal statement, three letters of recommendation, current academic transcripts, and a completed application (available at the federation's Web site). *Amount: $2,000 and $3,000. *Deadline: Typically in August.

National FFA Organization
Scholarship Office
6060 FFA Drive, PO Box 68960
Indianapolis, IN 46268-0960
317-802-6060

scholarships@ffa.org
http://www.ffa.org/programs/scholarships
Scholarship Name: BRIDGE Endowment. *Academic
Area: Agriculture. *Age Group: Undergraduate
students, graduate students. *Eligibility: Applicants
must be physically disabled students who are
members of the FFA and are planning to pursue or
are currently pursuing a two- or four-year degree in
any area of agriculture. *Application Process: Contact
the National FFA for application details. *Amount:
$5,000. *Deadline: February 15.

National Foundation for Ectodermal Dysplasias
410 East Main Street, PO Box 114
Mascoutah, IL 62258-0114
618-566-2020
info@nfed.org
http://www.nfed.org/College.htm
Scholarship Name: Ectodermal Dysplasias Memorial
College Scholarship. *Academic Area: Open. *Age
Group: Undergraduate students, graduate students.
*Eligibility: Applicants must be high school seniors
or college students with ectodermal dysplasias who
demonstrate academic achievement, community
service, and financial need. *Application Process:
Applicants must submit a completed application
and an essay on a designated topic. Contact the
foundation for further application details. *Amount:
Varies. *Deadline: Typically in March.

National Fraternal Society of the Deaf (NFSD)
1118 South Sixth Street
Springfield, IL 62703
217-789-7429, 217-789-7438 (TTY)
thefrat@nfsd.com
http://www.nfsd.com/scholarships.htm
The society offers scholarships to help finance college
training. *Academic Area: Open. *Age Group:
Undergraduate students, graduate students.
*Eligibility: Persons who have been a member of
the NFSD for at least one year are eligible to apply.
Hearing-impaired high school seniors and college
students may apply. *Application Process: Visit the
society's Web site to request an application. *Amount:
$1,000. *Deadline: Contact the society for details.

National Technical Institute for the Deaf (NTID)
Office of Financial Aid and Scholarships
52 Lomb Memorial Drive
Rochester, NY 14623

585-475-6700 (Voice/TTY)
http://www.ntid.rit.edu
The NTID is one of only a few postsecondary institutions
in the United States established exclusively to serve
the deaf. It offers financial aid to needy students.
*Academic Area: Open. *Age Group: Undergraduate
students, graduate students. *Eligibility: Deaf high
school seniors or college students in need of financial
assistance are eligible to apply. *Application Process:
Contact the institute for details. *Amount: Varies.
*Deadline: Contact the institute for details.

New England Hemophilia Association
Attn: Scholarship Committee Chairperson
347 Washington Street, Suite 402
Dedham, MA 02026
781-326-7645
scholarship@hemophiliahealth.com
http://www.newenglandhemophilia.org
The association provides a variety of scholarships and
grants to students. *Academic Area: Open. *Age
Group: Undergraduate students, graduate students.
*Eligibility: College students with hemophilia who
need financial assistance may apply. *Application
Process: Contact the association for details. *Amount:
Amounts vary according to need. *Deadline: Contact
the association for details.

North Dakota Association of the Blind (NDAB)
Attn: Carol Schmitt, Scholarship Committee Chairperson
1412 5th Street, SW
Minot, ND 58701
http://www.ndab.org/Scholarship.html
Scholarship Name: NDAB College Scholarship.
*Academic Area: Open. *Age Group: Undergraduate,
students, graduate students. *Eligibility: Applicant
must be legally blind, second-year through postgraduate students who are residents of North Dakota,
and have at least a 2.5 GPA. *Application Process:
Applicants must submit a completed application, a
personal statement, two letters of recommendation,
official transcripts, and a financial aid award letter. Visit
the association's Web site to download an application.
*Amount: $500 to $1,000. *Deadline: March 15.

North Dakota Association of the Blind (NDAB)
Attn: Carol Schmitt, Scholarship Committee Chairperson
1412 5th Street, SW
Minot, ND 58701
http://www.ndab.org/Scholarship.html

Scholarship Name: Emma Skogen Scholarship Fund. *Academic Area: Open. *Age Group: Undergraduate students, graduate students. *Eligibility: Applicants must be blind or visually impaired, at least 18 years old, attending a vocational or trade school, and demonstrate financial need. *Application Process: Applicants must submit a completed application, transcripts, and a letter of recommendation. Visit the association's Web site to download an application. *Amount: $400. *Deadline: March 15.

Northampton Community College
Services for Disabled
3835 Green Pond Road
Bethlehem, PA 18020
610-861-5342
http://www.northampton.edu/Finaid/Scholar_2.htm
Scholarship Name: Bethlehem Kiwanis Scholarship. *Academic Area: Open. *Age Group: Undergraduate students. *Eligibility: Full-time college students from the Bethlehem, Pennsylvania area who are learning disabled may apply. *Application Process: Contact the college for details. *Amount: Amounts vary according to need. *Deadline: Contact the college for details.

NuFACTOR
41093 County Center Drive, Suite B
Temecula, CA 92591
800-323-6832
http://www.nufactor.com/web_pages/edostie_scholarship.html
Scholarship Name: Eric Dostie Memorial College Scholarship. *Academic Area: Open. *Age Group: Undergraduate students, graduate students. *Eligibility: Applicants must have hemophilia or a related bleeding disorder or be a family member of a hemophiliac. They must also be U.S. citizens, enrolled full time in an accredited two- or four-year college program, and demonstrate scholastic achievement, community service, and financial need. *Application Process: Applicants must submit a completed application and essay describing how their education will be used to serve humankind and to encourage self-improvement and enrichment. Visit NuFACTOR's Web site to download an application. *Amount: $1,000. *Deadline: Varies.

Oklahoma State University
Office of Scholarships and Financial Aid
213 Student Union

Stillwater, OK 74078
405-744-7541, 404-744-6604
shuttic@okstate.edu
http://www.okstate.edu/ucs/stdis/scholarship.html
Scholarship Name: Hoyt E. James Endowed Scholarship. *Academic Area: Open. *Age Group: Undergraduate students, graduate students. *Eligibility: Applicants must be entering or attending Oklahoma State University and possess a physical, mental, visual, or hearing disability. Students with limiting health conditions are also eligible to apply. Applicants must be U.S. citizens with at least a 2.5 high school GPA who are not receiving any other state of federal financial aid. Residents of Haskell County, Oklahoma, are given first preference. *Application Process: Contact the Office of Scholarships and Financial Aid for application procedures. *Amount: Awards vary. *Deadline: Contact the Office of Scholarships and Financial Aid for details.

Oklahoma State University
Office of Disability Services
315 Student Union
Stillwater, OK 74078
405-744-7116
shuttic@okstate.edu
http://www.okstate.edu/ucs/stdis/scholarship.html
Scholarship Name: Margueritte Starr Scholarship. *Academic Area: Open. *Age Group: Undergraduate students, graduate students. *Eligibility: Applicants must be full-time, enrolled students who have a severe physical disability. *Application Process: Contact the Office of Disability Services for information about the application process. *Amount: Awards vary. *Deadline: Contact the Office of Disability Services for details.

Oklahoma State University
Office of Disability Services
315 Student Union
Stillwater, OK 74078
405-744-7116
shuttic@okstate.edu
http://www.okstate.edu/ucs/stdis/scholarship.html
Assistantship Name: Mary Jane Smothers Assistantship. *Academic Area: Library science. *Age Group: Undergraduate students, graduate students. *Eligibility: Applicants must have a documented disability on file with the Office of Disability Services and be interested in obtaining work experience

in a library setting. *Application Process: Contact the Office of Disability Services one month prior to the beginning of the fall semester for application information. *Amount: This is a paid work opportunity. Hours and assignments vary. *Deadline: Contact the Office of Disability Services for details.

Oklahoma State University
Office of Disability Services
315 Student Union
Stillwater, OK 74078
405-744-7116
shuttic@okstate.edu
http://www.okstate.edu/ucs/stdis/scholarship.html
Scholarship Name: McAlester Scottish Rite Scholarship for the Blind Scholarship. *Academic Area: Open. *Age Group: Undergraduate students, graduate students. *Eligibility: Applicants must be blind or visually impaired students who are attending Oklahoma State University. *Application Process: Visit the Office of Disability Services to receive an application and further information. *Amount: Varies. *Deadline: Applications are due in the spring of each year.

Oklahoma State University
Office of Scholarships and Financial Aid
213 Student Union
Stillwater, OK 74078
405-744-7541, 404-744-6604
shuttic@okstate.edu
http://www.okstate.edu/ucs/stdis/scholarship.html
Scholarship Name: Nate Fleming/Richey Lumpkin Academic Opportunity Scholarship. *Academic Area: Open. *Age Group: Undergraduate students, graduate students. *Eligibility: Applicants must be entering freshmen or transfer students who have overcome a significant obstacle, whether it be personal, economic, familial, or other. Applicants should possess a record of academic achievement and demonstrate financial need. They also must have graduated from a school in the state of Oklahoma with at least a 3.0 GPA. *Application Process: Contact the Office of Scholarships and Financial Aid for application procedures. *Amount: $1,200. *Deadline: Contact the Office of Scholarship and Financial Aid for details.

Oklahoma State University
Office of Disability Services
315 Student Union
Stillwater, OK 74078
405-744-7116
shuttic@okstate.edu
http://www.okstate.edu/ucs/stdis/scholarship.html
Scholarship Name: Oklahoma State University Foundation Scholarships for the Physically Limited. *Academic Area: Open. *Age Group: Undergraduate students, graduate students. *Eligibility: Applicants must be making progress towards a degree and must have a physically limiting disability. Preference is given to quadriplegic students. *Application Process: Applicants should visit the Office of Disability Services in the spring of each year to receive an application and further information. *Amount: Awards vary. *Deadline: Applications are accepted in the spring of each year.

Oklahoma, University of
Financial Aid Office
Buchanan Hall, 1000 Asp Avenue, Room 216
Norman, OK 73019-4078
405-325-4521
http://www.dsa.ou.edu/ods/resources.htm
Scholarship Name: Honorable Robert J. Dole Scholarship for Students with Disabilities. *Academic Area: Open. *Age Group: Undergraduate students, graduate students. *Eligibility: Students with disabilities who demonstrate strong academic performance and financial need may apply. Applicants must be certified by the Office of Disability Services as having a disability. They must also be high academic achievers who demonstrate leadership and service to the nation, state, community, or university.*Application Process: Contact the Financial Aid Office for details. *Amount: $1,200. *Deadline: October 1.

Oklahoma, University of
Financial Aid Office
Buchanan Hall
1000 Asp Avenue, Room 216
Norman, OK 73019-4078
405-325-4521, 405-325-6516 (TDD)
http://www.dsa.ou.edu/ods/resources.htm
Scholarship Name: Will Rogers Memorial Scholarship. *Academic Area: Open. *Age Group: Undergraduate students, graduate students. *Eligibility: Students who are mentally or physically handicapped, residents of Oklahoma, and in need of financial aid may apply. Non-disabled students preparing for

service in the field of educating individuals with disabilities may also apply. *Application Process: Contact the Financial Aid Office for details. *Amount: $1,000. *Deadline: March 1.

Oregon Council of the Blind
Attn: Jan Chance, Secretary, Board of Directors
3500 Summers Lane, #19
Klamath Falls, OR 97603
541-883-8227
http://www.acboforegon.org
*The council awards scholarships to help finance college study. *Academic Area: Open. *Age Group:* Undergraduate students. *Eligibility: High school seniors who are blind may apply. Oregon residents are given priority. *Application Process: Contact the council for details. *Amount: $2,500. *Deadline: Varies.

Oregon Student Assistance Commission
1500 Valley River Drive, Suite 100
Eugene, OR 97401
541-687-7400, 800-452-8807
awardinfo@mercury.osac.state.or.us
http://www.osac.state.or.us
http://www.getcollegefunds.org
Scholarship Name: Harry Ludwig Memorial Scholarship. *Academic Area: Open. *Age Group: Undergraduate students, graduate students. *Eligibility: Visually impaired students who are Oregon residents planning to enroll or currently enrolled in full-time undergraduate or graduate studies may apply. *Application Process: Contact the commission for details.. *Amount: Varies. *Deadline: Contact the commission for details.

P. Buckley Moss Society
20 Stoneridge Drive, Suite 102
Waynesboro, VA 22980
540-943-5678
society@mosssociety.org
http://www.mosssociety.org
Scholarship Name: Anne and Matt Harbison Scholarship. *Academic Area: Open. *Age Group: Undergraduate students. *Eligibility: Applicants must be graduating high school seniors with certified language-related learning disabilities who plan to pursue postsecondary education. *Application Process: Applicants must submit a completed application, a letter of nomination, verification of

language-related learning disability, transcripts, two letters of recommendation, and an essay. Visit the society's Web site to download an application. *Amount: $1,500. *Deadline: March 31.

Paralyzed Veterans of America (PVA)
Attn: Trish Hoover
801 18th Street, NW
Washington, DC 20006-3517
800-424-8200, ext. 619
TrishH@pva.org
http://www.pva.org/member/scholar.htm
Scholarship Name: PVA Education Scholarship (for full-time students). *Academic Area: Open. *Age Group: Undergraduate students, graduate students. *Eligibility: Applicants must be members of the organization or dependents of members of the organization (dependents must be under 24 years of age) who are pursuing college degrees full time. Contact the organization for further eligibility requirements. *Application Process: Information about the application process, as well as downloadable application forms, is made available on the organization's Web site in March of each year. Visit the organization's Web site or contact the organization for further application information. *Amount: $1,000. *Deadline: Contact the organization for details.

Paralyzed Veterans of America (PVA)
Attn: Trish Hoover, Membership/Volunteer Administrative Officer
801 18th Street, NW
Washington, DC 20006-3517
800-424-8200, ext. 619
TrishH@pva.org
http://www.pva.org/member/scholar.htm
Scholarship Name: PVA Educational Scholarship (for part-time students). *Academic Area: Open. *Age Group: Undergraduate students, graduate students. *Eligibility: Applicants must be members of the organization or dependents of members of the organization (dependents must be under 24 years of age) who are pursuing college degrees part time. Contact the organization for further eligibility requirements. *Application Process: Information about the application process, as well as downloadable application forms, is made available on the organization's Web site in March of each year. Visit the organization's Web site in March or contact

the organization for further application information. *Amount: $500 to $1,000. *Deadline: Contact PVA for details.

Patient Advocate Foundation
700 Thimble Shoals Boulevard, Suite 200
Newport News, VA 23606
800-532-5274
http://www.patientadvocate.org/index.php?p=69
Award Name: Cheryl Grimmel Award. *Academic Area: Open. *Age Group: Undergraduate students, graduate students. *Eligibility: Students who plan to resume a course of study that has been interrupted or delayed by a diagnosis of cancer or other critical or life threatening disease are eligible to apply. Applicants must pursue a course of study that renders them immediately employable after graduation. Applicants may enroll in a two- or four-year degree, or advanced studies if the regimen pursued satisfies the main employable criteria. Applicants must also enroll full-time, maintain at least a 3.0 GPA, demonstrate financial need, and complete 20 hours of community service for each year covered by a scholarship. High school seniors are also eligible for this award. *Application Process: Applicants must submit a completed application, written documentation from a physician of past medical diagnosis , last year's tax returns, official transcripts, and two letters of recommendation. Visit the foundation's Web site to download an application. *Amount: $2,000 per year (renewable). *Deadline: May 1.

Patient Advocate Foundation
700 Thimble Shoals Boulevard, Suite 200
Newport News, VA 23606
800-532-5274
http://www.patientadvocate.org/index.php?p=69
Award Name: Monica Bailes Award. *Academic Area: Open. *Age Group: Undergraduate students, graduate students. *Eligibility: Students who plan to resume a course of study that has been interrupted or delayed by a diagnosis of cancer or other critical or life-threatening disease are eligible to apply. Applicants must pursue a course of study that renders them immediately employable after graduation. Applicants may enroll in a two- or four-year degree, or advanced studies if the regimen pursued satisfies the main employable criteria. Applicants must also enroll full time, maintain at least a 3.0 GPA, demonstrate financial need, and complete 20 hours of community

service for each year covered by a scholarship. High school seniors are also eligible for this award. *Application Process: Applicants must submit a completed application, written documentation from a physician of past medical diagnosis, last year's tax returns, official transcripts, and two letters of recommendation. Visit the foundation's Web site to download an application. *Amount: $2,000 per year (renewable). *Deadline: May 1.

Patient Advocate Foundation
700 Thimble Shoals Boulevard, Suite 200
Newport News, VA 23606
800-532-5274
http://www.patientadvocate.org/index.php?p=69
Scholarship Name: Scholarship for Survivors. *Academic Area: Open. *Age Group: Undergraduate students, graduate students. *Eligibility: Students who plan to resume a course of study that has been interrupted or delayed by a diagnosis of cancer or other critical or life threatening disease are eligible to apply. Applicants must pursue a course of study that renders them immediately employable after graduation. Applicants may enroll in a two- or four-year degree, or advanced studies if the regimen pursued satisfies the main employable criteria. Applicants must also enroll full-time, maintain at least a 3.0 GPA, demonstrate financial need, and complete 20 hours of community service for each year covered by a scholarship. High school seniors are also eligible for this award. *Application Process: Applicants must submit a completed application, written documentation from a physician of past medical diagnosis, last year's tax returns, official transcripts, and two letters of recommendation. Visit the foundation's Web site to download an application. *Amount: $2,000 per year (renewable). *Deadline: May 1.

Pennsylvania State University
Office of Student Aid
314 Shields Building
University Park, PA 16802-1220
814-865-6301, 814-863-0585 (TDD)
http://www.psu.edu/dept/studentaid
Scholarship Name: Sy Barash Coaches vs. Cancer Scholarship. *Academic Area: Open. *Age Group: Undergraduate students. *Eligibility: Applicants must have had their studies interrupted by cancer, whether their own or that of an immediate family member. Applicants must also demonstrate

academic achievement, be a full-time undergraduate student, and be enrolled or plan to enroll at Penn State-University Park. *Application Process: Contact the Office of Student Aid for application details. *Amount: Varies. *Deadline: May 15.

Pfizer Epilepsy Scholarship Award Center

c/o The Eden Communications Group
515 Valley Street, Suite 200
Maplewood, NJ 07040
800-292-7373
czoppi@edencomgroup.com
http://www.epilepsy-scholarship.com
Scholarship Name: Pfizer Epilepsy Scholarship Award. *Academic Area: Open. *Age Group: Undergraduate students, graduate students. *Eligibility: Applicants must be high school seniors or college students who have overcome the challenges of epilepsy and who have been successful in school and in the community. *Application Process: Applicants must submit a completed application, two letters of recommendation, and transcripts. Visit the award center's Web site to download an application or submit an online application. *Amount: $3,000. *Deadline: March 1.

Pilot International Foundation

PO Box 4844
Macon, GA 31208-4844
478-743-7403
pifinfo@pilothq.org
http://www.pilotinternational.org/html/foundation/scholar.shtml
Scholarship Name: Marie Newton Sepia Memorial Scholarship. *Academic Area: Disability studies. *Age Group: Graduate students. *Eligibility: Applicants must be graduate students preparing for careers working with children with disabilities and/or brain-related disorders. Applicants must be sponsored by a Pilot Club in their hometown, or in the city in which their college or university is located. They must also have a GPA of 3.25 on a 4.0 scale or 4.01 on a 5.0 scale. *Application Process: Visit the foundation's Web site to download an application. *Amount: Up to $1,500. *Deadline: Contact the foundation for details.

Pilot International Foundation

PO Box 4844
Macon, GA 31208-4844
478-743-7403
pifinfo@pilothq.org
http://www.pilotinternational.org/html/foundation/scholar.shtml
Scholarship Name: Pilot International Foundation Scholarship. *Academic Area: Disability studies. *Age Group: Undergraduate students. *Eligibility: Applicants must be undergraduate students preparing for careers working directly with people with disabilities or training those who will. Applicants must be sponsored by a Pilot Club in their hometown, or in the city in which their college or university is located. They must also have a GPA of 3.25 on a 4.0 scale or 4.01 on a 5.0 scale. *Application Process: Visit the foundation's Web site to download an application. *Amount: Up to $1,500. *Deadline: Contact the foundation for details.

Portland State University

Office of Graduate Studies
117 Cramer Hall, Room 117
Portland, OR 97207-0751
503-725-8410
grad@pdx.edu
http://www.gsr.pdx.edu/ogs_funding_scholarships.html
Scholarship Name: Robert and Rosemary Low Memorial Scholarship. *Academic Area: Open. *Age Group: Graduate students. *Eligibility: Applicants must be full-time graduate students with physical disabilities and good academic records. *Application Process: Contact the Office of Graduate Studies for application details. *Amount: Varies. *Deadline: April 15.

Quota Club of Candlewood Valley

PO Box 565
Danbury, CT 06813
quota@quotacv.org
http://www.quotacv.org/community.htm
Scholarship Name: Quota Club of Candlewood Valley Scholarship. *Academic Area: Disability studies. *Age Group: Undergraduate students, graduate students. *Eligibility: Applicants must be either deaf or hard-of-hearing high school seniors or college students or hearing students preparing to work in the field of deafness. They must also be residents of the Danbury, Connecticut-area. *Application Process: Contact the Quota Club for application details. *Amount: $1,000 and $2,000. *Deadline: Varies.

Quota Club of the Mississippi Gulf Coast

Attn: Scholarship Chairperson
PO Box 8001

Gulfport, MS 39506

228-594-3738

http://www.orgsites.com/ms/quotamsgc

Scholarship Name: Quota Club of the Mississippi Gulf Coast Scholarship. *Academic Area: Disability studies. *Age Group: Undergraduate students, graduate students. *Eligibility: Applicants must be either deaf or hard-of-hearing high school seniors or college students or hearing students preparing to work in the field of deafness. They must also be residents of the Mississippi Gulf Coast. *Application Process: Contact the Quota Club for application details. *Amount: $750. *Deadline: April 1.

Quota International of Plantation, Florida

Attn: Scholarship Committee

1600 Northeast 49 Street

Oakland Park, FL 33334

QuotaPlantation@aol.com

http://members.aol.com/QuotaPlantation/Scholars.html

Scholarship Name: Quota International of Plantation, Florida. *Academic Area: Open. *Age Group: Undergraduate students. *Eligibility: Applicants must be deaf high school seniors or deaf graduates of South Florida high schools. They must also have a GPA of at least 2.7 and plan to attend college full time. *Application Process: Applicants must submit a completed application, most recent audiogram, a copy of their parents' income tax return(s) for the previous two years, two letters of recommendation, and a personal statement. Contact Quota International to request an application. *Amount: Varies. *Deadline: April 17.

Rhode Island, University of

Office of Financial Aid

Green Hall, 35 Campus Avenue

Kingston, RI 02881

401-874-9500

esmail@etal.uri.edu

http://www.uri.edu/catalog/cataloghtml/loansscholarshipawards.html

Scholarship Name: Paul DePace Scholarship Endowment. *Academic Area: Open. *Age Group: Undergraduate students, graduate students. *Eligibility: Applicants must be students who have a permanent disability. *Application Process: Contact the Office of Financial Aid for application details. *Amount: Varies. *Deadline: Varies.

Salisbury University

Financial Aid Office

1101 Camden Avenue

Salisbury, MD 21801

410-543-6165

finaid@salisbury.edu

http://www.salisbury.edu/admissions/finaid/UnivScholarships/part3.htm#dudley

Scholarship Name: Rick Dudley Scholarship Fund. *Academic Area: Open. *Age Group: Graduate students. *Eligibility: Applicants must be accepted into a graduate program at the university and must meet one or more of the following disability-required criteria: inability to ambulate without assistive devices, cerebral palsy, legally blind, profoundly deaf, inability of speech to be understood by the average person, or require personal assistance with daily living activities. *Application Process: Applicants must submit a completed application and personal statement. Visit the Salisbury's Web site to download an application. *Amount: $5,000 (full-time students), $3,000 (part-time students), and $1,500 (less than part-time students). *Deadline: June 15 and November 15.

San Jose State University

Financial Aid and Scholarships Office, Student Services Center

One Washington Square

San Jose, CA 95192-0036

408-283-7500

scholarships@sjsu.edu

http://www2.sjsu.edu/depts/finaid

Award Name: Donna Ellis Honorary Award. *Academic Area: Open. *Age Group: Undergraduate students, graduate students. *Eligibility: Applicants must be financially needy students with disabilities who are attending the university and have at least one semester of education remaining. Applicants must also maintain at least a 2.0 GPA. *Application Process: Contact the Financial Aid and Scholarship Office for application details. *Amount: Varies. *Deadline: Varies.

Scripps College

Office of Financial Aid

1030 Columbia Avenue

Claremont, CA 91711

909-621-8275

finaid@scrippscollege.edu

http://www.scrippscol.edu/dept/admission/financing.html

Scholarship Name: Juliet King Esterly '34 Scholarship. *Academic Area: Open. *Age Group: Undergraduate students. *Eligibility: Applicants must be female students who demonstrate financial need. Strong preference is given to those students who are visually impaired of blind. Applicants must also demonstrate scholastic achievement and possess character and personal qualities that indicate future success in her chosen field. Applicants who are not blind or visually handicapped may be considered if they have chosen a field of interest related to the service of those with physical challenges. *Application Process: Contact the Office of Financial Aid for application details. *Amount: Varies. *Deadline: Varies.

Sertoma International
Hearing Impaired Scholarship Program
1912 East Meyer Boulevard
Kansas City, MO 64132
816-333-8300
infosertoma@sertoma.org
http://www.sertoma.org/%5EScholarships/Scholarships.htm

Scholarship Name: Sertoma Hearing Impaired Scholarship. *Academic Area: Open. *Age Group: Undergraduate students. *Eligibility: Applicants must have documented hearing loss, be U.S. residents, have a GPA of at least 3.2, and plan to pursue, or be currently pursuing, a bachelor's degree. *Application Process: Applicants must submit one original application with all information completed and one copy (with applicant's personal information blanked out), personal statement, two letters of recommendation, transcripts, and a recent audiogram or statement from a hearing health professional (only one copy of audiogram required). Visit Sertoma International's Web site to download an application. *Amount: $1,000. *Deadline: May 1.

Sickle Cell Disease Association of America Inc.
Attn: Jeannine Knight
231 East Baltimore Street, Suite 800
Baltimore, MD 21202
410-528-1555, 800-421-8453
jknight@sicklecelldisease.org or scdaa@sicklecelldisease.org
http://www.sicklecelldisease.org/programs/nash_scholarship.phtml

Scholarship Name: Kermit B. Nash, Jr. Academic Scholarship. *Academic Area: Open. *Age Group: Undergraduate students. *Eligibility: Applicants must be graduating high school seniors who have sickle cell disease, are U.S. citizens, and plan to attend a four-year accredited college. *Application Process: Applicants must submit a completed application, a physician's certification of sickle cell status, and a personal essay. Contact the association for further application details. *Amount: $5,000 per year. *Deadline: June 10.

Sickle Cell Disease Foundation of California
Attn: Deborah Green, Program Administrator
6133 Bristol Parkway, Suite 240
Culver City, CA 90230
310-693-0247
deborahg@scdfc.org
http://www.scdfc.org/program_services/LifeSteps/Scott_Zuniga_Scholarship.htm

Scholarship Name: Scott Zuniga Memorial Scholarship. *Academic Area: Open. *Age Group: Undergraduate students, graduate students. *Eligibility: Applicants must be California residents of Los Angeles, Orange, Riverside, San Bernardino, or Ventura counties and have sickle cell disease. Awardees must maintain a GPA of at least 2.0 and complete at least 2.5 to 15 hours of community service at the foundation. *Application Process: Applicants must submit a completed application, a two-page autobiographical sketch, a cover letter, transcripts, three letters of recommendation, a letter of acceptance in a postsecondary institution, certification of sickle cell disease, and a copy of the most recent federal tax return. *Amount: $250 to $1,500. *Deadline: May 1 and December 1.

Sierra College
Financial Aid Office
5000 Rocklin Road
Rocklin, CA 95677
916-781-0568, 800-242-4004
http://www.sierra.cc.ca.us/ed_programs/student_support_services/financial_services/financial_aid/Inc_Scholarships.html

Scholarship Name: Billy Hanley Memorial Scholarship. *Academic Area: Open. *Age Group: Undergraduate students. *Eligibility: Applicants must be incoming college freshmen with disabilities who have a minimum GPA of 2.0 and meet enrollment requirements. *Application Process: Contact the Financial Aid Office for application details. *Amount: $1,000. *Deadline: February 3.

Sierra College
Financial Aid Office
5000 Rocklin Road
Rocklin, CA 95677
916-781-0568, 800-242-4004
http://www.sierra.cc.ca.us/ed_programs/student_
support_services/financial_services/financial_aid/
Misc_Scholarships.html
Scholarship Name: Ken Holt Memorial Scholarship.
*Academic Area: Open. *Age Group: Undergraduate students. *Eligibility: Applicants must be students with disabilities who are involved in athletics. They must also have a minimum GPA of 2.0, meet enrollment requirements, and be a member of Students Overcoming Challenges. *Application Process: Contact the Financial Aid Office for application details. *Amount: $200. *Deadline: February 3.

Sierra College
Financial Aid Office
5000 Rocklin Road
Rocklin, CA 95677
916-781-0568, 800-242-4004
http://www.sierra.cc.ca.us/ed_programs/student_
support_services/financial_services/financial_aid/
Inc_Scholarships.html
Scholarship Name: Success for the Physically Challenged Scholarship. *Academic Area: Open. *Age Group: Undergraduate students. *Eligibility: Applicants must be incoming college freshmen with learning or physical disabilities who have a minimum GPA of 2.75 and meet enrollment requirements. *Application Process: Contact the Financial Aid Office for application details. *Amount: $200. *Deadline: February 3.

Sigma Alpha Iota Philanthropies Inc.
Attn: Karen Louise Gearreald, Project Director
One Tunnel Road
Asheville, NC 28805
hadley@exis.net
http://www.sai-national.org/phil/philschs.html
Scholarship Name: Special Needs Scholarship.
*Academic Area: Performing arts (music). *Age Group: Undergraduate students, graduate students.

*Eligibility: Applicants must be Sigma Alpha Iota members with sensory or physical impairments, who are enrolled in an undergraduate or graduate degree program in music. *Application Process: A $25 non-refundable application fee is required. Contact Sigma Alpha Iota Philanthropies Inc. for application details. *Amount: $1,000. *Deadline: March 15.

Solvay Pharmaceuticals Inc.
Attn: CREON Family Scholarship Program Coordinator
901 Sawyer Road
Marietta, GA 30062
770-578-9000
http://www.solvaypharmaceuticals-us.com/products/
cfscholarships/0,,14635-2-0,00.htm
Scholarship Name: CREON Family Scholarship.
*Academic Area: Open. *Age Group: Undergraduate students, graduate students. *Eligibility: Applicants must be U.S. citizens with cystic fibrosis who are enrolled in higher education in the fall. They must also demonstrate academic achievement, financial need, and the ability to serve as a role model for others with cystic fibrosis *Application Process: Applicants must submit a completed application, original transcripts, a copy of applicant's/parent's/guardian's Federal Income Tax Return, a photograph, two letters of recommendation, and a creative representation addressing what the applicant has learned from living with cystic fibrosis. Visit the Solvay Pharmaceuticals Inc. Web site to download an application. *Amount: $2,000 per year. *Deadline: June 24.

Soroptimist International of the Americas
Attn: Venture Program Coordinator
1709 Spruce Street
Philadelphia, PA 19103-6103
215-893-9000
http://www.soroptimist.org
Award Name: Venture Student Aid Award for a Physically Disabled Student. *Academic Area: Open. *Age Group: Ages 15 to 40. *Eligibility: Applicants must be physically disabled students between 15 and 40 years old, who demonstrate financial need and the capacity to profit from further education. *Application Process: The scholarship is administered by local, participating Venture Clubs and is not available in all communities. Contact Soroptimist for application details. *Amount: $2,500 to $5,000. *Deadline: Varies.

Southern Indiana, University of
College of Business
8600 University Boulevard
Evansville, IN 47712
812-464-1718
http://business.usi.edu/awards.asp
Scholarship Name: Roy W. & Adelaide D. Daudistel
Sanders Scholarship. *Academic Area: Business.
*Age Group: Undergraduate students. *Eligibility:
Applicants must be high school seniors with
disabilities who have maintained a minimum high
school GPA of 3.5. They must also have scored at least
1800 on the SAT and 28 on the ACT and be enrolled
at the university for at least three-quarter time (nine
semester hours). *Application Process: Contact the
College of Business for application details. *Amount:
$2,000 per year. *Deadline: Varies.

Spina Bifida Association of America (SBAA)
4590 MacArthur Boulevard, NW, Suite 250
Washington, DC 20007-4226
202-944-3285, 800-621-3141
sbaa@sbaa.org
http://www.sbaa.org/site/DocServer?docID=1021
Scholarship Name: Lazof Family Foundation
Scholarship. *Academic Area: Open. *Age Group:
Undergraduate students. *Eligibility: Applicants
must be high school juniors and seniors with spina
bifida who maintain at least a 3.0 GPA and plan
to graduate from a four-year college or university
within four years. *Application Process: Applicants
must submit a completed application, official
transcripts, standardized test scores, a college
letter of acceptance, a statement of disability by
physician, two letters of recommendation, a personal
statement, and an FAFSA report. Visit the association's
Web site to download an application. *Amount:
$2,500 per year. *Deadline: March 1.

Spina Bifida Association of America (SBAA)
4590 MacArthur Boulevard, NW, Suite 250
Washington, DC 20007-4226
202-944-3285, 800-621-3141
sbaa@sbaa.org
http://www.sbaa.org/site/DocServer?docID=1021http
Scholarship Name: SBAA Four-Year Scholarship.
*Academic Area: Open. *Age Group: Undergraduate
students. *Eligibility: Applicants must be high school
juniors and seniors with spina bifida. *Application
Process: Applicants must submit a completed

application, official transcripts, standardized
test scores, a college letter of acceptance, a
statement of disability by physician, two letters
of recommendation, a personal statement, and
an FAFSA report. Visit the association's Web site to
download an application. *Amount: Up to $5,000 per
year. *Deadline: March 1.

Spina Bifida Association of America (SBAA)
4590 MacArthur Boulevard, NW, Suite 250
Washington, DC 20007-4226
202-944-3285, 800-621-3141
sbaa@sbaa.org
http://www.sbaa.org/site/DocServer?docID=1021
Scholarship Name: SBAA One-Year Scholarship.
*Academic Area: Open. *Age Group: Undergraduate
students. *Eligibility: Applicants must be graduating
high school seniors, GED recipients, or recent
graduates with spina bifida. *Application Process:
Applicants must submit a completed application,
official transcripts, standardized test scores, a college
letter of acceptance, a statement of disability by
physician, two letters of recommendation, a personal
statement, and an FAFSA report. Visit the association's
Web site to download an application. *Amount:
$2,000. *Deadline: March 1.

Spina Bifida Association of Connecticut
Attn: Allocations Committee
PO Box 2545
Hartford, CT 06146-2545
800-574-6274
sbac@sbac.org
http://www.sbac.org
Scholarship Name: Spina Bifida Association of
Connecticut Scholarship. *Academic Area: Open.
*Age Group: Undergraduate students. *Eligibility:
Applicants must reside within the state of Connecticut,
have spina bifida, and plan to or be currently enrolled
in a postsecondary institution. *Application Process:
Applicants must submit a completed application
and a physician statement of disability. Contact the
association for further application details. *Amount:
$1,000. *Deadline: April 15.

Stony Wold-Herbert Fund
Attn: Cheri Friedman, Executive Director
136 East 57th Street, Room 1705
New York, NY 10022
212-753-6565

director@stonywoldherbertfund.com
http://www.stonywoldherbertfund.com
Scholarship Name: Stony Wold-Herbert Direct
Service Grant. *Academic Area: Open. *Age Group:
Undergraduate students, graduate students.
*Eligibility: Applicants must be high school seniors
or college students with pulmonary diseases who
attend school in the New York City area (within 50-mile
radius) area. *Application Process: Contact Stony Wold-
Herbert Fund for application details. *Amount: $250
per month for up to four years. *Deadline: Varies.

Syracuse University
Office of Scholarship Programs
216 Archbold North
Syracuse, NY 13244
315-443-2443
scholar@syr.edu
http://financialaid.syr.edu/scholar-mattstauffer.htm
Scholarship Name: Matt Stauffer Memorial Scholarship.
*Academic Area: Open. *Age Group: Undergraduate
students, graduate students. *Eligibility: Students who
are battling or who have overcome cancer and who
display financial need may apply. *Application Process:
Applicants must submit two letters of recommendation,
a financial need form, and a 500-word essay. Contact
the Office of Scholarship Programs for additional
details.*Amount: $1,000. *Deadline: April 1.

Temple University
Disability Resources and Services
1300 Cecile Moore Avenue, 100 Ritter Annex (004-00)
Philadelphia, PA 19122
215-204-1280, 215-204-1786 (TTY)
drs@temple.edu
http://www.temple.edu/disability/scholarships.html
Scholarship Name: Charlotte W. Newcombe Scholarship.
*Academic Area: Open. *Age Group: Undergraduate
students. *Eligibility: Enrolled students with a
permanent disability are eligible to apply. Applicants
must have a minimum GPA of 2.0 and demonstrate
financial need. *Application Process: Applicants must
submit a written statement of need and a completed
application. *Amount: Varies. *Deadline: Applications
are due the first Friday of each semester.

**Tennessee Hemophilia and & Bleeding Disorders
Foundation**
Attn: Scholarship Committee
7003 Chadwick Drive

Brentwood, TN 37027
615-373-0351, 888-703-3269
mail@tennesseehemophilia.org
http://www.thbdf.org
Scholarship Name: Dudgale - Van Eys Scholarship.
*Academic Area: Open. *Age Group: Undergraduate
students. *Eligibility: Applicants must reside in
Tennessee and be students with a bleeding disorder
or the child, spouse, or guardian of someone with a
bleeding disorder. Applicants must be full-time students
and maintain at least a 2.5 GPA. The scholarship is
available for high school seniors and undergraduate
students. *Application Process: Applicants must
submit a completed application, a resume, an essay,
proof of enrollment, transcripts, three letters of
recommendation, a community service form, and a
photograph. Visit the foundation's Web site for further
application details and to download an application.
*Amount: $500 to $2,000. *Deadline: May 1.

Tennessee-Knoxville, University of
Office of Disability Services
191 Hoskins Library
Knoxville, TN 37996-4007
865-974-6087 (Voice/TTY)
ods@tennessee.edu
http://ods.utk.edu
Scholarship Name: Charles Jackson Scholarship.
*Academic Area: Open. *Age Group: Undergraduate
students. *Eligibility: Applicants must be students
with documented disabilities who maintain a
minimum GPA of 2.5, have been enrolled at the
University of Tennessee for at least two semesters,
and are classified as juniors or seniors. *Application
Process: Applicants must submit a completed
application, transcripts, medical documentation
of disability, a one-page essay, and a letter of
recommendation. Visit the Office of Disability
Services Web site to download an application.
*Amount: $500. *Deadline: May 1.

Tennessee-Knoxville, University of
Office of Disability Services
191 Hoskins Library
Knoxville, TN 37996-4007
865-974-6087 (Voice/TTY)
ods@tennessee.edu
http://ods.utk.edu
Scholarship Name: Robert L. and Helen Johnson
Scholarship. *Academic Area: Open. *Age Group:

Undergraduate students. *Eligibility: Applicants must be students with documented disabilities who maintain a minimum GPA of 2.0, have been enrolled at the University of Tennessee for at least two semesters, and are Knox County residents. *Application Process: Applicants must submit a completed application, transcripts, medical documentation of disability, and a one-page essay. Visit the Office of Disability Services Web site to download an application. *Amount: $750. *Deadline: May 1.

Tennessee-Knoxville, University of
Office of Disability Services
191 Hoskins Library
Knoxville, TN 37996-4007
865-974-6087 (Voice/TTY)
ods@tennessee.edu
http://ods.utk.edu
Scholarship Name: Scholarship for Students with Visual Impairments. *Academic Area: Open. *Age Group: Undergraduate students. *Eligibility: Applicants must be students with documented visual impairments who maintain a minimum GPA of 2.0 and are enrolled as full-time undergraduate students. *Application Process: Applicants must submit a completed application, transcripts, medical documentation of disability, and a one-page essay. Visit the Office of Disability Services Web site to download an application. *Amount: Varies. *Deadline: May 1.

Texas A&M University
Department of Student Financial Aid
PO Box 30016
College Station, TX 77842-3016
979-845-3982
http://financialaid.tamu.edu
Award Name: Opportunity Award Program. *Academic Area: Open. *Age Group: Undergraduate students, graduate students. *Eligibility: Applicants must be high school seniors or college students who have overcome significant traumatic life experiences, including, but not limited to, cancer, traumatic brain injury, leukemia, learning disabilities, orthopedic disabilities, and HIV/AIDS. *Application Process: Contact the Department of Student Financial Aid for application details. *Amount: Varies. *Deadline: Varies.

Texas at Austin, University of
Office of Student Financial Services
PO Box 7758, UT Station

Austin, TX 78713-7758
512-475-6282
http://bealonghorn.utexas.edu/bal/financial_aid. WBX
Scholarship Name: Carole Patterson Endowed Scholarship. *Academic Area: Open. *Age Group: Undergraduate students, graduate students. *Eligibility: Applicants must be physically disabled students taking at least six hours of credit at the university. *Application Process: Contact the Office of Student Financial Services for application details. *Amount: $500 to $2,000. *Deadline: Varies.

Texas at Austin, University of
Office of Student Financial Services
PO Box 7758, UT Station
Austin, TX 78713-7758
512-475-6282
http://finaid.utexas.edu/sources/scholarships
Scholarship Name: Will Rogers Scholarship. *Academic Area: Open. *Age Group: Undergraduate students, graduate students. *Eligibility: Applicants must be disabled students or those preparing to work with disabled children. They must also demonstrate financial need. *Application Process: Contact the Office of Student Financial Services for application details. *Amount: $400 to $1,000. *Deadline: Varies.

Texas Higher Education Coordinating Board
PO Box 12788
Austin, TX 78711-2788
512-427-6101, 800-242-3062
http://www.thecb.state.tx.us/
http://www.collegefortexans.com/cfbin/tofa2.cfm?ID=13
Grant Name: Blind/Deaf Student Exemption Program. *Academic Area: Open. *Age Group: Undergraduate students, graduate students. *Eligibility: Blind or deaf students planning to attend or currently attending public colleges and universities in Texas are eligible. Applicants must otherwise qualify for admission. *Application Process: Applicants must provide certification from the Department of Assistive and Rehabilitative Services of their status as a blind or deaf person, a written statement detailing which certificate, degree program, or professional enhancement they will pursue, a high school transcript, a letter of recommendation, and proof of admission. Visit the board's Web site for a list of Texas public colleges and universities. *Amount: Tuition and fees are waived. *Deadline: Contact the board for details.

Toledo, University of
Office of Student Financial Aid
2801 West Bancroft Street, Mail Stop 314
Toledo, OH 43606-3390
419-530-8700
utfinaid@utnet.utoledo.edu
http://www.financialaid.utoledo.edu/general_
    scholarships.htm
Scholarship Name: Paula Marie Kuehn Endowed
    Scholarship. *Academic Area: Open. *Age Group:
    Undergraduate students, graduate students.
    *Eligibility: Applicants must be blind, hearing
    impaired, or wheelchair-bound students who have a
    GPA of 2.5 or higher and demonstrate financial need.
    *Application Process: Contact the Office of Student
    Financial Aid for application details. *Amount: Varies.
    *Deadline: April 1.

Toledo, University of
Office of Student Financial Aid
2801 West Bancroft Street, Mail Stop 314
Toledo, OH 43606-3390
419-530-8700
utfinaid@utnet.utoledo.edu
http://www.financialaid.utoledo.edu/general_
    scholarships.htm
Scholarship Name: Toledo Host Lions Club Welfare Inc.
    Endowed Scholarship. *Academic Area: Open. *Age
    Group: Undergraduate students. *Eligibility: Applicants
    must be full-time students who are legally disabled
    due to sight impairment or blindness and U.S citizens
    who reside in Northwest Ohio or Southeast Michigan.
    Entering freshmen must have a high school GPA of 3.0
    or higher. *Application Process: Contact the Office of
    Student Financial Aid for application details. *Amount:
    Varies. *Deadline: April 1.

Tourism Cares for Tomorrow
Attn: Sarah Graham Mann, Program Manager
585 Washington Street
Canton, MA 02021
sarahm@tourismcaresfortomorrow.org
http://www.tourismcaresfortomorrow.org/
    TourismCares/What+We+Do/Students/Scholarships/
    2005+Scholarships.htm
Scholarship Name: Yellow Ribbon Scholarship.
    *Academic Area: Hospitality. *Age Group:
    Undergraduate students. *Eligibility: Applicants
    must have documentation of a physical or sensory
    disability, be enrolled in a two- or four-year degree
program, and maintain a minimum 3.0 GPA. This
    scholarship, sponsored by entertainer Tony Orlando,
    is for students who are pursing careers in the travel
    or tourism industry. *Application Process: Applicants
    should submit a completed application along with
    documentation from a physician of the disability,
    official transcripts, two letters of recommendation,
    and a signed, typewritten essay regarding their
    future plans for a travel or tourism career. Applicants
    can submit materials by email or mail. Visit the
    association's Web site to download an application.
    *Amount: $2,500. *Deadline: May 1.

Travelers Protective Association of America
c/o Scholarship Trust for the Deaf and Near Deaf
3755 Lindell Boulevard
St. Louis, MO 63108-3476
314-371-0533
support@tpahq.org
http://www.tpahq.org
Scholarship Name: Scholarship Trust for the Deaf and
    Near Deaf. *Academic Area: Open. *Age Group:
    Undergraduate students, graduate students, and
    adults. *Eligibility: Applicants must be deaf or hearing-
    impaired high school seniors, college students, and
    adults who need assistance in obtaining mechanical
    devices, medical or specialized treatment, or
    specialized education. *Application Process: Applicants
    must submit a completed application, a full release
    form, a medical authorization form, and a photograph.
    Visit the association's Web site to download an
    application and required forms. *Amount: Varies.
    *Deadline: March 1.

Twitty, Milsap, Sterban Foundation
600 Renaissance Center, Suite 1300, PO Box 43517
Detroit, MI 48243
313-567-1920
*The foundation offers scholarships to help finance
    undergraduate or graduate training. *Academic
    Area: Open. *Age Group: Undergraduate students,
    graduate students. *Eligibility: Blind or visually
    impaired students with strong academic records
    and achievements are eligible. *Application Process:
    Contact the foundation for details. *Amount: $500 or
    more. *Deadline: Contact the foundation for details.*

Ulman Cancer Fund for Young Adults
PMB #505, 4725 Dorsey Hall Drive, Suite A
Ellicott City, MD 21042

410-964-0202

scholarship@ulmanfund.org

http://www.ulmanfund.org/Services/Scholarship/
tabid/73/Default.aspx

Scholarship Name: Matt Stauffer Memorial Scholarship.
*Academic Area: Open. *Age Group: Undergraduate
students, graduate students. *Eligibility: Applicants
must be students between the ages of 15 and 40
who are battling, or have overcome, cancer and who
display financial need. Applicants must be seeking
postsecondary higher education. *Application
Process: Applicants must submit a completed
application, two letters of recommendation, a
financial need form (applicants and parents), and
an essay. Visit the fund's Web site to download an
application and required forms. *Amount: $1,000.
*Deadline: April 1.

Utah, University of

Center for Disability Services

162 Union Building, 200 South Central Campus Drive,
Room #162

Salt Lake City, UT 84112-9107

801-581-5020 (Voice/TDD)

info@disability.utah.edu

http://disability.utah.edu/scholarship.htm

Scholarship Name: Drake Briggs Scholarship. *Academic
Area: Open. *Age Group: Undergraduate students,
graduate students. *Eligibility: Applicants must be
residents of the state of Utah who are legally deaf and
maintain a minimum 2.5 GPA. They must also be high
school seniors planning to attend the University of
Utah on a full-time basis, or currently enrolled full-time
students. They must also demonstrate involvement in
leadership and/or community activities. *Application
Process: Applicants must submit a completed
application, transcripts, standardized test scores,
a most recent audiogram, a personal statement, a
letter of recommendation, and list of extracurricular
activities and/or community service. Visit the Center
for Disability Services Web site to download an
application. *Amount: $1,000 to $2,000. *Deadline:
February 1.

Utah, University of

Center for Disability Services

162 Union Building, 200 South Central Campus Drive,
Room #162

Salt Lake City, UT 84112-9107

801-581-5020 (Voice/TDD)

info@disability.utah.edu

http://disability.utah.edu/scholarship.htm

Scholarship Name: Keaton Walker Scholarship.
*Academic Area: Open. *Age Group: Undergraduate
students, graduate students. *Eligibility: Applicants
must be students with visual (or physical disabilities
who have a GPA of at least 2.5. They must also be
registered with the Center for Disability Services.
*Application Process: Applicants must submit
a completed application, transcripts, a letter of
recommendation, a copy of their most recent
tax return or financial statement, and a personal
statement. Visit the Center for Disability Services Web
site to download an application. *Amount: $500.
*Deadline: February 17.

Utah, University of

Center for Disability Services

162 Union Building, 200 South Central Campus Drive,
Room #162

Salt Lake City, UT 84112-9107

801-581-5020 (Voice/TDD)

info@disability.utah.edu

http://disability.utah.edu/scholarship.htm

Scholarship Name: Louise J. Snow Scholarship.
*Academic Area: Open. *Age Group: Undergraduate
students, graduate students. *Eligibility: Applicants
must be disabled students with a GPA of at least
2.5 and registered with the Center for Disability
Services. *Application Process: Applicants must
submit a completed application, transcripts, a letter
of recommendation, a copy of their most recent
tax return or financial statement, and a personal
statement. Visit the Center for Disability Services Web
site to download an application. *Amount: $400 to
$600. *Deadline: February 17.

Vermont Association for the Blind and Visually
Impaired (VABVI)

VABVI Scholarship

PO Box 2000, Champlain Mill

Winooski, VT 05404

http://www.vabvi.org/scholar.htm

Scholarship Name: Charles E. Leonard Memorial
Scholarship. *Academic Area: Open. *Age Group:
Undergraduate students, graduate students.
*Eligibility: Applicants must be blind or visually
impaired students or children of blind or visually
impaired parents who are Vermont residents and
demonstrate academic excellence and financial need.

Preference is given to those applicants pursuing engineering degrees or those who plan to enter other fields in which they will work with blind or visually impaired people. The scholarship is available to both high school seniors and college students. *Application Process: Contact the association for application details. *Amount: Approximately $2,000. *Deadline: May 1.

VSA arts

818 Connecticut Avenue, NW, Suite 600
Washington, DC 20006
202-628-2800, 800-933-8721, 202-737-0645 (TDD)
info@vsarts.org
http://www.vsarts.org/x244.xml
Contest Name: VSA arts Playwright Discovery Award. *Academic Area: Performing arts (theatre). *Age Group: Students in grades six through 12. *Eligibility: Young playwrights with and without disabilities are eligible to submit an original one-act script that explores any aspect of disability. Applicants must be U.S. citizens. *Application Process: Applicants must submit two copies of their script along with a completed application form. *Amount: Winners receive up to $1,500, plus a trip to Washington, DC, to view their production at the John F. Kennedy Center for the Performing Arts. *Deadline: April 14.

VSA arts

818 Connecticut Avenue, NW, Suite 600
Washington, DC 20006
202-628-2800, 800-933-8721, 202-737-0645 (TDD)
info@vsarts.org
http://www.vsarts.org
Contest Name: VSA arts Young Soloists Award. *Academic Area: Performing arts (general), performing arts (music-instrumental), performing arts (voice). *Age Group: Age 25 and under. *Eligibility: Young musicians with disabilities who have exhibited exceptional talents in any type of music as instrumentalists or vocalists may apply. *Application Process: Contact VSA for details. *Amount: $5,000, plus the chance to perform at the John F. Kennedy Center for the Performing Arts. *Deadline: Contact VSA for details.

Washington Council of the Blind (WCB)

Attn: Alan Bentson, WCB Scholarship Committee Chair
7356 34th Avenue, NW
Seattle, WA 98115

206-527-4527, 800-255-1147
info@wcbinfo.org
http://www.wcbinfo.org
Scholarship Name: The council offers educational scholarships to blind students. *Academic Area: Open. *Age Group: Undergraduate students, graduate students. *Eligibility: Blind high school seniors and college students planning to or currently attending a postsecondary education in Washington may apply. *Application Process: Contact the council for details. *Amount: At least $2,000. *Deadline: Typically in June.

Winston-Salem Foundation

Attn: Student Aid Committee
860 West Fifth Street
Winston-Salem, NC 27101-2506
336-725-2382
info@wsfoundation.org
http://www.wsfoundation.org
Scholarship Name: Marcus Raper Zimmerman Scholarship. *Academic Area: Open. *Age Group: Undergraduate students, graduate students. *Eligibility: Applicants must be high school seniors or college students with disabilities from Forsyth County, North Carolina. They must also have a minimum GPA of 2.5. Non-disabled persons who wish to prepare for careers serving persons with disabilities are also eligible. *Application Process: Applicants must submit a completed application, a copy of recent tax returns (parents and applicant), official transcripts, Student Aid Report (SAR), and a $20 application fee. Visit the foundation's Web site to download an application. *Amount: Up to $1,000. *Deadline: August 31.

Wisconsin Council of the Blind

Attn: Sue Barker
754 Williamson Street
Madison, WI 53703
800-783-5213
sue@wcblind.org
http://www.wcblind.org/Scholarships.htm
Scholarship Name: Lloyd P. Foote Scholarship. *Academic Area: Open. *Age Group: Undergraduate students, graduate students. *Eligibility: Applicants must be blind college students who reside in Wisconsin, have completed at least one year carrying a full academic load, and maintain a GPA of at least 2.5. *Application Process: Contact the council for application details. *Amount: $1,000. *Deadline: Varies.

Wisconsin Higher Educational Aids Board
Attn: Sandy Thomas
PO Box 7885
Madison, WI 53707-7885
608-267-2206
sandy.thomas@heab.state.wi.us
http://www.heab.state.wi.us
Scholarship Name: Hearing and Visually Handicapped
Student Grant. *Academic Area: Open. *Age Group:
Undergraduate students. *Eligibility: Wisconsin
residents with hearing- and/or vision-related
disabilities may apply. *Application Process: Contact
the board for details. *Amount: $250 to $1,800.
*Deadline: Contact the board for details.

Wisconsin-Madison, University of
McBurney Disability Resource Center
1305 Linden Drive
Madison, WI 53706
608-263-2741, 608-263-6393 (TTY)
FrontDesk@mcb.wisc.edu
http://www.mcburney.wisc.edu
Scholarship Name: McBurney Academic Scholarships.
*Academic Area: Open. *Age Group: Undergraduate
students, graduate students. *Eligibility: Applicants
must be high school seniors or college students with
a documented disability (physical, psychological,
sensory, or learning, as verified by the McBurney
Disability Resource Center). *Application Process:
Applicants must submit one original and four
copies of a completed application, two letters of
recommendation, and transcripts. They must also
submit one copy of documentation of disability (if
applicants are not current McBurney clients). Visit
the McBurney Disability Resource Center Web site to
download an application. *Amount: $500 to $2,500.
*Deadline: April 15.

Woodrow Wilson National Fellowship Foundation
PO Box 5281
Princeton, NJ 08543-5281
609-452-7007
http://www.woodrow.org/newcombe
Fellowship Name: Charlotte W. Newcombe Doctoral
Dissertation Fellowship. *Academic Area: Humanities,
religion, social sciences. *Age Group: Graduate
students. *Eligibility: Disabled students pursuing
doctoral degrees in the United States in humanities
and social sciences are encouraged to apply.
*Application Process: Applicants must submit a

completed application, a dissertation abstract,
graduate transcripts, a dissertation proposal, three
letters of recommendation, a bibliography, and a
timetable. Visit the foundation's Web site to submit an
online application. *Amount: Approximately $18,500.
*Deadline: November 7.

World TeamTennis
Attn: Diane Donnelly Stone
1776 Broadway, Suite 600
New York, NY 10019
212-586-3444
dstone@wtt.com
http://www.wtt.com/charities/donnelly.asp
Scholarship Name: Novo Nordisk Donnelly Award.
*Academic Area: Athletics. *Age Group: Ages 14 to
21. *Eligibility: Applicants must be students between
the ages 14 to 21 who have diabetes and play tennis
competitively in tournaments or on their school team.
They must also show strong personal character, values,
sportsmanship, and community involvement, as well
as demonstrate financial need. *Application Process:
Applicants must submit a completed application, an
essay, two letters of recommendation, and physician's
written confirmation of diabetes diagnosis. Visit
the World TeamTennis Web site to download an
application. *Amount: $5,000. *Deadline: May 1.

Wyoming, University of
University Disability Support Services
Department 3808, 1000 East University Avenue
Laramie, WY 82071
307-766-6189, 307-766-3073 (TTY)
udssc@uwyo.edu
http://ed.uwyo.edu/graduate/gradschols.htm
Scholarship Name: Bernadette Smith Memorial
Scholarship. *Academic Area: Open. *Age Group:
Undergraduate students, graduate students.
*Eligibility: Students with severe disabilities attending
the university may apply. *Application Process:
Contact University Disability Support Services for
more information. *Amount: Varies. *Deadline: Varies.

Yes I Can! Foundation for Exceptional Children
1110 North Glebe Road, Suite 300
Arlington, VA 22201-5704
800-224-6830, ext. 450
http://yesican.cec.sped.org/scholarship
Scholarship Name: Sara Conlon Memorial Scholarship.
*Academic Area: Education. *Age Group:

Undergraduate students. *Eligibility: Applicants must be disabled and enrolling in full-time, postsecondary education or training for the first time, demonstrate financial need, and be committed to pursuing a major in education. *Application Process: Applicants must submit two copies of a completed application, transcripts, three letters of recommendation, and a personal statement. They must also submit one copy of a statement verifying disability (from a physician or school counselor/administrator) and a statement indicating financial need. Visit the foundation's Web site to download an application. *Amount: $500. *Deadline: February 1.

Yes I Can! Foundation for Exceptional Children
1110 North Glebe Road, Suite 300
Arlington, VA 22201-5704
800-224-6830, ext. 450
http://yesican.cec.sped.org/scholarship/

Scholarship Name: Stanley E. Jackson Scholarship. *Academic Area: Open. *Age Group: Undergraduate students. *Eligibility: Applicants must be disabled and enrolling in full-time, postsecondary education or training for the first time. Applicants must also demonstrate financial need. Awards are granted in four categories, including students with disabilities, ethnic minority students with disabilities, talented and gifted students with disabilities, and talented and gifted ethnic minority students with disabilities. *Application Process: Applicants must submit two copies of a completed application, transcripts, three letters of recommendation, and a personal statement. They must also submit one copy of a statement verifying disability (from a physician or school counselor/administrator) and a statement indicating financial need. Visit the foundation's Web site to download an application. *Amount: $500. *Deadline: February 1.

THEOLOGICAL STUDIES AND MEMBERS OF RELIGIOUS DENOMINATIONS

The following undergraduate and graduate financial aid resources are available to students pursuing theological study and to members of religious denominations pursuing study in a variety of academic areas.

Acton Institute for the Study of Religion & Liberty
161 Ottawa, NW, Suite 301
Grand Rapids, MI 49503
616-454-3080
awards@acton.org
http://www.acton.org/programs/students/essay/2005
Award Name: Acton Essay Competition Award.
*Academic Area: Philosophy, religion. *Age Group: Undergraduate students, graduate students, postgraduate scholars, seminary students. *Eligibility: Applicants may be undergraduate students, graduate students, postgraduates, seminarians, or anyone interested in writing a scholarly essay on the proposed topic. *Application Process: Applicants should submit a completed application along with the 1,000- to 1,500-word scholarly reflective essay in response to the year's topic. Visit the institute's Web site for information on the essay topic. *Amount: $500 to $2,000. *Deadline: November 15.

Acton Institute for the Study of Religion & Liberty
161 Ottawa, NW, Suite 301
Grand Rapids, MI 49503
616-454-3080
programs@acton.org
http://www.acton.org/programs/students/calihan/r_and_l.html
Fellowship Name: Calihan Academic Fellowship. *Academic Area: Religion. *Age Group: Graduate students, seminary students. *Eligibility: Applicants should be pursuing a graduate or seminary degree at an accredited institution, demonstrate academic achievement, have an interest in the intersection of religious and classical liberal ideas, and believe in the advancement of a virtuous, free society. *Application Process: Applicants should submit a completed, signed application along with two essays (described on the application), two letters of reference, official transcripts (undergraduate and graduate), and a disclosure form showing additional funding sources the applicant is receiving. Visit the institute's Web site to download an application. *Amount: Up to $5,000. *Deadline: March 31.

Acton Institute for the Study of Religion & Liberty
161 Ottawa, NW, Suite 301
Grand Rapids, MI 49503
616-454-3080
homiletics@acton.org
http://www.acton.org/programs/students/homiletics/2005
Award Name: Homiletics Award. *Academic Area: Religion. *Age Group: Professionals. *Eligibility: Applicants must be Christian preachers who are interested in competing for an award. Applicants should demonstrate exceptional skill in preaching, including preparation and presentation. *Application Process: Each January, the institute posts on its Web site the topic and Bible passage upon which the sermon is to be based. Applicants should visit the institute's Web site in January for information on the contest. For additional information, applicants should contact the institute by e-mail. *Amount: $500 to $2,000. *Deadline: Contact the institute for deadline information.

Military Chaplains Association (MCA) of the United States
PO Box 7056
Arlington, VA 22207-7056
703-533-5890
chaplains@mca-usa.org
http://www.mca-usa.org
Scholarship Name: MCA Chaplain Candidate Scholarships. *Academic Area: Religion. *Age Group: Graduate students. *Eligibility: Applicants must want to be a military chaplain and already be approved as a chaplain candidate in one of the U.S. Armed Forces. Applicant must be enrolled full time in an accredited seminary. *Application Process: Applicants should complete the online Free Application for Federal Student Aid (FAFSA) before applying, as results are required for the application. Applicants should submit a completed application along with four letters of recommendation and a photo, preferably in military uniform, as well as the FAFSA results. Visit

the association's Web site to download an application.
*Amount: $2,000. *May 30.

CHRISTIANITY

American Baptist Financial Aid Program
American Baptist Churches USA
National Ministries
PO Box 851
Valley Forge, PA 19482-0851
610-768-2000, 800-ABC-3USA, ext. 2067
Financialaid.web@abc-usa.org
http://www.nationalministries.org/Education/Financial_
   Aid/student_info.cfm
Scholarship Name: Ellen Cushing Scholarship. *Academic
   Area: Human services, religion. *Age Group: Graduate
   students. *Eligibility: Applicants must be female
   students pursuing a graduate degree in religion and/
   or human services. Applicants should demonstrate
   active participation in their school, church, or region.
   *Application Process: Applicants should request an
   application by e-mail or phone from the financial
   aid office of the American Baptist Churches USA.
   Complete application instructions are available
   with the application form. *Amount: Awards vary.
   *Deadline: May 31.

American Baptist Financial Aid Program
American Baptist Churches USA
National Ministries
PO Box 851
Valley Forge, PA 19482-0851
610-768-2000, 800-ABC-3USA, ext. 2067
Financialaid.web@abc-usa.org
http://www.nationalministries.org/Education/Financial_
   Aid/student_info.cfm
Grant Name: Individual Seminarian Grant. *Academic
   Area: Religion. *Age Group: Seminary students.
   *Eligibility: Applicants must be American Baptist
   students who are attending a seminary not related
   to American Baptist Churches USA at least two-thirds
   time. They also must be pursuing one of the following
   degrees: M.Div., M.C.E., M.A.C.E., or M.R.E. *Application
   Process: Applicants should request an application by
   e-mail or phone from the financial aid office of the
   American Baptist Churches USA. Complete application
   instructions are available with the application
   form.*Amount: $750, renewable for two additional
   years. *Deadline: May 31.

American Baptist Financial Aid Program
American Baptist Churches USA
National Ministries
PO Box 851
Valley Forge, PA 19482-0851
610-768-2000, 800-ABC-3USA, ext. 2067
Financialaid.web@abc-usa.org
http://www.nationalministries.org/financial-aid/student_
   info.cfm
Scholarship Name: Seminarian Support Program.
   *Academic Area: Religion. *Age Group: Seminary
   students. *Eligibility: Applicants must be American
   Baptist students enrolled at least two-thirds time who
   are attending American Baptist-related seminaries.
   Applicants must be pursuing one of the following
   degrees: M. Div., M.C.E., M.A.C.E., or M.R.E. *Application
   Process: Applicants should request an application
   from the financial aid officer of his or her school.
   Complete application instructions are available with the
   application form. *Amount: Up to $1,000. *Deadline:
   Deadlines vary.

American Baptist Financial Aid Program
http://www.nationalministries.org/Education/Financial_
   Aid/student_info.cfm m
Scholarship Name: Undergraduate Scholarships.
   *Academic Area: Religion. *Age Group: Undergraduate
   students. *Eligibility: Applicants must be full-time
   American Baptist students and maintain a 2.75 GPA to
   renew the scholarship. *Application Process: Applicants
   should request an application by e-mail or phone
   from the financial aid office of the American Baptist
   Churches USA. Complete application instructions are
   available with the application form.*Amount: Students
   attending an American Baptist-related college are
   eligible for $2,000 per year, while students attending a
   non American Baptist college or university are eligible
   to receive $1,000 per year. *Deadline: May 31.

**Association of Theological Schools (ATS) in the
   United States and Canada**
Attn: William R. Myers
10 Summit Park Drive
Pittsburgh, PA 15275-1103
412-788-6505, ext. 252
myers@ats.edu
http://www.ats.edu/leadership_education/
   LuceFellowsInTheology.asp
Fellowship Name: Henry Luce III Fellows in Theology
   Program. *Academic Area: Religion. *Age Group:

Postdoctoral scholars. *Eligibility: Applicants must be full-time faculty members of an ATS-accredited or candidate school and must be eligible to take a 12-month leave of absence. Fellows must also receive matching support from their institution. Applicants must demonstrate a commitment to a specific research project, as outlined in the application booklet. *Application Process: Applicants should submit a completed application along with a 200-word abstract of their research proposal, a formal project proposal (three single-spaced pages), a budget, transcripts, a curriculum vitae, a one-page plan on how their research will affect others, and three letters of recommendation. Visit the association's Web site to download an application. *Amount: Up to $75,000. *Deadline: December 1.

Bethesda Lutheran Homes and Services Inc.
Attn: Thomas Heuer, Coordinator/NCRC
600 Hoffmann Drive
Watertown, WI 53094
800-369-4636, ext. 4449
ncrc@blhs.org
http://www.blhs.org/youth/scholarships
Scholarship Name: Scholarship for Lutheran College Students. *Academic Area: Disability studies. *Age Group: Undergraduate students. *Eligibility: Applicants must be active participants in the Lutheran church who have maintained a minimum GPA of 3.0 and are currently classified as college sophomores or juniors at an accredited college or university. They also must desire to work in the field of developmental disabilities. *Application Process: Applicants should submit a completed application along with a two-page essay on their career goals, four letters of recommendation, official transcripts, a one-page narrative detailing their academic and community activities, and documentation that they have completed a minimum of 100 hours of service to the developmentally disabled in the last two years. All materials should be placed in a folder and sent via U.S. mail. Visit the organization's Web site to download an application. *Amount: $1,500. *Deadline: March 15.

Bethesda Lutheran Homes and Services Inc.
Attn: Thomas Heuer, Coordinator/NCRC
600 Hoffmann Drive
Watertown, WI 53094
800-369-4636, ext. 4449

ncrc@blhs.org
http://www.blhs.org/youth/scholarships
Scholarship Name: Scholarship for Lutheran Nursing Students. *Academic Area: Nursing (developmental disabilities). *Age Group: Undergraduate students. *Eligibility: Applicants must be active participants in the Lutheran church who have maintained a minimum GPA of 3.0, have attained sophomore status or higher at a four-year college or university or completed one year of a two-year ADN program, and desire to work with the developmentally disabled. *Application Process: Applicants should submit a completed application along with a two-page essay on their career goals, four letters of recommendation, official transcripts, a one-page narrative detailing their academic and community activities, and documentation that they have completed a minimum of 100 hours of service to the developmentally disabled in the last two years. All materials should be placed in a folder and sent via U.S. mail. Visit the organization's Web site to download an application. *Amount: $1,500. *Deadline: March 15.

Catholic Aid Association
Scholarship Program
3499 Lexington Avenue North
St. Paul, MN 55126
651-490-0170, ext. 133, 800-568-6670
http://www.catholicaid.com
Scholarship Name: Catholic Aid Association Tuition Scholarship. *Academic Area: Open. *Age Group: Undergraduate students. *Eligibility: Applicants must be members of Catholic Aid (for a minimum of two years prior to application) who are entering their first or second year of post-high school education. They also must be enrolled either in a degree or a certificate program. *Application Process: Applicants should submit a completed application along with high school and college transcripts. Visit the association's Web site to download an application. *Amount: $500 (for students attending a Catholic college or university); $300 (for students attending a non-Catholic institution.) Deadline: February 15.

Catholic Kolping Society of America
Attn: Patricia Farkas
9 East 8th Street
Clifton, NJ 07011
877-659-7237

PatFarkas@aol.com
http://www.kolping.org/scholar.htm
Scholarship Name: Father Krewitt Scholarship.
*Academic Area: Open. *Age Group: Undergraduate students, graduate students. *Eligibility: Applicants must be members of the organization or children or grandchildren of members. They also must be enrolled in college or a postsecondary vocational program. *Application Process: Applicants should look for information in the organization's monthly newsletter, the Kolping Banner, each year in November, December, January, and February. Application information and current essay topics are published in the newsletter. Applicants may also visit the society's Web site to download an application. Applicants must submit a completed application along with an essay. *Amount: $1,000. *Deadline: February 28.

The Christian Connector Inc.

http://www.christianconnector.com
Scholarship Name: Christian College Scholarship.
*Academic Area: Religion. *Age Group: Undergraduate students. *Eligibility: Applicants must be interested in receiving information regarding Christian and Bible colleges. Applicants must enroll for the first time at a Christian college or Bible college within one year of receiving the scholarship. *Application Process: Visit the organization's Web site to fill out an online request for information from Christian and Bible colleges. By submitting a request for information, you will be entered into a drawing to receive a randomly drawn $1,000 scholarship. *Amount: $1,000. *Deadline: May 31.

The Christian Connector Inc.

http://www.christianconnector.com
Scholarship Name: Missions Scholarship. *Academic Area: Religion. *Age Group: Open. *Eligibility: Applicants must be interested in receiving information regarding missionary opportunities. Applicants must participate in a missions trip (long or short) or become employed by a missions agency within a year of receiving the scholarship. *Application Process: Visit the organization's Web site to fill out an online request for information from missions agencies. By submitting a request for information, you will be entered into a drawing to receive a randomly drawn $1,000 scholarship. *Amount: $1,000. *Deadline: May 31.

The Christian Connector Inc.

http://www.christianconnector.com
Scholarship Name: Seminary and Graduate School Scholarship. *Academic Area: Religion. *Age Group: Graduate students. *Eligibility: Applicants must be interested in receiving information from seminaries and Christian graduate schools. Applicants must enroll for the first time at a Christ-centered seminary or Christian graduate school within 12 months of winning. *Application Process: Visit the organization's Web site to fill out an online request for information from schools in the geographical areas in which you are interested. By submitting a request for information, you will be entered into a drawing to receive a randomly drawn $1,000 scholarship. *Amount: $1,000. *Deadline: May 31.

Colleges and Universities of the Anglican Communion

815 Second Avenue
New York, NY 10017-4594
212-716-6148
office@cuac.org
http://www.cuac.org/53810_57187_ENG_HTM. htm?menupage=53912
Scholarship Name: Charitable Service Scholarship.
*Academic Area: Open. *Age Group: Undergraduate students. *Eligibility: Applicants must be enrolled in one of the 11 colleges and universities of the Anglican Communion. Applicants must also be able to demonstrate financial need as well as a strong commitment to community service. Visit the organization's Web site for a listing of the colleges and their locations. Contact the organization or one of the college's financial aid offices for further eligibility information. *Application Process: Applicants should contact the organization or the financial aid office of their college or university for information on the application process. *Amount: Awards vary. *Deadline: Contact your financial aid office for deadline information.

Domestic and Foreign Missionary Society (the Episcopal Church Center)

Attn: Ms. Denise Coy, Convenor of the Scholarship Committee
Episcopal Church Center
c/o The Treasurer's Office
815 Second Avenue
New York, NY 10017

dcoy@episcopalchurch.org

http://www.episcopalchurch.org/1521_34194_ENG_
HTM.htm

Scholarship Name: Elizabeth Allison Hynson Memorial Scholarship Fund. *Academic Area: Religion. *Age Group: Undergraduate students. *Eligibility: Applicants must be under the age of 30 and attending, or planning to attend, one of the 11 accredited Episcopal seminaries. Applicants must have the intent to serve in the ministry. Applicants from East Carolina, Minnesota, Southwest Florida, and Atlanta, Georgia are given preference. Application Process: Applicants should contact the church headquarters for information on the application procedure. *Amount: $2,000. *Deadline: May 1.

Eastern Orthodox Committee on Scouting (EOCS)

Attn: EOCS Scholarship Chairperson

862 Guy Lombardo Avenue

Freeport, NY 11520

516-868-4050

http://www.eocs.org/Religious%20Awards/
Scholarship%20PR%202004_2005%20New.htm

Scholarship Name: Eastern Orthodox Committee on Scouting Scholarship. *Academic Area: Open. *Age Group: Undergraduate students. *Eligibility: Applicants must be high school seniors who are registered, active members of a Boy or Girl Scout unit. Applicants should also have earned the Eagle Scout Award (boys) or the Gold Award (girls) as well as be active members of an Eastern Orthodox Church. They also should be able to demonstrate participation in their church, school, or community and must also have earned the Alpha Omega Religious Scout Award. Two scholarships of $1,000 are given, and one scholarship of $500. A scout of Russian descent is awarded one of the $1,000 scholarships. *Application Process: Applicants should submit an application along with four letters of recommendation. Contact the organization by mail to receive a scholarship application. *Amount: $1,000 and $500. *Deadline: May 1.

Episcopal Association for College Work (EACW)

Attn: Scholarship Committee

1405 East Houghton Avenue

Houghton, MI 49931-2110

http://www.pasty.com/~eacw/downloads/EACW_
scholarship_brochure_2004_2005.pdf

Scholarship Name: EACW Undergraduate and Graduate Scholarships. *Academic Area: Open. *Age Group: Undergraduate students, graduate students. *Eligibility: Applicants must be Episcopal students who either graduated from a high school in the Upper Peninsula of Michigan (attending college anywhere in the United States) or anyone who graduated from a high school in another area of the United States and is attending a college or university in the Upper Peninsula of Michigan. Applicants must also be attending school full time, demonstrate academic achievement (2.5 GPA for undergraduate scholarships, 3.0 GPA for graduate scholarships), and demonstrate active participation in the Episcopal Church. *Application Process: Applicants should submit a completed application along with a letter of support from a church official, transcripts, a letter of college acceptance, and a statement of purpose and spiritual goals. Visit the association's Web site to download an application. *Amount: Awards average around $1,500, but can vary depending on availability of funds. *Deadline: June 30.

Episcopal Diocese of Bethlehem

Attn: Archdeacon Rick Cluett

333 Wyandotte Street

Bethlehem, PA 18015

610-691-5655

archdeacon@diabeth.org

http://www.diobeth.org/Ministries/gressle.html

Scholarship Name: Gressle Scholarship. *Academic Area: Open. *Age Group: Undergraduate students. *Eligibility: Applicants must be male children of diocesan clergy. *Application Process: Applicants should contact Archdeacon Rick Cluett for information on the application process. *Amount: Awards vary. *Deadline: Contact the Archdeacon for deadline information.

Episcopal Diocese of Bethlehem

Attn: Archdeacon Rick Cluett

333 Wyandotte Street

Bethlehem, PA 18015

610-691-5655

archdeacon@diabeth.org

http://www.diobeth.org/Ministries/gressle.html

Scholarship Name: Shannon Fund Scholarship. *Academic Area: Open. *Age Group: Undergraduate students. *Eligibility: Applicants must be female children of diocesan clergy. *Application Process: Applicants should contact Archdeacon Rick Cluett for information on the application process. *Amount: Awards vary. *Deadline: Contact the Archdeacon for deadline information.

Episcopal Diocese of Newark

Attn: Office of the Bishop
31 Mulberry Street
Newark, NJ 07102
973-430-9976
http://www.dioceseofnewark.org/rathfund01.html
Scholarship Name: George E. Roth Scholarship Fund.
*Academic Area: Open. *Age Group: Undergraduate
students. *Eligibility: Applicants must be the children
of canonically resident clergy (or deceased canonically
resident clergy at the time of death). They also must be
attending or planning to attend an accredited four-year
college or university. *Application Process: Applicants
should submit a completed application along with
an acceptance letter to college or official college
transcripts. Visit the diocese's Web site to download an
application. *Amount: Awards vary. *Deadline: April 15.

Evangelical Lutheran Church in America (ELCA)

Fund for Leaders in Mission
Attn: Cynthia Halverson, Director
8765 West Higgins Road
Chicago, IL 60631
800-638-3522, ext. 2119
cindy.halverson@elca.org
http://www.elca.org/fo/FundforLeaders/application_
    process.html
Scholarship Name: ELCA Fund for Leaders in Mission
Scholarship. *Academic Area: Religion. *Age Group:
Seminary students. *Eligibility: Applicants should
be entering seminary students who plan to study
full time at an ELCA seminary, demonstrate financial
need, and show promise for leadership in ministry.
*Application Process: Being nominated by your
seminary is the first step toward being considered,
so if you are interested in being a candidate, let your
seminary leaders know of your intentions. Once
nominated, candidates are asked to complete an
application, which includes a 500-word essay and
recommendations from the seminary director of
admissions. Scholarships are awarded based on funds
available. Contact the program director for further
information. *Amount: Full tuition for three years.
*Deadline: There are currently no deadlines in place.

First Catholic Slovak Ladies Association

Attn: Director of Fraternal Scholarship Aid
24950 Chagrin Boulevard
Beachwood, OH 44122
216-464-8015, 800-464-4642

info@fcsla.com
http://www.fcsla.com/scholarship.shtml
Scholarship Name: College and Graduate Scholarships.
*Academic Area: Open. *Age Group: Undergraduate
students, graduate students. *Eligibility: Applicants
must be members of the organization for at least
three years prior to application, who are at least
on a $1,000 legal reserve certificate. Applicants
should be able to demonstrate a commitment to
civic and volunteer activities as well as demonstrate
leadership potential. *Application Process: Applicants
should submit a completed application along
with a 500-word personal statement on their
goals and objectives. Applicants must also submit
a wallet-size photograph, a copy of their college
acceptance letter, and all relevant transcripts. Visit
the organization's Web site for additional information
on specific memorial scholarships and to download
an application. *Amount: $1,250 (undergraduate
students); $1,750 (graduate students). *Deadline:
March 1.

First Catholic Slovak Ladies Association

Attn: Director of Fraternal Scholarship Aid
24950 Chagrin Boulevard
Beachwood, OH 44122
216-464-8015, 800-464-4642
info@fcsla.com
http://www.fcsla.com/scholarship.shtml
Scholarship Name: High School Scholarship.
*Academic Area: Open. *Age Group: High school
students. *Eligibility: Applicants must be members
of the organization for at least three years prior
to application, who are at least on a $1,000 legal
reserve certificate. Applicants must attend or want to
attend a private or Catholic accredited high school
in the United States or Canada. Applicants should
be able to demonstrate involvement in civic and
volunteer activities. *Application Process: Applicants
should submit a completed application along with
a 250-word personal statement on "What this high
school scholarship will do for me." Applicants must
also submit a wallet-size photograph, a copy of their
high school acceptance letter, and school transcripts.
Visit the organization's Web site to download an
application. *Amount: $1,000. *Deadline: March 1.

First Catholic Slovak Ladies Association

Attn: Director of Fraternal Scholarship Aid
24950 Chagrin Boulevard

Beachwood, OH 44122
216-464-8015, 800-464-4642
info@fcsla.com
http://www.fcsla.com/scholarship.shtml
Scholarship Name: Seminarian (College) Scholarship. *Academic Area: Religion. *Age Group: Undergraduate students, graduate students, seminary students. *Eligibility: Applicants must be members of the organization for at least three years prior to application, who are at least on a $1,000 legal reserve certificate. Applicants should be able to demonstrate a commitment to civic and volunteer activities as well as demonstrate leadership potential. They also should be able to demonstrate a commitment to seminary study. *Application Process: Applicants should submit a completed application along with a 500-word personal statement on their goals and objectives. Applicants must also submit a wallet-size photograph, a copy of their college acceptance letter, and any relevant transcripts. Any member who is studying for the priesthood should apply, as scholarship funds will be automatic, pending satisfaction of all requirements. *Amount: Awards vary. *Deadline: March 1.

First Presbyterian Church
c/o San Antonio Area Foundation
Attn: Penny Simone
404 North Alamo
San Antonio, TX 78205
210-225-2243
info@saafdn.org
http://www.saafdn.org/scholarship/scholar_funds_detail.php
Scholarship Name: Ida V. Holland Missionary Scholarship. *Academic Area: Religion. *Age Group: Undergraduate students, graduate students, seminary students. *Eligibility: Applicants must be between the ages of 18 and 24 and preparing to enter the seminary or become a missionary. Applicants should also be attending a Moody School (or a school of equal standing). *Application Process: Applicants should submit a request for an application in writing. *Amount: Awards vary. *Deadline: Deadlines vary (determined by committee; additional information is typically available on the application).

Fund for Theological Education Inc.
Attn: Sharon Watson Fluker, Vice President for Doctoral Programs and Administration

825 Houston Mill Road, Suite 250
Atlanta, GA 30329
404-727-1450
http://www.thefund.org/programs
Fellowship Name: African American Ph.D./Th.D. Scholars Fellowships. *Academic Area: Religion. *Age Group: Graduate students. *Eligibility: Applicants must be currently enrolled in a Ph.D. or Th.D. program in theological or religious studies and must be African American. They also must be U.S. or Canadian citizens with a high record of academic achievement and a commitment to teaching. Two types of fellowships are awarded: dissertation fellowships and doctoral fellowships. Eligibility requirements for each differ slightly; visit the fund's Web site for further information about eligibility requirements. *Application Process: Applicants should submit a completed application along with a resume, a three-page essay, undergraduate/graduate transcripts, and two letters of reference. Additional materials, including a one-page prospectus and abstract, a budget statement form, and a statement regarding financial aid already received are required of applicants for the dissertation fellowship. Visit the fund's Web site to download an application. *Amount: Up to $15,000. *Deadline: February 1 (dissertation fellowship); March 1 (doctoral fellowship).

Fund for Theological Education Inc.
Attn: Nikol Reed, Fellowships Administrator
North American Doctoral Fellowship Program
825 Houston Mill Road, Suite 250
Atlanta, GA 30329
404-727-1450
http://www.thefund.org/programs
Fellowship Name: Racial/Ethnic Ph.D./Th.D. Scholars Fellowship. *Academic Area: Religion. *Age Group: Graduate students. *Eligibility: Applicants must be currently enrolled in a Ph.D. or Th.D. program in theological or religious studies and must be a member of a racial or ethnic group that is traditionally underrepresented in graduate programs. They also must be U.S. or Canadian citizens with a high record of academic achievement and a commitment to teaching. *Application Process: Applicants should submit a completed application along with a curriculum vitae, a two-page essay, graduate transcripts, an academic form, a budget statement form, and documentation showing the amount of financial aid already received. Visit the fund's Web

site to download all of the forms and an application. *Amount: $5,000 to $10,000. *Deadline: March 1.

Fund for Theological Education Inc.
Attn: Melissa Wiginton, Vice President for Ministry
  Programs and Planning
825 Houston Mill Road, Suite 250
Atlanta, GA 30329
404-727-1450
http://www.thefund.org/programs
Fellowship Name: Support for Seminary Students
  Fellowships. *Academic Area: Religion. *Age Group:
  Seminary students. *Eligibility: Applicants must have
  an intent to enter ministry as a profession, be U.S. or
  Canadian citizens, and be 35 years of age or younger.
  There are two kinds of fellowships available: ministry
  fellowships and congregational fellowships. Visit the
  fund's Web site for specific eligibility requirements
  for each. *Application Process: Applicants should
  submit a completed application along with a
  statement of intent to enter the ministry, a resume,
  a three-page essay, undergraduate transcripts, two
  letters of reference, and a profile of the congregation
  (congregational fellowships only). Application
  materials may vary slightly depending on whether
  the applicant is applying for a ministry fellowship
  or congregational fellowship. Visit the fund's Web
  site to download the applications, which outline
  specific requirements and procedures for each type of
  fellowship. *Amount: Awards vary. *Deadline: April 1.

Fund for Theological Education Inc.
Attn: Melissa Wiginton, Vice President for Ministry
  Programs and Planning
825 Houston Mill Road, Suite 250
Atlanta, GA 30329
404-727-1450
http://www.thefund.org/programs
Fellowship Name: Undergraduate Fellowships. *Academic
  Area: Religion. *Age Group: Undergraduate students.
  *Eligibility: Applicants must be college juniors or
  seniors in an accredited program at a North American
  college or university who have an interest in entering
  the ministry as a profession. They must be U.S. or
  Canadian citizens, have at least a 3.0 GPA, and have a
  love of God and a desire to share that faith with others.
  *Application Process: Applicants should submit a
  completed application along with a three-page essay,
  a resume, undergraduate transcripts, and two letters
  of reference. Visit the fund's Web site to download an

application. *Amount: $1,500, plus $500 to support a
mentoring relationship. *Deadline: March 1.

The Gertrude Butts Memorial Home Association
c/o The Episcopal Diocese of Newark
31 Mulberry Street
Newark, NJ 07102
973-430-9983
http://www.dioceseofnewark.org/buttsfun.html
Scholarship Name: Gertrude Butts Memorial Scholarship.
  *Academic Area: Open. *Age Group: Undergraduate
  students. *Eligibility: Applicants must be active
  members in the Episcopalian church who can
  demonstrate financial need. *Application Process:
  Applicants should request an application form by
  phone. Along with the application, applicants should
  submit a letter explaining why the scholarship
  funds will be of assistance, their involvement in their
  congregation, a letter of support from a rector or vicar,
  a list of any jobs they have held while in high school,
  and a copy of their high school grades. *Amount: Up
  to $2,000. *Deadline: April 30.

International Order of The King's Daughters and Sons
Attn: Student Ministry Department Director
PO Box 1040
Chautauqua, NY 14722-1040
http://www.iokds.org/scholarship.html
Scholarship Name: Student Ministry Scholarship.
  *Academic Area: Religion. *Age Group: Graduate
  students, seminary students. *Eligibility: Applicants
  must be U.S. or Canadian citizens who are enrolled
  full time in an accredited master of divinity program.
  They also must have maintained at least a 3.0 GPA
  in all previous course work. *Application Process:
  Applicants must request an application by mail.
  Applicants should send the request along with a self-
  addressed, stamped legal size envelope. Applicants
  should submit a completed application along with
  transcripts and a budget signed by the financial aid
  office at the school or seminary. *Amount: $1,000.
  *Deadline: April 30.

Knights of Columbus
1 Columbus Plaza
New Haven, CT 06510
203-752-4000
info@kofc.org
http://www.kofc.org/un/about/activities/church/
  vocations/index.cfm

Scholarship Name: Father McGivney and Bishop Daily Vocations Scholarship. *Academic Area: Religion. *Age Group: Seminary students. *Eligibility: Applicants must be U.S. or Canadian seminary students who are attending an accredited school of theology. Applicants must also either exhibit financial need or demonstrate academic achievement. Preference is given to members of the Knights of Columbus or sons of members. *Application Process: Contact the organization for information on the application process. *Amount: $2,500; renewable for up to four years. *Deadline: Contact the organization for deadline information.

Knights of Columbus
1 Columbus Plaza
New Haven, CT 06510
203-752-4000
info@kofc.org
http://www.kofc.org/un/about/activities/church/vocations/index.cfm
Grant Name: Refund Support Vocations Program (RSVP). *Academic Area: Religion. *Age Group: Seminary students. *Eligibility: Applicants must be seminarians or postulants in need of financial assistance. *Application Process: Applicants should contact the Knights of Columbus to receive information about the application process. Visit the organization's Web site for a complete description of the program. *Amount: Up to $2,000. *Deadline: Contact the organization for deadline information.

Knights of Lithuania
Attn: John P. Baltrus, Scholarship Committee Chair
118 Vine Street
Jefferson Hills, PA 15025
http://www.knightsoflithuania.com/scholarships.html
Scholarship Name: Knights of Lithuania Scholarship. *Academic Area: Open. *Age Group: Undergraduate students, graduate students. *Eligibility: Applicants must be active members of the organization who exhibit a commitment to the community as well as financial need. *Application Process: Applicants should contact the committee chair by mail to request an application. *Amount: Awards vary. *Deadline: Contact the committee chair for deadline information.

MHS Alliance
Attn: Wendy Rohn
234 South Main Street, Suite 1

Goshen, IN 46526
574-534-9689, 800-611-4007
info@mhsonline.org
http://www.mhsonline.org/php/services/scholarship.php
Scholarship Name: Elmer Ediger Memorial Scholarship Fund. *Academic Area: Disability studies, medicine (mental health). *Age Group: Graduate students. *Eligibility: Applicants should be U.S. or Canadian citizens who are active members of a Mennonite, Brethren in Christ, or Mennonite Brethren congregation. They also should demonstrate academic achievement by maintaining at least a 3.25 GPA and exhibit a commitment to volunteer and community service. Extra consideration is give to those attending church-related colleges and those with financial need. *Application Process: Applicants should submit a completed application, which includes references and answers to short essay questions, along with transcripts. Visit the organization's Web site to download an application. *Amount: $1,000 to $1,200. *Deadline: April 1.

MHS Alliance
Attn: Wendy Rohn
234 South Main Street, Suite 1
Goshen, IN 46526
574-534-9689, 800-611-4007
info@mhsonline.org
http://www.mhsonline.org/php/services/scholarship.php
Loan Name: Miller-Erb Nursing Development Fund. *Academic Area: Nursing (open). *Age Group: Undergraduate students, graduate students. *Eligibility: Applicants must be involved in some branch of the nursing profession and desire the opportunity to work on a research or writing project, attend graduate school, or attend leadership training. Recipients who publish their work and and/or present it to a Mennonite constituency or nursing forum will have their loan forgiven. *Application Process: Applicants should submit a completed application, which includes a project proposal. Visit the organization's Web site to download an application. *Amount: $1,000 to $2,000. *Deadline: April 1.

Mustard Seed Foundation
The Harvey Fellows Program
3330 North Washington Boulevard, Suite 100
Arlington, VA 22201

703-524-5620

http://www.harveyfellows.org/

Fellowship Name: Harvey Fellows Program. *Academic Area: Open. *Age Group: Graduate students. *Eligibility: Applicants must be of the Christian faith and must strive to pursue culturally influential careers in which they find themselves, as Christians, addressing modern societal issues with impact. Applicants need not choose a major directly relating to religion, but rather any major in which Christians are traditionally underrepresented. They should be able to express why there is a need for a Christian voice in their particular field of choice. They also should demonstrate commitment to their local church, maturity, and leadership abilities. *Application Process: Applicants should submit four unbound collated copies of the application packet, which includes a completed application along with a resume, essays (detailed on the application), four letters of recommendation, test scores required for the applicant's admission to degree program (GRE, LSAT, GMAT, etc.), undergraduate and graduate transcripts, and a significant piece of work from the applicant's field of study (up to 25 pages). Visit the organization's Web site to download an application and to read more about the program. The application process opens on August 1. *Amount: $15,000, renewable. *Deadline: November 1.

Omaha Presbyterian Seminary Foundation

2120 South 72nd Street, Suite 630

Omaha, NE 68124

402-397-5138

OPSF@omaha-sem-found.org

http://www.omaha-sem-found.org/07A-studentaid.html

Scholarship Name: Omaha Presbyterian Seminary Foundation Scholarships and Grants. *Academic Area: Religion. *Age Group: Seminary students. *Eligibility: Applicants must be members of the Presbyterian Church (USA), under the care of a Presbytery, and be an exceptional candidate for ministry. They also must be accepted or enrolled in one of the following approved seminary schools: Austin Seminary, Columbia Seminary, Dubuque Seminary, Johnson C. Smith Seminary, Louisville Seminary, McCormick Seminary, Pittsburgh Seminary, Princeton Seminary, San Francisco Seminary, or Union Seminary/PSCE. *Application Process: Applicants should submit a completed application along with official transcripts. The top four candidates will receive scholarship funds,

while 11 additional candidates will receive conditional grants. Applicants receiving the grants must graduate and serve at least three years in a church vocation approved by the Presbyterian General Assembly to avoid having to repay the funds. Visit the foundation's Web site to download an application. *Amount: $4,000, renewable for three additional years (scholarship); $2,500, renewable for two additional years (grant). *Deadline: May 1.

Opal Dancey Memorial Foundation

Attn: Betty D. Goddard, Chair

2637 North Revere Road

Akron, OH 44333

bethinbath@juno.com

http://www.opaldanceygrants.org

Scholarship Name: Opal Dancey Memorial Foundation Scholarship. *Academic Area: Religion. *Age Group: Seminary students. *Eligibility: Applicants must be full-time students who plan to pursue a master of divinity degree. Applicants must also reside in the Great Lakes region of the United States and be planning to attend an accredited theological seminary in the Great Lakes region as well. *Application Process: Applicants must request an application from the foundation chair by mail between the dates of January 15 and May 15. Applicants should submit an application along with a statement of acceptance from a seminary, a recent photo, and at least two letters of recommendation. Visit the foundation's Web site for the application address and additional information. *Amount: $3,000, renewable for three additional years. *Deadline: April 15.

Society for the Increase of the Ministry

920 Farmington Avenue

Hartford, CT 06107

860-233-1732

simministry@earthlink.net

http://www.simministry.org

Scholarship Name: Society for the Increase of the Ministry Scholarship. *Academic Area: Religion. *Age Group: Seminary students. *Eligibility: Applicants should be full-time candidates for holy orders in the Episcopal Church in the United States, be attending or planning to attend one of 11 select schools, and able to demonstrate financial need. Visit the society's Web site for a list of eligible schools. *Application Process: Applicants should request an application from the financial aid officer at their school. Applications should be submitted along with four letters of reference to the financial aid office (not the foundation). *Amount: $1,500 to $2,000. *Deadline: March 1.

United Methodist Division on Ministries with Young People

PO Box 340003
Nashville, TN 37203-0003
877-899-2780
umyouth@gbod.org
http://www.gbod.org
Scholarship Name: David W. Self Scholarship. *Academic Area: Religion. *Age Group: Undergraduate students. *Eligibility: Applicants must be United Methodist high school graduating seniors who have been active in their church for a least one year. They also must be U.S. citizens or permanent residents, admitted to a full-time degree program, maintaining a 2.0 high school GPA, planning to pursue a "church-related" career, and able to demonstrate financial need. *Application Process: Applicants should submit a completed application. Visit the organization's Web site to download an application. *Amount: $1,000. *Deadline: June 1.

United Methodist Division on Ministries with Young People

PO Box 340003
Nashville, TN 37203-0003
877-899-2780
umyouth@gbod.org
http://www.gbod.org
Scholarship Name: Richard S. Smith Scholarship. *Academic Area: Religion. *Age Group: Undergraduate students. *Eligibility: Applicants must be United Methodist high school graduating seniors who have been active in their church for a least one year. They also must be members of a racial or ethnic minority, U.S. citizens or permanent residents, admitted to a full-time degree program, maintaining a 2.0 high school GPA, planning to pursue a "church-related" career, and able to demonstrate financial need. *Application Process: Applicants should submit a completed application. Visit the organization's Web site to download an application. *Amount: $1,000. *Deadline: June 1.

Vance H. Havner Scholarship Fund Inc.

PO Box 9946
Greensboro, NC 27429

info@vancehavner.org
http://www.vancehavner.org/index.
    php?action=website-view&WebSiteID=74&WebPag
    eID=1283
Award Name: Vance H. Havner Preaching Award. *Academic Area: Religion. *Age Group: Seminary students. *Eligibility: Applicants must be third-year master of divinity students who demonstrate exceptional skill in preaching and who aspire to careers that emphasize preaching. *Application Process: Applicants should contact the organization for an application and further information on the application process. *Amount: $3,000. *Deadline: Contact the organization for deadline information.

Woman's Missionary Union (WMU) Foundation

Attn: Linda Lucas, Administrative Support
PO Box 11346
Birmingham, AL 35202-1346
205-408-5508, 877-482-4483
llucas@wmu.org
http://www.wmufoundation.com/scholar_summary.asp
Scholarship Name: WMU Foundation Scholarships. *Academic Area: Religion. *Age Group: Undergraduate students, graduate students. *Eligibility: This Christian foundation offers various scholarships with many different eligibility requirements. Applicants should visit the foundation's Web site for a complete list of scholarships and their respective eligibility requirements. *Application Process: Applicants should visit the foundation's Web site to download an application and to view the many scholarships available. Applicants should submit an application along with transcripts, a description of proposed project (if applicable), and a recent photograph. *Amount: Awards vary. *Deadline: Deadlines vary.

Women of the Evangelical Lutheran Church in America

Scholarship Program
8765 West Higgins Road
Chicago, IL 60631-4101
800-638-3522, ext. 2736
http://www.womenoftheelca.org
Scholarship Name: Amelia Kemp Scholarship. *Academic Area: Open. *Age Group: Undergraduate students, graduate students, professionals. *Eligibility: Evangelical Lutheran Church in America (ELCA) women of color in undergraduate, graduate, professional, or vocational courses of study may apply. Applicants

must be U.S. citizens, members of the ELCA, be at least 21 years of age, and have experienced an interruption in education of two or more years since graduating from high school. They also should be involved in Women of the ELCA. *Application Process: Applicants must submit an academic reference form, a completed application, a pastor's reference form, and a personal reference form. *Amount: $600 to $1,000. *Deadline: February 15.

Women of the Evangelical Lutheran Church in America
Scholarship Program
8765 West Higgins Road
Chicago, IL 60631-4101
800-638-3522, ext. 2736
http://www.womenoftheelca.org/whatwedo/arne.html
Scholarship Name: Arne Administrative Leadership Scholarship. *Academic Area: Business administration. *Age Group: Graduate students. *Eligibility: Applicants must be U.S. citizens, members of the Evangelical Lutheran Church in America (ELCA), and have at least a bachelor's degree. They also should be involved in Women of the ELCA and provide examples of their decision-making abilities and a commitment to their education. *Application Process: Applicants must submit an academic reference form, a completed application, a pastor's reference form, a personal reference form, and a letter of recommendation from a faculty member who has taught the applicant in the last three years. *Amount: $500 to $1,000. *Deadline: February 15.

Women of the Evangelical Lutheran Church in America
Scholarship Program
8765 West Higgins Road
Chicago, IL 60631-4101
800-638-3522, ext. 2736
http://www.womenoftheelca.org/whatwedo/belmer.html
Scholarship Name: Belmer, Flora Prince, and Kahler, Vickers/Raup, Wettstein Opportunity Scholarship for Lutheran Laywomen. *Academic Area: Open. *Age Group: Undergraduate students, graduate students. *Eligibility: Applicants must be U.S. citizens, members of the Evangelical Lutheran Church in America (ELCA), at least 21 years of age, and have experienced an interruption in education of two or more years since graduating from high school. They also should be

involved in Women of the ELCA and preparing for ELCA service abroad, either in general, or in health professions associated with ELCA projects abroad. *Application Process: Applicants must submit an academic reference form, a completed application, a pastor's reference form, and a personal reference form. *Amount: $800 to $1,000. *Deadline: February 15.

Women of the Evangelical Lutheran Church in America
Scholarship Program
8765 West Higgins Road
Chicago, IL 60631-4101
800-638-3522, ext. 2736
http://www.womenoftheelca.org/whatwedo/chilstrom.html
Scholarship Name: Chilstrom Scholarship for Ordained Ministry. *Academic Area: Religion. *Age Group: Seminary students. *Eligibility: Evangelical Lutheran Church in America (ELCA) women who are second career students in their final year of study at an ELCA seminary may apply. Applicants must be U.S. citizens, members of the ELCA, have been out of college at least five years, be endorsed by the Synodical Candidacy Committee, and be preparing for the ordained ministry in the ELCA. They also should be involved in Women of the ELCA. *Application Process: Applicants must submit an academic reference form, a completed application, letters from their academic dean or dean of students certifying that they are enrolled in a master of divinity program and in good academic standing, a letter of recommendation from a member of the seminary faculty, and a letter of endorsement from their Synodical Candidacy Committee. *Amount: Awards range from $600 to $2,000. *Deadline: February 15.

Women of the Evangelical Lutheran Church in America
Scholarship Program
8765 West Higgins Road
Chicago, IL 60631-4101
800-638-3522, ext. 2736
http://www.womenoftheelca.org/whatwedo/cronk.html
Scholarship Name: Cronk, First Triennium Board, General, Mehring, Paepke, Piero/Wade/Wade, Edwin/Edna Robeck Opportunity Scholarship for Lutheran Laywomen. *Academic Area: Open. *Age Group: Undergraduate students, graduate students. *Eligibility: Applicants must be U.S. citizens, members

of the Evangelical Lutheran Church in America (ELCA), be at least 21 years of age, and have experienced an interruption in education of two or more years since graduating from high school. They also should be involved in Women of the ELCA. *Application Process: Applicants must submit an academic reference form, a completed application, a pastor's reference form, and a personal reference form. *Amount: $1,000. *Deadline: February 15.

Women of the Evangelical Lutheran Church in America

Scholarship Program
8765 West Higgins Road
Chicago, IL 60631-4101
800-638-3522, ext. 2736
http://www.womenoftheelca.org/whatwedo/drinkall.html
Scholarship Name: Irene Drinkall Franke, Mary Seeley Knudstrup Opportunity Scholarship for Lutheran Laywomen. *Academic Area: Open. *Age Group: Undergraduate students, graduate students. *Eligibility: Applicants must be U.S. citizens, members of the Evangelical Lutheran Church in America (ELCA), be at least 21 years of age, and have experienced an interruption in education of two or more years since graduating from high school. They also should be involved in Women of the ELCA and preparing for occupations in Christian service. *Application Process: Applicants must submit an academic reference form, a completed application, a pastor's reference form, and a personal reference form. *Amount: $800 to $1,000. *Deadline: February 15.

ISLAM

Chicagoland Muslim Scholarship Fund

5901 North Cicero, Suite 309
Chicago, IL 60646
applicants@chicagomsf.org
http://www.chicagomsf.org
Scholarship Name: Chicagoland Muslim Scholarship Fund. *Academic Area: Business, communication, computer science, engineering (open), food science, Islamic studies. *Age Group: Undergraduate students. *Eligibility: Applicants must be U.S. citizens or permanent legal residents who are Muslim and are residing in the greater Chicagoland area. They also must be enrolled in an accredited

four-year U.S. university, maintain at least a 3.3 GPA, be able to demonstrate financial need, and show a commitment to involvement in the Islamic community. *Application Process: Applicants should submit a completed and signed application along with documentation of tuition costs, fees, and student loans and official transcripts. Applicants should enclose all information in one envelope and mail via U.S. mail. Visit the organization's Web site to download an application. *Amount: $1,000. *Deadline: July 1.

National Muslim Scholarship Fund

c/o The Freedom and Justice Foundation
PO Box 262366
Plano, TX 75026
972-365-8214
info@freeandjust.org
http://www.nmsf.us
Scholarship Name: National Muslim Scholarship Fund. *Academic Area: Open. *Age Group: Undergraduate students, graduate students. *Eligibility: Muslim American students who are interested in receiving scholarship funds should contact the organization regarding the availability of funds and eligibility requirements. This fund was established in 2004 and plans to have guidelines on eligibility requirements and disbursement of funds available soon. *Application Process: Contact the organization about how to apply for available funds. *Amount: Awards vary. *Deadline: Contact the organization for deadline information.

JUDAISM

American Sephardi Foundation

Broome & Allen Boys Camp & Scholarship Fund Inc.
American Sephardi Federation with Sephardic House
15 West 16th Street
New York, NY 10011
212-294-8301, ext. 8358
http://www.americansephardifederation.org
Scholarship Name: Broome and Allen Scholarship Fund. *Academic Area: Open, religion. *Age Group: Undergraduate students, graduate students. *Eligibility: Applicants must be attending college or university in the United States, but need not be U.S. citizens. Applicants must either be of Sephardic heritage or concentrating in Sephardic studies and must also demonstrate academic achievement and

a commitment to community service. *Application Process: Applicants should submit a completed application along with two letters of recommendation, a copy of their federal income tax return for the year immediately preceding the date of the application, and official school transcripts. Visit the organization's Web site for complete details regarding transcript submittal and additional application information. *Amount: Awards vary. *Deadline: May 15.

Memorial Foundation for Jewish Culture
50 Broadway, 34th Floor
New York, NY 10004
office@mfjc.org
http://www.memorialfoundation.org/scholarship/index.htm
Scholarship Name: International Community Service Scholarship. *Academic Area: Education, religion, social work. *Age Group: Undergraduate students, graduate students. *Eligibility: Applicants must be individuals enrolled in, or planning to enroll in, a college, university, teacher training seminary, or yeshiva. Applicants must commit to at least two years of service in a community of need in another country. The United States, Canada, and Israel are not options for this service. Applicants should have an understanding of the language and culture of the area they plan to serve in, or must be prepared to learn. *Application Process: Applicants should request a formal application by mail or e-mail. Contact the organization for further information. *Amount: Awards vary. *Deadline: November 30.

Memorial Foundation for Jewish Culture
50 Broadway, 34th Floor
New York, NY 10004
office@mfjc.org
http://www.memorialfoundation.org/scholarship/index.htm
Scholarship Name: International Doctoral Scholarship for Studies Specializing in Jewish Fields. *Academic Area: Religion. *Age Group: Graduate students. *Eligibility: Applicants must be graduate students enrolled in an accredited college or university doctoral program. They also should be pursuing a career in Jewish scholarship or research. Preference is given to applicants who are beginning work on their dissertations. *Application Process: Applicants should request a formal application by mail or e-mail. Applicants must submit a completed application along

with letters of reference. Contact the organization for further information. *Amount: Up to $7,500, renewable for up to four years. *Deadline: October 31.

Memorial Foundation for Jewish Culture
50 Broadway, 34th Floor
New York, NY 10004
office@mfjc.org
http://www.memorialfoundation.org/scholarship/index.htm
Fellowship Name: International Fellowships in Jewish Studies and Jewish Culture. *Academic Area: Religion. *Age Group: Open. *Eligibility: Applicants should be scholars, researchers, or artists who want to undertake a project that will, in some way, help contribute to the understanding and preservation of the Jewish culture. *Application Process: Applicants should request a formal application by mail. Applicants must submit a completed application along with a project proposal and letters of reference. Contact the organization by mail for further information. *Amount: Up to $7,500. *Deadline: October 31.

Wexner Foundation
Office of Graduate Fellowship Program
8000 Walton Parkway, Suite 110
New Albany, OH 43054
614-939-6060
info@wexlerfoundation.org
http://www.wexnerfoundation.org/GFA
Fellowship Name: Wexner Graduate Fellows/Davidson Scholars Program. Academic Area: Education, religion. *Age Group: Graduate students, seminary students. *Eligibility: Applicants must be between the ages of 21 and 40 with a commitment to serving the Jewish community as a Jewish professional in one of the following areas: Jewish education, Jewish communal leadership, the rabbinate, the cantorate, and Jewish studies. Applicants must demonstrate academic achievement and possess leadership potential. *Application Process: Applicants should submit a completed application, either in hard copy or online, along with transcripts, GRE scores, three letters of recommendation, and an acceptance letter from a graduate school. Visit the foundation's Web site to download an application or to apply online. *Amount: $5,000 to $20,000, depending on the applicant's area of study. (Renewable for two additional years.) *Deadline: February 1.

UNITED NEGRO COLLEGE FUND SCHOLARSHIPS

The United Negro College Fund (UNCF) is the nation's oldest and most successful African-American higher education assistance organization. It is a consortium of 39 private, accredited historically black colleges and universities. UNCF offers programs designed to enhance the quality of education for America's brightest young minds, and is committed to providing financial assistance to deserving students, raising operating funds for member colleges and universities, and supplying technical assistance to member institutions. UNCF oversees more than 450 scholarship programs; visit its Web site for a listing of opportunities and application information. A sampling of UNCF undergraduate and graduate scholarships is listed below. For more information, contact the United Negro College Fund (8260 Willow Oaks Corporate Drive, PO Box 10444, Fairfax, VA 22031-8044, 800-331-2244, http://www.uncf.org)

Abercrombie & Fitch Scholarship Program
Scholarship Name: Abercrombie and Fitch Scholarship Program. *Academic Area: Open. *Age Group: Undergraduate students. *Eligibility: Applicants must be college freshmen enrolled in an accredited four-year college or university and maintain a 3.0 GPA. Applicants must also be African Americans, Asian Americans, American Indians, or Hispanic Americans who are U.S. citizens or permanent residents of the United States. *Application Process: Applicants must submit a completed application along with a one-page essay, official transcripts, two letters of recommendation, and a headshot photo. *Amount: $3,000. *Deadline: October 28.

Alliant Techsystems Internship/Scholarship
Scholarship Name: Alliant Techsystems Internship/Scholarship. *Academic Area: Accounting. *Age Group: Undergraduate students. *Eligibility: Applicants must have a 3.0 GPA and be sophomores and juniors attending one of the 39 UNCF member colleges and universities. Application Process: Applicants must participate in a paid summer internship prior to receiving a scholarship the following academic year. Visit the UNCF's Web site to connect to the sponsor's Web site to download an application. *Amount: $5,000. *Deadline: Deadlines vary.

Alton and Dorothy Higgins MD Scholarship
Scholarship Name: Alton and Dorothy Higgins MD Scholarship. *Academic Area: Medicine (open). *Age Group: Undergraduate students, graduate students. *Eligibility: Applicants must maintain a 3.0 GPA, show financial need, and be attending one of the UNCF member colleges or universities. The scholarship is open to college juniors and seniors and graduate students. *Application Process: Applicants should submit a completed application along with two letters of recommendation, an essay, transcripts, a financial need statement, an acceptance notification from medical school (for incoming graduate students), and a small headshot photo. Visit the UNCF Web site to download an application. *Amount: $5,000 to $10,000. *Deadline: June 4.

American Hotel Foundation Scholarship
Scholarship Name: American Hotel Foundation Scholarship. *Academic Area: Management. *Age Group: Undergraduate students, graduate students. *Eligibility: Applicants must maintain a 2.5 GPA and attend one of the 39 UNCF member colleges or universities. *Application Process: Applicants must have unmet need as verified by the university financial aid office, complete the Free Application for Federal Student Aid (FAFSA), and must request that the Student Analysis Report (SAR) be sent to the financial aid office at their college or university. Students should complete their online student profiles at the UNCF Web site. *Amount: $1,500. *Deadline: Deadlines vary.

Athena Group L.L.C. Scholarship
Scholarship Name: Athena Group L.L.C. Scholarship. *Academic Area: Finance. *Age Group: Undergraduate students. *Eligibility: Applicants must be female residents of the New York City metropolitan area, college sophomores or juniors, attending one of the 39 UNCF member colleges or universities. Applicants must have a 3.0 GPA and have a declared finance major. *Application Process: Applicants should submit a completed application along with two nomination

letters, a 500-word essay (topic determined by the sponsoring company), undergraduate school transcripts, a resume, and a small headshot photograph. Visit the UNCF Web site to download an application. *Amount $7,000. *Deadline: March 4.

AXA Foundation Fund Achievement Scholarship
Scholarship Name: AXA Foundation Fund Achievement Scholarship. *Academic Area: Business. *Age Group: Undergraduate students, graduate students. *Eligibility: Applicants must be residents of New York who are attending or planning to attend one of the UNCF member colleges or universities. Applicants must also maintain a 3.0 GPA, show unmet financial need, demonstrate a commitment to community service, and exhibit high academic achievement and leadership ability. High school seniors are also eligible to apply for this scholarship. *Application Process: Applicants should contact the sponsoring organization directly for application materials. *Amount: $2,00 to $5,000. *Deadline: Deadlines vary.

Bank of America Scholarship
Scholarship Name: Bank of America Scholarship. *Academic Area: Business, computer science, education, finance, information technology, marketing. *Age Group: Undergraduate students, graduate students. *Eligibility: Applicants must maintain a 2.5 GPA and attend one of the following UNCF colleges or universities located in one of the Bank of America core states: Benedict College, Bennett College for Women, Bethune-Cookman College, Claflin University, Clark Atlanta University, Edward Waters College, Fisk University, Florida Memorial College, Huston-Tillotson College, Jarvis Christian College, Johnson C. Smith University, Lane College, LeMoyne-Owen College, Livingstone College, Morehouse College, Morris College, Paine College, Paul Quinn College, Philander Smith College, Saint Augustine's College, Saint Paul's College, Shaw University, Spelman College, Virginia Union University, Voorhees College, or Wiley College. *Application Process: Applicants should contact the sponsoring company directly for application information. *Amount: $1,000. *Deadline: November 25.

Benice Michaelson Diamond Fund
Scholarship Name: Benice Michaelson Diamond Fund. *Academic Area: Open. *Age Group: Undergraduate students, graduate students. *Eligibility: Applicants

must be attending one of the 39 UNCF member colleges or universities, maintain a 2.5 GPA, and demonstrate unmet financial need. Applicants also must be able to prove that their parents are or were members of a trade union. *Application Process: Applicants should submit a completed application, one letter of recommendation, and a personal statement detailing their career goals. Visit the UNCF Web site to download an application. *Amount: Awards vary. *Deadline: September 17.

Best Buy Scholarship Programs
Scholarship Name: Best Buy Scholarship Program. *Academic Area: Accounting, advertising, business, communications, computer science, finance, journalism, marketing, retail management. *Age Group: Undergraduate students. *Eligibility: Applicants must be attending one of the 39 UNCF member colleges or universities or Florida A&M University, maintain a 3.0 GPA, and show unmet financial need. Of the two types of scholarships offered (employee and nonemployee), the employee scholarship requires the student to have worked at Best Buy for at least six months. *Application Process: Applicants should submit a completed application along with a resume, official transcripts, two letters of recommendation, and a 500-word essay. Visit the UNCF Web site to download an application. *Amount: $2,500 (employee); $5,000 (nonemployee). *Deadline: November 5.

Cardinal Health Scholarship
Scholarship Name: Cardinal Health Scholarship. *Academic Area: Accounting, chemistry, computer science, engineering (computer), engineering (open), finance, information systems, information technology, marketing, operations management, pharmaceutical sciences. *Age Group: Undergraduate students. *Eligibility: Applicants must be freshmen, sophomores, or juniors attending accredited four-year colleges or universities, maintain a 3.0 GPA, demonstrate noncollegiate leadership experience, and unmet financial need. *Application Process: Applicants should submit a completed application along with official transcripts and a personal statement. Visit the UNCF's Web site to download an application. *Amount: $5,000. *Deadline: October 30.

Carolyn Bailey Thomas Scholarship
Scholarship Name: Carolyn Bailey Thomas Scholarship. *Academic Area: Open. *Age Group: Undergraduate

students, graduate students. *Eligibility: Applicants must maintain a 3.0 GPA, demonstrate financial need, and attend or plan to attend one of the 39 UNCF member colleges or universities. High school seniors are also eligible to apply for this scholarship. *Application Process: Applicants should contact the sponsoring institution directly for information on application procedures. *Amount: Awards vary, based on need. *Deadline: Deadlines vary.

Castle Rock Foundation Scholarship
Scholarship Name: Castle Rock Foundation Scholarship. *Academic Area: Business, engineering (open). *Age Group: Undergraduate students, graduate students. *Eligibility: Applicants must be attending or planning to attend one of the following participating schools: Bethune-Cookman College, LeMoyne-Owen College, Morehouse College, Shaw University, Spelman College, Tuskegee University, or Xavier University. Applicants must also maintain a 2.5 GPA. High school seniors are also eligible to apply for this scholarship. *Application Process: Applicants should contact the scholarship sponsor directly for application information. *Amount: $3,600. *Deadline: Deadlines vary.

Catherine W. Pierce Scholarship
Scholarship Name: Catherine W. Pierce Scholarship. *Academic Area: History, visual arts (open). *Age Group: Undergraduate students, graduate students. *Eligibility: Applicants must maintain a 3.0 GPA and demonstrate financial need. *Application Process: Applicants should submit an application along with supporting materials. Visit the UNCF Web site to download an application. *Amount: Up to $5,000. *Deadline: Deadlines vary.

CDM Scholarship/Internship
Scholarship Name: CDM Scholarship/Internship. *Academic Area: Engineering (open). *Age Group: Undergraduate students, graduate students. *Eligibility: Applicants must be attending one of the 39 participating UNCF colleges or universities, maintain a 3.0 GPA, and be willing to accept a paid summer internship with the sponsoring company. *Application Process: Applicants should submit a completed application along with two letters of recommendation, official transcripts, and an updated resume. Visit the UNCF Web site to download the application. *Amount: $5,000, plus a $2,000 living expenses stipend for the internship. *Deadline: March 1.

ChevronTexaco Scholars Program
Scholarship Name: ChevronTexaco Scholars Program. *Academic Area: Engineering (open). *Age Group: Undergraduate students. *Eligibility: Applicants must be sophomores and juniors attending one of the following participating UNCF schools: Clark Atlanta University, Morehouse College, Spelman College, or Tuskegee University. Applicants must also maintain a 2.5 GPA, demonstrate financial need, exhibit leadership skills, and have a commitment to community service. *Application Process: Applicants should submit a completed application along with transcripts, resume, a nomination letter from a faculty member, two personal references, and a one-page statement of career interest. Visit the UNCF Web site to download an application. *Amount: Up to $3,000. *Deadline: March 21.

Chrysler Corporation Scholarship
Scholarship Name: Chrysler Corporation Scholarship. *Academic Area: Open. *Age Group: Undergraduate students, graduate students. *Eligibility: Applicants must be attending or planning to attend one of the 39 UNCF member colleges or universities and maintain a 2.5 GPA. High school seniors are also eligible to apply for this scholarship. *Application Process: Applicants should download an application from the UNCF Web site and submit it along with supporting materials. *Amount: $3,900. *Deadline: Deadlines vary.

Cisco/United Negro College Fund Scholars Program
Scholarship Name: Cisco/United Negro College Fund Scholars Program. *Academic Area: Computer science, engineering (electrical). *Age Group: Undergraduate students. *Eligibility: Applicants must be sophomores attending one of the following UNCF member schools: Claflin University, Clark Atlanta University, Dillard University, Jarvis Christian College, Johnson C. Smith University, Livingstone College, Morehouse College, Paul Quinn College, Rust College, Saint Augustine's College, Shaw University, Spelman College, Wiley College, or Xavier University. Applicants also most maintain a 3.2 GPA and agree to participate in an internship with the sponsoring company. Preference is given to women and those who demonstrate a commitment to community service. *Application Process: Applicants should contact the scholarship sponsor for application information. *Amount: $4,000. *Deadline: Deadlines vary.

C.R. Bard Scholarship and Internship Program

Scholarship Name: C.R. Bard Scholarship and Internship Program. *Academic Area: Business. *Age Group: Undergraduate students. *Eligibility: Applicants must be residents of New Jersey who are sophomores attending one of the 39 UNCF member colleges or universities and must maintain a 3.0 GPA. Applicants also must accept a paid summer internship at the C. R. Bard headquarters in Murray Hill, New Jersey. *Application Process: Applicants should contact the scholarship sponsor directly for application information. *Amount: $4,000. *Deadline: Deadlines vary.

C-SPAN Scholarship Program

Scholarship Name: C-SPAN Scholarship Program. *Academic Area: Broadcasting, communication sciences, English/literature, film/video, history, political science, radio/TV. *Age Group: Undergraduate students. *Eligibility: Applicants must be college sophomores or juniors attending one of the 39 UNCF member colleges or universities, maintain a 3.0 GPA, and demonstrate unmet financial need. Accepting an internship with the sponsoring company is part of this scholarship opportunity. *Application Process: Applicants should submit a completed application along with two nomination letters from faculty members, transcripts, resume, a 300-word essay, and a small headshot photo. Visit the UNCF Web site to download an application. *Amount: $2,000 (one time), plus a $200 weekly stipend. *Deadline: April 8.

Doris and John Carpenter Scholarship

Scholarship Name: Doris and John Carpenter Scholarship. *Academic Area: Open. *Age Group: Undergraduate students. *Eligibility: Applicants must be undergraduate freshman attending, or high school seniors planning to attend, one of the 39 UNCF member colleges or universities. They must maintain a 2.5 and demonstrate financial need. The scholarship is awarded to students who demonstrate the greatest financial need. *Application Process: Applicants should contact the scholarship sponsor directly for application information. *Amount: $2,000 to $5,000. *Deadline: Deadlines vary.

Dorothy N. McNeal Scholarship

Scholarship Name: Dorothy N. McNeal Scholarship. *Academic Area: Open. *Age Group: Undergraduate students, graduate students. *Eligibility: Applicants must maintain a 2.5 GPA, demonstrate unmet financial need, and attend or plan to attend one of the 39 UNCF member colleges or universities. Applicants should be interested in pursuing careers related to community service. High school seniors are also eligible to apply for this scholarship. *Application Process: Applicants should contact the sponsoring institution for application procedures. *Amount: Awards vary, based on need. *Deadline: Deadlines vary.

Dr. James M. Rosin Scholarship

Scholarship Name: Dr. James M. Rosin Scholarship. *Academic Area: Medical (open). *Age Group: Undergraduate students, graduate students. *Eligibility: Applicants must maintain a 3.0 GPA, demonstrate financial need, and be committed to personal growth, to helping others, and to their education. *Application Process: Applicants should contact the sponsoring institution directly for information about application procedures. *Amount: $5,000. *Deadline: Deadlines vary.

Earl and Patricia Armstrong Scholarship

Scholarship Name: Earl and Patricia Armstrong Scholarship. *Academic Area: Biology, medicine (open). *Age Group: Undergraduate students, graduate students. *Eligibility: Applicants must maintain a 3.0 GPA, have unmet need as verified by their university's financial aid office, complete the Free Application for Federal Student Aid, and request that the Student Analysis Report be sent to their school's financial aid office. Students also must be attending one of the 39 UNCF member colleges or universities. Students can begin the application process by completing their online student profiles on the UNCF Web site. *Amount: Up to $3,000. *Deadline: Deadlines vary.

Ella Fitzgerald Charitable Foundation Scholarship

Scholarship Name: Ella Fitzgerald Charitable Foundation Scholarship. *Academic Area: Performing arts (music-general). *Age Group: Undergraduate students, graduate students. *Eligibility: Applicants must maintain a 2.5 GPA, show unmet financial need, and attend or be planning to attend one of the 39 UNCF member colleges or universities. High school seniors are also eligible to apply for this scholarship. *Application Process: Applicants should contact the sponsoring institution directly for application procedures. *Amount: Awards vary. *Deadline: Deadlines vary.

ESSENCE Scholars Program

Scholarship Name: ESSENCE Scholars Program. *Academic Area: Open. *Age Group: Undergraduate students. *Eligibility: Applicants must be female college sophomores or juniors attending one of the following UNCF member colleges or universities: Howard University or Hampton University. Applicants must also maintain a 3.0 GPA. *Application Process: Applicants should apply online via the UNCF Web site. *Amount: $10,000. *Deadline: October 15.

Fannie Mae Foundation Scholarship

Scholarship Name: Fannie Mae Foundation Scholarship. *Academic Area: Open. *Age Group: Undergraduate students. *Eligibility: Applicants must maintain a 3.0 GPA and be college juniors attending one of the following colleges or universities: Benedict College, Bethune-Cookman College, Johnson C. Smith University, LeMoyne-Owen College, and other UNCF participating schools. Applicants also must demonstrate financial need and be involved in community development programs. *Application Process: Applicants should submit a completed application along with a 500-word essay on their community service work, transcripts, two letters of recommendation, and a small headshot photograph. Visit the UNCF Web site to download an application. *Amount: Awards vary. *Deadline: November 5.

Financial Services Institution

Scholarship Name: Financial Services Institution Scholarship. *Academic Area: Finance. *Age Group: Undergraduate students, graduate students. *Eligibility: Applicants must maintain a 2.5 GPA, have unmet financial need, and be attending or planning to attend one of the 39 UNCF member colleges or universities. High school seniors are also eligible to apply for this scholarship. *Application Process: Applicants should contact the scholarship sponsor directly for application procedures. *Amount: Varies, based on need. *Deadline: Deadlines vary.

GAP Foundation Scholarship

Scholarship Name: GAP Foundation Scholarship. *Academic Area: Fashion, management. *Age Group: Undergraduate students, graduate students. *Eligibility: Applicants must maintain a 3.0 GPA, show unmet financial need, and attend or be planning to attend one of the 39 UNCF member colleges or universities. High school seniors are also eligible to apply for this scholarship. *Application Process: Applicants should submit a completed application along with transcripts, a resume, two nomination letters, a one-page essay on their career goals, and a financial need statement. Visit the UNCF Web site to download an application. *Amount: Up to $10,000. *Deadline: December 9.

Gates Millennium Scholarship

Scholarship Name: Gates Millennium Scholarship. *Academic Area: Mathematics, science. *Age Group: Undergraduate students. *Eligibility: Applicants must have at least a 3.3 GPA, show unmet financial need, and be entering freshman who are planning to attend one of the 39 UNCF member colleges or universities. The scholarship is open to African Americans, American Indians/Native Alaskans, Asian Pacific Islander Americans, and Hispanic Americans. *Application Process: Applicants should contact the scholarship sponsor directly for application procedures. *Amount: Awards vary. *Deadline: Deadlines vary.

General Mills Technology Scholars Award

Scholarship Name: General Mills Technology Scholars Award. *Academic Area: Engineering (open), food science. *Age Group: Undergraduate students. *Eligibility: Applicants must be U.S. citizens who are college juniors and seniors, maintain a 3.0 GPA, show unmet financial need, and are attending one of the UNCF member colleges and universities or selected Historically Black Colleges and Universities (HBCU) and majority institutions. Applicants must also show demonstrated leadership skills and academic achievement. *Application Process: Applicants should submit a completed application along with transcripts, resume, two recommendation letters, and a 500-word essay. Visit the UNCF Web site to download an application. *Amount: $5,000. *Deadline: November 4.

General Motors Sullivan Fellowship

Scholarship Name: General Motors Sullivan Fellowship. *Academic Area: Engineering (open). *Age Group: Undergraduate students. *Eligibility: Applicant must be college freshmen, sophomores, and juniors, maintain a 3.0 GPA, show unmet financial need, and attend or plan to attend one of the following schools: Clark Atlanta University, Morehouse College, Spelman

College, Tuskegee University. *Application Process: Applicants should contact the sponsoring institution directly for application procedures. *Amount: $5,000. *Deadline: Deadlines vary.

GlaxoSmithKline Company Science Achievement Award

Scholarship Name: GlaxoSmithKline Company Science Achievement Award. *Academic Area: Science. *Age Group: Graduate students. *Eligibility: Applicants must maintain a 3.0 GPA. Applicants can be attending any graduate school in the United States, but they must have graduated from a UNCF school. *Application Process: Applicants should submit a completed application along with an essay, transcripts, graduate school admission letter, two letters of recommendation, and a small headshot photo. Visit the UNCF Web site to download an application. *Amount: $3,000. *Deadline: January 23.

Houghton Mifflin Company Fellows Program/ Internship

Scholarship Name: Houghton Mifflin Company Fellows Program/Internship. *Academic Area: Publishing. *Age Group: Undergraduate students. *Eligibility: Applicants must be college juniors, maintain a 3.0 GPA, attend one of the 39 UNCF member colleges or universities, and have an interest in learning about the field of publishing. This scholarship is awarded in combination with a paid summer internship in publishing. *Application Process: Applicants should contact the sponsoring institution directly for application procedures. *Amount: $3,700 (scholarship), $3,300 (internship). *Deadline: Deadlines vary.

Intel Scholars Program

Scholarship Name: Intel Scholars Program. *Academic Area: Computer science, engineering (open). *Age Group: Undergraduate students. *Eligibility: Applicants must be college sophomores, maintain a 3.0 GPA, demonstrate financial need, and be attending one of the UNCF member colleges or universities or one of the following additional institutions: North Carolina A&T State University, North Carolina State University, Georgia Institute of Technology, or Tennessee State University. *Application Process: Applicants should apply online through a link on the UNCF Web site. *Amount: Up to $5,000. *Deadline: March 31.

Jack and Jill of America Foundation Scholarship

Scholarship Name: Jack and Jill of America Foundation Scholarship. *Academic Area: Open. *Age Group: Undergraduate students. *Eligibility: Applicants must be high school seniors, maintain a 3.0 GPA, have financial need, demonstrate leadership qualities, and must become and maintain full-time status at an accredited, postsecondary institution in the fall semester after receiving award. Applicants must also agree to complete 60 hours of community service in the year following the awarding of the scholarship. *Application Process: Applicants should submit a completed application along with a resume, high school transcripts, an essay, and two letters of recommendation. Visit the UNCF Web site to download an application. *Amount: $1,500 to $2,500. *Deadline: March 14.

Jeffry and Barbara Picower Foundation Scholarship

Scholarship Name: Jeffry and Barbara Picower Foundation Scholarship. *Academic Area: Open. *Age Group: Undergraduate students, graduate students. *Eligibility: Applicants must maintain a 3.0 GPA, demonstrate financial need, and attend or plan to attend one of the 39 UNCF member colleges or universities. High school seniors are also eligible to apply for this scholarship. *Application Process: Applicants should contact the sponsoring institution directly for application procedures. *Amount: $5,000. *Deadline: Deadlines vary.

Jesse Jones Jr. Scholarship

Scholarship Name: Jesse Jones, Jr. Scholarship. *Academic Area: Business. *Age Group: Undergraduate students. *Eligibility: Applicants must maintain a 2.5 GPA, demonstrate unmet financial need, and attend or be planning to attend one of the 39 UNCF member colleges or universities. High school seniors are also eligible to apply for this scholarship. *Application Process: Applicants should contact the sponsoring institution directly for application procedures. *Amount: $2,000 to $5,000. *Deadline: Deadlines vary.

Jimi Hendrix Endowment Fund Scholarship

Scholarship Name: Jimi Hendrix Endowment Fund Scholarship. *Academic Area: Performing arts (music-general). *Age Group: Undergraduate students. *Eligibility: Applicants must maintain a 2.5 GPA, show unmet financial need, and attend or be planning to attend one of the 39 UNCF member colleges or universities. High school seniors are also eligible to apply for this scholarship. *Application Process: Applicants should contact the sponsoring institution directly for application procedures. *Amount: $2,000 to $5,000. *Deadline: Deadlines vary.

John Lennon Scholarship
Scholarship Name: John Lennon Scholarship. *Academic Area: Communications, performing arts (music-general). *Age Group: Undergraduate students. *Eligibility: Applicants must maintain a 3.0 GPA, demonstrate financial need, and attend or plan to attend one of the 39 UNCF member colleges or universities. High school seniors are also eligible to apply for this scholarship. *Application Process: Applicants should submit a completed application along with transcripts, two references, an autobiographical essay, financial need statement, and a small headshot photo. Visit the UNCF Web site to download an application. *Amount: $5,000. *Deadline: February 13.

Mae Maxey Memorial Scholarship
Scholarship Name: Mae Maxey Memorial Scholarship. *Academic Area: Open. *Age Group: Undergraduate students. *Eligibility: Applicants must maintain a 2.5 GPA and be attending or planning to attend one of the 39 UNCF member colleges or universities. While the scholarship is open to all, students who express an interest in poetry are given priority. High school seniors are also eligible to apply for this scholarship. *Application Process: Applicants should contact the sponsoring institution directly for application procedures. *Amount: $1,000 to $5,000. *Deadline: Deadlines vary.

Malcolm X Scholarship for Exceptional Courage
Scholarship Name: Malcolm X Scholarship for Exceptional Courage. *Academic Area: Open. *Age Group: Undergraduate students. *Eligibility: Applicants must maintain a 2.5 GPA, demonstrate financial need, and attend or plan to attend one of the 39 UNCF member colleges or universities. They must also demonstrate academic excellence, and campus and community leadership. Applicants who have overcome tremendous obstacles, hardships, or special circumstances are encouraged to apply. High school seniors are also eligible to apply for this scholarship. *Application Process: Applicants should

submit a completed application along with an essay, transcripts, two recommendation letters, and a small headshot photo. Visit the UNCF Web site to download an application. *Amount: $4,000. *Deadline: March 7.

Mary E. Scott Memorial Scholarship
Scholarship Name: Mary E. Scott Memorial Scholarship. *Academic Area: Open. *Age Group: Undergraduate students. *Eligibility: Applicants must maintain a 2.5 GPA, demonstrate financial need, and attend or plan to attend one of the 39 UNCF member colleges or universities. High school seniors are also eligible to apply for this scholarship. *Application Process: Applicants should contact the sponsoring institution directly to obtain application procedures. *Amount: $1,500 to $5,000. *Deadline: Deadlines vary.

Maytag Company Scholarship
Scholarship Name: Maytag Company Scholarship. *Academic Area: Business, computer science, engineering (open), information technology. *Age Group: Undergraduate students, graduate students. *Eligibility: Applicants must maintain a 2.5 GPA, demonstrate unmet financial need, and attend one of the following schools: Benedict College, Claflin University, Lane College, Morris College, Paine College, Philander Smith College, Voorhees College, Wilberforce University, or Historically Black Colleges and Universities. *Application Process: Applicants should contact the sponsoring institution for application procedures. *Amount: $1,250. *Deadline: Deadlines vary.

Medtronic Foundation Internship/Scholarship
Scholarship Name: Medtronic Foundation Internship/ Scholarship. *Academic Area: Engineering (open), science. *Age Group: Undergraduate students. *Eligibility: Applicants must be college sophomores and juniors, maintain a minimum 3.3 GPA, and attend one of the 39 UNCF member colleges or universities. *Application Process: Applicants should submit a completed application along with transcripts, a resume, two letters of recommendation, an autobiographical essay including career aspirations, and a small headshot photograph. Visit the UNCF Web site to download an application. *Amount: $5,000. *Deadline: March 15.

Mike and Stephanie Bozic Scholarship
Scholarship Name: Mike and Stephanie Bozic Scholarship. *Academic Area: Open. *Age Group:

Undergraduate students. *Eligibility: Applicants must be attending or planning to attend one of the 39 UNCF member colleges or universities, maintain a 2.5 GPA, and demonstrate unmet financial need. High school seniors are also eligible to apply for this scholarship. *Application Process: Applicants should contact the sponsor directly for application information. *Amount: Awards vary. *Deadline: Deadlines vary.

Mitsubishi Motors U.S.A. Foundation Leadership Awards

Scholarship Name: Mitsubishi Motors U.S.A. Foundation Leadership Award. *Academic Area: Open. *Age Group: Undergraduate students. *Eligibility: Applicants must maintain a 2.5 GPA, demonstrate unmet financial need, and attend or plan to attend one of the 39 UNCF member colleges or universities. Applicants should also have community service experience that demonstrates their leadership in community activities. High school seniors are also eligible to apply for this scholarship. *Application Process: Applicants should submit a completed application along with transcripts, two letters of recommendation, a financial need statement, and answers to two short essay questions listed on the application. Visit the UNCF Web site to download an application. *Amount: $2,000. *Deadline: October 29.

Nathalia Bowser Scholarship

Scholarship Name: Nathalia Bowser Scholarship. *Academic Area: Open. *Age Group: Undergraduate students, graduate students. *Eligibility: Applicants must be African-American males attending Morris College or Voorhees College in South Carolina. Applicants also must maintain a 2.5 GPA. *Application Process: Applicants should contact the sponsor directly for application information. *Amount: $1,500. *Deadline: Deadlines vary.

National Association for the Advancement of Colored People (NAACP)/Agnes Jones Jackson Scholarship

Scholarship Name: NAACP/Agnes Jones Jackson Scholarship. *Academic Area: Open. *Age Group: Undergraduate and graduate students under the age of 25. *Eligibility: Applicants must be current (verifiable) NAACP members, U.S. citizens, full-time students in an accredited college (graduate students may be full- or part-time students), possess a 3.0 GPA (graduate students) or a 2.5 GPA

(undergraduates), and demonstrate financial need. *Application Process: Applicants should submit a completed application along with three letters of recommendation, transcripts, a financial verification letter, evidence of enrollment, and a one-page essay. Visit the UNCF Web site to download an application. *Amount: $1,500 (undergraduate); $2,500 (graduate). *Deadline: March 25.

National Association for the Advancement of Colored People (NAACP)/Earl G. Graves Scholarship

Scholarship Name: NAACP/Earl G. Graves Scholarship. *Academic Area: Business. *Age Group: Undergraduate students, graduate students. *Eligibility: Applicants must be college junior or seniors or graduate students, full-time students in good academic standing at an accredited college, and be in the top 20 percent of their class. *Application Process: Applicants should submit a completed application along with three letters of recommendation, transcripts, evidence of full-time enrollment, and a one-page essay. Visit the UNCF Web site to download an application. *Amount: $5,000. *Deadline: March 25.

National Association for the Advancement of Colored People (NAACP)/Historically Black College and University Scholarship Fund

Scholarship Name: NAACP/Historically Black College and University Scholarship Fund. *Academic Area: Open. *Age Group: Undergraduate students. *Eligibility: Applicants must be U.S. citizens who are incoming freshmen at a Historically Black College or University. Applicants must also maintain a 2.5 GPA and demonstrate financial need. *Application Process: Applicants should submit a completed application along with transcripts, three letters of recommendation, financial verification information, an essay, and evidence of full-time enrollment. Visit the UNCF Web site to download an application. *Amount: $2,000. *Deadline: March 25.

National Association for the Advancement of Colored People (NAACP)/Lillian and Samuel Sutton Education Scholarship

Scholarship Name: NAACP/Lillian and Samuel Sutton Education Scholarship. *Academic Area: Education. *Age Group: Undergraduate students graduate students. *Eligibility: Applicants must be U.S. citizens, full-time students in an accredited college in the

United States (graduate students may be full- or part-time students), possess a 3.0 GPA (graduate students) or a 2.5 GPA (undergraduate students), and demonstrate financial need. NAACP membership and participation is desirable. High school seniors are also eligible to apply for this scholarship. *Application Process: Applicants must submit a completed application along with two letters of recommendation, evidence of enrollment, transcripts, financial verification information, and a one-page essay. Visit the UNCF Web site to download an application. *Amount: $1,000 (undergraduate); $2,000 (graduate). *Deadline: March 25, 2005.

National Association for the Advancement of Colored People (NAACP)/Roy Wilkins Educational Scholarship

Scholarship Name: NAACP/Roy Wilkins Educational Scholarship. *Academic Area: Open. *Age Group: Undergraduate students. *Eligibility: Applicants must be U.S. citizens who are entering freshman, in an accredited college, have a 2.5 GPA, and demonstrate financial need. NAACP membership and participation is desirable. *Application Process: Applicants should submit a completed application along with transcripts, a letter verifying acceptance to college, a financial need statement, and proof of NAACP membership, if applicable. Visit the UNCF Web site to download an application. *Amount: $1,000. *Deadline: March 25.

National Association for the Advancement of Colored People (NAACP)/Willems, Hubertus W. V. Scholarship for Male Students

Scholarship Name: NAACP/Willems, Hubertus W. V. Scholarship for Male Students. *Academic Area: Chemistry, engineering (open), mathematics, science. *Age Group: Undergraduate students, graduate students. *Eligibility: Applicants must be male U.S. citizens who are planning to or are currently attending an accredited college as full-time students (graduate students may be part-time students). They must also have a 2.5 GPA (high school, undergraduates) or a 3.0 GPA (graduate students) and demonstrate financial need. NAACP membership and participation is highly desirable. High school seniors are also eligible to apply for this scholarship. *Application Process: Applicants should submit a completed application along with transcripts, evidence of enrollment, financial verification information, and a

one-page essay. Visit the UNCF Web site to download an application. *Amount: $2,000 (undergraduates); $3,000 (graduate students). *Deadline: March 25.

Nelnet Scholarship

Scholarship Name: Nelnet Scholarship. *Academic Area: Open. *Age Group: High school seniors, undergraduate students. *Eligibility: Applicants must maintain a 2.5 GPA, demonstrate unmet financial need, and attend or plan to attend one of the 39 UNCF member colleges or universities. *Application Process: Applicants should contact the sponsoring institution directly for application procedures. *Amount: $1,000. *Deadline: Deadlines vary.

Nicholas H. Noyes Jr. Memorial Foundation Scholarship

Scholarship Name: Nicholas H. Noyes Jr. Memorial Foundation Scholarship. *Academic Area: Open. *Age Group: Undergraduate students. *Eligibility: Applicants must possess a 2.5 GPA, demonstrate financial need, and attend or plan to attend one of the 39 UNCF member colleges or universities. High school seniors are also eligible to apply for this scholarship. *Application Process: Applicants should submit a completed application and supporting materials. Visit the UNCF Web site to download an application. *Amount: Awards vary, based on need. *Deadline: Deadlines vary.

Nissan/United Negro College Fund

Scholarship Name: Nissan/United Negro College Fund. *Academic Area: Business, communications, design, engineering (open), finance, law, marketing, public relations. *Age Group: Undergraduate students. *Eligibility: Applicants must be high school seniors enrolled in a Los Angeles Unified School District school and must be planning to attend a Historically Black College or University (HBCU). Applicants must also have a 3.0 GPA. *Application Process: Applicants should submit a completed application along with two recommendations, an essay (subject listed on application), high school transcripts, and a letter of acceptance from an HBCU. Visit the UNCF Web site to download an application. *Amount: $10,000. *Deadline: June 6.

Northrop Grumman Diversity Scholarship

Scholarship Name: Northrop Grumman Diversity Scholarship. *Academic Area: Computer science, engineering (computer), engineering (electrical), engineering (mechanical), and mathematics. *Age Group: Undergraduate students, graduate students. *Eligibility: Applicants should have a 3.0 GPA and attend or plan to attend selected HBCUs and majority institutions. This scholarship supports females and minorities in the technical disciplines. College sophomores, juniors and seniors and first-year graduate students may apply. *Application Process: Applicants should submit a resume along with transcripts, resume, two letters of recommendation, and answers to a few short essays (listed on application). Visit the UNCF Web site to download an application. *Amount: $1,500 and up. *Deadline: February 28.

Principal Financial Group Scholarship
Scholarship Name: Principal Financial Group Scholarship. *Academic Area: Business, finance, information technology, liberal arts. *Age Group: Undergraduate students. *Eligibility: Applicants must maintain a 3.0 GPA, demonstrate financial need, and attend or plan to attend one of the 39 UNCF member colleges or universities. Applicants must be residents of Iowa who value community involvement and academic achievement. High school seniors are also eligible to apply for this scholarship. *Application Process: Applicants should submit an application along with transcripts, a personal statement, two letters of recommendation, a letter of acceptance from a UNCF school, and their most recent tax return. Visit the UNCF Web site to download an application. *Amount: Up to $12,000, based on need. *Deadline: March 1.

Raymond W. Cannon Memorial Scholarship
Scholarship Name: Raymond W. Cannon Memorial Scholarship. *Academic Area: Law, pharmaceutical sciences. *Age Group: Undergraduate students. *Eligibility: Applicants must be college juniors attending one of the 39 UNCF member colleges or universities, maintain a 2.5 GPA, and possess demonstrated leadership skills in high school and college. *Application Process: Applicants should contact the scholarship sponsor directly for application information. *Amount: $2,000 to $5,000. *Deadline: Deadlines vary.

Reader's Digest Scholarship
Scholarship Name: Reader's Digest Scholarship. *Academic Area: Communication sciences, English/literature, journalism. *Age Group: Undergraduate students. *Eligibility: Applicants must be college juniors or seniors, maintain a 3.0 GPA, demonstrate financial need, attend one of the 39 UNCF member colleges or universities, and have an interest in print journalism. *Application Process: Applicants should submit a completed application along with transcripts, recommendations, a published writing sample, a personal statement, a financial need statement, and a small headshot photograph. Visit the UNCF Web site to download an application. *Amount: $5,000. *Deadline: November 18.

Robert Dole Scholarship
Scholarship Name: Robert Dole Scholarship. *Academic Area: Open. *Age Group: Undergraduate students. *Eligibility: Applicants must be attending or planning to attend one of the 39 UNCF member colleges or universities, maintain a 2.5 GPA, prove unmet financial need, and be either physically or mentally challenged. High school seniors are also eligible to apply for this scholarship. *Application Process: Applicants should submit a completed application along with a nomination letter from a faculty member, transcripts, a 500-word essay, and a financial need statement. Visit the UNCF Web site to download an application. *Amount: $3,500. *Deadline: October 31.

Robert Half International Scholarship
Scholarship Name: Robert Half International. *Academic Area: Accounting, business. *Age Group: Undergraduate students. *Eligibility: Applicants must maintain a 2.5 GPA, show unmet financial need, and be attending or planning to attend one of the 39 UNCF member colleges or universities. High school seniors are also eligible to apply for this scholarship. *Application Process: Applicants should contact the sponsoring institution directly for application procedures. *Amount: $1,000 to $1,750. *Deadline: Deadlines vary.

Sallie Mae Fund American Dream Scholarship
Scholarship Name: Sallie Mae Fund American Dream Scholarship. *Academic Area: Open. *Age Group: Undergraduate students. *Eligibility: Applicants must maintain a minimum 2.5 GPA and demonstrate financial need. High school seniors are also eligible to apply for this scholarship. *Application Process: Applicants should apply online via a link at the UNCF Web site. *Amount: $500 to $5,000. *Deadline: April 15.

Samuel Newhouse Scholarship

Scholarship Name: Samuel Newhouse Scholarship. *Academic Area: Open. *Age Group: Undergraduate students. *Eligibility: Applicants must maintain a 3.0 GPA, demonstrate financial need, and attend or plan to attend one of the following schools: Dillard University, Miles College, Oakwood College, Stillman College, Talladega College, Tuskegee University, or Xavier University. High school seniors are also eligible to apply for this scholarship. *Application Process: Applicants should contact the sponsoring institution directly for information on the application procedure. *Amount: Awards vary, based on need. *Deadline: Deadlines vary.

SBC Foundation Scholarship

Scholarship Name: SBC Foundation Scholarship. *Academic Area: Business, computer science, economics, engineering (open), finance, information technology. *Age Group: Undergraduate students. *Eligibility: Applicants must be college juniors, maintain a 3.0 GPA, demonstrate financial need, and attend one of the 39 UNCF member colleges or universities. Applicants must also be permanent residents of one of the following states: Arkansas, California, Illinois, Indiana, Kansas, Michigan, Missouri, Oklahoma, Ohio, Texas, or Wisconsin. *Application Process: Applicants should submit a completed application along with two nominating letters, a one-page personal statement, transcripts, a resume, and a small headshot photo. Visit the UNCF Web site to download an application. *Amount: $5,000. *Deadline: January 17.

Sodexho Scholarship

Scholarship Name: Sodexho Scholarship. *Academic Area: Medicine (open), political science, social work. *Age Group: Undergraduate students. Eligibility: Applicants must maintain a 3.0 GPA, demonstrate financial need, and attend or plan to attend one of the 39 UNCF member colleges or universities or a HBCU school. They should have an interest in careers that focus on health disciplines, government, or combating homelessness or other social welfare programs. Applicants may be high school seniors or college freshmen. *Application Process: Applicants should contact the sponsoring institution directly for application procedures. *Amount: Up to $3,500. *Deadline: Deadlines vary.

SouthTrust Scholarship/Internship

Scholarship Name: SouthTrust Scholarship/Internship. *Academic Area: Business. *Age Group: Undergraduate students. *Eligibility: Applicants must be college sophomores or juniors, maintain a 3.0 GPA, demonstrate financial need, and attend one of the 39 UNCF member colleges or universities. Applicants must also be willing to commit to a six- to eight-week summer internship. *Application Process: Applicants should submit a completed application along with transcripts, a 500-word essay, two letters of recommendation, a financial need statement, and a small headshot photograph. Visit the UNCF Web site to download an application. *Amount: $6,250. *Deadline: March 30.

Sterling Bank Scholarship

Scholarship Name: Sterling Bank Scholarship. *Academic Area: Open. *Age Group: Undergraduate students. *Eligibility: Applicants must maintain a 2.5 GPA, demonstrate financial need, and attend or plan to attend one of the 39 UNCF member colleges or universities. High school seniors are also eligible to apply for this scholarship. *Application Process: Applicants should contact the sponsoring institution directly to obtain application information. *Amount: Awards vary, based on need. *Deadline: Deadlines vary.

Terex/United Negro College Fund Scholarship

Scholarship Name: Terex/United Negro College Fund Scholarship. *Academic Area: Open. *Age Group: Undergraduate students, graduate students. *Eligibility: Applicants must be employees or children of employees of Terex Corporation. Applicants must also maintain a 3.0 GPA. *Application Process: Applicants should submit a completed application along with supporting materials. Visit the UNCF Web site to download an application. *Amount: $2,500. *Deadline: Deadlines vary.

Time Warner Scholars Program

Scholarship Name: Time Warner Scholars Program. *Academic Area: Open. *Age Group: Undergraduate students. *Eligibility: Applicants must be college sophomores, maintain a 3.0 GPA, demonstrate financial need, and attend one of the following participating Historically Black Colleges and Universities: Benedict College, Bennett College for Women, Bethune-Cookman College, Claflin University, Clark Atlanta University, Dillard University, Edward Waters College, Fisk University, Florida A&M University, Florida Memorial College, Huston-Tillotson College, Johnson C. Smith University, Lane College,

LeMoyne-Owen College, Livingstone College, Miles College, Morehouse College, Morris College, Norfolk State University, Oakwood College, Paine College, Paul Quinn College, Philander Smith College, Rust College, Saint Augustine's College, Saint Paul's College, Shaw University, Spelman College, Stillman College, Talladega College, Tougaloo College, Tuskegee University, Virginia Union University, Voorhees College, Wilberforce University, Wiley College, or Xavier University. *Application Process: Applicants should apply online via a link on the UNCF Web site. *Amount: $2,500. *Deadline: October 15.

Toyota/United Negro College Fund Scholarship
Scholarship Name: Toyota/United Negro College Fund Scholarship. *Academic Area: Business, communications science, computer science, engineering (open), English/literature, information technology. *Age Group: Undergraduate students. *Eligibility: Applicants must maintain a 3.0 GPA, demonstrate financial need, and attend one of the following schools: Bethune-Cookman College, Clark Atlanta University, Morehouse College, Spelman College, Tuskegee University, or Xavier University. Applicants may be high school seniors or college freshmen *Application Process: Applicants should submit a completed application along with recommendations, transcripts, one-page personal statement, resume, and a small headshot photograph. Visit the UNCF Web site to download an application. *Amount: $7,500, renewable through senior year. *Deadline: October 28.

TRW Information Technology Minority Scholarship
Scholarship Name: TRW Information Technology Minority Scholarship. *Academic Area: Computer science. *Age Group: Undergraduate students. *Eligibility: Applicants must be college sophomores or juniors, maintain a 3.0 GPA, demonstrate financial need, and attend one of the following schools: George Mason University, Howard University, Morgan State, Pennsylvania State, or Virginia Polytechnic Institute. *Application Process: Applicants should contact the sponsoring institution directly for application procedures. *Amount: $3,000. *Deadline: Deadlines vary.

UBS/PaineWebber Scholarship
Scholarship Name: UBS/PaineWebber Scholarship. *Academic Area: Business. *Age Group: Undergraduate students. *Eligibility: Applicants

must be college sophomores or juniors, maintain a 3.0 GPA, have unmet financial need, and attend one of the 39 UNCF member colleges or universities. *Application Process: Applicants should submit a completed application along with two letters of nomination, a three-page essay that describes their leadership abilities, resume, transcripts, and a headshot photograph. Visit the UNCF Web site to download an application. *Amount: $8,000. *Deadline: March 18.

United Negro College Fund/Foot Locker Foundation Inc. Scholarship
Scholarship Name: United Negro College Fund/Foot Locker Foundation Inc. Scholarship. *Academic Area: Open. *Age Group: Undergraduate students, graduate students. *Eligibility: Applicants must maintain a 2.5 GPA, demonstrate financial need, and attend one of the 39 UNCF member colleges or universities. *Application Process: Applicants should submit a completed application along with transcripts, two nomination letters, a financial need statement, and a one-page autobiographical essay. Visit the UNCF Web site to download an application. *Amount: $5,000. *Deadline: April 1.

United Parcel Service Foundation
Scholarship Name: United Parcel Service Foundation Scholarship. *Academic Area: Open. *Age Group: Undergraduate students, graduate students. *Eligibility: Applicants must maintain a 2.5 GPA, demonstrate unmet financial need, and attend one of the 39 UNCF member colleges or universities. *Application Process: Applicants should submit a completed application along with supporting materials. Visit the UNCF Web site to download an application. *Amount: Awards vary, based on need. *Deadline: Deadlines vary.

USENIX Association Scholarship
Scholarship Name: USENIX Association Scholarship. *Academic Area: Computer science, information technology. *Age Group: Undergraduate students, graduate students. *Eligibility: Applicants must maintain a 3.5 GPA, demonstrate unmet financial need, and attend one of the 39 UNCF member colleges or universities. *Application Process: Applicants should contact the sponsoring institution directly for information about application procedures. *Amount: Up to $10,000. *Deadline: Deadlines vary.

WOMEN

The following financial aid resources are available to female students. Aid for undergraduate, graduate, and medical students is listed.

Alpha Chi Omega Foundation Inc.
Attn: Jen Nuckles Stafford, Foundation Programs
    Coordinator
5939 Castle Creek Parkway, North Drive
Indianapolis, IN 46250-4343
317-579-5050
jstafford@alphachiomega.org
http://www.alphachiomega.org/foundation/
    scholarships_grants/main.asp
Scholarship Name: Alpha Chi Omega Scholarships.
    *Academic Area: Open. *Age Group: Undergraduate
    students, graduate students. *Eligibility: Applicants
    must be members of Alpha Chi Omega with a strong
    record of academic achievement. Scholarships are
    merit based. *Application Process: Members only
    can log into the scholarship application portion of
    the organization's Web site. *Amount: Awards vary.
    *Deadline: March 15.

Alpha Chi Omega Foundation Inc.
Attn: Foundation Director
5939 Castle Creek Parkway, North Drive
Indianapolis, IN 46250-4343
317-579-5050
foundation@alphachiomega.org
http://www.alphachiomega.org/foundation/
    scholarships_grants/educational_assistance_grants.
    asp
Grant Name: Educational Assistance Grant. *Academic
    Area: Open. *Age Group: Undergraduate students,
    graduate students, alumnae. *Eligibility: Members and
    alumna of Alpha Chi Omega who are seeking funds to
    continue their undergraduate or graduate education
    are eligible to apply. *Application Procedure: Sorority
    members can visit the foundation's Web site to
    download an application. *Amount: Varies. *Deadline:
    Applications are accepted throughout the year and
    reviewed quarterly.

Alpha Delta Kappa International
1615 West 92nd Street
Kansas City, MO 64114-3296
816-363-5525, 800-247-2311
dfrost@alphadeltakappa.org
http://www.alphadeltakappa.org
Scholarship Name: International Teacher Education
Scholarship. *Academic Area: Education. *Age Group:
Undergraduate students. *Eligibility: Applicants must
be between the ages of 20 and 35 in the year study
is to begin. They must be non-U.S. citizens living
outside of the United States, maintain that residency
status from the time of application to awarding of
the scholarship, be single with no dependents, and
rank academically in the top 25 percent of their class.
They must also have completed at least one year of
college, agree to purchase health insurance as well
as fund their own travel expenses, and maintain full-
time student status. *Application Process: Visit Alpha
Delta Kappa's Web site to download an application.
*Amount: $10,000 per year, divided into installments
at designated intervals according to the college/
university attended. *Deadline: January 1.

Alpha Delta Pi
1386 Ponce de Leon Avenue, NE
Atlanta, GA 30306
404-378-3164, ext. 123
foundation@alphadeltapi.org
http://www.alphadeltapi.org/contentmanager/page.
    asp?webpageid=172
Grant Name: Alpha Delta Pi Foundation Academic
    Scholarship. *Academic Area: Open. *Age Group:
    Undergraduate students, graduate students, adults.
    *Eligibility: Members and alumnae of Alpha Delta Pi
    who are experiencing financial difficulties are eligible
    to apply. *Application Procedure: Visit the foundation's
    Web site to download an application. *Amount: Varies
    by need. *Deadline: March 1.

Alpha Delta Pi
1386 Ponce de Leon Avenue, NE
Atlanta, GA 30306
404-378-3164, ext. 156
foundation@alphadeltapi.org
http://www.alphadeltapi.org
Scholarship Name: Abigail Davis Emergency Grant.
    *Academic Area: Open. *Age Group: Undergraduate
    students. *Eligibility: Applicants who are experiencing
    unforeseen financial difficulties that will force them to
    withdraw from school may apply. Applicants must be
    members of Alpha Delta Pi. *Application Process: Visit
    the sorority's Web site to download an application,

or request more information by phone or e-mail. *Amount: $1,500. *Deadline: There is no deadline; applications are accepted throughout the year.

Alpha Epsilon Phi Foundation

Attn: Bonnie Wunsch, Executive Director
11 Lake Avenue Extension, Suite 1A
Danbury, CT 06811
203-748-0029
execdir@aephi.org
http://www.aephi.org
Scholarship Name: This organization offers multiple memorial scholarships to women. *Academic Area: Open. *Age Group: Varies by scholarship. *Eligibility: Varies. Application Process: Submit an application via Alpha Epsilon Phi's Web site. *Amount: Varies. *Deadline: Varies.

Alpha Gamma Delta Foundation

8701 Founders Road
Indianapolis, IN 46268-1392
317-872-2655
scholarships@alphagammadelta.org
http://www.alphagammadelta.org/content/foundation/scholarship.htm
Scholarship Name: Alpha Gamma Delta Foundation Scholarship. *Academic Area: Open. *Age Group: Undergraduate students, graduate students. *Eligibility: Applicants must be members of Alpha Gamma Delta who are pursuing full-time academic studies. They must be at least sophomores in college to apply for the awards. Applicants are judged on scholastic achievement, chapter contributions, campus honors and activities, volunteer experiences, and financial need. *Application Process: Applicants should submit a completed four-page application form, complete with narrative, along with an original transcript of grades, one letter of recommendation from an Alpha Gamma Delta advisory member, and two letters of recommendation from nonmembers. *Amount: Scholarships range from $500 to $2,000. *Deadline: March 1.

Alpha Gamma Delta Foundation

8701 Founders Road
Indianapolis, IN 46268-1392
317-879-9328
foundation@alphagammadelta.org
http://www.alphagammadelta.org/content/foundation/scholarship.htm
Grant Name: Continuing Education Grant Program.

*Academic Area: Open. *Age Group: Adults. *Eligibility: Alumnae members of Alpha Gamma Delta who are seeking funds to return to school are eligible to apply. Applicants must demonstrate financial need and involvement in the community. *Application Procedure: Applicants must submit two letters of recommendation and a completed application form. Visit the foundation's Web site to download an application. *Amount: $500. *Deadline: Contact the foundation for details.

Alpha Kappa Alpha Educational Advancement Foundation Inc.

Attn: Scholarship Application Enclosed
5656 South Stoney Island Avenue
Chicago, IL 60637
773-947-0026
akaeaf@aol.com
http://www.akaeaf.org
Scholarship Name: This sorority offers a variety of merit-based and need-based scholarships for women. *Academic Area: Open. *Age Group: Undergraduate students, graduate students. *Eligibility: Applicants must be members of Alpha Kappa Alpha and have a 2.5 or 3.0 GPA, depending upon the scholarship. *Application Process: Applicants should submit a completed application (available for download in November of each year), a personal statement, three letters of recommendation, and official transcripts. Graduate students should also include a current resume and documentation of project and/or research plans. All applications should have the applicant's social security number on each page. Visit the sorority's Web site to download an application. *Amount: Scholarships range from $750 to $1,500. *Deadline: January 15.

Alpha Kappa Alpha Educational Advancement Foundation Inc.

Attn: Scholarship Application Enclosed
5656 South Stoney Island Avenue
Chicago, IL 60637
773-947-0026
akaeaf@aol.com
http://www.akaeaf.org
Scholarship Name: Youth-P.A.C. Scholarship. *Academic Area: Open. *Age Group: Undergraduate students. *Eligibility: Female students of at least sophomore status may apply. Applicants must be members of Alpha Kappa Alpha, demonstrate exceptional academic achievement or financial need, and participate in leadership, volunteer, civic, or campus

activities. They must also have at least a 3.0 GPA. *Application Process: Applicants should submit two letters of recommendation, a personal statement, a completed application form, and official unopened transcripts in one packet. Visit Alpha Kappa Alpha's Web site to download an application. *Amount: Awards vary. *Deadline: January 15.

Alpha Omicron Pi Foundation

Attn: Grace Day
c/o Diamond Jubilee Scholarship Committee
PO Box 395
Brentwood, TN 37024-0395
615-370-0920
gday@alphaomicronpi.org
http://www.aoiifoundation.org/scholarships.html

Scholarship Name: Diamond Jubilee Scholarships (various scholarships for women). *Academic Area: Open. *Age Group: Undergraduate students, graduate students. *Eligibility: Applicants must be members of Alpha Omicron Pi in good standing who are attending school full time. Visit the foundation's Web site for a complete listing of named scholarships and specific eligibility requirements. *Application Process: Applicants should submit an application along with an official transcript, a personal letter of reference from a professor, and a recommendation form to be filled out by someone from within the fraternity. All materials should be mailed in one envelope, and the same form is used for all scholarships that are offered. Visit the foundation's Web site to download an application, and contact Grace Day for further information about specific awards. *Amount: Awards vary. *Deadline: March 1.

Alpha Phi Foundation

1930 Sherman Avenue
Evanston, IL 60201
847-475-4532
foundation@alphaphi.org

Grant Name: Emergency Aid Program and Forget-Me-Not Fund. *Academic Area: Open. *Age Group: Undergraduate students, graduate students, adults. *Eligibility: Members and alumnae of Alpha Phi who are experiencing financial difficulties or other crises are eligible to apply. *Application Procedure: Visit the foundation's Web site to download an application. *Amount: Varies by need. *Deadline: There is no deadline; applications are accepted as need arises from members and alumna.

Alpha Phi Foundation

1930 Sherman Avenue
Evanston, IL 60201
847-475-4932
foundation@alphaphi.org
http://www.alphaphi.org/foundation/
  ScholarAwardOpps.html

Scholarship Name: This organization offers numerous scholarships for women. *Academic Area: Open. *Age Group: Undergraduate students, graduate students. *Eligibility: Applicants must be members of Alpha Phi who demonstrate an exceptional scholastic record, service to Alpha Phi and the community, and campus involvement. The applicant's essays and alumnae recommendations must also be exceptional. All scholarships awarded are merit based, with no regard to financial need. *Application Process: Applicants should submit a completed application along with alumna recommendation, official transcripts, and typed essays by mail. Visit the foundation's Web site to download an application. *Amount: Awards vary. *Deadline: March 15.

Alpha Sigma Alpha Foundation

Attn: Executive Director
9550 Zionsville Road, Suite 160
Indianapolis, IN 46268
317-871-2920
fndstaff@alphasigmaalpha.org
http://www.alphasigmaalpha.org/asa/foundation/
  programs.htm

Grant Name: Alpha Sigma Alpha Career Enhancement Grant. *Academic Area: Open. *Age Group: Adults. *Eligibility: Alumnae of Alpha Sigma Alpha who are interested in continuing their education are eligible to apply. *Application Procedure: Applicants should submit two letters of recommendation, promotional literature describing the program (including costs), a personal essay that describes how the educational opportunity will assist their personal or professional goals, and a completed application (available at the foundation's Web site). *Amount: Varies. *Deadline: Although applications are accepted throughout the year, they should be submitted at least 60 days prior to need.

Alpha Sigma Alpha Foundation

9550 Zionsville Road, Suite 160
Indianapolis, IN 46268
317-871-2920

foundation@alphasigmaalpha.org
http://www.alphasigmaalpha.org/asa/foundation/
    programs.htm
Scholarship Name: Alpha Sigma Alpha Foundation
    Scholarships. *Academic Area: Open. *Age Group:
    Undergraduate students, graduate students. *Eligibility:
    Applicants must be members of Alpha Sigma Alpha
    who exhibit leadership potential and a dedication to
    volunteerism and meaningful participation in Alpha
    Sigma Alpha and/or other activities. All awards are merit
    based with no regard to financial need. *Application
    Process: Applications are available for download from
    the foundation's Web site in September of each year.
    Applicants should submit a completed application
    along with all supporting materials. *Amount: Awards
    vary. *Deadline: February 10.

Alpha Sigma Alpha Foundation

9550 Zionsville Road, Suite 160
Indianapolis, IN 46268
317-871-2920
foundation@alphasigmaalpha.org
http://www.alphasigmaalpha.org/asa/foundation/
    programs.htm
Scholarship Name: The Marjorie Anderson Thompson
    Scholarship and the Alpha Sigma Alpha Special
    Education Scholarship. *Academic Area:
    Education. *Age Group: Undergraduate students,
    graduate students. *Eligibility: Applicants should
    exhibit leadership potential and a dedication to
    volunteerism and meaningful participation in
    Alpha Sigma Alpha and/or other community and
    school activities. They do not need to be members
    of Alpha Sigma Alpha. Note: applicants for the
    Marjorie Anderson Thompson Scholarship must
    have moderate to severe hearing loss. *Application
    Process: Applications are available for download
    from the organization's Web site in September of
    each year. Applicants should submit a completed
    application along with all supporting materials.
    *Amount: Awards vary. *Deadline: February 10.

Alpha Sigma Tau Foundation

Attn: Pamela Wales Szafarczyk, National Foundation
    Scholarships/Grant Chairman
11 Fawn Meadows Court
Getzville, NY 14068
irmingham, AL 35216
716-639-8834
http://www.alphasigmatau.org

Grant Name: Mary Alice Peterson American Indian Grant.
    *Academic Area: Open. *Age Group: Undergraduate
    students, graduate students. *Eligibility: Members
    and alumnae of Alpha Sigma Tau who are Native
    American may apply. Applicants must have a GPA of
    least 3.0 and must have sophomore, junior, senior, or
    graduate status. *Application Procedure: Applicants
    must submit official transcripts, two letters of
    recommendation, and a one-page essay detailing
    why they should receive the scholarship. Applicants
    should visit the foundation's Web site to download an
    application. *Amount: $250. *Deadline: March 1.

Alpha Sigma Tau Foundation

Attn: Pamela Wales Szafarczyk, National Foundation
    Scholarships/Grant Chairman
11 Fawn Meadows Court
Getzville, NY 14068
716-639-8834
http://www.alphasigmatau.org
Scholarship Name: Alpha Sigma Tau Foundation
    Scholarships. *Academic Area: Open. *Age Group:
    Undergraduate students, graduate students. *Eligibility:
    Applicants must be members of Alpha Sigma Tau who
    demonstrate scholastic achievement and involvement
    in sorority and campus activities. They must also
    have a GPA of least 3.0 and have sophomore, junior,
    senior, or graduate status. *Application Process:
    Applicants must submit official transcripts, two letters
    of recommendation, and a one-page essay detailing
    why they should receive the scholarship. Visit the
    foundation's Web site to download an application.
    *Amount: Awards vary. *Deadline: March 1.

Alpha Xi Delta Foundation

8702 Founders Road
Indianapolis, IN 46268
317-872-3500
ehannan@alphaxidelta.org
http://www.alphaxidelta.org/scholarships.asp
Scholarship Name: Alpha Xi Delta Foundation Alumnae
    Scholarship. *Academic Area: Open. *Age Group: Adults.
    *Eligibility: Applicants must be alumnae members of
    Alpha Xi Delta who are returning to school and who
    were in good financial standing with their chapter as
    collegiate members. *Application Process: Applicants
    should submit official transcripts, a recommendation
    form from an alumna in good standing, a letter of
    recommendation from a current or former employer or
    academician, and a completed application. Applicants

should explain their professional work experience as well as demonstrate a record of academic achievement and commitment to community involvement. Applicants should also exhibit need and have clearly defined career goals. Visit Alpha Xi Delta's Web site to download an application. *Amount: Scholarships range from $750 to $2,000. *Deadline: March 15.

Alpha Xi Delta Foundation

8702 Founders Road
Indianapolis, IN 46268
317-872-3500
fhq@alphaxidelta.org
http://www.alphaxidelta.org/scholarships.asp
Scholarship Name: Alpha Xi Delta Foundation Undergraduate Scholarship. *Academic Area: Open. *Age Group: Undergraduate students. *Eligibility: Applicants must be members of Alpha Xi Delta and have a strong record of academic achievement and community involvement. Applicants should also demonstrate financial need and have clearly defined career goals. *Application Process: Applicants should submit a completed application, official transcripts, a recommendation form from an alumna in good standing, and a letter of recommendation from a college or university faculty member or administrator. Visit Alpha Xi Delta's Web site to download an application. *Amount: Scholarships range from $750 to $2,000. *Deadline: March 15.

Alpha Xi Delta Foundation

8702 Founders Road
Indianapolis, IN 46268
317-872-3500
fhq@alphaxidelta.org
http://www.alphaxidelta.org/scholarships.asp
Grant Name: The foundation provides grants to members and alumnae. *Academic Area: Open. *Age Group: Undergraduate students, graduate students, adults. *Eligibility: Members and alumnae of Alpha Xi Delta who are interested in continuing their education or who need emergency financial assistance are eligible to apply. *Application Procedure: Visit the foundation's Web site to download an application. *Amount: Varies. *Deadline: Applications are accepted throughout the year.

Altrusa International Foundation

332 South Michigan Avenue, Suite 1123
Chicago, IL 60604
312-427-4410
foundation@altrusa.com
http://www.altrusa.com/Foundation/FoundationMain. asp
Grant Name: Altrusa International Foundation, a philanthropic corporation, supplements its direct contributions to society through a program of cash grants to individuals and Altrusa clubs that support its interests, including the well-being of women and families. *Academic Area: Open. *Age Group: Open. *Eligibility: Projects must involve members of Altrusa International. *Application Procedure: Visit the foundation's Web site for a sample grant application. *Amount: Varies. *Deadlines: Contact the foundation for details. .

America's Junior Miss Foundation

PO Box 2786
Mobile, AL 36602
251-438-3621, 800-256-5435
foundation@ajm.org
http://www.ajm.org
Scholarship Name: America's Junior Miss Foundation awards various scholarships to its contest winners. *Academic Area: Open. *Age Group: Undergraduate students. *Eligibility: To receive scholarship funds, applicants must win at some level in America's Junior Miss competitions. Competitions are judged on the following criteria: scholastics (20 percent), interview (25 percent), talent (25 percent), fitness (15 percent), and poise (15 percent). *Application Process: Inquire during your sophomore year of high school as to the starting point for applicants in your particular state. State-by-state contact information can be found on the foundation's Web site. *Amount: Varies. Ranges up to full tuition for four years at select schools. *Deadline: Varies.

America's National Teenager

808 Deer Crossing Court
Nashville, TN 37220
615-370-4338, 866-NAT-TEEN
telwar@comcast.net
http://www.nationalteen.com
Contest Name: America's National Teenager. *Academic Area: Open. *Age Group: Undergraduate students. *Eligibility: Applicants must be female high school students who are planning on attending college after high school graduation. There are two divisions, one for girls ages 12 through 15 and another for girls ages

16 through 18. Applicants are judged on academic excellence, school and community involvement, social and conversational skills, poise and personality in an evening gown, personal expression, and ability to answer an on-state question. Applicants should visit the organization's Web site to locate the office in their state where they should begin their inquiry. *Application Process: State representatives will advise applicants of the local and state procedures and deadlines for application. *Amount: Awards vary. *Deadline: Deadlines vary by state. Contact your state office for deadline information.

American Agricultural Economics Association Foundation
c/o Committee on Women in Agricultural Economics
415 South Duff Avenue, Suite C
Ames, IA 50010-6600
515-233-3202
foundation@aaea.org
http://www.aaea.org/sections/cwae
Fellowship Name: Sylvia Lane Fellowship Fund. The fund offers short-term (up to one year) grants for women conducting innovative research, with an established expert, about food, agricultural, or natural resources issues. *Academic Areas: Agricultural economics, agriculture, food sciences, natural resources. *Age Group: Graduate students, recent Ph.D.'s. *Eligibility: Applicants must have completed an academic year in an accredited American graduate degree program in agricultural economics or closely related discipline and must have initiated a mentor association with an expert in the field. Women with recent Ph.D. degrees are also encouraged to apply. *Application Procedure: Contact the foundation for more information. *Amount: Varies. *Deadline: Varies. Contact the foundation for details.

American Agri-Women
Attn: Peggy Clark
Daughters of American Agriculture
2274 East Lytle Five Points Road
Dayton, OH 45458
info@americanagriwomen.org
http://americanagriwomen.org/scholarships.htm
Scholarship Name: Daughters of American Agriculture Scholarship. *Academic Area: Agriculture, communications science, Medicine (open), sociology. *Age Group: Ages 18 to 23. *Eligibility: Applicants must be a farmer, rancher, or the wife, daughter, or

close relative of a farmer, rancher, or person employed in agriculture, and must demonstrate financial need. They must also be high school graduates and be knowledgeable about or have work experience in agriculture. Grade point average and placement tests are considered. Applicants must plan to pursue study in one of the academic areas listed above as they relate to agriculture. *Application Process: Applicants must agree to give personal and family financial information and submit application that can be downloaded from the American Agri-Women's Web site. *Amount: $500. *Deadline: June 1.

American Agri-Women
Attn: Mary Graff
Daughters of American Agriculture
PO Box 7506
Visalia, CA 93290
info@americanagriwomen.org
http://americanagriwomen.org/scholarships.htm
Scholarship Name: Sister Thomas More Bertels Scholarship. *Academic Area: Agriculture, communications science, medicine (open), sociology. *Age Group: Ages 24 and over. *Eligibility: Applicants must be a farmer, rancher, or the wife, daughter, or close relative of a farmer, rancher, or person employed in agriculture and must demonstrate financial need. They must also be high school graduates and be knowledgeable about or have work experience in agriculture. Grade point average and placement tests are considered. Applicants must plan to pursue study in one of the academic areas listed above as they relate to agriculture. *Application Process: Applicants must agree to give personal and family financial information and submit an application that can be downloaded from the American Agri-Women's Web site. *Amount: $500. *Deadline: June 1.

American Association of Critical-Care Nurses (AACN)
101 Columbia
Aliso Viejo, CA 92656-4109
800-899-2226
info@aacn.org
http://www.aacn.org
Scholarship Name: BSN Educational Advancement Scholarship. *Academic Area: Nursing (critical care). *Age Group: Professionals. *Eligibility: Applicant must be an AACN member in good standing, have an active RN license, maintain a cumulative GPA of at least 3.0, and currently work in critical care or have

worked in critical care for at least one year in the last three years. They must also currently be enrolled in an accredited nursing program and have junior or upper division status. *Application Process: Applicants must submit a completed application by mail, followed by final grade reports. They must also send letters of verification from their place of employment and school. Visit the association's Web site to download an application. *Amount: $1,500. *Deadline: April 1.

American Association of Critical-Care Nurses (AACN)

101 Columbia
Aliso Viejo, CA 92656-4109
800-899-2226
info@aacn.org
http://www.aacn.org

Scholarship Name: Graduate Educational Advancement Scholarship. *Academic Area: Nursing (critical care). Age Group: Professionals. *Eligibility: Applicants must be AACN members in good standing, have an active RN license, maintain a cumulative GPA of at least 3.0, and currently work in critical care or have worked in critical care for at least one year in the last three years. They also must be graduates of a baccalaureate degree program and be currently enrolled in a graduate program leading to a master's or doctorate in nursing. Alternately, they may also be enrolled in a faculty supervisor's clinical practicum leading to eligibility for the CCNS exam. *Application Process: Applicants must submit a completed application by mail, followed by final grade reports. They must also send letters of verification from their place of employment and school. *Amount: $1,500. *Deadline: April 1.

American Association of Family and Consumer Sciences (AAFCS)

AAFCS Fellowship Program
400 North Columbus Street, Suite 202
Alexandria, VA 22314
703-706-4600, 800-424-8080
http://www.aafcs.org/programs/fellowships.html

Fellowship Name: The National Graduate Fellowship Program provides a variety of individually named fellowships. *Academic Area: Family and consumer sciences. *Age Group: Graduate students. *Eligibility: Full-time graduate students planning to study or currently studying family and consumer science are eligible to apply. Applicants must also be U.S. citizens. *Application Procedure: Applicants should complete

the online Fellowship and Scholarship Payment Form and submit a nonrefundable application fee of $40. An application will be sent upon receipt of this fee. *Amount: Fellowships range from $3,500 to $5,000. *Deadline: January 13.

American Association of Family and Consumer Sciences (AAFCS)

AAFCS Scholarships Program
400 North Columbus Street, Suite 202
Alexandria, VA 22314
800-424-8080
scholarships@aafcs.org
http://www.aafcs.org/programs/scholarships.htm

Scholarship Name: Jewell L. Taylor National Scholarship. *Academic Area: Family and consumer sciences. *Age Group: Undergraduate students. *Eligibility: Applicants must be citizens or permanent residents of the United States who are planning to or pursuing a degree in family and consumer sciences or its specialties on a full-time basis. Award criteria includes applicant's ability to pursue undergraduate study, experience in relation to preparation for study in proposed field, special recognition and awards, voluntary participation in community organizations and activities, evidence of professional commitment and leadership, significance of proposed area of study to families and individuals, professional goals, written communication skills, recommendations, and membership in the AAFCS. High school seniors may also apply for this scholarship. *Application Process: Applicants must submit a request for an application, along with a $40 fee, via the association's Web site. Once the applicant has paid the fee and received the application, five hard copies of the application package (which includes application, recommendations, and transcripts) should be mailed. The application should also be e-mailed. *Amount: $5,000. *Deadline: January 13.

American Association of Nurse Anesthetists (AANA)

Attn: Mary Collins
AANA Foundation
222 South Prospect Avenue
Park Ridge, IL 60068-4011
847-692-7050
foundation@aana.com
http://www.aana.com/uploadedFiles/Professional_Development/AANA_Foundation/Applications/2006studentscholapp_final.pdf

Scholarship Name: Dean and Fred Hayden Student Research Scholarship. *Academic Area: Nursing (anesthesia). *Age Group: Professionals. *Eligibility: Applicants must be members of the AANA with a demonstrated interest in research. *Application Process: Applicants must submit a completed abstract, a copy of institutional investigation committee/review board approval, a letter of support from the research advisor or program director, and an estimate of the anticipated value of their research findings. Visit the association's Web site for detailed information about the abstract and application process. *Amount: $1,000. *Deadline: June 1.

American Association of Nurse Anesthetists (AANA)
Attn: Mary Collins
AANA Foundation
222 South Prospect Avenue
Park Ridge, IL 60068-4011
847-692-7050, ext. 1171
foundation@aana.com
http://www.aana.com
Scholarship Name: Al Jarvis Research Scholarship. *Academic Area: Nursing (anesthesia). *Age Group: Undergraduate students, graduate students. *Eligibility: Applicants must be members of the AANA and enrolled in a nurse anesthesia educational program in Michigan. *Application Process: Applicants must submit a completed abstract, a copy of institutional investigation committee/review board approval, a letter of support from the research advisor or program director, and an estimate of the anticipated value of their research findings. Visit the association's Web site for detailed information about the abstract and application process. *Amount: $2,500. *Deadline: August 1.

American Association of University Women (AAUW)
AAUW Educational Foundation
Dept. 60
301 ACT Drive
Iowa City, IA 52243-4030
info@aauw.org
http://www.aauw.org/fga
Grant Name: Career Development Grant. *Academic Area: Open. *Age Group: Adults. *Eligibility: Applicants must be women who hold a bachelor's degree and are preparing to advance their careers, change careers, or re-enter the work force. They must also be U.S. citizens and plan to attend an accredited two- or four-year institution. *Application Procedure: Visit the association's Web site for an application. *Amount: Grants range from $2,000 to $8,000. *Deadline: December 15. Contact the association for details.

American Association of University Women (AAUW)
AAUW Educational Foundation
Dept. 60
301 ACT Drive
Iowa City, IA 52243-4030
info@aauw.org
http://www.aauw.org/fga
Fellowship Name: This association offers various American fellowships to support women doctoral candidates completing dissertations or scholars seeking funds for postdoctoral research leave from accredited institutions. *Academic Area: Open. *Age Group: Graduate students, post-doctoral scholars.*Eligibility: Applicants must be U.S. citizens or permanent residents. Candidates are evaluated on the basis of scholarly excellence, teaching experience, and active commitment to helping women and girls through service in their communities, professions, or fields of research. *Application Process: Visit the Association's Web site to request an application. Applications are available between August 1 and November 15. *Amount: $6,000 to $30,000. *Deadline: November 15.

American Association of Women Podiatrists Inc.
Attn: Dr. Holly Sheets
PO Box 1962
Palatka, FL 32177
http://www.aawpinc.com/scholarship_app.pdf
Scholarship Name: Founder's Scholarship. *Academic Area: Podiatry. *Age Group: Podiatry students. *Eligibility: Female podiatry students with a GPA of at least 3.0 may apply. Applicants must be at least college juniors. *Application Process: Applicants must submit a completed application, official transcripts, and a personal statement. Visit the association's Web site to download an application. *Amount: $1,000. *Deadline: June 1.

American College of Nurse-Midwives (ACNM) Foundation
ACNM Foundation Fellowship for Graduate Education
8403 Colesville Road, Suite 1550
Silver Spring, MD 20910
240-485-1800
http://www.midwife.org/support.cfm?id=278

Fellowship Name: ACNM Foundation Fellowship for Graduate Education. *Academic Area: Nursing (midwifery). *Age Group: Graduate students, postdoctoral scholars. *Eligibility: Applicant must be actively enrolled in a doctoral or postdoctoral studies program, a certified nurse-midwife or a certified midwife, and a member of the ACNM. Applicant must also demonstrate good standing in her academic program, agree to submit periodic progress reports, and acknowledge and promote the ACNM Foundation in professional activities that result from receiving the fellowship. *Application Process: Applicants must submit a statement of academic and career goals and plans, two academic letters of recommendation, and a completed application. Visit the college's Web site to download an applicant information form. *Amount: Awards vary. *Deadline: March 17.

American College of Nurse-Midwives (ACNM) Foundation
ACNM Basic Midwifery Student Scholarship
8403 Colesville Road, Suite 1550
Silver Spring, MD 20910
240-485-1800
http://www.midwife.org/support.cfm?id=274
Scholarship Name: Basic Midwifery Student Scholarship. *Academic Area: Nursing (midwifery). *Age Group: Undergraduate students. *Eligibility: Applicants must be enrolled in an accredited basic midwifery program and have successfully completed one clinical semester or module. They must also be members of the ACNM, show academic achievement, and demonstrate financial need. *Application Process: Applicants must submit a completed application, a brief statement of career goals and plans, a financial assessment form, a statement of financial need, and one letter of recommendation from a faculty member. Visit the college's Web site to download an application. *Amount: Varies. *Deadline: March 17.

American College of Nurse-Midwives (ACNM) Foundation
8403 Colesville Road, Suite 1550
Silver Spring, MD 20910
240-485-1800
http://www.midwife.org/support.cfm?id=275
Scholarship Name: Mary Keller Scholarship Fund Award. *Academic Area: Nursing (midwifery). *Age Group: Undergraduate students. *Eligibility: Applicants

must be current residents of Michigan, enrolled in the nurse-midwife program at Case Western Reserve University, and agree to submit a data collection form to the ACNM Foundation within one year of scholarship award. They must also be members of the ACNM, show academic achievement, and demonstrate financial need. *Application Process: Applicants must submit a completed application, a brief statement of their career goals and plans, a financial assessment form, a statement of financial need, and one letter of recommendation from a faculty member. Visit the college's Web site to download an application. *Amount: Awards vary. *Deadline: March 17.

American College of Nurse Practitioners (ACNP)
1111 19th Street, NW, Suite 404
Washington, DC 20036
202-659-2190
acnp@acnpweb.org
http://www.nurse.org/acnp/awards/acnp.scholar.shtml
Scholarship Name: ACNP Nurse Practitioner Student Scholarship Award. *Academic Area: Nursing (nurse practitioner). *Age Group: Graduate students. *Eligibility: Applicants must show proof of membership in the ACNP, proof of enrollment in an accredited nurse practitioner program, and maintain a 3.4 or higher grade point average. Applicants should also demonstrate evidence of distinction by participation in professional organizations, promotion of research, participation in legislative or policy-making activities, and community service. *Application Process: Applicants should submit proof of membership in the ACNP, two letters of support from professional colleagues, a current curriculum vitae, an official transcript, a 200-word personal statement, and a completed application. Visit the college's Web site to download an application. *Amount: $1,000. *Deadline: June 30.

American Congress on Surveying and Mapping (ACSM)
6 Montgomery Village Avenue, Suite 413
Gaithersburg, MD 20879
240-632-9716
pat.canfield@acsm.net
http://www.acsm.net/scholar.html
Scholarship Name: Cady McDonnell Memorial Scholarship. *Academic Area: Surveying. *Age Group: Undergraduate students. *Eligibility: Students

enrolled in the field of surveying in either a two- or four-year surveying program may apply. Applicants must be residents of one of the following western states: Alaska, Arizona, California, Colorado, Hawaii, Idaho, Montana, Nevada, New Mexico, Oregon, Utah, Washington, or Wyoming. They must also be members of the ACSM. *Application Process: Applicants must submit a completed application along with a statement indicating their educational objectives, future plans of study or research, professional activities, and financial need. Three letters of recommendation are also required (at least two from faculty members). A complete, original transcript is also required. Visit the ACSM's Web site to download an application. *Amount: $1,000. *Deadline: December 1.

American Library Association (ALA)
ALA Scholarship Clearinghouse
50 East Huron Street
Chicago, IL 60611
800-545-2433, ext. 4277
scholarships@ala.org
http://www.ala.org/hrdr/scholarship
Scholarship Name: This organization offers multiple scholarships to individuals pursuing careers in librarianship. *Academic Area: Library sciences. *Age Group: Graduate students. *Eligibility: Applicants must be U.S. or Canadian citizens currently enrolled in an ALA-accredited master's program. They must have completed no more than 12 semester hours toward a MLS/MLIS/MIS. *Application Process: An online application must be submitted, which includes a personal statement and three references. Official transcripts from your undergraduate university must be submitted by mail. Visit the association's Web site to submit an application. *Amount: Scholarships range from $3,000 to $5,000. *Deadline: March 1.

American Medical Women's Association (AMWA)
801 North Fairfax Street, Suite 400
Alexandria, VA 22314
info@amwa-doc.org
http://www.amwa-doc.org
Scholarship Name: Wilhelm-Frankowski Scholarship. *Academic Area: Medicine (physicians). *Age Group: Medical students. *Eligibility: AMWA members who are first-, second-, or third-year medical or osteopathic medical students at an accredited school in the United States may apply. They must

demonstrate considerable involvement in their community, in AMWA's student branch and national membership activities, and in a women-in-medicine group or medical student group(s) other than the AMWA. *Application Process: Applicants must download an application from the association's Web site and submit a completed application by mail. Other documents required include two letters of recommendation from administrators associated with the applicant's involvement in community and women's health issues, two personal references, a letter from the dean stating the applicant has met all academic requirements to date, and a 300- to 500-word personal statement. Visit the association's Web site to download an application. *Amount: $4,000. *Deadline: April 30 for application, May 15 for supporting documentation.

American Nephrology Nurses' Association (ANNA)
East Holly Avenue
Box 56
Pitman, NJ 08071-0056
888-600-2662
anna@ajj.com
http://www.annanurse.org
Scholarship Name: This association offers a variety of Career Mobility Scholarships for women. *Academic Area: Nursing (nephrology). *Age Group: Professionals. *Eligibility: Applicants must be current full members of the ANNA for at least two years, accepted or enrolled in a baccalaureate or higher degree program in nursing, and currently employed in nephrology nursing. *Application Process: Applicants must submit an application, documentation that eligibility has been fulfilled, certified transcripts of academic records, a letter from the academic institution confirming acceptance into a course of study, three letters of recommendation, and a 250-word personal statement detailing their career and education goals. Visit the association's Web site to download applications for specific Career Mobility Scholarships. *Amount: Scholarships range from $2,000 to $2,500. *Deadline: October 15.

American News Women's Club (ANWC)
1607 22nd Street, NW
Washington, DC 20008
202-332-6770
anwclub@covad.net
http://www.anwc.org/scholarships.html

The club offers a scholarship program for female students studying journalism or communications at one of the following postsecondary institutions: American University, Gallaudet University, George Washington University, Howard University, and University of Maryland. *Academic Area: Communications science, journalism. *Age Group: Undergraduate students, graduate students. *Eligibility: Contact the ANWC for information. *Application Process: Contact the club for information. *Amount: Varies. *Deadline: Contact the club for details.

American Nuclear Society (ANS)
Attn: Scholarship Coordinator
555 North Kensington Avenue
LaGrange Park, IL 60526-5592
708-352-6611
http://www.ans.org/honors/scholarships
Scholarship Name: Delayed Education Scholarship for Women. *Academic Area: Engineering (nuclear), nuclear science. *Age Group: Adults. *Eligibility: Mature women whose undergraduate studies in nuclear science, nuclear engineering, or a nuclear-related field have been delayed may apply. *Application Process: Contact the ANS outreach department via an online form for information about the scholarship process. *Amount: $4,000. *Deadline: February 1.

American Nurses Association (ANA)
SAMHSA Minority Fellowship Program
Attn: Janet Jackson, Program Manager
8515 Georgia Avenue, Suite 400
Silver Spring, MD 20910-3492
301-628-5349, 800-274-4ANA
http://www.nursingworld.org/emfp/fellowships/
Fellowship Name: Clinical Research Pre-Doctoral Fellowship. *Academic Area: Nursing (substance abuse and mental health). *Age Group: Graduate students. *Eligibility: Applicants must be master's-prepared nurses who are members of a minority group and committed to pursuing doctoral study on minority psychiatric-mental health and substance abuse issues. They must also be U.S. citizens and members of the ANA. *Application Process: Applicants must complete and electronically submit an application form, a scientifically based essay, and a curriculum vita. Additionally, four letters of recommendation, official copy of sealed transcripts, a copy of the applicant's active RN license, published articles or scholarly writing, and proof of admittance to a Ph.D. program

must all be sent via mail. Visit the association's Web site for more information and to submit an application. *Amount: Fellowship awards vary. *Deadline: March 1.

American Planning Association (APA)
Attn: Kriss Blank, Leadership Affairs Associate
APA Judith McManus Scholarship
122 South Michigan Avenue, Suite 1600
Chicago, IL 60603-6107
312-431-9100
kblank@planning.org
http://www.planning.org/institutions/scholarship.htm
Scholarship Name: Judith McManus Scholarship. *Academic Area: Planning. *Age Group: Undergraduate students, graduate students. *Eligibility: Applicants must be women, U.S. citizens, and African American, Hispanic American, or Native American. They must demonstrate a commitment to planning, strong academic achievement and/or improvement, professional presentation, and financial need. The scholarship is open to both high school seniors and college students. *Application process: Applicants must submit a completed application along with a two- to five-page personal background statement describing their career goals, two letters of recommendation, official transcripts of college work completed, written verification from their school of the average cost per academic year, a resume (optional), a copy of their acceptance letter (incoming students only), and a notarized statement of financial independence signed by their parent(s), also optional. Visit the APA's Web site to download an application. *Amount: Scholarships range from $2,000 to $4,000. *Deadline: April 30.

American Psychiatric Nurses Association (APNA)
1555 Wilson Boulevard, Suite 602
Arlington, VA 22209
703-243-2443
http://www.apna.org
This association offers scholarships for women. *Academic Area: Nursing (psychiatric). *Age Group: Undergraduate students. *Eligibility: Varies by scholarship. *Application Process: contact the association for more information about available scholarships and application procedures. *Amount: Awards vary. *Deadline: Deadlines vary.

American Society for Microbiology (ASM)
ASM Microbiology Undergraduate Research Fellowship Education Board

1752 N Street, NW
Washington, DC 20036
202-942-9283
fellowships-careerinformation@asmusa.org
http://www.asm.org/Education/index.asp?bid=4322
Fellowship Name: Microbiology Undergraduate
Research Fellowship. *Academic Area: Microbiology.
*Age Group: Undergraduate students. *Eligibility:
Underrepresented and historically excluded
undergraduate students who have lab experience,
demonstrate a strong interest in obtaining a Ph.D. or
MD/Ph.D. in the microbiological sciences, and agree
to participate in an undergraduate summer research
program are eligible to apply. Applicants must also be
U.S. citizens. *Application Procedure: Visit the society's
Web site to download an application. *Amount: Up
to $3,500 for student stipend; up to $850 for student
lodging; up to $500 for roundtrip travel to the host
institution (if applicable); and up to $1,000 in travel
support to attend the ASM's General Meeting.
*Deadline: February 1.

American Society of PeriAnesthesia Nurses (ASPAN)
10 Melrose Avenue, Suite 110
Cherry Hill, NJ 08003-3696
877-737-9696
jcerto@aspan.org
http://www.aspan.org/ScholarshipProgram.htm
The society offers various scholarships for women.
*Academic Area: Nursing (anesthesia). *Age Group:
Professionals. *Eligibility: Applicants must be active
ASPAN members for two full years prior to the
application deadline, be registered RNs, employed in
any phase of the perianesthesia setting, and have a
minimum of two years experience in perianesthesia.
*Application Process: Applicants should submit
four copies (one original and three copies) of the
application and supporting materials via mail.
Supporting materials include photocopies of the
applicant's ASPAN membership card and nursing
license, a curriculum vitae, a letter from the dean
of nursing verifying the applicant's enrollment and
GPA, a statement of need and expense projection,
two letters of recommendation, and a one-page
narrative statement (heavily weighted in selection
process) describing the applicant's level of activity
and involvement in any phase of perianesthesia
nursing as well as community involvement. *Amount:
Scholarships range from $260 to $1,000. *Deadline:
July 1.

American Society of Women Accountants (ASWA)
8405 Greensboro Drive, Suite 800
McLean, VA 22102
703-506-3265, 800-326-2163
aswa@aswa.org
http://www.aswa.org/i4a/pages/Index.
cfm?pageid=3412#top
Scholarship Name: Certification Scholarship. *Academic
Area: Accounting, finance. *Age Group: Professionals.
*Eligibility: Applicants must have passed any of the
following exams: CPA, CFP, CFE, CIA, CMA or CVA.
*Application Process: Applicants must submit a
completed application form, a copy of the letter
indicating a passing score (the receipt indicating
proof of payment for the certification exam fees must
accompany the application form), a 75-word essay
about their career goals and objectives, and one
personal reference. Applicants must visit the ASWA's
Web site to request an application from the correct
regional chapter. *Amount: Varies. *Deadline: Contact
the chapter in your region for more information.

American Society of Women Accountants (ASWA)
8405 Greensboro Drive, Suite 800
McLean, VA 22102
703-506-3265, 800-326-2163
aswa@aswa.org
http://www.aswa.org/i4a/pages/Index.
cfm?pageid=3412#top
Scholarship Name: Two-Year College Scholarship. *Academic
Area: Accounting, finance. *Age Group: Undergraduate
students. *Eligibility: Applicants must be in their
second year of an associate degree program, and must
have completed 15 semester hours, with a minimum
cumulative grade point average of 3.0 on a 4.0 scale (or
the equivalent). They should also demonstrate good
leadership, character, communication skills, and financial
need. *Application Process: Applicants must submit
a completed application, a 75-word essay about their
career goals and objectives, one original and two copies
of academic transcripts, one personal reference, and two
references from accounting faculty. Applicants must visit
the ASWA's Web site to request an application from the
correct regional chapter. *Amount: Varies. *Deadline:
Contact the chapter in your region for more information.

American Society of Women Accountants (ASWA)
8405 Greensboro Drive, Suite 800
McLean, VA 22102
703-506-3265, 800-326-2163

aswa@aswa.org

http://www.aswa.org/i4a/pages/Index.
cfm?pageid=3412#top

Scholarship Name: Undergraduate Scholarship. *Academic Area: Accounting, finance. *Age Group: Undergraduate students. *Eligibility: Applicants must have completed 60 semester hours (or the equivalent), with a minimum cumulative grade point average of 3.0 on a 4.0 scale (or the equivalent). They should demonstrate good leadership, character, communication skills, and financial need. *Application Process: Applicants must submit a completed application, a 75-word essay about their career goals and objectives, one original and two copies of academic transcripts, one personal reference, and two references from accounting faculty. Applicants must visit the ASWA's Web site to request an application from the correct regional chapter. *Amount: Varies. *Deadline: Contact the chapter in your region for more information.

American Statistical Association

Attn: Holly B. Shulman, Chair, Gertrude M. Cox
Scholarship Committee

205 College Avenue

Swarthmore, PA 19081

610-690-0861, 888-231-3473

hbs1@cdc.gov

http://www.amstat.org/awards

Scholarship Name: Gertrude M. Cox Scholarship. *Academic Area: Statistics. *Age Group: Graduate students. *Eligibility: Applicants must be citizens or permanent residents of the United States or Canada and be admitted to full-time study in a graduate statistical program by July 1 of the award year. *Application Process: Applicants must submit the original plus two copies of the completed application, original plus two copies of all academic transcripts, three academic reference letters, and a one-page, double-spaced essay. Visit the association's Web site to download an application. *Amount: $1,000. *Deadline: April 1.

American Water Works Association (AWWA)

Attn: Scholarship Coordinator

6666 West Quincy Avenue

Denver, CO 80235

303-347-6206

swheeler@awwa.org

http://www.awwa.org

Scholarship Name: Holly A. Cornell Scholarship. *Academic Area: Engineering (water supply and treatment). *Age Group: Graduate students. *Eligibility: Female and/or minority students may apply. Applicants must be in pursuit of advanced training in the field of water supply and treatment, demonstrate a quality academic record, and have potential to provide leadership in the field of water supply and treatment. *Application Process: Applicants must submit a completed application, official transcripts of all university education, official copies of GRE scores, three letters of recommendation, a proposed curriculum of study, and a one- to two-page statement describing their career objectives. Visit the AWWA's Web site to download an application. *Amount: $5,000. *Deadline: January 15.

American Woman's Society of Certified Public Accountants (AWSCPA)

136 South Keowee Street

Dayton, OH 45402

937-222-1872, 800-297-2721

info@awscpa.org

http://www.awscpa.org

Scholarship Name: National Scholarship. *Academic Area: Accounting. *Age Group: Undergraduate students, graduate students, professionals. *Eligibility: College seniors, fifth-year students, graduate students, and graduates who are eligible to take a CPA review course within on year of scholarship award may apply. Applicants must aspire to become a certified public accountant, have a 3.0 GPA in accounting and a 3.0 GPA overall, be citizens or permanent residents of the United States, and demonstrate high scholastic aptitude as well as financial need. *Application Process: Applicants must submit official transcripts from all college course work, an essay, and a completed application. Visit the association's Web site to download and/or submit an application as well as to find out additional information about regional affiliate scholarships. *Amount: Approximately $2,200. *Deadline: March 15.

American Women in Radio and Television Inc. (AWRT)

8405 Greensboro Drive, Suite 800

McLean, VA 22102

703-506-3290

info@awrt.org

http://www.awrt.org

Scholarship Name: AWRT provides a variety of scholarships through its regional chapters. *Academic Area: Broadcasting, media arts. *Age Group: Varies by scholarship. *Eligibility: Varies. *Application Process: Applicants should visit the AWRT's Web site to locate contact information for their local chapter. *Amount: Varies. *Deadline: Varies.

American Women's Hospitals Service (AWHS)
c/o American Medical Women's Association (AMWA)
801 North Fairfax Street, Suite 400
Alexandria, VA 22314
703-838-0500
info@amwa-doc.org
http://www.amwa-doc.org/index.
cfm?objectId=E1D4E40B-D567-0B25-
574CAFD0BB526D9B
Grant Name: AWHS Overseas Assistance Grants. *Academic Area: Medicine (physicians). *Age Group: Medical students. *Eligibility: Women who are completing their second, third, or fourth year at an accredited U.S. medical school who plan to pursue medical studies in an overseas setting where the medically neglected will benefit are eligible to apply. Applicants must be student members of the AMWA and plan to spend a minimum of six weeks and no longer than one year in a sponsored program that assists the medically neglected. *Application Procedure: Applicants must submit a letter of recommendation, an 800- to 1,000-word statement of interest at least three months prior to departure, and a completed application (available at the organization's Web site). *Amount: Up to $1,500. *Deadline: Applications are accepted on a rolling basis.

Appraisal Institute
Attn: Olivia Carreon
550 West Van Buren Street, Suite 1000
Chicago, IL 60607
312-335-4100
ocarreon@appraisalinstitute.org
http://www.appraisalinstitute.org/education/scolarshp.
asp
Scholarship Name: Educational Scholarship Program. *Academic Area: Real estate. *Age Group: Undergraduate students, graduate students. *Eligibility: Applicants must be female minorities who are pursing degrees in real estate appraisal or a related field. *Application Process: Applicants should visit the institute's Web site for updated information

about the application process. Contact the institute for an application. *Amount: Awards vary. *Deadline: Contact the institute for deadline information.

Appraisal Institute
Attn: Olivia Carreon
550 West Van Buren Street, Suite 1000
Chicago, IL 60607
312-335-4100
http://www.appraisalinstitute.org/education/scolarshp.
asp
Scholarship Name: Regional Scholarship Matching Program. *Academic Area: Real estate. *Age Group: Open. *Eligibility: Applicants must be female minorities who are associate members of the institute and are actively working in the field of real estate appraisal. Applicants should be interested in taking courses through the Appraisal Institute, leading to the SRA or MAI designations. *Application Process: Applicants should visit the institute's Web site for updated information about the application process. Contact the institute for an application. *Amount: Awards vary. *Deadline: Contact the institute for deadline information.

Arkansas Single Parent Scholarship Fund
Attn: Kelley Bradley
614 East Emma Avenue, Suite 119
Springdale, AR 72764
479-927-1402
http://www.aspsf.org/students.html
Scholarship Name: Single Parent Scholarship. *Academic Area: Open. *Age Group: Undergraduate students, graduate students. *Eligibility: Applicants must be economically disadvantaged single parents living in Arkansas with a child (or children) under the age of 18 in custodial care. Applicants must be pursuing an undergraduate degree at a four-year college or university or a master's degree in teaching. *Application Process: Visit the organization's Web site for a detailed map and listing of appropriate contacts, which are assigned by county. Contact your county representative for information about the scholarship application procedures in your area. *Amount: Awards vary. *Deadline: Contact the organization for deadline information.

Association for Feminist Anthropology (AFA)
Attn: Florence Babb, AFA President-Elect
Center for Women's Studies and Gender Research

University of Florida
PO Box 117352
Gainesville, FL 32611
fbabb@wst.ufl.edu
http://sscl.berkeley.edu/~afaweb/Scholarship%20&%20
 Grant%20Information.htm
Award Name: Sylvia Forman Prize. *Academic Area:
 Anthropology. *Age Group: Undergraduate students,
 graduate students. *Eligibility: Undergraduate or
 graduate anthropology students may compete for the
 prize by submitting essays in feminist anthropology.
 *Application Procedure: Essays should be no more than
 35 double-spaced pages, include a bibliography, and
 be written using the American Anthropologist style.
 Contact the AFA President-Elect for further application
 details.. *Amount: $400. *Deadline: August 1.

Association for Women Geoscientists
Chrysalis Scholarship
PO Box 30645
Lincoln, NE 68503-0645
chrysalis@awg.org
http://www.awg.org/eas/scholarships.html
Scholarship Name: Chrysalis Scholarship. *Academic
 Area: Geosciences. *Age Group: Graduate students.
 *Eligibility: Graduate students whose education has
 been interrupted for at least one year may apply.
 Applicants must be students who have contributed
 and plan to continue to contribute to both the
 geosciences and the larger world community through
 their academic and personal strengths. *Application
 Process: Applicants must submit a letter of application
 describing their background, career goals and
 objectives, how the scholarship will be used, and
 the nature and length of the interruption to their
 education. They must also submit letters of reference
 from their thesis advisor and another scientist.
 Applicants must apply by e-mail, with "Chrysalis
 Scholarship" in the subject line. *Amount: $2,000.
 *Deadline: March 15.

Association for Women Geoscientists (AWG)
Attn: Minority Scholarship
PO Box 30645
Lincoln, NE 68503-0645
awgscholarship@yahoo.com
http://www.awg.org/eas/scholarships.html
Scholarship Name: AWG Minority Scholarship.
 *Academic Area: Earth science, geochemistry,
 geology, geophysics, geosciences, hydrology,

meteorology, oceanography. *Age Group:
 Undergraduate students. *Eligibility: Applicants must
 be African American, Hispanic American, or Native
 American and be pursuing or planning to pursue a
 degree full time in earth science, geology, geophysics,
 geochemistry, hydrology, meteorology, physical
 oceanography, planetary geology, or education at an
 accredited college or university. High school seniors
 may also apply. *Application Process: Applicants must
 submit a completed application, a statement detailing
 their academic and career goals, two letters of
 recommendation, high school and college transcripts,
 and SAT or ACT scores. Visit the association's Web
 site to download an application as well as to find
 information about additional scholarships in the
 geosciences available in select regional areas.
 *Amount: $5,000. *Deadline: May 27.

**Association for Women Geoscientists-Salt Lake
 Chapter**
Attn: Scholarship Committee
Attn: Janae Wallace Boyer
PO Box 58691
Salt Lake City, UT 84158-0691
801-537-3387
janaewallace@utah.gov
http://www.awg.org/eas/scholarships.html
Award Name: Outstanding Woman Geologist Award.
 *Academic Area: Geology, geosciences. *Age Group:
 Undergraduate students. *Eligibility: Undergraduate
 women with a declared major in geology who are
 attending a postsecondary institution in Utah or Idaho
 are eligible to apply. Applicants must demonstrate
 strong academic achievement in geology related
 course work and good achievement in other course
 work. This award is not based on financial need.
 *Application Process: Applicants must submit an
 academic transcript and a written recommendation
 from their geology professor. *Amount: $500.
 *Deadline: Typically in March. Contact the association
 for more information.

Association for Women in Architecture-Los Angeles
Attn: Scholarship Committee
22815 Frampton Avenue
Torrance, CA 90501-5034
310-534-8466
scholarship@awa-la.org
http://www.awa-la.org/scholarships.php
Scholarship Name: Association for Women in

Architecture Scholarship. *Academic Area: Architecture, engineering (civil, engineering (electrical), engineering (mechanical), engineering (structural), illustration, interior design, landscape architecture, planning. *Age Group: Undergraduate students, graduate students. *Eligibility: Applicants must be residents of California or attending a California school and must be enrolled in one of the qualifying majors (listed earlier) for the next school term. Applicants must have completed a minimum of 18 units in their major by the application due date. *Application Process: Applicants should mail a completed application form, two letters of recommendation from instructors, official transcripts, a one-page personal statement, a completed financial statement, and a self-addressed stamped envelope. Visit the association's Web site to download the application. *Amount: Scholarships range from $1,000 to $2,500. *Deadline: April 21.

Association for Women in Aviation Maintenance (AWAM)
PO Box 1030
Edgewater, FL 32132-1030
386-416-0248
scholarships@awam.org
http://www.awam.org/awards.htm
Award Name: AWAM Beyond All Odds Award. *Academic Area: Aviation maintenance. *Age Group: Undergraduate students, graduate students *Eligibility: Female aviation maintenance professionals who have become successful despite enormous challenges are eligible to apply. Applicants must be members of the AWAM and demonstrate a commitment to community service. *Application Process: Visit the association's Web site for more information and to download an application. *Amount: Contact the association for details. *Deadline: December 31.

Association for Women in Aviation Maintenance (AWAM)
AWAM Scholarships
PO Box 1030
Edgewater, FL 32132-1030
386-416-0248
scholarships@awam.org
http://www.awam.org
The association offers many scholarships for women. *Academic Area: Aviation maintenance. *Age Group: Varies by scholarship. *Eligibility: Applicants must be

current members of the AWAM or officially join when they submit their scholarship application. *Application Process: Applicants should submit a completed application, two letters of recommendation, a 200-word essay, and their AWAM membership number by mail. Two copies are necessary for each individual scholarship application. Visit the association's Web site to download the application. *Amount: Awards vary. *Deadline: December 31.

Association for Women in Aviation Maintenance (AWAM)
PO Box 1030
Edgewater, FL 32132-1030
386-416-0248
http://www.awam.org/awards.htm
Award Name: Student of the Year Award. *Academic Area: Aviation maintenance. *Age Group: Undergraduate students, graduate students. *Eligibility: Female aviation maintenance students are eligible to apply. Applicants must be members of the AWAM and demonstrate a commitment to community service. *Application Process: Visit the association's Web site for more information and to download an application. *Amount: Contact the association for details. *Deadline: December 31.

Association for Women in Computing
41 Sutter Street, Suite 1006
San Francisco, CA 94104
415-905-4663
info@awc-hq.org
http://www.awc-hq.org
Scholarship Name: This organization offers various scholarships at the regional level. *Academic Area: Computer science. *Age Group: Varies by scholarship. *Eligibility: Varies by scholarship. Application Process: Visit the association's Web site for a listing of regional offices, and to inquire about scholarship opportunities within your geographic region. *Amount: Varies. *Deadline: Varies.

Association for Women in Science (AWIS)
Attn: Dr. Barbara Filner, President, AWIS Educational Foundation
1200 New York Avenue, Suite 650
Washington, DC 20005
202-326-8940
awisedfd@awis.org
http://www.awis.org

Scholarship Name: Association for Women in Science College Scholarship. *Academic Area: Behavioral sciences, engineering (open), life sciences, physical sciences, social sciences. *Age Group: Undergraduate students. *Eligibility: Applicants must be female students who are U.S. citizens. They must plan to attend a college or university in the United States, and have a 3.75 grade point average (on a 4.0 scale), SAT scores (math plus verbal) of at least 1200, or ACT composite scores of 25. Eligible fields of study include the behavioral, life, and physical sciences, and engineering. Applicants must plan a career in research and/or teaching. Competition for the award is strong, and applicants must demonstrate excellent academic achievement, commitment to a career in research or teaching, involvement in community activities, and any economic, social, or other barriers that they have overcome. *Application Process: Applicants must submit five copies of: an essay describing their research experience, scientific interests, and career aspirations; two recommendation letters from science teachers or research advisors; a high school transcript; reports of standardized test scores; and a completed application. Visit the association's Web site to download an application and other required forms. *Amount: $1,000. *Deadline: January 19.

Association for Women in Science (AWIS)
Attn: Dr. Barbara Filner, President, AWIS Educational Foundation
1200 New York Avenue, Suite 650
Washington, DC 20005
202-326-8940
awisedfd@awis.org
http://www.awis.org
Scholarship Name: Association for Women in Science Graduate Fellowship. *Academic Area: Behavioral sciences, engineering (open), life sciences, physical sciences, social sciences. *Age Group: Graduate students. *Eligibility: Female students enrolled in a program leading to a Ph.D. at a U.S. institution may apply. Applicants should have passed their department's qualifying exam and expect to complete their degree by June, demonstrate high academic achievement, illustrate the importance of the research question they are addressing, and explain the importance of their future contributions to science or engineering. *Application Process: Applicants must submit five copies of the following: a completed application, a five-page research plan,

two recommendation letters (including one from their thesis adviser), and transcripts of undergraduate and graduate course work. Visit the association's Web site to download an application and other required forms. *Amount: $1,000. *Deadline: January 26.

Association for Women in Science
1200 New York Avenue, Suite 650
Washington, DC 20005
202-326-8940
awisedfd@awis.org
http://www.awis.org
Scholarship Name: Kirsten R. Lorentzen Award. *Academic Area: Geosciences, physics. *Age Group: Undergraduate students. *Eligibility: Females in their sophomore or junior year of college may apply. Applicants must be U.S. citizens or permanent residents who attend a college or university in the United States and are exceptionally well-rounded students who excel academically as well as in outdoor activities, service, sports, music, or other non-academic pursuits. *Application Process: Applicants must submit a resume form, an essay describing their academic and nonacademic interests and goals, three reference letters, college transcripts, and a completed application. Significant barriers an applicant has had to overcome should also be addressed in the essay. Visit the association's Web site to download an application and relevant forms. *Amount: $1,000. *Deadline: February 2.

Association for Women in Sports Media (AWSM)
PO Box 11897
College Station, TX 77842
AWSMIntern@hotmail.com
http://www.awsmonline.org
Scholarship Name: Association for Women in Sports Media Scholarship and Internship. *Academic Area: Athletics, broadcasting, English/literature, media arts, public relations, visual arts (photography). *Age Group: Undergraduate students, graduate students. *Eligibility: Applicants must be full-time undergraduate or graduate female students pursuing careers in sports writing, copy editing, public relations, broadcasting, Internet, or photography. *Application Process: Applicants must submit a letter explaining their reasons for pursuing a career in sports media (and specifying an interest category), a resume highlighting their journalism experience, three reverences with contact information, two

letters of recommendation, up to five samples of their work, and a $15 application fee (waived for AWSM members). Visit the association's Web site for more information about internship options in various categories. *Amount: $1,000 plus an internship. *Deadline: Contact AWSM for deadline information.

Association for Women Veterinarians (AWV)
Magnolia Association Management Affiliates
310 North Indian Hill Boulevard, Box 337
Claremont, CA 91711-4611
mama.la@verizon.net
http://www.vet.ksu.edu/AWV/docs/awards.html
Scholarship Name: AWV Student Scholarship. *Academic Area: Medicine (veterinary). *Age Group: Veterinary students. *Eligibility: Current second- or third-year veterinary students may apply. Applicants must be attending a college or school of veterinary medicine in the United States or Canada and demonstrate proof of academic achievement and leadership ability. *Application Process: Applicants must submit three completed application packets, which will include a 500-word essay, a resume, a letter of recommendation from a faculty member, and an official transcript (copies acceptable in two packets). Visit the association's Web site for more detailed information about application packets. *Amount: $1,500. *Deadline: January 31.

Association of Black Women Historians
Attn: Wanda A. Hendricks, Ph.D., Graduate Director, Women's Studies Program
University of South Carolina
204 Flinn Hall
Columbia, SC 29208
803-777-4007
nationaldirector@abwh.org
http://www.abwh.org
Scholarship Name: Drusilla Dunjee Houston Memorial Scholarship Award. *Academic Area: History. *Age Group: Graduate students. *Eligibility: Candidates must be African American females who are graduate students of history. *Application Process: Candidates must be nominated for the award. *Amount: $300. *Deadline: August 1.

Association of Black Women Historians (ABWH)
Attn: Wanda A. Hendricks, Ph.D., Graduate Director, Women's Studies Program
University of South Carolina
204 Flinn Hall

Columbia, SC 29208
803-777-4007
nationaldirector@abwh.org
http://www.abwh.org
Award Name: Lillie M. Newton Hornsby Memorial Award. *Academic Area: History. *Age Group: Undergraduate students. *Eligibility: African American females with accomplishments in historical research may be nominated. Applicants must be either at the end of their junior year or beginning their senior year. *Application Process: Candidates must be nominated for the award. Contact the association for more information. *Amount: $250. *Deadline: September 1.

Association of Black Women Lawyers of New Jersey Inc. (ABWLNJ)
PO Box 22524
Trenton, NJ 08607
abwlnj@yahoo.com
http://www.abwlnj.org
Scholarship Name: ABWLNJ Scholarship. *Academic Area: Law. *Age Group: Law students. *Eligibility: Contact the association for eligibility requirements. *Application Process: Contact the association for information on application requirements. *Amount: Awards vary. *Deadline: Deadlines vary.

Association of College and Research Libraries
Attn: Megan Bielefeld
50 East Huron Street
Chicago, IL 60611
312-280-2514, 800-545-2433
mbielefeld@ala.org
http://www.ala.org/Template.cfm?Section=grantfellowship
Fellowship Name: Doctoral Dissertation Fellowship. *Academic Area: Library sciences. *Age Group: Graduate students. *Eligibility: Female and male doctoral students in academic librarianship who have completed all course work and have had a dissertation proposal accepted by their academic institution are eligible to apply. *Application Procedure: Applicants must submit a maximum 10-page, double-spaced proposal and a recent curriculum vitae. *Amount: $1,500. *Deadline: Typically in December. Contact the fellowship chair for details.

Association of Home-Based Women Entrepreneurs Inc.
11330 Olive Boulevard, Suite 106
St. Louis, MO 63141-7161

314-995-1455
aschaefer@advbizsol.com
http://www.hbwe.org/forms/2005/HBWE%20Entreprene
ur%20App.doc
Scholarship Name: Association of Home-Based Women
Entrepreneurs Entrepreneurial Scholarship. *Academic
Area: Entrepreneurism. *Age Group: Open. *Eligibility:
Applicants must be members in good standing of the
association for a minimum of six months. *Application
Process: Applicants should submit a completed
application along with a brief statement on how the
funds will help them develop their at-home business.
Visit the association's Web site to download an
application. *Amount: $500. *Deadline: September 1.

Association of Professional Insurance Women (APIW)

Attn: Laura White, APIW Scholarship Chair
646-227-4200
lwhite@navigantconsulting.com
http://www.apiw.org/scholars.asp
Scholarship Name: APIW Scholarships. *Academic Area:
finance, insurance, risk management. *Age Group:
Undergraduate students. *Eligibility: The association
awards scholarships to women attending either St.
John's University in Queens, New York (APIW Memorial
Scholarship), or the Katie School of Insurance and
Financial Services at Illinois State University (APIW Lana
James Memorial Scholarship) . *Application Process:
Contact the scholarship chair for further information
about the application process. *Amount: Varies.
*Deadline: Varies.

Association of Rehabilitation Nurses (ARN)

Attn: Gayle Elliott, Scholarship Coordinator
4700 West Lake Avenue
Glenview, IL 60025-1485
800-229-7530
gelliott@amctec.com
http://www.rehabnurse.org
Scholarship Name: BSN Scholarship. *Academic Area:
Nursing (rehabilitation). *Age Group: Professionals.
*Eligibility: Applicants must be involved members of
the ARN, enrolled in a BSN program in good standing
and have completed at least one course, and current
practicing rehabilitation nurses with a minimum of
two years of experience in rehabilitation nursing.
*Application Process: Applicants must submit a
completed application form, a transcript documenting
enrollment in a BSN degree program, a typed summary
of their professional and educational goals and

achievements, and two letters of recommendation.
*Amount: $1,000. *Deadline: June 1.

Association of Rehabilitation Nurses

c/o Rehabilitation Nursing Foundation
4700 West Lake Avenue
Glenview, IL 60025-1485
800-229-7530, 847-375-4710
info@rehabnurse.org
http://www.rehabnurse.org/awards/allgrants.html
Grant Name: Mentor Grant. *Academic Area: Nursing
(rehabilitation). *Age Group: Graduate students,
professionals. *Eligibility: Graduate students and
registered nurses who plan to pursue research
in rehabilitation nursing are eligible to apply.
*Application Procedure: Visit the organization's Web
site to download an application. *Amount: $13,500.
*Deadline: February 1.

AVS Science and Technology Society

120 Wall Street, 32nd Floor
New York, NY 10005-3993
212-248-0200
angela@avs.org
http://www.avs.org/popup.aspx?FileName=whetten
Award Name: Nellie Yeoh Whetten Award. *Academic
Area: Science, technology. *Age Group: Graduate
students. *Eligibility: Female graduate students
are eligible to apply. *Application Process:
Applicants must submit a statement detailing their
current research activity, a resume, at least two
recommendations, and a completed application
(available for download at the society's Web site). Five
finalists are invited to present their research at the
society's International Symposium; the trustees then
choose the winner. *Amount: $1,500, plus reimbursed
travel support to attend the symposium. *Deadline:
Typically in late March. Contact the society for more
information.

Bell Labs

c/o Lucent Technologies Foundation
600 Mountain Avenue, Room 6F4
Murray Hill, NJ 07974
908-582-7906
foundation@lucent.com
http://www.lucent.com/news/foundation/blgrfp
The Bell Labs Graduate Research Fellowship Program
seeks to increase the number of women and minorities
pursuing Ph.D.'s in science, math, engineering and

technology. Fellows will be exposed to a variety of research environments by participating in ongoing research activities at Bell Laboratories. *Academic Areas: Communications science, computer science, engineering (chemical), engineering (computer), engineering (electrical), engineering (open), engineering (mechanical), information science, materials science, mathematics, operations research, Physics, statistics. *Age Group: Graduate students. *Eligibility: Women and/or minorities pursuing full-time doctoral studies in chemical engineering, chemistry, communications science, computer science, computer engineering, electrical engineering, information science, materials science, mathematics, mechanical engineering, operations research, physics, or statistics are eligible to apply. Candidates are selected based on their academic achievement and their potential as research scientists. The fellowship is geared toward graduating college seniors, but is open to first-year graduate students. *Application Procedure: Contact the foundation for guidelines. *Amount: The fellowship provides an annual stipend of $17,000, a $250 book allotment per semester, and $1,000 annually for travel expenses to conferences. *Deadline: Contact the foundation for more information.

Beta Pi Sigma Sorority Inc.
8831 South Michigan Avenue
Chicago, IL 60619
bpssi@betapisigmasorority.org
http://www.betapisigmasorority.org/Scholarships.html
This organization offers local and national scholarships for women. *Academic Area: Open. *Age Group: Undergraduate students. *Eligibility: Eligibility varies by scholarship and region. Visit the organization's Web site for a listing of local chapters and specific national scholarship eligibility requirements. The scholarships are available to both high school seniors and college students. *Application Process: Contact the national office by e-mail for information. *Amount: Awards vary. *Deadline: Deadlines vary.

Black Women Lawyers Association of Greater Chicago Inc.
Attn: Marla Shade Harris
321 South Plymouth Court, Suite 600
Chicago, IL 60604
312-554-2088
scholarshipbd@bwla.org
http://www.bwla.org
Scholarship Name: Black Women Lawyers Association of Greater Chicago Scholarship. *Academic Area: Law. *Age Group: Law students. *Eligibility: Applicants must be enrolled in an accredited law school in Illinois and be in good academic standing. *Application Process: Applicants must submit one official law school transcript, one letter of recommendation from a law school professor or staff member, a resume listing their contact information and community service involvement, and a 1,000-word essay on a specific topic. Visit the association's Web site for further information on current essay topics. *Amount: Awards vary. *Deadline: February 17.

Black Women Lawyers Association of Los Angeles Inc.
Attn: Karen E. Pointer
Scholarship Selection Committee
PO Box 8179
Los Angeles, CA 90008
213-538-0137
kpointer@lpclawyers.com
http://www.blackwomenlawyersla.org
Scholarship Name: Black Women Lawyers Association of Los Angeles Scholarship. *Academic Area: Law. *Age Group: Law students. *Eligibility: Second- and third-year full-time law students or fourth-year night program law students may apply. Applicants must have passed the California first year student's examination, demonstrate financial need, be involved in community service projects, and exhibit strong academic achievement as well as legal writing ability. *Application Process: Applicants must submit a completed application along with required documents. Visit the association's Web site to request an application and submission instructions. *Amount: Awards vary. *Deadline: April 9.

Blue Grass Community Foundation
Attn: Barbara A. Fischer, Grants Officer
250 West Main Street, Suite 1220
Lexington, KY 40507-1714
859-225-3343, 877-500-2423
bfischer@bgcf.org
http://www.bgcf.org/scholarships.html
Scholarship Name: John T. and Willie Hedges Scholarship. *Academic Area: Open. *Age Group: Undergraduate students. *Eligibility: Applicants must be female, high school seniors who reside in Bourbon County, Kentucky. *Application Process: Contact the Blue Grass Community Foundation

for application procedures. *Amount: $1,450.
*Deadline: Deadlines vary.

Business and Professional Women/New York State

Attn: Cynthia B. Gillmore, GLG Fellowship Chair
PO Box 200
Johnstown, NY 12095-0200
866-335-9304
BPWNYS@si.rr.com
http://www.bpwnys.org/glg_s.html
Fellowship Name: Grace LeGendre Fellowship. *Academic
Area: Business. *Age Group: Graduate students.
*Eligibility: Women who are permanent residents of
New York State, U.S. citizens, hold a bachelor's degree,
and are currently registered full time in graduate studies
at an accredited college or university in New York State
are eligible to apply. Applicants must demonstrate
academic ability and financial need. *Application
Procedure: Applicants should submit two letters of
recommendation, post-high school transcripts, and
a completed application to the fellowship chair. Visit
the foundation's Web site to download an application.
*Amount: $1,000. *Deadline: February 28.

Business and Professional Women/USA

1900 M Street, NW, Suite 310
Washington, DC 20036
202-293-1100, 800-525-3729
bpwfoundation@act.org
http://www.bpwusa.org
Scholarship Name: Career Advancement Scholarship.
*Academic Area: Open. *Age Group: Adults.
*Eligibility: Applicants must be U.S. citizens, 25 years
of age or older, officially accepted into an accredited
program or course of study at a U.S. institution
(including American Samoa, Puerto Rico, and the
U.S. Virgin Islands), demonstrate clear career plans,
graduate within 12 to 24 months from the date of
the award, demonstrate critical financial need, and
not be earning a Ph.D., M.D., D.D.S., D.V.M., or J.D.
*Application Process: Applicants must submit a
completed application. Visit the association's Web site
after August 1 to download an application. *Amount:
Awards vary. *Deadline: April 15.

Calgon

c/o Maddenmedia
1650 East Ft. Lowell Road, Suite 100
Tucson, AZ 85719
http://www.takemeaway.com/scholarship/index.html

Scholarship Name: Calgon "Take Me Away!" to College
Scholarship. *Academic Area: Open. *Age Group:
Undergraduate students. *Eligibility: Applicants
must be at least 18 years of age (by a specified
date) and enrolled and matriculating full time in an
undergraduate program by the fall of the next year.
Applicants must demonstrate academic achievement
by having a 3.0 GPA, either in high school or already
completed college work. *Application Process:
Applicants should apply online via the company's Web
site. Two short answer essays are required. Calgon
will select individuals from this first-round online
competition to compete in a final essay contest. Visit
the company's Web site to apply. *Amount: $5,000
(first place); $3,500 (second place); $1,500 (third place);
$500 (six runners up). *Deadline: February 28.

Canadian Federation of University Women (CFUW)

Attn: CFUW Fellowships Program Manager
251 Bank Street, Suite 600
Ottawa, ON K2P 1X3 Canada
613-234-2732
cfuwfls@rogers.com
http://www.cfuw.org/index.php?option=com_content
&task=category&sectionid=7&id=85&Itemid=88&la
ng=eng
The federation offers fellowships to support female
graduate students. *Academic Area: Open. *Age
Group: Graduate students. *Eligibility: Women
who hold a bachelor's degree or the equivalent
and who have been accepted into or are currently
enrolled in a graduate program are eligible to apply.
Applicants must be Canadian citizens or have held
immigrant status for one year. *Application Process:
The applicant must submit a completed application
(available for download at the federation's Web site),
a letter of intent, and transcripts. An application fee
of $45 CDN is required per fellowship application.
*Amount: Fellowships range from $2,000 to $12,000.
*Deadline: November 1.

Carrie Chapman Catt Center for Women and Politics

Iowa State University
309 Carrie Chapman Catt Hall
Ames, IA 50011-1305
515-294-3181
cattcntr@iastate.edu
http://www.iastate.edu/~cccatt
Award Name: Carrie Chapman Catt Prize for Research on
Women and Politics. *Academic Area: Political science.

*Age Group: Graduate students, professionals.
*Eligibility: Female junior and senior academic professionals may apply. *Application Process: Applicants should submit a cover sheet, a one-page (or less) biographical statement, and a detailed description (five to 10 pages) of their research project. *Amount: $1,000 for the grand prize; $500 for honorable mentions. *Deadline: October 1. Contact the center for more information.

Carrie Chapman Catt Center for Women and Politics
Iowa State University
309 Carrie Chapman Catt Hall
Ames, IA 50011
515-294-3181
cattcntr@iastate.edu
http://www.iastate.edu/~cccatt/
  legacy%20of%20heroines.html
Scholarship Name: Legacy of Heroines Scholarship Program. *Academic Area: Open. *Age Group: Undergraduate students. *Eligibility: Applicants must be attending or planning to attend Iowa State University (ISU) and should possess a strong involvement in and knowledge of the political process and public service. Scholarships are awarded on the basis of academic merit, contributions to campus and community, leadership ability, and specific criteria established by scholarship donors. Recipients will be required to participate in Carrie Chapman Catt Center for Women & Politics activities each semester. *Application Process: Applicants should submit a completed application and two letters of recommendation from ISU faculty or staff, or two letters of recommendation from high school teachers or counselors (for incoming freshmen only). Visit the center's Web site to download an application. E-mail the center for additional information. *Amount: Awards vary. *Deadline: Application review is ongoing.

Central States Anthropological Society (CSAS)
http://www.iupui.edu/%7Ecsas/Awards.htm
Award Name: Beth Wilder Dillingham Award. *Academic Area: Anthropology. *Age Group: Undergraduate students, graduate students. *Eligibility: Undergraduate or graduate anthropology students of either gender who are responsible for the care of one or more children may apply. Applicants do not need to be married and they do not need to be the legal guardian of the children. *Application Procedure: Visit the society's Web site for application requirements.

*Amount: Award amounts vary each year. *Deadline: May 10.

Chi Eta Phi Sorority Inc.
3029 13th Street, NW
Washington, DC 20009
202-232-3858
chietaphi@erols.com
http://www.chietaphi.com/scholar.html
Scholarship Name: Aliene Carrington Ewell Scholarship. *Academic Area: Nursing (open). *Age Group: Undergraduate students. *Eligibility: Applicants must be currently pursuing a nursing degree and demonstrate scholastic ability, financial need, and leadership potential. Application Process: Contact the organization via e-mail for information on application availability. *Amount: Awards vary. *Deadline: Deadlines vary.

Chi Eta Phi Sorority Inc.
3029 13th Street, NW
Washington, DC 20009
202-232-3858
chietaphi@erols.com
http://www.chietaphi.com/scholar.html
Scholarship Name: Mabel Keaton Staupers Scholarship. *Academic Area: Nursing (open). *Age Group: Undergraduate students, graduate students. *Eligibility: Students pursuing a baccalaureate, master's, or doctoral degree in nursing may apply. Applicants must have contributed to the recruitment and retention of minorities into nursing and the advancement of minority nurses in education and nursing, and have demonstrated leadership skills. Applicants must also be members of both Chi Eta Phi and the American Nurses Association. *Application Process: Contact Chi Eta Phi via e-mail for information on application availability. *Amount: Awards vary. *Deadline: Deadlines vary.

Chi Omega Fraternity
3395 Players Club Parkway
Memphis, TN 38125-8817
901-748-8600
foundation@chiomega.com
http://www.chiomega.com
Scholarship Name: Alumnae Educational Grant. *Academic Area: Open. *Age Group: Adults. *Eligibility: Applicants must be alumna of Chi Omega Fraternity ages 24 years or older who have found it necessary

to interrupt their education, exhibit need and merit, and demonstrate specific individual goals for study at a college, university, vocational, or technical school. *Application Process: Applicants must submit a completed application, official transcripts, official course or program description, a personal letter describing why they need a grant, and two letters of recommendation. Applicants should request further information and application forms by mail or e-mail. *Amount: $1,000. *Deadline: February 3.

Chi Omega Fraternity
3395 Players Club Parkway
Memphis, TN 38125-8817
901-748-8600
foundation@chiomega.com
http://www.chiomega.com/everyday
Scholarship Name: Elizabeth Carmichael Orman Scholarship. *Academic Area: Open. *Age Group: Undergraduate students. *Eligibility: Applicants must be members of Chi Omega Fraternity who are enrolled in their junior year and demonstrate financial need in order to complete their senior year. *Application Process: Applicants must submit a completed application, official transcripts, a written statement of financial need from the institution's financial aid officer, three letters of recommendation, and an essay, not to exceed 200 words. Applicants should request further information by mail or e-mail. Visit the organization's Web site to download an application. *Amount: Awards vary. *Deadline: Typically in early March.

Chi Omega Fraternity
3395 Players Club Parkway
Memphis, TN 38125-8817
901-748-8600
foundation@chiomega.com
http://www.chiomega.com/everyday
Scholarship Name: Mary Love Collins Memorial Scholarship. *Academic Area: Open. *Age Group: Graduate students. *Eligibility: Applicants must be members of Chi Omega fraternity, enrolled full time in a graduate program, demonstrate personal and professional goals, and exhibit a record of academic achievement and aptitude, contribution and service to Chi Omega, their university, and the community. *Application Process: Applicants must submit official transcripts, official GRE or GMAT scores, evidence of admission into a graduate degree program, four

letters of recommendation, a completed application, and an essay, not to exceed 500 words. Applicants should request further information by mail or e-mail. Visit the organization's Web site to download an application. *Amount: Awards vary. *Deadline: Typically in early March.

Computing Research Association (CRA)
Committee on the Status of Women in Computing Research
1100 17th Street, NW, Suite 507
Washington, DC 20036-4632
dmp@cs.tamu.edu
http://www.cra.org/Activities/craw/dmp
The Distributed Mentor Project, funded by the National Science Foundation, seeks to increase the number of women entering graduate school in computer science. The project brings together computer science/engineering undergraduates and professors for 10 weeks of summer research at the mentor's research institution. Students will be involved in research, learn how a research university operates, and meet and interact with graduate students and successful researchers. *Academic Area: Computer science, engineering (computers). *Age Group: Undergraduate students. *Eligibility: College students who are interested in pursuing advanced education and careers in computer science and engineering are eligible to apply. *Application Procedure: Visit the association's Web site to download an application. *Amount: $600 per week for research, plus relocation travel assistance when appropriate. *Deadline: February 15.

Computing Research Association (CRA)
1100 17th Street, NW, Suite 507
Washington, DC 20036-4632
202-234-2111
awards@cra.org
http://www.cra.org/Activities/awards/undergrad/home.html
Award Name: CRA Outstanding Undergraduate Award. *Academic Area: Computer science, engineering (computer). Age Group: Undergraduate students. *Eligibility: Exceptional female and male undergraduates in computer science and engineering may apply. Applicants must demonstrate strong research skills, academic achievement, and service to the community, and be attending schools located in the United States or Canada. *Application Process:

Computer science and engineering departments in the United States and Canada submit nominations. Preference is given to college seniors (or the equivalent). *Amount: $1,000. *Deadline: Typically mid-October. Contact the association for more information.

Coordinating Council for Women in History (CCWH)

Attn: Professor Ann Le Bar, Department of History
Eastern Western University
Patterson Hall 200
Cheney, WA 99004
alebar@mail.ewu.edu
http://www.theccwh.org/awards.htm
Fellowship Name: CCWH/Berkshire Conference of Women Historians Graduate Student Fellowship. *Academic Area: History. *Age Group: Graduate students. *Eligibility: Applicants must be female graduate students in a history department at a U.S. college who are completing a dissertation. They must be members of the CCWH and have passed to ABD status by time of application. *Application Procedure: Applicants must submit a curriculum vitae, a statement describing their proposed dissertation, two letters of recommendation, an application form (available at the council's Web site), and other support materials. Direct fellowship inquiries to Professor Ann Le Bar. *Amount: $500. *Deadline: September 1.

Coordinating Council for Women in History (CCWH)

Attn: Professor Ann Le Bar, Department of History
Eastern Western University
Patterson Hall 200
Cheney, WA 99004
alebar@mail.ewu.edu
http://www.theccwh.org/awards.htm
Fellowship Name: CCWH/Ida B. Wells Award. *Academic Areas: Ethnic studies, history, women's studies. *Age Group: Graduate students. *Eligibility: Applicants must be female graduate students in a history department at a U.S. college who are completing a dissertation in history or interdisciplinary area, such as women's studies or ethnic studies. They must be members of the CCWH and have passed to ABD status. *Application Procedure: Applicants must submit a curriculum vitae, a statement describing their proposed dissertation, two letters of recommendation, an application form (available at the council's Web site), and other support materials. Direct award inquiries to Professor Ann Le Bar. *Amount: $500. *Deadline: September 1.

Daughters of Penelope Foundation Inc.

c/o The American Hellenic Educational Progressive Association (AHEPA)
1909 Q Street, NW, Suite 500
Washington, DC 20009
202-232-6300
daughters@ahepa.org
http://www.ahepa.org/ahepa/Document.aspx?d=1&rd=19682599&f=35&rf=1324245299&m=73&rm=8027069
Scholarship Name: Daughters of Penelope Foundation Scholarship Program. *Academic Area: Open. *Age Group: Undergraduate students, graduate students. *Eligibility: The foundation awards a number of scholarships to undergraduate and graduate students. Financial need is a requirement for some scholarships, but not for others. Academic merit is a necessity for all scholarships. *Application Process: Applicants should contact the foundation for information about the application process. Visit the organization's Web site for periodic updates on additional scholarships that may become available. *Amount: $1,000 to $1,500. *Deadline: Contact the foundation for deadline information.

Delta Delta Delta (Tri Delta) Foundation

Attn: Cindy McSpadden
PO Box 5987
Arlington, TX 76005-5987
817-633-8001
cmcspadden@trideltaeo.org
http://www.trideltafoundation.org
Scholarship Name: Graduate Scholarship. *Academic Area: Open. *Age Group: Graduate students. *Eligibility: Applicants must be members of Tri Delta in good standing who exhibit strong academic merit as well as chapter, campus, and community involvement. Various awards are available at the graduate level through Tri Delta—review criteria for specific individual awards can be found on its official application. *Application Process: Applicants must submit a completed application, two academic recommendations, a personal statement outlining their educational and vocational goals, and official transcripts. Visit the foundation's Web site to download an application. *Amount: Up to $3,000. *Deadline: February 15.

Delta Delta Delta (Tri Delta) Foundation

Attn: Cindy McSpadden
PO Box 5987

Arlington, TX 76005-5987
817-633-8001
cmcspadden@trideltaeo.org
http://www.trideltafoundation.org
Scholarship Name: Undergraduate Scholarship.
*Academic Area: Open. *Age Group: Undergraduate
students. *Eligibility: Applicants must be college
sophomores or juniors who are initiated members
of Tri Delta in good standing. They must remain
on campus as full-time students and active dues-
paying chapter members during the full academic
year. Applicants must also demonstrate chapter and
campus involvement, financial need, a commitment
to community service, and strong academic
achievement. *Application Process: Applicants must
submit an alumna advisor checkoff list, a personal
statement, one letter of recommendation, official
transcripts, and a completed application. Visit the
foundation's Web site to download an application.
*Amount: Awards vary. *Deadline: February 15.

Delta Gamma (DG)
Attn: Jacque Everson, Director, Scholarships, Fellowships,
and Loans
PO Box 7237
The Woodlands, TX 77387
DGScholarships@aol.com
http://www.deltagamma.org/scholarships_fellowships_
and_loans_2.shtml
Scholarship Name: DG Foundation Scholarships for
Undergraduate Study. *Academic Area: Open.
*Age Group: Undergraduate students. *Eligibility:
Applicants must be members of Delta Gamma,
maintain a 3.0 GPA, and participate in chapter,
campus, and community leadership activities.
*Application Process: Visit the sorority's Web site for
specific information about these scholarships and
to download an application form. *Amount: $1,000.
*Deadline: February 1

Delta Gamma (DG)
3250 Riverside Drive
PO Box 21397
Columbus, OH 43221-0397
614-481-8169
http://www.deltagamma.org
Fellowship Name: DG Fellowships for Graduate Study.
*Academic Area: Open. *Age Group: Graduate
students. *Eligibility: Applicant must be a member of
Delta Gamma, demonstrate scholastic excellence, and

illustrate commitment and contribution to her chosen
field. *Application Process: Visit the sorority's Web site
for specific information and to download an official
application form. *Amount: $2,500. *Deadline: April 1.

Delta Kappa Gamma Society International
Attn: International Scholarship Committee
PO Box 1589
Austin, TX 78767-1589
512-478-5748, 888-762-4885
corleap@deltakappagamma.org
http://www.deltakappagamma.org
Scholarship Name: International Scholarship. *Academic
Area: Education. *Age Group: Graduate students.
*Eligibility: Applicants must be active members of
Delta Kappa Gamma for at least three years and
demonstrate leadership skills. They should also
have completed a master's degree, be pursuing a
doctoral degree, and exhibit excellence in scholarship
and service to community. *Application Process:
Applicants should request a full application packet
from the society, and submit a completed application,
three letters of recommendation, sealed transcripts,
and a signed status of program letter in one packet.
*Amount: $5,000. *Deadline: Contact the Committee
for details. .

Delta Phi Epsilon Educational Foundation
16A Worthington Drive
Maryland Heights, MO 63043
314-275-2626
info@dphie.org
http://www.dphie.org/foundation/apply.shtml
Scholarship Name: Delta Phi Epsilon Graduate
Scholarship. *Academic Area: Open. *Age Group:
Graduate students. *Eligibility: Applicants must be
graduate students who are members of Delta Phi
Epsilon or the daughter of a member, demonstrate
academic achievement, financial need, and a
commitment to service and community involvement.
*Application Process: Applicants must submit a
completed application, official transcripts, letters
of introduction and need for scholarship, a typed
1,000-word autobiographical sketch, two recent
photos suitable for publication (for use in press
releases), three letters of recommendation, and
contact information for their school's financial aid
director. Visit the foundation's Web site to download
an application. *Amount: Awards vary. *Deadline:
March 15.

Delta Phi Epsilon Educational Foundation
16A Worthington Drive
Maryland Heights, MO 63043
314-275-2626
info@dphie.org
http://www.dphie.org/foundation/apply.shtml
Scholarship Name: Delta Phi Epsilon Undergraduate
Scholarship. *Academic Area: Open. *Age Group:
Undergraduate students. *Eligibility: Applicants must
be members of Delta Phi Epsilon or the daughter
of a member, demonstrate academic achievement,
financial need, and a commitment to service and
community involvement. High school seniors and
undergraduate students may apply. *Application
Process: Applicants must submit official transcripts
of grades, letters of introduction and need for
scholarship, a typed 1,000-word autobiographical
sketch, two recent photos suitable for publication (for
use in press releases), two letters of recommendation,
a completed application, and the name and address
of the financial aid director for the school they plan to
attend or are currently attending. Visit the foundation's
Web site to download an official application. *Amount:
Awards vary. *Deadline: March 15.

Educational Foundation for Women in Accounting (EFWA)
Attn: Cynthia Hires, Foundation Administrator
Laurels Scholarships
PO Box 1925
Southeastern, PA 19399-1925
610-407-9229
info@efwa.org
http://www.efwa.org/scholarships.htm
Scholarship Name: Laurels Fund Scholarship. *Academic
Area: Accounting. *Age Group: Graduate students.
*Eligibility: Students pursuing a doctoral degree may
apply. Applicants should exhibit academic excellence,
commitment to volunteer work, and financial need.
*Application Process: Applicants should submit
a current curriculum vitae, one copy of an official
transcript, one copy of the abstract and citations of
articles published and/or presented at academic
conferences, one copy of any cases or materials they
have developed (either single- or co-authored), one
letter of reference based on scholarship (addressing
both scholarship and teaching potential), a second
letter of reference detailing their character and
leadership potential, and a statement detailing their
personal and career goals and objectives. Visit the

foundation's Web site to download an application.
*Amount: $1,000 to $5,000. *Deadline: May 1.

Educational Foundation for Women in Accounting (EFWA)
Attn: Cynthia Hires, Foundation Administrator
PO Box 1925
Southeastern, PA 19399-1925
610-407-9229
info@efwa.org
http://www.efwa.org/scholarships.htm
Scholarship Name: Women in Need Scholarship. *Academic
Area: Accounting. *Age Group: Undergraduate students,
adults. *Eligibility: Incoming or current juniors, or those
returning to school with sufficient credits to qualify for
junior status, may apply. Applicants should be committed
to the goal of pursuing a degree in accounting (including
evidence of continued commitment after receiving the
award), aptitude for accounting, clear evidence that they
have established goals and a plan for achieving those
goals (both personal and professional), and financial
need. *Application Process: Applicants should submit a
completed application along with copies of tax returns
for three prior years. They must also submit references:
two personal reference letters (from individuals who
are not related to applicant), two or more professional
reference letters, and a statement from the applicant's
academic advisor assessing the overall quality of their
work and the likelihood of their successful completion
of the degree program. If the applicant is not currently
enrolled in an academic program, a similar statement
from a career counselor or other person who has aided
her in setting goals will suffice. Applicants should review
the application for responsibilities required of award
recipients. Visit the foundation's Web site to download
an application. *Amount: $2,000 per year (for two years).
*Deadline: April 15.

Educational Foundation for Women in Accounting (EFWA)
Attn: Cynthia Hires, Foundation Administrator
PO Box 1925
Southeastern, PA 19399-1925
610-407-9229
info@efwa.org
http://www.efwa.org/scholarships.htm
Scholarship Name: Women in Transition Scholarship.
*Academic Area: Accounting. *Age Group:
Undergraduate students, adults. *Eligibility: Incoming
or current freshman and women returning to school

with a freshman status may apply. Applicants should be committed to the goal of pursuing a degree in accounting (including evidence of continued commitment after receiving the award), aptitude for accounting, clear evidence that they have established goals and a plan for achieving those goals (both personal and professional), and financial need. *Application Process: Applicants should submit a completed application along with copies of tax returns for three prior years. They must also submit references: two personal reference letters (from individuals who are not related to applicant), two or more professional reference letters, and a statement from the applicant's academic advisor assessing the overall quality of their work and the likelihood of their successful completion of the degree program. If the applicant is not currently enrolled in an academic program, a similar statement from a career counselor or other person who has aided her in setting goals will suffice. Applicants should review the application for responsibilities required of award recipients. Visit the foundation's Web site to download an application. *Amount: $4,000. *Deadline: April 15.

Epsilon Sigma Alpha (ESA) Foundation
Attn: Lynn Hughes, Scholarship Director
PO Box 270517
Fort Collins, CO 80527
970-223-2824
orcycler@vsisp.net
http://www.esaintl.com
Scholarship Name: ESA Foundation Scholarships. *Academic Area: Open. *Age Group: Varies by scholarship. *Eligibility: Varies by scholarship and region. *Application Process: Applicants should submit a completed application to their state's counselor or directly to the scholarship director if there is no counselor for their state. Visit Epsilon Sigma Alpha's Web site for a complete listing of scholarships by state and for state counselor contacts. E-mail your state's counselor or the scholarship director for further information about application availability. *Amount: $500 and up. *Deadline: February 1.

Epsilon Sigma Alpha (ESA) Foundation
Attn: Lynn Hughes, Scholarship Director
PO Box 270517
Fort Collins, CO 80527
970-223-2824
orcycler@vsisp.net
http://www.esaintl.com

Scholarship Name: ESA Foundation Graduate Study Scholarship. *Academic Area: Open. *Age Group: Graduate students. *Eligibility: Any student attending an accredited graduate school in the United States may apply. Applicants must show proof of a minimum GPA of 3.5 on a 4.0 scale and submit verification of enrollment in a graduate studies program. Applicants must also demonstrate financial need and have a background in service and leadership. *Application Process: Applicants must submit a completed application, a $5 processing fee, a one-page personal statement about their studies and how they will benefit the community in the field, two current letters of recommendation, and official transcripts. Applicants should be sure to include the name, address, and phone number of the college or university they are attending. Visit ESA's Web site to download an application. *Amount: $7,500. *Deadline: February 1.

Executive Women International
515 South 700 East, Suite 2A
Salt Lake City, UT 84102
801-355-2800
ewi@executivewomen.org
http://www.executivewomen.org/ScriptContent/scholarships/asist.cfm
Scholarship Name: Adult Students in Scholastic Transition Scholarship. *Academic Area: Open. *Age Group: Adults. *Eligibility: Adults at transitional points in their lives who are at least 18 years old may apply. Applicants may be single parents, individuals just entering the workforce, or displaced workers. Applicants must demonstrate financial need and may be socially, physically, and economically challenged with displaced households and small children. Criteria differ according to individual chapters. Visit the organization's Web site for contact information for your regional chapter. *Application Process: Applicants must submit a completed application, federal and state tax returns for the most recent year, two letters of recommendation, and any school transcripts or test scores. Visit the organization's Web site to download an application. *Amount: Up to $2,500. *Deadline: Deadlines vary according to regional chapter.

Executive Women International
515 South 700 East, Suite 2A
Salt Lake City, UT 84102

801-355-2800

ewi@executivewomen.org

http://www.executivewomen.org/ScriptContent/
scholarships/ewisp.cfm

Scholarship Name: Executive Women International
Scholarship. *Academic Area: Open. *Age Group:
Undergraduate students. *Eligibility: Applicants
must be female, high school juniors. Criteria vary
with each regional chapter. Visit the organization's
Web site for contact information for your regional
chapter. *Application Process: Applicants must submit
a completed application, an essay, two letters of
recommendation, and school transcripts. Visit the
organization's Web site to download an application.*
Amount: Up to $10,000. *Deadline: Deadlines vary
according to regional chapter.

Financial Women International (FWI) Foundation

1027 West Roselawn Avenue

Roseville, MN 55113

651-487-7632, 866-236-2007

info@fwifoundation.org

http://www.fwifoundation.org/fwi_scholarships.php

Scholarship Name: The Graduate School of Banking,
University of Wisconsin-Madison Scholarship.
*Academic Area: Finance. *Age Group: Graduate
students. *Eligibility: This organization matches the
funds issued by the Herbert V. Prochnow Educational
Foundation Scholarship awarded through the
Graduate School of Banking at the University of
Wisconsin-Madison. To receive these matching funds
from Financial Women International, applicants must
be members of FWI. Contact FWI to find out about
other eligibility criteria. *Application Process: Visit the
FWI Web site for application information. *Amount:
The FWI Foundation pays one third of the student's
tuition fees and the Graduate School of Banking also
pays one third. *Deadline: July 1.

Founders' Foundation of Theta Phi Alpha

Attn: Scholarships

27025 Knickerbocker Road

Bay Village, OH 44140-2300

440-899-9282

info@thetaphialpha.org

http://www.thetaphialpha.org/foundation_scholarship.
php

Scholarship Name: Founders' Foundation Scholarship.
*Academic Area: Open. *Age Group: Undergraduate
students, graduate students. *Eligibility: Applicants

must be members of Theta Phi Alpha in good
standing who demonstrate good academic
performance, financial need, and service to Theta
Phi Alpha. *Application Process: Applicants must
submit a completed application form, an official
transcript, and one recommendation letter. They
must also demonstrate a strong history of academic
achievement, financial need, and service to sorority
and campus. Visit the foundation's Web site to
download an application. *Amount: Awards vary.
*Deadline: April 30.

Friday Morning Music Club (FMMC) Inc.

2233 Wisconsin Avenue, NW, Suite 326

Washington, DC 20007-4126

202-333-2075

fmmc@fmmc.org

http://www.fmmc.org/wic/index.shtml

Award Name: Washington International Competition.
*Academic Area: Performing arts (music-open. *Age
Group: High school students, college students, young
adults. *Eligibility: FMWC offers several competitions
for young women and men singers, composers,
pianists, and string players who are preparing for a
professional career are eligible to compete for awards.
*Application Process: Competitions are announced
through secondary and postsecondary institutions,
music teachers, and music publications. Applicants
must submit an audition CD. Those who are accepted
compete in Washington, D.C., before a panel of judges
who determine category winners. *Amount: Varies.
Past awards ranged from $2,000 to $7,000. *Deadline:
Contact the club for more information.

Friends of Lulu

13210 Michigan Avenue

Dearborn, MI 48126

info@friends-lulu.org

http://www.friends-lulu.org/awards.html

Friends of Lulu, a national organization aimed at getting
more women and girls involved in comic books,
offers several awards to recognize outstanding comic
book artists. *Academic Area: Illustration, visual arts
(open). *Age Group: Open. *Eligibility: Nominees must
have had their work published, whether company-
published, Internet-published, or self-published.
The awards are open to both women and men.
*Application Process: Nominations can be made at the
organization's Web site or via e-mail. *Amount: This is
not a monetary award, but an excellent opportunity

for comic book artists to gain professional recognition and expand their profile at the national level. *Deadline: Varies. Contact Friends of Lulu for more information.

Gamma Phi Beta
12737 East Euclid Drive
Centennial, CO 80111
303-799-1874
info@gammaphibeta.org
http://www.gammaphibeta.org
This sorority offers fellowships for women. *Academic Area: Open. *Age Group: Undergraduate students, graduate students. *Eligibility: Applicants must be members of Gamma Phi Beta to apply for funds or to log on to the scholarship/fellowship section of the sorority's Web site. *Application Process: Applicants should use their membership information to log onto the sorority's Web page to download information about available funds. *Amount: Amounts vary. *Deadline: Deadlines vary.

Gamma Phi Delta Sorority Inc.
Attn: Katie Broughton, Scholarship Chair
PO Box 450672
Houston, TX 77245-0672
713-433-2031
Kbroug5603@aol.com
http://www.gammaphideltasorority.com
This sorority offers four national scholarships and two national endowments as well as local-level scholarships for women. *Academic Area: Open. *Age Group: Varies by scholarship. *Eligibility: Varies by scholarship. *Application Process: Applicants should contact the scholarship chair via e-mail for further information on the application process. *Amount: Awards vary. *Deadline: Deadlines vary.

George Washington University Summer Program for Women in Mathematics
Attn: Professor Murli M. Gupta, Program Director
Mathematics Department (Old Main 102)
1922 F Street, NW
Washington, DC 20052
202-994-4857
mmg@gwu.edu
http://www.gwu.edu/~math/spwm.html
Grant Name: Summer Program for Women in Mathematics. Goals of the program are to build enthusiasm, develop research skills, cultivate mathematical self-confidence, and promote success in graduate school. (Note: No course credits or grades will be given.) *Academic Area: Mathematics. *Age Group: Undergraduate students. *Eligibility: Mathematically talented women who are contemplating graduate study in the mathematical sciences are eligible to apply for this five-week intensive program. Applicants must have completed their junior year by the time of the program. *Application Procedure: Interested parties should submit an application form (which includes a list of mathematics courses taken or in progress and a statement of interest), two letters of faculty recommendation, and academic transcripts. *Amount: $1,500, plus a travel allowance and campus room and board. *Deadline: March 1.

Girls Incorporated
Scholarships and Awards
120 Wall Street
New York, NY 10005-3902
800-374-4475
http://www.girlsinc.org
This organization offers scholarships for young women. *Academic Area: Open. *Age Group: Undergraduate students. *Eligibility: Applicants must be high school juniors or seniors who are members of a Girls Incorporated affiliate. *Application Process: Visit the organization's Web site for information on joining local affiliate groups. Information about scholarships is distributed to members only. *Amount: $2,500 and $15,000 scholarships are available. *Deadline: Deadlines vary.

Graduate Women in Science (GWS)
Sigma Delta Epsilon (SDE)
Attn: Dr. Jennifer Ingram, SDE/GWS Fellowships Coordinator
CIIT Centers for Health Research
PO Box 12137
Research Triangle Park, NC 27709-2137
919-558-1444
jingram@ciit.org
http://www.gwis.org
This organization offers numerous fellowships to women. *Academic Area: Science. *Age Group: Graduate students. *Eligibility: Applicants must be members of Sigma Delta Epsilon who are enrolled in a graduate program and who show outstanding ability and promise in research. *Application Process:

Applicants should send four copies of their completed application to the appropriate award chair (listed at GWS's Web site). Visit the organization's Web site to download the appropriate application for each fellowship. *Amount: $300 to $4,000. *Deadline: January 15.

Guardian Life Insurance Company of America
Attn: Girls Going Places
7 Hanover Square, Mailstop 26-J
New York, NY 10004-2616
diana_acevedo@glic.com
http://www.guardianlife.com/womens_channel/girls_
going_places/girls_going_places.html
Contest Name: Girls Going Places Entrepreneurship Award Program. *Academic Area: Entrepreneurism. *Age Group: Ages 12 through 18. *Eligibility: Applicants must be females between the ages of 12 and 18 as of December 31, who demonstrate having taken steps towards financial independence. Applicants must be nominated by an adult U.S. citizen (family members are acceptable). Applicants also must have demonstrated a commitment to their school and community, and are NOT currently enrolled in any form of postsecondary educational institution. *Application Process: Applicants should submit a completed application form, signed by a nominating party, along with a 750- to 1,000-word essay (written by the nominator). Visit the company's Web site to download an application form and to view specific information regarding the essay question. *Amount: $10,000 (first prize); $5,000 (second prize); $3,000 (third prize); $1,000 (12 runners up). *Deadline: February 24.

Henry Luce Foundation Inc.
111 West 50th Street, Suite 4601
New York, NY 10020
212-489-7700
hlf@hluce.org
http://www.hluce.org/3cblfm.html
Fellowship Name: Clare Booth Luce Program. *Academic Areas: Engineering (open), mathematics, science. *Age Group: Undergraduate and graduate students. *Eligibility: Female undergraduate or graduate students who are U.S. citizens are eligible to apply to the program, which encourages women to pursue study and careers in fields that are typically male-dominated. Fellowships are awarded based on the applicant's academic excellence and

professional potential. *Application Procedure: Fellowships are made only through four-year degree-granting institutions, not directly to individuals. Thirteen institutions (Boston University, Colby College, Creighton University, Fordham University, Georgetown University, Marymount University, Mount Holyoke College, St. John's University, Santa Clara University, Seton Hall University, Trinity College, University of Notre Dame, and Villanova Preparatory School) have been designated permanent participants, and other colleges are invited to participate on a temporary basis. *Amount: Varies. Awards must be used exclusively in the United States. *Deadline: Contact the foundation for more information.

Independent Means Inc.
Attn: Meghan Kerner
126 East Haley Street, #A16
Santa Barbara, CA 93101
800-350-1816
mkerner@independentmeans.com
http://www.independentmeans.com/imi/dollardiva/
bizplan
Independent Means is a national organization that seeks to instill in teenagers and young women the desire and the means to attain financial independence and maintain it throughout adult life. It offers the annual National Business Plan Competition. *Academic Area: Business, entrepreneurism. * Age Group: High school students, undergraduate students. *Eligibility: Young women ages 13 to 21, who are interested in business and/or entrepreneurship are eligible to apply. *Application Process: Applicants must submit an application and a business plan. Visit the organization's Web site for more information and tips on writing a business plan. *Amount: $2,000, plus a scholarship to Camp $tart-Up, an entrepreneurial camp for young women. *Deadline: November 15.

INTEL Corporation
Corporate U.S Headquarters
2200 Mission College Boulevard
Santa Clara, CA 95052
408-765-8080
http://www.intel.com/community
This company offers scholarships to women. *Academic Area: Computer science, engineering (computer), engineering (electrical), information technology. *Age Group: Undergraduate students. *Eligibility:

Intel awards renewable scholarships for women and underrepresented minority high school seniors who plan to attend a collaborating university at an Intel site in the United States. These scholarship programs are administered at the relevant Intel sites and are available only for study at the designated collaborating universities. Visit the company's Web site for more information. *Application Process: Applicants must apply for scholarships through the collaborating universities. Applications should be requested from these organizations. Visit Intel's Web site for a complete list of participating institutions in the United States and abroad. *Amount: Awards vary. *Deadline: Deadlines vary.

International Federation of University Women (IFUW)
8 rue de l'Ancien-Port
CH-1201 Geneva, Switzerland
info@ifuw.org
http://ifuw.org/fellowships
This organization offers a variety of grants to women. *Academic Area: Open. *Age Group: Varies by grant. *Eligibility: Applicants should visit the organization's Web site for specific information regarding grants offered by IFUW's international affiliates for primary, secondary, undergraduate, and postgraduate studies. Contact the IFUW affiliate in your respective country to ask about available funding. *Application Process: Varies depending on affiliate's process. Visit the affiliate directly at the IFUW's Web site for further information. *Amount: Awards vary. *Deadline: Deadlines vary.

International Society of Women Airline Pilots (ISA +21)
Attn: Beverly Sinclair
ISA +21 Scholarship
2457-F South Victor Street
Aurora, CO 80114
isa21scholarbev@aol.com
http://www.iswap.org/html/scholarship_info.html
Scholarship Name: ISA +21 Airline Scholarship. *Academic Area: Aviation. *Age Group: Adults. *Eligibility: Applicants must possess a United States FAA Commercial Pilot Certificate with an instrument rating, a first-class medical certificate, and an airline transport pilot rating. Applicants must have a current FE written and also demonstrate financial need. *Application Process: Applicants must submit a completed application form, copies of income tax forms, logbook

pages, pilot licenses and medical certificates, a descriptive essay, and at least three recommendations. Visit the society's Web site to download an application. *Amount: Awards include necessary instruction to achieve aircraft type ratings such as B727, MD-80, and B737. *Deadline: December 10.

International Society of Women Airline Pilots (ISA +21)
Attn: Beverly Sinclair
ISA +21 Scholarship
2457-F South Victor Street
Aurora, CO 80114
isa21scholarbev@aol.com
http://www.iswap.org
Scholarship Name: ISA +21 Financial Scholarship. *Academic Area: Aviation. *Age Group: Professionals. *Eligibility: Applicants must possess a United States FAA Commercial Pilot Certificate with an instrument rating and a first-class medical certificate, as well as flight time in a fixed wing aircraft commensurate with the rating sought. Applicants must also demonstrate financial need. *Application Process: Applicants must submit a completed application form, copies of income tax forms, logbook pages, pilot licenses and medical certificates, a descriptive essay, and at least three recommendations. Visit the society's Web site to download an application. *Amount: Awards vary according to funds available. Visit the society's Web site for a listing of specific scholarships. *Deadline: December 10.

Iota Sigma Pi
Attn: Kathryn A. Thomasson, Director for Student Awards
University of North Dakota, Department of Chemistry
PO Box 9024
Grand Forks, ND 58202-9024
701-777-3199
kthomasson@chem.und.edu
http://www.iotasigmapi.info/ISPstudentawards/ISPstudentawards.htm
Award Name: Iota Sigma Pi (a national honor society for women in chemistry) offers several awards to recognize academic and professional excellence. *Academic Area: Biochemistry, chemistry. *Age Group: Undergraduate students, graduate students, professionals. *Eligibility: Varies by award. *Application Process: Varies by award. Visit Iota Sigma Pi's Web site for contact information for and details about specific awards. *Amount: Awards range from

$500 to $1,000. *Deadline: Varies by award. (Note: Not all awards are offered annually.) Contact Iota Sigma Pi for more information.

Iota Sigma Pi
Attn: Kathryn A. Thomasson, Director for Student Awards
University of North Dakota, Department of Chemistry
PO Box 9024
Grand Forks, ND 58202-9024
701-777-3199
kthomasson@chem.und.edu
http://www.iotasigmapi.info/ISPstudentawards/
    ISPstudentawards.htm
Scholarship Name: Gladys Anderson Emerson
    Scholarship. *Academic Area: Biochemistry, chemistry.
    *Age Group: Undergraduate students. *Eligibility:
    Applicants who have attained a minimum junior
    standing at the college level may be nominated.
    They must have at least one semester of work to
    complete and be a member of Iota Sigma Phi at
    the time of their nomination. Nomination for the
    scholarship must be made by a member of Iota Sigma
    Pi and supported by members of the faculty of the
    nominee's institution. *Application Process: Applicants
    must submit information on their chapter status,
    official transcripts from all colleges and universities
    they have attended, a list of all academic honors and
    professional memberships they have earned or hold,
    a letter of nomination from a member of Iota Sigma
    Pi, at least two letters of recommendation from faculty
    members, a completed application, and a short essay
    detailing their goals in chemistry, hobbies and talents,
    and financial need. Five copies should be sent to
    the director for student awards. Visit the Iota Sigma
    Pi's Web site to download an application. *Amount:
    $2,000. *Deadline: February 15.

Jewish Foundation for Education of Women (JFEW)
Attn: Marge Goldwater, Executive Director
135 East 64th Street
New York, NY 10021
212-288-3931
FdnScholar@aol.com
http://www.jfew.org
Scholarship Name: Biller/JFEW Scholarship.*Academic
    Area: Open. *Age Group: Undergraduate students,
    graduate students. *Eligibility: Applicants must
    be Jewish students with financial need, who are
    permanent residents of and attending school in
    New York City, or the New York counties of Nassau,

Suffolk, or Westchester. This scholarship is offered
through a joint program with UJA-Federation that
is administered by the Hebrew Free Loan Society.
*Application Process: Contact the foundation for an
application and instructions after March 15. *Amount:
$5,000 and up. *Deadline: Deadlines vary.

Jewish Foundation for Education of Women (JFEW)
Attn: Marge Goldwater, Executive Director
135 East 64th Street
New York, NY 10021
212-288-3931
FdnScholar@aol.com
http://www.jfew.org
Scholarship Name: Emigres in the Health Sciences
    Scholarship. *Academic Area: Medicine (dental
    hygiene), medicine (dentistry), medicine
    (open), medicine (physician assisting), medicine
    (sonography), nursing (open), pharmaceutical
    sciences, therapy (occupational), therapy (physical)
    *Age Group: Undergraduate students, graduate
    students, dental students. *Eligibility: Applicants
    must be Jewish, live within a 50-mile radius of New
    York City, and be an emigrant from the former
    Soviet Union. They must be enrolled in or about to
    enroll in a health sciences program, and also show
    financial need. (Note: Premedical students are not
    eligible to apply.) *Application Process: Contact
    the foundation for an application and instructions
    after March 15. *Amount: $5,000 and up. *Deadline:
    Deadlines vary.

Kappa Alpha Theta Fraternity Foundation
Attn: Cindy Thoennes, Coordinator of Programs
8740 Founders Road
Indianapolis, IN 46268
888-526-1870, ext. 119
cthoennes@kappaalphatheta.org
http://www.kappaalphatheta.org
The foundation provides leadership and educational
    grants. *Academic Area: Open. *Age Group:
    Undergraduate students, adults. *Eligibility: Members
    and alumna of Kappa Alpha Theta Fraternity (a
    Greek-letter fraternity for women) are eligible to
    apply. *Application Procedure: Visit the foundation's
    Web site to download an application. *Amount:
    Varies. *Deadline: Applicants should submit their
    applications no later than 90 days before the start
    date of the leadership or educational program they
    wish to attend.

Kappa Alpha Theta Fraternity Foundation

Attn: Cindy Thoennes, Coordinator of Programs
8740 Founders Road
Indianapolis, IN 46268
888-526-1870, ext. 119
cthoennes@kappaalphatheta.org
http://www.kappaalphatheta.org
Kappa Alpha Theta offers many undergraduate and graduate scholarships for women. *Academic Area: Open. *Age Group: Undergraduate students, graduate students. *Eligibility: Graduate students and undergraduate freshmen, sophomore, and juniors may apply. Applicants must be members in good standing of Kappa Alpha Theta. All Kappa Alpha Theta scholarships are merit based. *Application Process: Applicants should submit, in one envelope, two sets (one original and one copy) of: a completed application, two letters of reference, official transcripts, a personal statement, and a current resume. Visit Kappa Alpha Theta's Web site to download an application. *Amount: $1,000 and up. *Deadline: February 1.

Kappa Delta Sorority

Attn: Foundation Manager
3205 Players Lane
Memphis, TN 38125
901-748-1897, 800-536-1897
foundation@kappadelta.org
http://www.kappadelta.org
Scholarship Name: Founders' Scholarship. *Academic Area: Open. *Age Group: Undergraduate students. *Eligibility: Undergraduate collegiate initiated members of Kappa Delta Sorority may apply. Scholarships are awarded on the basis of academic excellence and the applicant's service to chapter. Applicants also must illustrate a commitment to service on campus and in the community, strong personal objectives, and future career goals. *Application Process: Applicants should submit a completed application, a personal statement, two letters of recommendation, an official transcript, and a professional-quality photograph. *Amount: $4,000. *Deadline: February 1.

Kappa Delta Sorority

Attn: Foundation Manager
3205 Players Lane
Memphis, TN 38125
901-748-1897, 800-536-1897

foundation@kappadelta.org
http://www.kappadelta.org
The sorority offers numerous undergraduate and graduate memorial scholarships for women. *Academic Area: Open. *Age Group: Undergraduate students, graduate students. *Eligibility: All applicants will be judged on academic excellence, service to the chapter, alumnae association or national Kappa Delta participation, service to the campus and community, financial need, and personal objectives and goals. Please note that some scholarships have restrictions on major or class in school, and others weigh financial need. Visit the sorority's Web site for an extensive list of specific scholarships that are available. *Application Process: Applicants must submit an application, a personal statement, two recommendations, an official transcript, and a professional-quality photograph. Visit the sorority's Web site to download an application form. *Amount: Awards vary, but most are between $1,000 and $2,000. *Deadline: February 1.

Kappa Kappa Gamma Foundation

Attn: Brenda Landry, Foundation Administrator
PO Box 38
Columbus, OH 43216-0038
614-228-6515, 866-KKG-1870
blandry@kappakappagamma.org
http://www.kappakappagamma.org
This fraternity for women offers numerous undergraduate and graduate scholarships for women. *Academic Area: Open. *Age Group: Undergraduate students, graduate students. *Eligibility: All applicants must be initiated members of Kappa Kappa Gamma in good standing, with a GPA of at least 3.0 on a 4.0 scale. Graduate students must be pursuing full-time study. *Application Process: Applicants must submit an original plus two copies of application and supporting materials. These materials should include a personal essay expressing the applicant's educational and career goals and financial need, official transcripts from all colleges attended, two letters of recommendation, and one self-addressed stamped postcard. Visit the fraternity's Web site to download an application form. *Amount: Awards vary. *Deadline: February 1.

Kappa Omicron Nu Honor Society

Awards Committee
4990 Northwind Drive, Suite 140
East Lansing, MI 48823-5031

517-351-8335
http://www.kon.org/awards/grants.html
Fellowship Name: Eileen C. Maddex Fellowship.
  *Academic Area: Family and consumer sciences.
  *Age Group: Graduate students. *Eligibility: Women pursuing graduate study in the family and consumer sciences or related disciplines are eligible to apply. Applicants must be current, active members of the society and demonstrate academic ability, an interest in research related to family and consumer sciences, and leadership skills. *Application Procedure: Applicants must submit a completed application (available at the organization's Web site) and three letters of recommendation. *Amount: $2,000. *Deadline: April 1.

Kappa Omicron Nu Honor Society
Attn: Awards Committee
4990 Northwind Drive, Suite 140
East Lansing, MI 48823-5031
517-351-8335
http://www.kon.org/awards/grants.html
Fellowship Name: Hettie M. Anthony Fellowship.
  *Academic Area: Family and consumer sciences.
  *Age Group: Graduate students. *Eligibility: Women pursuing doctoral study in the family and consumer sciences or related disciplines are eligible to apply. Applicants must be current, active members of the society and demonstrate academic ability, an interest in research related to family and consumer sciences, and leadership skills. *Application Procedure: Applicants must submit a completed application (available at the organization's Web site) and three letters of recommendation. *Amount: $2,000. *Deadline: January 15.

Kappa Omicron Nu Honor Society
Attn: Awards Committee
4990 Northwind Drive, Suite 140
East Lansing, MI 48823-5031
517-351-8335
http://www.kon.org/awards/grants.html
Fellowship Name: Kappa Omicron Nu Marjorie M. Brown Dissertation Fellowship Program. *Academic Area: Family and consumer sciences. *Age Group: Graduate students. *Eligibility: Women seeking doctoral degrees in the family and consumer sciences are eligible to apply. Applicants must be current, active members of the society and seek to continue, via her dissertation, Dr. Marjorie M. Brown's philosophical

work using critical social theory. *Application Procedure: Applicants must submit five copies of a dissertation research application. Visit the society's Web site for details. *Amount: $3,000 is awarded upon approval of the applicant's dissertation proposal and $7,000 upon completion of the applicant's dissertation. *Deadline: March 15.

Kappa Omicron Nu Honor Society
Attn: Awards Committee
4990 Northwind Drive, Suite 140
East Lansing, MI 48823-5031
517-351-8335
http://www.kon.org/awards/grants.html
Fellowship Name: National Alumni Fellowship.
  *Academic Area: Family and consumer sciences.
  *Age Group: Graduate students. *Eligibility: Women pursuing graduate study in the family and consumer sciences or related disciplines are eligible to apply. Applicants must be current, active members of the society and demonstrate academic ability, an interest in research related to family and consumer sciences, and leadership skills. *Application Procedure: Applicants must submit a completed application (available at the organization's Web site) and three letters of recommendation. The fellowship is awarded biennially. *Amount: $2,000. *Deadline: April 1.

Kappa Omicron Nu Honor Society
Attn: Awards Committee
4990 Northwind Drive, Suite 140
East Lansing, MI 48823-5031
517-351-8335
http://www.kon.org/awards/grants.html
Fellowship Name: Omicron Nu Research Fellowship.
  *Academic Area: Family and consumer sciences. *Age Group: Graduate students. *Eligibility: Women pursuing doctoral study in the family and consumer sciences or related disciplines are eligible to apply. Applicants must be current, active members of the society and demonstrate academic ability, an interest in research related to family and consumer sciences, and leadership skills. *Application Procedure: Applicants must submit a completed application (available at the organization's Web site) and three letters of recommendation. *Amount: $2,000. *Deadline: January 15.

Kappa Omicron Nu Honor Society
Attn: Dr. Dorothy I. Mitstifer, Executive Director
4990 Northwind Drive, Suite 140

East Lansing, MI 48823-5031
517-351-8335
dmitstifer@kon.org
http://www.kon.org/awards/grants.html
Scholarship Name: Chapter Scholar Program (scholarships for undergraduates and graduates at the local chapter level). *Academic Area: Family and consumer sciences. *Age Group: Undergraduate students, graduate students. *Eligibility: Applicants must be current, active members of Kappa Omicron Nu, with an interest in research, excellent communication skills, and an overall record of achievement. They should also exhibit leadership skills in a campus or unit project. *Application Process: Applicants should contact their local units for more information. Visit the society's Web site for a list of eligible chapters. *Amount: Scholarships range from $150 to $500. *Deadline: Deadlines vary.

Kappa Phi Iota Sorority Inc.
kappa_phi_iota@hotmail.com
http://www.angelfire.com/nj/kappaphiiota
This historically black sorority with a strong literary focus offers scholarships to women. *Academic Area: English (literature, writing). *Age Group: Varies by award. *Eligibility: Applicants must be members of Kappa Phi Iota and exhibit excellence and potential in writing. *Application Process: Applicants should contact their local chapters for more information about scholarship funds available, or contact the national office by e-mail for application information. *Amount: Awards vary. *Deadline: Deadlines vary.

Kentucky Foundation for Women (KFW)
1215 Heyburn Building, 332 West Broadway
Louisville, KY 40202
502-562-0045
http://www.kfw.org/grants.html
Grant Name: Artist Enrichment Grant Program (helps feminist artists and arts organizations enhance their skills and abilities). *Academic Area: Visual arts (open). *Age Group: Open. *Eligibility: Kentucky-based women artists and organizations are eligible to apply. Applicants must demonstrate artistic ability, a commitment to feminism, and an understanding of how the creation of art relates to social change. *Application Procedure: Applicants must submit a completed grant proposal, which will then be reviewed by a panel that makes funding recommendations to the KFW Board of

Directors. *Amount: Awards range from $1,000 to $7,500—grants typically average from $3,000 to $5,000. Awards may be used for artistic development, artist residencies, the exploration of new areas or techniques, and the creation of new art. *Deadline: September 1.

Kentucky Foundation for Women (KFW)
1215 Heyburn Building, 332 West Broadway
Louisville, KY 40202
502-562-0045
http://www.kfw.org/grants.html
Grant Name: Art Meets Activism Grant (supports the work of women in Kentucky who create art for social change). *Academic Area: Visual arts (open). *Age Group: Open. *Eligibility: Kentucky-based women artists and organizations are eligible to apply. Applicants must demonstrate artistic ability, a commitment to feminism, and an understanding of how the creation of art relates to social change. *Application Procedure: Applicants must submit a completed grant proposal, which will then be reviewed by a panel that makes funding recommendations to the KFW Board of Directors. *Amount: Awards range from $1,000 to $7,500—grants typically average from $3,000 to $5,000. Awards may be used for arts education programs focused on women or girls, community participation in the creation of new art forms, artist-centered projects involving nontraditional venues or new partnerships between artists and activists, and artist-centered projects with social change themes or contents. *Deadline: Typically in early March.

Lambda Theta Nu Sorority Inc.
1220 Rosecrans, #543
San Diego, CA 92106
community@lamdathetanu.org
http://www.lambdathetanu.org
Scholarship Name: Lambda Scholarships are available to women at the local chapter level. *Academic Area: Open. *Age Group: Undergraduate students. *Eligibility: Students of Latina heritage with a dedication to community service and empowerment of the Latino community may apply. Applicants must be high school seniors planning to attend an accredited community college, university, or technical or vocational school. *Application Process: Applicants must submit a completed application to the appropriate local chapter (which

can be found on the sorority's Web site). A personal statement addressing family background, scholastic achievements, educational and career goals, commitment to the Latina community, and financial need should also be enclosed, along with one letter of recommendation from a high school administrator, teacher, or community leader and official high school transcripts. Visit the sorority's Web site to download an application. *Amount: Awards vary. *Deadline: May 1.

Latin American Professional Women's Association
3514 North Broadway, PO Box 31532
Los Angeles, CA 90031
213-227-9060
Scholarship Name: Latin American Professional Women's Association Scholarship. *Academic Area: Open. *Age Group: Age 23 and up. *Eligibility: Applicants must be of Hispanic heritage and planning to return to school. *Application Process: Applicants should contact the association by mail for an application. *Amount: $500. *Deadline: April 1.

League of Canadian Poets
920 Yonge Street, Suite 608
Toronto, ON M4W 3C7 Canada
416-504-1657
readings@poets.ca
http://www.poets.ca/linktext/awards/lowther.htm
Award Name: Pat Lowther Memorial Award (for the best book of poetry, which is at least 48 pages, published in the previous calendar year). *Academic Area: English (literature, writing). *Age Group: Professionals. *Eligibility: Applicants must be women who are Canadian citizens or landed immigrants. Contact the league for more details regarding eligibility. *Application Process: Applicants should submit four copies of their book, a brief biography and bibliography, and a handling fee of $15 per title. *Amount: $1,000. *Deadline: November 1.

Leeway Foundation
123 South Broad Street, Suite 2040
Philadelphia, PA 19109
215-545-4078
info@leeway.org
http://www.leeway.org
Grant Name: Art and Change Grant (allows female artists to take advantage of opportunities for art and change). *Academic Area: Visual arts (open). *Age Group: Adults. *Eligibility: Women artists ages 18 and over, in the Philadelphia five-county (Bucks, Chester, Delaware, Montgomery, and Philadelphia) region, who need financial assistance are eligible to apply. Applicants must use their art to promote individual or community change and collaborate with a Change Partner such as a mentor, editor, gallery, community art space, theatre, nonprofit organization, film studio, or club. Full-time or matriculated students in arts degree programs are ineligible for the grant. *Application Procedure: Applicants should submit a short description of their opportunity, a brief overview of their artistic experience, a description of their project, and a project budget. *Amount: Up to $2,500 *Deadlines: February 11, April 11, June 20, and October 31. Contact the foundation for more information.

Leeway Foundation
123 South Broad Street, Suite 2040
Philadelphia, PA 19109
215-545-4078
info@leeway.org
http://www.leeway.org
Award Name: Leeway Transformation Award (given to female artists "whose art engages in change and has an impact on the artist herself or a larger group, audience, or community"). *Academic Area: English (literature), film/video) media arts, performing arts (open), visual arts (open), visual arts (photography). *Age Group: Adults. *Eligibility: Women artists ages 18 and over who have lived in the Philadelphia five-county (Bucks, Chester, Delaware, Montgomery, and Philadelphia) region for the past two years are eligible to apply. Applicants must also demonstrate financial need and have a body of work that spans at least five years and focuses on the theme of change. (Note: Full-time or matriculated students in arts degree programs are ineligible for the Award). *Application Procedure: Visit the foundation's Web site for a detailed overview of application guidelines. *Amount: $15,000. *Deadline: Deadlines vary. Contact the foundation for more information.

Margaret McNamara Memorial Fund (MMMF)
World Bank Family Network
1818 H Street, NW, MSN H2-204
Washington, DC 20433
202-473-8751
MMMF@worldbank.org
http://www.wbfn.org

Award Name: The Margaret McNamara Memorial Fund, administered by the World Bank Family Network, seeks to strengthen the role of women in any aspect of their country's life. *Academic Area: Open. *Age Group: Graduate students. *Eligibility: Women from developing countries who are engaged in graduate studies in the United States or Canada are eligible to apply. Applicants must be citizens of a specified country (visit the network's Web site to view a country eligibility list), full-time students, at least 25 years old, have financial need and record of service to women and children in the developing world, and plan to return to their home country within two years of the award. U.S. residents are not eligible. *Application Process: Applicants must submit a personal statement form, recent transcripts, a copy of the applicant's fall registration, an official estimate of expenses, a passport-size photograph, two recommendations, a copy of a Visa, copy of an I-20, and a completed application form. Visit the network's Web site to download an application form, personal statement form, and a recommendation form. *Amount: $11,000. *Deadline: February 1.

McKenzie River Gathering (MRG) Foundation
2705 East Burnside, Suite 210
Portland, OR 97214
503-289-1517
info@mrgfoundation.org
http://www.mrgfoundation.org/html/apply/grant_detail.php?id=441
Award Name: Lilla Jewel Award. *Academic Area: English (literature), media arts, performing arts (open). *Age Group: Open. *Eligibility: Women artists in Oregon may apply. Awards are given based on the artistic impact of the work presented, the degree to which the work challenges the status quo (the MRG has a mission of progressive social change), and whether the artist is a member of another traditionally underfunded group. *Application Process: Award categories rotate annually. Contact the foundation to request an application and learn its current focus. *Amount: Up to $4,000 (Note: The award may be divided among several artists.) *Deadline: Varies. Contact the foundation for more information.

Miss America Organization
Attn: Miss America Scholarship Department
Two Miss America Way, Suite 1000
Atlantic City, NJ 08401
609-345-7571, ext. 27
info@MissAmerica.org
http://www.missamerica.org
Contest Name: Miss America Scholarship. *Academic Area: Open. *Age Group: Ages 17 to 24. *Eligibility: Applicants must be United States citizens between the ages of 17 and 24 who meet the residency requirements for competing in their town or state. Applicants must be of good character, as deemed by the Miss America Organization, be in good health, and be able to meet the time commitment and job responsibilities of the local, state, and national programs in which the applicant chooses to compete. Contact the organization for information about local competition eligibility. *Application Process: Applicants should contact the organization for information about the local, state, and national contest structure. *Amount: Awards vary. *Deadline: Contact the organization for deadline information.

National Association of Black Women Entrepreneurs
One Ford Place
Detroit, MI 48202
313-874-6284
info@nabwe.org
http://www.nabwe.org
This association offers scholarships to women based on available funding. *Academic Area: Athletics. *Age Group: Varies by award. *Eligibility: Women who are interested in pursuing education in athletics administration may apply. Contact the association for information on scholarships available and eligibility requirements. *Application Process: Contact the association for an application. *Amount: Awards vary. *Deadline: Deadlines vary.

National Association of Insurance Women (NAIW)
Attn: Billie Sleet, NAIW Liaison
Insurance Scholarship Foundation of America
PO Box 866
Hendersonville, NC 28793-0866
828-890-3328
billie@inssfa.org
http://www.inssfa.org/site/PageServer?pagename=college_scholarships
Scholarship Name: NAIW College Scholarship. *Academic Area: Actuarial science, insurance, risk management. *Age Group: Undergraduate students, graduate students. *Eligibility: Applicants must have successfully completed two insurance, risk

management, or actuarial science courses, having a minimum of three credit hours each. They also must be currently attending a college or university and be completing or have completed their third year of college, have a GPA of at least 3.75 on a 4.0 scale, and be a NAIW student member. They must not be receiving full reimbursement for the expenses of college from an employer or any other outside source. *Application Process: Applicants must submit a completed application, official transcripts, three letters of recommendation, and a 500-word essay describing their chosen career path and goals. Visit the association's Web site to download an application. *Amount: Scholarships range from $2,500 to $5,000. *Deadline: March 1.

National Association of Railway Business Women (NARBW)

16507 Hilo Circle
Papillion, NE 68046
narbwinfo@narbw.org
http://www.narbw.org
This organization offers scholarships to women. *Academic Area: Railroad sciences. *Age Group: Varies. *Eligibility: Applicants must be members of the NARBW or relatives of a member of the organization, exhibit scholastic ability, ambition and potential, and financial need. *Application Process: Applicants should visit the association's Web site and sign the guest book for information about the organization and available scholarships. *Amount: Scholarships range from $500 to $1,000. *Deadline: Deadlines vary.

National Association of Women Artists (NAWA)

Attn: Anna Walinska Award
80 Fifth Avenue, Suite 1405
New York, NY 10011-8002
212-675-1616
office@nawanet.org
http://www.nawanet.org
Scholarship Name: Anna Walinska Memorial Scholarship. *Academic Area: Visual arts (open). *Age Group: Varies. *Eligibility: Applicants must be members of NAWA who exhibit artistic excellence and commitment and/or promise. Artists may use the award to pursue their artistic work or study in a workshop situation in the United States or elsewhere. *Application Process: Applicants must submit 10 slides of current work completed within the last three years (or 20 slides if their work is three-dimensional), three copies of a

one-page artist's resume, three copies of an artist's statement, and three copies of a proposal of 150 words or less indicating the requested award amount, the intended use of the award, and how it would benefit the artistic career of the applicant. Applicants should include a self-addressed, stamped envelope for acknowledgement of receipt of application. Visit the association's Web site for details, including specifications about slides. *Amount: Up to $5,000. *Deadline: April 30.

National Association of Women in Construction (NAWIC)

Attn: Theresa Price
327 South Adams Street
Fort Worth, TX 76104-1002
800-552-3506
theresap@nawic.org
http://www.nawic.org/eduinfo.htm
Scholarship Name: Undergraduate Scholarship and the Construction Trades Scholarship. *Academic Area: Construction. *Age Group: Undergraduate students, professionals. *Eligibility: Applicants should visit the association's Web site after October 1 for information about eligibility. *Application Process: Applicants can download an application after October 1 from the association's Web site. Contact NAWIC via e-mail for more information on additional local scholarships that are available. *Amount: Scholarships range from $1,000 to $2,000. *Deadline: March 15.

National Black Nurses' Association (NBNA)

Scholarship Committee
8630 Fenton Street, Suite 330
Silver Spring, MD 20910-3803
301-589-3200, 800-575-6298
NBNA@erols.com
http://www.nbna.org
This organization offers various scholarships for women in nursing programs. *Academic Area: Nursing (open). *Age Group: Undergraduate students. *Eligibility: Applicants must be currently enrolled in a nursing program (BSN, AD, diploma, LPN, or LVN) and in good scholastic standing. They must also be members of the NBNA (including a local-chapter member) and have at least one full year of school remaining. *Application Process: Applicants should submit a completed application form, official transcripts from an accredited school of nursing, a two-page essay, and two letters of recommendation—one from their

school of nursing and one from their local chapter. Applicants may also choose to send supporting materials that document their participation in student nursing activities and involvement in the African American community. Visit the association's Web site to download an application. *Amount: Scholarships range from $500 to $2,000. *Deadline: April 15.

National Collegiate Athletic Association (NCAA)

Attn: Teresa Smith, NCAA Office for Diversity and Inclusion
PO Box 6222
Indianapolis, IN 46206-6222
317-917-6222
tsmith@ncaa.org
http://www1.ncaa.org/membership/ed_outreach/prof_ development/minority-womens_scholarships.html
Scholarship Name: Ethnic Minority and Women's Enhancement Postgraduate Scholarship for Careers in Athletics. *Academic Area: Athletics administration. *Age Group: Graduate students. *Eligibility: Applicants must be female and/or minorities entering a graduate program in sports management or administration. Anyone already enrolled in a graduate program is not eligible. Applicants must also be U.S. citizens who have demonstrated academic achievement as well as involvement in extracurricular activities, and they should be able to demonstrate commitment to a future career in sports. *Application Process: Applicants should visit the organization's Web site to apply online. *Amount: $6,000. *Deadline: January 18.

National Federation of Press Women (NFPW)

PO Box 5556
Arlington, VA 22205
800-780-2715
presswomen@aol.com
http://www.nfpw.org/competitions.htm
Contest Name: High School Communications Competition. *Academic Area: Graphic design, illustration, journalism, visual arts (photography). *Age Group: High school students. *Eligibility: High school students may enter work (completed between March 1 of the previous year and February 28 of the year applying for award) in editorial, opinion, news, feature, sports, column, feature photography, sports photography, cartooning, reviews, graphics, and single-page layout categories. *Application Process: Students compete at the state level, and may advance to the national contest. Visit NFPW's Web

site for application guidelines and to download the entry form. *Amount: $100 for first place, plaques for second and third place, and certificates for honorable mention. Deadline: Varies. Contact the federation for more information.

National Federation of the Blind

Attn: Peggy Elliott, Chairman of Scholarship Committee
805 Fifth Avenue
Grinnell, IA 50112
641-236-3366
http://www.nfb.org
Scholarship Name: Hermione Grant Calhoun Scholarship. *Academic Area: Open. *Age Group: Undergraduate students. *Eligibility: Applicants must be legally blind females and demonstrate scholastic excellence, financial need, and a commitment to community service. They must be pursuing or planning to pursue full-time, postsecondary course of study. *Application Process: Applicants must submit a personal letter stating why they should receive the award, two letters of recommendation, official transcripts, a letter from a federation state president or designee, standardized test scores (for high school students), and a completed application. *Amount: $3,000. *Deadline: March 31.

National Museum of Women in the Arts

Library and Research Center
1250 New York Avenue, NW
Washington, DC 20005-3970
202-783-5000, 800-222-7270
http://www.nmwa.org/library/pdf/Submission_ guidelinesV2.pdf
Grant Name: Library Fellows Artist Book Grant (provides funding for the creation of an artist book in the edition of 125). *Academic Area: Visual arts (open). *Age Group: Professionals. *Eligibility: Women artists are eligible to apply. Applicants must be working on a new project to be eligible for the grant. *Application Procedure: Applicants should submit a proposal that includes a completed application form, a detailed description of the proposed book, a mockup/dummy of the proposed book, up to 20 slides of book-related artwork, a resume, and an estimated, itemized budget. The proposal will be evaluated based on its aesthetic and intellectual value, originality, quality, potential market, appropriateness of budget, and other criteria. *Amount: Up to $12,000, plus $1,000 for creation of promotional brochure, and $1,000 for

travel to annual the Library Fellows' annual meeting to present the completed book. *Deadline: January 31. Contact the Library and Research Center for more information.

National Physical Science Consortium (NPSC)

Attn: Joretta Joseph, Program Administrator
3716 South Hope, Suite 348
Los Angeles, CA 90007-4344
213-743-2409, 800-854-6772
npschq@npsc.org
http://npsc.org

Fellowship Name: National Physical Science Consortium Fellowship. *Academic Areas: Biochemistry, computer science, engineering (open), physical sciences, science. *Age Group: Graduate students, professionals. *Eligibility: Students, especially women and underrepresented minorities, who are interested in earning a Ph.D. are eligible to apply. Applicants must be U.S. citizens who plan to or who are currently pursuing graduate work at an NPSC member institution. *Application Procedure: Applicants should apply online at the consortium's Web site. Required documents include academic transcripts and three to five letters of recommendation from professors and employers. *Amount: Up to $200,000. *Deadline: November 5. Contact the consortium for details.

National Society of Professional Engineers

Education Services
1420 King Street
Alexandria, VA 22314-2794
703-684-2800
ed@nspe.org
http://www.nspe.org

Scholarship Name: Auxiliary Scholarship. *Academic Area: Engineering (open). *Age Group: Undergraduate students. *Eligibility: Applicant must be female high school seniors who plan to enroll in a program that is accredited by the Engineering Accreditation Commission of the Accreditation Board for Engineering and Technology, have a GPA of at least 3.5 on a scale of 4.0, and SAT scores of 700 in math, 600 in reading, 500 in writing, or ACT scores of 29 in both math and English. This scholarship is awarded strictly on the basis of achievement. *Application Process: Applicants must submit a completed application, high school transcripts, two teacher recommendations, a 500-word essay discussing their interest in engineering and long-term career goals, and a copy of either

their SAT or ACT scores. Visit the society's Web site to download an application. *Amount: $2,000 ($1,000 per year for two years). *Deadline: December 1.

National Society of Professional Engineers

Education Services
1420 King Street
Alexandria, VA 22314-2794
703-684-2800
ed@nspe.org
http://www.nspe.org

Scholarship Name: Virginia D. Henry Memorial Scholarship. *Academic Area: Engineering (open). *Age Group: Undergraduate students. *Eligibility: Applicants must be high school seniors who plan to enroll in a program that is accredited by the Engineering Accreditation Commission of the Accreditation Board for Engineering and Technology, have a GPA of at least 3.5 on a 4.0 scale, and SAT scores of 700 in math, 600 in reading, 500 in writing, or ACT scores of 29 in both math and English. This scholarship is awarded strictly on the basis of achievement. *Application Process: Applicants must submit a completed application, high school transcripts, two teacher recommendations, a 500-word essay discussing their interest in engineering and long-term career goals, and a copy of SAT or ACT scores. Visit the association's Web site to download an application. *Amount: $1,000 for freshman year only. *Deadline: December 1.

National Strength and Conditioning Association (NSCA) Foundation

Attn: Grants and Scholarships
1885 Bob Johnson Drive
Colorado Springs, CO 80906
719-632-6722, 800-815-6826
nsca@nsca-lift.org
http://www.nsca-lift.org/Foundation

Scholarship Name: Women's Scholarship. *Academic Area: Wellness (strength and conditioning). *Age Group: Graduate students. *Eligibility: Applicants must be women, ages 17 and older, who plan to enter the field of strength and conditioning. They also must demonstrate they have been accepted into an accredited institution and are working toward a graduate degree in the strength and conditioning field. Applicants must be NSCA members for at least one year prior to the application deadline date. College seniors and graduate students may apply for this scholarship. *Application Process: Applicants must submit a covering letter of application, an application form including information listed on the foundation's Web site, a resume, original transcripts, three letters of recommendation, and a personal statement. Visit the foundation's Web site for further details. *Amount: $1,000. *Deadline: March 15.

National Student Nurses' Association (NSNA)

45 Main Street, Suite 606
Brooklyn, NY 11201
718-210-0705
nsna@nsna.org
http://www.nsna.org

Scholarship Name: Nursing Student Scholarship. *Academic Area: Nursing (open). *Age Group: Undergraduate students, graduate students. *Eligibility: Applicants must be U.S. citizens currently enrolled in state-approved schools of nursing or prenursing in associate degree, baccalaureate, diploma, generic doctorate, and generic master's programs. Funds are not available for graduate study unless it is for a first degree in nursing. Awards are based on academic achievement, financial need, and involvement in nursing student organizations and community activities related to health care. Graduating high school seniors are not eligible. *Application Process: Applicants must submit a completed application, along with a $10 processing fee. The application is available from August though January at the association's Web site. *Amount: Scholarships range from $1,000 to $2,500. *Deadline: January 22.

National Women's Studies Association (NWSA)

University of Maryland
7100 Baltimore Avenue, Suite 502
College Park, MD 20740
301-403-0524
nwsaoffice@nwsa.org
http://www.nwsa.org/scholarship/index.php

Scholarship Name: NWSA Graduate Scholarship Award. *Academic Area: Women's studies. *Age Group: Graduate students. *Eligibility: Applicants must be engaged in the research or writing stages of a master's thesis or Ph.D. dissertation in the interdisciplinary field of women's studies. The research project must enhance the NWSA's mission. Applicants must be members of the NWSA at the time of application. *Application Process: Applicants must submit a completed application form, a two- to three-page abstract of the work in progress, and three letters of recommendation. Visit the association's Web site to

download an application. Amount: $1,000. *Deadline: February 15.

National Women's Studies Association (NWSA)

University of Maryland
7100 Baltimore Avenue, Suite 502
College Park, MD 20740
301-403-0524
nwsaoffice@nwsa.org
http://www.nwsa.org/scholarship/index.php

Scholarship Name: NWSA Graduate Scholarship in Lesbian Studies. *Academic Area: Women's studies. *Age Group: Graduate students. *Eligibility: Students must be attending graduate school full time and working on a thesis or dissertation in lesbian studies. They must also be able to demonstrate financial need. *Application Process: Applicants should submit a completed application form, a two- to three-page abstract of the work in progress, and three letters of recommendation. Visit the association's Web site to download an application. *Amount: $500. *Deadline: Typically in February.

National Women's Studies Association (NWSA)

Attn: Phyllis Holman Weisbard, Scholarship Chair
University of Maryland
7100 Baltimore Avenue, Suite 502
College Park, MD 20740
301-403-0524
jewishchair@nwsa.org
http://www.nwsa.org/scholarship/index.php

Scholarship Name: NWSA Jewish Caucus Prize. *Academic Area: Women's studies. *Age Group: Graduate students. *Eligibility: Applicants must be attending school full time and working on a thesis or dissertation. They should also have a special interest in the lives, work, and culture of Jewish women. *Application Process: Applicants should submit a completed application form, up to five pages answering three biographical essay questions as stated on the application, and two letters of recommendation. Visit the association's Web site to download an application. *Amount: $1,000. *Deadline: March 1.

Naval Academy Women's Club (NAWC)

Attn: Maryada Ritchie, NAWC Scholarship Co-Chairman
PO Box 826
Annapolis, MD 21404-0826
NavyScholars@aol.com

http://www.nadn.navy.mil/WomensClub/
nawcscholarship.html

Scholarship Name: Naval Academy Women's Club
Scholarship. *Academic Area: Open. *Age Group:
Undergraduate students, adults. *Eligibility: Applicants
must be U.S. citizens who are enrolled full time in a two-
or four-year undergraduate college or university, visual
or performing arts school, or a vocational-technical
school. Applicants must also be one of the following
to meet eligibility requirements: (1) A dependent, less
than 23 years old, of active duty, retired, or deceased
member of the U.S. Armed Forces who was/is stationed
at the Naval Academy Complex; (2) A dependent, less
than 23 years old, of civilian staff or faculty member
who is currently employed, retired, or deceased after
employment at the Naval Academy Complex for a
minimum of three consecutive years; (3) A dependant,
less than 23 years old, of a current NAWC Board
Member; (4) A current regular member of NAWC for at
least one year. This award is 100 percent merit based.
High school seniors are eligible to apply. *Application
Process: Applicants should submit a completed
application along with a 500- to 1,000-word essay,
official transcripts, and a copy of official USNA orders.
*Amount: Awards vary. *Deadline: March 31.

Nevada Women's Fund
770 Smithridge Drive, Suite 300
Reno, NV 89502
775-786-2335
info@nevadawomensfund.org
http://www.nevadawomensfund.org/scholarships

Scholarship Name: Nevada Women's Fund Scholarship.
*Academic Area: Open. *Age Group: Undergraduate
students, graduate students. *Eligibility: Applicants
must be attending or planning to attend an educational
institution in Nevada; preference is given to northern
Nevada residents and applicants attending educational
institutions in northern Nevada. Selection is based
on the applicant's need, commitment to community
service, and plans for the future. *Application Process:
Applicants must submit a completed five-page
application and certified transcripts of completed
course work. Visit the fund's Web site to download an
application (available each January for the upcoming
year). *Amount: $500 and up. *Deadline: February 27.

The Newberry Library
Attn: Committee on Awards
60 West Walton Street

Chicago, IL 60610-7324
312-255-3666
research@newberry.org
http://www.newberry.org/research/L3rfellowships.html

Fellowship Name: Frances C. Allen Fellowship (a one-
month to one-year fellowship that encourages
Native American women to pursue advanced
study). *Academic Area: Open (special emphasis on
the humanities and social sciences). *Age Group:
Graduate students. *Eligibility: Women of Native
American heritage are eligible to apply. Allen Fellows
are expected to spend a large part of their tenure
in residence at the Newberry's D'Arcy McNickle
Center for American Indian History. *Application
Procedure: Applicants should submit a cover sheet,
a project description, a curriculum vitae, and letters
of reference. Visit the Newberry's Web site for more
information. *Amount: Up to $8,000 (may include
travel expenses). *Deadline: March 1.

**New Jersey State Federation of Women's Clubs of the
General Federation of Women's Clubs**
Attn: Margaret Yardley Fellowship Fund Chairman
55 Labor Center Way
New Brunswick, NJ 08901
732-249-5474
http://www.njsfwc.org/MYFellowship.html

Fellowship Name: Margaret Yardley Fellowship. *Academic
Area: Open. *Age Group: Graduate students. *Eligibility:
Female graduate students from New Jersey who are
enrolled in a master's or doctoral program are eligible
to apply. Applicants must demonstrate financial
need. *Application Procedure: Applicants should
submit an official college transcript, at least two
letters of recommendation from college faculty and
other sources, a completed application (available for
download at the federation's Web site), an essay, and
a self-addressed stamped envelope. *Amount: $1,000.
*Deadline: Contact the federation for more information.

Newswomen's Club of New York
Attn: Joan O'Sullivan, President, Scholarship Fund
15 Gramercy Park South, 2nd Floor
New York, NY 10003
212-777-1610
joanandarchie@aol.com
http://www.newswomensclubnewyork.com/
scholarships.html

Scholarship Name: Ann O'Hare McCormick Scholarship
Fund. *Academic Area: Journalism. *Age Group:

Graduate students. *Eligibility: Applicants must be attending Columbia University's Graduate School of Journalism. *Application Process: Applicant should submit a completed application along with a brief statement of financial resources and need, two letters of recommendation, an autobiographical essay mentioning their family, educational background, journalistic experience, and goals, one example of what they consider their best writing to date, and a list of job-related experiences including on-campus journalism jobs, summer jobs, freelance gigs, internships, and full-time jobs. Visit the club's Web site to download an application. *Amount: Scholarships range from $5,000 to $7,500. *Deadline: June 8.

The Ninety-Nines Inc.
Attn: Dr. Jacque Boyd, AEMSF Chairman
4300 Amelia Earhart Road
Oklahoma City, OK 73159
505-377-3166, 800-994-1929
AEChair@ninety-nines.org
http://www.ninety-nines.org/aemsf.html
The Ninety-Nines, an international organization of licensed women pilots, offers the Amelia Earhart Memorial Future Woman Pilot Award to student pilots to help them complete their Private Pilot Certificate. *Academic Area: Aviation. *Age Group: Open. *Eligibility: Women student pilots are eligible to apply. Applicant must be a Future Woman Pilot Member of The Ninety-Nines. *Application Process: Visit the organization's Web site for an application. *Amount: Up to $1,000. *Deadline: December 1.

The Ninety-Nines Inc.
Attn: Dr. Jacque Boyd, AEMSF Chairman
Ninety-Nines Headquarters
4300 Amelia Earhart Road
Oklahoma City, OK 73159-1140
505-377-3166, 800-994-1929
AEChair@ninety-nines.org
http://www.ninety-nines.org/aemsf.html
Scholarship Name: Amelia Earhart Memorial Scholarship. *Academic Area: Aviation. *Age Group: Undergraduate students, professionals. *Eligibility: Applicants must be enrolled in an aviation training course such as a multi-engine rating or jet-type rating course, a flight instructor or airline transport pilot certificate program, or a college course. They must also be members of The Ninety-Nines for at least one year. *Application Process: Applicants should

visit the organization's Web site to download an application and to find additional information about regional chapter scholarships. *Amount: Awards vary. *Deadline: December 1.

Omega Phi Beta Sorority Inc.
Attn: Director of Reach for the Gold Book Scholarship
Grand Central Station, PO Box 3352
New York, NY 10163
reachforgold@omegaphibeta.org
http://www.omegaphibeta.org/serving/scholarship.htm
Scholarship Name: Reach for the Gold Book Scholarship (Academic). *Academic Area: Open. *Age Group: Undergraduate students. *Eligibility: Applicants must be female students of color graduating from high school in May/June and accepted to a full-time college or university program for the fall semester. Applicants must also be U.S. citizens or legal residents with a high school GPA of at least 3.7 on a 4.0 scale and a minimum ACT score of 23 or SAT score of 900. *Application Process: Applicants must submit an official high school transcript, a copy of their ACT or SAT score report, one letter of recommendation from a teacher, guidance counselor, or school official, a 500-word personal essay, and a business-size, self-addressed stamped envelope. *Amount: $500, to cover the cost of books. *Deadline: Must be postmarked between April 1 and May 15.

Omega Phi Beta Sorority Inc.
Attn: Director of Reach for the Gold Book Scholarship
Grand Central Station, PO Box 3352
New York, NY 10163
reachforgold@omegaphibeta.org
http://www.omegaphibeta.org/serving/scholarship.htm
Scholarship Name: Reach for the Gold Book Scholarship (Community Service). *Academic Area: Open. *Age Group: Undergraduate students. *Eligibility: Applicants must be female students of color graduating from high school in May/June and accepted to a full-time college or university program for the fall semester. Applicants must also be U.S. citizens or legal residents with a high school GPA of at least 2.7 on a 4.0 scale and a demonstrated involvement in community service projects. *Application Process: Applicants must submit an official high school transcript, one letter of recommendation from a teacher, guidance counselor, or school official, one letter of recommendation from a community service agency verifying involvement,

a 500-word personal essay, and a business-size, self-addressed stamped envelope. *Amount: $500, to cover the cost of books. *Deadline: Must be postmarked between April 1 and May 15.

Organization of American Historians

112 North Bryan Avenue
PO Box 5457
Bloomington, IN 47408-5457
812-855-7311
http://www.oah.org/activities/awards/lernerscott
Award Name: The Lerner-Scott Dissertation Prize is awarded annually for the best doctoral dissertation in U.S. women's history. *Academic Area: History. *Age Group: Graduate students. *Eligibility: Female graduate students who are working on their doctoral dissertations are eligible to apply. *Application Process: Each application must contain a letter of support from a faculty member, an abstract, a table of contents, and a sample chapter. *Amount: $1,000. *Deadline: October 1.

P.E.O. International

3700 Grand Avenue
Des Moines, IA 50312
515-255-3153
http://www.peointernational.org/projects/overview.php
Loan Name: The P.E.O. Educational Loan Fund is a revolving loan fund to assist worthy female students in securing a higher education. *Academic Area: Open. *Age Group: Undergraduate students, graduate students. *Eligibility: Applicants must be citizens or legal permanent residents of the United States or Canada, high school graduates (or the equivalent), enrolled full time in an accredited school (at the time loan is drawn), and recommended by a local P.E.O. chapter. *Application Process: Applications are mailed from the P.E.O. Executive Office upon receipt of the recommendation from the local P.E.O. chapter. *Amount: Up to $9,000 at 2 percent interest. *Loan Repayment Deadline: Due six years from the date of issue. *Application Deadline: Applications are accepted throughout the year.

P.E.O. International

3700 Grand Avenue
Des Moines, IA 50312
515-255-3153
http://www.peointernational.org/projects/overview.php
Scholarship Name: P.E.O. International Peace Scholarship.
*Academic Area: Open. *Age Group: Undergraduate students, graduate students. *Eligibility: Graduate students or students attending Cottey College, a two-year college in Nevada, Missouri, are eligible to apply. Applicants must be citizens of a country other than the United States or Canada and must agree to return to their home countries within 60 days of their completion of their degree program to pursue their professional careers. *Application Process: Once eligibility is established, application materials will be mailed to the applicant. Required materials to support the application include four recommendations, official transcripts, and confirmation of admission to graduate study. Contact P.E.O. International after July 1 for specific eligibility requirements. *Amount: Up to $8,000. *Deadline: January 31.

P.E.O. International

3700 Grand Avenue
Des Moines, IA 50312
515-255-3153
http://www.peointernational.org/projects/overview.php
Grant Name: P.E.O. Program for Continuing Education.
*Academic Area: Open. *Age Group: Adults. *Eligibility: Women in the United States and Canada whose education has been interrupted and who would like to return to school are eligible to apply. Applicants must be citizens of the United States or Canada, sponsored by a P.E.O. chapter, demonstrate financial need, have spent at least 24 consecutive months as a nonstudent sometime in her adult life, and not enrolled in a doctoral degree program. *Application Procedure: Contact your local P.E.O. chapter for information on the application process. *Amount: Up to $1,500 for educational expenses (e.g., tuition, books, transportation, and childcare). *Deadline: Applications are accepted throughout the year.

P.E.O. International

3700 Grand Avenue
Des Moines, IA 50312
515-255-3153
http://www.peointernational.org/projects/overview.php
Award Name: P.E.O. Scholar Award. *Academic Area: Open. *Age Group: Graduate students. *Eligibility: Female U.S. and Canadian citizens who are pursuing advanced degrees or are engaged in advanced study and research are eligible to apply. Applicants must be full-time students and sponsored by a local P.E.O. chapter. *Application Process: Contact your local P.E.O.

chapter for information on the application process. *Amount: Varies. *Deadline: Applications are accepted from September 1 through December 31.

P3-Partnership in Print Production

Attn: Katerina Caterisano, Executive Director
276 Bowery
New York, NY 10012
212-334-2106
admin@p3-ny.org
http://www.p3-ny.org/scholarships.html
Scholarship Name: Foundation for P3 Scholarship. *Academic Area: Graphic communications, publishing. *Age Group: Varies. *Eligibility: Applicants must be members of P3 in good standing who plan to register for a course to maintain currency with emerging technologies or to enhance their business management skills. *Application Process: Applicants should submit a completed application along with a one-page letter or essay describing the course they want to take, what they expect to learn from it, and how this knowledge will benefit their career. P3-Partnership In Print Production is the result of a merger between Women In Production and the Association of Publication Managers. Visit the organization's Web site to download an application. *Amount: $500. *Deadline: July 29.

The Pen and Brush Inc.

Pen Contests
16 East 10th Street
New York, NY 10003
212-475-3669
penbrush99@aol.com
http://www.penandbrush.org
Contest Name: Poetry, Prose and Playwriting Contest. *Academic Area: English (literature, writing), performing arts (theatre). *Age Group: Open. *Eligibility: Women writers are eligible to apply. *Application Process: Each submission should include one title page with name, address, phone/e-mail and one title page with title only. A $15 entry fee is required for the prose and playwriting contests; a $10 application fee is required for the poetry contest. *Amount: Varies. *Deadline: September 30.

Phi Chi Theta Educational Foundation

Attn: Mary Ellen Lewis, Scholarship Committee Chair
1886 South Poplar Street
Denver, CO 80224-2271
303-757-2535
FoundationScholarship@phichitheta.org
http://www.phichitheta.org/foundation/programs.htm
Scholarship Name: Naomi Satterfield Memorial Scholarship. *Academic Area: Business, economics. *Age Group: Undergraduate students, graduate students. *Eligibility: Applicants must be national members in good standing of Phi Chi Theta who have completed at least one semester or two quarters of college. *Application Process: Applicants should submit a completed application along with supporting materials, which include a statement of career goals, official transcripts, two letters of recommendation, contributions to Phi Chi Theta, and a list of courses they have enrolled in for the upcoming semester. Visit the foundation's Web site to download an application. *Amount: $1,000. *Deadline: May 1.

Phi Mu Foundation

Attn Kimberly Tramel
400 Westpark Drive
Peachtree City, GA 30269
770-632-2122
ktramel@phimu.org
http://www.phimu.org/foundation/schol.asp
This fraternity offers undergraduate and graduate scholarships to women. *Academic Area: Open. *Age Group: Undergraduate students, graduate students. *Eligibility: Applicants must be initiated members in good standing of Phi Mu Fraternity. They must also have a cumulative GPA of at least 3.0 on a 4.0 scale and remain in an accredited college or university working toward a degree. Note: Some scholarships require specific fields of study. *Application Process: Applicants must submit a completed application and official transcripts from each college or university they have attended. Undergraduate applicants must submit two recommendations, one from the chapter adviser and another from an employer or academic source. Graduate applicants or alumnae returning as undergraduates should submit two recommendations from academic or professional sources. Visit the foundation's Web site to download an application and recommendation forms. *Amount: Awards vary. *Deadline: March 1.

Pi Beta Phi Foundation

1154 Town & Country Commons Drive
Town & Country, MO 63017
636-256-0680

FNDN@piphico.org
http://www.pibetaphi.org
This organization awards graduate fellowships.
*Academic Area: Open. *Age Group: Graduate students. *Eligibility: Applicants must be members in good standing of Pi Beta Phi Fraternity, have a minimum GPA of 3.0, and have a record of service to Pi Beta Phi, campus and community. *Application Process: Applicants must submit a financial disclosure form, an undergraduate transcript, a personal letter of introduction, three current references, and a completed application form. Visit the fraternity's Web site to download applications and forms. *Amount: Awards vary. *Deadline: January 31.

Pi Beta Phi Foundation
1154 Town & Country Commons Drive
Town & Country, MO 63017
636-256-0680
FNDN@piphico.org
http://www.pibetaphi.org
This organization awards scholarships to women at the undergraduate and graduate levels. *Academic Area: Open. *Age Group: Undergraduate students, graduate students, adults. *Eligibility: Applicants must be members in good standing of Pi Beta Phi Fraternity, have a minimum GPA of 3.0 (Canadian student must have a 70 percent GPA), and have a record of service to Pi Beta Phi, campus, and community. Alumnae continuing education applicants must have been out of school more than two academic years prior to application. Note: some scholarships require specific fields of study. *Application Process: Applicants must submit an application form, a financial disclosure form, transcripts, a personal letter of introduction, and three current references. Visit the fraternity's Web site to download applications and forms. *Amount: Awards vary. *Deadline: January 31.

Print and Graphics Scholarship Foundation
200 Deer Run Road
Sewickley, PA 15143-2600
800-910-4283
pgsf@piagatf.org
http://www.gain.net/eweb/DynamicPage.
aspx?webcode=lower35&wps_key=7CA2C42E-AEF4-4351-9139-A5BB554604EA
This organization offers more than 300 scholarships annually, including several female memorial scholarships. *Academic Area: Graphic

communications, publishing. *Age Group: Undergraduate students. *Eligibility: Applicants must be or intend to be full-time students and interested in a career in graphic communication. High school seniors and undergraduate students may apply. *Application Process: Applicants must submit a completed application, SAT or ACT scores, high school transcripts, two letters of recommendation, a photocopy of their intended program of study, and a self-addressed stamped envelope. Visit the foundation's Web site to download an application. *Amount: Scholarships range from $1,000 to $1,500. *Deadline: March 1 (high school students) and April 1 (enrolled college students).

Professional Women of Color (PWC)
Dream Grant
PO Box 5196
New York, NY 10185
212-714-7190
TLawr64783@aol.com
http://www.pwcnetwork.org/dreamgrant.html
Grant Name: Professional Women of Color Dream Grant (helps women start a business, attend an educational program, finish a research project, or introduce a new product). *Academic Area: Open. *Age Group: Undergraduate students, graduate students, professionals. *Eligibility: Current members of PWC are eligible to apply. *Application Procedure: Applicants should submit a 300- to 1,000-word essay that details their project/venture, a resume, a one-page bio, and a 3 ½ " x 5" black-and-white headshot. An application fee of $50 is required. *Amount: Grants range from $3,000 to $5,000. *Deadline: Varies. Contact PWC for more information.

Radcliffe Institute for Advanced Study
34 Concord Avenue
Cambridge, MA 02138
617-496-1324
fellowships@radcliffe.edu
http://www.radcliffe.edu/fellowships
Fellowship Name: Radcliffe Institute Fellowship Program. *Academic Area: Open. *Age Group: Graduate students, professionals. *Eligibility: Female and male students and academic professionals are eligible to apply. *Application Procedure: Applicants can apply online at the institute's Web site. Applications are available after April 30. *Amount: Up to $55,000. Fellows also receive reimbursement for travel and

office or studio space, computers and high-speed Internet links, and access to libraries and other resources at Harvard University. *Deadline: Varies. Contact the institute for details.

Roscoe Pound Institute
Attn: Publications and Awards Coordinator
1054 31st Street, NW, Suite 260
Washington, DC 20007
pound@roscoepound.org
http://www.roscoepound.org/new/programs/eoj06.htm
Award Name: Elaine Osborne Jacobson Award.
    *Academic Area: Law. *Age Group: Law students. *Eligibility: Applicants must be female law students who can demonstrate a commitment to health care advocacy on behalf of women, children, the elderly, and the disabled. *Application Process: Applicants should submit a completed application along with a letter from the dean of their program or program director, a curriculum vitae, a personal statement, an essay, and up to three letters of recommendation. Visit the institute's Web site to download an application and to view details on the personal statement and essay topic. *Amount: $3,000, plus an all-expenses paid trip to the award ceremony in Seattle, Washington. *Deadline: February 13.

Sigma Sigma Sigma
225 North Muhlenberg Street
Woodstock, VA 22664
540-459-4212
foundation@trisigma.org
http://www.sigmasigmasigma.org
This sorority awards scholarships to both undergraduate and graduate women. *Academic Area: Open. *Age Group: Undergraduate students, graduate students. *Eligibility: Sigma Sigma Sigma's scholarships are entirely merit based. Applicants must be members in good standing, enrolled as full-time students with the minimum GPA required for participation in Sigma Sigma Sigma, and demonstrate leadership and service to chapter, campus, and community. *Application Process: Applicants must submit official transcripts, documentation of academic achievements or accomplishments, a summary of service involvement and leadership, an outline of their professional and career objectives, three letters of recommendation, and a completed application. Visit the sorority's Web site to download an application. *Amount: $1,000. *Deadline: May 1.

Society for Historians of American Foreign Relations (SHAFR)
Department of History
Ohio State University
106 Dulles Hall
230 West 17th Avenue
Columbus, OH 43210
614-292-1951
shafr@osu.edu
http://www.shafr.org/prizes.htm
Fellowship Name: Myrna F. Bernath Fellowship Award.
    *Academic Area: History. *Age Group: Graduate students. *Eligibility: Female graduate students who wish to do research in American foreign relations history or aspects of international history are eligible to apply. *Application Procedure: Applications should be submitted in triplicate and include a letter of intent, a curriculum vitae, and three copies of a detailed research proposal. The fellowship is awarded biannually. Contact the SHAFR business office for the name of the current fellowship chair. *Amount: $2,500. *Deadline: December 1.

Society of Lesbian and Gay Anthropologists (SOLGA)
Attn: Ellen Lewin
Department of Women's Studies
University of Iowa
210 Jefferson Building
Iowa City, IA 52242
319-335-1610
ellen-lewin@uiowa.edu
http://sscl.berkeley.edu/~afaweb/
    Payne%20Prize%20SOLGA.htm
Award Name: Kenneth W. Payne Student Prize.
    *Academic Area: Anthropology. *Age Group: Graduate students. *Eligibility: Graduate students who have completed an outstanding work on a lesbian, gay, bisexual, or transgendered topic in anthropology are eligible to apply. *Application Procedure: Papers should be no more than 40 typed, double-spaced pages. Visit the society's Web site for updated information. . *Amount: $300. *Deadline: August 1.

Society of Women Engineers
230 East Ohio Street, Suite 400
Chicago, IL 60611-3265
312-596-6223, 877-SWE-INFO
scholarshipapplication@swe.org
http://www.swe.org/stellent/idcplg?IdcService=SS_GET_
    PAGE&nodeId=118&ssSourceNodeId=9

Scholarship Name: Freshman Scholarships. *Academic Area: Engineering (open). *Age Group: Undergraduate students. *Eligibility: A variety of freshman scholarships are available to applicants who have a minimum GPA of 3.5, are entering freshman in the fall of a new academic year, and meet all of the additional eligibility requirements for individual scholarships. Applicants should visit the society's Web site for a complete list of freshman scholarships. Some have additional requirements such as residence in a particular state, while others simply require the 3.5 GPA. *Application Process: Applications are available for download at the society's Web site starting February 1 of each year. *Amount: $1,000 to $5,000. *Deadline: May 15.

Society of Women Engineers
230 East Ohio Street, Suite 400
Chicago, IL 60611-3265
312-596-6223, 877-SWE-INFO
scholarshipapplication@swe.org
http://www.swe.org/stellent/idcplg?IdcService=SS_GET_PAGE&nodeId=124&ssSourceNodeId=119
Scholarship Name: Graduate Scholarship. *Academic Area: Computer science, engineering (open). *Age Group: Graduate students. *Eligibility: A variety of scholarships are available to graduate students. Applicants should have a minimum GPA of 3.0 for most scholarships, though a few require slightly higher averages. Applicants should visit the society's Web site for a complete list of graduate scholarships and their specific requirements. Some require specific engineering specialties declared, attendance at particular schools, and/or U.S. citizenship. *Application Process: Visit the society's Web site to apply online. *Amount: $1,000 to $63,000. *Deadline: February 1.

Society of Women Engineers
230 East Ohio Street, Suite 400
Chicago, IL 60611-3265
312-596-6223, 877-SWE-INFO
scholarshipapplication@swe.org
http://www.swe.org/stellent/idcplg?IdcService=SS_GET_PAGE&nodeId=120&ssSourceNodeId=119s, engineering (open).
Scholarship Name: Reentry Scholarship. *Academic Area: Computer s, engineering (open). *Age Group: Undergraduate students, graduate students. *Eligibility: Several scholarships are available to

students who are returning to college after an absence of at least two years from school and the engineering workforce. Applicants should visit the society's Web site for a complete list of scholarships and their specific requirements. *Application Process: Visit the society's Web site to apply online. *Amount: $2,000. *Deadline: February 1.

Society of Women Engineers
230 East Ohio Street, Suite 400
Chicago, IL 60611-3265
312-596-6223, 877-SWE-INFO
scholarshipapplication@swe.org
http://www.swe.org/stellent/idcplg?IdcService=SS_GET_PAGE&nodeId=121&ssSourceNodeId=120
Scholarship Name: SWE Section Scholarships. *Academic Area: Computer science, engineering (open). *Age Group: Undergraduate students, graduate students. *Eligibility: Several scholarships are available to students in particular geographical areas. Applicants should visit the society's Web site for a geographical listing of additional scholarships by state. *Application Process: Visit the society's Web site to find contact information for local scholarship opportunities. *Amount: Awards vary. *Deadline: Contact your state office for deadline information.

Society of Women Engineers
230 East Ohio Street, Suite 400
Chicago, IL 60611-3265
312-596-6223, 877-SWE-INFO
scholarshipapplication@swe.org
http://www.swe.org/stellent/idcplg?IdcService=SS_GET_PAGE&nodeId=119&ssSourceNodeId=118
Scholarship Name: Undergraduate Scholarship. *Academic Area: Computer science, engineering (open). *Age Group: Undergraduate students, graduate students. *Eligibility: A variety of scholarships are available to college sophomores, juniors, and seniors; some are also available to graduate students Applicants should have a minimum GPA of 3.0 for most scholarships, though a few require slightly higher averages. Applicants should visit the association's Web site for a complete list of undergraduate scholarships and their specific requirements. Some require specific engineering specialties declared and/or financial need. *Application Process: Visit the association's Web site to apply online. *Amount: $1,000 to $6,000. *Deadline: February 1.

Sociologists for Women in Society

Attn: Professor Myra Marx Ferree
University of Wisconsin-Madison
Department of Sociology
1180 Observatory Drive
Madison, WI 53706
mferree@ssc.wisc.edu
http://newmedia.colorado.edu/~socwomen/
    awardschol/hessScholarship.html
Scholarship Name: Beth B. Hess Memorial Scholarship.
    *Academic Area: Sociology. *Age Group: Graduate
    students. *Eligibility: Applicants must have started
    their academic careers in a community college or
    technical school and must have completed at least
    one full academic year at such a two-year college in
    the United States before transferring to complete
    a bachelor of arts. They must also demonstrate a
    commitment to teaching at a community college,
    a background in research or activism in issues of
    social inequality or social justice with a focus on
    gender and/or gerontology, and service to academic
    and/or local community that includes mentoring.
    *Application Process: Applicants should submit a
    letter of application that describes their decision
    to study sociology, career goals, research and
    activism, and service; a letter confirming enrollment
    in or admission to a sociology graduate program;
    a letter of recommendation from a sociologist in
    a sealed envelope; a full curriculum vitae; and a
    one-page letter describing a community college
    faculty member who particularly contributed to
    their decision to study sociology or pursue higher
    education. Additionally, applicants must submit
    a cover sheet complete with name and contact
    information, current academic or organizational
    affiliation (with years), future graduate school and
    date of entry (if not currently enrolled), community
    college attended (with years), name, and contact
    information for references. Six copies of this
    application packet should be submitted by mail.
    *Amount: $1,000. *Deadline: May 15.

Sociologists for Women in Society (SWS)

University of Akron
Sociology Department, Olin 251
Akron, OH 44325-1905
330-972-7918
sws@uakron.edu
http://newmedia.colorado.edu/~socwomen/
    awardschol/miller.html

Award Name: Cheryl Allyn Miller Award (recognizes a
    women whose activism or research constitutes a
    major contribution to the field of women and work).
    *Academic Area: Sociology. *Age Group: Graduate
    students, recent Ph.D.'s. *Eligibility: Graduate students
    and recent Ph.D.'s who are members of SWS are
    eligible to apply. *Application Process: Applicants
    should submit three copies of the following materials:
    a curriculum vitae; a cover page with the author's
    name, affiliation, and contact information; and an
    abstract and paper of article length (no more than
    30 double-spaced pages, including bibliography).
    *Amount: $500, plus reimbursement for travel to the
    annual meeting of the SWS. *Deadline: May 15.

Soroptimist International of the Americas

1709 Spruce Street
Philadelphia, PA 19103-6103
215-893-9000
siahq@soroptimist.org
http://www.soroptimist.org/woa/woa.asp
The Women's Opportunity Awards program assists
    women who, as head of their households, must
    enter or return to the workforce or upgrade their
    employment status. *Academic Area: Open. *Age
    Group: Adults. *Eligibility: Women who have been
    accepted into a vocational/skills training program
    or an undergraduate degree program are eligible to
    apply. *Application Process: The program begins on
    the local level, after which recipients become eligible
    for region-level and national awards. Applications are
    available from local Soroptimist clubs or by visiting
    the organization's Web site. *Amount: Awards range
    from $3,000 to $10,000. *Deadline: Applications are
    accepted from July 1 through December 1.

Talbots Charitable Foundation

Scholarship Management Services, Scholarship America
One Scholarship Way
PO Box 297
Saint Peter, MN 56082
507-931-1682
http://www1.talbots.com/about/scholar/scholar.asp
Scholarship Name: Talbots Women's Scholarship Fund.
    *Academic Area: Open. *Age Group: Undergraduate
    students. *Eligibility: Applicants must be females who
    graduated from high school or received a GED at least
    10 years ago. They should also be currently residing
    in the United States, enrolled in or plan to enroll in a
    two- or four-year degree program or vocational-tech

program, and should also have at least two semesters of school remaining. *Application Process: Applicants should submit a completed application form along with official college transcripts, proof of high school graduation date, and a personal essay. Visit the company's Web site to download an application. *Amount: Up to $10,000. *Deadline: January 3.

United Daughters of the Confederacy
Attn: Mrs. Robert C. Kraus, Second Vice President General
328 North Boulevard
Richmond, VA 23220-4009
804-355-1636
hqudc@rcn.com
http://www.hqudc.org
Scholarship Name: Undergraduate Scholarship.
*Academic Area: Open. *Age Group: Undergraduate students. *Eligibility: Applicants must be of lineal descent of an eligible Confederate soldier, maintain at least a 3.0 GPA, and be admitted to an accredited college or university. They also should visit the organization's Web site for specific details about acceptable Confederate lineage as well as additional eligibility requirements for individual scholarships. *Application Process: Applicants should submit a completed, original application along with original transcripts, recommendation forms, a copy of their birth certificate, and a lineage form. One complete set of originals should be included (with the exception of a photocopied birth certificate) along with four additional photocopied sets of these materials. Additionally, a wallet-sized photograph, a completed checklist, and Confederate ancestor's proof of service are required. Visit the organization's Web site to download an application. *Amount: Awards vary. *Deadline: March 15.

Whirly-Girls Inc.
Attn: Bev Vetter
PO Box 16446
Missoula, MT 59808-6446
209-369-6187
scholarships@whirlygirls.org
http://www.whirlygirls.org
Whirly-Girls Inc. offers numerous scholarships to women. *Academic Area: Aviation. *Age Group: Undergraduate students, professionals. *Eligibility: Information about eligibility for individual scholarships will be posted each August on the organization's Web site. For many scholarships,

applicants must be a member in good standing of Whirly-Girls for at least one year prior to time of scholarship application, and possess a pilot's license. *Application Process: Visit the organization's Web site after August 1 for an updated list of available scholarships as well as a downloadable application form. *Amount: Awards vary (most are between $4,000 and $5,000). *Deadline: October 1.

Woman's National Farm and Garden Association–New Jersey
Attn: Claudia Scioly
1634 East Stadium
Ann Arbor, MI 48104
cscioly@hotmail.com
http://wnfga.org/code/scholarships.htm
Scholarship Name: Burlingame/Gerrity Horticultural Therapy Scholarship. *Academic Area: Therapy (horticultural). *Age Group: Undergraduate students. *Eligibility: Applicants must be enrolled in a bachelor's degree program in horticultural therapy. *Application Process: There is no formal application for this scholarship. Please contact the association via e-mail for information on how to apply for this scholarship as well as any additional regional scholarships. *Amount: $500. *Deadline: Deadlines vary.

Woman's National Farm and Garden Association–New Jersey
Attn: Markie Philips
83 Webster Road
Weston, MA 02493
http://wnfga.org/code/scholarships.htm
Scholarship Name: Warren/Sanders/McNaughton Oceanographic Scholarship. *Academic Area: Oceanography. *Age Group: Undergraduate students, graduate students. *Eligibility: Applicants must agree to complete the program of study or research as outlined in the application and to communicate with the scholarship chair any changes in the program, as well as give periodic progress reports. The scholarship is available to high school seniors and college students. *Application Process: There is no formal application for this scholarship. Applicants should submit a letter that includes their name and address, and a statement of their career objectives and interests, along with a resume that includes references, two letters of recommendation, academic transcripts, and a description of their planned academic program. This information should be mailed to Markie Philips at

the address listed above. *Amount: Scholarships range from $1,000 to $1,500. *Deadline: May 25.

Women Band Directors International (WBDI)

Attn: Diane Gorzycki, WBDI Scholarship Chair
7424 Whistletop Drive
Austin, TX 79749
dgorzycki@austin.rr.com
http://www.womenbanddirectors.org

Scholarship Name: Women Band Directors International Memorial Scholarships. *Academic Area: Performing arts (music-directing), performing arts (music-instrumental). *Age Group: Undergraduate students, graduate students. *Eligibility: Any female college student pursuing a degree in instrumental music studying to be a band director should apply. *Application Process: Applicants should submit a completed application, two letters of recommendation, current transcripts, and a philosophy statement on why they want to be a band director. Visit the association's Web site to download an application. *Amount: $300. *Deadline: December 1.

Women Executives in Public Relations Foundation

FDR Station
PO Box 7657
New York, NY 10150-7657
212-859-7375
http://www.wepr.org/foundation_scholarships.asp

This organization offers five annual undergraduate scholarships for women. *Academic Area: Public relations. *Age Group: Undergraduate students. *Eligibility: Contact the foundation via e-mail for specific eligibility requirements. Scholarships are available for students attending Cornell University or City College of New York. *Application Process: Contact the foundation via e-mail to request an application. *Amount: Awards vary. *Deadline: Deadlines vary.

Women Grocers of America

1005 North Glebe Road, Suite 250
Arlington, VA 22201-5758
703-516-0700
wga@nationalgrocers.org
http://www.nationalgrocers.org/WGA.html

Scholarship Name: Mary Macey Scholarship. *Academic Area: Business, management. *Age Group: Undergraduate students, graduate students. *Eligibility: Applicants must be attending a U.S.

college or university, maintain a 2.0 GPA, and be pursuing a career in the independent sector of the grocery industry. Applicants must be at least college sophomores. *Application Process: Applicants should submit a letter of recommendation from a sponsor in the grocery industry, official transcripts, a completed application, and a personal statement outlining their scholastic achievements, leadership awards, and extracurricular activities. Visit the association's Web site to download an application. *Amount: $1,000. *Deadline: June 1.

Women In Film (WIF) Foundation

8857 West Olympic Boulevard, Suite 201
Beverly Hills, CA 90211
310-657-5144
http://www.wif.org/info_page.cfm?id=6

This organization offers numerous scholarships for women. *Academic Area: Film/video. *Age Group: Varies by award. *Eligibility: Applicants must be attending select film schools in the Los Angeles area, including (but not limited to) University of California-Los Angeles, University of Southern California, Chapman University, and American Film Institute. *Application Process: This scholarship program is unique in that the foundation does not award these scholarships directly, but rather school instructors and faculty choose enrolled students. Students should ask their advisors if these scholarships are available to them, or, if applying to film schools, ask them directly if they offer WIF Foundation scholarships. *Amount: Awards vary. *Deadline: Deadlines vary.

Women in Government Relations (WGR) LEADER Foundation

Attn: Tiffany D. Nice
Washington, DC 20005
LeaderFoundation@hotmail.com
FAX: 703-698-1694
http://www.leaderfoundation.org

Scholarship Name: WGR LEADER Foundation Fellowships for Our Future. *Academic Area: Government, Public policy. *Age Group: Undergraduate students, graduate students. *Eligibility: Applicants must demonstrate financial need, a history of community involvement, and proof of enrollment or acceptance into a degree program or nondegree training program that supports a career in public policy. Applicants must also be permanent or scholastic residents of the greater Washington,

D.C. area. *Application Process: Applicants should submit a completed application, a 200-word statement on community involvement, a 200-word statement on how they plan to use their degree to pursue a career in a public policy-related field, a 50-word statement on financial need, a copy of their FAFSA report, proof of enrollment or acceptance in program, and proof of residency in the greater D.C. area. Visit the foundation's Web site to download an application. Applications are accepted by fax or e-mail only.. *Amount: $5,000. *Deadline: May 31.

Women Marines Association (WMA)

Attn: Luann Weeks, Scholarship Chair
18 Maple Court
New Hyde Park, NY 11040-3105
ldweeks@pocketmail.com
http://www.womenmarines.org/scholarships.php
This organization offers numerous scholarships for
    women. *Academic Area: Open. *Age Group:
    Undergraduate students. *Eligibility: Applicants
    must fall into one of the following four categories: (1)
    Have served or be serving in the U.S. Marine Corps or
    Reserves. (2) Be a direct descendant of a marine on
    active duty, or of one who has served honorably. (3)
    Be a sibling or descendant of a sibling of a Marine. (4)
    Have completed two years in a Marine Corps JROTC
    program. High school seniors and undergraduate
    students who meet one of the above requirements
    may apply for this scholarship. Applicants must also
    have a WMA sponsor. Visit the association's Web
    site for specific academic eligibility requirements
    for both high school students and college students.
    *Application Process: Applicants should submit a
    completed application, official transcripts, letters,
    essays, and copy of sponsor's membership card. Visit
    the association's Web site to download an application.
    *Amount: Most are $1,500; other amounts are
    available as well. *Deadline: March 31.

Women's Basketball Coaches Association (WBCA)

Attn: Amy Lowe, WBCA Awards Program Manager
4646 Lawrenceville Highway
Lilburn, GA 30047-3620
770-279-8027, ext. 102
alowe@wbca.org
http://www.wbca.org/WBCAScholarAward.asp
WBCA Scholarship Award. *Academic Area: Open. *Age
    Group: Undergraduate students, graduate students.
    *Eligibility: Applicants must demonstrate outstanding
commitment to the sport of women's basketball as well as to academic excellence. Applicants must be basketball players in any of the intercollegiate divisions of the National Collegiate Athletic Association and the National Association of Intercollegiate Athletics. Awards are based on sportsmanship, commitment to excellence as a student athlete, honesty, ethical behavior, courage, and dedication to purpose. *Application Process: Applicants must be nominated by coaches. Visit the association's Web site for information on the nomination process, and request further information about the scholarship application process by e-mail. *Amount: $1,000. *Deadline: Nomination forms for coaches are available in January. Deadlines, as noted on these forms, are firm.

Women's International Network of Utility Professionals (WiNUP)

PO Box 335
Whites Creek, TN 37189
http://www.winup.org/prof_dev_scholarships.htm
Fellowship Name: Julia Kiene Fellowship in Electrical
    Energy. *Academic Area: Electrical energy. *Age
    Group: Graduate students. *Eligibility: Students
    who are pursuing graduate work toward a degree
    in any phase of electrical energy are eligible to
    apply. *Application Procedure: Visit the WiNUP Web
    site to download an application. *Amount: $2,000.
    *Deadline: Varies. Contact the network for more
    information.

Women's International Network of Utility Professionals (WiNUP)

PO Box 335
Whites Creek, TN 37189
http://www.winup.org/prof_dev_scholarships.htm
Fellowship Name: Lyle Mamer Fellowship. *Academic
    Area: Electrical energy. *Age Group: Graduate
    students. *Eligibility: Students who are pursuing
    graduate work toward a degree in any phase of
    electrical energy are eligible to apply. *Application
    Procedure: Visit the network's Web site to download
    an application. *Amount: $1,000. *Deadline: Varies.
    Contact the network for more information.

Women's Jewelry Association (WJA)

Attn: Scholarship Committee
Building E, 373 Route 46 West, Suite 215
Fairfield, NJ 07004
973-575-7190

info@womensjewelry.org

http://www.womensjewelry.org/scholarships.html

Scholarship Name: WJA Student Scholarship. *Academic Area: Jewelry design. *Age Group: Varies. *Eligibility: Applicants must be enrolled in fine jewelry and watch design courses in the United States. *Application Process: Applicants should submit a completed application, two letters of recommendation, a short essay, three slides of recent ranked work, and a self-addressed envelope for the return of their slides. Visit the association's Web site to download an application. *Amount: $500 and up. *Deadline: May 1.

Woman's National Farm and Garden Association Inc. (WFNGA)

Attn: Frysinger Exchange

PO Box 1175

Midland, MI 48641-1175

http://www.wnfga.org

Fellowship Name: The Grace E. Frysinger Exchange Fellowship allows the recipient to participate in a one-month foreign exchange program. *Academic Areas: Agriculture, horticulture. *Age Group: Open. *Eligibility: Applicants must have an outgoing personality, an interest in the rural and urban life of other women of the world, knowledge of the mission of the organization she represents, and be in good health. All members of the association are eligible to apply. *Application Procedure: Applicants must submit the following information in resume form: two recent photos and detailed personal information. Visit the association's Web site for detailed information on application requirements. The fellowship is awarded every four years. *Amount: Travel expenses are paid in full. *Deadline: Varies. Contact the association for more information.

Woman's National Farm and Garden Association Inc.

Attn: Tyson Scholarship Chair

PO Box 1175

Midland, MI 48641-1175

http://www.wnfga.org/code/fellowships.htm

Fellowship Name: Sarah Bradley Tyson Fellowship. *Academic Areas: Agriculture, horticulture. *Age Group: Undergraduate students. *Eligibility: Female undergraduate students are eligible to apply. *Application Procedure: There is no application form. A letter of application containing an account of the applicant's educational training, plan of study, certification of degrees held, and testimonials as to character, ability, personality, and scholarship should be sent to the scholarship chair. *Amount: Varies. *Deadline: Varies. Contact the association for more information.

Women's Research and Education Institute

WREI Congressional Fellowship Program

1750 New York Avenue, NW, Suite 350

Washington, DC 20006

202-628-0444

wrei@wrei.org

http://www.wrei.org/fellowships

Fellowship Name: Congressional Fellowships on Women and Public Policy allow women to work for eight months as congressional legislative aides in Washington, D.C. *Academic Areas: Government, public policy. *Age Group: Graduate students, recent graduates of graduate or professional degree programs in the United States. *Eligibility: Female graduate students or recent graduates with an interest in the public policy process are eligible to apply. Applicants must have a strong academic background, be articulate, and have strong writing skills. *Application Procedure: Applications are available by sending a self-addressed, 60-cent-stamped envelope to the above address. *Amount: Fellows receive stipends for tuition and living expenses. *Deadline: May 20.

Women's Sports Foundation

Eisenhower Park

East Meadow, NY 11554

800-227-3988

info@womenssportsfoundation.org

http://www.womenssportsfoundation.org/cgi-bin/iowa/funding/featured.html?record=3

Scholarship Name: Dorothy Harris Endowed Scholarship. *Academic Area: Athletics, business, education, psychology, sociology. *Age Group: Graduate students. *Eligibility: Applicants must be U.S. citizens or legal residents and pursuing a full-time course of study in a sports-related major at an accredited postgraduate institution. They also must demonstrate financial need. *Application Process: Applicants should submit four stapled copies of the application packet, which includes a completed application, official transcripts (one official, the rest copies), and two letters of recommendation. Visit the foundation's Web site to download an application form. *Amount: $1,500. *Deadline: December 31.

Women's Sports Foundation

Eisenhower Park

East Meadow, NY 11554

800-227-3988

info@womenssportsfoundation.org

http://www.womenssportsfoundation.org/cgi-bin/iowa/
funding/featured.html?record=8

Scholarship Name: Linda Riddle/SGMA Endowed
Scholarship. *Academic Area: Open. *Age Group:
Undergraduate students. *Eligibility: Applicants must
be high school seniors planning to pursue a full-time
course of study at an accredited two- or four-year
college and must have participated on an officially
recognized high school athletic team. Applicants also
must have a minimum cumulative GPA of 3.5 on a 4.0
scale. *Application Process: Applicants should visit
the foundation's Web site for more information on
the availability of this scholarship. *Amount: $1,500.
*Deadline: Deadlines vary.

Women's Studio Workshop

PO Box 489

Rosendale, NY 12472

845-658-9133

info@wsworkshop.org

http://www.wsworkshop.org/_art_opp/fellowships.htm

The Women's Studio Workshop, an alternative space
for artists to create new work and come together to
share skills, provides fellowships in several mediums,
including intaglio, silkscreen, hand papermaking,
photography, letterpress, and ceramics. *Academic
Areas: Visual arts (ceramics), visual arts (open), visual
arts (photography). *Age Group: Open. *Eligibility:
Female artists may apply. *Application Procedure:
Applicants should submit a one-page letter of intent
detailing their planned project, a resume, a completed
application form (available at the workshop's Web
site), slides of recent work, and a self-addressed,
stamped envelope for return of materials. *Amount:
Approximately $200 to $300 a week. *Deadline: Varies
by fellowship. Contact the workshop for details.

Women's Studio Workshop

PO Box 489

Rosendale, NY 12472

845-658-9133

info@wsworkshop.org

http://www.wsworkshop.org/_art_opp/grants.htm

The Women's Studio Workshop, an alternative space
for artists to create new work and come together to
share skills, provides residency grants. *Academic
Area: Visual arts (ceramics, visual arts (open), visual
arts (photography). *Age Group: Open. *Eligibility:
Female printmakers, papermakers, photographers,
book artists, and ceramic artists may apply. (Note:
One grant program is open only to New Jersey
artists.) *Application Procedure: Applicants should
submit a one-page letter of intent detailing their
planned project, a resume, a completed application
form (available at the workshop's Web site), slides of
recent work, and a self-addressed, stamped envelope
for return of materials. *Amount: Grant recipients
receive 24-hour studio access, on-campus housing,
technical and production assistance, a travel per diem,
a materials stipend, and a weekly personal stipend
during their stay. *Deadline: Varies by grant. Contact
the workshop for details.

Woodrow Wilson (WW) National Fellowship Foundation

PO Box 5281

Princeton, NJ 08543-5281

609-452-7007

http://www.woodrow.org/womens-studies

Fellowship Name: The Woodrow Wilson Dissertation
Fellowships in Women's Studies encourage original
research about women that crosses disciplinary,
regional, or cultural boundaries. *Academic Area: Open.
*Age Group: Graduate students. *Eligibility: Doctoral
students who have completed all pre-dissertation
requirements in any field of study are eligible to apply.
*Application Procedure: Visit the foundation's Web site
to download an application. *Amount: $3,000 (which
must be used for research expenses such as travel,
books, taping, and computer services). *Deadline:
Typically in October. Contact the foundation for details.

Zeta Phi Beta Sorority Inc.

National Educational Foundation

1734 New Hampshire Avenue, NW

Washington, DC 20009

202-387-3103

IHQ@zphib1920.org

http://www.zpbnef1975.org

Fellowship Name: Deborah Partridge Wolfe International
Graduate Fellowship. *Academic Area: Open. *Age
Group: Undergraduate students, graduate students.
*Eligibility: Female undergraduate and graduate
students who are studying abroad are eligible to
apply. The fellowship is also open to foreign students

studying in the United States. Women who are not members of the sorority may apply. *Application Procedure: Applicants should submit proof of academic study, three letters of recommendation, an academic transcript, a completed application (available for download at Zeta Phi Beta's Web site), and an essay detailing their educational goals, professional aspirations, and why they should receive the fellowship. *Amount: $500 to $1,000. *Deadline: Applications are accepted September 1 through February 1. Contact the sorority for details.

Zeta Phi Beta Sorority Inc.
National Educational Foundation
1734 New Hampshire Avenue, NW
Washington, DC 20009
202-387-3103
IHQ@zphib1920.org
http://www.zpbnef1975.org
Scholarship Name: General Graduate Scholarship. *Academic Area: Open. *Age Group: Graduate students, post-doctoral scholars. *Eligibility: Women pursuing a master's, doctoral, or postdoctoral degree may apply. Applicants do not have to be members of the sorority, but must be full-time students. *Application Process: Applicants must submit a 150-word personal essay describing their educational goals and professional aspirations, three letters of recommendation, and a completed application. Visit the foundation's Web site to download an application. *Amount: Up to $2,500. *Deadline: February 1.

Zeta Phi Beta Sorority Inc.
National Educational Foundation
1734 New Hampshire Avenue, NW
Washington, DC 20009
202-387-3103
IHQ@zphib1920.org
http://www.zpbnef1975.org
Scholarship Name: General Undergraduate Scholarship. *Academic Area: Open. *Age Group: Undergraduate students. *Eligibility: Applicants do not have to be members of the sorority, but must be full-time students or high school seniors who are enrolled as full-time students for the upcoming fall semester. *Application Process: Applicants must submit a 150-word personal essay describing their educational goals and professional aspirations, three letters of recommendation, and a completed application. Visit the foundation's Web site to download an application.

*Amount: Scholarships range from $500 to $1,000. *Deadline: February 1.

Zeta Phi Beta Sorority Inc.
National Educational Foundation
1734 New Hampshire Avenue, NW
Washington, DC 20009
202-387-3103
IHQ@zphib1920.org
http://www.zpbnef1975.org
Scholarship Name: Isabel M. Herson Scholarship in Education. *Academic Area: Education. *Age Group: Undergraduate students, graduate students. *Eligibility: Any woman pursuing an undergraduate or graduate degree in elementary or secondary education may apply. Applicants do not have to be members of the sorority but must be full-time students. *Application Process: Applicants must submit a completed application, a 150-word personal essay describing their educational goals and professional aspirations, and three letters of recommendation. Proof of enrollment is also required. Visit the foundation's Web site to download an application. *Amount: Scholarships range from $500 to $1,000. *Deadline: February 1.

Zeta Phi Beta Sorority Inc.
National Educational Foundation
1734 New Hampshire Avenue, NW
Washington, DC 20009
202-387-3103
IHQ@zphib1920.org
http://www.zpbnef1975.org
Scholarship Name: Lullelia W. Harrison Scholarship in Counseling. *Academic Area: Counseling. *Age Group: Undergraduate students, graduate students. *Eligibility: Applicant does not have to be a member of the sorority but must be a full-time student enrolled in a degree program in counseling. *Application Process: Applicants must submit a completed application, a 150-word personal essay describing their educational goals and professional aspirations, and three letters of recommendation. Visit the foundation's Web site to download an application. *Amount: Scholarships range from $500 to $1,000. *Deadline: February 1.

Zeta Phi Beta Sorority Inc.
National Educational Foundation
1734 New Hampshire Avenue, NW

Washington, DC 20009
202-387-3103
IHQ@zphib1920.org
http://www.zpbnef1975.org
Fellowship Name: Mildred Cater Bradham Social Work Fellowship. *Academic Area: Social work. *Age Group: Graduate students. *Eligibility: Female students who are pursuing a graduate or professional degree in social work at an accredited college or university are eligible to apply. The fellowship is open only to members of the sorority. *Application Procedure: Applicants should submit proof of academic study, three letters of recommendation, an academic transcript, a completed application (available for download at Zeta Phi Beta's Web site), and an essay detailing their educational goals, professional aspirations, and why they should receive the fellowship. *Amount: $500 to $1,000. *Deadline: Applications are accepted September 1 through February 1. Contact the sorority for details.

Zeta Phi Beta Sorority Inc.
National Educational Foundation
1734 New Hampshire Avenue, NW
Washington, DC 20009
202-387-3103
IHQ@zphib1920.org
http://www.zpbnef1975.org
Fellowship Name: Nancy B. Woolridge McGee Graduate Fellowship. *Academic Area: Open. *Age Group: Graduate students. *Eligibility: Female graduate students who are pursuing a graduate or professional degree at an accredited college or university are eligible to apply. Applicants must demonstrate scholarly distinction in their field of study. The fellowship is open only to members of the sorority. *Application Procedure: Applicants should submit proof of academic study, three letters of recommendation, an academic transcript, a completed application (available for download at Zeta Phi Beta's Web site), and an essay detailing their educational goals, professional aspirations, and why they should receive the fellowship. *Amount: $500 to $1,000. *Deadline: Applications are accepted September 1 through February 1. Contact the sorority for details.

Zeta Phi Beta Sorority Inc.
National Educational Foundation
1734 New Hampshire Avenue, NW

Washington, DC 20009
202-387-3103
IHQ@zphib1920.org
http://www.zpbnef1975.org
Scholarship Name: S. Evelyn Lewis Memorial Scholarship in Medical Health Sciences. *Academic Area: Medicine (open). *Age Group: Undergraduate students, graduate students. *Eligibility: Any woman pursuing an undergraduate or graduate degree in medicine or health sciences may apply. Applicants do not have to be members of the sorority, but must be full-time students. *Application Process: Applicants must submit a150-word personal essay describing their educational goals and professional aspirations, three letters of recommendation, and a completed application. Visit the foundation's Web site to download an application. *Amount: Scholarships range from $500 to $1,000. *Deadline: February 1.

Zeta Phi Beta Sorority Inc.
National Educational Foundation
1734 New Hampshire Avenue, NW
Washington, DC 20009
202-387-3103
IHQ@zphib1920.org
http://www.zpbnef1975.org
Scholarship Name: Zora Neale Hurston Scholarship. *Academic Area: Anthropology. *Age Group: Graduate students. *Eligibility: Any woman pursuing a graduate degree in anthropology or a related field may apply. Applicant does not have to be a member of the sorority, but must be a full-time student. *Application Process: Applicants must submit a 150-word personal essay describing their educational goals and professional aspirations, three letters of recommendation, and a completed application. Visit the foundation's Web site to download an application. *Amount: Scholarships range from $500 to $1,000. *Deadline: February 1.

Zeta Tau Alpha (ZTA)
3450 Founders Road
Indianapolis, IN 46268
317-872-0540
zetataualpha@zetataualpha.org
http://www.zetataualpha.org/content/achievement/programs.asp
Scholarship Name: Achievement Scholarship. *Academic Area: Open. *Age Group: Undergraduates students, graduate students. *Eligibility: Applicants must

be members of Zeta Tau Alpha, maintain a high scholastic average, and exhibit outstanding leadership skills in their ZTA chapter or alumnae group, campus, or community. They must also demonstrate financial need. *Application Process: Applicants must submit a completed application, which is available in January from collegiate chapter presidents or alumnae. *Amount: Minimum of $1,000. *Deadline: March 1.

Zeta Tau Alpha (ZTA)

3450 Founders Road
Indianapolis, IN 46268
317-872-0540
zetataualpha@zetataualpha.org
http://www.zetataualpha.org/content/achievement/
    programs.asp
Scholarship Name: Founders Grant. *Academic Area: Open. *Age Group: Graduate students. *Eligibility: Applicants must be members of Zeta Tau Alpha and demonstrate outstanding leadership skills, exceptional academic achievement, and financial need. *Application Process: Applicants must submit a completed application, which is available in January from collegiate chapter presidents or alumnae. *Amount: $6,000. *Deadline: March 1.

Zeta Tau Alpha (ZTA)

3450 Founders Road
Indianapolis, IN 46268
317-872-0540
zetataualpha@zetataualpha.org
http://www.zetataualpha.org/content/achievement/
    programs.asp
Scholarship Name: Recognition Scholarship. *Academic Area: Open. *Age Group: Undergraduate students, graduate students. *Eligibility: Applicants must be members of Zeta Tau Alpha and exhibit outstanding academic and personal achievement. These scholarships are established for specific chapters or areas only, and applicants must be recommended by a local alumna or chapter advisor. *Amount: Minimum of $1,300. *Deadline: March 1.

Zeta Tau Alpha (ZTA)

3450 Founders Road
Indianapolis, IN 46268
317-872-0540
zetataualpha@zetataualpha.org
http://www.zetataualpha.org/content/achievement/
    programs.asp

Scholarship Name: Zeta Tau Alpha Service Scholarship. *Academic Area: Medicine (open), social work, special education. *Age Group: Undergraduate students, graduate students. *Eligibility: Applicants must be members of Zeta Tau Alpha. *Application Process: Applicants must submit a completed application, which is available in January from collegiate chapter presidents or alumnae. *Amount: Minimum of $1,000. *Deadline: March 1.

Zonta International Foundation

557 West Randolph Street
Chicago, IL 60661
312-930-5848
zontaintl@zonta.org
http://www.zonta.org/site/PageServer?pagename=zi_
    ae_fellowships
Fellowship Name: Amelia Earhart Fellowship. *Academic Areas: Aerospace, engineering (aerospace). *Age Group: Graduate students. *Eligibility: Women pursuing graduate study in aerospace-related sciences and engineering are eligible to apply. Applicants must be registered in an accredited doctoral program and demonstrate superior academic ability. The fellowship is open to women from throughout the world. *Application Procedure: Applicants must submit the following materials: biographical information, academic transcripts, a list of schools they have attended and degrees received, an essay on their academic and professional goals, three letters of recommendation, and a completed application (available at the organization's Web site). *Amount: $6,000. *Deadline: November 15.

Zonta International Foundation

557 West Randolph Street
Chicago, IL 60661
312-930-5848
zontaintl@zonta.org
http://www.zonta.org/site/PageServer?pagename=zi_
    scholarships_fellowships_awards
Scholarship Name: Jane M. Klausman Women in Business Scholarship. *Academic Area: Business. *Age Group: Undergraduate students. *Eligibility: Students of any nationality pursuing an undergraduate business degree who demonstrate outstanding potential in the field and who have achieved an outstanding academic record during their first two or three years of academic study in college should apply. *Application Process: Applicants must contact the Zonta Club nearest them

to apply. Visit the foundation's Web site to do this. Or. e-mail your name and contact information to Zonta International headquarters and you will be given instructions on how to proceed with the application process. Applicants must be nominated by a local Zonta Club. An application packet should include one letter of recommendation from a faculty member, one letter of recommendation from an employer, volunteer supervisor, or academic advisor, an essay in 500 words or less that describes your academic and professional goals, and verification of enrollment from the university or college registrar is required. Visit Zonta's Web site to download an application and to contact your local Zonta Club. *Amount: $5,000. *Deadline: Deadlines vary by Zonta Club, though all applications are due during the month of April.

Zonta International Foundation
557 West Randolph Street
Chicago, IL 60661

312-930-5848
zontaintl@zonta.org
http://www.zonta.org/site/PageServer?pagename=zi_ywpa

Grant Name: Young Women in Public Affairs Award. *Academic Area: Government, public policy. *Age Group: Undergraduate students. *Eligibility: Young women ages 16 to 20 who are interested in pursuing careers and leadership positions in public policy, government, and volunteer organizations are eligible to apply. *Application Process: The awards program operates at the club, district, and international levels. Each club selects a winner and submits her name to the district. The application of the district winner is forwarded to the international headquarters for international competition. Visit Zonta's Web site to complete an online application. *Amount: Awards range from $500 to $1,000. *Deadline: Varies.

OTHER TYPES OF
FINANCIAL AID

ATHLETIC SCHOLARSHIPS— UNDERGRADUATE

The following scholarships are available to athletes at the undergraduate level. Check also with specific colleges for athletic scholarships specific to those schools.

Columbia 300 Inc.
Attn: Dale Garner
PO Box 13430
San Antonio, TX 78213
http://columbia300.com/jjowdy.pdf
Scholarship Name: Columbia 300 John Jowdy Scholarship. *Academic Area: Open. *Age Group: Undergraduate students. *Eligibility: Applicants must be graduating high school seniors who have been actively involved in the sport of bowling. *Application Process: Applicants should submit a completed application along with optional letters of recommendation. Finalists will be notified and instructed to submit their high school transcripts. Visit the organization's Web site to download an application. *Amount: $500. *Deadline: April 1.

Harness Horse Youth Foundation
Attn: Ellen Taylor, Executive Director
16575 Carey Road
Westfield, IN 46074
317-867-5877
ellen@hhyf.org
http://www.hhyf.org/scholarships.html
Scholarship Name: Harness Horse Youth Foundation Scholarships. *Academic Area: Open. *Age Group: Undergraduate students *Eligibility: Applicants should be high school seniors or undergraduate students (preferably under age 25) with a background in harness horse racing. They also should be able to demonstrate both academic achievement and financial need. This foundation offers several scholarships, each with additional eligibility requirements. Visit the foundation's Web site to view additional eligibility requirements for the scholarships. *Application Process: Applicants should contact the foundation by mail or e-mail to request a scholarship application. *Amount: $500 to $3,000. *Deadline: April 30.

Patrick Kerr Skateboard Scholarship
PO Box 2054
Jenkintown, PA 19046
http://www.skateboardscholarship.org/index.html

Scholarship Name: Patrick Kerr Skateboard Scholarship. *Academic Area: Open. *Age Group: Undergraduate students. *Eligibility: Applicants must be graduating high school seniors who possess at least a 2.5 GPA, are U.S. citizens, and who are planning to enroll full time in a two- or four-year undergraduate program in the fall. They must also be passionate skateboarders. *Application Process: Applicants should submit a page of personal information (as detailed on the organization's Web site), a 300-word essay about skateboarding (topic posted on Web site), two letters of recommendation from school administrators, official transcripts, and documentation of any skateboard activist activities the applicant may have initiated or participated in. Visit the organization's Web site for additional information. *Amount: $5,000 (one winner); $1,000 (three winners). *Deadline: April 20.

Salute to Education Inc.
PO Box 833425
Miami, FL 33283
305-476-7709
steinfo@stescholarships.org
http://www.stescholarships.org/SC_categories.html
Scholarship Name: Salute to Education Athletics Scholarship. *Academic Area: Open. *Age Group: Undergraduate students. *Eligibility: Applicants must be graduating high school seniors who attend a Miami-Dade or Broward County, Florida, high school and who also reside in one of these counties. They also must be legal residents of the United States, have a minimum weighted GPA of 3.0, demonstrate a commitment to service by participating in at least one school or community organization, and intend to pursue a college degree at an accredited institution after graduation. Applicants must have participated in varsity athletics for at least two years, while demonstrating good leadership skills, a positive attitude, and good sportsmanship. *Application Process: Applicants must apply online. Supporting materials should be mailed as detailed on the online application. *Amount: $1,000. *Deadline: Visit the organization's Web site for updated deadline information.

ATHLETICS—GRADUATE

The following graduate financial aid resources are available to students who compete in high school and/or college athletics, as well as those who do not compete in athletics, but who are interested in pursuing careers in athletics-related fields (such as athletics administration, athletic training, golf course management, and turfgrass science).

Golf Course Superintendents Association of America (GCSAA)
Attn: Amanda Howard
1421 Research Park Drive
Lawrence, KS 66049-3859
800-472-7878, ext. 4424
ahoward@gcsaa.org
http://www.gcsaa.org/students/scholarships/default.asp
Contest Name: GCSAA Student Essay Contest. *Academic Area: Agronomy, golf course management, turfgrass science. *Age Group: Graduate students. *Eligibility: Contest applicants must be pursuing degrees in turfgrass science, agronomy, or any other field related to golf course management. The contest is also open to undergraduate students. *Application Process: Essays should be seven to 12 pages in length. Contact Amanda Howard for application details. *Amount: Up to $4,500. *Deadline: March 31.

National Athletic Trainers Association (NATA) Foundation
Contact: Barbara Niland
2952 Stemmons
Dallas, TX 75247
800-TRY-NATA, ext. 121
barbaran@nata.org
http://www.natafoundation.org/scholarship.html
Scholarship Name: NATA Research & Education Foundation Scholarship. *Academic Area: Athletics training. *Age Group: Graduate students. *Eligibility: Applicants must be at least juniors in college. They also must be NATA members, maintain at least a 3.2 GPA, and be sponsored by a certified athletic trainer. The scholarship is also available to undergraduate students. *Application Process: Applicants must submit a completed application and official transcripts. Visit the foundation's Web site for further application details and to download an application. *Amount: $2,000. *Deadline: February 10.

National Collegiate Athletic Association (NCAA)
Attn: Teresa Smith
700 West Washington Street
PO Box 6222
Indianapolis, IN 46206-6222
317-917-6222
tksmith@ncaa.org
http://www1.ncaa.org/membership/ed_outreach/prof_development/minority-womens_scholarships.html
Scholarship Name: Ethnic Minority and Women's Enhancement Postgraduate Scholarship for Careers in Athletics. *Academic Area: Athletics administration, athletics. *Age Group: Graduate students. *Eligibility: Applicants must be in their senior year of undergraduate studies and already accepted into graduate program in sports administration or a similar major leading to a career in intercollegiate athletics. An equal number of scholarships are awarded to (13) women and (13) minority candidates. *Application Process: Applicants must submit an online application and forward their transcripts by mail. Visit the NCAA's Web site for additional information and to submit your application. *Amount: $6,000. *Deadline: January 18.

National Collegiate Athletic Association (NCAA)
Walter Byers Scholarship Committee Staff Liaison
700 West Washington Street
PO Box 6222
Indianapolis, IN 46206-6222
317-917-6222
http://www1.ncaa.org/membership/scholarships/byers/index.html
Scholarship Name: Walter Byers Postgraduate Scholarship. *Academic Area: Open. *Age Group: Graduate students. *Eligibility: Applicants must be student athletes who are in their senior year of intercollegiate athletics, or who have enrolled in graduate study at a NCAA-member institution while completing their last year of eligibility. They also must have performed exceptionally as a member of a varsity team, excelled academically by maintaining a 3.5 GPA, and demonstrate exceptional character and leadership potential. *Application Process: Applicants must be nominated by the faculty athletics representative and/or department. Along with an application, an essay, four recommendations, and official transcripts must be submitted. *Amount: $21,500. *Deadline: January 13.

National Collegiate Athletic Association
Attn: Teresa Smith
700 West Washington Street
PO Box 6222
Indianapolis, IN 46206-6222
317-917-6222
tksmith@ncaa.org
http://www1.ncaa.org/membership/ed_outreach/prof_
    development/postgrad_scholarships.html
Scholarship Name: NCAA Postgraduate Scholarship
    Program. *Academic Area: Open. *Age Group:
    Graduate students. *Eligibility: Applicants must
    be student athletes who are in their final year of
    intercollegiate athletics and who have performed
    exceptionally as a member of a varsity team. They
    must also excel academically by maintaining a 3.2
    GPA. Applicants must intend to pursue graduate
    study. *Application Process: Applications are mailed
    to athletic department personnel periodically. An
    applicant must be nominated in order to apply.
    Contact your head coach or athletic director to let
    them know your intentions on pursuing a graduate
    education. *Amount: $7,500. *Deadline: February 24,
    May 5, and December 9.

Professional Bowlers Association
Attn: Billy Welu Bowling Scholarship
719 Second Avenue, Suite 701
Seattle, WA 98104
206-332-9688
http://www.pba.com/corporate/scholarships.asp
Scholarship Name: Billy Welu Scholarship. *Academic
    Area: Open. *Age Group: Graduate students.
    *Eligibility: Applicants must be amateur bowlers
who are matriculating college students maintaining
at least a 2.5 GPA. They also should demonstrate
academic achievement and a love of bowling. The
scholarship is also open to undergraduate students.
*Application Process: Applicants should submit a
completed application along with transcripts and
an essay that does not exceed 500 words. Visit the
organization's Web site to download an application.
*Amount: $1,000. *Deadline: May 31.

Safer Athletic Field Environments (SAFE)
c/o Sports Turf Managers Association
SAFE Scholarship
805 New Hampshire, Suite E
Lawrence, KS 66044
800-323-3875
stmainfo@sportsturfmanager.org
http://www.sportsturfmanager.org/Professionalism/
    SCHOL/INTRO
Scholarship Name: Safer Athletic Field Environments
    Scholarship. *Academic Area: Turfgrass science. *Age
    Group: Graduate students. *Eligibility: Applicants must
    be enrolled in two- or four-year programs in sports
    turf management, with at least one semester of study
    remaining. They must also be Sports Turf Managers
    Association student members planning careers in
    the sports turf industry (golf course management
    excluded). Undergraduate students may also apply for
    this scholarship. *Application Process: Applicants must
    submit a completed application, official transcripts,
    a personal statement, faculty advisor form, and an
    employer reference form. Visit the association's Web
    site to download an application and forms. *Amount:
    At least $1,000. *Deadline: October 1.

EARLY AWARENESS PROGRAMS

A college degree opens doors to career opportunities and economic mobility in a way that few can deny. It is commonplace for middle- and upper-income families in America to assume their children will earn a college degree. Many would not dream otherwise. However, the fact remains: attending college is not a right-of-passage that all Americans view as possible. Poverty, social conditions, and public schools that produce underprepared students all contribute to a widespread problem: a large population of students in America simply assume from a very young age that their future does not include a college education. Nobody in their family has gone to college—how can they?

Federal, state, and private organizations have funded early awareness programs to address this issue and attempt to open the door for low-income students to begin thinking about attending college at a very young age. The idea is to remove the barriers that are traditionally keeping them from attending college. Some programs focus on providing scholarship funds for students who demonstrate academic achievement. Others focus on educating families about the types of aid their children can receive if they stay motivated and perform well in school. Others attempt to make sure students in inner-city schools are being challenged in such a way that they will be ready for a college education. The following sections provide an overview of major early awareness programs.

FEDERAL EARLY AWARENESS PROGRAMS

Federal TRIO Programs

U.S. Department of Education
1990 K Street, NW, 7th Floor
Washington, DC 20006-8510
OPE_TRIO@ed.gov
http://www.ed.gov/about/offices/list/ope/trio/index.html

Through six different outreach programs (some of which are available solely to adults or academic institutions), Federal TRIO Programs aim to motivate students from disadvantaged backgrounds to pursue higher education. Services and funds are provided through these programs to encourage low-income students to become the first generation of college graduates in their families.

GEAR UP (Gaining Early Awareness and Readiness for Undergraduate Programs)

Office of Postsecondary Education
U.S. Department of Education
1990 K Street, NW
Washington, DC 20006-8524
202-502-7676
gearup@ed.gov
http://www.ed.gov/programs/gearup/index.html

This federal grant program provides funding in low-income schools in which students are mentored and tutored, typically in grades 7 through 12, in an effort to affect the students' readiness, desire, and ability to enter postsecondary education. Part of the money in this grant program is distributed in the form of scholarships for students who are involved in the program.

Talent Search

c/o Federal TRIO Programs
1990 K Street, NW, 7th Floor
Washington, DC 20006-8510
http://www.ed.gov/programs/triotalent/index.html

This program, an outreach area of the TRIO Programs, identifies students from disadvantaged backgrounds and focuses on academic and financial counseling, mentoring, and career exploration at the sixth, seventh, and eighth grade levels.

Think College Early

U.S. Department of Education
400 Maryland Avenue, SW
Washington, DC 20202
http://www.ed.gov/students/prep/college/thinkcollege/early/edlite-index.html

This initiative's goal is to educate both students and parents, while students are still in elementary school, on how to finance a college education. With a family plan of action in place, students are more likely to strive to attend college.

Upward Bound

c/o Federal TRIO Programs
1990 K Street, NW, 7th Floor
Washington, DC 20006-8510
http://www.ed.gov/programs/trioupbound/index.html

This program, an outreach area of the TRIO Programs,

serves students in high school who come from low-income families in which the parents did not attend college. It also serves disabled students and first-generation military veterans. Its goal is to prepare students for college by providing tutoring, mentoring, and counseling services as well as a precollegiate curriculum of courses in math, science, literature, composition, and foreign language. There is also a special division of this program that is focused solely on preparing students for higher education in math and science.

STATE EARLY AWARENESS PROGRAMS

Individuals who are interested in learning about early awareness programs that are being implemented in their states should contact their state's department of education. Many of the federally funded programs may be operating at select sites within your state and your children might be able to participate. Keep in mind that most of these programs begin during the elementary school years. Check with your state's department of education for these programs and any others that are designed to benefit college-bound students.

PRIVATE EARLY AWARENESS PROGRAMS

Advancement Via Individual Determination (AVID)
AVID Center
5120 Shoreham Place, Suite 120
San Diego, CA 92122
858-623-2843
http://www.avidonline.org
This program is targeted to low-income and minority students in grades 5 through 12 who are achieving B, C, and D grades. Emphasizing a student's potential and the need for increased motivation, particularly in students who might not view college as a viable option for them, AVID challenges these individuals to become prepared for college admittance by placing them in challenging courses and steering them away from remediation.

America's Promise: The Alliance for Youth
909 North Washington Street, Suite 400
Alexandria, VA 22314-1556
703-684-4500
http://www.americaspromise.org
This program focuses on creating environments for children that include five important fundamentals—caring adults, safe places, healthy lifestyles, effective education, and opportunities to help others—so that all students will be able to pursue a higher education. Community partnerships and collaborative efforts are created to make sure these "promises" become a reality for all students.

"I Have a Dream" Foundation
330 Seventh Avenue, 20th Floor
New York, NY 10001
212-293-5480
info@ihad.org
http://www.ihad.org
This program serves to mentor and tutor a select group of low-income students from the time they are elementary students through college students in an effort to increase the students' chances of completing a college education. Students of similar age groups are "adopted" by organized volunteer groups, which stay involved in the students' educational development throughout their elementary, middle, high school, and college years.

Project GRAD USA
Attn: Robert Rivera, President and CEO
1100 Louisiana, Suite 450
Houston, TX 77002
713-986-0499
rrivera@projectgradusa.org
http://www.projectgrad.org
Students who fall behind academically in the late elementary years are seldom able to catch up to the academic level needed to pursue postsecondary education. This program aims to rectify this situation in the populations it most often affects—low-income and minority students—by implementing programs that focus on a variety of areas including (but not limited to) literacy, social services and parental involvement, and classroom management.

MILITARY SCHOLARSHIPS— UNDERGRADUATE

The following undergraduate financial aid resources are available to active, reserve, and retired military personnel. Visit the section "Dependents of Veterans" for resources for children and spouses of military personnel who have died or who were disabled as a result of military service, as well as those who have been declared prisoners of war or missing in action.

Air Force Reserve Officer Training Corps (AFROTC)

AFROTC Admissions
551 East Maxwell Boulevard
Maxwell AFB, AL 36112-5917
866-423-7682
http://www.afrotc.com

Scholarship Name: Air Force Reserve Officer Training Corps Scholarship. *Academic Area: Open. *Age Group: Undergraduate students. *Eligibility: Applicants must be U.S. citizens or persons who will be able to obtain citizenship by the end of their first term of study. They also must graduate from a high school or have an equivalent certificate. Applicants must be at least 17 years old prior to scholarship activation and under 31 years old as of December 31 of the commission year. They also must pass a Physical Fitness Assessment and submit a letter of verification. Normally scholarship recipients have achieved an SAT composite of 1100 (Math and Verbal portion only) or ACT composite of 24, a cumulative GPA of 3.0 or higher, and a class ranking in the top 40 percent. *Application Process: Applicants must submit a completed application, SAT and/or ACT scores, a counselor letter, a personal statement, a resume, and evidence of academic credentials. Visit the AFROTC Web site in the spring to apply online and download required forms. *Amount: Varies. *Deadline: December 1.

Army Aviation Association of America (AAAA)

755 Main Street, Suite 4D
Monroe, CT 06468-2830
203-268-2450
aaaa@quad-a.org
http://www.quad-a.org

Grant/Loan Name: AAAA Scholarship Grant and Loan Program. *Academic Area: Open. *Age Group: Undergraduate students. *Eligibility: Applicants must be members of AAAA for at least one year prior to applying, spouses of AAAA members or a deceased member, or unmarried children, siblings, or grandchildren of AAAA members or deceased members. They also should demonstrate academic achievement and exceptional character. The program is also available to graduate students. Certain grants under this program are specifically reserved for enlisted, warrant officer, company grade, and Department of the Army civilian members. *Application Process: Applicants should submit a completed application along with official transcripts, a photograph, proof of college admission, two references, school recommendation, a teacher recommendation, and an academic reporting form. Visit the organization's Web site to download an application and additional forms. *Amount: $1,000 to $4,000. Applicants who don't receive grants will qualify for no-interest loans. *Deadline: May 1.

Army Reserve Officer Training Corps (ROTC)

U.S. Army ROTC Cadet Command
Attn: Army ROTC Scholarship
Ft. Monroe, VA 23651-1052
800-USA-ROTC
atccps@usacc.army.mil
http://www.goarmy.com/rotc/college_students.jsp

Scholarship Name: College Four-Year Scholarship. *Academic Area: Open. *Age Group: Undergraduate students. *Eligibility: Applicants must be U.S. citizens between the ages of 17 and 26 who are college freshmen in their first year of an undergraduate program. They also must maintain at least a minimum 2.5 GPA, have a high school diploma or equivalent, score at least 920 on the SAT or 19 on the ACT, and meet physical standards. Applicants must also agree to accept a commission and serve in the Army on active duty or in a reserve component (U.S. Army Reserve or Army National Guard). (Note: Three-Year and Two-Year College Scholarships are also available for those already enrolled in college; the eligibility requirements are identical to the College Four-Year Scholarship except that applicants must be between the ages of 17 and 27. *Application Process:

Applicants must submit a completed application, SAT/ACT scores, and official transcripts. Contact the Army ROTC directly to learn more about additional application requirements. Visit the Army ROTC's Web site to submit an online application. *Amount: Varies. *Deadline: December 1.

Army Reserve Officer Training Corps (ROTC)
U.S. Army ROTC Cadet Command
Attn: Army ROTC Scholarship
Ft. Monroe, VA 23651-1052
800-USA-ROTC
atccps@usacc.army.mil
http://www.goarmy.com/rotc/high_school_students.jsp
Scholarship Name: Green to Gold Scholarship.
*Academic Area: Open. *Age Group: Undergraduate students. *Eligibility: Enlisted soldiers, under 31, who would like to complete their baccalaureate degree and obtain a commission as a second lieutenant by participating in the ROTC may apply. Options exist for those who would like to leave the Army and pursue their education and for those who would like to remain in the service while pursuing their degree. Contact the Army ROTC for additional information on eligibility requirements. *Application Process: Visit the Army ROTC's Web site to submit an online application. *Amount: Varies. *Deadline: Contact the Army ROTC for details.

Army Reserve Officer Training Corps (ROTC)
U.S. Army ROTC Cadet Command
Attn: Army ROTC Scholarship
Ft. Monroe, VA 23651-1052
800-USA-ROTC
atccps@usacc.army.mil
http://www.goarmy.com/rotc/high_school_students.jsp
Scholarship Name: High School Four-Year Scholarship.
*Academic Area: Open. *Age Group: Undergraduate students. *Eligibility: Applicants must be U.S. citizens between the ages of 17 and 26. They also must maintain at least a minimum 2.5 GPA, have a high school diploma or equivalent, score at least 920 on the SAT or 19 on the ACT, and meet physical standards. However, the most best candidates for an Army ROTC Four-Year Scholarship will have at least a SAT score of 1100 or an ACT score of 24. Applicants must also agree to accept a commission and serve in the Army on active duty or in a reserve component (U.S. Army Reserve or Army National Guard). *Application Process: Applicants must submit

a completed application, SAT/ACT scores, and official transcripts. Contact the Army ROTC directly to learn more about additional application requirements. Visit the Army ROTC's Web site to submit an online application. *Amount: Varies. *Deadline: December 1.

Coast Guard Mutual Assistance (CGMA)
Attn: CWO Kimberly A. Smith
2100 2nd Street, SW, Room B-442
Washington, DC 20593-0001
202-267-2085, 800-881-2462
kasmith@comdt.uscg.mil
http://www.cgmahq.org/Assistance/Frame.htm
Grant Name: Supplemental Education Grant. *Academic Area: Open. *Age Group: Undergraduate students. *Eligibility: Applicants must be enrolled in an undergraduate degree program or vocational/tech program approved by the U.S. Department of Veteran Affairs or Department of Education. They also may be seeking a GED, with intentions of pursuing a college education. The following groups are eligible for this grant: active duty members of the U.S. Coast Guard, retired U.S. Coast Guard military personnel, civilian employees of the U.S. Coast Guard, U.S. Coast Guard Reserve members, U.S. Coast Guard Auxiliary members, public health service officers serving with the U.S. Coast Guard, and family members of the aforementioned groups. *Application Process: Applicants should submit a completed application, receipts for qualifying items (the grant pays for specific school-related expenses), and proof of enrollment. Visit the organization's Web site for a complete list of eligible expenses and to download an application. Applicants should submit their completed documents to their nearest CGMA representative. A complete list of CGMA representatives, by state, is available at the organization's Web site. *Amount: $160. *Deadline: Contact your local CGMA representative for deadline information.

Coast Guard Mutual Assistance (CGMA)
Attn: CWO Kimberly A. Smith
2100 2nd Street, SW, Room B-442
Washington, DC 20593-0001
202-267-2085, 800-881-2462
kasmith@comdt.uscg.milhttp://www.cgmahq.org/Assistance/Frame.htm
Loan Name: Supplemental Student Loan Program.
*Academic Area: Open. *Age Group: Undergraduate students. *Eligibility: Applicants must demonstrate

unmet financial need after other sources of maximum assistance from the Coast Guard Tuition Assistance (CGTA) have been utilized. The following groups are eligible for this program: active duty members of the U.S. Coast Guard, retired U.S. Coast Guard military personnel, civilian employees of the U.S. Coast Guard, U.S. Coast Guard Reserve members, U.S. Coast Guard Auxiliary members, public health service officers serving with the U.S. Coast Guard, and family members of the aforementioned groups. *Application Process: Applicants should submit a completed application along with a copy of the front and back of the member's valid Coast Guard identification card, a copy of a signed tuition assistance authorization form, or a copy of documentation that shows that other sources of Coast Guard assistance have been temporarily suspended. Visit the organization's Web site to download an application. Applications should be turned in to the nearest CGTA representative. A complete list of CGTA representatives is available at the organization's Web site. *Amount: Up to $700. *Deadline: None.

Coast Guard Mutual Assistance (CGMA)
Attn: CWO Kimberly A. Smith
2100 2nd Street, SW, Room B-442
Washington, DC 20593-0001
202-267-2085, 800-881-2462
kasmith@comdt.uscg.milhttp://www.cgmahq.org/
    Assistance/Frame.htm
Loan Name: Vocational and Technical Training Student Loan Program. *Academic Area: Vocational education. *Age Group: Undergraduate students. *Eligibility: Applicants must be CGMA members, their spouses, or their dependent children who are enrolled in a vocational education program and who demonstrate financial need. *Application Process: Applicants should submit a completed application along with proof of enrollment and a copy of the front and back of the member's Coast Guard identification card. Visit the organization's Web site to download an application. Applications should be submitted to the closest CGMA representative. Visit the Web site for a list of CGMA representatives by state. *Amount: Up to $1,500. *Deadline: Applicants must submit the application no longer than 30 days after the course began.

Fleet Reserve Association (FRA)
Attn: FRA Scholarship Administration
125 North West Street
Alexandria, VA 22314-2754

703-683-1400, 800-FRA-1924
http://www.fra.org/Content/fra/AboutFRA/Scholarships/
    default.htm
Scholarship Name: Fleet Reserve Association Scholarship. *Academic Area: Open. *Age Group: Undergraduate students. *Eligibility: Applicants must be FRA members or the children, dependents, grandchildren, or spouses of FRA members (current and former members of the Navy, Marine Corps, and Coast Guard) in good standing or of a member in good standing at the time of death. Applicants must demonstrate academic achievement, leadership potential, and financial need. The scholarship is also available to graduate students. *Application Process: Applicants should submit a completed application along with completed transcript request forms and an essay. Financial information on the application (along with all other sections) should be completed in its entirety to be considered. Visit the association's Web site to download an application. *Amount: $5,000. *Deadline: April 15.

Fleet Reserve Association (FRA)
Attn: FRA Scholarship Administrator
125 North West Street
Alexandria, VA 22314-2754
703-683-1400, 800-FRA-1924
http://www.fra.org/Content/fra/AboutFRA/Scholarships/
    default.htm
Scholarship Name: Schuyler S. Pyle Scholarship. *Academic Area: Open. *Age Group: Undergraduate students. *Eligibility: Applicants must be FRA members or the children, dependents, grandchildren, or spouses of FRA members (current and former members of the Navy, Marine Corps, and Coast Guard) in good standing or of a member in good standing at the time of death. Applicants must demonstrate academic achievement, leadership potential, and financial need. The scholarship is also available to graduate students. *Application Process: Applicants should submit a completed application along with completed transcript request forms and an essay. Financial information on the application (along with all other sections) should be completed in its entirety to be considered. Visit the association's Web site to download an application. *Amount: $5,000. *Deadline: April 15.

Fleet Reserve Association (FRA)
Attn: W. R. Holcombe
Walter E. Beale Scholarship

4911 Fennell Court
Suffolk, VA 23435
800-FRA-1924
prp.inc2@verizon.net
http://www.fra.org/Content/fra/AboutFRA/Scholarships/
    default.htm
Scholarship Name: Walter E. Beale Scholarship.
    *Academic Area: Aviation, engineering (aeronautical).
    *Age Group: Undergraduate students. *Eligibility:
    Applicants must be FRA members (current and
    former members of the Navy, Marine Corps, and Coast
    Guard), or their spouses, children, or grandchildren
    who are majoring in aeronautical engineering or
    aviation. They also must demonstrate academic
    achievement, leadership potential, and financial
    need. The scholarship is also available to graduate
    students. *Application Process: Applicants must
    request an application by mail or email. Applications
    must be submitted along with any additional required
    documentation the deadline. *Amount: Awards vary.
    *Deadline: April 15.

Force Recon Association
Scholarship Committee
Attn: Dr. Wayne M. Lingenfelter, Chairman
2992 Calle Gaucho
San Clemente, CA 92673
http://www.forcerecon.com
Scholarship Name: Force Recon Association Scholarship.
    *Academic Area: Open. *Age Group: Undergraduate
    students. *Eligibility: Applicants must members
    in good standing of the Force Recon Association,
    family members of members, or family members of
    a deceased member. They also must be pursuing any
    kind of postsecondary education and demonstrate
    academic achievement and exceptional character.
    The scholarship is also available to graduate
    students. *Application Process: Applicants should
    submit a completed application along with a
    personal statement detailing their career plans,
    copies of official transcripts, and three letters of
    recommendation. Visit the association's Web site to
    download an application. *Amount: Awards vary.
    *Deadline: Two weeks prior to the annual meeting.

Grantham University
7200 NW 86th Street, Suite M
Kansas City, MO 64153
800-955-2527
admissions@grantham.edu
http://www.grantham.edu/scholarships.htm

Scholarship Name: Military Education Scholarship for
    Service Members. *Academic Area: Open. *Age Group:
    Undergraduate students. *Eligibility: Applicants
    must be military service members in any branch
    of the United States military (including reserves).
    They also must intend to pursue a degree program
    at Grantham University and be eligible for military
    tuition assistance. The scholarship is also available to
    graduate students. *Application Process: Applicants
    should visit the university's Web site to download
    an application packet. Application forms are
    downloadable as zip files; you'll need the appropriate
    program to open the files. Contact the university
    if you would like an application mailed to you. An
    application and additional supporting materials
    should be submitted. *Amount: Books, software, and
    remaining tuition after tuition assistance benefits
    have been applied. *Deadline: Contact the university
    for deadline information.

Grantham University
7200 NW 86th Street, Suite M
Kansas City, MO 64153
800-955-2527
admissions@grantham.edu
http://www.grantham.edu/scholarships.htm
Scholarship Name: Military Education Scholarship
    for Veterans. *Academic Area: Open. *Age Group:
    Undergraduate students. *Eligibility: Applicants
    must be veterans of the United States military who
    have served honorably. They must also intend to
    pursue higher education at Grantham University. The
    scholarship is also available to graduate students.
    *Application Process: Applicants should visit the
    university's Web site to download an application
    packet. Application forms are downloadable as
    zip files; you'll need the appropriate program to
    open the files. Contact the university if you would
    like an application mailed to you. An application
    and additional supporting materials should be
    submitted. *Amount: 25 percent of standard tuition
    costs. *Deadline: Contact the university for deadline
    information.

**Horatio Alger Association of Distinguished
    Americans**
Attn: Military Veterans Scholarship
99 Canal Plaza
Alexandria, VA 22314
703-684-9444
https://www.horatioalger.com//scholarships_military/

Scholarship Name: Horatio Alger Military Veterans Scholarship. *Academic Area: Open. *Age Group: Undergraduate students. *Eligibility: Applicants must have served in the U.S. military in either Operation Enduring Freedom in Afghanistan or Operation Iraqi Freedom, post-September 11, 2001. They also must possess an honorable service record, demonstrate extreme financial need, and intend to pursue a bachelor's degree in the United States. Applicants must not have accumulated more than 60 semester hours prior to applying, maintain at least a 2.0 GPA, and demonstrate perseverance in the face of adversity. The scholarship is available to both active duty military personnel and those who have been discharged and met the aforementioned eligibility requirements. *Application Process: Applicants should apply online via the association's Web site. Additional documentation including college transcripts or proof of college enrollment (for those who haven't completed any coursework), a copy of tax returns, and proof of military service must be mailed. Visit the association's Web site to apply online. *Amount: Awards vary. *Deadline: February 1.

Illinois Department of Veterans' Affairs
c/o Illinois Student Assistance Commission
1755 Lake Cook Road
Deerfield, IL 60015
847-948-8550, 800-899-ISAC
http://www.state.il.us/agency/dva/vetben.htm
Scholarship Name: Illinois National Guard Scholarship. *Academic Area: Open. *Age Group: Undergraduate students. *Eligibility: Applicants must be enlisted National Guard lieutenants or captains with at least one year of service in the Illinois Army/Air National Guard. Applicants must also enroll in an Illinois state-sponsored university or community college. The scholarship is also available to graduate students. *Application Process: Applicants should contact the Illinois Student Assistance Commission (ISAC) for an application. Visit the ISAC online at http://www.collegezone.com. *Amount: Paid tuition and fees for eight semesters of full-time study or 12 semesters of part-time study. *Deadline: Contact the commission for deadline information.

Illinois Department of Veterans' Affairs
c/o Illinois Student Assistance Commission
1755 Lake Cook Road
Deerfield, IL 60015
847-948-8550, 800-899-ISAC
http://www.state.il.us/agency/dva/vetben.htm
Grant Name: Veterans' Grant. *Academic Area: Open. *Age Group: Undergraduate students. *Eligibility: Applicants must be honorably discharged veterans who resided in Illinois at least six months before entering the service and who also have at least one year of active duty service in the U.S. armed forces. *Application Process: Applicants should contact their local field office of the Illinois Department of Veterans' Affairs, their college financial aid office, or the Illinois Student Assistance Commission (ISAC) to receive information on the application process. Visit http://www.collegezone.com for more information about the ISAC. *Amount: Full tuition at Illinois state-supported institutions. *Deadline: Contact the commission for deadline information.

ITT Technical Institute
Locations nationwide
http://www.itt-tech.edu/military.cfm
Scholarship Name: ITT Tech Military Scholarship. *Academic Area: Open. *Age Group: Undergraduate students. *Eligibility: Applicants must be first-time students who have been enrolled in an ITT Technical institute for at least one quarter. They also must have maintained a 2.0 GPA during that first quarter. Applicants must be past or current members of the military. Army, Navy, Air Force, Marines, Coast Guard, National Guard and military reservists are eligible to apply. Most of the institute's 75 locations nationwide offer this scholarship, but applicants should visit the school's Web site to make sure the institution that they plan to attend offers the scholarship. *Application Process: Applicants should visit the financial aid office at their local ITT Technical Institute to apply. A valid DD214 form or current military ID card will be required. *Amount: 10 percent discount on tuition. *Deadline: Contact your local ITT Technical Institute for deadline information.

Massachusetts Department of Veterans' Services
600 Washington Street, Suite 1100
Boston, MA 02111
617-210-5480
http://www.state.ma.us/veterans
Grant Name: Massachusetts National Guard Education Assistance Program. *Academic Area: Open. *Age Group: Undergraduate students. *Eligibility: Members of the Massachusetts National Guard may apply.

Applicants must plan to attend a public institution in the state of Massachusetts. The program is also open to graduate students.*Application Process: Visit the department's Web site for more information.*Amount: Full tuition. *Deadline: Contact the department for details.

Massachusetts Department of Veterans' Services
600 Washington Street, Suite 1100
Boston, MA 02111
617-210-5480
veted@bhe.mass.edu
http://www.state.ma.us/veterans
Grant Name: Tuition Waiver. *Academic Area: Open. *Age Group: Undergraduate students. *Eligibility: Veterans of Massachusetts, as well as active duty personnel, may apply. Applicants must plan to attend a public institution in the state of Massachusetts. *Application Process: Visit the department's Web site for more information. *Amount: Up to full tuition. *Deadline: Contact the department for details.

Minnesota Department of Veterans Affairs
State Veterans Service Building
20 West 12th Street, Room 206C
St. Paul, MN 55155-2006
651-296-2562
http://www.mdva.state.mn.us
Grant Name: Veterans Grant. *Academic Area: Open. *Age Group: Undergraduate students. *Eligibility: Disabled Minnesota veterans who have exhausted all federal education benefits may apply. Applicants must plan to or currently attend a public college or university in Minnesota. The grant is also available to graduate students. *Application Process: Visit the department's Web site for details.*Amount: Contact the department for details. *Deadline: Contact the department for details.

Naval Reserve Officers Training Corps (NROTC)
Attn: Director, Candidate Guidance
U.S. Naval Academy
117 Decatur Road
Annapolis, MD 21402-5017
410-293-4361, 800-NAV-ROTC
PNSC_NROTC.scholarships@navy.mil
https://www.nrotc.navy.mil/scholarships_application.cfm
Scholarship Name: Four-Year Scholarship. *Academic Area: Open. *Age Group: Undergraduate students.

*Eligibility: Applicants must be U.S. citizens who are not younger than 17 year old and not older than 27, who will have graduated from high school by August 1, prior to entering a four-year NROTC program. They also must pass physical ability standards of the Navy or Marine corps, gain admission to a NROTC-affiliated college, and meet minimum set scores on the SAT or ACT (minimums by section are detailed on the organization's Web site). Certain academic standards are also set, such as the necessity of enrolling in one naval course each semester. Applicants should visit the corps' Web site to determine further academic requirements. *Application Process: Applicants must apply online. *Amount: Full tuition, plus a stipend for books, paid uniforms, and a subsistence monthly allowance. *Deadline: Contact the corps for details.

Naval Reserve Officers Training Corps (NROTC)
Attn: Director, Candidate Guidance
U.S. Naval Academy
117 Decatur Road
Annapolis, MD 21402-5017
410-293-4361, 800-NAV-ROTC
PNSC_NROTC.scholarships@navy.mil
https://www.nrotc.navy.mil/scholarships.cfm
Scholarship Name: Historically Black College (HBC) Scholarship Program. *Academic Area: Open. *Age Group: Undergraduate students. *Eligibility: Applicants must be U.S. citizens who are not younger than 17 year old and not older than 27, who will have graduated from high school by August 1, prior to entering a four-year NROTC program. They also must pass physical ability standards of the Navy or Marine corps, gain admission to a NROTC-affiliated college, and meet minimum set scores on the SAT or ACT (minimums by section detailed on the organization's Web site). Certain academic standards are also set, such as the necessity of enrolling in one naval course each semester. Applicants must attend one of the following Historically Black Colleges: Florida A & M, Hampton University, Morehouse College, Norfolk State University, Prairie View A&M University, Savannah State University, Southern University and A&M College. Applicants should visit the corps' Web site to determine further academic requirements. *Application Process: Applicants should contact the financial aid office directly at the individual schools. *Amount: Full tuition, plus a stipend for books, paid uniforms, and a subsistence monthly allowance. *Deadline: Contact the corps for details.

Naval Reserve Officers Training Corps (NROTC)
Attn: Director, Candidate Guidance
U.S. Naval Academy
117 Decatur Road
Annapolis, MD 21402-5017
410-293-4361, 800-NAV-ROTC
PNSC_NROTC.scholarships@navy.mil
https://www.nrotc.navy.mil/scholarships_application.cfm
Scholarship Name: Naval Reserve Officers Training Corps College Program. *Academic Area: Naval science. *Age Group: Undergraduate students. *Eligibility: Applicants must be U.S. citizens who are not younger than 17 year old and not older than 27, who are either college freshmen (four-year applicants) or college sophomores (two-year applicants) at the time of application. Applicants must pass physical ability standards of the Navy or Marine corps, be enrolled in a NROTC-affiliated college, and upon graduation be commissioned to the U.S. Naval Reserve or second lieutenant in the U.S. Marine Corps Reserve. Eight years of total military service is required, with at least three years of active duty. Applicants must also participate in a six-week summer training institute. Applicants should visit the corps' Web site to determine further academic requirements. *Application Process: Applicants should apply through their naval science professors as college freshmen (four-year applicants) or college sophomores (two-year applicants). *Amount: Paid tuition for naval courses (two years or four years, depending on which scholarship is applied for), paid uniforms, and a possible subsistence allowance for up to 20 months. *Deadline: Contact the corps for details.

Naval Reserve Officers Training Corps (NROTC)
Attn: Director, Candidate Guidance
U.S. Naval Academy
117 Decatur Road
Annapolis, MD 21402-5017
410-293-4361, 800-NAV-ROTC
PNSC_NROTC.scholarships@navy.mil
https://www.nrotc.navy.mil/scholarships_application.cfm
Scholarship Name: Navy Nurse Corps NROTC Program. *Academic Area: Nursing (open). *Age Group: Undergraduate students. *Eligibility: Applicants must be U.S. citizens who are not younger than 17 year old and not older than 27, who will have graduated from high school by August 1, prior to entering a four-year NROTC program. They also must pass physical ability standards of the Navy or Marine corps, gain admission to a NROTC-affiliated college, and meet minimum set scores on the SAT or ACT (minimums by section detailed on the organization's Web site). Applicants must enroll in a bachelor of science in nursing program. Certain academic standards are also set. Applicants should visit the corps' Web site to determine further academic requirements. *Application Process: Applicants should apply through their Navy recruiting office. *Amount: Full tuition, plus a stipend for books, paid uniforms, and a subsistence monthly allowance. *Deadline: Contact the corps for details.

Naval Reserve Officers Training Corps (NROTC)
Attn: Director, Candidate Guidance
U.S. Naval Academy
117 Decatur Road
Annapolis, MD 21402-5017
410-293-4361, 800-NAV-ROTC
PNSC_NROTC.scholarships@navy.mil
https://www.nrotc.navy.mil/scholarships.cfm
Scholarship Name: Tweedale Scholarship. *Academic Area: Computer science, chemistry, engineering (open), mathematics, physics. *Age Group: Undergraduate students. *Eligibility: Applicants must have completed one college semester, but not more than four semesters, and have maintained at least a 3.0 GPA and must not have received a grade lower than a C in any course. They also must have received at least a B in high school calculus. Applicants must have taken a math or science course and will be required to complete "Naval Science 101" immediately. They also must demonstrate leadership potential and physical fitness. *Application Process: Applicants must submit a degree plan for review to the unit professor of naval science (PNS). The student's faculty adviser must verify that the plan can be completed in order for the student to graduate with his or her class. Contact your PNS for additional information. *Amount: Awards vary. *Deadline: Contact your PNS for deadline information.

Naval Reserve Officers Training Corps (NROTC)
Attn: Director, Candidate Guidance
U.S. Naval Academy
117 Decatur Road
Annapolis, MD 21402-5017
410-293-4361, 800-NAV-ROTC
PNSC_NROTC.scholarships@navy.mil
https://www.nrotc.navy.mil/scholarships_application.cfm

Scholarship Name: Two-Year Scholarship. *Academic Area: Open. *Age Group: Undergraduate students. *Eligibility: Applicants must be U.S. citizens who are not younger than 17 year old and not older than 27, who have completed their sophomore year or third year in a five-year program. They also must pass physical ability standards of the Navy or Marine corps, be enrolled in a NROTC-affiliated college, and upon graduation be commissioned to the U.S. Naval Reserve or second lieutenant in the U.S. Marine Corps Reserve. Eight years of total military service is required, with four years of active duty. Applicants should visit the corps' Web site to determine further academic requirements. *Application Process: Applicants must apply online. *Amount: Full tuition for final two years of college, plus a stipend for books, paid uniforms, and a subsistence allowance for up to 20 months. *Deadline: March 15.

Naval Reserve Officers Training Corps (NROTC)
Attn: Director, Candidate Guidance
U.S. Naval Academy
117 Decatur Road
Annapolis, MD 21402-5017
410-293-4361, 800-NAV-ROTC
PNSC_NROTC.scholarships@navy.mil
https://www.nrotc.navy.mil/scholarships_application.cfm
Scholarship Name: U.S. Naval Academy Scholarship. *Academic Area: Naval science. *Age Group: Undergraduate students. *Eligibility: Applicants must be between 17 and 23 years of age, single, childless, and desire a naval career. Applicants must seek nomination from U.S. senators or representatives, the Secretary of the Navy, or the vice president or president of the United States. Awardees are required to serve a minimum of five years of active duty Navy or Marine Corps Reserve service. *Application Process: High school juniors should inquire about receiving a precandidate questionnaire. *Amount: Full four-year tuition, plus a monthly salary. *Deadline: Contact the corps for deadline information.

Navy-Marine Corps Relief Society (NMCRS)
NMCRS Education Division
4015 Wilson Boulevard, 10th Floor
Arlington, VA 22203
703-696-4960
education@hq.nmcrs.org
http://www.nmcrs.org/education.html
Scholarship Name: Admiral Mike Boorda Scholarship.

*Academic Area: Medicine (open), military. *Age Group: Undergraduate students. *Eligibility: Applicants must be enrolled in either the Marine Enlisted Commissioning Education Program or the Medical Enlisted Commissioning Program. They also should be full-time undergraduate students in a program that participates in the U.S. Department of Education's Title IV financial aid program. Applicants must maintain at least a 2.0 GPA and demonstrate financial need. *Application Process: Applicants must submit a completed application along with an eligibility application form, a completed application, a family financial data form, a grade point average verification form, transcripts, and a copy of their current Navy or Marine Corps identification card. The application must be endorsed by the student's commanding officer. Visit the organization's Web site to download the application and forms. *Amount: Up to $2,000. *Deadline: May 1.

New Mexico Veterans' Services
PO Box 2324
Santa Fe, NM 87504
505-827-6300, 866-433-8387
alan.martinez@state.nm.us
http://www.state.nm.us/veterans/vschome.html
Scholarship Name: Vietnam Veterans Scholarship. *Academic Area: Open. *Age Group: Undergraduate students. *Eligibility: Applicants must be Vietnam veterans who have been honorably discharged and who have been awarded the Vietnam Campaign or the Vietnam Service Medal. Applicants must have been residents of the state of New Mexico for at least 10 years, as well as at the time they entered the Armed Forces, and must attend a state-supported college or university to receive funds. *Application Process: Applicants should contact the Veterans' Services office for details on the application process. *Amount: Tuition, fees, and books. *Deadline: Contact the Department of Veterans' Services for deadline information.

North Dakota Department of Veterans Affairs
1411 32nd Street South, PO Box 9003
Fargo, ND 58106-9003
701-239-7165, 866-634-8387
http://www.nd.gov/veterans/benefits/waiver.html
Grant Name: National Guard Tuition Waiver. *Academic Area: Open. *Age Group: Undergraduate students. *Eligibility: Members of the North Dakota National Guard are eligible. *Application Process: Contact

the department for details. *Amount: Full tuition. *Deadline: Contact the department for details.

South Dakota Division of Veterans Affairs
Soldiers & Sailors Memorial Building, 425 East Capitol
   Avenue
Pierre, SD 57501-5070
605-773-3269
andy.gerlach@state.sd.us
http://mva.sd.gov/Default.asp?navid=11
Scholarship Name: Free Tuition for Veterans. *Academic
   Area: Open. *Age Group: Undergraduate students.
   *Eligibility: Applicants must be veterans of the U.S.
   Armed Forces who have been discharged honorably
   and who currently reside in South Dakota. Applicants
   must also meet one of the following qualifications:
   served in active duty status on or after August 2,
   1990, to present; received a medal for participation
   in combat operations against hostile forces outside
   of the United States; or obtained a disability of at
   least 10 percent from a service-related incident.
   *Application Process: Applicants should request an
   application from their school's financial aid office,
   their local veterans representative, or the Division of
   Veterans Affairs. The completed application should be
   submitted to the Sioux Falls VA Regional Office along
   with a copy of the veteran's DD-214. *Amount: One
   month of paid tuition for each month of "qualifying"
   service. *Deadline: Contact the Veterans Affairs office
   for deadline information.

South Dakota Division of Veterans Affairs
Soldiers & Sailors Memorial Building, 425 East Capitol
   Avenue
Pierre, SD 57501-5070
605-773-3269
andy.gerlach@state.sd.us
http://mva.sd.gov/Default.asp?navid=11
Scholarship Name: Reduced Tuition for South Dakota
   National Guardmembers. *Academic Area: Open. *Age
   Group: Undergraduate students. *Eligibility: Applicants
   must be residents of South Dakota and members
   of the South Dakota Army or Air Guard during each
   semester he or she applies for benefits. Applicants
   must also have completed the required active duty
   training, attend 90 percent of drills and training
   periods, and maintain satisfactory academic standing.
   *Application Process: Applicants should request an
   application from their school's financial aid office,
   their local veterans representative, or the Division of
   Veterans Affairs. The completed application should

be submitted to the Sioux Falls VA Regional Office.
   *Amount: Half-paid tuition at state-supported college
   or vocational schools. *Deadline: Contact the Division
   of Veterans Affairs office for deadline information.

Tailhook Educational Foundation
9696 Businesspark Avenue
San Diego, CA 92131-1643
858-689-9223, 800-269-8267
thookassn@aol.com
http://www.tailhook.org
Scholarship Name: Tailhook Educational Foundation
   Scholarship. *Academic Area: Open. *Age Group:
   Undergraduate students. *Eligibility: Applicants must
   be individuals who are serving or have served on a
   U.S. Navy aircraft carrier in the ship's company or the
   air wing, or their dependent children. They also must
   already be accepted into an undergraduate program
   at a college or university, and have demonstrated
   academic achievement in their high school careers.
   *Application Process: Applicants should submit a
   completed application along with SAT or ACT scores,
   a personal essay detailing their career goals, high
   school and college transcripts, an acceptance letter
   to college, and summary of achievements. Visit the
   foundation's Web site to download an application.
   *Amount: $2,000. *Deadline: March 15.

Texas Veterans Commission
PO Box 12277
Austin, TX 78711-2277
512-463-6564, 800-252-8387
info@tvc.state.tx.us
http://www.tvc.state.tx.us/Hazlewood_Act.htm
Grant Name: The commission provides tuition waivers for
   the purpose of college study. *Academic Area: Open.
   *Age Group: Undergraduate students. *Eligibility:
   Veterans of the Spanish-American War through the
   Persian Gulf War who were legal residents of Texas
   at the time they entered military service are eligible
   to apply. Applicants must have exhausted all federal
   educational benefits, be current residents of Texas,
   and plan to attend a public college or university in the
   state. The grant is also available to graduate students.
   *Application Process: Contact the commission for
   details. *Amount: Full tuition. *Deadline: Contact the
   commission for details.

Wisconsin Department of Veterans Affairs
30 West Mifflin Street, PO Box 7843
Madison, WI 53703

608-266-1311, 800-947-8387
wdvaweb@dva.state.wi.us
http://dva.state.wi.us/Ben_personalloans.asp
Loan Name: Personal Loan Program. *Academic
Area: Open. *Age Group: Undergraduate students.
*Eligibility: Veterans, spouses of deceased veterans,
and children of deceased veterans who are seeking a
loan to pursue postsecondary education may apply.
Applicants must plan to attend a public institution in
the state of Wisconsin. The loan program is also open
to graduate students. *Application Process: Visit the
department's Web site to download an application.
*Amount: Up to $25,000. *Deadline: Contact the
department for details.

Wisconsin Department of Veterans Affairs
30 West Mifflin Street, PO Box 7843
Madison, WI 53703
608-266-1311, 800-947-8387
wdvaweb@dva.state.wi.us
http://dva.state.wi.us/Ben_education.asp
Grant Name: Tuition Residency for Wisconsin Veterans.
*Academic Area: Open. *Age Group: Undergraduate
students. *Eligibility: Veterans who entered active
duty as Wisconsin residents may apply. Applicants
must plan to or currently attend a University of
Wisconsin System institution. The program is also
open to graduate students. *Application Process:
Visit the department's Web site to download an
application. *Amount: Eligibility for in-state tuition
rates. *Deadline: Contact the department for details.

Wisconsin Department of Veterans Affairs
30 West Mifflin Street, PO Box 7843
Madison, WI 53703
608-266-1311, 800-947-8387
wdvaweb@dva.state.wi.us
http://dva.state.wi.us/Ben_VetEd.asp
Grant Name: Veterans Education Reimbursement Grant.
*Academic Area: Open. *Age Group: Undergraduate
students. *Eligibility: Wisconsin veterans who have not
yet earned a bachelor's degree may apply. Applicants
must plan to attend a public institution in the state
of Wisconsin; have a 2.0 GPA or C average during
the semester(s) for which they plan to seek aid; have
a household income below $50,000, plus $1,000
for each dependent in excess of two dependents;
and apply within 10 years of leaving active duty
(exceptions are made for those pursuing part-time
study). *Application Process: Visit the department's
Web site to download an application or to apply

online. *Amount: Up to 100 percent of tuition and
fees. (Note: Reimbursement is based on the amount of
active duty time served by the applicant.) *Deadline:
Contact the department for details.

Wisconsin Department of Veterans Affairs
30 West Mifflin Street, PO Box 7843
Madison, WI 53703
608-266-1311, 800-947-8387
wdvaweb@dva.state.wi.us
http://dva.state.wi.us/Ben_education.asp
Grant Name: Wisconsin G.I. Bill. *Academic Area: Open.
*Age Group: Undergraduate students. *Eligibility:
Veterans who have substantial service-connected
disabilities may apply. Applicants must plan to
attend a public institution in the state of Wisconsin.
The program is also open to graduate students.
*Application Process: Visit the department's Web
site to download an application. *Amount: Tuition
reduced by 50 percent. *Deadline: Contact the
department for details.

Wyoming Commission of Veterans Affairs
5905 Cy Avenue, Room 101
Casper, WY 82604
307-265-7372
wvac@bresnan.net
http://www.nasdva.com/wyoming.html
Grant Name: The commission provides tuition waivers
for the purpose of college study. *Academic Area:
Open. *Age Group: Undergraduate students.
*Eligibility: Residents of Wyoming who served in the
U.S. military during the Vietnam War are eligible to
apply. Applicants must be residents of Wyoming and
attend a public college or university in the state either
full or part time. Tuition waivers are also available to
graduate students. *Application Process: Contact the
commission for details. *Amount: Full tuition for no
more than 10 semesters of credit classes. *Deadline:
Contact the commission for details.

Wyoming, University of
Contact: Mary Candelaria
Office of Student Financial Aid
1000 East University Avenue, Department 3335
Laramie, WY 82071
307-766-3015
http://uwadmnweb.uwyo.edu/sfa/Vet/PDF/kuehne.pdf
Scholarship Name: Marna M. Kuehne Scholarship
for Disabled Veterans. *Academic Area: Open.
*Age Group: Undergraduate students. *Eligibility:

Disabled veterans who are residents of Wyoming may apply. Applicants should have applied for admission to the University of Wyoming (UW) at the time of their scholarship request and be in good academic standing. *Application Process: Applicants should submit a completed application along with documentation of veteran status (DD-214) and documentation of their current disability rating. (Note: They should also submit the FAFSA by March 31.) Visit the UW's Office of Student Financial Aid for further details. *Amount: Up to $10,000. *Deadline: May 31.

MILITARY SCHOLARSHIPS—GRADUATE

The following graduate financial aid resources are available to active, reserve, and retired military personnel. Visit the "Dependents of Veterans" section for resources for children and spouses of military personnel who have died or who were disabled as a result of military service, as well as those who have been declared prisoners of war or missing in action.

Air Force Aid Society
National Headquarters
241 18th Street, Suite 202
Arlington, VA 22202
800-769-8951
dvosburg@afas.org
http://www.afas.org/Education/body_stap.cfm
Grant Name: General George S. Brown Spouse Tuition Assistance Program. *Academic Area: Open. *Age Group: Graduate students. *Eligibility: Applicants must be spouses of active duty officers who intend to pursue higher education that will lead to better employment opportunities. They also must be living overseas with their spouses. Applicants must attend institutions that have been contracted for on-base programs and must be able to demonstrate financial need and career goals. Visit the society's Web site an in-depth explanation of the program. The program is also open to undergraduate students. *Application Process: Applicants should pick up AFAS Form 90A at their base education office. The base office will be able to inform the applicant of additional information that may be required along with the application (this varies by office). *Amount: Up to $1,500. *Deadline: Deadlines vary. Contact your base education office for deadlines.

Army Aviation Association of America (AAAA)
755 Main Street, Suite 4D
Monroe, CT 06468-2830
203-268-2450
aaaa@quad-a.org
http://www.quad-a.org
Grant/Loan Name: AAAA Scholarship Grant & Loan Program. *Academic Area: Open. *Age Group: Graduate students. *Eligibility: Applicants must be members of AAAA for at least one year prior to applying, spouses of AAAA members or a deceased member, or unmarried children, siblings, or grandchildren of AAAA members or deceased members. Applicants should demonstrate academic achievement and exceptional character. Undergraduates may also apply. *Application Process: Applicants should submit a completed application

along with official transcripts, a photograph, proof of college admission, two references, a school recommendation, a teacher recommendation, an essay, and an academic reporting form. Visit the organization's Web site to download an application and additional forms. *Amount: $1,000 to $4,000. Applicants who don't receive grants will qualify for no-interest loans. *Deadline: May 1.

Fleet Reserve Association (FRA)
Attn: FRA Scholarship Administrator
125 North West Street
Alexandria, VA 22314
703-683-1400, 800-FRA-1924
http://www.fra.org/Content/fra/AboutFRA/Scholarships/
default.htm
Scholarship Name: FRA Scholarship. *Academic Area: Open. *Age Group: Graduate students. *Eligibility: Applicants must be members of the FRA or children, dependents, grandchildren, or spouses of FRA members in good standing or of a member in good standing at the time of death. Applicants must demonstrate academic achievement, leadership potential, and financial need. The scholarship is also available to undergraduate students. *Application Process: Applicants should submit a completed application along with completed transcript request forms and an essay. Financial information on the application (along with all other sections) should be completed in its entirety to be considered. Visit the association's Web site to download an application. *Amount: $5,000. *Deadline: April 15.

Fleet Reserve Association (FRA)
Attn: FRA Scholarship Administrator
125 North West Street
Alexandria, VA 22314-2754
703-683-1400, 800-FRA-1924
http://www.fra.org/Content/fra/AboutFRA/Scholarships/
default.htm
Scholarship Name: Glenn F. Glezen Scholarship. *Academic Area: Open. *Age Group: Graduate students. *Eligibility: Applicants must be members of FRA or the children, grandchildren, or spouses of

FRA members in good standing. Applicants must demonstrate academic achievement, leadership potential, and financial need. Preference is given to students pursuing master's or doctorate degrees. *Application Process: Applicants should submit a completed application along with completed transcript request forms and an essay. Financial information on the application (along with all other sections) should be completed in its entirety to be considered. Visit the association's Web site to download an application. *Amount: $5,000. *Deadline: April 15.

Fleet Reserve Association (FRA)
Attn: FRA Scholarship Administrator
125 North West Street
Alexandria, VA 22314-2754
703-683-1400, 800-FRA-1924
http://www.fra.org/Content/fra/AboutFRA/Scholarships/
    default.htm
Scholarship Name: Joseph R. Baranski Scholarship.
    *Academic Area: Open. *Age Group: Graduate
    students. *Eligibility: Applicants must be the children,
    grandchildren, or spouses of FRA members in good
    standing, or members of FRA themselves. Applicants
    must demonstrate academic achievement, leadership
    potential, and financial need. Preference is given to
    students pursuing master's or doctorate degrees.
    *Application Process: Applicants should submit
    a completed application along with completed
    transcript request forms and an essay. Financial
    information on the application (along with all
    other sections) should be completed in its entirety
    to be considered. Visit the association's Web site
    to download an application. *Amount: $5,000.
    *Deadline: April 15.

Fleet Reserve Association (FRA)
Attn: FRA Scholarship Administrator
125 North West Street
Alexandria, VA 22314-2754
703-683-1400, 800-FRA-1924
http://www.fra.org/Content/fra/AboutFRA/Scholarships/
    default.htm
Scholarship Name: Robert W. Nolan Emeritus
    Scholarship. *Academic Area: Open. *Age Group:
    Graduate students. *Eligibility: Applicants must be
    members of FRA or the children, grandchildren, or
    spouses of FRA members in good standing. They
    must also demonstrate academic achievement,
    leadership potential, and financial need. Preference

is given to students pursuing master's or doctorate degrees. *Application Process: Applicants should submit a completed application along with completed transcript request forms and an essay. Financial information on the application (along with all other sections) should be completed in its entirety to be considered. Visit the association's Web site to download an application. *Amount: $5,000. *Deadline: April 15.

Fleet Reserve Association (FRA)
Attn: FRA Scholarship Administrator
125 North West Street
Alexandria, VA 22314-2754
703-683-1400, 800-FRA-1924
http://www.fra.org/Content/fra/AboutFRA/Scholarships/
    default.htm
Scholarship Name: Schuyler S. Pyle Scholarship.
    *Academic Area: Open. *Age Group: Graduate
    students. *Eligibility: Applicants may be members of
    the FRA or the children, dependents, grandchildren,
    or spouses of FRA members in good standing or of
    a member in good standing at the time of death.
    They must also demonstrate academic achievement,
    leadership potential, and financial need. The
    scholarship is also available to undergraduate
    students. *Application Process: Applicants should
    submit a completed application along with
    completed transcript request forms and an essay.
    Financial information on the application (along
    with all other sections) should be completed in its
    entirety to be considered. Visit the association's Web
    site to download an application. *Amount: $5,000.
    *Deadline: April 15.

Fleet Reserve Association (FRA)
Attn: W. R. Holcombe
Walter E. Beale Scholarship
4911 Fennell Court
Suffolk, VA 23435
prp.inc2@verizon.net
http://www.fra.org/Content/fra/AboutFRA/Scholarships/
    default.htm
Scholarship Name: Walter E. Beale Scholarship.
    *Academic Area: Engineering (aeronautical),
    aviation. *Age Group: Graduate students.
    *Eligibility: Applicants must be FRA members or
    spouses, children, or grandchildren of members
    who are majoring in aeronautical engineering
    or aviation. Applicants must demonstrate
    academic achievement, leadership potential, and

financial need. The scholarship is also available to undergraduate students. *Application Process: Applicants must request an application by mail or e-mail. Applications must be submitted along with any additional required documentation by the deadline. *Amount: Awards vary. *Deadline: April 15.

Force Recon Association (FRA)
Scholarship Committee
Attn: Dr. Wayne M. Lingenfelter, Chairman
2992 Calle Gaucho
San Clemente, CA 92673
http://www.forcerecon.com
Scholarship Name: FRA Scholarship. *Academic Area: Open. *Age Group: Graduate students. *Eligibility: Applicants must members in good standing of Force Recon Association or family members of members. They may also be family members of a deceased member. Applicants must be pursuing any kind of postsecondary education and demonstrate academic achievement and exceptional character. The scholarship is also available to undergraduate students. *Application Process: Applicants should submit a completed application along with a personal statement detailing their career plans, copies of official transcripts, and three letters of recommendation. Visit the association's Web site to download an application. *Amount: Awards vary. *Deadline: Two weeks prior to the annual meeting.

Grantham University
7200 NW 86th Street, Suite M
Kansas City, MO 64153
800-955-2527
admissions@grantham.edu
http://www.grantham.edu/scholarships.htm
Scholarship Name: Military Education Scholarship for Service Members. *Academic Area: Open. *Age Group: Graduate students. *Eligibility: Applicants must be military service members in any branch of the United States military (including reserves) who intend to pursue a degree program at Grantham University. Applicants should be eligible for military tuition assistance or DANTES to receive this scholarship. The scholarship is also available to undergraduate students. *Application Process: Applicants should visit the university's Web site to download an application packet. Application forms are downloadable as zip files; you'll need an appropriate program to open the files. Contact the university if you would like an application mailed to you. An application and

additional supporting materials should be submitted. *Amount: Books, software, and remaining tuition after tuition assistance/DANTES benefits have been applied. *Deadline: Contact the university for deadline information.

Grantham University
7200 NW 85th Street, Suite M
Kansas City, MO 64153
800-955-2527
admissions@grantham.edu
http://www.grantham.edu/scholarships.htm
Scholarship Name: Military Education Scholarship for Veterans. *Academic Area: Open. *Age Group: Graduate students. *Eligibility: Applicants must be veterans of the United States military who have served honorably. They must also intend to pursue higher education at Grantham University. The scholarship is also available to undergraduate students. *Application Process: Applicants should visit the university's Web site to download an application packet. Application forms are downloadable as zip files; you'll need an appropriate program to open the files. Contact the university if you would like an application mailed to you. An application and additional supporting materials should be submitted. *Amount: 25 percent of standard tuition costs. *Deadline: Contact the university for deadline information.

Illinois Department of Veterans' Affairs
c/o Illinois Student Assistance Commission
1755 Lake Cook Road
Deerfield, IL 60015
847-948-8550, 800-899-ISAC
http://www.state.il.us/agency/dva/vetben.htm
Scholarship Name: Illinois National Guard Scholarship. *Academic Area: Open. *Age Group: Graduate students. *Eligibility: Applicants must be enlisted National Guard lieutenants or captains with at least one year of service in the Illinois Army/Air National Guard. They must also enroll in an Illinois state-sponsored university or community college. The scholarship is also available to undergraduate students. *Application Process: Applicants should contact the Illinois Student Assistance Commission (ISAC) for an application. Visit the ISAC online at http://www.collegezone.com. *Amount: Paid tuition and fees for eight semesters of full-time study or 12 semesters of part-time study. *Deadline: Contact the commission for deadline information.

Massachusetts Department of Veterans' Services
600 Washington Street, Suite 1100
Boston, MA 02111
617-210-5480
http://www.state.ma.us/veterans
Grant Name: Massachusetts National Guard Education
Assistance Program. *Academic Area: Open. *Age
Group: Graduate students. *Eligibility: Members
of the Massachusetts National Guard who plan
to attend a public institution in the state of
Massachusetts may apply. The program is also
open to undergraduate students.*Application
Process: Visit the department's Web site for more
information.*Amount: Full tuition. *Deadline:
Contact the department for details.

Minnesota Department of Veterans Affairs
State Veterans Service Building
20 West 12th Street, Room 206C
St. Paul, MN 55155-2006
651-296-2562
http://www.mdva.state.mn.us
Grant Name: Veterans Grant. *Academic Area: Open.
*Age Group: Graduate students. *Eligibility: Disabled
Minnesota veterans who have exhausted all federal
education benefits may apply. Applicants must
plan to or currently attend a public college or
university in Minnesota. The grant is also available to
undergraduate students. *Application Process: Visit the
department's Web site for details. *Amount: Contact
the department for details. *Deadline: Contact the
department for details.

Texas Veterans Commission
PO Box 12277
Austin, TX 78711-2277
512-463-6564, 800-252-8387
info@tvc.state.tx.us
http://www.tvc.state.tx.us/Hazlewood_Act.htm
Grant Name: The commission provides tuition waivers
for the purpose of college study. *Academic Area:
Open. *Age Group: Graduate students. *Eligibility:
Veterans of the Spanish-American War through the
Persian Gulf War who were legal residents of Texas
at the time they entered military service are eligible
to apply. Applicants must have exhausted all federal
educational benefits, be current residents of Texas,
and plan to attend a public college or university
in the state. Tuition waivers are also available to
undergraduate students. *Application Process:

Contact the commission for details. *Amount: Full
tuition. *Deadline: Contact the commission for
details.

Wisconsin Department of Veterans Affairs
30 West Mifflin Street, PO Box 7843
Madison, WI 53703
608-266-1311, 800-947-8387
wdvaweb@dva.state.wi.us
http://dva.state.wi.us/Ben_personalloans.asp
Loan Name: Personal Loan Program. *Academic Area:
Open. *Age Group: Graduate students. *Eligibility:
Veterans who are seeking a loan to pursue
postsecondary education may apply. Applicants
must plan to attend a public institution in the state
of Wisconsin. Spouses of deceased veterans, and
children of deceased veterans may also apply. The
program is also open to undergraduate students.
*Application Process: Visit the department's Web site
to download an application. *Amount: Up to $25,000.
*Deadline: Contact the department for details.

Wisconsin Department of Veterans Affairs
30 West Mifflin Street, PO Box 7843
Madison, WI 53703
608-266-1311, 800-947-8387
wdvaweb@dva.state.wi.us
http://dva.state.wi.us/Ben_education.asp
Grant Name: Tuition Residency for Wisconsin Veterans.
*Academic Area: Open. *Age Group: Graduate
students. *Eligibility: Veterans who entered active
duty as Wisconsin residents may apply. Applicants
must plan to or currently attend a University of
Wisconsin System institution. The program is also
open to undergraduate students. *Application
Process: Visit the department's Web site to download
an application. *Amount: Eligibility for in-state tuition
rates. *Deadline: Contact the department for details.

Wisconsin Department of Veterans Affairs
30 West Mifflin Street, PO Box 7843
Madison, WI 53703
608-266-1311, 800-947-8387
wdvaweb@dva.state.wi.us
http://dva.state.wi.us/Ben_education.asp
Grant Name: Wisconsin G.I. Bill. *Academic Area: Open.
*Age Group: Graduate students. *Eligibility: Veterans
who have substantial service-connected disabilities
may apply. Applicants must plan to attend a public
institution in the state of Wisconsin. The program is

also open to undergraduate students. *Application Process: Visit the department's Web site to download an application. *Amount: Tuition reduced by 50 percent. *Deadline: Contact the department for details.

Wyoming Commission of Veterans Affairs
5905 Cy Avenue, Room 101
Casper, WY 82604
307-265-7372
wvac@bresnan.net
http://www.nasdva.com/wyoming.html

Grant Name: The commission provides tuition waivers for the purpose of college study. *Academic Area: Open. *Age Group: Graduate students. *Eligibility: Residents of Wyoming who served in the U.S. military during the Vietnam War are eligible to apply. Applicants must be residents of Wyoming and attend a public college or university in the state either full or part time. The program is also open to undergraduate students. *Application Process: Contact the commission for details. *Amount: Full tuition for no more than 10 semesters of credit classes. *Deadline: Contact the commission for details.

STUDY ABROAD—UNDERGRADUATE

The following financial aid resources are available to undergraduate students who are interested in pursuing study abroad.

American Institute for Foreign Study
AIFS College Division
River Plaza
9 West Broad Street
Stamford, CT 06902-3788
800-727-2437
http://www.aifsabroad.com/ays/scholarships.htm
Scholarship Name: American Institute for Foreign Study Diversity Scholarship. *Academic Area: Open. *Age Group: Undergraduate students. *Study Abroad Country: Open. *Eligibility: Applicants must be African American, Asian American, Hispanic American, Native American, or Pacific Islander. They also must meet the minimum requirements for the program to which they are applying, have at least a 3.0 minimum cumulative GPA, show leadership potential, and be involved in extracurricular activities centered on multicultural or international issues. *Application Process: Applicants should submit a completed application along with a $95 application fee, one letter of reference, and an essay of up to 1,000 words on "How studying abroad will change my life." Visit the institute's Web site to download an application. *Amount: Full program fees plus round trip airfare for the winner; three runners up receive $2,000 each. *Deadline: April 15, October 15.

American Institute for Foreign Study
AIFS College Division
River Plaza
9 West Broad Street
Stamford, CT 06902-3788
800-727-2437
http://www.aifsabroad.com/ays/scholarships.htm
Scholarship Name: American Institute for Foreign Study Study Abroad Scholarship. *Academic Area: Open. *Age Group: Undergraduate students. *Study Abroad Country: Open. *Eligibility: Applicants must meet the minimum requirements for the program to which they are applying, have at least a 3.0 minimum cumulative GPA, show leadership potential, and be involved in extracurricular activities centered on multicultural or international issues. *Application Process: Applicants should submit a completed application along with a $95 application fee, one letter of reference, and an essay of up to 1,000 words on "How studying abroad will impact my academic

and personal growth." Visit the institute's Web site to download an application. *Amount: $1,000 to $2,000. *Deadline: April 15, October 15.

American Swedish Institute
2600 Park Avenue
Minneapolis, MN 55407-1090
612-871-4907
information@americanswedishinst.org
http://www.americanswedishinst.org/scholarship.htm
Scholarship Name: Malmberg Scholarship. *Academic Area: Open. *Age Group: Open. *Study Abroad Country: Sweden. *Eligibility: Applicants must be U.S. residents who are either enrolled in a degree-granting institution or are scholars whose work can be enhanced by study in Sweden. They also must have chosen a university in Sweden and have attained an acceptance letter or an invitation from the school prior to applying. Applicants are responsible for attaining their own visas. *Application Process: Applicants should submit a completed application along with two letters of recommendation, a copy of an acceptance letter from a Swedish institution, a 1,000-word summary of the applicant's research topic/project, and a proposed budget. Visit the organization's Web site to download an application. Applications are accepted only after September 1 of each year. *Amount: Up to $10,000. *Deadline: November 15.

Augsburg College
Center for Global Education
2211 Riverside Avenue
Minneapolis, MN 55454
612-330-1159, 800-299-8899
globaled@augsburg.edu
http://www.augsburg.edu/global/seminfo.html
Scholarship Name: Scholarship for Students from Historically Disadvantaged Groups. *Academic Area: Open. *Age Group: Undergraduate students. *Study Abroad Country: El Salvador, Guatemala, Mexico, Namibia, Nicaragua. *Eligibility: Applicants must be currently enrolled as an undergraduate in a college or university in the United States, be accepted into the Center for Global Education's study abroad program, have funding beyond the scholarship (financial aid, loans, etc.), and be able to demonstrate membership

in an underrepresented minority group. Applicants should also demonstrate their reasons for wanting to participate in the program, how they will share their experiences with others, and demonstrate financial need. Priority is given to U.S. citizens and permanent residents. Although open to all majors, students will be studying predetermined subjects for college credit while participating in the program. For example, students in the Central American program will take classes in Spanish language, history, religion, and political science. *Application Process: Applicants should submit a completed application along with answers to two essay questions and proof of additional funding sources other than the scholarship. Visit the center's Web site for additional information on the travel abroad semesters. *Amount: Awards vary. *Deadline: May 1, November 1.

AustraLearn Scholarship
12050 North Pecos Street, Suite 320
Westminster, CO 80234
303-446-2214, 800-980-0033
studyabroad@australearn.org
http://www.australearn.org/Programs/StudyAbroad/
    Scholarship/GeneralScholarship.htm
Scholarship Name: AustraLearn Scholarship. *Academic Area: Open. *Age Group: Undergraduate students. *Study Abroad Country: Australia, New Zealand. *Eligibility: Applicants must be enrolled in a college or university in the United States and must be already accepted to study abroad at an AustraLearn program university in Australia or New Zealand. Applicants cannot apply for the scholarship prior to being accepted into the study abroad program. They also must maintain at least a 2.5 GPA. The scholarship is also available to graduate students. *Application Process: Applicants should submit a completed application along with a statement of financial need, a statement of their extracurricular activities and career plans, and an essay discussing how studying abroad will impact that future career. Visit the organization's Web site to learn more about their study abroad programs. Applications are distributed to individuals once they have been accepted into the study abroad program only. *Amount: $1,000 to $2,500. *Deadline: April 30, November 30.

Ben-Gurion University of the Negev
Center for International Student Programs (CISP)
342 Madison Avenue, Suite 1224

New York, NY 10173
800-962-2248
osp@aabgu.org
http://www.bgu.ac.il/cgi-bin/osp/bgu.
    pl?side1=finances/side1.htm&side2=finances/side6b.
    htm&main=finances/6b.htm
Scholarship Name: Ginsburg-Ingerman Scholarship Fund. *Academic Area: Open. *Age Group: Undergraduate students. *Study Abroad Country: Israel. *Eligibility: Applicants must be accepted into or enrolled in a college or university in the United States, never have been to Israel, and must want to learn about the people of Israel by living there for a period of time. They must also demonstrate financial need and must commit to working as a recruiter and representative for the CISP upon their return to the United States. *Application Process: Applicants should contact the center for information on how to apply. *Amount: Awards vary. *Deadline: Contact the center for deadline information.

British Council
British Embassy
3100 Massachusetts Avenue, NW
Washington, DC 20008-3600
202-588-7844
info@marshallscholarship.org
http://www.marshallscholarship.org
Scholarship Name: Marshall Scholarship. *Academic Area: Open. *Age Group: Undergraduate students. *Study Abroad Country: United Kingdom. *Eligibility: Applicants must be U.S. citizens who have attained an undergraduate degree in the U.S. and have maintained at least a 3.7 GPA. Applicants should have received their undergraduate degree within the past two years and want to study in the United Kingdom in order to strengthen relationships between U.S. and British people and governments. The scholarship is also available to graduate students. *Application Process: Applicants should visit the council's Web site to determine where the regional office in their area is located. Applications must be submitted online, but supporting materials should be sent to the applicant's regional office. Applicants must state in their application their first and second choices of universities and courses of proposed study. Supporting materials include four letters of recommendation and academic transcripts. Visit the council's Web site to apply online. This scholarship is for a two-year period of study. *Amount: University

fees, cost of living expenses, annual book grant, thesis grant, research and daily travel grants, fares to and from the United States and, where applicable, a contribution toward the support of a dependent spouse.*Deadline: October 5.

CIEE
7 Custom House Street, 3rd Floor
Portland, ME 04101
207-553-7600, 800-40-STUDY
scholarships@ciee.org
http://www.ciee.org/study/scholarships.aspx
Scholarship Name: CIEE International Study Programs (CIEE-ISP) Scholarship. *Academic Area: Open. *Age Group: Undergraduate students. *Study Abroad Country: Open. *Eligibility: Applicants must be U.S. residents applying to a CIEE Study Center program, whose school is also an academic consortium member (a complete list can be viewed at the organization's Web site), and who demonstrate both financial need and academic achievement. The scholarship is also available to graduate students. *Application Process: Applicants should submit a completed application online. Additional application materials, including a personal statement that touches on the student's achievements and financial circumstances, should be mailed. Recommendations and academic transcripts must be submitted also. Visit the organization's Web site to view a complete list of study abroad programs. *Amount: $500, $1000. *Deadline: April 1, November 1.

CIEE
7 Custom House Street, 3rd Floor
Portland, ME 04101
207-553-7600, 800-40-STUDY
scholarships@ciee.org
http://www.ciee.org/study/scholarships.aspx
Scholarship Name: Jennifer Ritzmann Scholarship for Studies in Tropical Biology. *Academic Area: Biology. *Age Group: Undergraduate students. *Study Abroad Country: Costa Rica. *Eligibility: Applicants must be attending the CIEE Tropical Biology Program at Monteverde, Costa Rica, and aim to work in forestry and rainforest preservation. *Application Process: This memorial scholarship is awarded to one student each year who applies to the program in Costa Rica. All applicants to this program are considered, and the one whose application materials most match the goals of Jennifer Ritzmann is chosen for the scholarship. There are no additional application

requirements. Visit the organization's Web site to read about the life of Jennifer Ritzmann and the scholarship established in her name. *Amount: $1,000. *Deadline: April 1, November 1.

CIEE
7 Custom House Street, 3rd Floor
Portland, ME 04101
207-553-7600, 800-40-STUDY
scholarships@ciee.org
http://www.ciee.org/study/scholarships.aspx
Grant Name: John E. Bowman Travel Grant. *Academic Area: Open. *Age Group: Undergraduate students. *Study Abroad Area: Africa, Asia, Eastern Europe, Latin America. *Eligibility: Applicants must be U.S. citizens or permanent residents who are participating in a CIEE study or volunteer program and who have financial need. Applicants must attend a school that is a CIEE member or academic consortium member. Visit the organization's Web site for complete list of college and university members. Applicants must be traveling to a nontraditional destination in Africa, Asia, Eastern Europe, or Latin America. The scholarship is also available to graduate students. *Application Process: Applicant should apply online and send additional application materials, including a personal statement essay (not to exceed 500 words), letters of recommendation, and academic transcripts. *Amount: $500, $1000. *Deadline: April 1, November 1.

CIEE
7 Custom House Street, 3rd Floor
Portland, ME 04101
207-553-7600, 800-40-STUDY
scholarships@ciee.org
http://www.ciee.org/study/scholarships.aspx
Scholarship Name: Robert B. Bailey Scholarship. *Academic Area: Open. *Age Group: Undergraduate students. *Study Abroad Country: Open. *Eligibility: Applicants should be applying to a CIEE Study Center program, be U.S. citizens, and be members of an underrepresented minority group. They also must demonstrate financial need and academic achievement. The scholarship is also available to graduate students. *Application Process: Applicants should submit a completed application online. Additional application materials, including a personal statement that touches on the impact of the student's minority status on his or her choice of study abroad program, should be submitted by mail. Recommendations and academic transcripts must

also be submitted. Visit the organization's Web site to view a complete list of study abroad programs. *Amount: $500. *Deadline: April 1, November 1.

CIEE
7 Custom House Street, 3rd Floor
Portland, ME 04101
207-553-7600, 800-40-STUDY
scholarships@ciee.org
http://www.ciee.org/study/scholarships.aspx
Scholarship Name: U.S. Department of Education Fulbright-Hays Group Projects Abroad Program. *Academic Area: Foreign languages. *Age Group: Undergraduate students. *Study Abroad Country: China. *Eligibility: Applicants must be U.S. citizens or permanent residents who want to attend a Chinese language program at one of the following universities: University of Beijing, East China Normal University (Shanghai), Nanjing University, or National Chengchi University (Taipei). Applicants must be undergraduate juniors or seniors who intend to pursue careers in foreign language teaching. They also must have completed at least two years of college-level Mandarin Chinese, demonstrate academic achievement, financial need, and an interest in pursuing a graduate degree in Chinese studies. The scholarship is also available to graduate students. *Application Process: Applicants should apply online, and mail additional application materials, including official transcripts, recommendations, an application fee, and a 250- to 500-word personal statement. Visit the organization's Web site for more specific information about the application process. *Amount: $500 to $8,000. *Deadline: April 1, November 1.

Cultural Experiences Abroad (CEA)
1400 East Southern Avenue, Suite B-108
Tempe, AZ 85282-8011
800-266-4441
http://www.gowithcea.com/financing/scholarships.html
Scholarship Name: Cultural Experiences Abroad Academic Development Scholarship. *Academic Area: Open. *Age Group: Undergraduate students. *Study Abroad Country: Open. *Eligibility: Applicants must be accepted into a CEA program, currently enrolled as an undergraduate student in a U.S. or Canadian college or university, maintain at least a 2.7 GPA, and adhere to the CEA Code of Conduct. Visit the organization's Web site to read the CEA Code of Conduct. Applicants must be attending a trimester, semester, or year-long CEA program. *Application Process: Applicants

should submit a completed application along with an unofficial transcript and a 400- to 500-word essay answering a specific question relating to the scholarship. Visit the organization's Web site to view the current essay question. *Amount: $500. Deadline: March 1, April 15, October 15.

Cultural Experiences Abroad (CEA)
1400 East Southern Avenue, Suite B-108
Tempe, AZ 85282-8011
800-266-4441
info@GOWithCEA.com
http://www.gowithcea.com/financing/scholarships.html
Scholarship Name: Cultural Experiences Abroad Affiliate Scholarship. *Academic Area: Open. *Age Group: Undergraduate students. *Study Abroad Country: Open. *Eligibility: Applicants must be accepted into a CEA program, currently enrolled as an undergraduate student in a U.S. or Canadian college or university, maintain at least a 3.0 GPA, and adhere to the CEA Code of Conduct. Visit the organization's Web site to read the CEA Code of Conduct. Applicants must attend a home institution that is a member of the CEA Affiliate Program. *Application Process: Applicants should submit a completed application along with an unofficial transcript and a 400- to 500-word essay answering a specific question relating to the scholarship. Visit the organization's Web site to view the current essay question. *Amount: $1,000. Deadline: March 1, April 15, October 15.

Cultural Experiences Abroad (CEA)
1400 East Southern Avenue, Suite B-108
Tempe, AZ 85282-8011
800-266-4441
info@GoWithCEA.com
http://www.gowithcea.com/financing/scholarships.html
Scholarship Name: Cultural Experiences Abroad Alumni Go-Again Scholarship. *Academic Area: Open. *Age Group: Undergraduate students. *Study Abroad Country: Open. *Eligibility: Applicants must be accepted into a CEA program, currently enrolled as an undergraduate student in a U.S. or Canadian college or university, maintain at least a 3.0 GPA, and adhere to the CEA Code of Conduct. Visit the organization's Web site to read the CEA Code of Conduct. Applicants must have already completed a CEA program and want to attend a second trimester, semester, or year program. *Application Process: Applicants should submit a completed application along with an unofficial transcript and a 400- to 500-word

essay answering a specific question relating to the scholarship. Visit the organization's Web site to view the current essay question. *Amount: $500. Deadline: March 1, April 15, October 15.

Cultural Experiences Abroad (CEA)
1400 East Southern Avenue, Suite B-108
Tempe, AZ 85282-8011
800-266-4441
info@GoWithCEA.com
http://www.gowithcea.com/financing/scholarships.html
Scholarship Name: Cultural Experiences Abroad Arts Scholarship. *Academic Area: Visual arts (history), visual arts (open). *Age Group: Undergraduate students. *Study Abroad Country: Open. *Eligibility: Applicants must be accepted into a CEA program, currently enrolled as an undergraduate student in a U.S. or Canadian college or university, maintain at least a 3.0 GPA, and adhere to the CEA Code of Conduct. Visit the organization's Web site to read the CEA Code of Conduct. Applicants must be attending a trimester, semester, or year-long CEA program in which they study art history or studio or fine arts. *Application Process: Applicants should submit a completed application along with an unofficial transcript and a 400- to 500-word essay answering a specific question relating to the scholarship. Visit the organization's Web site to view the current essay question. *Amount: $1,000. Deadline: March 1, April 15, October 15.

Cultural Experiences Abroad (CEA)
1400 East Southern Avenue, Suite B-108
Tempe, AZ 85282-8011
800-266-4441
info@GoWithCEA.com
http://www.gowithcea.com/financing/scholarships.html
Scholarship Name: Cultural Experiences Abroad Business Scholarship. *Academic Area: Business. *Age Group: Undergraduate students. *Study Abroad Country: Open. *Eligibility: Applicants must be accepted into a CEA program, currently enrolled as an undergraduate student in a U.S. or Canadian college or university, maintain at least a 3.0 GPA, and adhere to the CEA Code of Conduct. Visit the organization's Web site to read the CEA Code of Conduct. Applicants must be attending a trimester, semester, or year-long CEA program in which they study business. *Application Process: Applicants should submit a completed application along with an unofficial transcript and a

400- to 500-word essay answering a specific question relating to the scholarship. Visit the organization's Web site to view the current essay question. *Amount: $1,000. Deadline: March 1, April 15, October 15.

Cultural Experiences Abroad (CEA)
1400 East Southern Avenue, Suite B-108
Tempe, AZ 85282-8011
800-266-4441
info@GoWithCEA.com
http://www.gowithcea.com/financing/scholarships.html
Scholarship Name: Cultural Experiences Abroad Chris Towns France Scholarship. *Academic Area: Open. *Age Group: Undergraduate students. *Study Abroad Country: France. *Eligibility: Applicants must be accepted into a CEA program, be currently enrolled as an undergraduate student in a U.S. or Canadian college or university, maintain at least a 3.0 GPA, and adhere to the CEA Code of Conduct. Visit the organization's Web site to read the CEA Code of Conduct. Applicants must be applying for a trimester, semester, or year program in France and also must demonstrate involvement in extracurricular activities that are multicultural or international in nature. *Application Process: Applicants should submit a completed application along with an unofficial transcript and a 400- to 500-word essay answering a specific question relating to the scholarship. Visit the organization's Web site to view the current essay question. *Amount: $1,000. Deadline: March 1, April 15, October 15.

Cultural Experiences Abroad (CEA)
1400 East Southern Avenue, Suite B-108
Tempe, AZ 85282-8011
800-266-4441
info@GoWithCEA.com
http://www.gowithcea.com/financing/scholarships.html
Scholarship Name: Cultural Experiences Abroad Liberal Arts and Sciences Scholarship. *Academic Area: Liberal arts, sciences. *Age Group: Undergraduate students. *Study Abroad Country: Open. *Eligibility: Applicants must be accepted into a CEA program, currently enrolled as an undergraduate student in a U.S. or Canadian college or university, maintain at least a 3.0 GPA, and adhere to the CEA Code of Conduct. Visit the organization's Web site to read the CEA Code of Conduct. Applicants must be attending a trimester, semester, or year-long CEA program in which they study liberal arts and sciences.

*Application Process: Applicants should submit a completed application along with an unofficial transcript and a 400- to 500-word essay answering a specific question relating to the scholarship. Visit the organization's Web site to view the current essay question. *Amount: $1,000. Deadline: March 1, April 15, October 15.

Cultural Experiences Abroad (CEA)
1400 East Southern Avenue, Suite B-108
Tempe, AZ 85282-8011
800-255-4441
info@GoWithCEA.com
http://www.gowithcea.com/financing/scholarships.html
Scholarship Name: Cultural Experiences Abroad Spanish Language Scholarship. *Academic Area: Foreign languages. *Age Group: Undergraduate students. *Study Abroad Country: Open. *Eligibility: Applicants must be accepted into a CEA program, currently enrolled as an undergraduate student in a U.S. or Canadian college or university, maintain at least a 3.0 GPA, and adhere to the CEA Code of Conduct. Visit the organization's Web site to read the CEA Code of Conduct. Applicants must be attending a trimester, semester, or year-long Spanish Language CEA program. *Application Process: Applicants should submit a completed application along with an unofficial transcript and a 400- to 500-word essay answering a specific question relating to the scholarship. Visit the organization's Web site to view the current essay question. *Amount: $1,000. Deadline: March 1, April 15, October 15.

German Academic Exchange Service/Deutscher Akademischer Austausch Dienst (DAAD)
Undergraduate Scholarships
871 UN Plaza
New York, NY 10017
212-758-3223
huntscott@daad.org
http://www.daad.org/?p=47220
Scholarship Name: Undergraduate Scholarship. *Academic Area: Open. *Age Group: Undergraduate students. *Eligibility: Applicants must be college sophomores or juniors who are seeking DAAD support for a four- to 10-month period in Germany during the German academic year. They must also demonstrate academic achievement, be U.S. or Canadian citizens, be able to receive credit at their home institution for their study in Germany, and

have a well-defined project or internship plans for their stay in Germany. Applicants must be younger than 32 and should demonstrate an interest in German and European affairs. German language proficiency is not required. *Application Process: Applicants should submit a completed application along with a curriculum vitae/resume, project proposal, at least one letter of recommendation (three maximum), a statement of support from the student's study abroad office, proof of acceptance into a study abroad program or a letter of invitation from a German institution, transcripts, and a DAAD language certificate. Visit the organization's Web site to download an application. *Amount: 615 Euro per month. *Deadline: January 31.

Golden Key
Attn: Scholarship Program Administrators
Golden Key Scholarships/Awards
PO Box 23737
Nashville, TN 37202-3737
404-377-2400, 800-377-2401
memberservices@goldenkey.org
http://www.goldenkey.org/GKweb/
    ScholarshipsandAwards/
    ScholarshipandAwardListing/
    MemberScholarshipsandAwards.htm
Scholarship Name: Golden Key Study Abroad Scholarship. *Academic Area: Open. *Age Group: Undergraduate students. *Study Abroad Country: Open. *Eligibility: Applicants should be undergraduate members of the Golden Key International Honour Society who demonstrate academic achievement and whose plans to study abroad will enhance their major field of study. *Application Process: Applicants must first register their intent to apply online at the society's Web site. Once registered, applicants will be prompted to print a cover page to the application, which must be mailed. Additional required documents to mail include a description of the applicant's planned academic program at the host university (up to five pages), a one-page statement of the relevance of the study abroad to the applicant's degree (signed by a professor), and an official academic transcript. *Amount: $1,000. *Deadline: April 15.

Golden Key
Macquarie Abroad
Macquarie International Building, E3A

Macquarie University
North Ryde NSW 2109 Australia
404-377-2400, 800-377-2401
memberservices@goldenkey.org
http://www.goldenkey.org/GKweb/
    ScholarshipsandAwards/
    ScholarshipandAwardListing/PartnerScholarships.
    htm
Scholarship Name: Macquarie University Study Abroad
    Scholarship. *Academic Area: Open. *Age Group:
    Undergraduate students. *Study Abroad Country:
    Australia. *Eligibility: Applicants should be U.S. or
    Canadian citizens who are undergraduate members
    of the Golden Key International Honour Society.
    Applicants should demonstrate involvement in their
    Golden Key chapter as well as academic achievement.
    *Application Process: Applicants must first register
    their intent to apply online at the society's Web site.
    Once registered, applicants will be prompted to
    print a cover page that is to accompany the official
    application, . This should be mailed along with the
    cover page, personal essay (500-word maximum),
    two letters of recommendation, an official transcript,
    and a personal resume that lists extracurricular
    activities, work history, universities attended, and
    any special circumstances. *Amount: One semester
    of paid tuition. All other related expenses are the
    responsibility of the applicant. *Deadline: October 20.

Institute of Current World Affairs
Attn: Peter B. Martin, Executive Director
4 West Wheelock Street
Hanover, NH 03755
603-643-5548
icwa@valley.net
http://www.icwa.org
Fellowship Name: John O. Crane Memorial Fellowship.
    *Academic Area: Open. *Age Group: Adults. *Study
    Abroad Area: East-Central Europe, Middle East.
    *Eligibility: Applicants must be under the age of 36
    and interested in participating in a self-designed
    independent study for two years in East-Central
    Europe or the Middle East. They also should be
    finished with academic study, or at least currently
    not pursuing academic study. This fellowship does
    not fund academic study, but rather independent
    study of the applicant's design. *Application
    Process: Applicants should submit a letter of interest
    outlining their proposed area of study, personal
    background, and professional experience along with

a resume. Candidates who are chosen to proceed
to the next round will be provided with a detailed
application. Visit the institute's Web site for an in-
depth description of the fellowship and its purpose.
*Amount: Awards vary. Full funding for two years.
*Deadline: February 28.

Institute of Current World Affairs
Attn: Peter B. Martin, Executive Director
4 West Wheelock Street
Hanover, NH 03755
603-643-5548
icwa@valley.net
http://www.icwa.org
Fellowship Name: Target-of-Opportunity Fellowship.
    *Academic Area: Open. *Age Group: Adults. *Study
    Abroad Country: Open. *Eligibility: Applicants must be
    under the age of 36 and interested in participating in a
    self-designed independent study for two years in the
    country of their choice. Applicants should be finished
    with academic study, or at least currently not pursuing
    academic study. This fellowship does not fund academic
    study, but rather independent study of the applicant's
    design. A list of countries has been designated by the
    institute as areas of interest; however, applicants can
    propose an area of study in any country that he or
    she believes has a topic worthy of study. *Application
    Process: Applicants should submit a letter of interest
    outlining their proposed area of study, personal
    background, and professional experience along with a
    resume. Candidates who are chosen to proceed to the
    next round will be provided with a detailed application.
    Visit the institute's Web site for an in-depth description
    of the fellowship and its purpose. *Amount: Awards
    vary. Full funding for two years. *Deadline: February 28.

Institute of International Education Inc.
Fulbright Program
809 United Nations Plaza
New York, NY 10017-3580
212-984-5400
http://www.iie.org//TemplateFulbright.
    cfm?section=Fulbright1
Grant Name: Fulbright Grant. *Academic Area: Open.
    *Age Group: Undergraduate students. *Study
    Abroad Country: Open. *Eligibility: Applicants must
    be interested in studying abroad for any number of
    purposes. Visit the institute's Web site for eligibility
    requirements for individual placements in various
    countries. Graduate students and recent college

graduates may also apply for this grant. *Application Process: Students enrolled in undergraduate or graduate programs in the United States must apply through the Fulbright Program Adviser (FPA) on their campuses. College graduates should contact the FPA at their alma mater. Applicants must collect all supporting documents, including a foreign language report, references, and transcripts, and submit them with a hard copy application to their campus FPA. Visit the institute's Web site to locate the name of the FPA at your campus. *Amount: Awards vary. *Deadline: Deadlines vary by college campus, but are usually between mid-September and early October.

Institute of International Education Inc.
Attn: Transcripts
520 Post Oak Boulevard, Suite 740
Houston, TX 77027
713-621-6300, ext. 25
gilman@iie.org
http://www.iie.org/programs/gilman/index.html
Scholarship Name: Benjamin A. Gilman International Scholarship. *Academic Area: Open. *Age Group: Undergraduate students. *Study Abroad Country: Open. *Eligibility: Applicants must be undergraduate students at two- or four-year colleges who are receiving federal Pell Grants. They also must be U.S. citizens and should have applied to or been accepted into a study abroad program (in any country except Cuba or any country on the State Department's travel warning list). Applicants must demonstrate financial need, and priority is given to students who are seeking nontraditional destinations (outside of Western Europe and Australia). Candidates from two-year colleges are encouraged to apply as are ethnic minority or disabled students. Scholarships are offered for the fall and spring semesters only. Summer scholarships are not offered. *Application Process: Applicants must apply online, completing the student section, and should tell their advisers of their intent to apply. After a student applies online, an e-mail is sent to the student's adviser requesting that he or she fill out an online application. Applicants need to send three paper copies of their transcripts (one original and two photocopies) by mail. Visit the organization's Web site to apply online. *Amount: Up to $5,000. *Deadline: April 4, September 26.

International Education Finance Corporation (IEFC)
222 Forbes Road, Suite 406
Braintree, MA 02184

781-843-5334, 888-296-4332
contact@iefc.com
http://www.iefc.com
Loan Name: International Education Finance Corporation Loans. *Academic Area: Open. *Age Group: Undergraduate students. *Study Abroad Country: Open. *Eligibility: Applicants must be U.S. citizens who want to study outside of the United States either for a designated period of time or for a full degree. Some loans require school participation. Visit the organization's Web site to determine if your school is eligible. Graduate students may also apply for these loans. *Application Process: Applicants should visit the organization's Web site to apply online. *Amount: Awards vary. Loans must be repaid. *Deadline: There is no deadline.

International Student Exchange Program (ISEP)
Attn: Jennifer Precht, Sr. Program Officer (Germany), or Léa Senn, Program Officer (France)
1616 P Street, NW, Suite 150
Washington, DC 20036
202-667-8027
jprecht@isep.org; lsenn@isep.org
http://www.isep.org/scholarship/kade.html
Scholarship Name: New York Community Trust-Annette Kade Scholarship. *Academic Area: Open. *Age Group: Undergraduate students. *Study Abroad Country: France, Germany. *Eligibility: Applicants must apply and be qualified for a full-year ISEP placement and must demonstrate financial need. Students must choose an ISEP member institution in France or Germany. Visit the organization's Web site to read in-depth about full-year programs and to view lists of member institutions. Students may elect to enter programs with paid language lessons or not. Larger scholarships are awarded to those taking paid language classes. The scholarship is also available to graduate students. *Application Process: Applicants should submit a completed ISEP application signed by an ISEP coordinator, as well as an essay. Visit the organization's Web site to view the current essay question. *Amount: Up to $3,000. *Deadline: May 15.

International Student Loan Program Center
15 Cottage Avenue, Fifth Floor
Quincy, MA 02169
617-535-7710, 866-229-8900
http://www.internationalstudentloan.com
Loan Name: Study Abroad Loan. *Academic Area: Open.

*Age Group: Undergraduate students. *Study Abroad Country: Open. *Eligibility: Applicants must be U.S. citizens who have good credit. Even with good credit, most applicants require a cosigner. Applicants must show proof of acceptance or enrollment in a study abroad program at an approved institution. Visit the organization's Web site to view approved institutions and/or programs. Graduate students may also apply for these loans. *Application Process: Applicants can apply online, over the phone, or by mail. Visit the organization's Web site to apply. This is a loan program, and all funds must be repaid. *Amount: Up to $30,000. *Deadline: There are no deadlines for this program.

Jerome Foundation

400 Simbley Street, Suite 125
St. Paul, MN 55101-1928
651-224-9431, 800-995-3766
info@jeromefdn.org
http://www.jeromefdn.org/IV~Grant_Programs/
  C~Travel_and_Study

Grant Name: Travel and Study Grant Program. *Academic Area: English/literature, writing, film/television, performing arts (choreography). *Age Group: Adults. *Study Abroad Country: Open. *Eligibility: Applicants must be emerging creative artists who live in either the 11-county metropolitan area of the Twin Cities in Minnesota or the five boroughs of New York City. Most undergraduate and graduate students do not qualify. Visit the organization's Web site for exceptions to this rule. *Application Process: Applicants should submit a cover sheet and a project proposal (limited to one discipline). Visit the organization's Web site to read more about the program. *Amount: Up to $5,000. *Deadline: January 13.

My Travel Bug

Attn: Amanda O'Neil, Executive Director
60 Elm Street
Westerly, RI 02891
Amanda@MyTravelBug.org
http://www.mytravelbug.org

Fellowship Name: My Travel Bug Fellowship. *Academic Area: Open. *Age Group: Age 16 and up. *Study Abroad Country: Open. *Eligibility: Applicants must be U.S. citizens over the age of 16 who can demonstrate financial need, intellectual curiosity, and a desire to travel. They also must be in good health and have a U.S. passport. Applicants must agree to write two travelogues and take four photographs

for each month abroad, which will be published on the organization's Web site. *Application Process: Applicants should submit a personal information form, an itinerary and budget (with specific activities), three 1,000-word essays, and a small application fee. Visit the organization's Web site for further information and to download necessary forms. *Amount: Awards vary. *Deadline: Deadlines vary. Visit the organization's Web site for the next scheduled deadline.

National Italian American Foundation

1860 19th Street, NW
Washington, DC 20009
202-387-0600
info@niaf.org
https://www.niaf.org/scholarships/index.asp

Scholarship Name: National Italian American Foundation Scholarships. *Academic Area: Open, Italian studies. *Age Group: Undergraduate students. *Study Abroad Country: Italy. *Eligibility: Applicants must be high school seniors or college students who belong to one of two eligibility categories: Italian American students who demonstrate academic achievement and potential or students from any ethnic background who are majoring or minoring in Italian studies or Italian language and who also exhibit academic achievement. Some scholarships require financial need, while others focus more on academic achievement. Applicants must be enrolled or accepted into an accredited U.S. college or university for the fall semester, maintain a GPA of at least 3.5, and be U.S. citizens. Some scholarships are also available to graduate students. *Application Process: Applicants should submit an application online at the organization's Web site. Students must ask one of their teachers to submit an online evaluation form. Official transcripts, as well as the Free Application for Federal Student Aid (for financial need scholarships), must be submitted by mail. *Amount: $2,500 to $10,000. *Deadline: March 1.

National Security Education Program

c/o Academy for Educational Development
1825 Connecticut Avenue, NW
Washington, DC 20009
202-884-8285, 800-498-9360
nsep@aed.org
http://worldstudy.gov/overview.html

Scholarship Name: David L. Boren Scholarship. *Academic Area: Open. *Age Group: Undergraduate students. *Study Abroad Country: Countries critical to U.S. national security, including countries in Africa, Asia, Eastern and Central Europe, Latin America, the Caribbean, and the Middle East. *Eligibility: Applicants must be U.S. citizens who are matriculating in an accredited degree program in the United States. Applicants must be pursuing a program/major/career that has a "justifiable connection" with national security. Applicants also must include the study of foreign language as part of their programs and must agree to a service requirement upon completion of the program. The service requirement consists of equal amount of time (as what was spent overseas) working for the U.S. government or a U.S. college or university. David L. Boren Fellowships are also available to graduate students. *Application Process: Applicants can apply online or request a printed application. Visit the organization's Web site to apply online and to learn more about the program. *Amount: Up to $20,000. *Deadline: Deadlines vary. Contact the organization for deadline information.

National Society of Collegiate Scholars
1900 K Street, NW, Suite 890
Washington, DC 20006
202-265-9000, 800-989-6727
http://www.nscs.org/memberbenefits/
ScholarshipOpportunities/Abroad/index.cfm
Scholarship Name: National Society of Collegiate Scholars Scholar Abroad Scholarship. *Academic Area: Open. *Age Group: Undergraduate students. *Eligibility: Applicants must be NSCS members and full-time students who wish to study abroad for a semester. The scholarship is also available to graduate students. *Application Process: Applicants should visit the society's Web site to apply online *Amount: $5,000 (fall, spring); $2,500 (summer). *Deadline: Deadlines vary by semester.

National Welsh-American Foundation
143 Sunny Hillside Road
Benton, PA 17814-7822
570-925-NWAF
nwaf@dfnow.com
http://www.wales-usa.org/projects.html
Scholarship Name: National Welsh-American Foundation Exchange Scholarship Program. *Academic Area: Welsh studies. *Age Group: Undergraduate students. *Study Abroad Country: Wales. *Eligibility: Applicants must be Welsh-American students who wish to participate in an exchange program by which they can

have the opportunity to study Welsh history, language, and culture in Wales. Applicants should contact the organization for additional eligibility requirements. The scholarship is also available to graduate students. *Application Process: Applicants should contact the organization for information about the application process. *Amount: Awards vary. *Deadline: Contact the organization for deadline information.

Phi Kappa Phi
Louisiana State University
PO Box 16000305
Baton Rouge, LA 70893-6000
225-388-4917, 800-804-9880, ext. 13
awards@phikappaphi.org
http://www.phikappaphi.org/Web/Scholarships/
studyabroad.html
Grant Name: Study Abroad Grant Competition. *Academic Area: Open. *Age Group: Undergraduate students. *Study Abroad Country: Open. *Eligibility: Applicants may be Phi Kappa Phi members or non-members, but they must attend a college or university with an active chapter of Phi Kappa Phi. They also must have completed at least 56 semester hours, but not more than 90 semester hours, and they must have at least two semesters remaining once they return from studying abroad. Applicants must have applied and been accepted into a study abroad program and it must relate to the applicant's major. They also must have a GPA of at least 3.5 on a 4.0 scale. *Application Process: Applicants should submit a completed application along with two completed recommendation forms, a personal statement, a letter of acceptance into a study abroad program, and transcripts. Applicants must submit six copies of this application packet. Visit the organization's Web site to download an application. *Amount: $1,000. *Deadline: February 15.

Rotary International
One Rotary Center
1560 Sherman Avenue
Evanston, IL 60201
847-866-3000
inquiriess@rotary.org
http://www.rotary.org/foundation/educational/amb_
scho/index.html
Scholarship Name: Ambassadorial Scholarships. *Academic Area: Open. *Age Group: Undergraduate students. *Eligibility: Applicants must be citizens of

a country in which there are Rotary clubs. They also must have completed at least two years of college-level course work or have equivalent professional experience before commencing their scholarship studies. Applicants for Academic-Year and Multi-Year Ambassadorial Scholarships must be proficient in the language of the proposed host country. Cultural Ambassadorial Scholarship applicants must have completed at least one year of college-level course work or equivalent in the proposed language of study. Graduate students and professionals may also apply for these scholarships. *Application Process: Applicants must submit a completed application, a personal statement, a statement of intent, a language ability form, and official transcripts. Visit Rotary International's Web site to download an application. Applicants should submit this application to their local or district Rotary Club. *Amount: Varies. *Deadline: Contact your local Rotary Club for details.

Sons of Norway Foundation
c/o Sons of Norway
1455 West Lake Street
Minneapolis, MN 55408-2666
612-827-3611, 800-945-8851
foundation@sofn.com
http://www.sofn.com/aboutus/Foundation/
GrantsScholarships.html
Scholarship Name: Astrid G. Cates Scholarship Fund and Myrtle Beinhauer Fund. *Academic Area: Open. *Age Group: Undergraduate students. *Eligibility: Applicants must be current members of Sons of Norway or children or grandchildren of current members in districts 1-6. They also must demonstrate academic achievement and financial need and be enrolled or accepted into a postsecondary institution. *Application Process: Applicants should submit a completed application along with a personal statement outlining their plan and location of study, a statement of financial need, transcripts, and one letter of recommendation. Visit the organization's Web site to download an application. *Amount: $500 to $750. *Deadline: March 1.

Sons of Norway Foundation
c/o Sons of Norway
1455 West Lake Street
Minneapolis, MN 55408-2666
612-827-3611, 800-945-8851
foundation@sofn.com

http://www.sofn.com/aboutus/Foundation/
GrantsScholarships.html
Scholarship Name: Nancy Lorraine Jensen Memorial Scholarship. *Academic Area: Chemistry, engineering (chemical), engineering (electrical), engineering (mechanical), physics. *Age Group: Undergraduate students. *Eligibility: Applicants must be female U.S. citizens between the ages of 17 and 35 who are pursuing degrees in chemistry, physics, or chemical, electrical, or mechanical engineering. They must also be members of Sons of Norway or children or grandchildren of members. Alternately, applicants' parents or grandparents may be employed at the NASA Goddard Space Flight Center in Greenbelt, Maryland. The scholarship is also available to graduate students. *Application Process: Applicants should contact the organization to receive an application and further information about the application process. *Amount: Awards vary. *Deadline: March 1.

Sons of Norway Foundation
c/o Sons of Norway
1455 West Lake Street
Minneapolis, MN 55408-2666
612-827-3611, 800-945-8851
foundation@sofn.com
http://www.sofn.com/aboutus/Foundation/
GrantsScholarships.html
Scholarship Name: Oslo International Summer School Scholarship. *Academic Area: Open. *Age Group: Undergraduate students. *Study Abroad Country: Norway. *Eligibility: Applicants must be current members of Sons of Norway or children or grandchildren of current members in districts 1-6. They must also be accepted into the Oslo International Summer School program and demonstrate academic potential, financial need, and participation in school activities. *Application Process: Applicants should submit a completed application along with answers to two essays found on the application, three letters of recommendation, and official transcripts. Visit the organization's Web site to download an application. *Amount: $1,500. *Deadline: March 1.

Woman's National Farm and Garden Association Inc. (WFNGA)
Attn: Frysinger Exchange
PO Box 1175
Midland, MI 48641-1175
http://www.wnfga.org

Fellowship Name: The Grace E. Frysinger Exchange Fellowship allows the recipient to participate in a one-month foreign exchange program. *Academic Areas: Agriculture, horticulture. *Age Group: Open. *Study Abroad Country: Varies. *Eligibility: Applicants must be women with outgoing personalities who have an interest in the rural and urban life of other women of the world, knowledge of the mission of the organization she represents, and are in good health. All members of the association are eligible to apply. *Application Procedure: Applicants must submit, in resume form, detailed personal information and two recent photos. Visit the association's Web site for detailed information on application requirements. The fellowship is awarded every four years. *Amount: Travel expenses are paid in full. *Deadline: Varies. Contact the association for more information.

Youth For Understanding USA
American Overseas Office
6400 Goldsboro Road, Suite 100
Bethesda, MD 20817
800-TEENAGE
http://www.yfu-usa.org

Scholarship Name: Youth For Understanding Scholarships. *Academic Area: Open. *Age Group: High school students. *Study Abroad Country: Varies; applicants must select from a list of participating countries. *Eligibility: Applicants must be between the ages of 15 and 18 who want to live and study abroad for a period of a semester, year, or summer. They also must demonstrate academic achievement by maintaining at least a 3.0 GPA (summer and year programs) or a 2.0 GPA for summer programs. Eligibility requirements differ for each scholarship awarded. Visit the organization's Web site to see if you qualify for national, regional, or employer sponsored scholarships. *Application Process: Applicants should submit a completed application along with a $35 application fee, transcripts, and any additional supporting materials required for the specific scholarship. Visit the organization's Web site to download applications and to find out more about the different programs offered. *Amount: Paid tuition, travel, and living expenses for a designated period of time. *Deadline: Deadlines vary.

STUDY ABROAD—GRADUATE

The following financial aid resources are available to graduate and medical students who are interested in pursuing study abroad.

American Swedish Institute
2600 Park Avenue
Minneapolis, MN 55407-1090
612-871-4907
information@americanswedishinst.org
http://www.americanswedishinst.org/scholarship.htm
Scholarship Name: Malmberg Scholarship. *Academic Area: Open. *Age Group: Open. *Study Abroad Country: Sweden. *Eligibility: Applicants must be U.S. residents who are either enrolled in a degree-granting institution or are scholars whose work can be enhanced by study in Sweden. They also must have chosen a university in Sweden and have attained an acceptance letter or an invitation from the school prior to applying. Applicants are responsible for attaining their own visas. *Application Process: Applicants should submit a completed application along with two letters of recommendation, a copy of an acceptance letter from a Swedish institution, a 1,000-word summary of the applicant's research topic/project, and a proposed budget. Visit the organization's Web site to download an application. Applications are accepted only after September 1 of each year. *Amount: Up to $10,000. *Deadline: November 15.

American Women's Hospitals Service
c/o American Medical Women's Association (AMWA)
801 North Fairfax Street, Suite 400
Alexandria, VA 22314
703-838-0500
info@amwa-doc.org
http://www.amwa-doc.org/index.
    cfm?objectId=E1D4E40B-D567-0B25-
    574CAFD0BB526D9B
Grant Name: American Women's Hospitals Service Overseas Assistance Grant. *Academic Area: Medicine (physicians). *Age Group: Medical students. *Eligibility: Women who are completing their second, third, or fourth year at an accredited U.S. medical school who plan to pursue medical studies in an overseas setting where the medically neglected will benefit are eligible to apply. Applicants must be student members of the AMWA and plan to spend a minimum of six weeks and no longer than one year in a sponsored program that assists the medically

neglected. *Application Procedure: At least three months prior to departure, applicants should submit a completed application (available on the organization's Web site) along with a letter of recommendation a travel budget, and an 800- to 1,000-word statement of interest. *Amount: Up to $1,500. *Deadline: Applications are accepted on a rolling basis.

AustraLearn Scholarship
12050 North Pecos Street, Suite 320
Westminster, CO 80234
303-446-2214, 800-980-0033
studyabroad@australearn.org
http://www.australearn.org/Programs/StudyAbroad/
    Scholarship/GeneralScholarship.htm
Scholarship Name: AustraLearn Scholarship. *Academic Area: Open. *Age Group: Graduate students. *Study Abroad Country: Australia, New Zealand. *Eligibility: Applicants must be enrolled in a college or university in the United States and must be already accepted to study abroad at an AustraLearn program university in Australia or New Zealand. Applicants cannot apply for the scholarship prior to being accepted into the study abroad program. They also must maintain at least a 2.5 GPA. The scholarship is also available to undergraduate students. *Application Process: Applicants should submit a completed application along with a statement of financial need, a statement detailing their extracurricular activities and career plans, and an essay discussing how studying abroad will impact that future career. Visit the organization's Web site to learn more about their study abroad programs. Applications are distributed to individuals once they have been accepted into the study abroad program only. *Amount: $1,000 to $2,500. *Deadline: November 30, April 30.

British Council
British Embassy
3100 Massachusetts Avenue, NW
Washington, DC 20008-3600
202-588-7844
info@marshallscholarship.org
http://www.marshallscholarship.org
Scholarship Name: Marshall Scholarship. *Academic Area: Open. *Age Group: Graduate students. *Study

Abroad Country: United Kingdom. *Eligibility: Applicants must be U.S. citizens who have attained an undergraduate degree within the last two years in the United States and have maintained at least a 3.7 GPA. They must also want to study in the United Kingdom (U.K.) to strengthen relationships between U.S. and British people and governments. Persons already studying for or holding a British degree are not eligible to apply. *Application Process: Applicants should visit the council's Web site to determine the location of their regional office. Applications must be submitted online, but supporting materials should be sent to the applicant's regional office. Applicants must state in their application their first and second choices of universities and courses of proposed study. Supporting materials include four letters of recommendation and academic transcripts. Visit the council's Web site to apply online. This scholarship is for a two-year period of study. *Amount: University fees, cost of living expenses, annual book grant, thesis grant, research and daily travel grants, fares to and from the United States and, where applicable, a contribution towards the support of a dependent spouse. *Deadline: Early October.

CIEE
7 Custom House Street, 3rd Floor
Portland, ME 04101
207-553-7600, 800-40-STUDY
scholarships@ciee.org
http://www.ciee.org/study/scholarships.aspx
Scholarship Name: CIEE International Study Programs Scholarships. *Academic Area: Open. *Age Group: Graduate students. *Study Abroad Country: Open. *Eligibility: Applicants must be U.S. residents applying to a CIEE Study Center program, whose school is also an academic consortium member (a complete list can be viewed at the organization's Web site), and who demonstrate both financial need and academic achievement. The scholarship is also available to undergraduate students. *Application Process: Applicants should submit a completed application online. Additional application materials, including a personal statement that touches on the student's achievements and financial circumstances, should be mailed. Recommendations and academic transcripts also must be submitted. Visit the organization's Web site to view a complete list of study abroad programs. *Amount: $500, $1,000. *Deadline: April 1, November 1.

CIEE
7 Custom House Street, 3rd Floor
Portland, ME 04101
207-553-7600, 800-40-STUDY
scholarships@ciee.org
http://www.ciee.org/study/scholarships.aspx
Grant Name: John E. Bowman Travel Grant. *Academic Area: Open. *Age Group: Graduate students. *Study Abroad Area: Africa, Asia, Eastern Europe, Latin America. *Eligibility: Applicants must be U.S. citizens or permanent residents who are participating in a CIEE study or volunteer program and who have financial need. They also must attend a school that is a CIEE member or academic consortium member. Visit the organization's Web site for a complete list of college and university members. Applicants must be traveling to a nontraditional destination in Africa, Asia, Eastern Europe, or Latin America. The grant is also available to undergraduate students. *Application Process: Applicant should apply online and send additional application materials, including a personal statement essay (not to exceed 500 words), letters of recommendation, and academic transcripts. *Amount: $500, $1,000. *Deadline: April 1, November 1.

CIEE
7 Custom House Street, 3rd Floor
Portland, ME 04101
207-553-7600, 800-40-STUDY
scholarships@ciee.org
http://www.ciee.org/study/scholarships.aspx
Scholarship Name: Robert B. Bailey Scholarship. *Academic Area: Open. *Age Group: Graduate students. *Study Abroad Country: Open. *Eligibility: Applicants should be U.S. citizens who are applying to a CIEE Study Center program and are members of an underrepresented minority group. They must also demonstrate financial need and academic achievement. The scholarship is also available to undergraduate students. *Application Process: Applicants should submit a completed application online. Additional application materials, including a personal statement that touches on the impact of the student's minority status on his or her choice of study abroad program, should be submitted by mail. Recommendations and academic transcripts must also be submitted. Visit the organization's Web site to view a complete list of study abroad programs. *Amount: $500. *Deadline: April 1, November 1.

CIEE

7 Custom House Street, 3rd Floor

Portland, ME 04101

207-553-7600, 800-40-STUDY

scholarships@ciee.org

http://www.ciee.org/study/scholarships.aspx

Scholarship Name: U.S. Department of Education Fulbright-Hays Group Projects Abroad Program. *Academic Area: Foreign languages. *Age Group: Graduate students. *Study Abroad Country: China. *Eligibility: Applicants must be U.S. citizens or permanent residents who want to attend a Chinese language program at one of the following universities: University of Beijing, East China Normal University (Shanghai), Nanjing University, or National Chengchi University (Taipei). Applicants must be graduate students who intend to pursue careers in foreign language teaching, have completed at least two years of college-level Mandarin Chinese, and demonstrate academic achievement, financial need, and an interest in pursuing a graduate degree in Chinese studies. The program is also available to undergraduate students. *Application Process: Applicants should apply online, and mail additional material, including official transcripts, recommendations, an application fee, and a 250- to 500-word personal statement. Visit the organization's Web site for more specific information about the application process. *Amount: $500 to $8,000. *Deadline: April 1, November 1.

German Academic Exchange Service/Deutscher Akademischer Austausch Dienst (DAAD)

871 UN Plaza

New York, NY 10017

212-758-3223

huntscott@daad.org

http://www.daad.org/?p=73215

Scholarship Name: Study Scholarship. *Academic Area: Open. *Age Group: Graduate students. *Eligibility: Applicants must be graduating college seniors or graduate students in the United States or Canada who have a well-defined study project that requires studying abroad in Germany. They also must be younger than age 32, and applicants in the arts, humanities, and social sciences should have German language fluency. Applicants should know where they want to study and should be taking steps toward application. *Application Process: Applicants should submit a completed application along with a curriculum vitae/resume, a study proposal, two

letters of recommendation, evidence of contact with a German institution, a DAAD Language evaluation form, and transcripts. If their university is a DAAD partner, applicants should submit materials to their campus coordinator. Visit the organization's Web site to find out if your school is a DAAD partner. If your school is not a DAAD partner, materials should be submitted to the New York office. Five copies of the packet, in addition to the original set, should be submitted in collated, unstapled stacks. *Amount: 715 to 795 Euro per month. *Deadline: November 1 (applicants in music, visual arts, performing arts), November 15 (all other applicants).

Henry Luce Foundation

111 West 50th Street

New York, NY 10020

212-480-7700

http://www.hluce.org/3scholfm.html

Scholarship Name: Luce Scholars Program. *Academic Area: Open. *Age Group: Graduate students. *Study Abroad Country: Open, but it must be an Asian country. *Eligibility: Applicants must be U.S. citizens who have earned at least a bachelor's degree and who are not older than 29 at the time they enter the program. Applicants should not be Asian studies majors and should not have had much exposure to Asian culture. Applicants can have any other undergraduate background. *Application Process: Applicants must be attending or be alumni of one of 67 predetermined participating colleges and universities, and be nominated by their academic institution. Visit the foundation's Web site for a complete list and the name of the contact person at each institution. If your academic institution is a participating member, contact a representative directly to inform him or her of your interest in being nominated. Candidates will be contacted after the nomination process for interviews. Placements are for one year in any number of Asian countries. *Amount: Tuition and expenses, plus a stipend for one year. *Deadline: First Monday in December.

Institute of Current World Affairs

Attn: Peter B. Martin, Executive Director

4 West Wheelock Street

Hanover, NH 03755

603-643-5548

icwa@valley.net

http://www.icwa.org

Fellowship Name: John Miller Musser Memorial Forest & Society Fellowship. *Academic Area: Environmental Science. *Age Group: Postgraduates. *Study Abroad Country: Open. *Eligibility: Applicants must be younger than the age of 36 and interested in participating in a self-designed independent study for two years in the country of their choice. Applicants should hold graduate degrees or special training in forest-related disciplines and desire the opportunity to study a related topic in a country other than the United States. They also should be finished with academic study, or at least currently not pursuing academic study. This fellowship does not fund academic study, but rather independent study of the applicant's design. *Application Process: Applicants should submit a letter of interest outlining their proposed area of study, personal background, and professional experience along with a resume. Candidates who are chosen to proceed to the next round will be provided with a detailed application. Visit the institute's Web site for an in-depth description of the fellowship and its purpose. *Amount: Awards vary. Full funding for two years. *Deadline: February 28.

Institute of Current World Affairs
Attn: Peter B. Martin, Executive Director
4 West Wheelock Street
Hanover, NH 03755
603-643-5548
icwa@valley.net
http://www.icwa.org
Fellowship Name: John O. Crane Memorial Fellowship. *Academic Area: Open. *Age Group: Adults. *Study Abroad Area: East-Central Europe, Middle East. *Eligibility: Applicants must be under the age of 36 and interested in participating in a self-designed independent study for two years in East-Central Europe or the Middle East. They also should be finished with academic study, or at least currently not pursuing academic study. This fellowship does not fund academic study, but rather independent study of the applicant's design. *Application Process: Applicants should submit a letter of interest outlining their proposed area of study, personal background, and professional experience along with a resume. Candidates who are chosen to proceed to the next round will be provided with a detailed application. Visit the institute's Web site for an in-depth description of the fellowship and its purpose. *Amount: Awards vary. Full funding for two years. *Deadline: February 28.

Institute of Current World Affairs
Attn: Peter B. Martin, Executive Director
4 West Wheelock Street
Hanover, NH 03755
603-643-5548
icwa@valley.net
http://www.icwa.org
Fellowship Name: Target-of-Opportunity Fellowship. *Academic Area: Open. *Age Group: Adults. *Study Abroad Country: Open. *Eligibility: Applicants must be under the age of 36 and interested in participating in a self-designed independent study for two years in the country of their choice. Applicants should be finished with academic study, or at least currently not pursuing academic study. This fellowship does not fund academic study, but rather independent study of the applicant's design. A list of countries has been designated by the institute as "areas of interest;" however, applicants can propose an area of study in any country that he or she believes has a topic worthy of study. *Application Process: Applicants should submit a letter of interest outlining their proposed area of study, personal background, and professional experience along with a resume. Candidates who are chosen to proceed to the next round will be provided with a detailed application. Visit the institute's Web site for an in-depth description of the fellowship and its purpose. *Amount: Awards vary. Full funding for two years. *Deadline: February 28.

Institute of International Education Inc.
Fulbright Program
809 United Nations Plaza
New York, NY 10017-3580
212-984-5400
fulbrightonline@iie.org
http://www.iie.org//TemplateFulbright.cfm?section=Fulbright1
Grant Name: Fulbright Grant. *Academic Area: Open. *Age Group: Graduate students, recent college graduates. *Eligibility: Applicants must be interested in studying abroad for any number of purposes. Visit the institute's Web site for eligibility requirements for individual placements in various countries. Undergraduate students may also apply for this grant. *Application Process: Students enrolled in undergraduate or graduate programs in the United States must apply through the Fulbright Program Adviser (FPA) on their campuses. College graduates should contact the FPA at their alma mater. Applicants

must collect all supporting documents, including a foreign language report, references, and transcripts, and submit them with a hard copy application to their campus FPA. Visit the institute's Web site to locate the name of the FPA at your campus. *Amount: Awards vary. *Deadline: Deadlines vary by college campus, but are usually between mid-September and early October.

International Education Finance Corporation (IEFC)
222 Forbes Road, Suite 406
Braintree, MA 02184
781-843-5334, 888-296-4332
contact@iefc.com
http://www.iefc.com
Loan Name: IEFC Loans. *Academic Area: Open. *Age Group: Graduate students. *Study Abroad Country: Open. *Eligibility: Applicants must be U.S. citizens who want to study outside of the United States either for a designated period of time or for a full degree. Some loans require school participation. Visit the organization's Web site to determine if your school is eligible. Undergraduate students may also apply for these loans. *Application Process: Applicants should visit the organization's Web site to apply online. *Amount: Awards vary. Loans must be repaid. *Deadline: There is no deadline.

International Student Exchange Program (ISEP)
Attn: Jennifer Precht, Sr. Program Officer (Germany), or Léa Senn, Program Officer (France)
1616 P Street, NW, Suite 150
Washington, DC 20036
202-667-8027
jprecht@isep.org; lsenn@isep.org
http://www.isep.org/scholarship/kade.html
Scholarship Name: New York Community Trust-Annette Kade Scholarship. *Academic Area: Open. *Age Group: Graduate students. *Study Abroad Country: France, Germany. *Eligibility: Applicants must apply and be qualified for a full-year ISEP placement and must demonstrate financial need. Students must choose an ISEP member institution in France or Germany. Visit the organization's Web site to read in-depth about full-year programs and to view lists of member institutions. Students may elect to enter programs with paid language lessons or not. Larger scholarships are awarded to those taking paid language classes. The scholarship is also available to undergraduate students. *Application Process: Applicants should

submit a completed ISEP application signed by an ISEP coordinator, as well as an essay. Visit the organization's Web site to view the current essay question. *Amount: Up to $3,000. *Deadline: May 15.

International Student Loan Program Center
15 Cottage Avenue, Fifth Floor
Quincy, MA 02169
617-535-7710, 866-229-8900
http://www.internationalstudentloan.com
Loan Name: Study Abroad Loans. *Academic Area: Open. *Age Group: Graduate students. *Study Abroad Country: Open. *Eligibility: Applicants must be U.S. citizens who have good credit. Even with good credit, most applicants require a cosigner. Applicants must show proof of acceptance or enrollment in a study abroad program at an approved institution. Visit the organization's Web site to view approved institutions and/or programs. Undergraduate students may also apply for these loans. *Application Process: Applicants can apply online, over the phone, or by mail. Visit the organization's Web site to apply. This is a loan program, and all funds must be repaid. *Amount: Up to $30,000. *Deadline: There are no deadlines for this program.

Jerome Foundation
400 Simbley Street, Suite 125
St. Paul, MN 55101-1928
651-224-9431, 800-995-3766
info@jeromefdn.org
http://www.jeromefdn.org/IV~Grant_Programs/ C~Travel_and_Study
Grant Name: Travel and Study Grant Program. *Academic Area: English/literature, writing, film/television, performing arts (choreography). *Age Group: Adults. *Study Abroad Country: Open. *Eligibility: Applicants must be emerging creative artists who live in either the 11-county metropolitan area of the Twin Cities in Minnesota or the five boroughs of New York City. Most undergraduate and graduate students do not qualify. Visit the organization's Web site for exceptions to this rule. *Application Process: Applicants should submit a cover sheet and a project proposal (limited to one discipline). Visit the organization's Web site to read more about the program. *Amount: Up to $5,000. *Deadline: January 13.

My Travel Bug
Attn: Amanda O'Neil, Executive Director
60 Elm Street

Westerly, RI 02891
Amanda@MyTravelBug.org
http://www.mytravelbug.org
Fellowship Name: My Travel Bug Fellowship. *Academic Area: Open. *Age Group: Age 16 and up. *Study Abroad Country: Open. *Eligibility: Applicants must be U.S. citizens older than the age of 16 who can demonstrate financial need, intellectual curiosity, and a desire to travel. They also must be in good health and have a U.S. passport. Applicants must agree to write two travelogues and take four photographs for each month abroad, which are to be published on the organization's Web site. *Application Process: Applicants should submit a personal information form, an itinerary and budget (with specific activities), three 1,000-word essays, and a small application fee. Visit the organization's Web site for further information and to download necessary forms. *Amount: Awards vary. *Deadline: Deadlines vary. Visit the organization's Web site for the next scheduled deadline.

National Italian American Foundation

1860 19th Street, NW
Washington, DC 20009
202-387-0600
info@niaf.org
https://www.niaf.org/scholarships/index.asp
Scholarship Name: National Italian American Foundation Scholarship. *Academic Area: Open, Italian studies. *Age Group: Graduate students. *Study Abroad Country: Italy. *Eligibility: Applicants must be high school seniors or college students who belong to one of two eligibility categories: Italian American students who demonstrate academic achievement and potential, or students from any ethnic background who are majoring or minoring in Italian studies or Italian language and who also exhibit academic achievement. Some scholarships require financial need, while others focus more on academic achievement. Applicants must be enrolled or accepted into an accredited U.S. college or university for the fall semester, maintain a GPA of at least 3.5, and be U.S. citizens. Some scholarships are also available to undergraduate students. *Application Process: Applicants should submit an application online. Visit the organization's Web site to submit an online application. Students must request that one of their teachers submits an online evaluation form. Official transcripts, as well as the Free Application for Federal Student Aid (for financial need scholarships), must

be submitted by mail. *Amount: $2,500 to $10,000. *Deadline: March 1.

National Security Education Program

c/o Academy for Educational Development
1825 Connecticut Avenue, NW
Washington, DC 20009
202-884-8285, 800-498-9360
nsep@aed.org
http://worldstudy.gov/overview.html
Fellowship Name: David L. Boren Fellowship. *Academic Area: Open. *Age Group: Graduate students. *Study Abroad Country: Countries critical to U.S. national security, including countries in Africa, Asia, Eastern and Central Europe, Latin America, the Caribbean, and the Middle East. *Eligibility: Applicants must be U.S. citizens who are matriculating in an accredited degree program in the United States. Applicants must be pursuing a program/major/career that has a "justifiable connection" with national security. Applicants also must include the study of foreign language as part of their programs and must agree to a service requirement upon completion of the program. The service requirement consists of equal amount of time (as what was spent overseas) working for the U.S. government or a U.S. college or university. David L. Boren Scholarships are also available to undergraduate students. *Application Process: Applicants can apply online or request a printed application. Visit the organization's Web site to apply online and to learn more about the program. *Amount: Up to $28,000. *Deadline: Deadlines vary. Contact the organization for deadline information.

National Society of Collegiate Scholars

1900 K Street, NW, Suite 890
Washington, DC 20006
202-265-9000, 800-989-6727
http://www.nscs.org/memberbenefits/ScholarshipOpportunities/Abroad/index.cfm
Scholarship Name: National Society of Collegiate Scholars Scholar Abroad Scholarship. *Academic Area: Open. *Age Group: Graduate students. *Eligibility: Applicants must be NSCS members and full-time students who wish to study abroad for a semester. The scholarship is also available to undergraduate students. *Application Process: Applicants should visit the society's Web site to apply online *Amount: $5,000 (fall, spring); $2,500 (summer). *Deadline: Deadlines vary by semester.

National Welsh-American Foundation

143 Sunny Hillside Road

Benton, PA 17814-7822

570-925-NWAF

nwaf@dfnow.com

http://www.wales-usa.org/projects.html

Scholarship Name: National Welsh-American Foundation Exchange Scholarship Program. *Academic Area: Welsh studies. *Age Group: Graduate students. *Study Abroad Country: Wales. *Eligibility: Applicants must be Welsh-American students who wish to participate in an exchange program by which they can have the opportunity to study Welsh history, language, and culture in Wales. Applicants should contact the organization for additional eligibility requirements. The scholarship is also available to undergraduate students. *Application Process: Applicants should contact the organization for information about the application process. *Amount: Awards vary. *Deadline: Contact the organization for deadline information.

The Rhodes Trust

Attn: Elliott F. Gerson, American Secretary

8229 Boone Boulevard, Suite 240

Vienna, VA 22182

amsec@rhodesscholar.org

http://www.rhodesscholar.org

Scholarship Name: Rhodes Scholarship. *Academic Area: Open. *Age Group: Graduate students. *Study Abroad Country: United Kingdom. *Eligibility: Applicants must be U.S. citizens who are at least 18, but not yet 24, who have completed most of their undergraduate degree requirements (see specifications noted on application). They also must demonstrate intellectual and academic achievement, and leadership ability and participation in college and community activities. Applicants must desire to attend graduate school at Oxford University in England. *Application Process: Applicants should submit a completed application along with an institutional endorsement from their undergraduate institution, recommendation letters, a signed personal statement, transcripts, a list of their college honors and activities, a headshot photo, and a photocopy of their birth certificate. With the exception of the birth certificate, 10 copies of all other materials must be submitted. The program is intended to last for two years, with the possibility of renewal for a third year. Applicants must submit an application to the appropriate district office. Visit the organization's Web site to download an application. *Amount: Full

tuition and expenses for two years, plus a stipend. *Deadline: October 3.

Rotary International

One Rotary Center

1560 Sherman Avenue

Evanston, IL 60201

847-866-3000

inquiriess@rotary.org

http://www.rotary.org/foundation/educational/amb_scho/index.html

Scholarship Name: Ambassadorial Scholarships. *Academic Area: Open. *Age Group: Graduate students, professionals. *Eligibility: Applicants must be citizens of a country in which there are Rotary clubs and have completed at least two years of college-level course work or have equivalent professional experience before commencing their scholarship studies. Applicants for Academic-Year and Multi-Year Ambassadorial Scholarships must be proficient in the language of the proposed host country. Cultural Ambassadorial Scholarship applicants must have completed at least one year of college-level course work or equivalent in the proposed language of study. Undergraduate students may also apply for these scholarships. *Application Process: Applicants must submit a completed application, a personal statement, a statement of intent, a language ability form, and official transcripts. Visit Rotary International's Web site to download an application. Applicants should apply to their local or district Rotary Club. *Amount: Varies. *Deadline: Contact your local Rotary Club for details.

Sons of Norway Foundation

c/o Sons of Norway

1455 West Lake Street

Minneapolis, MN 55408-2666

612-827-3611, 800-945-8851

foundation@sofn.com

http://www.sofn.com/aboutus/Foundation/GrantsScholarships.html

Scholarship Name: Nancy Lorraine Jensen Memorial Scholarship. *Academic Area: Chemistry, engineering (chemical), engineering (electrical), engineering (mechanical), physics. *Age Group: Graduate students. *Eligibility: Applicants must be female U.S. citizens between the ages of 17 and 35 who are pursuing degrees in chemistry, physics, or chemical, electrical, or mechanical engineering. They also must be members of Sons of Norway or children or grandchildren of members. Alternately, applicants' parents or grandparents may be employed at the NASA Goddard Space Flight Center in Greenbelt, Maryland. The scholarship is also available to undergraduate students. *Application Process: Applicants should contact the organization to receive an application and further information about the application process. *Amount: Awards vary. *Deadline: March 1.

Student American Veterinary Medical Association (SAVMA)

1931 North Meacham Road, Suite 100
Schaumburg, IL 60173
847-925-8070
avmainfo@avma.org
http://www.avma.org/noah/members/savma/
  committees/ivsrc_scholarship_guidelines.pdf
Scholarship Name: International Veterinary Student Relations Committee International Exchange Scholarship. *Academic Area: Medicine (veterinary). *Age Group: Veterinary students. *Eligibility: Applicants must demonstrate a strong desire to participate in a veterinary-related international exchange. They also must be SAVMA members. *Application Procedure: Applicants must submit a completed application, a letter of intention, a letter of recommendation, and an estimated budget. They also must contact the SAVMA international exchange officer prior to application submittal. Visit the association's Web site to download an application. *Amount: $500. *Deadline: January 15.

US-Ireland Alliance

Attn: Mary Lou Hartman, Director of George J. Mitchell Scholarship Program
2800 Clarendon Boulevard, #502
Arlington, VA 22201
703-841-5843
hartman@us-irelandalliance.org
http://www.us-irelandalliance.org/scholarships.html
Scholarship Name: George J. Mitchell Scholarship Program. *Academic Area: Open. *Age Group: Graduate students. *Study Abroad Country: Ireland. *Eligibility: Applicants must be U.S. citizens between the ages of 18 and 30 who intend to pursue a graduate degree at a university in Ireland. Applicants may choose from any discipline, but must have demonstrated academic achievement during their undergraduate education, a commitment to community service, and leadership potential. *Application Process: Applicants must apply online. In addition to the online application, between five and eight letters of recommendation, transcripts, and a personal essay are required. Visit the alliance's Web site in March to complete an application. *Amount: Full tuition, housing, travel, plus a $12,000 living expenses stipend. Program is for one year only. *Deadline: October 6.

Winston Churchill Foundation

Attn: Harold Epstein, Executive Director
PO Box 1240, Gracie Station
New York, NY 10028
212-879-3480
churchillf@aol.com
http://www.thechurchillscholarships.com
Scholarship Name: Churchill Foundation Scholarship. *Academic Area: Engineering (open), mathematics, science. *Age Group: Graduate students. *Study Abroad Country: United Kingdom. *Eligibility: Applicants must be U.S. citizens who are enrolled at a participating institution in the United States, between the ages of 19 and 26, and hold a bachelor's degree. They also must demonstrate academic achievement and leadership qualities, be in good health, and desire to complete a one-year master's degree at Cambridge University. Applicants must commit to completing their program of study at Cambridge or agree to pay back the funds. They also must agree to write two narratives for the foundation about their experience. *Application Process: Applicants should visit the foundation's Web site to determine if their undergraduate institution is a participating institution. If an applicant qualifies, they must submit a completed application along with additional forms, which are downloadable from the foundation's Web site. Additional forms include an application for admission as a graduate student to Cambridge, a medical certificate, and a reference report. Four letters of recommendation, Graduate Record Examination scores, official academic transcripts, and six full copies of the application packet are also required. Visit the foundation's Web site to download the forms. *Amount: Full tuition for one year, plus $500 travel allowance and up to 7,500 pounds living stipend. *Deadline: Contact the organization or a participating academic institution for deadline information.

Woman's National Farm and Garden Association Inc. (WFNGA)
Attn: Frysinger Exchange
PO Box 1175
Midland, MI 48641-1175
http://www.wnfga.org/code/fellowships.htm
Fellowship Name: The Grace E. Frysinger Exchange Fellowship allows the recipient to participate in a one-month foreign exchange program. *Academic Areas: Agriculture, horticulture. *Age Group: Open. *Study Abroad Country: Varies. *Eligibility: Applicants must be women with outgoing personalities who have an interest in the rural and urban life of other women of the world, knowledge of the mission of the organization they represent, and who are in good health. All members of the association are eligible to apply. *Application Procedure: Applicants must submit , in resume form, detailed personal information and two recent photos. Visit the association's Web site for detailed information on application requirements. The fellowship is awarded every four years. *Amount: Travel expenses are paid in full. *Deadline: Varies. Contact the association for more information.

PART IV

FURTHER RESOURCES

FEDERAL FINANCIAL AID PROGRAMS AND OFFICES

This section lists federal financial aid options (scholarships, loans, grants, savings account programs, saving bond programs, and work study) that are available to finance undergraduate study.

Internal Revenue Service (IRS)

800-829-1040

http://www.irs.gov/taxtopics/tc310.html http://www.irs.gov/newsroom/article/0,,id=107636,00.html

Program Name: The Coverdell Education Savings Account is a savings program to help parents and students save for education-related expenses. *Academic Area: Open. *Age Group: Undergraduate students. *Eligibility: All individuals, known as beneficiaries, planning to go to college are eligible for this program. Beneficiaries must be under the age of 18, or have a special need. Anyone can contribute to this account, including the beneficiary, but must meet income limitations. According to the IRS, a contributor's annual income should be less than $110,000 (modified adjusted gross income) or $220,000 if filing jointly. The program is also available to individuals who are planning graduate study. *Application Process: Contact the IRS for enrollment information. *Amount: Money saved in this account may be applied tax free towards tuition at an eligible educational institution, or for related expenses. *Deadline: There is no deadline.

U.S. Department of Education

Federal Student Aid Office Programs

800-433-3243

http://www.studentaid.ed.gov

http://www.fafsa.ed.gov

Grant Name: Academic Competitiveness Grant. *Academic Area: Open. *Age Group: Undergraduate students. *Eligibility: Applicants must be U.S. citizens or eligible noncitizens, full-time students, and complete a rigorous high school academic program (which is determined by their state or local education agency and recognized by the Secretary of Education). They must also be eligible for a Federal Pell Grant (i.e., demonstrate financial need). The grant may be used for first- and second-year undergraduate study. *Application Process: Applicants must submit the Free Application for Federal Student Aid (FAFSA). *Amount: $750 for the first year of undergraduate study; $1,300 for the second year of undergraduate study. *Deadline: June 30 (FAFSA).

U.S. Department of Education

Attn: Darryl Davis

Office of Postsecondary Education

1990 K Street, NW, 6th Floor
Washington, DC 20006-8512

202-502-7657

Darryl.Davis@ed.gov

http://www.ed.gov/programs/iduesbyrd

Loan Name: The Robert C. Byrd Honors Scholarship is a federal program that is administered at the state level. *Academic Area: Open. *Age Group: Undergraduate students. *Eligibility: Applicants must be high school seniors, U.S. citizens or eligible noncitizens, legal residents of the state in which they apply, and have applied to or been accepted into a postsecondary institution. *Application Process: Applicants should contact their state education agency for details. *Amount: Varies; the average award per scholar is $1,500. *Deadline: Applicants should contact their state education agency for details.

U.S. Department of Education

Federal Student Aid Office Programs

800-433-3243

http://www.studentaid.ed.gov

http://www.fafsa.ed.gov

Loan Name: Federal Family Education Loan or Direct PLUS Loan. *Academic Area: Open. *Age Group: Undergraduate students. *Eligibility: Applicants must be parents of dependent students who are enrolled in school at least half time. *Application Process: Students must submit the Free Application for Federal Student Aid (FAFSA). Loans are made through participating schools; contact your school's financial aid department for details. *Amount: Cost of attendance, minus other financial aid that the student has received. *Deadline: June 30 (FAFSA).

U.S. Department of Education

Federal Student Aid Office Programs

800-433-3243

http://www.studentaid.ed.gov

http://www.fafsa.ed.gov

Grant Name: Federal Pell Grant. *Academic Area: Open. *Age Group: Undergraduate students. *Eligibility: Applicants must be U.S. citizens or eligible noncitizens and demonstrate financial need. *Application Process: Applicants must submit the Free Application for Federal Student Aid (FAFSA); amount of grant money will depend on cost of school and student's status. *Amount: $400 to $4,050 a year. *Deadline: June 30 (FAFSA).

U.S. Department of Education
Federal Student Aid Office Programs
800-433-3243
http://www.studentaid.ed.gov
http://www.fafsa.ed.gov
Loan Name: Federal Perkins Loan. *Academic Area: Open. *Age Group: Undergraduate students. *Eligibility: Applicants must be U.S. citizens or eligible noncitizens and attend school at least half time. Graduate students may also apply for this loan program. *Application Process: Applicants must submit the Free Application for Federal Student Aid (FAFSA). Loans are made through participating schools; contact your school's financial aid department for details. *Amount: Up to $4,000 a year for undergraduates, 5 percent interest rate, up to 10 years to repay. *Deadline: June 30 (FAFSA).

U.S. Department of Education
Federal Student Aid Office Programs
800-433-3243
http://www.studentaid.ed.gov
http://www.fafsa.ed.gov
Grant Name: Federal Supplemental Educational Opportunity Grant. *Academic Area: Open. *Age Group: Undergraduate students. *Eligibility: Applicants must be U.S. citizens or eligible noncitizens and demonstrate exceptional financial need. Pell Grant recipients receive priority for this grant. *Application Process: Applicants must submit the Free Application for Federal Student Aid (FAFSA); amount of grant money will depend on cost of school and student's status. *Amount: $100 to $4,000 a year. *Deadline: June 30 (FAFSA).

U.S. Department of Education
Federal Student Aid Office Programs
800-433-3243
http://www.studentaid.ed.gov
http://www.fafsa.ed.gov

Program Name: Federal Work Study. *Academic Area: Open. *Age Group: Undergraduate students. *Eligibility: Applicants must be U.S. citizens or eligible noncitizens who are willing to work on or off campus during college in exchange for college funding. Graduate students may also apply for this program. *Application Process: Applicants must submit the Free Application for Federal Student Aid (FAFSA). Select colleges and universities participate in this program; contact your school's office of financial aid for details. *Amount: Varies depending on total amount of aid student receives. Students must be paid at least minimum wage. *Deadline: June 30 (FAFSA).

U.S. Department of Education
Federal Student Aid Office Programs
800-433-3243
http://www.studentaid.ed.gov
http://www.fafsa.ed.gov
Grant Name: National Science and Mathematics Access to Retain Talent Grant (National Smart Grant). *Academic Area: Computer science, foreign language, life sciences, physical sciences. *Age Group: Undergraduate students. *Eligibility: Applicants must be U.S. citizens or eligible noncitizens, full-time students with a GPA of at least 3.0, and be majoring in physical, life, or computer sciences, mathematics, technology, or engineering or in a foreign language determined critical to national security. They must also be eligible for a Federal Pell Grant (i.e., demonstrate financial need). The grant may be used for third- and fourth-year undergraduate study. *Application Process: Applicants must submit the Free Application for Federal Student Aid (FAFSA). *Amount: $4,000 per year. *Deadline: June 30 (FAFSA).

U.S. Department of Education
Federal Student Aid Office Programs
800-433-3243
http://www.studentaid.ed.gov
http://www.fafsa.ed.gov
Loan Name: Subsidized Federal Family Educational Loan or Direct Student Loan. *Academic Area: Open. *Age Group: Undergraduate students. *Eligibility: Applicants must be U.S. citizens or eligible noncitizens, demonstrate financial need, and attend school at least part time. Graduate students may also apply for these loans. *Application Process: Applicants must submit the Free Application for Federal Student Aid (FAFSA). Contact the U.S. Department of Education for details.

*Amount: $3,500 to $20,500 a year. The U.S. Department of Education pays interest on the loan while the borrower is in school and during grace and deferment periods. After this, the interest rate varies annually; borrowers have between 10 and 30 years to repay, depending on the loan. *Deadline: June 30 (FAFSA).

U.S. Department of Education
Federal Student Aid Office Programs
800-433-3243
http://www.studentaid.ed.gov
http://www.fafsa.ed.gov
Loan Name: Federal Graduate PLUS Loan. *Academic Area: Open. *Age Group: Graduate students. *Eligibility: Graduate students who are enrolled at least half time may apply. Applicants must be U.S. citizens or noncitizen permanent residents and have an acceptable credit history. *Application Process: Students must submit the Free Application for Federal Student Aid (FAFSA). Loans are made through private loan providers. *Amount: Cost of attendance, minus other financial aid that the student has received. *Deadline: June 30 (FAFSA).

U.S. Department of Education
Federal Student Aid Office Programs
800-433-3243
http://www.studentaid.ed.gov
http://www.fafsa.ed.gov
Loan Name: Unsubsidized Federal Family Educational Loan or Direct Stafford Loan. *Academic Area: Open. *Age Group: Undergraduate students. *Eligibility: Applicants must be U.S. citizens or eligible noncitizens and attend school at least half time. Graduate students may also apply for these loans. *Application Process: Applicants must submit the Free Application for Federal Student Aid (FAFSA). Contact the U.S.

Department of Education for details. *Amount: $3,500 to $20,500 a year. The borrower pays interest (rates change annually) during the life of the loan. Borrower has between 10 and 30 years to repay, depending on the loan. *Deadline: June 30 (FAFSA).

U.S. Department of the Treasury
Series EE and I
Bureau of the Public Debt
Division of Customer Assistance
PO Box 1328
Parkersburg, WV 26106-1328
http://savingsbonds.gov/indiv/indiv.htm
Program Name: The Education Savings Bond Program, also known as the Tax-Free Interest for Education Program, comes in the form of U.S. Savings Bonds. These bonds are a very safe form of investment because the U.S. federal government backs them. Bonds must be a Series EE or I and can be purchased from any bank, savings and loan, or through employer programs. *Academic Area: Open. *Age Group: Undergraduate students. *Eligibility: Anyone may purchase bonds that can be used to save for college. The program is also available to individuals who are planning to pursue graduate study. *Application Process: Contact the U.S. Department of the Treasury for enrollment information. *Amount: Bonds earn a flexible or set rate of interest depending on when they were purchased. The interest-earning period for both types of bonds is 30 years. Bonds are non-taxable, but must be used to pay for educational expenses—tuition and fees—at approved colleges and universities or vocational schools. Room and board, books, and other such expenses are not covered. Eligible institutions are those that participate in federally assisted programs. *Deadline: There is no deadline.

STATE FINANCIAL AID PROGRAMS AND OFFICES

This section lists state financial aid resources (scholarships, loans, grants, and awards) that are available to undergraduate students. Eligibility requirements vary, although most states require applicants to reside in and attend a postsecondary educational program in the state. Some state educational organizations offer dozens of financial aid resources to students, while others offer one or just a handful of programs. The following list of financial aid resources by state is not comprehensive; visit your state education assistance organization's Web site for a complete list of financial aid programs.

ALABAMA

Alabama Commission on Higher Education
PO Box 302000
Montgomery, AL 36130-2000
334-242-1998
http://www.ache.state.al.us/StudentAsst/Programs.htm
Scholarship Name: Alabama Student Assistance Program. *Academic Area: Open. *Age Group: Undergraduate students. *Eligibility: Applicants must be Alabama residents who are attending one of 80 eligible Alabama institutions of higher education. They also must be able to demonstrate financial need. *Application Process: Applicants should submit the Free Application for Federal Student Aid. Contact your high school guidance office or college financial aid office for further information. *Amount: $300 to $2,500 a year. *Deadline: Contact your guidance counselor or financial aid office for deadline information.

Alabama Commission on Higher Education
PO Box 302000
Montgomery, AL 36130-2000
334-242-1998
http://www.ache.state.al.us/StudentAsst/Programs.htm
Grant Name: Alabama Student Grant Program. *Academic Area: Open. *Age Group: Undergraduate students. *Eligibility: Applicants must be Alabama residents who are attending one of the following colleges: Birmingham-Southern College, Concordia College, Faulkner University, Huntingdon College, Judson College, Miles College, Oakwood College, Samford University, Selma University, Southeastern Bible College, Southern Vocational College, Spring Hill College, Stillman College, or the University of Mobile. Applicants do not need to demonstrate financial need. *Application Process: Applicants should contact the financial aid office at the school they plan to

attend to request an application. *Amount: Up to $1,200 per year. *Deadline: Contact the financial aid office at your school for deadline information.

Alabama Commission on Higher Education
Attn: Dr. William E. Goodwin, Jr.
State Department of Education
PO Box 302101
Montgomery, AL 36130-2101
334-242-9935
http://www.ache.state.al.us/StudentAsst/Programs.htm
Scholarship Name: Mathematics and Science Scholarship For Alabama Teachers. *Academic Area: Education. *Age Group: Undergraduate students. *Eligibility: Applicants must be full-time students pursuing teaching certificates in biology, mathematics, physics, or science (general). They also must attend an Alabama public university and agree to teach for five years in a school system designated as having critical need. *Application Process: Applicants should contact the Alabama Commission on Higher Education to request an application. *Amount: $4,000. *Deadline: Contact your school's financial aid office for deadline information.

Alabama Commission on Higher Education (ACHE)
PO Box 302000
Montgomery, AL 36130-2000
334-242-2273
http://www.ache.state.al.us/StudentAsst/Programs.htm
Scholarship Name: Police Officer's and Firefighter's Survivor's Educational Assistance Program. *Academic Area: Open. *Age Group: Undergraduate students. *Eligibility: Applicants must be the dependent children or spouses of police officers or firefighters who were killed in the line of duty in the state of Alabama. They must attend a public college or university in Alabama. Additional eligibility requirements may apply. Contact the ACHE for further

information. *Application Process: Applicants should contact the ACHE to request an application form. *Amount: Paid tuition, books, fees, and supplies. *Deadline: Contact the ACHE for deadline information.

Alabama Commission on Higher Education
PO Box 302000
Montgomery, AL 36130-2000
334-242-1998
http://www.ache.state.al.us/StudentAsst/Programs.htm
Scholarship Name: Two-Year College Academic Scholarship. *Academic Area: Open. *Age Group: Undergraduate students. *Eligibility: Applicants must be accepted into a public two-year postsecondary institution in the state of Alabama and must demonstrate academic achievement. In-state applicants are given priority. *Application Process: Applicants should contact the financial aid office at the public two-year school they are attending to request an application. *Amount: In-state tuition, plus books. *Deadline: Contact the financial aid office for deadline information.

ALASKA

Alaska Commission on Postsecondary Education
AlaskAdvantage Programs
3030 Vintage Boulevard
Juneau, AK 99801-7100
907-465-2962, 800-441-2962
customer_service@acpe.state.ak.us
http://alaskaadvantage.state.ak.us/page/225
Grant Name: AlaskAdvantage Education Grant. *Academic Area: Open. *Age Group: Undergraduate students. *Eligibility: Applicants must be Alaskan residents and U.S. citizens or permanent resident aliens who are admitted to an undergraduate or vocational certificate program at an approved educational institution in Alaska. They must also be enrolled in a program that qualifies as having a workforce shortage. These programs may change from year to year; in 2005/2006, the eligible programs included allied health science, teaching, and community or social services. Applicants must demonstrate unmet financial need of at least $500 and strong academic achievement. *Application Process: Applicants must submit the Free Application for Federal Student Aid (FAFSA) by April 15 and list at least one qualifying Alaska college or university.

Eligible students will receive notification of their eligibility after they've submitted the FAFSA and the results indicate they have at least $500 in unmet financial need. Contact the commission for further information. *Amount: $500 to $2,000. *Deadline: April 15 (FAFSA application).

Alaska Commission on Postsecondary Education
3030 Vintage Boulevard
Juneau, AK 99801-7100
907-465-6741
http://www.eed.state.ak.us/gearup/scholarship.html
Scholarship Name: GEAR UP Scholarship. *Academic Area: Open. *Age Group: Undergraduate students. *Eligibility: Applicants must have participated in the GEAR UP Programs as a 6th, 7th, or 8th grade student. When these students are high school graduating seniors, they are eligible to apply for this scholarship. Applicants must be less than 22 years old, possess an Alaska high school diploma or GED, and demonstrate financial need. *Application Process: Applicants should complete and submit the Free Application for Federal Student Aid, as well as a completed application. The applicant's Student Aid Report and a copy of their parents' federal income tax form should be submitted along with the application. Visit the commission's Web site to download an application. *Amount: Up to $7,000 a year for four years (full-time students), up to $3,500 a year (half-time students). *Deadline: May 31.

ARIZONA

Arizona Commission for Postsecondary Education
2020 North Central Avenue, Suite 550
Phoenix, AZ 85004
602-258-2435
judi@azhighered.gov
http://www.azhighered.org/acpe_default.aspx?pageid=21
Scholarship Name: Arizona Private Postsecondary Education Student Financial Assistance. *Academic Area: Open. *Age Group: Undergraduate students. *Eligibility: Applicants must be graduates of an Arizona community college who are enrolling full time in a baccalaureate degree-granting private educational institution. They also must demonstrate financial need. *Application Process: Applicants should contact the financial aid office at their private

college or university for details. Individual schools handle applications directly. *Amount: Up to $2,000. *Deadline: Contact the college or university financial aid office for deadline information.

ARKANSAS

Arkansas Department of Higher Education
114 East Capitol Avenue
Little Rock, AR 72201
501-371-2050, 800-54-STUDY
finaid@adhe.arknet.edu
http://www.arkansaschallenge.com
Scholarship Name: Academic Challenge Scholarship. *Academic Area: Open. *Age Group: Undergraduate students. *Eligibility: Applicants must be Arkansas high school graduates (or soon to be graduates) who have taken a core set of requirements during their high school careers and who also meet GPA and ACT score requirements. They must have a family income of less than $60,000 for a family with one child (add $5,000 for each additional child and $10,000 for children in college). Applicants must have taken the following in high school: four units of English, two units of the same foreign language (i.e., two years of Spanish or two years of French, but not one year of each), three units of natural science (with labs), four units of math (one unit beyond algebra II and geometry), and three units of social studies. Applicants should contact their guidance counselor for additional information. Eligibility requirements for GPA and ACT scores are on a sliding scale. The higher your ACT score, the lower the necessary GPA. If you have a lower ACT score, you need to make up for it by demonstrating a higher GPA. Visit the department's Web site to view a complete list of GPA and corresponding ACT requirements. *Application Process: Applicants should apply online. Visit the department's Web site to apply online. *Amount: Up to $12,000 (over four years of college). *Deadline: June 1.

Arkansas Department of Higher Education
Governor's Scholars Program
114 East Capitol Avenue
Little Rock, AR 72201
501-371-2050, 800-54-STUDY
finaid@adhe.arknet.edu
http://www.arkansasgovernorsscholarship.com
Scholarship Name: Governor's Scholar Program. *Academic Area: Open. *Age Group: Undergraduate students. *Eligibility: Applicants must have maintained at least a 3.5 high school GPA or received an ACT composite score of 27 (or a combined SAT score of 1220). They must also demonstrate leadership skills and enroll full time at a public or private college or university in Arkansas. The student or one parent must be a resident of the state of Arkansas for at least six months prior to the deadline, and the applicant must be a U.S. citizen or permanent resident alien. *Application Process: Applicants must apply online. Visit the department's Web site to apply online. *Amount: $4,000 to $10,000. *Deadline: February 1.

CALIFORNIA

California Student Aid Commission
PO Box 419027
Rancho Cordova, CA 95741-9027
888-224-7268
http://www.csac.ca.gov/doc.asp?ID=20
Grant Name: Cal Grant Entitlement Award. *Academic Area: Open. *Age Group: Undergraduate students. *Eligibility: Applicants must be residents of the state of California who are pursuing or intend to pursue a college degree. They must also be able to demonstrate financial need and academic achievement. *Application Process: Applicants must submit the Free Application for Federal Student Aid by March 2 of each year. Applicants must also file a verified grade point average with the California Student Aid Commission no later than March 2. Check with your school to see if it automatically files your verified grade point average. If it does not, you must request a verified form be sent to the commission. Contact the commission for additional information. *Amount: Awards vary. *Deadline: March 2.

California Student Aid Commission
PO Box 419027
Rancho Cordova, CA 95741-9027
888-224-7268
http://www.csac.ca.gov/doc.asp?id=110
Grant Name: Child Development Grant Program. *Academic Area: Education. *Age Group: Undergraduate students. *Eligibility: Applicants must plan to enroll at least part time in a child development program with the intention of pursuing a career as a teacher, site supervisor, or program director.

Applicants must commit to serving at least one year of full-time service in a licensed children's center for each year they receive the grant. A contract must be signed, and duty must be met to avoid having to repay the funds. Applicants must be able to demonstrate financial need. *Application Process: Applications are available for download from the commission's Web site in early spring of each year. Visit the commission's Web site to download an application. *Amount: Awards vary. *Deadline: Contact the commission for deadline information.

COLORADO

Colorado Commission on Higher Education
c/o CollegeInvest
1801 Broadway, Suite 1300
Denver, CO 80202
303-295-1981, 800-COLLEGE
cic@collegeinvest.org
http://www.collegeinvest.org/Scholarships/CICgeneral.htm
Scholarship Name: College in Colorado Scholarship. *Academic Area: Open. *Age Group: Undergraduate students. *Eligibility: Applicants must apply during their eighth, ninth, or 10th grade years of junior high or high school. Applicants must be legal Colorado residents who will qualify for in-state resident college tuition and must maintain a minimum 2.5 GPA for all classes taken in grades nine through 12. They must meet all of the state higher education admissions requirements. Visit the organization's Web site to view a complete list of high school course requirements, or contact your guidance counselor for additional information. Applicants must demonstrate financial need and attend a public college or university in Colorado. *Application Process: Applicants must submit a completed application during their 8th, 9th, or 10th grade years of junior high or high school. They must also complete the Free Application for Federal Student Aid upon graduating from high school and must be eligible for a Pell Grant (family income approximately $40,000 or less for a family of four). Applicants must also apply (after graduating high school) for a College Opportunity Fund stipend and attend a college or university in Colorado that accepts this stipend. Visit the organization's Web site to download an application. *Amount: Up to $1,500 per year. *Deadline: June 1.

Colorado Commission on Higher Education
1380 Lawrence Street, Suite 1200
Denver, CO 80204
303-866-2723
CCHE@state.co.us
http://www.state.co.us/cche/finaid/students/stateaid/eligibility.html
Grant Name: Colorado Student Grant. *Academic Area: Open. *Age Group: Undergraduate students. *Eligibility: Applicants must be residents of the state of Colorado and enrolled in or planning to enroll in an eligible program at an eligible Colorado college or university. They must also demonstrate financial need. *Application Process: Applicants should contact their college or university for information about the application process. All applications are distributed through the financial aid offices of individual institutions. *Amount: Awards vary. *Deadline: Contact your financial aid office for deadline information.

Colorado Commission on Higher Education
1380 Lawrence Street, Suite 1200
Denver, CO 80204
303-866-2723
CCHE@state.co.us
http://www.collegeincolorado.org/FinAid/Steps/colorado_scholarships.asp
Scholarship Name: Colorado Undergraduate Merit Scholarship. *Academic Area: Open. *Age Group: Undergraduate students. *Eligibility: Applicants must be residents of the state of Colorado and enrolled in or planning to enroll in an eligible program at an eligible Colorado college or university. They also must demonstrate exceptional academic achievement by having a GPA of at least 3.0. *Application Process: Applicants should contact their college or university for information about the application process. All applications are distributed through the financial aid offices of individual institutions. *Amount: Awards vary. *Deadline: Contact your financial aid office for deadline information.

Colorado Commission on Higher Education
1380 Lawrence Street, Suite 1200
Denver, CO 80204
303-866-2723
gos@cche.state.co.us
http://www.state.co.us/cche/finaid/gos/brochure.pdf
Scholarship Name: Governor's Opportunity Scholarship. *Academic Area: Open. *Age Group: Undergraduate

students. *Eligibility: Applicants must be Colorado residents and U.S. citizens or permanent residents who can demonstrate high financial need, as shown on the student's Student Aid Report by an Expected Family Contribution of 0. Applicants must enroll as full-time, degree seeking students at one of 30 participating two- and four-year colleges and universities in Colorado. They must also agree not to take out any student loans while receiving the Governor's Opportunity Scholarship. *Application Process: Applicants should apply for admission at a participating college and complete the Free Application for Federal Student Aid (FAFSA). The financial aid office at the participating school will automatically consider you for the scholarship if the FAFSA requirements, and additional requirements, are met. The financial aid award letter from the college will tell you if you have been awarded a Governor's Opportunity Scholarship. Visit the commission's Web site to view a complete list of participating colleges and universities. *Amount: Up to $10,700 per year. *Deadline: May 1 (FAFSA).

CONNECTICUT

Connecticut Department of Higher Education
61 Woodland Street
Hartford, CT 06105-2326
860-947-1855, 800-842-0229
csp@ctdhe.org
http://www.ctdhe.org/SFA/sfa.htm
Scholarship Name: Capitol Scholarship. *Academic Area: Open. *Age Group: Undergraduate students. *Eligibility: Applicants must be high school graduating seniors or recent high school graduates with a class rank in the top 20 percent of their class or an SAT score of at least 1800. They must also be residents of Connecticut and U.S. citizens who plan to attend a college in Connecticut or a college located outside of Connecticut that has a reciprocity agreement with Connecticut. Applicants must be able to demonstrate financial need. *Application Process: Applicants should contact their high school guidance counselor. All applications must be filed through a high school guidance office. *Amount: Up to $3,000. *Deadline: February 15.

Connecticut Department of Higher Education
61 Woodland Street
Hartford, CT 06105-2326

860-947-1855, 800-842-0229
csp@ctdhe.org
http://www.ctdhe.org/SFA/sfa.htm
Scholarship Name: Connecticut Aid for Public College Students. *Academic Area: Open. *Age Group: Undergraduate students. *Eligibility: Applicants must be residents of the state of Connecticut who are attending (or planning to attend) a Connecticut public college or university and who can demonstrate unmet financial need. *Application Process: Applicants should contact the financial aid office at the college or university they are attending (or plan to attend). All applications are handled directly through the college financial aid office. Applicants should submit the Free Application for Federal Student Aid by the deadline in order to demonstrate their financial need. *Amount: Awards vary. *Deadline: Contact the college financial aid office for deadline information.

Connecticut Department of Higher Education
61 Woodland Street
Hartford, CT 06105-2326
860-947-1855, 800-842-0229
csp@ctdhe.org
http://www.ctdhe.org/SFA/sfa.htm
Grant Name: Connecticut Independent College Student Grant Program. *Academic Area: Open. *Age Group: Undergraduate students. *Eligibility: Applicants must be residents of the state of Connecticut who are attending (or planning to attend) an independent college or university in Connecticut. They must also be able to demonstrate unmet financial need. *Application Process: Applicants should contact the financial aid office at the college or university they are attending (or plan to attend). All applications are handled directly through the college financial aid office. Applicants should submit the Free Application for Federal Student Aid by the deadline in order to demonstrate their financial need. *Amount: Up to $8,500. *Deadline: Contact the college financial aid office for deadline information.

Connecticut Department of Higher Education
61 Woodland Street
Hartford, CT 06105-2326
860-947-1855, 800-842-0229
mtip@ctdhe.org
http://www.ctdhe.org/SFA/pdfs/MTIP%20Brochure%20and%20Form.pdf

Grant Name: Minority Teacher Incentive Grant Program. *Academic Area: Education. *Age Group: Undergraduate students. *Eligibility: Applicants must be full-time college juniors or seniors who belong to a minority group and who are enrolled in a Connecticut college or university teacher preparation program. They must intend to teach within the public school system in Connecticut and be nominated by the dean of their department. *Application Process: Applicants should contact the dean of the education department and request that he or she submit a nomination form for the application. The nomination form is available for download from the Connecticut Department of Higher Education's Web site. For further information, applicants should contact the department. *Amount: Up to $5,000/year for two years (grant). This award will also provide a loan reimbursement of $2,500/year for up to four years of teaching in a Connecticut public school. *Deadline: October 1.

DELAWARE

Delaware Higher Education Commission
Carvel State Office Building, 820 North French Street
Wilmington, DE 19801
302-577-5240, 800-292-7935
DHEC@doe.k12.de.us
http://www.doe.k12.de.us/high-ed/barnes.htm
Scholarship Name: B. Bradford Barnes Memorial Scholarship. *Academic Area: Open. *Age Group: Undergraduate students. *Eligibility: Applicants must be graduating high school seniors in the upper quarter of their classes who are legal residents of the state of Delaware, and who have achieved a combined SAT score of 1800. They must also intend on enrolling full time at the University of Delaware. *Application Process: Applicants should apply online or request a paper application by mail. Visit the department's Web site to apply online. *Amount: Full tuition, fees, room, board, and books. *Deadline: February 6.

Delaware Higher Education Commission
Carvel State Office Building, 820 North French Street
Wilmington, DE 19801
302-577-5240, 800-292-7935
DHEC@doe.k12.de.us
http://www.doe.k12.de.us/high-ed/hebner.htm
Scholarship Name: Charles L. Hebner Memorial Scholarship. *Academic Area: Humanities, political science, social sciences. *Age Group: Undergraduate students. *Eligibility: Applicants must be graduating high school seniors in the upper half of their classes who have achieved a combined SAT score of 1350. Applicants must be legal residents of Delaware and intend on enrolling full time at the University of Delaware or Delaware State University in a humanities or social sciences degree program. Preference is given to political science majors. *Application Process: Applicants should apply online or request a paper application by mail. Visit the commission's Web site to apply online. *Amount: Full tuition, fees, room, board, and books. *Deadline: March 13.

Delaware Higher Education Commission
Carvel State Office Building, 820 North French Street
Wilmington, DE 19801
302-577-5240, 800-292-7935
DHEC@doe.k12.de.us
http://www.doe.k12.de.us/high-ed/christa.htm
Loan Name: Christa McAuliffe Teacher Scholarship Loan. *Academic Area: Education. *Age Group: Undergraduate students. *Eligibility: Applicants must be U.S. citizens, legal residents of Delaware, and enrolled as full-time students (or planning to enroll) at a Delaware college or university in a teacher certification program. Applicants who are high school graduating seniors must be in the upper half of their class, with a combined SAT score of at least 1570, while enrolled undergraduate students must have maintained at least a 2.75 cumulative GPA in any completed college course work. Applicants who plan to teach in critical needs areas (as defined by the Delaware Department of Education) are given preference. Visit the department's Web site for a current list of critical needs areas. *Application Process: Applicants should apply online or request a paper application by mail. Visit the department's Web site to apply online. *Amount: Tuition, fees, and expenses. The award is distributed as a loan. For each year of teaching in a Delaware public school, one year of the loan is forgiven (need not be paid back). *Deadline: March 31.

Delaware Higher Education Commission
Carvel State Office Building, 820 North French Street
Wilmington, DE 19801
302-577-5240, 800-292-7935
DHEC@doe.k12.de.us
http://www.doe.k12.de.us/high-ed/nursing.htm

Scholarship Name: Delaware Nursing Incentive Program. *Academic Area: Nursing (open). *Age Group: Undergraduate students, professionals. *Eligibility: Applicants must be legal residents of Delaware who are enrolled as full-time students (or planning to enroll as full-time students) in an accredited program leading to a registered nurse (RN) or licensed practical nurse (LPN) certification. Registered nurses may also enroll in bachelor of science in nursing (B.S.N.) programs. High school graduating seniors must rank in the upper half of their class and possess a 2.5 minimum GPA. Employed RNs with five or more years of experience, who are working in the state of Delaware, may enroll in a BSN program on a part-time basis, and do not have to be Delaware residents to qualify. *Application Process: Applicants should apply online or request a paper application by mail. Visit the commission's Web site to apply online. *Amount: Full tuition, fees, and expenses. This award is distributed as a loan. The loan will be forgiven (meaning it doesn't have to be paid back) under the following condition: for each year the loan was received, the recipient must work for a year in a state-owned hospital or clinic. *Deadline: March 31.

Delaware Higher Education Commission
Carvel State Office Building, 820 North French Street
Wilmington, DE 19801
302-577-5240, 800-292-7935
DHEC@doe.k12.de.us
http://www.doe.k12.de.us/high-ed/diamond.htm
Scholarship Name: Diamond State Scholarship. *Academic Area: Open. *Age Group: Undergraduate students. *Eligibility: Applicants must be graduating high school seniors who rank in the upper quarter of their high school class. Applicants must also be legal residents of the state of Delaware, have a combined SAT score of at least 1800, and enroll as full-time students in a degree program at a nonprofit, regionally accredited college or university. *Application Process: Applicants should apply online or request a paper application by mail. Visit the commission's Web site to apply online. *Amount: $1,250. *Deadline: March 31.

Delaware Higher Education Commission
Carvel State Office Building, 820 North French Street
Wilmington, DE 19801
302-577-5240, 800-292-7935
DHEC@doe.k12.de.us
http://www.doe.k12.de.us/high-ed/holloway.htm

Scholarship Name: Herman M. Holloway, Sr. Memorial Scholarship. *Academic Area: Open. *Age Group: Undergraduate students. *Eligibility: Applicants must be graduating high school seniors who are U.S. citizens and legal residents of the state of Delaware. They also must intend to enroll full time at Delaware State University and possess a combined SAT score of at least 1350. *Application Process: Applicants must either apply online or request a paper application by mail. The Free Application for Federal Student Aid must be filed prior to the application deadline. Visit the commission's Web site to apply online. *Amount: Full tuition, fees, room, and board for one year. *Deadline: March 13.

Delaware Higher Education Commission
Carvel State Office Building, 820 North French Street
Wilmington, DE 19801
302-577-5240, 800-292-7935
DHEC@doe.k12.de.us
http://www.doe.k12.de.us/high-ed/essay.htm
Scholarship Name: Legislative Essay Scholarship. *Academic Area: Open. *Age Group: Undergraduate students. *Eligibility: Applicants must be graduating high school seniors in public, private, or home school programs in Delaware who are planning to enroll full time at a public college or university in Delaware. *Application Process: Applicants should submit an essay addressing the current year's topic, which can be found on the commission's Web site. *Amount: $750 (62 district award winners); $7,500, $3,750, and $2,250 for first through third place, statewide. *Deadline: December 1.

Delaware Higher Education Commission
Carvel State Office Building, 820 North French Street
Wilmington, DE 19801
302-577-5240, 800-292-7935
DHEC@doe.k12.de.us
http://www.doe.k12.de.us/high-ed/scip.htm
Scholarship Name: Scholarship Incentive Program. *Academic Area: Open. *Age Group: Undergraduate students. *Eligibility: Applicants must be legal residents of the state of Delaware who can demonstrate financial need (according to their Free Application for Federal Student Aid report). Applicants must be enrolled as full-time students at nonprofit, regionally accredited colleges or universities in Delaware or Pennsylvania. Applicants must also maintain a GPA of at least 2.5. Exceptions will be made for students attending schools outside of this

region if a student's major isn't available at a public college in the region. The program is also open to graduate students. *Application Process: Applicants should submit the Free Application for Federal Student Aid no later than April 15. Residents of Delaware are automatically considered for this award. Eligible candidates will be notified of the deadline to submit their college information, major, and grades. *Amount: $700 to $2,200. *Deadline: April 15.

Delaware Higher Education Commission
Carvel State Office Building
820 North French Street
Wilmington, DE 19801
302-577-5240, 800-292-7935
DHEC@doe.k12.de.us
http://seedscholarship.delaware.gov
Scholarship Name: Student Excellence Equals Degree Scholarship. *Academic Area: Open. *Age Group: Undergraduate students. *Eligibility: Applicants must be Delaware graduating high school seniors who have a GPA of at least 2.5 and do not have any felony convictions. Applicants must intend to enroll as full-time students in an associate degree program at Delaware Technical and Community College or the Associate of Arts program at the University of Delaware. *Application Process: Applicants must complete the Free Application for Federal Student Aid to be eligible—even if the student doesn't think he or she will be eligible for need-based aid. Applicants should then apply for admission to the institution of their choice. Students should contact the college's financial aid office for further information. *Amount: Full tuition. *Deadline: Contact the school's financial aid office for deadline information.

Delaware Higher Education Commission
Carvel State Office Building, 820 North French Street
Wilmington, DE 19801
302-577-5240, 800-292-7935
DHEC@doe.k12.de.us
http://www.doe.k12.de.us/high-ed/teacher.corps.htm
Loan Name: Teacher Corps Loans. *Academic Area: Education. *Age Group: Undergraduate students. *Eligibility: Applicants must be legal residents of Delaware who are enrolled (or planning to enroll) as full-time students at a public Delaware college or university in a teacher certification program in an area that has critical need. Students intending to teach middle or high school math or science are given first priority, while special education is given second priority. Applicants who are high school graduating seniors must be in the upper half of their class, with a combined SAT score of at least 1570, while enrolled undergraduate students must have maintained at least a 2.75 cumulative GPA in any completed college course work. Visit the department's Web site for a current list of critical needs areas. *Application Process: Applicants should apply online or request a paper application by mail. Visit the department's Web site to apply online. *Amount: Paid tuition. The award is distributed as a loan. For each year of teaching in a Delaware public school, one year of the loan is forgiven (need not be paid back). *Deadline: March 31.

FLORIDA

Florida Department of Education
Office of Student Financial Assistance-State Programs
1940 North Monroe Street, Suite 70
Tallahassee, FL 32303-4759
888-827-2004
osfa@fldoe.org
http://www.firn.edu/doe/bin00065/ablefactsheet.htm
Grant Name: Access to Better Learning and Education Grant. *Academic Area: Open. *Age Group: Undergraduate students. *Eligibility: Applicants must be Florida residents for at least 12 months prior to receiving funding, have no other bachelor's degrees, and enroll full time in an eligible Florida college or university baccalaureate program. Visit the department's Web site for a complete listing of eligible institutions. Each institution has additional eligibility requirements. Applicants should contact the financial aid office at their college or university for eligibility information. *Application Process: Applicants should contact the financial aid office at their college or university to receive an application. A complete listing of eligible Florida colleges and universities can be found at the Florida Department of Education's Web site. *Amount: Awards vary. *Deadline: Contact your school's financial aid office for deadline information.

Florida Department of Education
Office of Student Financial Assistance-State Programs
1940 North Monroe Street, Suite 70
Tallahassee, FL 32303-4759
888-827-2004
osfa@fldoe.org

http://www.firn.edu/doe/bin00065/ethicfactsheet.htm

Scholarship Name: Ethics in Business Scholarship Program. *Academic Area: Open. *Age Group: Undergraduate students. *Eligibility: Applicants must be Florida residents for at least 12 months prior to receiving funding and must enroll in an eligible community college or private Florida college or university. Visit the department's Web site for a complete listing of eligible institutions. Each institution has additional eligibility requirements. Applicants should contact the financial aid office at their college or university for further eligibility information. *Application Process: Applicants should contact the financial aid office at their college or university to request additional information. A complete listing of eligible Florida colleges and universities can be found at the Florida Department of Education's Web site. *Amount: Awards vary. *Deadline: Contact your school's financial aid office for deadline information.

Florida Department of Education

Office of Student Financial Assistance-State Programs

1940 North Monroe Street, Suite 70

Tallahassee, FL 32303-4759

888-827-2004

osfa@fldoe.org

http://www.firn.edu/doe/brfutures/bffactsheet.htm

Scholarship Name: Florida Bright Futures Scholarship Program. *Academic Area: Open. *Age Group: Undergraduate students. *Eligibility: Applicants must be Florida residents for at least 12 months prior to the first day of classes, U.S. citizens or eligible noncitizens (as determined by the college or university), and they must demonstrate academic achievement by maintaining a GPA of at least 2.75. Applicants must also complete the Florida Financial Aid Application during their senior year of high school (at any time after December 1 and before graduation). Three different awards are distributed under this program. The Florida Academic Scholars Award (FAS) is the highest honor and award. Applicants must have a 3.0 GPA to be eligible. The Florida Medallion Scholars Award (FMS) and the Florida Gold Seal Vocational Scholars Award (GSV) both require a minimum 2.75 GPA. *Application Process: Applicants must visit http://www.FloridaStudentFinancialAid.org to complete the online application for financial aid. This must be done after December 1, but before high school graduation. Submitting this application allows the Florida Department of Education to evaluate an applicant's high school transcripts and standardized test scores. Tuition awards are based on public institutions' tuition rates. If an applicant chooses to attend a private institution, he or she will receive tuition based on a public institution's rates only. *Amount: Full tuition and up to $300 per semester in fees, plus a $300 stipend. The top scholars in each county will receive an extra $750 per semester (FAS); 75 percent tuition, plus up to $300 in fees (FMS and GSV). *Deadline: Contact the department for specific deadline information. Applicants must apply prior to high school graduation.

Florida Department of Education

Office of Student Financial Assistance-State Programs

1940 North Monroe Street, Suite 70

Tallahassee, FL 32303-4759

888-827-2004

osfa@fldoe.org

http://www.firn.edu/doe/bin00065/fsagfactsheet.htm

Grant Name: Florida Student Assistance Grant. *Academic Area: Open. *Age Group: Undergraduate students. *Eligibility: Applicants must be Florida residents for at least 12 months prior to receiving funding, have no other bachelor's degrees, and enroll full time in an eligible Florida college or university baccalaureate program. This grant is divided into three areas that include state universities and public community colleges, private (nonprofit) colleges and universities, and private universities that are not covered by the Florida Private Student Assistance Grant. Applicants must demonstrate financial need in order to receive this grant. Visit the department's Web site for a complete listing of eligible institutions. Each institution also has additional eligibility requirements. Applicants should contact the financial aid office at their college or university for further eligibility information. Additionally, the Talented Twenty Program guarantees students in the top 20 percent of their classes (who also qualify financially for this program) admission to one of the 11 state universities as well as priority funding under this program. *Application Process: Applicants should submit the Free Application for Federal Student Aid by the deadline. They should also contact the financial aid office at their college or university to request additional information. A complete listing of eligible Florida colleges and universities can be found at the Florida Department of Education's Web site. *Amount: Awards vary. *Deadline: Contact your school's financial aid office for deadline information.

Florida Department of Education

Office of Student Financial Assistance-State Programs
1940 North Monroe Street, Suite 70
Tallahassee, FL 32303-4759
888-827-2004
osfa@fldoe.org
http://www.firn.edu/doe/bin00065/jmfactsheet.htm

Grant Name: José Martí Scholarship Challenge Grant. *Academic Area: Open. *Age Group: Undergraduate students. *Eligibility: Applicants must be residents of Florida for at least 12 months prior to receiving the scholarship and be of Hispanic descent, born in or having at least one parent born in Mexico, Spain, or any other Caribbean, Central, or South American country. They must also be U.S. citizens or eligible noncitizens (individual colleges can provide information on what it means to be an eligible non-citizen). Applicants must enroll in full-time study, and demonstrate academic achievement by maintaining at least a 3.0 GPA. Preference is given to high school graduating seniors, but students up to graduate level can apply. *Application Process: Applicants should submit a Florida Financial Aid Application by April 1 of the year prior to college enrollment. They must also submit the Free Application for Federal Student Aid (FAFSA) no later than May 15. Qualified applicants will be notified of further instructions to receive the award. Contact your school's financial aid office with questions or to request further information. Questions can also be directed to the Florida Department of Education's hotline. *Amount: $2,000. *Deadline: April 1 (Florida Financial Aid Application), May 15 (FAFSA).

Florida Department of Education

Office of Student Financial Assistance-State Programs
1940 North Monroe Street, Suite 70
Tallahassee, FL 32303-4759
888-827-2004
osfa@fldoe.org
http://www.firn.edu/doe/bin00065/mmbfactsheet.htm

Scholarship Name: Mary McLeod Bethune Scholarship. *Academic Area: Open. *Age Group: Undergraduate students. *Eligibility: Applicants must attend one of four colleges in the state of Florida: Bethune-Cookman College, Edward Waters College, Florida A&M University, or Florida Memorial University. They must also demonstrate financial need, reside in Florida for at least 12 months before attending college, and demonstrate academic achievement by maintaining a 3.0 GPA. *Application Process: Applicants should contact their college of choice's

financial aid office to request an application and any additional information on the application process. *Amount: $3,000. *Deadline: Contact the college or university financial aid office for deadline information.

Florida Department of Education

Office of Student Financial Assistance-State Programs
1940 North Monroe Street, Suite 70
Tallahassee, FL 32303-4759
888-827-2004
osfa@fldoe.org
http://www.firn.edu/doe/bin00065/fragfactsheet.htm

Grant Name: William L. Boyd, IV, Florida Resident Access Grant. *Academic Area: Open. *Age Group: Undergraduate students. *Eligibility: Applicants must be Florida residents for at least 12 months prior to receiving funding, have no other bachelor's degrees, and enroll full time in an eligible Florida college or university baccalaureate program. This grant funds education at private, nonprofit institutions in Florida. Applicants must not be majoring in theology or divinity. Visit the department's Web site for a complete listing of eligible institutions. Each institution also has additional eligibility requirements. Applicants should contact the financial aid office at their college or university for eligibility information. *Application Process: Applicants should contact the financial aid office at their college or university to receive an application. A complete listing of eligible Florida colleges and universities can be found at the Florida Department of Education's Web site. *Amount: Awards vary. *Deadline: Contact your school's financial aid office for deadline information.

GEORGIA

Georgia Student Finance Commission

2082 East Exchange Place, Suite 230
Tucker, GA 30084
770-724-9000, 800-505-4732
http://gacollege411.org/FinAid/ScholarshipsAndGrants/mcdaniel_teacher_scholarship.asp

Scholarship Name: Charles McDaniel Teacher Scholarship. *Academic Area: Education. *Age Group: Undergraduate students. *Eligibility: Applicants must be full-time college juniors or seniors who are attending a public college or university in Georgia, have attended a public high school in Georgia, been admitted to the department of education's teacher education program, and have a minimum 3.25 cumulative GPA. They must also be legal residents of Georgia; U.S. citizens, nationals, or permanent resident aliens who are registered with the Selective Service (if required to do so); and not be in default in any financial aid program. *Application Process: Applicants should contact their department head to request an application, or they can visit the commission's Web site to download an application. Each institution can only have one applicant per year, so interested candidates should make known their intentions to the department head in the education department as soon as possible. The application requires sections to be completed by the education department, financial aid office, and the applicant. *Amount: $1,000. *Deadline: July 15.

Georgia Student Finance Commission
2082 East Exchange Place, Suite 230
Tucker, GA 30084
770-724-9000, 800-505-4732
http://gacollege411.org/FinAid/ScholarshipsAndGrants/
    governors_scholarship.asp
Scholarship Name: Governor's Scholarship Program. *Academic Area: Open. *Age Group: Undergraduate students. *Eligibility: Applicants must be graduating high school seniors in Georgia who are either the valedictorians of their classes or STAR Students. They must enroll full time in a college or university in Georgia within nine months of graduation and must not be receiving financial aid that totals more than the cost of college. Applicants must be legal residents of Georgia; U.S. citizens, nationals, or permanent resident aliens who are registered with the Selective Service (if required to do so); and not be in default in any financial aid program. *Application Process: Applications are mailed to every valedictorian and STAR student. Applicants must return the completed application to the financial aid office of the Georgia college or university they plan to attend. If you believe you should have received an application and did not, contact your high school guidance counselor. *Amount: Up to $900. *Deadline: Contact your guidance counselor for deadline information.

Georgia Student Finance Commission
2082 East Exchange Place, Suite 230
Tucker, GA 30084
770-724-9000, 800-505-4732
http://gacollege411.org/FinAid/ScholarshipsAndGrants/
    HOPEScholarship/default.asp

Scholarship Name: Helping Outstanding Pupils Educationally (HOPE) Scholarship. *Academic Area: Open. *Age Group: Undergraduate students. *Eligibility: Applicants must be graduating high school seniors or first-time entering freshmen who are Georgia residents and who are enrolled (or planning to enroll) in an eligible Georgia college, university, or technical school. They must be legal residents of Georgia; U.S. citizens, nationals, or permanent resident aliens who are registered with the Selective Service (if required to do so); and not be in default in any financial aid program. Applicants must have maintained a 3.0 high school GPA (or a 3.2 GPA for technical school applicants). There is no financial need requirement. Visit the commission's Web site to view a complete list of eligible institutions. *Application Process: Applicants who are attending a public college or university should file the Free Application for Federal Student Aid as early after January 1 as possible. If you file this application, you are automatically considered for the Hope Scholarship as well as Pell Grants and more. If you do not wish to be considered for other forms of aid, but still want to apply for the Hope Scholarship, you can submit an online application for the Hope Scholarship only, or download a paper application at the commission's scholarship Web site. Applicants attending private colleges in Georgia must complete a separate application that can be filed online or downloaded from the commission's Web site. *Amount: Full tuition, plus $150/semester book allowance (public institutions), $1,500/semester (private institutions). *Deadline: Contact the financial aid office of your college or university for priority filing dates and deadline information.

HAWAII

University of Hawaii Board of Regents
Student Equity, Excellence and Diversity Office
University of Hawaii-Manoa
Queen Liliuokalani Center for Student Services, 2600
    Campus Road, #413
    Honolulu, HI 96822
808-956-4642
seed@hawaii.edu
http://www.hawaii.edu/diversity/scholarships/index.htm
Scholarship Name: The University of Hawaii Board of Regents serves as the student financial assistance agency in Hawaii. It awards Presidential Scholarships for two years of undergraduate study. *Academic Area: Open. *Age Group: Undergraduate students.

*Eligibility: Applicants must be incoming college juniors who have a GPA of at least 3.7 and demonstrate superior academic achievement or creativity. They must also be residents of Hawaii. *Application Process: The scholarship program is administered by the Student Equity, Excellence and Diversity Office at the University of Hawaii-Manoa. Contact the office for application details. *Amount: Tuition waiver, $2,000 per semester, plus a one-time travel grant of $2,000 (must be used before graduation). *Deadline: Contact the office for deadline information.

University of Hawaii Board of Regents

Student Equity, Excellence and Diversity Office
University of Hawaii-Manoa
Queen Liliuokalani Center for Student Services, 2600
    Campus Road, #413
    Honolulu, HI 96822
808-956-4642
seed@hawaii.edu
http://www.hawaii.edu/diversity/scholarships/index.htm
Scholarship Name: The University of Hawaii Board of Regents serves as the student financial assistance agency in Hawaii. It awards Regents Scholarships for four years of undergraduate study. *Academic Area: Open. *Age Group: Undergraduate students. *Eligibility: Applicants must be high school seniors who have at least a 1300 combined mathematics and verbal ACT score, have at least a 3.5 GPA for grades nine through 11, and demonstrate "remarkable" achievement in extracurricular activities. They must also be residents of Hawaii. *Application Process: The scholarship program is administered by the Student Equity, Excellence and Diversity Office at the University of Hawaii-Manoa. Contact the office for application details. *Amount: Tuition waiver, $2,000 per semester, plus a one-time travel grant of $2,000 (must be used before graduation). *Deadline: Contact the office for deadline information.

IDAHO

Idaho State Board of Education

Attn: Dana Kelly, Student Affairs Program Manager
PO Box 83720
Boise, ID 83720-0037
208-332-1574
dana.kelly@osbe.idaho.gov
http://www.boardofed.idaho.gov/scholarships/
    challenge.asp

Scholarship Name: Governor's Challenge Scholarship. *Academic Area: Open. *Age Group: Undergraduate students. *Eligibility: Applicants must be graduating high school seniors of an Idaho high school, who intend to enroll as full-time students in an academic or professional-technical program at an Idaho college or university. They must also demonstrate academic achievement by maintaining at least a 2.8 GPA as well as a commitment to community service (participation in volunteer work and public service must be documented). *Application Process: Applicants should visit the department's Web site to apply online. *Amount: $3,000. *Deadline: February 14.

Idaho State Board of Education

Attn: Dana Kelly, Student Affairs Program Manager
PO Box 83720
Boise, ID 83720-0037
208-332-1574
dana.kelly@osbe.idaho.gov
http://www.boardofed.idaho.gov/scholarships/minority.
    asp
Scholarship Name: Minority and At-Risk Student Scholarship. *Academic Area: Open. *Age Group: Undergraduate students. *Eligibility: Applicants must be U.S. citizens and residents of the state of Idaho as well as graduates of an Idaho high school. They must also meet three of the following criteria: be a first-generation college student, be disabled, be a migrant farm worker or a dependent of a migrant farm worker, demonstrate substantial financial need, or be a member of a traditionally underrepresented (in higher education) ethnic minority. Applicants must also attend one of the following eight eligible institutions in Idaho: Albertson College, Boise State University, Idaho State University, Lewis-Clark State College, University of Idaho, College of Southern Idaho, North Idaho College, or Eastern Idaho Technical College. *Application Process: Applicants should contact the financial aid office at their college of choice to request additional information and a scholarship application. *Amount: Up to $3,000. *Deadline: Contact the financial aid office at the college or university of your choice for deadline information.

Idaho State Board of Education

Contact: Dana Kelly, Student Affairs Program Manager
PO Box 83720
Boise, ID 83720-0037
208-332-1574
dana.kelly@osbe.idaho.gov

http://www.boardofed.idaho.gov/scholarships/
promisea.asp

Scholarship Name: Robert R. Lee Promise Category A Scholarship. *Academic Area: Open. *Age Group: Undergraduate students. *Eligibility: Applicants must be graduating high school seniors of an Idaho high school who intend to enroll as full-time students in an academic or professional-technical program at an eligible Idaho college or university. They must also be Idaho residents who are in the top 10 percent of their graduating class, with a GPA of at least 3.5, and an ACT score of at least 28. *Application Process: Applicants should apply visit the board's Web site to apply online. *Amount: $3,000. *Deadline: February 14.

ILLINOIS

Illinois Student Assistance Commission
Attn: Marcia Franklin
c/o Illinois Department of Public Health
Center for Rural Health
535 West Jefferson Street
Springfield, IL 62761-0001
217-782-1624
http://www.collegezone.com/studentzone/416_1502.htm

Scholarship Name: Allied Health Care Professional Scholarship. *Academic Area: Medicine (physician assisting), nursing (nurse practitioner), nursing (midwifery). *Age Group: Undergraduate students. *Eligibility: Applicants must be pursuing an education that will prepare them to work as nurse practitioners, physician assistants, or nurse midwives at accredited institutions in Illinois. They must be residents of Illinois, enrolled or accepted into a program, and able to demonstrate financial need. Applicants must agree to work in the state of Illinois (in an area designed as having critical need) an equal number of years for which funds were received in order to avoid having to repay the funds. *Application Process: Applicants should apply through their school's financial aid department by the school's predetermined deadline. Applicants must also submit a completed application. Visit the commission's Web site to download an application. *Amount: $7,500 (for up to two years). *Deadline: June 30.

Illinois Student Assistance Commission
c/o Illinois State Board of Education
100 North First Street

Springfield, IL 62777
866-262-6663
http://www.collegezone.com/studentzone/416_1496.htm

Scholarship Name: General Assembly Scholarship. *Academic Area: Open. *Age Group: Undergraduate students. *Eligibility: Applicants must be enrolled at an Illinois four-year, state-supported college or university and must meet additional eligibility standards set by the legislative member of their district. Interested candidates should contact their district legislative member for additional eligibility requirements. Applicants must apply only through the district in which they maintain residence. Visit the commission's Web site for a complete list of county officials and contact instructions. *Application Process: Applicants must contact the appropriate legislative official for their district of residence to apply. *Amount: Awards vary. *Deadline: Contact your district legislator for deadline information.

Illinois Student Assistance Commission
1755 Lake Cook Road
Deerfield, IL 60015-5209
847-948-8500, 800-899-4722
http://www.collegezone.com/studentzone/416_945.htm

Scholarship Name: Illinois Future Teacher Corps Program. *Academic Area: Education. *Age Group: Undergraduate students. *Eligibility: Applicants must be Illinois residents and U.S. citizens or eligible noncitizens who can demonstrate financial need. They must also be high school graduates or GED certificate holders, be enrolled in a teacher certification program, and maintain at least a 2.5 GPA. Applicants must commit to teaching in the state of Illinois for a period of five years in order to receive these funds as a scholarship. If the obligation is not fulfilled, the funds turn into a loan that must be repaid. The grant is also available to graduate students. *Application Process: Applicants must apply online. Visit the organization's Web site to complete the interactive online application. Before completing the scholarship application process, applicants should submit the Free Application for Federal Student Aid. *Amount: Up to $10,000. *Deadline: March 1.

Illinois Student Assistance Commission
1755 Lake Cook Road
Deerfield, IL 60015-5209
847-948-8500, 800-899-4722
http://www.collegezone.com/studentzone/416_949.htm

Scholarship Name: Merit Recognition Scholarship Program. *Academic Area: Open. *Age Group: Undergraduate students. *Eligibility: Applicants must be high school graduating seniors who either are in the top 5 percent of their classes or who earn an ACT or SAT score in the top 5 percent of Illinois test takers. They must attend an eligible college or university in the state of Illinois, and be legal residents of the state of Illinois, as well as U.S. citizens or eligible noncitizens. *Application Process: There is no formal application process for this scholarship award. Candidate test scores and academic ranks are filed automatically with the state and awardees will receive an award letter letting them know they have qualified for the award. Applicants will then have to prove their enrollment in a college or university program to receive the award. *Amount: $1,000. *Deadline: There is no formal deadline for this award.

Illinois Student Assistance Commission
1755 Lake Cook Road
Deerfield, IL 60015-5209
847-948-8500, 800-899-4722
http://www.collegezone.com/studentzone/416_947.htm
Scholarship Name: Minority Teachers of Illinois Scholarship Program. *Academic Area: Education. *Age Group: Undergraduate students. *Eligibility: Applicants must be residents of the state of Illinois, U.S. citizens or eligible noncitizens, and minority students of African American/ Black, Hispanic, Asian, or Native American origin. They must also be high school graduates or GED certificate holders, be enrolled in a teacher certification program, maintain at least a 2.5 GPA, and commit to teaching in the state of Illinois for a period of time equal to that for which funds are received. The scholarship is also available to graduate students. *Application Process: Applicants must apply online. Visit the commission's Web site to complete an interactive online application. *Amount: Up to $5,000. *Deadline: March 1.

Illinois Student Assistance Commission
1755 Lake Cook Road
Deerfield, IL 60015-5209
847-948-8500, 800-899-4722
http://www.collegezone.com/studentzone/416_891.htm
Scholarship Name: Monetary Award Program. *Academic Area: Open. *Age Group: Undergraduate students. *Eligibility: Applicants must be residents of Illinois who are also U.S. citizens or eligible noncitizens. They must also demonstrate financial need, be enrolled in at least three credit hours at an approved college or university in Illinois, and be admitted to a degree or certificate program. Applicants cannot be in default on any other loan, must not have attained a bachelor's degree, and cannot be incarcerated. Visit the commission's Web site for a complete list of eligible colleges and universities. *Application Process: Applicants should complete and submit the Free Application for Federal Student Aid (FAFSA) and list the eligible Illinois colleges or universities they plan to attend. If an applicant's FAFSA shows that he or she qualifies for the award, the financial aid office of the college or university will notify the applicant of the dollar amount the applicant is granted. *Amount: Awards vary. *Deadline: September 30 (first-time applicants).

Illinois Student Assistance Commission
c/o Illinois Department of Public Health
Center for Rural Health
535 West Jefferson Street
Springfield, IL 62761-0001
217-782-1624
http://www.collegezone.com/studentzone/416_1503.htm
Scholarship Name: Nursing Education Scholarship Program. *Academic Area: Nursing. *Age Group: Undergraduate students. *Eligibility: Applicants must be pursuing an associate, certificate, or undergraduate degree in nursing. They must be residents of Illinois, enrolled or accepted into a nursing education program, and able to demonstrate financial need. Applicants must agree to work in Illinois for a determined number of years (according to the type of degree they are pursuing) in order to avoid having to repay the funds. Nursing professionals may also apply for this program. *Application Process: Applicants should submit a completed application along with transcripts, a copy of their Student Aid Report, and a copy of their professional license (if licensed already). Visit the commission's Web site to download an application. *Amount: Awards vary depending on the degree the applicant is seeking. Visit the commission's Web site for a detailed explanation of the award amounts. *Deadline: May 31.

INDIANA

State Student Assistance Commission of Indiana
Grant Division
150 West Market Street, Suite 500

Indianapolis, IN 46204

317-232-2350

grants@ssaci.state.in.us

http://www.in.gov/ssaci/programs/hea.html

Grant Name: Frank O'Bannon Grant. *Academic Area: Open. *Age Group: Undergraduate students. *Eligibility: Applicants must be high school graduates (or hold a GED), residents of Indiana, U.S. citizens (or eligible noncitizens), and plan to or currently attend an approved Indiana institution of higher education (list available at the commission's Web site) as full-time students. *Application Process: Applicants should complete the Free Application for Federal Student Aid. *Amount: Varies. *Deadline: March 10.

State Student Assistance Commission of Indiana

Attn: Ada Sparkman

150 West Market Street, Suite 500

Indianapolis, IN 46204

317-232-2350

asparkman@ssaci.in.gov

http://www.in.gov/ssaci/programs/hsa.html

Award Name: Hoosier Scholar Award. *Academic Area: Open. *Age Group: Undergraduate students. *Eligibility: High school seniors who are high academic achievers (ranking in the top 20 percent of their class), residents of Indiana, and plan to attend an approved Indiana institution of higher education (as full-time students) are eligible for the award. *Application Process: High school guidance staff members select one to three winners of the award per high school. *Amount: $500. *Deadline: There is no deadline; nomination is based on academic achievement.

State Student Assistance Commission of Indiana

150 West Market Street, Suite 500

Indianapolis, IN 46204

317-232-2350

special@ssaci.state.in.us

http://www.in.gov/ssaci/programs/m-teach.html

Scholarship Name: Minority Teacher/Special Education Services Scholarship. *Academic Area: Education, special education, therapy (occupational), therapy (physical). *Age Group: Undergraduate students. *Eligibility: Applicants must be minority students (defined as black or Hispanic) who are planning to pursue or currently pursuing full-time study in education, occupational therapy, physical therapy, or special education at an approved Indiana institution of higher education. They must also be

Indiana residents and U.S. citizens and have a GPA of at least 2.0 on a 4.0 scale. Recipients must agree to meet education/service requirements specific to their career field after completion of study. *Application Process: Applicants should complete the Free Application for Federal Student Aid and a scholarship application (available for download at the commission's Web site). *Amount: Up to $1,000 (up to $4,000 for applicants who demonstrate strong financial need). *Deadline: Contact the commission for details.

State Student Assistance Commission of Indiana

150 West Market Street, Suite 500

Indianapolis, IN 46204

317-232-2350

special@ssaci.state.in.us

http://www.in.gov/ssaci/programs/nur.html

Scholarship Name: Nursing Scholarship Fund. *Academic Area: Nursing (open). *Age Group: Undergraduate students. *Eligibility: Applicants must be planning to pursue or currently pursuing study in nursing at an approved Indiana institution of higher education. They must also be residents of Indiana and U.S. citizens, demonstrate financial need, and have a GPA of at least 2.0 on a 4.0 scale. Recipients must agree to work as a nurse in Indiana for at least the first two years following graduation. *Application Process: Applicants should complete the Free Application for Federal Student Aid and a scholarship application (available for download at the commission's Web site). *Amount: $5,000. *Deadline: Contact the commission for details.

State Student Assistance Commission of Indiana

150 West Market Street, Suite 500

Indianapolis, IN 46204

888-528-4719

21stScholars@ssaci.in.gov

http://www.in.gov/ssaci/programs/21st/index.html

Scholarship Name: Twenty-First Century Scholars Program. *Academic Area: Open. *Age Group: Undergraduate students. *Eligibility: High school seniors and college students from low- and moderate-income families who seek college financial assistance may apply. Applicants must be planning to pursue or currently pursuing full-time study at an approved Indiana institution of higher education (visit the commission's Web site for a list of approved programs). They must also be residents of Indiana and U.S. citizens or eligible noncitizens. Applicants must take a pledge that states that they will graduate from an accredited Indiana high school; attain a cumulative high school GPA of at least 2.0; apply for admission to an Indiana college as a high school senior; not use illegal drugs, alcohol, or commit a crime; and apply on time for state and federal aid. *Application Process: Applicants should complete the Free Application for Federal Student Aid, a pledge affirmation, and a scholarship application (available for download at the commission's Web site). *Amount: Full tuition and fees at approved Indiana public colleges; partial tuition and fees at approved Indiana private colleges. *Deadline: March 10.

IOWA

Iowa College Student Aid Commission
200 Tenth Street, 4th Floor
Des Moines, IA 50309-3609
515-242-3344
http://www.iowacollegeaid.org/scholarshipsandgrants/index.html
Scholarship Name: Governor Terry E. Branstad Iowa State Fair Scholarship. *Academic Area: Open. *Age Group: Undergraduate students. *Eligibility: Applicants must be graduating high school seniors in Iowa who have actively participated at the Iowa State Fair, who plan to enroll in an Iowa college or university, and who demonstrate financial need. They should be well-rounded individuals with significant involvement in extracurricular school and community activities as well as a record of academic achievement. *Application Process: Applicants should submit a completed application along with a 400-word essay (details listed on the application), a list of state fair involvements, three letters of recommendation, and academic transcripts. Applicants must also submit the Free Application for Federal Student Aid no later than April 1. Visit the organization's Web site to download an application. *Amount: $500 to $1,000. *Deadline: May 2.

Iowa College Student Aid Commission
200 Tenth Street, 4th Floor
Des Moines, IA 50309-3609
515-242-3344
http://www.iowacollegeaid.org/scholarshipsandgrants/grantlist.html
Grant Name: Iowa Grant. *Academic Area: Open. *Age Group: Undergraduate students. *Eligibility:

Applicants must be residents of Iowa; U.S. citizens, nationals, or permanent residents of the U.S.; and currently enrolled or planning to enroll at least half time in a degree program at a state university, independent college or university, or community college in Iowa. Applicants must be able to demonstrate financial need. *Application Process: Applicants must complete and submit the Free Application for Federal Student Aid (FAFSA) as soon after January 1 as possible, and no later than July 1. Candidates whose FAFSA reports demonstrate the required financial need—and if adequate funding is available—will receive an award notification from the financial aid office of their choice college or university. *Amount: Up to $1,000. *Deadline: July 1.

Iowa College Student Aid Commission
200 Tenth Street, 4th Floor
Des Moines, IA 50309-3609
515-242-3344
http://www.iowacollegeaid.org/scholarshipsandgrants/grantlist.html
Grant Name: Iowa Tuition Grant. *Academic Area: Open. *Age Group: Undergraduate students. *Eligibility: Applicants must be Iowa residents; U.S. citizens, nationals, or permanent residents of the U.S.; and currently enrolled or planning to enroll at least half time in a degree program at an eligible Iowa college or university. They must also demonstrate financial need. Visit the commission's Web site for a list of eligible colleges and universities. *Application Process: Applicants must submit the Free Application for Federal Student Aid (FAFSA) as soon after January 1 as possible, and no later than July 1. Candidates whose FAFSA reports demonstrate the required financial need will receive an award notification from the financial aid office of the college or university of their choice. *Amount: Up to $4,000. *Deadline: July 1.

Iowa College Student Aid Commission
200 Tenth Street, 4th Floor
Des Moines, IA 50309-3609
515-242-3344
http://www.iowacollegeaid.org/scholarshipsandgrants/grantlist.html
Grant Name: Iowa Vocational-Technical Tuition Grant. *Academic Area: Vocational education. *Age Group: Undergraduate students. *Eligibility: Applicants must be Iowa residents; U.S. citizens, nationals, or permanent residents of the United States; and currently enrolled or planning to enroll at least

half time in a career education or career option course or program of study at a community college in Iowa. They must also be able to demonstrate financial need. *Application Process: Applicants must complete and submit the Free Application for Federal Student Aid (FAFSA) as soon after January 1 as possible, and no later than July 1. Candidates whose FAFSA reports demonstrate the required financial need will receive an award notification from the community college's financial aid office. *Amount: Up to $1,200. *Deadline: July 1.

KANSAS

Kansas Board of Regents
1000 SW Jackson Street, Suite 520
Topeka, KS 66612-1368
785-296-3421
http://www.kansasregents.org/financial_aid/awards.
html
Grant Name: Kansas Comprehensive Grant. *Academic Area: Open. *Age Group: Undergraduate students. *Eligibility: Applicants must be enrolled or planning to enroll full time at an eligible private or public college or university in Kansas. Applicants must be able to demonstrate financial need. Visit the board's Web site to determine which schools are eligible. *Application Process: Applicants must submit the Free Application for Federal Student Aid (FAFSA), listing one or more eligible institutions. The financial aid offices at their college of choice will notify applicants who are awarded funds. *Amount: $200 to $3,000 (private colleges), $100 to $1,100 (public institutions). *Deadline: March 15 (FAFSA filing).

Kansas Board of Regents
1000 SW Jackson Street, Suite 520
Topeka, KS 66612-1368
785-296-3421
http://www.kansasregents.org/financial_aid/minority.
html
Scholarship Name: Kansas Ethnic Minority Scholarship. *Academic Area: Open. *Age Group: Undergraduate students. *Eligibility: Applicants must be members of an ethnic or racial minority (African American, American Indian or Alaskan Native, Asian or Pacific Islander, or Hispanic) who can demonstrate both academic achievement (3.0 GPA; 990 SAT; 21 ACT) and financial need. They must also attend or plan to attend a college or university in Kansas. *Application Process: Applicants must submit the Free Application for Federal Student Aid, listing one or more eligible institutions. They must also submit the State of Kansas Student Aid Application. Visit the board's Web site to download a copy, or to apply online. *Amount: Up to $1,850. *Deadline: May 1.

Kansas Board of Regents
1000 SW Jackson Street, Suite 520
Topeka, KS 66612-1368
785-296-3421
http://www.kansasregents.org/financial_aid/nursing.
html
Scholarship Name: Kansas Nursing Service Scholarship. *Academic Area: Nursing (open). *Age Group: Undergraduate students. *Eligibility: Applicants must be accepted into a Kansas nursing program and have obtained a sponsor (hospital or long-term care facility) that will fund up to half of the scholarship and provide full-time employment after the applicant has earned a nursing license. Applicants must sign an agreement to practice nursing within the state of Kansas, at a predetermined institution, for each year of funding that is received. If the recipient does not fulfill the agreement, the funding must be repaid as a loan. *Application Process: Applicants must submit the Free Application for Federal Student Aid. They must also submit the State of Kansas Student Aid Application. Visit the board's Web site to download a copy, or to apply online. *Amount: $2,500 (licensed practical nursing programs), $3,500 (registered nursing programs). *Deadline: May 1.

Kansas Board of Regents
1000 SW Jackson Street, Suite 520
Topeka, KS 66612-1368
785-296-3421
http://www.kansasregents.org/financial_aid/teacher.
html
Scholarship Name: Kansas Teacher Service Scholarship. *Academic Area: Education. *Age Group: Undergraduate students. *Eligibility: Applicants should be in enrolled in or accepted into a college or university teacher education program in Kansas. They must sign an agreement to serve as teachers within designated underserved geographic regions in subject areas that have a relative shortage of teachers. They must also commit to teaching in an underserved school in Kansas for one year for each year of funding

that is received. If the recipient does not fulfill the agreement, the funding must be repaid as a loan. Applicants should visit the board's Web site for a list of current geographic areas and subject areas. *Application Process: Applicants must submit the State of Kansas Student Aid Application along with ACT or SAT scores, high school GPA and class rank, high school and college transcripts, and a letter of recommendation from a college or university official (high school seniors do not need to submit this). Applicants should also submit the Free Application for Federal Student Aid. Visit the board's Web site to download an application or to apply online. *Amount: $5,000. *Deadline: May 1.

Kansas Board of Regents
1000 SW Jackson Street, Suite 520
Topeka, KS 66612-1368
785-296-3421
http://www.kansasregents.org/financial_aid/math.html
Scholarship Name: Math and Science Teacher Service Scholarship. *Academic Area: Education. *Age Group: Undergraduate students. *Eligibility: Applicants should be in enrolled in a college or university math or science teacher education program in Kansas. Applicants are eligible to receive this award during their junior and senior years of college and should apply by the deadline of the year preceding this status. They must sign an agreement to serve as teachers within the state of Kansas, two years for each year of funding that is received. If the recipient does not fulfill the agreement, the funding must be repaid as a loan. *Application Process: Applicants must submit the State of Kansas Student Aid Application along with ACT or SAT scores, high school GPA and class rank, high school and college transcripts, and a letter of recommendation from a college or university official. Visit the board's Web site to download an application or to apply online. *Amount: $5,000. *Deadline: May 1.

Kansas Board of Regents
1000 SW Jackson Street, Suite 520
Topeka, KS 66612-1368
785-296-3421
http://www.kansasregents.org/financial_aid/state.html
Scholarship Name: State Scholars Scholarship. *Academic Area: Education. *Age Group: Undergraduate students. *Eligibility: Applicants should be Kansas residents who are currently in their

senior year of high school. Applicants should have taken the ACT prior to December of their senior year, as well as completed the Kansas Scholars Curriculum. The top 20 to 40 percent of students (calculated with a formula that combines test scores and GPA) are awarded this scholarship (pending availability of funds). *Application Process: Applicants must submit the State of Kansas Student Aid Application. Visit the board's Web site to download an application or to apply online. *Amount: $1,000. *Deadline: May 1.

Kansas Board of Regents
1000 SW Jackson Street, Suite 520
Topeka, KS 66612-1368
785-296-3421
http://www.kansasregents.org/financial_aid/awards.html
Scholarship Name: Vocational Scholarship. *Academic Area: Vocational education. *Age Group: Undergraduate students. *Eligibility: Applicants must be high school graduating seniors or enrolled students in an approved vocational program at a community or technical college in Kansas. *Application Process: Applicants must submit a completed application and register to take the vocational exam (form included as part of the application). The test is offered at various sites across the state on the first Saturday in November and March. Contact your high school guidance counselor or your college's financial aid adviser to receive an application and additional information. *Amount: $500. *Deadline: Contact your counselor or financial aid adviser for deadline information.

KENTUCKY

Kentucky Higher Education Assistance Authority (KHEAA)
PO Box 798
Frankfort, KY 40602-0798
800-928-8926
http://www.kheaa.com/prog_cap.html
Scholarship Name: College Access Program (CAP). *Academic Area: Open. *Age Group: Undergraduate students. *Eligibility: Applicants must be Kentucky residents who are attending eligible private colleges, universities, proprietary schools, or technical colleges within the state of Kentucky. They must also be attending school at least part time in programs that

take two years to complete. and demonstrate financial need. The Expected Family Contribution that is computed when filing the Free Application for Federal Student Aid (FAFSA) must not be greater than $3,850. *Application Process: Applicants should complete the FAFSA. Contact your high school counselor or college financial aid office for a hard-copy application or apply online. The college you are attending or plan to attend will notify you if you have been awarded a CAP scholarship. *Amount: Up to $1,700. *Deadline: Contact the financial aid office for deadline information. The FAFSA can be submitted anytime after January 1.

Kentucky Higher Education Assistance Authority (KHEAA)
PO Box 798
Frankfort, KY 40602-0798
800-928-8926
http://www.kheaa.com/prog_ecds.html
Scholarship Name: Early Childhood Development Scholarship. *Academic Area: Education. *Age Group: Undergraduate students. *Eligibility: Applicants must be pursuing an associate or bachelor's degree, certificate, or child development associate credential from an eligible institution in Kentucky. They must be Kentucky residents; U.S. citizens, nationals, or permanent residents; enrolled part time (up to nine credit hours), employed part time (at least 20 hours per week) in a participating early childhood facility, not be eligible for other state or federal training funds, and agree to a service commitment based on the credentials being pursued. *Application Process: Applicants should submit a completed application to their regional professional development counselor. Visit the authority's Web site to download an application and to view a complete list of professional development counselors. *Amount: Up to $1,400. *Deadline: Contact your professional development counselor for deadline information.

Kentucky Higher Education Assistance Authority (KHEAA)
PO Box 798
Frankfort, KY 40602-0798
800-928-8926
http://www.kheaa.com/prog_keeshome.html
Scholarship Name: Kentucky Educational Excellence Scholarship. *Academic Area: Open. *Age Group: Undergraduate students. *Eligibility: Applicants

must be Kentucky residents who have demonstrated academic achievement throughout their high school careers by maintaining at least a 2.5 GPA. They must attend an eligible college or university within the state of Kentucky (or a school listed in the Academic Common Marketplace). Applicant's ACT or SAT scores are also taken into account. Visit the authority's Web site for a complete chart of GPAs and test scores, to configure the amount for which you are eligible. A complete list of eligible colleges and universities can also be found at its Web site. *Application Process: There is no formal application process for this award. Your school submits your scores and once you enroll in an eligible institution, the school's financial aid office will notify you of the award you will receive. *Amount: Awards vary. *Deadline: There is no formal deadline for this scholarship.

Kentucky Higher Education Assistance Authority (KHEAA)
PO Box 798
Frankfort, KY 40602-0798
800-928-8926
http://www.kheaa.com/prog_ktg.html
Grant Name: Kentucky Tuition Grant. *Academic Area: Open. *Age Group: Undergraduate students. *Eligibility: Applicants must be Kentucky residents who are attending eligible private, independent colleges in Kentucky. They must be full-time students pursing an associate or bachelor's degree, not be in default on any other student aid accounts, and demonstrate financial need. Visit the authority's Web site for a complete list of eligible schools. *Application Process: Applicants should complete the Free Application for Federal Student Aid. Contact your high school counselor or college financial aid office for a hard-copy application or apply online. The college you are attending or plan to attend will notify you if you have been awarded a grant. *Amount: Up to $200 to $2,800. *Deadline: Contact your school's financial aid office for deadline information. The FAFSA can be submitted anytime after January 1.

Kentucky Higher Education Assistance Authority (KHEAA)
PO Box 798
Frankfort, KY 40602-0798
800-928-8926
http://www.kheaa.com/prog_tchschl.html
Scholarship Name: KHEAA Teacher Scholarship. *Academic Area: Education. *Age Group:

Undergraduate students. *Eligibility: Applicants must be Kentucky residents, attending eligible colleges or universities in Kentucky, and pursing an initial teacher certification. They must also be full-time college juniors or seniors who can demonstrate financial need. Applicants must commit to teach in Kentucky for a period of time. If the commitment is not honored, the awarded funds revert to a loan rather than a scholarship. Visit the authority's Web site for a complete list of eligible schools. The scholarship is also available to graduate students. *Application Process: Applicants should complete the Free Application for Federal Student Aid. Contact your college financial aid office for a hard-copy application or apply online. Applicants must also submit a Teacher Scholarship application, which can be completed online. Visit the organization's Web site to complete the application. *Amount: Up to $5,000. *Deadline: May 1.

LOUISIANA

Louisiana Office of Student Financial Assistance
Attn: Bonnie Lavergne
PO Box 91202
Baton Rouge, LA 70821-9202
225-922-3258, 800-259-5626, ext. 1012
http://www.osfa.state.la.us
Scholarship Name: Rockefeller State Wildlife Scholarship. *Academic Area: Marine sciences, natural resources. *Age Group: Undergraduate students. *Eligibility: Applicants must be U.S. citizens or eligible non-citizens who are enrolled full time in a degree program at a Louisiana public college or university in one of the following fields: forestry, marine science, wildlife science. They must also have been Louisiana residents for at least one year prior to receiving the award, not have any criminal convictions, and maintain a 2.5 GPA. Applicants must complete the degree program they are in, or they risk having to pay back the funds as a loan, with interest. The scholarship is also available to graduate students. *Application Process: Applicants must submit the Free Application for Federal Student Aid by July 1. A completed application along with college transcripts (if credit has been earned), and/or ACT/SAT scores (if fewer than 24 college credit hours have been earned) should be submitted. Visit the organization's Web site to download an application. *Amount: $1,000. *Deadline: July 31.

MAINE

Finance Authority of Maine
5 Community Drive, PO Box 949
Augusta, ME 04332-0949
207-623-3263, 800-228-3734
http://www.famemaine.com/html/education/grants.html
Grant Name: Maine State Grant Program. *Academic Area: Open. *Age Group: Undergraduate students. *Eligibility: Applicants must be Maine residents, demonstrate financial need, and plan to or currently attend a postsecondary institution in Maine, Connecticut, the District of Columbia, Massachusetts, New Hampshire, Pennsylvania, Rhode Island, or Vermont. *Application Process: Applicants must complete and submit the Free Application for Federal Student Aid. *Amount: $500 to $1,250. *Deadline: May 1.

MARYLAND

Maryland Higher Education Commission
839 Bestgate Road, Suite 400
Annapolis, MD 21401
410-260-4500, 800-974-0203
http://www.mhec.state.md.us/financialAid/ProgramDescriptions/prog_delegate.asp
Scholarship Name: Delegate Scholarship. *Academic Area: Open. *Age Group: Undergraduate students. *Eligibility: Applicants must be high school seniors or degree-seeking college students who are Maryland residents and who are enrolled or planning to enroll in a Maryland college or university. Applicants should contact their delegates for instructions. Some delegates ask the Maryland Office of Student Financial Assistance to make the awards for them, in which case the applicant must demonstrate financial need. The scholarship is also available to graduate students. *Application Process: Applicants should contact their delegates in February for instructions. Some delegates create their own awards, so you should call or write your delegate for instructions. Contact the Maryland Office of Student Financial Assistance for a list of state delegates. Applicants should file the Free Application for Federal Student Aid prior to applying. *Amount: Awards vary. *Deadline: March 1.

Maryland Higher Education Commission
839 Bestgate Road, Suite 400
Annapolis, MD 21401

410-260-4500, 800-974-0203
http://www.mhec.state.md.us/financialAid/
    ProgramDescriptions/prog_ds.asp
Scholarship Name: Distinguished Scholar Scholarship.
    *Academic Area: Open. *Age Group: Undergraduate
    students. *Eligibility: Applicants must be current high
    school juniors who are Maryland residents and who
    intend to enroll full time in a Maryland college or
    university. Applicants must apply in the "academic
    achievement" category (3.7 GPA required) or the
    "talent in the arts" category. Visit the commission's
    Web site to find out how to be nominated by your
    school in these categories. National Merit Scholarship
    and National Achievement Scholarship finalists
    will automatically receive the award if they attend
    an institution in Maryland. *Application Process:
    Applicants should contact their high school guidance
    counselor to request an application. *Amount: $3,000.
    *Deadline: February. Contact your guidance counselor
    for details.

Maryland Higher Education Commission
839 Bestgate Road, Suite 400
Annapolis, MD 21401
410-260-4500, 800-974-0203
http://www.mhec.state.md.us/financialAid/
    ProgramDescriptions/prog_ea.asp
Grant Name: Educational Assistance Grant. *Academic
    Area: Open. *Age Group: Undergraduate students.
    *Eligibility: Applicants must be graduating high school
    seniors or full-time, degree-seeking college students
    who are attending (or planning to attend) a college
    or university in the state of Maryland. They must also
    be Maryland residents who can demonstrate financial
    need. *Application Process: Applicants should submit
    the Free Application for Federal Student Aid (FAFSA)
    between January 1 and March 1. *Amount: $400 to
    $2,700 (35 percent of financial need as determined on
    the FAFSA). *Deadline: March 1.

Maryland Higher Education Commission
Attn: Theresa Lowe
839 Bestgate Road, Suite 400
Annapolis, MD 21401
410-260-4555, 800-974-0203
tlowe@rnhec.state.md.us
http://www.mhec.state.md.us/financialAid/
    ProgramDescriptions/prog_ga.asp
Grant Name: Guaranteed Access (GA) Grant. *Academic
    Area: Open. *Age Group: Undergraduate students.
    *Eligibility: Applicants must be high school

graduating seniors who are ontrack to complete
a college preparatory program and who plan to
enroll full time in a two- or four-year college or
university in Maryland. They must also be residents of
Maryland, maintain a 2.5 high school GPA, and able
to demonstrate financial need. *Application Process:
Applicants should submit the Free Application for
Federal Student Aid along with a completed GA
Grant application. Visit the commission's Web site to
download an application. *Amount: $400 to $13,800
(100 percent of student's financial need). *Deadline:
March 1.

Maryland Higher Education Commission
839 Bestgate Road, Suite 400
Annapolis, MD 21401
410-260-4500, 800-974-0203
http://www.mhec.state.md.us/financialAid/
    ProgramDescriptions/prog_tolbert.asp
Grant Name: Jack F. Tolbert Memorial Student Grant
    Program. *Academic Area: Open. *Age Group:
    Undergraduate students. *Eligibility: Applicants
    (or their parents, if they are dependents) must be
    Maryland residents who are enrolled in or planning
    to enroll in a private career school (for at least 18
    clock hours per week). They must also demonstrate
    financial need. *Application Process: Applicants must
    submit the Free Application for Federal Student
    Aid by March 1. Applicants must also apply to the
    financial aid office of the private career school they
    are attending. Contact the financial aid office for
    additional information. *Amount: $400. *Deadline:
    Rolling deadline.

Maryland Higher Education Commission
Attn: Gerrie Rogers
839 Bestgate Road, Suite 400
Annapolis, MD 21401
410-260-4574, 800-974-0203
grogers@rnhec.state.md.us
http://www.mhec.state.md.us/financialAid/
    ProgramDescriptions/prog_otpt.asp
Grant Name: Physical and Occupational Therapists and
    Assistants Grants Program. *Academic Area: Therapy
    (occupational), therapy (physical). *Age Group:
    Undergraduate students. *Eligibility: Applicants
    must be graduating high school seniors or full-time,
    degree-seeking college students who are majoring
    in physical or occupational therapy. They must also
    be residents of Maryland and enrolled (or planning
    to enroll) at a two- or four-year Maryland college

or university leading to licensure. Applicants must demonstrate academic achievement and commit to a service obligation to practice in Maryland. Visit the commission's Web site for further information on the service obligation. The grant is also available to graduate students. *Application Process: Applicants must submit a completed application along with transcripts (high school, college, or GED scores—whatever is applicable) and a statement from a Maryland college certifying enrollment. Visit the commission's Web site to download an application. *Amount: $2,000. *Deadline: July 1.

Maryland Higher Education Commission
839 Bestgate Road, Suite 400
Annapolis, MD 21401
410-260-4500, 800-974-0203
http://www.mhec.state.md.us/financialAid/
ProgramDescriptions/prog_senatorial.asp
Scholarship Name: Senatorial Scholarship. *Academic Area: Open. *Age Group: Undergraduate students. *Eligibility: Applicants must be high school seniors or degree-seeking college students who are Maryland residents, enrolled or planning to enroll in a Maryland college or university, and able to demonstrate financial need. The scholarship is also available to graduate students. *Application Process: Applicants should contact their senator in February for instructions. Some senators create their own awards, so you should contact your senator for instructions. Applicants should file the Free Application for Federal Student Aid prior to applying. SAT or ACT scores are also required for students who have not yet completed 24 hours of college credit. Those with more than 24 hours of college credit should submit transcripts. *Amount: $200 to $2,000. *Deadline: March 1.

Maryland Higher Education Commission
839 Bestgate Road, Suite 400
Annapolis, MD 21401
410-260-4500, 800-974-0203
http://www.mhec.state.md.us/financialAid/
ProgramDescriptions/prog_nurse.asp
Scholarship/Grant Name: State Nursing Scholarship and Living Expenses Grant. *Academic Area: Nursing (open). *Age Group: Undergraduate students. *Eligibility: Applicants must be current high school seniors or degree-seeking college students who are Maryland residents, maintain a 3.0 GPA, and are enrolled (or plan to enroll) in a Maryland college or university. Financial need is not required for the

scholarship, but it is a factor in the Living Expenses Grant. Applicants must commit to fulfilling a service agreement to receive this award. Visit the commission's Web site for a detailed description of the service agreement. The scholarship/grant program is also available to graduate students. (Note: To receive the Living Expenses Grant, applicants must first receive the State Nursing Scholarship.) *Application Process: Applicants should submit a completed scholarship application along with transcripts and an official acceptance letter into a nursing program. Those who are also applying for the Living Expenses Grant should complete the Free Application for Federal Student Aid (FAFSA) by March 1. Visit the commission's Web site to download a scholarship application. *Amount: Up to $1,500/semester (scholarship) and $1,500/semester (grant). *Deadline: June 30 (scholarship application), March 1 (FAFSA application for the grant).

Maryland Higher Education Commission
839 Bestgate Road, Suite 400
Annapolis, MD 21401
410-260-4500, 800-974-0203
http://www.mhec.state.md.us/financialAid/
ProgramDescriptions/prog_WDS.asp
Scholarship Name: William Donald Schaefer Scholarship. *Academic Area: Government, public policy. *Age Group: Undergraduate students. *Eligibility: Applicants must be graduating high school seniors or full-time college students who are attending (or planning to attend) an eligible college or university in Maryland that offers programs leading to a career in public service. They must also be residents of Maryland and demonstrate financial need. The scholarship is also available to graduate students. *Application Process: Applicants should file the Free Application for Federal Student Aid and submit the scholarship application along with applicable transcripts, a copy of the Student Aid Report, a 1,000-word essay, three letters of recommendation, and a one-page resume. Visit the commission's Web site to download an application. *Amount: Up to $8,550. *Deadline: March 1.

MASSACHUSETTS

Massachusetts Office of Student Financial Assistance
454 Broadway, Suite 200
Revere, MA 02151

617-727-9420
osfa@osfa.mass.edu
http://www.osfa.mass.edu/programs.
   asp?program=agnes_lindsay
Scholarship Name: Agnes M. Lindsay Scholarship.
   *Academic Area: Open. *Age Group: Undergraduate
   students. *Eligibility: Applicants must be permanent
   legal residents of Massachusetts for at least one year
   prior to receiving the scholarship, U.S. citizens or
   eligible noncitizens, and enrolled full time in a degree
   program at an eligible public college or university in
   Massachusetts. They also must be from a rural area
   of Massachusetts and able to demonstrate financial
   need. *Application Process: Applicants should
   contact the Massachusetts Office of Student Financial
   Assistance for information on the application process.
   *Amount: Awards vary. *Deadline: Contact the
   Massachusetts Office of Student Financial Services for
   deadline information.

Massachusetts Office of Student Financial Assistance
454 Broadway, Suite 200
Revere, MA 02151
617-727-9420
osfa@osfa.mass.edu
http://www.osfa.mass.edu/programs.
   asp?program=early_child_educators_scholarship
Scholarship Name: Early Childhood Educators
   Scholarship. *Academic Area: Education, psychology,
   sociology. *Age Group: Undergraduate students.
   *Eligibility: Applicants must be permanent legal
   residents of Massachusetts, U.S. citizens or eligible
   noncitizens, and enrolled in a degree program in
   Massachusetts that will lead to a career in early
   childhood education. Applicants must demonstrate
   financial need (and be eligible for Title IV aid), and be
   employed as an early childhood educator or a licensed
   family child care provider for at least one year while
   attending school. Applicants must also sign a service
   agreement in which they agree to serve for a length
   of time in Massachusetts, to avoid having to repay the
   funds. Visit the office's Web site to read more about the
   service agreement. *Application Process: Applicants
   must submit the Free Application for Federal Student
   Aid along with a completed scholarship application.
   Visit the office's Web site to download an application.
   *Amount: Up to $4,050/semester (depending on
   student status and type of institution attending).
   *Contact the Massachusetts Office of Student Financial
   Assistance for deadline information.

Massachusetts Office of Student Financial Assistance
454 Broadway, Suite 200
Revere, MA 02151
617-727-9420
osfa@osfa.mass.edu
http://www.osfa.mass.edu/programs.
   asp?program=massgrant
Grant Name: MASS Grant. *Academic Area: Open.
   *Age Group: Undergraduate students. *Eligibility:
   Applicants must be permanent legal residents of
   Massachusetts for at least one year prior to receiving
   the grant, U.S. citizens or eligible noncitizens,
   and enrolled full time in a degree program in
   Massachusetts or in an eligible institution in a state
   that has a reciprocity agreement with Massachusetts.
   They must also demonstrate financial need (and
   be eligible for Title IV aid) by having an Expected
   Family Contribution of $0 to $3,850. *Application
   Process: Applicants must submit the Free Application
   for Federal Student Aid (FAFSA). Applicants should
   contact their financial aid office or guidance counselor
   for additional application requirements. *Amount:
   $300 to $2,300. *Deadline: May 1 (FAFSA).

Massachusetts Office of Student Financial Assistance
454 Broadway, Suite 200
Revere, MA 02151
617-727-9420
osfa@osfa.mass.edu
http://www.osfa.mass.edu/programs.
   asp?program=part_time_grant
Grant Name: Massachusetts Part-Time Grant. *Academic
   Area: Open. *Age Group: Undergraduate students.
   *Eligibility: Applicants must be permanent legal
   residents of Massachusetts for at least one year
   prior to receiving the grant, U.S. citizens or eligible
   noncitizens, and enrolled part time in a degree or
   certificate program in Massachusetts. They must
   also demonstrate financial need (and be eligible for
   Title IV aid). *Application Process: Applicants must
   submit the Free Application for Federal Student Aid.
   Applicants should contact their financial aid office
   or guidance counselor for additional application
   requirements. *Amount: Awards vary (from $200 and
   up). *Deadline: Contact your financial aid office for
   deadline information.

Massachusetts Office of Student Financial Assistance
454 Broadway, Suite 200
Revere, MA 02151

617-727-9420

osfa@osfa.mass.edu

http://www.osfa.mass.edu/programs.
asp?program=paul_tsongas

Scholarship Name: Paul Tsongas Scholarship. *Academic Area: Open. *Age Group: Undergraduate students. *Eligibility: Applicants must be permanent legal residents of Massachusetts for at least one year prior to receiving the scholarship, U.S. citizens or eligible noncitizens, and enrolled full time in a degree program in one of the nine state colleges or universities in Massachusetts. They also must have graduated from high school within the last three years and demonstrated academic achievement by achieving a 3.75 GPA and a 1200 combined SAT score. Some exceptions apply for the residency and time (three-year) requirements. Visit the organization's Web site for further information. *Application Process: Applicants should contact the financial aid office at the state college they are attending for additional information about the application process. *Amount: Full tuition. *Deadline: Contact your college financial aid office for deadline information.

MICHIGAN

Michigan Bureau of Student Financial Assistance

Office of Scholarships and Grants

PO Box 30462

Lansing, MI 48909-7962

888-447-2687

osg@michigan.gov

http://www.michigan.gov/mistudentaid/0,1607,7-128-
38193_39939-6189--,00.html

Scholarship Name: Michigan Competitive Scholarship. *Academic Area: Open. *Age Group: Undergraduate students. *Eligibility: Applicants must be Michigan residents (since July 1 of the previous year); U.S. citizens, permanent residents, or approved refugees; and accepted into or enrolled in an approved degree-granting college or university in Michigan. They should also demonstrate both financial need and academic achievement. A 2.0 GPA is required as well as a competitive score on the ACT (the required score changes). Visit the bureau's Web site for an explanation of how the ACT score affects the application. Applicants should have completed any bachelor's degree. They should not be incarcerated, nor in default on an educational loan, and they should

not be pursuing a degree in theology, divinity, or religion. *Application Process: Applicants should file the Free Application for Federal Student Aid (FAFSA). Contact the bureau or your school's financial aid office for additional information. *Amount: Up to $1,300. *Deadline: March 1 (FAFSA).

Michigan Bureau of Student Financial Assistance

Office of Scholarships and Grants

PO Box 30462

Lansing, MI 48909-7962

888-447-2687

osg@michigan.gov

http://www.michigan.gov/mistudentaid/0,1607,7-128-
38193_38212_39079_39081-6153--,00.html

Grant Name: Michigan Educational Opportunity Grant. *Academic Area: Open. *Age Group: Undergraduate students. *Eligibility: Applicants must be Michigan residents, U.S. citizens or permanent residents, and attend (or plan to attend) a Michigan public community college or university. They must not be in default on an educational loan or incarcerated. They must also demonstrate they are making satisfactory academic progress, and have financial need. *Application Process: Applicants should file the Free Application for Federal Student Aid. The financial aid award letter that the student receives from the college financial aid office will inform them of their eligibility for the grant. *Amount: Up to $1,000. *Deadline: Contact your college financial aid office for deadline information.

Michigan Bureau of Student Financial Assistance

Office of Scholarships and Grants

PO Box 30462

Lansing, MI 48909-7962

888-447-2687

osg@michigan.gov

http://www.michigan.gov/mistudentaid/0,1607,7-128-
38193_39284---,00.html

Scholarship Name: Michigan Merit Award. *Academic Area: Open. *Age Group: Undergraduate students. *Eligibility: Applicants must be graduates of a Michigan high school (or GED recipients) or Michigan residents who are graduates of an out-of-state high school. They must also enroll at an approved college or university and have demonstrated academic achievement as proven by their scores on the Michigan Educational Assessment Program or the Michigan Merit Exam (class of 2007 and after).

*Application Process: There is no formal application process. Student test scores for all four years of high school are tabulated electronically and notification letters are mailed to students during their senior year if they qualify. Alternately, ACT or SAT scores can be used to receive the award as well. Visit the bureau's Web site for alternate eligibility explanations. *Amount: Up to $3,000. *Deadline: There is no formal deadline for this program.

Michigan Bureau of Student Financial Assistance
Office of Scholarships and Grants
PO Box 30462
Lansing, MI 48909-7962
888-447-2687
osg@michigan.gov
http://www.michigan.gov/mistudentaid/0,1607,7-128-38193_39939-54524--,00.html
Scholarship Name: Michigan Nursing Scholarship. *Academic Area: Nursing (open). *Age Group: Undergraduate students. *Eligibility: Applicants must be residents of Michigan (for at least one year prior to receiving the award) who are enrolled in an LPN, AND, or BSN program in the state. They must also be U.S. citizens or permanent residents who agree to work in Michigan after receiving their degrees (or face paying the funds back as a loan). *Application Process: Applicants should contact the financial aid office of their school in Michigan to receive information about the application process. Some schools may have additional eligibility requirements, including academic achievement or financial need. *Amount: Up to $4,000 (full-time students); $3,000 (3/4-time students); $2,000 (half-time students). *Deadline: Contact the financial aid office at your school for deadline information.

Michigan Bureau of Student Financial Assistance
Office of Scholarships and Grants
PO Box 30462
Lansing, MI 48909-7962
888-4GRANTS
osg@michigan.gov
http://www.michigan.gov/mistudentaid/0,1607,7-128-38193_39940_39949-6155--,00.html
Grant Name: Michigan Tuition Grant. *Academic Area: Open. *Age Group: Undergraduate students. *Eligibility: Applicants must be Michigan residents (since July 1 of the previous calendar year); U.S. citizens, permanent residents, or approved refugees; and attend (or plan to attend) an approved

independent, degree-granting Michigan college or university. They must not be in default on an educational loan or incarcerated, and also must not be pursuing a degree in theology, divinity, or religion. Applicants must be able to demonstrate financial need. *Application Process: Applicants should file the Free Application for Federal Student Aid (FAFSA) by March 1. Contact the bureau for additional information. *Amount: Up to $2,000. *Deadline: March 1 (FAFSA).

MINNESOTA

Minnesota Office of Higher Education
1450 Energy Park Drive, Suite 350
St. Paul, MN 55108-5227
651-642-0567, 800-657-3529
info@ohe.state.mn.us
http://www.getreadyforcollege.org/pdfGR/FocusSumEng.pdf
Grant Name: Minnesota State Grant. *Academic Area: Open. *Age Group: Undergraduate students. *Eligibility: Applicants must be Minnesota residents who are high school graduates or GED holders who are attending college (or planning to attend) at an eligible Minnesota institution. They must also be U.S. citizens or eligible noncitizens who are not in default on any educational loans or child support payments. Applicants must demonstrate financial need. *Application Process: Applicants should file the Free Application for Federal Student Aid within 30 days of the start of their current term. Contact your school's financial aid office for additional information. If you qualify, the amount you receive is based on your financial need and the cost of tuition at your school. *Amount: Up to $7,861. (The average award is $1,656.) *Deadline: Contact your school's financial aid office for deadline information.

MISSISSIPPI

Mississippi Office of Student Financial Aid
Attn: Susan Eckels, Program Administrator
3825 Ridgewood Road
Jackson, MS 39211-6453
601-432-6997, 800-327-2980
seckels@ihl.state.ms.us
http://www.ihl.state.ms.us/financialaid/hcp.html
Loan/Scholarship Name: Health Care Professions

Loan/Scholarship. *Academic Area: Psychology, speech pathology, therapy (occupational), therapy (physical). *Age Group: Undergraduate students. *Eligibility: Applicants must be college juniors or seniors at a Mississippi college or university who are also Mississippi residents. They must also agree to a service commitment as part of this scholarship. For every year of funding received, applicants must agree to work in a state-operated health institution. If the commitment is not honored, the funds will revert to a loan. The program is also available to graduate students. *Application Process: Applicants should submit an online application as well as an e-mail certifying that they have reviewed and agreed to the service requirements. Applicants must also submit verification of residency and their college transcripts. Visit the department's Web site to apply online. *Amount: $1,500. *Deadline: March 31.

Mississippi Office of Student Financial Aid
3825 Ridgewood Road
Jackson, MS 39211-6453
601-432-6997, 800-327-2980
sfa@ihl.state.ms.us
http://www.ihl.state.ms.us/financialaid/mesg.html
Grant Name: Mississippi Eminent Scholars Grant. *Academic Area: Open. *Age Group: Undergraduate students. *Eligibility: Applicants must be Mississippi residents for at least one year prior to college enrollment who are accepted into or enrolled in a two- or four-year eligible institution in Mississippi. They must be full-time students who have demonstrated academic achievement by maintaining a 3.5 GPA. High school applicants should have received a 29 on the ACT or a 1280 on the SAT. Visit the office's Web site for a list of eligible institutions and more detailed eligibility requirements for high school and college applicants. *Application Process: Applicants should submit an online application and supporting documents. Supporting documents include a copy of the applicant's or parents' (if applicant is a dependent) tax return from the prior year, official transcripts, official ACT or SAT scores, and a notification letter (for students who were National Merit Scholarship or National Achievement Scholarship semi-finalists or finalists). Visit the office's Web site to apply online. *Amount: Up to $2,500. *Deadline: September 15.

Mississippi Office of Student Financial Aid
3825 Ridgewood Road
Jackson, MS 39211-6453

601-432-6997, 800-327-2980
sfa@ihl.state.ms.us
http://www.ihl.state.ms.us/financialaid/mtag.html
Grant Name: Mississippi Resident Tuition Assistance Grant. *Academic Area: Open. *Age Group: Undergraduate students. *Eligibility: Applicants must be residents of the state of Mississippi for at least one year prior to college enrollment, who are accepted into or enrolled in a two- or four-year eligible institution in Mississippi. They must be high school seniors or full-time college students who have demonstrated academic achievement by maintaining a 2.5 GPA. High school applicants must have received a minimum score of 15 on the ACT. Applicants must have received less than the full federal Pell Grant. Visit the organization's Web site for a list of eligible institutions and more detailed eligibility requirements for high school and college applicants. *Application Process: Applicants should submit an online application and supporting documents. Supporting documents include a copy of the applicant's or parents' (if applicant is a dependent) tax return from the prior year, official transcripts, and official ACT or SAT scores (if applicable). Visit the organization's Web site to apply online. *Amount: Up to $500 (freshman, sophomores), $1,000 (juniors, seniors). *Deadline: September 15.

Mississippi Office of Student Financial Aid
3825 Ridgewood Road
Jackson, MS 39211-6453
601-432-6997, 800-327-2980
sfa@ihl.state.ms.us
https://www.state.ms.us/sfa/nissanEntry.jsp
Scholarship Name: Nissan North America Inc. Scholarship. *Academic Area: Open. *Age Group: Undergraduate students. *Eligibility: Applicants must attend a two-year or public four-year college or university in Mississippi, be graduates of a Mississippi high school, achieved a 2.5 GPA, and earned a minimum score of 20 on the ACT (or 940 on the SAT). They must also be accepted for enrollment as a full-time student at a Mississippi public community college or university, demonstrate financial need, and exhibit leadership qualities as proven by their involvement in extracurricular activities. *Application Process: Applicants should submit an online application. Submission of the Free Application for Federal Student Aid is also required. *Amount: Awards vary. *Deadline: Contact the organization for deadline information.

MISSOURI

Missouri Department of Higher Education
3515 Amazonas Drive
Jefferson City, MO 65109
573-751-2361
info@dhe.mo.gov
http://www.dhe.mo.gov/hsstudentscharlesgallagher.
  shtml
Scholarship Name: Charles Gallagher Student Financial
  Assistance Program. *Academic Area: Open.
  *Age Group: Undergraduate students. *Eligibility:
  Applicants must be Missouri residents, U.S. citizens or
  eligible noncitizens, and demonstrate financial need.
  They must also be enrolled full time (or planning to
  enroll full time) at a participating Missouri college or
  university. Visit the department's Web site to view a
  complete list of participating colleges and universities.
  *Application Process: Applicants should submit the
  Free Application for Federal Student Aid by April 1
  in order to be considered for this award. *Amount:
  Applicants can receive their remaining demonstrated
  financial need, up to $1,500. *Deadline: Contact the
  department for deadline information.

Missouri Department of Higher Education
3515 Amazonas Drive
Jefferson City, MO 65109
573-751-2361
info@dhe.mo.gov
http://www.dhe.mo.gov/hsstudentsrossbarnett.shtml
Scholarship Name: Marguerite Ross Barnett Memorial
  Scholarship. *Academic Area: Open. *Age Group:
  Undergraduate students. *Eligibility: Applicants must
  be Missouri residents, U.S. citizens or eligible noncitizens, enrolled in a Missouri college or university
  on a part-time basis, employed (in a paid position)
  for at least 20 hours per week, and demonstrate
  financial need. They cannot be pursuing a degree
  in theology or divinity. Visit the department's Web
  site for a complete list of participating colleges and
  universities. *Application Process: Applicants should
  file the Free Application for Federal Student Aid to
  illustrate their financial need. They should do this
  as early as possible after January 1. Applicants must
  also submit an employment verification form to be
  considered for this award. Visit the department's Web
  site to download the form. *Amount: Full tuition (or
  the equivalent of part-time tuition at the University
  of Missouri-Columbia). *Deadline: Contact the

department or your school's financial aid office for
deadline information.

Missouri Department of Higher Education
3515 Amazonas Drive
Jefferson City, MO 65109
573-751-2361
info@dhe.mo.gov
http://www.dhe.mo.gov/hsstudentscollegeguarantee.
  shtml
Scholarship Name: Missouri College Guarantee Program.
  *Academic Area: Open. *Age Group: Undergraduate
  students. *Eligibility: Applicants must be graduating
  high school seniors or enrolled college students
  who are attending (or plan to attend) a participating
  college in the state of Missouri. They must be
  Missouri residents, U.S. citizens or eligible noncitizens,
  pursuing a degree in any field except theology or
  divinity, and demonstrate financial need. Applicants
  must have maintained a high school GPA of 2.5 and
  received an ACT score of 20 or an SAT score of 950.
  Visit the department's Web site for a complete list of
  participating colleges and universities. *Application
  Process: Applicants should file the Free Application
  for Federal Student Aid. Applicants must also receive
  a qualifying ACT score by April of the year preceding
  the award. *Amount: Awards vary *Deadline: April
  1 (FAFSA). Contact the department or your school's
  financial aid office for additional deadline information.

Missouri Department of Higher Education
3515 Amazonas Drive
Jefferson City, MO 65109
573-751-2361
info@dhe.mo.gov
http://www.dhe.mo.gov/hsstudentsbrightflight.shtml
Scholarship Name: Missouri Higher Education
  Academic "Bright Flight" Scholarship. *Academic
  Area: Open. *Age Group: Undergraduate students.
  *Eligibility: Applicants must be graduating high
  school seniors who are enrolling as first-time, full-
  time freshmen at a participating Missouri college
  or university. They must be Missouri residents and
  U.S. citizens or eligible noncitizens and cannot
  be pursuing a degree in theology or divinity.
  Applicants must have received a composite ACT
  or SAT score in the top 3 percent of all students
  in Missouri. Applicants should contact their high
  school counselor to determine what score they
  need to receive. Visit the department's Web site

for a complete list of participating colleges and universities. *Application Process: There is no formal application process for this award. Applicants must have received a qualifying test score by the June test date. Eligible students will be notified by mail by the Missouri Department of Higher Education. *Amount: $2,000. *Deadline: Typically in June. Applicants must have a qualifying test score by the June test date.

MONTANA

Montana Office of the Commissioner of Higher Education
46 North Last Chance Gulch
Helena, MT 59620-3201
406-444-6570
http://mus.montana.edu
Grant Name: Indian Student Fee Waiver. *Academic Area: Open. *Age Group: Undergraduate students. *Eligibility: Applicants must be at least one-quarter Native American, residents of Montana, demonstrate financial need, and plan to or currently attend a two- or four-year school in the Montana University System. *Application Process: Applicants will need to file the Free Application for Federal Student Aid in order to determine financial need. They also must provide documentation of tribal enrollment. *Amount: Tuition and registration fees. *Deadline: Contact the office for details.

NEBRASKA

Nebraska Coordinating Commission for Postsecondary Education
PO Box 95005
Lincoln, NE 68509-5005
402-471-2847
http://www.ccpe.state.ne.us/publicdoc/ccpe
Grant Name: Nebraska State Grant. *Academic Area: Open. *Age Group: Undergraduate students. *Eligibility: Applicants must be residents of Nebraska. *Application Process: The commission disburses grant money in this program to colleges and universities in Nebraska that award funds to eligible students. Contact the financial aid office of your chosen Nebraska school for details. *Amount: Varies. *Deadline: Contact the financial aid office of your

chosen Nebraska school for details.

NEVADA

Nevada Office of the State Treasurer
Attn: Susan Moore
555 East Washington Avenue, Suite 4600
Las Vegas, NV 89101
702-486-3383, 888-477-2667
http://nevadatreasurer.gov/millennium
Scholarship Name: Governor Guinn Millennium Scholarship. *Academic Area: Open. *Age Group: Undergraduate students. *Eligibility: Applicants must graduate from a Nevada high school, and be a Nevada resident for at least two years. Applicants must have a 3.25 GPA and must attend an eligible college or university in the state of Nevada. *Application Process: There is no formal application for this award. High schools submit the names of qualified student to the Nevada State Treasurer's Office, and students will be notified of their award, pending acceptance to a qualified institution. Contact your high school guidance counselor or college's financial aid office for additional information. Visit the Treasurer's Office Web site for an explanation of eligibility institutions. *Amount: $40 to $80 per credit hour, depending on type of college student attends (community college, state college, private college). A maximum of $10,000 can be applied to an undergraduate degree. *Deadline: There is no formal deadline for this award.

NEW HAMPSHIRE

New Hampshire Postsecondary Education Commission
3 Barrell Court, Suite 300
Concord, NH 03301-8543
603-271-2555
http://www.state.nh.us/postsecondary/fin.html
Grant Name: Leveraged Incentive Grant Program. *Academic Area: Open. *Age Group: Undergraduate students. *Eligibility: Applicants must be college sophomores, juniors, or seniors who are residents of New Hampshire, are attending an accredited New Hampshire college or university, and who can demonstrate academic achievement and financial need. *Application Process: Applicants should contact the financial aid office at their New Hampshire

college or university for information about the application process. Applicants will need to file the Free Application for Federal Student Aid in order to determine financial need. *Amount: Awards vary. *Deadline: Contact your school's financial aid office for deadline information.

New Hampshire Postsecondary Education Commission

Attn: Sherrie Tucker
3 Barrell Court, Suite 300
Concord, NH 03301-8543
603-271-2555, ext. 255
http://www.state.nh.us/postsecondary/fin.html
Scholarship Name: New Hampshire Incentive Program. *Academic Area: Open. *Age Group: Undergraduate students. *Eligibility: Applicants must be residents of New Hampshire who can demonstrate financial need and who are enrolled (or intend to enroll) as part-time or full-time undergraduate students at an eligible college or university in New England. Applicants must not have earned a previous bachelor's degree. *Application Process: Applicants should file the Free Application for Federal Student Aid (FAFSA) in order to determine financial need. Contact the commission for additional information, including eligible colleges and universities. *Amount: $125 to $1,000. *Deadline: May 1 (FAFSA).

NEW JERSEY

New Jersey Higher Education Student Assistance Authority

PO Box 540
Trenton, NJ 08625
800-792-8670
http://www.nj.gov/highereducation/njhesaa.htm
Scholarship Name: Edward J. Bloustein Distinguished Scholars. *Academic Area: Open. *Age Group: Undergraduate students. *Eligibility: Applicants must be U.S. citizens or eligible noncitizens, New Jersey residents for at least one year prior to receiving the award, ranked in the top 10 percent of their high school class at the end of their junior year, and scored a combined critical reading and math SAT score of 1260. Alternately, applicants may rank in first, second, or third place in their graduating class and rank in the top 10 percent at the end of the junior year (without regard to SAT score). Applicants must attend a college

or university in New Jersey as full-time students to receive this award. *Application Process: There is no formal application process for this merit-based award. Contact your high school guidance counselor for information about your candidacy for the award. *Amount: $1,000. *Deadline: There is no formal deadline for this award.

New Jersey Higher Education Student Assistance Authority

PO Box 540
Trenton, NJ 08625
800-792-8670
http://www.nj.gov/highereducation/njhesaa.htm
Scholarship Name: NJ STARS Program. *Academic Area: Open. *Age Group: Undergraduate students. *Eligibility: Applicants must be New Jersey residents for at least one year prior to receiving the award, be U.S. citizens or eligible noncitizens, and have graduated in the top 20 percent of their high school class. They must also attend a New Jersey county college as full-time students to receive this award. Applicants who postponed college attendance for one year may also be considered. Applicants must demonstrate financial need in addition to academic merit. *Application Process: There is no formal application process for this award. Applicants must submit the Free Application for Federal Student Aid (FAFSA) within established deadlines—the earlier the better. Their county college will notify eligible candidates of their award . *Amount: Up to five semesters of paid full-time tuition. *Deadline: Current FAFSA deadline.

New Jersey Higher Education Student Assistance Authority

PO Box 540
Trenton, NJ 08625
800-792-8670
http://www.nj.gov/highereducation/njhesaa.htm
Grant Name: Tuition Aid Grant. *Academic Area: Open. *Age Group: Undergraduate students. *Eligibility: Applicants must be residents of New Jersey for at least one year prior to receiving the award and U.S. citizens or eligible noncitizens. They must also be able to demonstrate financial need as well as enrollment in an approved degree-granting institution in New Jersey. Applicants must be full-time students who have not previously earned a baccalaureate degree (or an associate degree if enrolled in a two-year college) and who are in good academic standing, not in default

on any student loan, and not enrolled in a theology or divinity degree program. *Application Process: Applicants should complete the Free Application for Federal Student Aid (FAFSA) either by mail or online. Eligible candidates will be notified if they receive the grant. *Amount: Up to $9,026 (independent colleges); up to $5,220 (state colleges); up to $2,030 (county colleges). *Deadline: March 1, October 1 (FAFSA, depending on semester you are applying for).

New Jersey Higher Education Student Assistance Authority
PO Box 540
Trenton, NJ 08625
800-792-8670
http://www.nj.gov/highereducation/njhesaa.htm
Scholarship Name: Urban Scholars Program. *Academic Area: Open. *Age Group: Undergraduate students. *Eligibility: Applicants must be residents of New Jersey for at least one year prior to receiving the award and U.S. citizens or eligible noncitizens who attend high school in the state's urban and economically distressed areas. They must also be able to demonstrate exceptional academic achievement by ranking in the top 10 percent of their class and having a minimum GPA of 3.0 at the end of their junior year of high school. Applicants must enroll as full-time students in approved colleges and universities within the state of New Jersey. Contact your high school guidance counselor for additional information. *Application Process: There is no formal application process for this merit-based award. Eligible students will be notified of their award, pending enrollment in an eligible institution. *Amount: $1,000. *Deadline: There is no formal deadline for this program.

NEW MEXICO

New Mexico Higher Education Department
Attn: Ofelia A. Morales, Director, Financial Aid
1068 Cerrillos Road
Santa Fe, NM 87505-1650
505-476-6500, 800-279-9777
ofelia.morales@state.nm.us
http://hed.state.nm.us/collegefinance/loansforservice.asp
Scholarship Name: Health Professional Loans-For-Service Scholarships. *Academic Area: Medicine (general), medicine (nursing), medicine (osteopathy), medicine

(physician). *Age Group: Undergraduate students. *Eligibility: Applicants must be seeking a degree in a selected health care field at a public college or university in New Mexico. (Note: Some scholarships allow for acceptance or enrollment to accredited public schools in the United States.) They must be residents of New Mexico and agree to a service agreement to work within the state, once licensure is obtained, for a designated period of time in a designated shortage area within the state. If applicants do not fulfill their commitment, penalties apply. Visit the department's Web site or call its help line for additional information about the service agreement for each field of study, and for more details about eligibility. The scholarship is also available to graduate students and medical students. *Application Process: Applicants should submit a completed application along with supporting documents, which include a letter of acceptance from the college or university and official transcripts. Applicants also must file the Free Application for Federal Student Aid. *Amount: Up to $12,000. *Deadline: Varies by field of study.

New Mexico Higher Education Department
Attn: Ofelia A. Morales, Director, Financial Aid
1068 Cerrillos Road
Santa Fe, NM 87505-1650
505-476-6500, 800-279-9777
ofelia.morales@state.nm.us
http://hed.state.nm.us/collegefinance/legislative.asp
Scholarship Name: Legislative Endowment Scholarship. *Academic Area: Open. *Age Group: Undergraduate students. *Eligibility: Applicants must be graduating high school seniors or college undergraduates who are residents of New Mexico. They may attend, either part time or full time, any public college or university within the state of New Mexico. Preference is given to returning adult students and transfer students from two-year New Mexico community colleges who are entering four-year institutions. Applicants must be able to demonstrate financial need. *Application Process: Applicants should contact the financial aid office of their chosen college or university for information on the application process. All applicants must file the Free Application for Federal Student Aid. *Amount: Up to $2,500 (four-year schools, prorated for part-time students); up to $1,000 (two-year schools, prorated for part-time students). *Deadline: Deadlines vary by institution. Contact your financial aid office for deadline information.

New Mexico Higher Education Department
Attn: Ofelia A. Morales, Director, Financial Aid
1068 Cerrillos Road
Santa Fe, NM 87505-1650
505-476-6500, 800-279-9777
ofelia.morales@state.nm.us
http://hed.state.nm.us/collegefinance/lotto.asp
Scholarship Name: Lottery Success Scholarship.
  *Academic Area: Open. *Age Group: Undergraduate
  students. *Eligibility: Applicants must be graduating
  high school seniors who are residents of New Mexico
  and who are accepted into a public college or
  university in New Mexico. They must hold a diploma
  from a New Mexico high school or a New Mexico
  GED, enroll full time in college, and earn a 2.5 GPA
  during the first semester of college. Applicants
  begin to receive funds after the first semester of
  college has been completed and they have fulfilled
  all requirements. Call the department's help line
  for additional information. *Application Process:
  Applicants should contact the financial aid office
  of their college or university for information on the
  application process. *Amount: Up to full tuition.
  *Deadline: Deadlines vary by institution. Contact your
  financial aid office for deadline information.

New Mexico Higher Education Department
Attn: Ofelia A. Morales, Director, Financial Aid
1068 Cerrillos Road
Santa Fe, NM 87505-1650
505-476-6500, 800-279-9777
ofelia.morales@state.nm.us
http://hed.state.nm.us/collegefinance/scholars.asp
Scholarship Name: New Mexico Scholars' Program.
  *Academic Area: Open. *Age Group: Undergraduate
  students. *Eligibility: Applicants must be graduating
  high school seniors or college undergraduates who
  have not yet turned 22, and who are residents of
  New Mexico. They must attend any public college
  or university within New Mexico or one of a select
  group of private colleges. The combined family
  income of the applicant's family must be less than
  $30,000 (or $40,000 if two or more family members
  are enrolled in postsecondary education), and the
  applicants must have graduated in the top 5 percent
  of their high school class or have scored a 25 on the
  ACT. Visit the department's Web site to view a list
  of private schools that are eligible for this program.
  *Application Process: Applicants should contact
  the financial aid office of their chosen college or
  university for information on the application process.

All applicants must complete the Free Application for
Federal Student Aid. *Amount: Paid tuition, books,
and fees (subject to availability of funds). *Deadline:
Deadlines vary by institution. Contact your financial
aid office for deadline information.

New Mexico Higher Education Department
Attn: Ofelia A. Morales, Director, Financial Aid
1068 Cerrillos Road
Santa Fe, NM 87505-1650
505-476-6500, 800-279-9777
ofelia.morales@state.nm.us
http://hed.state.nm.us/collegefinance/choice.asp
Grant Name: Student Choice Grant. *Academic Area:
  Open. *Age Group: Undergraduate students. *Eligibility:
  Applicants must be graduating high school seniors
  or college undergraduates who are residents of New
  Mexico. Applicants must attend one of the following
  private colleges within New Mexico: the College
  of Santa Fe, St. John's College in Santa Fe, or the
  College of the Southwest. Applicants must be able to
  demonstrate financial need. Call the department's help
  line for additional information. *Application Process:
  Applicants should contact the financial aid office of their
  college or university for information on the application
  process. All applicants must file the Free Application for
  Federal Student Aid. *Amount: Awards vary. *Deadline:
  Deadlines vary by institution. Contact your financial
  office for deadline information.

New Mexico Higher Education Department
Attn: Ofelia A. Morales, Director, Financial Aid
1068 Cerrillos Road
Santa Fe, NM 87505-1650
505-476-6500, 800-279-9777
ofelia.morales@state.nm.us
http://hed.state.nm.us/collegefinance/incentive.asp
Grant Name: Student Incentive Grant. *Academic
  Area: Open. *Age Group: Undergraduate students.
  *Eligibility: Applicants must be graduating high school
  seniors or college undergraduates who are residents
  of New Mexico. They must attend any public college or
  university within New Mexico or one of a select group
  of private colleges and may attend school part time
  or full time. Applicants must be able to demonstrate
  financial need. Visit the department's Web site to
  view a list of private schools that are eligible for this
  program or call its help line for additional information.
  *Application Process: Applicants should contact the
  financial aid office of their college or university for
  information on the application process. All applicants

must file the Free Application for Federal Student Aid. *Amount: $200 to $2,500. *Deadline: Deadlines vary by institution. Contact your financial aid office for deadline information.

NEW YORK

New York State Higher Education Services Corporation
99 Washington Avenue
Albany, NY 12255
518-473-1574, 888-697-4372
http://www.hesc.com/bulletin.nsf/0/9229D337BEFE8
    BBC85256D97004EBF47?OpenDocument
Scholarship Name: Aid for Part-Time Study. *Academic Area: Open. *Age Group: Undergraduate students. *Eligibility: Applicants must be New York State high school graduates or GED holders who are enrolled in or accepted into an approved New York State college or university. Applicants must be residents of the state of New York, U.S. citizens or qualifying noncitizens, maintain a 2.0 GPA, not be in default on any students loans, and attend college part time. Income limits apply. For a detailed explanation of family income limits, visit the department's Web site. Contact your college's financial aid office to determine if your school is a participating institution. *Application Process: Applicants should request an application from their college financial aid office. Applicants will also need to file the Free Application for Federal Student Aid. *Amount: Up to $2,000. *Deadline: Contact your financial aid office for deadline information.

New York State Higher Education Services Corporation
New York Lottery LOT Scholarship
One Broadway Center
PO Box 7540
Schenectady, NY 12301-7540
518-388-3415
lotscholar@lottery.state.ny.us
http://www.hesc.com/bulletin.nsf/0/9229D337BEFE8
    BBC85256D97004EBF47?OpenDocument
Scholarship Name: New York Lottery Leaders of Tomorrow Scholarship. *Academic Area: Open. *Age Group: Undergraduate students. *Eligibility: Applicants must be graduating high school seniors attending a public or private high school in the state of New York who have demonstrated involvement in extracurricular and community activities, academic achievement (3.0 GPA minimum), and leadership potential. Applicants must attend a college, university, or trade school in the state of New York, and their school must nominate them for the scholarship. Their parents or guardians must not work for the New York Lottery or any of its contractors. One scholarship is awarded to each school in the state of New York. *Application Process: Applicants should contact their high school guidance counselor to let him or her know they are interested in being nominated for the scholarship. Students must be nominated by their school to receive the award. *Amount: $4,000 ($1,000 per year). *Deadline: March 10.

New York State Higher Education Services Corporation
Bureau of HEOP/VATEA/Scholarships
Education Building Addition, Room 1071
Albany, NY 12234
518-486-1319
http://www.hesc.com/bulletin.nsf/0/9229D337BEFE8
    BBC85256D97004EBF47?OpenDocument
Scholarship Name: New York State Regents Professional Opportunity Scholarship. *Academic Area: Open (select range of 39 professional degree programs). *Age Group: Undergraduate students, graduate students. *Eligibility: Applicants must be New York State residents studying in a degree program in a New York State college or university. They must be studying in a particular field, as described on the department's Web site. Applicants must be U.S. citizens or qualifying noncitizens who are attending school full time. Priority is given to those who are economically disadvantaged, members of a minority group traditionally underrepresented in their chosen profession, and those enrolled in or graduates of SEEK, College Discovery, EOP, or HEOP. Applicants must also commit to a service agreement in which they work for one year in the state of New York, in their chosen profession, for each year that funds are received. If this obligation is not fulfilled, the funds revert to a loan. *Application Process: Applicants should request an application and further information by phone or mail. *Amount: $1,000 to $5,000. *Deadline: Contact the Bureau of Scholarships for deadline information.

New York State Higher Education Services Corporation
99 Washington Avenue
Albany, NY 12255
518-473-1574, 888-697-4372

http://www.hesc.com/bulletin.nsf/0/9229D337BEFE8
BBC85256D97004EBF47?OpenDocument

Scholarship Name: New York State Scholarships for
Academic Excellence. *Academic Area: Open. *Age
Group: Undergraduate students. *Eligibility: Applicants
must be New York State high school graduates who are
enrolled in or accepted into a New York State college or
university. They must be residents of the state of New
York, U.S. citizens or qualifying noncitizens, in good
academic standing and not in default on any student
loans, and attend college full time. Applicants must
demonstrate academic achievement and be nominated
by their high school. *Application Process: Applicants
should contact their high school guidance counselor for
information about the scholarships. Eligible candidates
who are nominated by their schools and chosen for the
award will be notified by the New York State Education
Department. Once notified, applicants must submit
an application for payment, with proof of college
acceptance/enrollment. *Amount: $500 and $1,500.
*Deadline: May 1 (deadline for eligible applicants
to return their application after they've received
notification of their eligibility).

**New York State Higher Education Services
Corporation**
Native American Education Unit
New York State Education Department, Room 374 EBA
Albany, NY 12234
518-474-0537
http://www.hesc.com/bulletin.nsf/0/9229D337BEFE8
BBC85256D97004EBF47?OpenDocument

Scholarship Name: State Aid to Native Americans.
*Academic Area: Open. *Age Group: Undergraduate
students. *Eligibility: Applicants must be enrolled
members of a New York State tribe and/or their children
who are attending, or plan to attend, a college or
university in the state of New York. Applicants must be
residents of the state of New York. All eligible applicants
receive the award. Applicants may enroll in two-, four-,
or five-year undergraduate programs. *Application
Process: Applicants should request additional
information and an application from the New York State
Education Department. *Amount: $1,000/semester.
*Deadline: May 20, July 15, and December 31.

**New York State Higher Education Services
Corporation**
99 Washington Avenue
Albany, NY 12255

518-473-1574, 888-697-4372
http://www.hesc.com/bulletin.nsf/0/9229D337BEFE8
BBC85256D97004EBF47?OpenDocument

Scholarship Name: Tuition Assistance Program (TAP).
*Academic Area: Open. *Age Group: Undergraduate
students. *Eligibility: Applicants must be New York
State high school graduates or GED holders who are
enrolled in or accepted into an approved New York
State college or university. They must be residents of
the state of New York, U.S. citizens or qualifying noncitizens, maintain a 2.0 GPA, not be in default on any
student loans, and attend college full time. Applicants
must also be in good academic standing and meet
income eligibility limitations. Visit the corporation's
Web site for a complete list of participating eligible
institutions. TAP is also available to graduate and
professional students. *Application Process: Applicants
should file the Free Application for Federal Student Aid
(FAFSA) online. After the FAFSA has been completed,
they will be given a link to complete the TAP
application. *Amount: Up to $5,000. *Deadline: May 1.

NORTH CAROLINA

North Carolina State Education Assistance Authority
PO Box 14103
Research Triangle Park, NC 27709
919-549-8614, 800-700-1775, ext. 313
http://www.cfnc.org/Gateway?command=GetBased
ProgramDetail&note=yes&type=8&vocType=11&
vocational=yes&id=142

Scholarship Name: Future Teachers of North Carolina
Scholarship/Loan. *Academic Area: Education. *Age
Group: Undergraduate students. *Eligibility: Applicants
must be residents of North Carolina who are college
juniors or seniors enrolled in a full-time program
leading to teacher certification in math, science,
special education, or English as a second language.
They must be attending a four-year institution in North
Carolina and demonstrate academic achievement
by maintaining at least a 3.0 GPA. Applicants must
commit to teach one of the aforementioned subjects
at a North Carolina public school for a minimum of
three years in order to avoid having to repay these
funds as a loan. *Application Process: Applicants
should notify the dean of the education department
of their college or university of their desire to be
considered for the award. The dean must nominate
individuals from their school. There is no other formal

application process until an individual has received this nomination. Once an applicant has been nominated, he or she will be required to sign a promissory note indicating that he or she will repay the funds if the teaching obligation is not met. *Amount: $6,500. *Deadline: Contact the North Carolina State Education Assistance Authority for deadline information.

North Carolina State Education Assistance Authority
PO Box 14103
Research Triangle Park, NC 27709
866-866-CFNC
http://www.cfnc.org/Gateway?command=GetBased ProgramDetail&note=no&type=7&vocType=10& vocational=no&id=47
Scholarship Name: Jagannathan Scholarship. *Academic Area: Open. *Age Group: Undergraduate students. *Eligibility: Applicants must be graduating high school seniors who plan to enroll as college freshmen in a full-time degree program at the University of North Carolina. Applicants must be North Carolina residents who can demonstrate both academic merit and financial need. Priority consideration is given to applicants who have a parent employed by TIEPET Inc. or Universal Fibers. *Application Process: Applicants should obtain an application from their high school guidance counselor, college financial aid office, or from the corporate offices of TIEPET Inc. or Universal Fibers. Applicants must be nominated by a counselor or company official. They should also take the SAT early enough to submit their scores by the deadline. *Amount: $3,500. *Deadline: February 15.

North Carolina State Education Assistance Authority
PO Box 14103
Research Triangle Park, NC 27709
866-866-CFNC
http://www.cfnc.org/Gateway?command=GetBasedPro gramDetail&note=no&type=7&vocType=10&vocatio nal=no&id=24
Grant Name: North Carolina Community College Grant and Loan Program. *Academic Area: Open. *Age Group: Undergraduate students. *Eligibility: Applicants must be U.S. citizens and North Carolina residents who are enrolled in or attending a community college in North Carolina as part-time or full-time students. They must be able to demonstrate financial need, and eligibility is based on the same criteria as the Federal Pell Grant. Students who do not receive the Pell Grant should still apply. Applicants

who have already earned a baccalaureate degree are not eligible to apply. *Application Process: Applicants must file the Free Application for Federal Student Aid. Contact the financial aid office at your community college for additional information. *Amount: Awards vary. *Deadline: Contact the financial aid office at your community college for deadline information.

North Carolina State Education Assistance Authority
PO Box 14103
Research Triangle Park, NC 27709
866-866-CFNC
http://www.cfnc.org/Gateway?command=GetBasedProg ramDetail&note=no&type=7&vocType=10&vocation al=yes&id=136
Scholarship Name: North Carolina Millennium Teacher Scholarship Loan Program. *Academic Area: Education. *Age Group: Undergraduate students. *Eligibility: Applicants must be North Carolina residents who are graduating high school seniors who intend to enroll in a teacher education program at one of the following three schools in North Carolina: Elizabeth City State University, Fayetteville State University, or Winston-Salem State University. Applicants must have a minimum SAT score of 900 and a 2.5 GPA, as well as demonstrate at least $3,000 in unmet financial need (as determined by their college financial aid office). Applicants who choose to teach in a critical shortage area are given priority. Applicants must commit to teach one year in a North Carolina public school for each year that funds are received in order to avoid having to repay these funds as a loan. *Application Process: Applicants should contact the school of education and the financial aid office at the school they plan to attend for information on the application process. Applicants should also file the Free Application for Federal Student Aid as soon after January 1 as possible. *Amount: $6,500. *Deadline: Contact the financial aid office at your school for deadline information.

North Carolina State Education Assistance Authority
PO Box 14103
Research Triangle Park, NC 27709
866-866-CFNC
http://www.cfnc.org/Gateway?command=GetBasedPro gramDetail&note=no&type=7&vocType=10&vocatio nal=no&id=31
Grant Name: North Carolina Student Incentive Grant. *Academic Area: Open. *Age Group: Undergraduate

students. *Eligibility: Applicants must be U.S. citizens and North Carolina residents who are enrolled in or accepted into a college or university in North Carolina as full-time students. They must not be pursing a religious vocation, and they must be able to demonstrate financial need. *Application Process: Applicants must file the Free Application for Federal Student Aid, listing North Carolina as the state of residence and also listing at least one postsecondary school in North Carolina. Applicants are encouraged to apply well before the official deadline as funds are typically exhausted before the deadline occurs. *Amount: $700. *Deadline: March 15.

North Carolina State Education Assistance Authority
PO Box 14103
Research Triangle Park, NC 27709
866-866-CFNC
http://www.cfnc.org/Gateway?command=GetBasedPro
    gramDetail&note=no&type=7&vocType=10&vocatio
    nal=yes&id=32
Scholarship Name: Nurse Education Scholarship Loan Program. *Academic Area: Nursing (open). *Age Group: Undergraduate students. *Eligibility: Applicants must be North Carolina residents who are graduating high school seniors or enrolled undergraduates who intend to complete programs leading to licensure as a registered nurse or licensed practical nurse. Applicants should be U.S. residents and able to demonstrate financial need and academic merit. Applicants must commit to work as a licensed nurse in North Carolina for a set period of time to avoid having to repay these funds as a loan. Visit the department's Web site for additional information about the service agreement. *Application Process: Applicants should contact the financial aid office at the school they plan to attend for information on the application process. If chosen to receive the award, applicants must sign a promissory note to repay the funds if the service obligation is not met. *Amount: $1,200 to $5,000. *Deadline: Contact the financial aid office at your school for deadline information.

North Carolina State Education Assistance Authority
PO Box 14103
Research Triangle Park, NC 27709
800-700-1775, ext. 313
http://www.cfnc.org/Gateway?command=GetBasedProg
    ramDetail&note=yes&type=8&vocType=11&vocation
    al=yes&id=143

Scholarship Name: Physical Education-Coaching Scholarship Loan Fund. *Academic Area: Education. *Age Group: Undergraduate students. *Eligibility: Applicants must be residents of North Carolina who are college juniors or seniors enrolled in a full-time program leading to teacher certification and to coaching. They must be attending a four-year institution in the state of North Carolina and demonstrate academic achievement by maintaining at least a 2.8 GPA. Applicants must commit to teach full time and serve as a head coach or an assistant coach in a North Carolina public school for however many years the funds are received to avoid having to repay these funds as a loan. *Application Process: Applicants should notify the dean of the education department of their college or university of their desire to be considered for the award. The dean must nominate individuals from their school. There is no other formal application process until an individual has received this nomination. Once an applicant has been nominated, he or she will be required to sign a promissory note indicating that he or she will repay the funds if the teaching and coaching obligation is not met. *Amount: $4,000. *Deadline: Contact the North Carolina State Education Assistance Authority for deadline information.

North Carolina State Education Assistance Authority
PO Box 14103
Research Triangle Park, NC 27709
800-700-1775, ext. 313
http://www.cfnc.org/paying/loan/career/teaching_
    prospective.jsp
Scholarship Name: Prospective Teacher Scholarship-Loan. *Academic Area: Education. *Age Group: Undergraduate students. *Eligibility: Applicants must be North Carolina residents who are graduating high school seniors or enrolled undergraduates who are pursuing a degree leading to teacher certification. Applicants must be attending an approved institution in the state of North Carolina and demonstrate academic achievement by maintaining at least a 3.0 GPA and an SAT score of at least 900. They must also commit to teach full time in a North Carolina public school for each year that the funds are received to avoid having to repay these funds as a loan. *Application Process: Applicants should notify their high school guidance counselor, principal, or college department head of their intentions to pursue the award, as a letter of recommendation is required from such an individual. Applicants should

visit the Education Assistance Authority's Web site to complete an online application and to view a list of eligible institutions. Once a candidate has been chosen, he or she will be required to sign a promissory note indicating that he or she will repay the funds if the teaching obligation is not met. *Amount: $2,500 (four-year schools); $1,200 (community colleges). *Deadline: February 28.

NORTH DAKOTA

North Dakota University System
Attn: Rhonda Schauer, Coordinator of Multicultural Education
North Dakota Student Financial Assistance Program
600 East Boulevard Avenue, Department 215
Bismarck, ND 58505-0230
701-328-9661
rhonda.schauer@ndus.nodak.edu
http://www.ndus.edu/students/default.asp?ID=252
Scholarship Name: North Dakota Indian Scholarship Program. *Academic Area: Open. *Age Group: Undergraduate students. *Eligibility: Applicants must either be residents of North Dakota who are at least one-quarter degree Indian blood or enrolled members of a tribe that is now located in North Dakota. They must be accepted for admission at a North Dakota college, university, or trade school, enrolled as full-time students, and maintain at least a 2.0 GPA. *Application Process: Applicants should submit a completed application along with verification of tribal enrollment, most recent transcript, and a budget completed by the financial aid officer at the institution the applicant is attending. Visit the organization's Web site to download an application. *Amount: $500 to $2,000. Deadline: July 15.

North Dakota University System
Attn: Director of Financial Aid
North Dakota Student Financial Assistance Program
919 South 7th Street, Suite 206
Bismarck, ND 58504-5881
701-328-4114
peggy.wipf@ndus.nodak.edu
http://www.ndus.edu/students/default.asp?ID=252
Scholarship Name: North Dakota Scholars Program. *Academic Area: Open. *Age Group: Undergraduate students. *Eligibility: Applicants must be graduating high school seniors who are residents of North Dakota and U.S. citizens or permanent residents who

enroll in full-time study at a college or university in North Dakota. They must receive an ACT score in the top five percent of all students in the state of North Dakota to qualify, and maintain a 3.5 college GPA in order to renew the scholarship. *Application Process: Applicants should contact their high school guidance counselors for information about their status as top five ACT scorers. There is no formal application process—eligible candidates will be notified and given further instructions. *Amount: Full tuition at a public college (or the equivalent of full tuition at a state college if the student chooses to attend a private college). Deadline: There is no formal deadline for this program.

North Dakota University System
Attn: Director of Financial Aid
North Dakota Student Financial Assistance Program
600 East Boulevard Avenue, Department 215
Bismarck, ND 58505-0230
701-328-4114
peggy.wipf@ndus.nodak.edu
http://www.ndus.edu/students/default.asp?ID=252
Grant Name: North Dakota State Student Incentive Grant. *Academic Area: Open. *Age Group: Undergraduate students. *Eligibility: Applicants must be residents of North Dakota, U.S. citizens or permanent residents, and high school graduates (or GED holders) who intend to use the grant at an eligible college in North Dakota. Applicants must enroll in full-time study, be first-time undergraduate students, and not be in default on any financial aid loans. They must also be able to demonstrate financial need. Contact the system for information on eligible colleges and universities. *Application Process: Applicants must submit the Free Application for Federal Student Aid. *Amount: $600 to $1,000. *Deadline: March 15.

OHIO

Ohio Board of Regents
30 East Broad Street, 36th Floor
Columbus, OH 43215-3414
888-833-1133
nealp_admin@regents.state.oh.us
http://www.regents.state.oh.us/sgs/nealp.htm
Loan Name: Nurse Education Assistance Loan Program. *Academic Area: Nursing (open). *Age Group: Undergraduate students. *Eligibility: Applicants must be residents of Ohio who are enrolled in a nursing

education program at an Ohio college or university. Applicants may need to demonstrate financial need if funding isn't available to award all eligible students. They must also agree to work as a nurse in Ohio to receive a 20 percent per year loan cancellation rate, up to 100 percent loan forgiveness. If this obligation is not met, applicants must repay the funds as a loan with 8 percent interest. The program is also available to graduate students. *Application Process: Applicants must apply online. Visit the board's Web site to apply online. *Amount: $3,000. *Deadline: June 1, November 1.

Ohio Board of Regents
Attn: Financial Aid Office
30 East Broad Street, 36th Floor
Columbus, OH 43215-3414
888-833-1133
bmetheney@regents.state.oh.us
http://www.regents.state.oh.us/sgs/OAS.htm
Scholarship Name: Ohio Academic Scholarship.
*Academic Area: Open. *Age Group: Undergraduate students. *Eligibility: Applicants must be academically outstanding Ohio high school graduates who enroll full time in a college or university in Ohio. Applicants must demonstrate exceptional academic achievement, as shown in their high school GPA and ACT scores. *Application Process: There is no formal application process for students. Each school submits their students' GPAs and ACT scores, and at least one applicant from each chartered school in the state receives the award. Contact your high school guidance counselor to confirm that your scores have been submitted by the deadline. *Amount: $2,205. *Deadline: February 23.

Ohio Board of Regents
Attn: Financial Aid Office
30 East Broad Street, 36th Floor
Columbus, OH 43215-3414
888-833-1133
bmetheney@regents.state.oh.us
http://www.regents.state.oh.us/sgs/oig.htm
Grant Name: Ohio Instructional Grant. *Academic Area: Open. *Age Group: Undergraduate students. *Eligibility: Applicants must be residents of Ohio who can demonstrate some level of financial need. They must enroll full time at a college in the state of Ohio. *Application Process: Applicants should complete the Free Application for Federal Student Aid. Contact your high school guidance counselor or college financial aid officer for additional information. *Amount: $174 to $5,466. *Deadline: October 1.

Ohio Board of Regents
Attn: Financial Aid Office
30 East Broad Street, 36th Floor
Columbus, OH 43215-3414
888-833-1133
bmetheney@regents.state.oh.us
http://www.regents.state.oh.us/sgs/choicegrant.htm
Grant Name: Ohio Student Choice Grant Program.
*Academic Area: Open. *Age Group: Undergraduate students. *Eligibility: Applicants must be residents of Ohio who are accepted into or enrolled in private nonprofit colleges in Ohio. Applicants do not need to exhibit any level of academic merit or financial need. *Application Process: There is no formal application process for students. Contact your college financial aid office for additional information on this award. *Amount: $900. *Deadline: Contact the financial aid office for deadline information.

Ohio Board of Regents
Attn: Financial Aid Office
30 East Broad Street, 36th Floor
Columbus, OH 43215-3414
888-833-1133
bmetheney@regents.state.oh.us
http://www.regents.state.oh.us/sgs/parttimegrant.htm
Grant Name: Part-Time Student Instructional Grant.
*Academic Area: Open. *Age Group: Undergraduate students. *Eligibility: Applicants must be residents of Ohio who can demonstrate financial need. They must enroll part time at a participating college or university in Ohio. Contact the Board of Regents for information on participating institutions. *Application Process: Applicants should contact the financial aid office at the Ohio college or university they attend or plan to attend for additional information. They should also complete the Free Application for Federal Student Aid. *Amount: Awards vary. *Deadline: Contact the financial aid office at your school for deadline information.

OKLAHOMA

Oklahoma State Regents for Higher Education
PO Box 108850
Oklahoma City, OK 73104-8850
405-225-9100, 800-858-1840
aharris@oshre.edu
http://www.okhighered.org/academic-scholars
Scholarship Name: Academic Scholars Program.
*Academic Area: Open. *Age Group: Undergraduate

students. *Eligibility: Applicants must be graduating high school seniors who are residents of Oklahoma who plan to enroll in a college or university in Oklahoma. Applicants may also be out-of-state students. All applicants must demonstrate academic excellence by being National Merit Scholar, National Merit Finalist or United States Presidential Scholar or by scoring in the 99.5 percentile on the ACT or SAT. They may also be nominated by their college or university based on their own set of criteria. *Application Process: Applicants should submit a completed application along with ACT or SAT scores or a copy of the appropriate scholar award. *Amount: Up to $5,500. Awards vary depending on the type of institution the student attends. *Deadline: Contact the board for deadline information.

Oklahoma State Regents for Higher Education
Future Teachers Scholarship
PO Box 108850
Oklahoma City, OK 73104-8850
405-225-9239, 800-858-1840
studentinfo@osrhe.edu
http://www.okhighered.org/student-center/financial-aid/future-teach.shtml
Scholarship Name: Future Teachers Scholarship. *Academic Area: Education. *Age Group: Undergraduate students. *Eligibility: Applicants must be Oklahoma residents attending a college or university in Oklahoma who are enrolled in teacher certification programs in a critical needs area, as designated by the state. Applicants must agree to teach in a public school within the state for a minimum of three consecutive years upon graduation and must be nominated by the college they are attending, based on high school GPA or class rank, ACT or SAT score, admission to the school's educational program, or a college record of academic success. Full-time students are given priority in the distribution of funds, and students must maintain a 2.5 GPA during their course of study. *Application Process: Applicants must submit a completed application along with their most recent official transcripts. First-time freshmen also must submit ACT or SAT scores. An essay is also required of all applicants. For additional information on the application process as well as areas that are designated as critical needs, contact the Oklahoma State Regents for Higher Education (OSRHE). *Amount: $500 to $1,500 (dependent on part-time or full-time status and the number of hours completed). *Deadline: Contact the OSRHE for deadline information.

Oklahoma State Regents for Higher Education
Oklahoma Higher Learning Access Program
PO Box 108850
Oklahoma City, OK 73181-8850
405-225-9100, 800-858-1840
ohlapinfo@osrhe.edu
http://www.okhighered.org/ohlap
Scholarship Name: Oklahoma Higher Learning Access Program-Oklahoma's Promise. *Academic Area: Open. *Age Group: Undergraduate students. *Eligibility: Applicants must be Oklahoma residents who are currently in the 8th, 9th, or 10th grade in Oklahoma and whose family income is less than $50,000 at the time of college enrollment. Applicants must take a required set of college preparatory classes in high school and maintain a 2.5 GPA in these courses. They must also make a decision to be upstanding students by not becoming involved in any troublemaking, attending school and handing in homework, and abstaining from the use of alcohol or drugs. *Application Process: Applicants should submit the Free Application for Federal Student Aid during their senior year in high school. Contact your high school guidance counselor for additional information. *Amount: Full tuition at a public two- or four-year college or university in Oklahoma. Individuals attending private colleges receive an amount equal to the full tuition rate at a public institution. *Deadline: Contact your guidance counselor for enrollment and deadline information.

Oklahoma State Regents for Higher Education
Oklahoma Tuition Aid Grant
PO Box 108850
Oklahoma City, OK 73101-8850
877-662-6231
otaginfo@otag.org
http://www.okhighered.org/student-center/financial-aid/otag.shtml
Grant Name: Oklahoma Tuition Aid Grant Program. *Academic Area: Open. *Age Group: Undergraduate students. *Eligibility: Applicants must be residents of Oklahoma who are enrolled in or accepted into an Oklahoma college, university, or trade school as full-time or part-time students. Applicants must be able to demonstrate financial need. Undocumented immigrants can also apply by filling out an additional application form. *Application Process: Applicants should submit the Free Application for Federal Student Aid as early after January 1 as possible. Because not everyone who applies receives funds,

early submission is important. Contact your high school guidance counselor or college financial aid officer for additional information. *Amount: $1,000 (public institutions), $1,300 (private institutions). *Deadline: June 30.

Oklahoma State Regents for Higher Education
Oklahoma Tuition Equalization Grant
PO Box 108850
Oklahoma City, OK 73101-8850
877-662-6231
studentinfo@osrhe.edu
http://www.okhighered.org/student-center/financial-aid/oteg.shtml
Scholarship Name: Oklahoma Tuition Equalization Grant Program. *Academic Area: Open. *Age Group: Undergraduate students. *Eligibility: Applicants must be Oklahoma residents who are accepted into full-time undergraduate study at private or independent colleges or universities in Oklahoma. They must be first-time freshmen with a family income that does not exceed $50,000. *Application Process: Applicants should file the Free Application for Federal Student Aid, listing their state of residence and the school they plan to attend. Eligible applicants will be notified of their receipt of the award by the financial aid office of the college or university they plan to attend. *Amount: $2,000. *Deadline: Contact the financial aid office at your college or university for deadline information.

Oklahoma State Regents for Higher Education
655 Research Parkway, Suite 200
Oklahoma City, OK 73104
800-858-1840
studentinfo@osrhe.edu
http://www.okhighered.org/student percent2Dcenter/financial percent2Daid/rubs.shtml
Scholarship Name: Regional University Baccalaureate Scholarship. *Academic Area: Open. *Age Group: Undergraduate students. *Eligibility: Applicants must be graduating high school seniors who are residents of Oklahoma who plan to enroll in one of the 11 participating public four-year universities in Oklahoma. Applicants must demonstrate academic excellence by achieving an ACT score of 30 or by being a National Merit Semifinalist or Commended Student. *Application Process: Applicants must contact the financial aid office of the school they plan to attend to inquire about the application process.

*Amount: Resident tuition waiver, plus $3,000. *Deadline: Contact the financial aid office of your college or university for deadline information.

OREGON

Oregon Student Assistance Commission
1500 Valley River Drive, Suite 100
Eugene, OR 97401
800-452-8807
http://www.getcollegefunds.org/ong.html
Grant Name: Oregon Opportunity Grant. *Academic Area: Open. *Age Group: Undergraduate students. *Eligibility: Applicants must be Oregon residents who are enrolled (or plan to enroll) full time at an Oregon college or university. They must be able to demonstrate financial need, and applicants may not enroll in a theology, divinity, or religious studies program if they are seeking this grant. *Application Process: Applicants should file the Free Application for Federal Student Aid (FAFSA) as soon after January 1 as possible. Applicants will be notified of their eligibility to receive funds once the FAFSA has been reviewed. *Amount: Awards vary by need and by the type of institution (public or private) the applicant will be attending. *Deadline: Contact your college or university financial aid office for preferred filing deadlines.

PENNSYLVANIA

Pennsylvania Higher Education Assistance Agency
New Economy Technology Scholarship
State Grant and Special Programs
1200 North Seventh Street
Harrisburg, PA 17105-1444
800-692-7392
http://www.pheaa.org/specialprograms/nets/New_Economy_Technology_Scholarship.shtml
Scholarship Name: New Economy Technology Scholarship. *Academic Area: Science, technology. *Age Group: Undergraduate students. *Eligibility: Applicants must be high school graduates and Pennsylvania residents who are enrolled in (or accepted into) a participating Pennsylvania college or university. They must pursue a degree in an eligible science or technology field and commit to working in this field in Pennsylvania for one year for each year

of funding received. If the service commitment isn't fulfilled, award recipients must repay the funds as a loan. *Application Process: Applicants should submit a completed application along with a master promissory note. Visit the agency's Web site to determine if your field of study is covered, as well as which institutions in Pennsylvania are eligible. Applicants should also submit the Free Application for Federal Student Aid before applying (applicants must attempt to receive need-based aid prior to receiving this award). Applicants may apply for the scholarship online or download a paper education from the agency's Web site. *Amount: Up to $3,000 (science); up to $1,000 (technology). *Deadline: December 31.

Pennsylvania Higher Education Assistance Agency (PHEAA)

Academic Excellence Scholarship Award Program
State Grant and Special Programs
PO Box 8114
Harrisburg, PA 17105-8114
800-692-7392
http://www.pheaa.org/specialprograms/Academic_
    Excellence.shtml
Scholarship Name: PHEAA Academic Excellence Scholarship Award. *Academic Area: Open. *Age Group: Undergraduate students. *Eligibility: Applicants must have fully qualified for the federal Robert C. Byrd Scholarship Program, but not received the award. They must be outstanding high school seniors within the state of Pennsylvania who have been accepted into a college or university and who demonstrate academic achievement. Applicants must have a 3.5 high school GPA or above, an ACT score of at least 25 or an SAT score of at least 1150 (critical reading and math), and rank in the top 5 percent of their graduating class (or hold the first, second, or third place in a class with fewer than 60 people). *Application Process: Applicants should submit a completed application for the Robert C. Byrd (federal) Scholarship along with a copy of their college acceptance letter and a form that has been certified by their high school guidance counselor. Visit the agency's Web site to download an application. *Amount: $1,500. *Deadline: May 1.

Pennsylvania Higher Education Assistance Agency (PHEAA)

1200 North Seventh Street
Harrisburg, PA 17105

800-692-7392
http://www.pheaa.org/stategrants/index.shtml
Grant Name: State Grant. *Academic Area: Open. *Age Group: Undergraduate students. *Eligibility: Applicants must be Pennsylvania residents who meet a designated level of financial need and who enroll at least half time in a PHEAA-approved institution. Applicants must not have earned a previous undergraduate degree. They must also demonstrate academic progress toward a degree in order to receive continued aid. Contact the PHEAA for information on approved colleges and universities. *Application Process: Applicants should file the Free Application for Federal Student Aid as early as possible after January 1. The financial aid offices of the schools they list will notify eligible applicants. *Amount: Up to $3,500. *Deadline: May 1.

RHODE ISLAND

Rhode Island Higher Education Assistance Authority

560 Jefferson Boulevard
Warwick, RI 02886
401-736-1170, 800-922-9855
collegeboundfund@riheaa.org
http://www.riheaa.org/borrowers/scholarships/
    academic_promise.html
Scholarship Name: CollegeBoundfund Academic Promise Scholarship. *Academic Area: Open. *Age Group: Undergraduate students. *Eligibility: Applicants must be graduating high school seniors who are Rhode Island residents planning to enroll in a college or university as full-time students. They must show academic promise and demonstrate financial need; a formula combining both of these elements is used to determine scholarship recipients. *Application Process: Applicants must file the Free Application for Federal Student Aid as well as take the ACT or SAT. Visit your high school guidance counselor for additional information. *Amount: Up to $2,500. *Deadline: March 1.

Rhode Island Higher Education Assistance Authority

560 Jefferson Boulevard
Warwick, RI 02886
401-736-1170, 800-922-9855
grants@riheaa.org
http://www.riheaa.org/borrowers/grants
Grant Name: Rhode Island State Grant. *Academic

Area: Open. *Age Group: Undergraduate students. *Eligibility: Applicants must be U.S. citizens or eligible non-citizens who have been residents of Rhode Island since January 1 of the previous academic year and who are enrolled in or accepted into a college or university program that leads to a degree or certificate. They must not owe a refund on a federal Title IV grant and must not be in default on a Title IV loan. Applicants must not have previously earned a bachelor's degree and must meet all Title IV eligibility requirements (no drug convictions and registered with the Selective Service). Applicants must attend school at least half time and be able to demonstrate financial need. *Application Process: Applicants must file the Free Application for Federal Student Aid. No other formal application must be filed. Students will be notified by mail or e-mail if they have been awarded a grant. *Amount: $250 to $1,400. *Deadline: March 1.

SOUTH CAROLINA

South Carolina Commission on Higher Education
Attn: Sandra Rhyne, Coordinator
1333 Main Street, Suite 200
Columbia, SC 29201
803-737-2280, 877-349-7183
srhyne@che.sc.gov
http://www.che.sc.gov/New_Web/GoingToCollege/
    LIFE_Hm.htm
Scholarship Name: Legislative Incentive for Future Excellence Scholarship. *Academic Area: Open. *Age Group: Undergraduate students. *Eligibility: Applicants must be graduating high school seniors or students enrolling for the first time in a degree program. They must be residents of South Carolina during high school and during the time of college enrollment, attend an eligible institution in South Carolina, and be U.S. citizens or permanent legal residents who have not received other select state scholarships and who have not been convicted of a felony. For this merit-based scholarship, applicants should demonstrate academic achievement by having a 3.0 GPA, 1100 SAT or 24 ACT score, and should have been in the top 30 percent of their high school graduating class. *Application Process: There is no formal application for this scholarship. Applicants should contact the financial aid office of the school they are attending if they feel they are eligible, but have not received notification from the office. *Amount: Up to $4,700, plus $300 book allowance.

*Deadline: Contact the financial aid office of your college or university for deadline information.

South Carolina Commission on Higher Education
Attn: Ms. Karen Wham
1333 Main Street, Suite 200
Columbia, SC 29201
803-737-4544, 877-349-7183
kwham@che.sc.gov
http://www.che.sc.gov/New_Web/GoingToCollege/
    LTA_Hm.htm
Scholarship Name: Lottery Tuition Assistance Program. *Academic Area: Open. *Age Group: Undergraduate students. *Eligibility: Applicants must be graduating high school seniors or students enrolling in an eligible South Carolina two-year college. They must be residents of South Carolina and U.S. citizens or permanent legal residents who have not received other select state scholarships. Applicants do not have to demonstrate financial need for this award, but they must file for federal aid since the amount an applicant is eligible for in this program is dependent on the amount of federal aid the applicant receives. *Application Process: There is no formal application for this scholarship. Applicants should file the Free Application for Federal Student Aid as soon after January 1 as possible. Contact your high school guidance counselor or college financial aid office for additional information. *Amount: Up to $936/term (full-time students), up to $78/credit hour (part-time students) *Deadline: Contact the financial aid office of your college or university for deadline information.

South Carolina Commission on Higher Education
Attn: Sherry Hubbard
1333 Main Street, Suite 200
Columbia, SC 29201
803-737-2262, 877-349-7183
shubbard@che.sc.gov
http://www.che.sc.gov/New_Web/GoingToCollege/
    PF_Hm.htm
Scholarship Name: Palmetto Fellows Scholarship. *Academic Area: Open. *Age Group: Undergraduate students. *Eligibility: Applicants should be graduating high school seniors who are accepted into an eligible four-year institution in South Carolina. They must be residents of South Carolina during high school and during the time of college enrollment, U.S. citizens or permanent legal residents who have not received other select state scholarships, and have not been convicted of a felony. This is a merit-based scholarship,

and priority is given to students who are members of an ethnic or racial minority. For further information on eligibility requirements or participating institutions, contact the commission. *Application Process: Contact the commission for information on the application process. *Amount: Up to $6,700. *Deadline: Contact the financial aid office of your college or university or the commission for deadline information.

South Carolina Commission on Higher Education

Attn: Ms. Karen Wham
1333 Main Street, Suite 200
Columbia, SC 29201
803-737-4544, 877-349-7183
kwham@che.sc.gov
http://www.che.sc.gov/New_Web/GoingToCollege/
    HOPE_Hm.htm
Scholarship Name: South Carolina HOPE Scholarship. *Academic Area: Open. *Age Group: Undergraduate students. *Eligibility: Applicants must be first-time entering freshmen enrolling in an eligible four-year South Carolina institution. They must be residents of South Carolina during high school and during the time of college enrollment, U.S. citizens or permanent legal residents who have not received other select state scholarships, and have not been convicted of a felony. For this merit-based scholarship, applicants should demonstrate academic achievement by having a 3.0 GPA. *Application Process: There is no formal application for this scholarship. Applicants' final GPAs are forwarded by their high school, and applicants are contacted if they receive the award. Applicants should contact the financial aid office of the school they are attending if they feel they are eligible but have not received notification from the office. *Amount: $2,650. *Deadline: Contact the financial aid office of your college or university for deadline information.

South Carolina Higher Education Tuition Grants Commission

Attn: Sandra Rhyne, Coordinator
1333 Main Street, Suite 200
Columbia, SC 29201
803-737-2280, 803-737-2280
srhyne@che.sc.gov
http://www.che.sc.gov/StudentServices/NeedBased/
    NBG.htm
Scholarship Name: South Carolina Need-Based Grant Program. *Academic Area: Open. *Age Group: Undergraduate students. *Eligibility: Applicants must be graduating high school seniors or students enrolling for the first time in a degree program. They must be residents of South Carolina during high school and during the time of college enrollment, attend an eligible South Carolina institution, U.S. citizens or permanent legal residents who have not received other select state scholarships, and have not been convicted of a felony. Applicants must maintain a 2.0 GPA and must be able to demonstrate extreme financial need. *Application Process: Applicants should submit the Free Application for Federal Student Aid as soon as possible after January 1. If applicants are attending private colleges, they should contact the commission at 803-896-1120 for further instructions. Applicants attending public institutions do not need to do anything further. Contact your financial aid office for any additional information. *Amount: Up to $2,500 (full-time students); up to $1,250 (part-time students). *Deadline: Contact the financial aid office of your college or university for priority deadline information. Apply as soon after January 1 as possible.

SOUTH DAKOTA

South Dakota Board of Regents

Attn: Scholarship Committee
306 East Capitol Avenue, Suite 200
Pierre, SD 57501-3159
http://www.sdbor.edu/administration/academics/
    documents/fowler_info_sheet-06.doc
Scholarship Name: Annis Irene Fowler/Kaden Scholarship. *Academic Area: Education. *Age Group: Undergraduate students. *Eligibility: Applicants must be entering college freshman majoring in elementary education at Black Hills State University, Dakota State University, Northern State University, or the University of South Dakota. They must have a cumulative high school GPA of at least 3.0. Winners are chosen based on GPA, high school course work (especially science and mathematics), letters of recommendation, and an essay. Applicants who demonstrate motivational ability, have a disability, or who are self-supporting will receive special consideration. *Application Process: Applicants should submit an original typed, double-spaced essay (1,000 to 1,500 words, topic picked by scholarship donors each year), ACT scores, two letters of recommendation from teachers, an official high school transcript, and a completed application (available at the board's Web site). *Amount: $1,000. *Deadline: February 9.

South Dakota Board of Regents

Attn: Scholarship Committee
306 East Capitol Avenue, Suite 200
Pierre, SD 57501-3159
http://www.sdbor.edu/administration/academics/
documents/bjugstad_info_sheet-06.doc
Scholarship Name: Ardell Bjugstad Scholarship Program
for Native American High School Seniors. *Academic
Area: Agriculture, natural resources. *Age Group:
Undergraduate students. *Eligibility: Applicants must
be enrolled members of a federally recognized Indian
tribe in South Dakota or North Dakota, residents
of South Dakota or North Dakota, and high school
seniors planning to pursue a degree in agriculture,
natural resources, or a related field. They must also be
academic achievers. *Application Process: Applicants
should submit two letters of recommendation, an
official high school transcript, verification of tribal
enrollment, and a completed application (available at
the board's Web site and from high school guidance
counselors). Contact your high school guidance
counselor for applications and additional information.
*Amount: $500. *Deadline: February 9.

South Dakota Board of Regents

Attn: Scholarship Committee
306 East Capitol Avenue, Suite 200
Pierre, SD 57501-3159
http://www.sdbor.edu/administration/academics/
documents/haines_info_sheet-06.doc
Scholarship Name: Haines Memorial Scholarship.
*Academic Area: Education. *Age Group:
Undergraduate students. *Eligibility: Applicants must
be college students enrolled in a teacher education
program at a South Dakota public university and
classified as a sophomore, junior, or senior as of January
1 of the year in which they seek the award. They must
have a GPA of at least 2.5 on a 4.0 scale. *Application
Process: Applicants should submit a typed resume
(which includes graduating high school and high school
activities, memberships, and services and a listing
of university memberships and activities), a typed
two-page double-spaced statement describing their
personal philosophy, a typed two-page double-spaced
statement describing their philosophy of education,
and a completed application (available at the board's
Web site). *Amount: $2,150. *Deadline: February 9.

South Dakota Board of Regents

Attn: Scholarship Committee
306 East Capitol Avenue, Suite 200

Pierre, SD 57501-3159
http://www.sdbor.edu/administration/academics/
documents/scarborough_info_sheet-06_000.doc
Scholarship Name: Marlin R. Scarborough Memorial
Scholarship. *Academic Area: Open. *Age Group:
Undergraduate students. *Eligibility: Applicants
must be juniors at a South Dakota public university
and have a college GPA of at least 3.5. They must be
classified as juniors at the time the funding is awarded
*Application Process: Applicants should submit a
completed application (available at the board's Web
site) and a typed, three-page, double-spaced essay
explaining their leadership and academic qualities,
educational interests, and career plans. These
documents should be submitted to the financial aid
office of the applicant's school. *Amount: $1,500.
*Deadline: Contact the board for details.

South Dakota Board of Regents

Attn: Scholarship Committee
306 East Capitol Avenue, Suite 200
Pierre, SD 57501-3159
http://www.sdbor.edu/SDOpportunityScholarship.htm
Award Name: South Dakota Opportunity Scholarship.
*Academic Area: Open. *Age Group: Undergraduate
students. *Eligibility: Applicants must be residents of
South Dakota, have an ACT score of 24 or higher or a
combined verbal/mathematics SAT score of at least
1070, and plan to attend an approved South Dakota
postsecondary institution. They must complete high
school course requirements (known as the Regents
Scholar curriculum), which require four units of
English, three units of social studies, four units of
algebra or higher mathematics, four units of science,
one-half unit of computer science, one unit of fine
arts, and two units of the same modern or classical
language. Applicants must have a GPA of at least 2.0 in
the Regents Scholar curriculum, and a cumulative GPA
of at least 3.0. *Application Process: Applicants should
submit high school transcripts, SAT/ACT scores, and a
completed application (available at the board's Web
site) to the admissions office of the school in which
they plan to attend. *Amount: $5,000 (over four years).
*Deadline: June 1.

TENNESSEE

Tennessee Student Assistance Corporation

Parkway Towers, 404 James Robertson Parkway, Suite 1950
Nashville, TN 37243-0820

615-741-1346, 800-342-1663
http://www.collegepaystn.com/mon_college/ned_mc_
shcolar.htm
Scholarship Name: Ned McWherter Scholars Program.
*Academic Area: Open. *Age Group: Undergraduate
students. *Eligibility: Applicants must be recent high
school graduates or high school seniors starting their
last semester of school, U.S. citizens, and Tennessee
residents (whose parents are also Tennessee
residents). They must have a GPA of at least 3.5 and
an ACT or SAT score in the top 5 percent of all test
takers. *Application Process: Students can obtain an
application from their high school guidance office or
at the corporation's Web site. *Amount: Up to $6,000.
*Deadline: February 15.

Tennessee Student Assistance Corporation
Parkway Towers, 404 James Robertson Parkway, Suite
1950
Nashville, TN 37243-0820
615-741-1346, 800-342-1663
http://www.collegepaystn.com/mon_college/lottery_
scholars.htm
Scholarship Name: Tennessee Education Lottery
Scholarship Program. *Academic Area: Open. *Age
Group: Undergraduate students. *Eligibility: Applicants
must be residents of Tennessee for at least one year
prior to application and be enrolled, or accepted for
enrollment, at an eligible postsecondary educational
institution in Tennessee. Visit the corporation's Web
site for a list of eligible colleges. Note: Several different
scholarships and grants are available via this program;
contact the corporation for eligibility requirements
for each scholarship and grant. *Application
Process: Applicants must have their completed Free
Application for Federal Student Aid processed by the
federal processor by February 1 (spring and summer
semesters) and September 1 (fall semester). Contact
the corporation for details. *Amount: $1,000 to $3,300.
*Deadline: February 1 (spring and summer semesters);
September 1 (fall semester).

Tennessee Student Assistance Corporation
Parkway Towers, 404 James Robertson Parkway, Suite
1950
Nashville, TN 37243-0820
615-741-1346, 800-342-1663
http://www.collegepaystn.com/mon_college/tsa_award.
htm
Award Name: Tennessee Student Assistance Award.
*Academic Area: Open. *Age Group: Undergraduate

students. *Eligibility: Applicants must be enrolled,
or accepted for enrollment, at a public or an eligible
non-public postsecondary educational institution in
Tennessee. They must also attend school at least part
time. Depending on funding, preference is given to
U.S. citizens. *Application Process: Applicants must
have their completed Free Application for Federal
Student Aid processed by the federal processor by
May 1. Contact the corporation for details. *Amount:
Up to full tuition and mandatory fees. *Deadline:
Contact the corporation for deadline information.

TEXAS

Texas Higher Education Coordinating Board
PO Box 12788
Austin, TX 78711-2788
800-242-3062
http://www.collegefortexans.com/cfbin/tofa2.cfm?ID=11
Scholarship Name: Professional Nursing Scholarship.
*Academic Area: Nursing (open). *Age Group:
Undergraduate students. *Eligibility: Texas residents
who demonstrate financial need may apply. Applicants
must pursue at least part-time study in course work at
a private or public Texas college or university that leads
to licensure as a professional nurse. Some funds under
this scholarship program are specifically targeted to
students from rural backgrounds. The scholarship
is also available to graduate students. *Application
Process: Students should obtain an application from
their college's financial aid office. *Amount: Up to
$3,000. *Deadline: Contact the board for details.

Texas Higher Education Coordinating Board
PO Box 12788
Austin, TX 78711-2788
800-242-3062
http://www.collegefortexans.com/cfbin/tofa2.cfm?ID=93
Grant Name: Texas Educational Opportunity Grant.
*Academic Area: Open. *Age Group: Undergraduate
students. *Eligibility: Applicants must demonstrate
financial need and be enrolled at least half time a
two-year public community college, public technical
college, or public state college in Texas. They must not
have been convicted of a felony or a crime involving a
controlled substance. Students who receive the grant
must meet their institution's satisfactory academic
progress requirements after their first year of study.
After their second year, they must have completed at
least 75 percent of credit hours attempted and have a

GPA of at least 2.5 on a 4.0 scale. *Application Process: Applicants must complete the Free Application for Federal Student Aid; they will be notified by their college's financial aid office if they are eligible for the grant. *Amount: Full tuition and required fees. *Deadline: Contact the board for details.

Texas Higher Education Coordinating Board
PO Box 12788
Austin, TX 78711-2788
800-242-3062
http://www.collegefortexans.com/cfbin/tofa2.cfm?ID=10
Grant Name: Texas Public Educational Grant. *Academic Area: Open. *Age Group: Undergraduate students. *Eligibility: Applicants must demonstrate financial need and be enrolled at a public college or university in Texas. Texas residents, nonresidents, and foreign students may apply. The grant is also available to graduate students. *Application Process: Applicants must complete the Free Application for Federal Student Aid; they will be notified by their college's financial aid office if they are eligible for the grant. *Amount: Varies by academic institution. *Deadline: Contact the board for details.

Texas Higher Education Coordinating Board
PO Box 12788
Austin, TX 78711-2788
800-242-3062
http://www.collegefortexans.com/TEXASGrant/TEXASGrant.cfm
Grant Name: TEXAS (Towards EXcellence, Access and Success) Grant. *Academic Area: Open. *Age Group: Undergraduate students. *Eligibility: Applicants must be high school seniors or college students, demonstrate financial need, and plan to attend (or be attending) a Texas public college or university. They must not have been convicted of a felony or a crime involving a controlled substance. Students who receive the grant must complete at least 75 percent of course hours attempted each year and have a minimum GPA of 2.5. *Application Process: Applicants must complete the Free Application for Federal Student Aid; they will be notified by their college's financial aid office if they are eligible for the grant. *Amount: Full tuition and required fees. *Deadline: Contact the board for details.

Texas Higher Education Coordinating Board
PO Box 12788
Austin, TX 78711-2788

800-242-3062
http://www.collegefortexans.com/cfbin/tofa2.cfm?ID=6
Grant Name: Tuition Equalization Grant Program. *Academic Area: Open. *Age Group: Undergraduate students. *Eligibility: Applicants must be residents of Texas or nonresident National Merit finalists, demonstrate financial need, maintain a GPA of at least 2.5 on a 4.0 scale, and enrolled full time at a private, nonprofit college or university in Texas. *Application Process: Applicants must complete the Free Application for Federal Student Aid; they will be notified by their college's financial aid office if they are eligible for the grant. *Amount: Up to $3,444. *Deadline: Contact the board for details.

Texas Higher Education Coordinating Board
PO Box 12788
Austin, TX 78711-2788
800-242-3062
http://www.collegefortexans.com/cfbin/tofa2.cfm?ID=12
Scholarship Name: Vocational Nursing Scholarship. *Academic Area: Nursing (open). *Age Group: Undergraduate students. *Eligibility: Texas residents who demonstrate financial need may apply. Applicants must pursue at least part-time study in course work at a private or public Texas college or university that leads to licensure as a vocational nurse. *Application Process: Students should obtain an application from their college's financial aid office. *Amount: Up to $1,500. *Deadline: Contact the board for details.

UTAH

Utah Higher Education Assistance Authority
PO Box 45202
Salt Lake City, UT 84101-0202
801-321-7200, 877-336-7378
uheaa@utahsbr.edu
http://www.uheaa.org/parentStudent02c.html
Loan Name: Terrel H. Bell Teaching Incentive Loan Program. *Academic Area: Education. *Age Group: Undergraduate students. *Eligibility: Applicants must be high school seniors or college students who have completed a specified number of course credits (varies by academic institution) and who are pursuing a degree in teacher education. They must be Utah residents and plan to or currently attend full time one of the following Utah colleges or universities: Brigham Young University, Dixie State College, College

of Eastern Utah, University of Phoenix, Salt Lake Community College, Snow College, Southern Utah University, University of Utah, Utah State University, Utah Valley State College, Weber State University, or Westminster College. *Application Process: High school seniors should obtain an application at their counselor's office, the state Office of Education, or online at the authority's Web site. College students can obtain an application from their school's financial aid office or online at the authority's Web site. *Amount: Varies; all or a portion of the loan is forgiven based on the number of years the student teaches in a Utah public or private school after graduation. *Deadline: March 31.

Utah Higher Education Assistance Authority
PO Box 45202
Salt Lake City, UT 84101-0202
801-321-7200, 877-336-7378
uheaa@utahsbr.edu
http://www.uheaa.org/parentStudent02c.html
Scholarship Name: The Centennial Scholarship is awarded to students who graduate early from high school. *Academic Area: Open. *Age Group: Undergraduate students. *Eligibility: Contact the authority for details. *Application Process: Contact the authority for details. *Amount: $250 for each quarter graduated early by the applicant. *Deadline: Contact the authority for details.

Utah Higher Education Assistance Authority
Board of Regents Building, The Gateway
60 South 400 West
Salt Lake City, UT 84101-1284
801-321-7107
http://www.utahsbr.edu/html/new_century.html
Scholarship Name: The New Century Scholarship is offered to students who complete an associate degree by the year their class graduates from high school; it helps students pay for the last two years of education that will culminate in the awarding of a baccalaureate degree. *Academic Area: Open. *Age Group: Undergraduate students. *Eligibility: Applicants must complete an associate degree at one of the following Utah System of Higher Education institutions by September 1 of the year their class graduates from high school: Dixie State College of Utah, College of Eastern Utah, Salt Lake Community College, Snow College, Southern Utah University, University of Utah, Utah State University, Utah Valley State College, or Weber State University.

Students may use the New Century Scholarship for baccalaureate study at Brigham Young University, Dixie State College of Utah, Southern Utah University, the University of Utah, Utah State University, Utah Valley State College, Weber State University, or Westminster College. Applicants must maintain a B average during baccalaureate study. *Application Process: Applicants must submit a completed application (available for download at the board's Web site), official high school and college transcripts, and verification of enrollment in a four-year program. *Amount: Up to 75 percent of tuition. *Deadline: Contact the board for details.

Utah Higher Education Assistance Authority
PO Box 45202
Salt Lake City, UT 84101-0202
801-321-7200, 877-336-7378
uheaa@utahsbr.edu
http://www.uheaa.org/parentStudent02b.html
Grant Name: Utah Centennial Opportunity Program for Education Grant. *Academic Area: Open. *Age Group: Undergraduate students. *Eligibility: Applicants must be Utah residents who are attending postsecondary institutions in Utah. Not all Utah schools offer these grants; contact the authority for information on eligible schools. *Application Process: Applicants must complete the Free Application for Federal Student Aid. Contact the authority for details. *Amount: Contact the authority for details. *Deadline: Contact the authority for details.

VERMONT

Vermont Student Assistance Corporation
PO Box 2000
Winooski, VT 05404
802-654-3798, 888-253-4819
info@vsac.org
http://services.vsac.org/ilwwcm/connect/VSAC/Pay+for+College
Scholarship Name: The corporation offers more than 100 scholarships. *Academic Area: Open. *Age Group: Undergraduate students. *Eligibility: Applicants must be Vermont high school seniors, undergraduate students, or graduate students. *Application Process: Applicants must complete the Free Application for Federal Student Aid (FAFSA) and a unified scholarship application, which is available at the corporation's Web site. Select scholarships are also available to

332 State Financial Aid Programs and Offices

graduate students. *Amount: Varies. *Deadline: Applicants must submit their completed application and FAFSA as soon as possible after January 1.

Vermont Student Assistance Corporation
PO Box 2000
Winooski, VT 05404
800-882-4166
info@vsac.org
http://services.vsac.org/ilwwcm/connect/VSAC/
    Pay+for+College
Grant Name: Vermont Incentive Grant. *Academic Area: Open. *Age Group: Undergraduate students. *Eligibility: Applicants must be Vermont residents who do not have a bachelor's degree (unless they are enrolled in the University of Vermont's College of Medicine or any accredited Doctor of Veterinary Medicine program), and who plan to attend (or currently attend) a postsecondary institution full time. They must also be U.S. citizens or eligible non-citizens, and demonstrate financial need. The grants may be used at in-state or out-of-state schools. *Application Process: Applicants must complete the Free Application for Federal Student Aid (FAFSA) and a grant application, which, along with a list of participating schools, is available at the corporation's Web site. Contact the corporation for details. *Amount: $500 to $9,800. *Deadline: Applicants must submit their application as soon as possible after January 1, and the FAFSA as soon as possible after February 1.

Vermont Student Assistance Corporation
PO Box 2000
Winooski, VT 05404
802-654-3750, 800-882-4166
info@vsac.org
http://services.vsac.org/ilwwcm/connect/VSAC/
    Pay+for+College
Grant Name: Vermont Part-Time Grant. *Academic Area: Open. *Age Group: Undergraduate students. *Eligibility: Applicants must be Vermont residents who do not have a bachelor's degree, and who plan to attend or are currently attending a postsecondary institution part time (fewer than 12 credits). They must be U.S. citizens or eligible non-citizens, and demonstrate financial need. The grants may be used at in-state or out-of-state schools. *Application Process: Applicants must complete the Free Application for Federal Student Aid (FAFSA) and a grant application, which, along with a list

of participating schools, is available at the corporation's Web site. Contact the corporation for details. *Amount: Varies by the number of credit hours taken. *Deadline: Applicants must submit their application as soon as possible after January 1, and the FAFSA as soon as possible after February 1.

VIRGINIA

State Council of Higher Education for Virginia
James Monroe Building, 101 North 14th Street
Richmond, VA 23219
804-225-2600
http://www.schev.edu/Students/factsheetCSAP.
    asp?from=students
Scholarship Name: College Scholarship Assistance Program. *Academic Area: Open. *Age Group: Undergraduate students. *Eligibility: Applicants must be residents of Virginia, citizens or eligible non-citizens of the United States, demonstrate extreme financial need, and be admitted to a Virginia public two- or four-year college or university. They must also attend college at least half time. Visit the council's Web site for further eligibility requirements. *Application Process: Applicants should complete the Free Application for Federal Student Aid (and if attending a private institution, file a Tuition Assistance Grant Program); applicants will be notified if they qualify for the program. *Amount: $400 to $5,000. *Deadline: Contact the council for details.

State Council of Higher Education for Virginia
James Monroe Building, 101 North 14th Street
Richmond, VA 23219
804-225-2600
http://www.schev.edu/Students/
    undergradfinancialAidPrograms.asp?from=students
Scholarship Name: Granville P. Meade Scholarship. *Academic Area: Open. *Age Group: Undergraduate students. *Eligibility: Applicants must be high school seniors and residents of Virginia who plan to attend a Virginia postsecondary institution. *Application Process: Applicants should obtain an application from their high school guidance office. *Amount: $2,000. *Deadline: Contact the council for details.

State Council of Higher Education for Virginia
James Monroe Building, 101 North 14th Street
Richmond, VA 23219

804-225-2600

http://www.schev.edu/Students/factsheetHETAP.
asp?from=students

Scholarship Name: Higher Education Teacher Assistance Program. *Academic Area: Education. *Age Group: Undergraduate students. *Eligibility: Applicants must be enrolled or plan to enroll in a K-12 teacher education program at a Virginia public two- or four-year college or university. They must be residents of Virginia, citizens or eligible non-citizens of the United States, demonstrate financial need, have a GPA of at least 2.5, and enrolled or plan to enroll full time. Priority will be given to applicants who are pursuing study in teacher shortage areas; contact the council for a list of current shortage areas. *Application Process: Applicants should contact the financial aid office or the education department at the college they plan to or currently attend for details. A faculty member must nominate applicants. *Amount: $2,000 (four-year institutions); $1,000 (two-year institutions). *Deadline: Contact the financial aid office for details.

State Council of Higher Education for Virginia
James Monroe Building, 101 North 14th Street
Richmond, VA 23219
804-225-2600
http://www.schev.edu/Students/factsheetVTAG.
asp?from=students

Grant Name: Tuition Assistance Grant Program. *Academic Area: Open. *Age Group: Undergraduate students. *Eligibility: Virginia residents who are pursuing nontheological-related degrees at accredited private, nonprofit colleges and universities in Virginia may apply. The grant is also available to graduate students. *Application Process: Applicants should contact the financial aid office at their college for details. *Amount: $2,500. *Deadline: July 31.

State Council of Higher Education for Virginia
James Monroe Building, 101 North 14th Street
Richmond, VA 23219
804-225-2600
http://www.schev.edu/Students/factsheetCOMMA.
asp?from=students

Award Name: Virginia Commonwealth Award. *Academic Area: Open. *Age Group: Undergraduate students. *Eligibility: Applicants must be residents of Virginia, U.S. citizens or eligible noncitizens, demonstrate financial need, and plan to enroll or be enrolled at least half time at a Virginia public two- or four-year college or university. The award is also available to graduate students. *Application Process: Applicants should contact the financial aid office at the college they plan to or currently attend for details. *Amount: Varies. *Deadline: Contact the financial aid office for details.

WASHINGTON

Washington Higher Education Coordinating Board
PO Box 43430
Olympia, WA 98504-3430
360-753-7843
ales@hecb.wa.gov
http://www.hecb.wa.gov/paying/waaidprgm/aies.asp

Scholarship Name: American Indian Endowed Scholarship. *Academic Area: Open. *Age Group: Undergraduate students. *Eligibility: Applicants must demonstrate financial need, be Washington residents, and plan to enroll or be enrolled full time pursuing any major (except theology) at a Washington college or university. High school seniors and college students may apply for this scholarship. Applicants must have close social and cultural ties to a Native American tribe. The scholarship is also available to graduate students. *Application Process: Applicants must complete the Free Application for Federal Student Aid and submit a scholarship application (available for download at the board's Web site), academic transcripts, three or more letters of recommendation, and a statement describing their close relationship with a Native American tribe and how they will serve this group upon graduation. *Amount: $500 to $2,000. *Deadline: May 15.

Washington Higher Education Coordinating Board
PO Box 43430
Olympia, WA 98504-3430
360-753-7861
eog@hecb.wa.gov
http://www.hecb.wa.gov/paying/waaidprgm/eog.asp

Grant Name: Educational Opportunity Grant. *Academic Area: Open. *Age Group: Undergraduate students, graduate students. *Eligibility: Applicants must demonstrate financial need, be Washington residents, and have already earned an associate degree or achieved junior class standing. They must have "placebound" circumstances (defined by the board as "having personal barriers, such as family or employment commitments, health concerns, financial inability, or other similar factors, that make it difficult to continue an education at a four-year college"). Placebound students typically have to relocate or are unable to relocate to attend college as a result of personal barriers. Eligible Washington schools in this grant program include: Antioch University, Bastyr University, Central Washington University, Cornish College of the Arts, Eastern Washington University, Evergreen State College, Gonzaga University, Heritage University, Northwest University, Pacific Lutheran University, Saint Martin's University, Seattle Pacific University, Seattle University, University of Puget Sound, University of Washington, Walla Walla College, Washington State University, Western Washington University, Whitman College, and Whitworth College. The grant is also available to graduate students. *Application Process: Applicants must complete the Free Application for Federal Student Aid and submit a scholarship application (available for download at the board's Web site). *Amount: $2,500. *Deadline: Varies.

Washington Higher Education Coordinating Board
Attn: Mary Knutson
PO Box 43430
Olympia, WA 98504-3430
360-753-7845, 888-535-0747
futureteachers@hecb.wa.gov
http://www.hecb.wa.gov/paying/waaidprgm/future.asp
Scholarship Name: Future Teachers Conditional Scholarship and Loan Repayment Program. *Academic Area: Education. *Age Group: Undergraduate students, professionals. *Eligibility: Applicants must be students who are planning to pursue careers in education, paraprofessionals who are interested in becoming teachers, and teachers who are interested in seeking additional endorsements in teacher shortage subjects. They must be residents of Washington, plan to attend school at least part time, and not pursue a degree in theology. In exchange for funding, participants agree to work in Washington K-12 public schools. Applicants are judged based on academic ability, contributions to the public school system, potential to serve as a positive role model for students, length of time until completion of their educational program, and commitment to serve as a Washington classroom teacher. Priority will be given to those seeking additional endorsements in math, science,

or special education, and those with bilingual ability in languages needed in Washington schools. *Application Process: Visit the board's Web site for more information on the application process. *Amount: $2,445 to $5,446. *Deadline: Contact the board for details.

Washington Higher Education Coordinating Board
Attn: Kathy McVay
c/o Washington State Department of Health
310 Israel Road SE
Tumwater, WA 98501
360-236-2816
kathy.mcvay@doh.wa.gov
http://www.hecb.wa.gov/paying/waaidprgm/health.asp
Scholarship Name: Health Professional Loan Repayment and Scholarship. *Academic Area: Medicine (dental hygiene), medicine (dentistry), medicine (physician), medicine (physician assisting), nursing (education), nursing (midwifery), nursing (nurse practitioner), nursing (open), pharmaceutical sciences. *Age Group: Undergraduate students, medical students. *Eligibility: Applicants must be students who are training to enter one of the following primary health care professions: physician (M.D./D.O., N.D.), physician assistant, nurse practitioner, midwife (certified-nurse and licensed), pharmacist, dentist, dental hygienist, or licensed nurse (all levels including faculty). Applicants must be U.S. citizens, but do not need to be residents of Washington. In addition to this scholarship, a loan repayment option is also available to licensed primary health care professionals. Participants in both programs agree to work in primary health care in rural or underserved urban areas for at least three years in exchange for scholarship funds. *Application Process: Visit the board's Web site to download an application. *Amount: Awards vary. *Deadline: Typically in April.

Washington Higher Education Coordinating Board
PO Box 43430
Olympia, WA 98504-3430
360-753-7850
finaid@hecb.wa.gov
http://www.hecb.wa.gov/paying/waaidprgm/sng.asp
Grant Name: State Need Grant. *Academic Area: Open. *Age Group: Undergraduate students, adults. *Eligibility: Applicants must be low-income residents of Washington who are interested in pursuing degrees, honing their skills, or retraining for new careers. They must have a family income of equal to

or less than 65 percent of the state median (a chart is available on the board's Web site), be a resident of Washington, enroll at least half time in an eligible program, and not be pursuing a degree in theology. *Application Process: Students who complete the Free Application for Federal Student Aid are automatically considered for this grant. *Amount: Varies by level of family income. *Deadline: Contact the board for details.

Washington Higher Education Coordinating Board
c/o Washington Workforce Training and Education
    Coordinating Board
128 10th Avenue SW, PO Box 43105
Olympia, WA 98504-3105
360-753-0892
ddonahoo@wtb.wa.gov
http://www.hecb.wa.gov/paying/waaidprgm/wave.asp
Award Name: The Washington Award for Vocational Excellence (WAVE) provides education grants to three high school students from each of Washington's 49 state legislative districts. *Academic Area: Open. *Age Group: Undergraduate students. *Eligibility: Applicants must demonstrate achievement in vocational/technical education, financial need, and plan to pursue any major except theology at a public or independent Washington college or university. Applicants should be enrolled in a Washington State high school, skills center, or public community or technical college at the time of application, and graduate from high school with at least 360 hours in a single, approved vocational program or be enrolled in a public technical or community college and have completed at least one year in an approved vocational program by June 30 of the award year. *Application Process: Applicants should obtain a nomination form from their school vocational administrator, WAVE coordinator, or counselor. An application is also available at the Washington Workforce Training and Education Coordinating Board's Web site: http://www.wtb.wa.gov. *Amount: $2,445 to $5,506. *Deadline: February 15.

Washington Higher Education Coordinating Board
PO Box 43430
Olympia, WA 98504-3430
360-753-7843
wascholars@hecb.wa.gov
http://www.hecb.wa.gov/paying/waaidprgm/wsp.asp
Grant Name: The Washington Scholars program awards

education grants to two high school students from each of Washington's 49 state legislative districts. *Academic Area: Open. *Age Group: Undergraduate students. *Eligibility: Applicants must demonstrate financial need, be Washington residents, and plan to pursue any major (except theology) at a public or independent Washington college or university. They must attend school full time. *Application Process: High school principals nominate the top 1 percent of their graduating class based on academic achievement, leadership, and community service. A committee of high school principals and college admissions staff chooses the winners. *Amount: $2,445 to $5,506. *Deadline: May 15.

WEST VIRGINIA

West Virginia Higher Education Policy Commission
1018 Kanawha Boulevard, East, Suite 700
Charleston, WV 25301
877-WVPROMISE
promise@hepc.wvnet.edu
http://www.promisescholarships.org/promise/home.aspx
Scholarship Name: PROMISE (Providing Real Opportunities for Maximizing In-State Student Excellence) Scholarship. *Academic Area: Open. *Age Group: Undergraduate students. *Eligibility: Applicants must be high school seniors who plan to pursue academic study at a West Virginia college or university. They must have been legal residents of West Virginia for at least one year prior to applying. Applicants must have a minimum GPA of 3.0, and an ACT score of at least 20 or an SAT score of at least 1000. *Application Process: Students should complete the Free Application for Federal Student Aid and the Promise Scholarship application, which is available online at http://www.wvapply.com. A printable scholarship application is available at http://www.wvapply.com/commonapp.pdf. *Amount: Full tuition and mandatory fees at public colleges or the average equivalent dollar amount at a private college ($3,326 in 2005-06). *Deadline: March 1.

West Virginia Higher Education Policy Commission
1018 Kanawha Boulevard, East, Suite 700
Charleston, WV 25301
304-558-4614, 888-825-5707

promise@hepc.wvnet.edu

http://www.hepc.wvnet.edu/students/index.html

Grant Name: West Virginia Higher Education Grant. *Academic Area: Open. *Age Group: Undergraduate students. *Eligibility: Applicants must plan to or currently attend a college or university in West Virginia or Pennsylvania, have been legal residents of West Virginia for at least one year prior to applying, demonstrate financial need, and be U.S. citizens. *Application Process: Students should complete the Free Application for Federal Student Aid and the Higher Education Grant application, which is available online at http://www.wvapply.com. A printable scholarship application is available at http://www.wvapply.com/commonapp.pdf. *Amount: $350 to $2,756. *Deadline: March 1.

WISCONSIN

Wisconsin Higher Educational Aids Board

Attn: Nancy Wilkison

PO Box 7885

Madison, WI 53707-7885

608-267-2213

nancy.wilkison@heab.state.wi.us

http://www.heab.state.wi.us/programs.html

Scholarship Name: Academic Excellence Scholarship. *Academic Area: Open. *Age Group: Undergraduate students. *Eligibility: Applicants must be high school seniors who have the highest grade point average in their high school, residents of Wisconsin, enrolled full time in a Wisconsin undergraduate degree program by the fall of the year in which they receive the scholarship, and demonstrate financial need. *Application Process: Students must be nominated by their high school. *Amount: Up to $2,250. *Deadline: February 15.

Wisconsin Higher Educational Aids Board

Attn: John Whitt

PO Box 7885

Madison, WI 53707-7885

608-266-1665

john.whitt@heab.state.wi.us

http://www.heab.state.wi.us/programs.html

Grant Name: Talent Incentive Program Grant. *Academic Area: Open. *Age Group: Undergraduate students. *Eligibility: Applicants must be residents of Wisconsin, have a high school diploma or GED, and be enrolled in an undergraduate degree or certificate program at a nonprofit college or university in Wisconsin. They must be first-time freshman students, attend school at least part time, and demonstrate financial need. *Application Process: Students must complete the Free Application for Federal Student Aid and be nominated by their schools' financial aid offices or counselors of the Wisconsin Educational Opportunity Programs. *Amount: $600 to $1,800. *Deadline: Contact the board for details.

Wisconsin Higher Educational Aids Board

Attn: Sandy Thomas

PO Box 7885

Madison, WI 53707-7885

608-266-0888

sandy.thomas@heab.state.wi.us

http://www.heab.state.wi.us/programs.html

Grant Name: Wisconsin Higher Education Grant. *Academic Area: Open. *Age Group: Undergraduate students. *Eligibility: Applicants must be residents of Wisconsin, have a high school diploma or GED, and be enrolled in an undergraduate degree or certificate program at a nonprofit college or university in Wisconsin. They must attend school at least part time and demonstrate financial need. *Application Process: Students who complete the Free Application for Federal Student Aid are automatically considered for this grant. *Amount: $250 to $2,500. *Deadline: Contact the board for details.

Wisconsin Higher Educational Aids Board

Attn: Mary Lou Kuzdas

PO Box 7885

Madison, WI 53707-7885

608-267-2212

mary.kuzdas@heab.state.wi.us

http://www.heab.state.wi.us/programs.html

Grant Name: Wisconsin Tuition Grant. *Academic Area: Open. *Age Group: Undergraduate students. *Eligibility: Applicants must be residents of Wisconsin, have a high school diploma or GED, be enrolled in an undergraduate degree or certificate program, and attending degree or certificate programs at nonprofit, independent colleges or universities in Wisconsin. They must attend school at least part time and demonstrate financial need. *Application Process: Students who complete the Free Application for Federal Student Aid are automatically considered for this grant. *Amount: At least $250. *Deadline: Contact the board for details.

WYOMING

Wyoming Community College Commission
2020 Carey Avenue, 8th Floor
Cheyenne, WY 82002
307-777-7763
http://communitycolleges.wy.edu/whatsnew/wiin.htm
Loan Name: Wyoming Investment in Nursing Program.
*Academic Area: Nursing (open). *Age Group:
Undergraduate students. *Eligibility: Applicants
must be accepted into a nursing program at one of
the following Wyoming postsecondary institutions:
Casper College, Central Wyoming College, Laramie
County Community College, Northwest College,
Sheridan College, Western Wyoming Community
College, or the University of Wyoming. They must also
demonstrate financial need. Loan recipients must
agree to work as nurses in Wyoming after graduation.
Graduate students and current nurses may also apply
for this program. *Application Process: Students must
complete the Free Application for Federal Student
Aid and a scholarship application (available at the
commission's Web site or at college nursing education
departments and financial aid offices). *Amount:
Varies. *Deadline: Contact the commission for details.

Wyoming Community College Commission
2020 Carey Avenue, 8th Floor
Cheyenne, WY 82002
307-777-7763
http://communitycolleges.wy.edu/whatsnew/tslrp.htm
Loan Name: Wyoming Teacher Shortage Loan
Repayment Program. *Academic Area: Education.
*Age Group: Undergraduate students. *Eligibility:
Applicants must be at least juniors enrolled in the
teacher education program at the University of
Wyoming, which leads to certification in mathematics,
science, or special education. They must also
demonstrate financial need. Loan recipients must
agree to work in a Wyoming public school teaching
mathematics, science, or special education for at
least 50 percent of the time. *Application Process:
Students must complete the Free Application for
Federal Student Aid and an application (available at
the commission's Web site). *Amount: Up to $6,000.
*Deadline: Last Friday in April.

Wyoming Department of Education
Attn: Bruce Hayes
Hathaway Building, 2nd Floor, 2300 Capitol Avenue
Cheyenne, WY 82002-0050
307-777-7690
http://www.k12.wy.us/grants.asp
Scholarship Name: Douvas Memorial Scholarship.
*Academic Area: Open. *Age Group: Undergraduate
students. *Eligibility: Applicants must be first
generation U.S. citizens who plan to attend one of
the following Wyoming postsecondary institutions:
Casper College, Central Wyoming College, Eastern
Wyoming College, Laramie County Community
College, Northwest Wyoming Community College,
Sheridan College, Western Wyoming Community
College, or the University of Wyoming. They must
be residents of Wyoming and high school seniors or
between the ages of 18 and 22. *Application Process:
Students should submit a completed application
(available for download at the department's Web
site) to their school's guidance office. The applicant's
guidance counselor or principal is required to
complete a portion of the application and submit
it to a screening/application committee within the
Wyoming Department of Education. *Amount: $500.
*Deadline: April 18.

BIBLIOGRAPHY/FURTHER READING

Antonoff, Steven R., and Friedmann, Marie A. *College Match: A Blueprint for Choosing the Best School for You,* 8th ed. Alexandria, Va.: Octameron Associates, 2003. This guidebook offers a formulaic approach to figuring out your true interests, finding a college that suits your personality and needs, and even writing the college essay. Worksheets and questionnaires help students determine where their true interests lie and what is really important to them in choosing a school. In addition to the 13 worksheets for getting ideas down on paper, the book offers practical advice on the entire admissions process.

Asher, Donald. *Cool Colleges for the Hyper-Intelligent, Self-Directed, Late Blooming, and Just Plain Different.* Berkeley, Calif.: Ten Speed Press, 2000. Selling itself on its uniqueness, this book caters to those who are seeking an unconventional (non-Ivy League) education. Schools with unique majors and specialties are covered in a chapter (computer game studies, comedy school, AmeriCorps), as are schools with innovative curricula and schedules. You'll even find schools that de-emphasize grades!

Avery, Christopher, Andrew Fairbanks, and Richard Zeckhauser. *The Early Admissions Game: Joining the Elite.* Cambridge, Mass.: Harvard University Press, 2004. This book, written for high school students and their parents, discusses the good and bad aspects of the early admissions "game." The book, which reads more like a novel than a guidebook, covers 14 of the most elite U.S. colleges, outlining the process of early admissions. The book does not advocate that early admissions is fair or even the best option—it, in fact, takes a stance against the corruption in the game.

Berent, Polly. *Getting Ready for College: Everything You Need to Know Before You Go From Bike Locks to Laundry Baskets, Financial Aid to Health Care.* New York: Random House Trade Paperbacks, 2003. This publication is appropriate for precollege teens as they are about to embark on their college experience. Providing truthful, accurate advice on the new experiences they will encounter, the book discusses a range of appropriate topics.

Chatfield, Carlyn Foshee. *Financial Aid 101.* Lawrenceville, N.J.: Petersons, 2003. This publication will walk students and parents through the process of applying for financial aid, including detailed instructions on filling out the required Free Application for Federal Student Aid) FAFSA application. It provides the latest information on federal tax laws and the negotiation process with colleges, as well as sample applications that help simplify the financial aid application process for readers.

College Cost & Financial Aid Handbook 2006, 26th ed. New York: College Board, 2005. Expect to find worksheets, itemized charts, and articles in this guide, which helps readers calculate the cost to attend specific colleges—more than 3,600—in the United States. Answers to almost any question about financial aid will be featured in this comprehensive handbook.

Colleges with a Conscience: 81 Great Schools with Outstanding Community Involvement. New York: The Princeton Review, 2005. Profiling 81 schools across the United States, the publishers of this book highlight schools that include an above-average quantity (and quality) of programs and activities for students who are interested in civic involvement, activism, and community service. Each school listing includes sections on getting involved, campus culture, connecting service with the classroom, impact on community and students, and student financial support for service. Of additional interest are 13 profiles of actual students who are attending some of these schools.

Combs, Patrick. *Major in Success: Make College Easier, Fire Up Your Dreams, and Get a Very Cool Job,* 4th ed. Berkeley, Calif.: Ten Speed Press, 2003. This publication aims to help students decide what their true passion is and then to transform that passion into a lucrative career. Students will receive advice on choosing a major, facing the six big fears, getting an internship, making bold decisions, and landing the ultimate interview, among other chapter highlights.

Cote, Elizabeth. *Conquer the Cost of College: Strategies for Financial Aid (Straight Talk on Paying for College).* New York: Kaplan, 2001. This book teaches students and parents how to make their own plan of action for paying for their college education. Not only does it cover the financial aid process and ensure you get your fair share of aid, but it also discusses the hidden costs of college—the expenses people often forget about.

Chronicle Financial Aid Guide 2005-2006: Scholarships And Loans For High School Students, College Under-

graduates, Graduates, and Adult Learners. Moravia, N.Y.: Chronicle Guidance Publications, 2005. This 466-page directory provides listings of scholarships and loans for anyone planning to attend, or attending, college.

11 Practice Tests for the New SAT & PSAT. New York: The Princeton Review, 2005. This book delivers just what the title says it does—practice tests. Ten SAT tests and one PSAT test are included, along with the answers and explanations. Students who want to know what to expect when taking the new-format SAT will find this book very informative.

Fisk, Edward B., and Robert Logue. *Fiske Guide to Colleges*, 22nd ed. Naperville, Ill.: Sourcebooks, 2005. This comprehensive guide to colleges lists more than 300 schools, providing information on everything from the town or city where the college is located to "scores" on the quality of academics, social life, dollar value, and more. The programs that are most highly regarded at each school are also included.

Fisk, Edward B., and Bruce G. Hammond. *The Fiske Guide to Getting into the Right College*, 3rd ed. Naperville, Ill.: Sourcebooks, 2002. This publication divides its chapters into four major categories: finding the right college, getting in, paying the bill, and reflecting on your options. "The One Hour College Finder" chapter is particularly helpful in providing descriptions of many of America's top schools, including which schools have the strongest programs in select majors. Students are subsequently guided through the application process, the campus tour, and writing the admissions essay.

Franek, Robert, ed. et al. *The Best 361 Colleges: The Smart Student's Guide to Colleges*, 2006 ed. New York: The Princeton Review, 2005. This book is an annual publication that ranks schools based on student surveys. Students will find lists of schools that rank student interest in "studying" as high and those that rank it low. Sample lists include schools with good and bad dorms, dorm food, and quality of social life opportunities in college towns. You'll also find alternative-lifestyle friendly schools, stone-cold sober schools, and schools that like to party.

Freer, Alexandra, and Nancy Redd. *Girls' Guide to the SAT: Tips and Techniques for Closing the Gender Gap.* New York: The Princeton Review, 2003. The fact that girls score lower on the SAT than boys is discussed in this publication, offering insight into the problem, reasons for it, and

advice on how to perform your best. With an emphasis on preparing for the SAT (versus simply believing there is no way to study for a standardized test), this book examines the importance of knowing what to expect and how to use that knowledge to your advantage when taking the SAT.

Gallant, Michael. *Getting the Most From Study Abroad.* New York: Natavi Guides, 2002. This concise guidebook, with contributions from students who have studied abroad, prepares students for the realities of what the experience really provides. From the basics of registering for credit courses to what to bring with you, how to deal with culture shock, and embracing the experience, the book is full of practical advice. A "Helpful Resources" section lists many relevant Web sites to visit.

Get a Jump! The Financial Aid Answer Book, 3rd ed. Lawrenceville, N.J.: Peterson's Guides, 2005. This publication includes chapters on need and non–need-based aid, getting your share of the money, tips from the pros, and questions parents and students should ask when applying for financial aid.

Getzel, Elizabeth Evans, and Paul H. Wehman, eds. *Going to College: Expanding Opportunities for People with Disabilities.* Baltimore, Md.: Brookes Publishing Company, 2005. This resource book provides a valuable look at the extra challenges that students with disabilities face when entering college life. Covering a range of disabilities—from physical to mental to learning—the book offers support and strategic advice for disabled students. Each chapter in this book reads like a research paper, addressing issues of importance to the disabled community as well as those that coordinate disabled services at colleges and universities.

Gibbs, George. *Campus Daze: Easing the Transition from High School to College*, 8th ed. Alexandria, Va.: Octameron Associates, 2003. This book starts at the day you pack your car to go away to college and guides you through the trials and tribulations of freshman year. Covering homesickness (and tips for commuter students), stress, academic life, and social adjustments, the book gives students an accurate glance at what is to come. Advice to freshmen, from those who have just lived through it, is also included in a "Reflections" chapter.

Guernsey, Lisa. *College.edu: On-Line Resources for the Cyber-Savvy Student.* Alexandria, Va.: Octameron Associates, 2005. This publication guides readers through the

Internet world of financial aid and college admissions Web sites. The book's goal is to help students find objective, factual, and useful information about pre-college admissions and financial aid activities.

Guide to College Majors. New York: The Princeton Review, 2005. This publication profiles more than 250 college majors. In addition to a brief description of the major, readers are given lists of sample careers and average salaries, closely related career options to consider, courses to take in high school to prepare for the major, sample college curriculums, and fun facts relating to the field.

Katzman, John, and Adam Robinson. *Cracking the New SAT,* 2006 ed. New York: The Princeton Review, 2005. This book focuses on the techniques that students can use to score better on the SAT, no matter the level of a person's intelligence. This edition is especially important because it addresses the new SAT—now divided into the three sections of math, critical reading, and writing. Included in the book are three complete practice tests, with answers and explanations, as well as a CD-ROM with four additional tests.

Kristof, Kathy. *Taming the Tuition Tiger: Getting the Money to Graduate—With 529 Plans, Scholarships, Financial Aid, and More.* New York: Bloomberg Press, 2003. Whether you're a parent, grandparent, or relative of a newborn or of a child about to enter college, this publication will tell you how to approach saving for his or her education, while maximizing your tax benefits.

Laurenzo, Peter V. *College Financial Aid: How To Get Your Fair Share,* 6th ed. Albany, N.Y.: Hudson Financial Press, 2002. This book explains the process of applying for financial aid in easy-to-understand terminology, defining key words and concepts along the way. The publication serves as a reference for anyone applying for financial aid for the first time, trying to make sense of the various options.

LaVeist, Thomas, Will LaVeist, and Tom Joyner. *Eight Steps to Help Black Families Pay for College: A Crash Course in Financial Aid.* New York: The Princeton Review, 2003. This publication covers everything you need to know about paying for a college education. In addition to loans, scholarships, grants, and other related topics, the book also discusses the role of affirmative action in the college admissions process.

Leider, Anna. *The A's and B's of Academic Scholarships: 100,000 Scholarships for Top Students,* 25th ed. Alexan-

dria, Va.: Octameron Associates, 2005. Students with a B average or better who are seeking merit-based financial aid will find this resource book of approximately 100,000 available scholarships very useful. Most scholarships are tied to individual schools, however, rather than being open for use at any college or university.

Leider, Anna. *Loans and Grants from Uncle Sam: Am I Eligible and for How Much?,* 13th ed. Alexandria, Va.: Octameron Associates, 2005. Defining all of the different kinds of loans that are available, as well as informing readers how to find grants that may seem hard to find, is the focus of this important resource book for college students. When faced with unknowns about individual lenders and repayment options, students spend too much time analyzing their options. This information-packed book tells you everything you need to know to make the best, informed decisions.

Leider, Anna, and Robert Leider. *Don't Miss Out: The Ambitious Student's Guide to Financial Aid,* 30th ed. Alexandria, Va.: Octameron Associates, 2005. With a new edition published yearly, this publication details the latest news and trends in the financial aid world to help students and parents find and receive the most money, fast. Estimate worksheets and companion software are included.

Light, Richard J. *Making the Most of College: Students Speak Their Minds.* Cambridge, Mass.: Harvard University Press, 2004. This handbook for students presents, in essay form, some obvious—yet important—advice. Students learn how to make powerful connections with students and professors, judge which classes will be most effective for them, and seek out diverse environments. The "Suggestions From Students" chapter provides down-to-earth advice from peers on daily college life.

Machado, Julio. *Fishing for a Major.* New York: Natavi Guides, 2002. This guidebook aims to provide practical advice for students who are not yet sure what they want to major in. The importance of accessing your strengths and weaknesses, determining your life goals, talking with other students and department insiders, and knowing when you should change your mind are all discussed frankly and honestly.

Maleson, Sandra, and Janet Spencer. *Visiting College Campuses,* 7th ed. New York: The Princeton Review, 2004. This book is a guide—literally—to making your way to, from, and around 299 most-toured colleges and universities in the United States. Each school listing includes airport transportation logistics, driving directions, and nearby hotel accommodations in addition to a range of advice on whether or not to make an appointment, when to go, length of tour, and more. Basic academic rankings are also included.

McGrath, Anne, ed. *U.S. News & World Report Ultimate College Directory 2005*. Naperville, Ill.: Sourcebooks, 2004. This 1,763-page mammoth of a directory contains facts and figures on more than 1,400 colleges and universities in the United States. Each school's listing contains contact information, student body statistics, admissions facts and figures, academics (majors), campus life and extracurricular activities, services and facilities, and costs and financial aid.

Moore, Donald. *Financial Aid Officers: What They Do— To You and for You,* 11th ed. Alexandria, Va.: Octameron Associates, 2005. The focus of this book is on when and how to approach and ask financial aid officers (FAOs) about your financial aid package to obtain the best results. The book also demystifies whom the FAO is, how he or she determines financial aid awards, and helps parents understand their rights in the negotiation process.

Navigating Your Freshman Year: How to Make the Leap to College Life and Land on Your Feet. New York: Prentice Hall Press, 2005. This practical guidebook covers everything an entering freshman needs to be aware of—even those things most books leave out. Touching on weight gain, dating, drugs, and "avoiding living hell" by being truthful on your roommate questionnaire, this book provides a down-to-earth, realistic picture of college life—written for students, by students.

Nist, Sherrie, and Jodi Patrick Holschuh. *College Rules! How to Study, Survive, and Succeed in College.* Berkeley, Calif.: Ten Speed Press, 2002. This book focuses on the transition from high school to college, noting the differences students will face as they become more independent. With tips on how to manage your time, handle stress, and improve your study habits, the book covers important topics that will play a large role in students' success and happiness in college.

100 Successful College Application Essays, 2nd ed. New York: New American Library, 2002. This publication provides sample college admissions essays as well as admissions counselors' comments about them. The book also includes a section advising students what to, and what not to, write about; but the bulk of the book is sample essays divided by subject. Serving as models for those who need guidance in developing their own essay to get into college, the major essay categories included in the book are about family, death and dying, coming to America, self-portraits, sports and activities, and more.

Orzechowski, Alice. *101 Tips for Maximizing College Financial Aid: Definitive Guide to Completing the 2005-2006 FAFSA*. Frederick, Md.: Financial Education Institute, LLC, 2005. This publication, written by a tax professional, focuses on informing readers about how to make the best tax-based decisions as they save and apply for financial aid. The text provides a detailed explanation of the Free Application for Federal Student Aid (FAFSA) and lets readers know how they can maximize their financial aid award.

Owens, Eric. *America's Best Value Colleges*, 2006 ed. New York: The Princeton Review, 2005. This publication profiles 81 colleges across the United States that offer above-average academics, at a cost that is lower than average. Schools are given an academic rating, financial aid rating, and a tuition GPA (or an average cost after the average scholarship and grant package is subtracted). Detailed information about the school's location, most popular majors, student/faculty ratios, and more is included.

Re, Joseph M. *Financial Aid Financer: Expert Answers to College Financing Questions,* 17th ed. Alexandria, Va.: Octameron Associates, 2005. Students with unique family circumstances will find this resource book helpful in unraveling the financial aid process. The effects of divorce, job loss, and much more on financial aid are discussed at length.

Ripple, G. Gary. *Campus Pursuit: Making the Most of Your Visit and Interview*, 9th ed. Alexandria, Va.: Octameron Associates, 2001. If you haven't gone on a college campus tour or had an admissions interview, you don't know what to expect. This booklet will prepare students for the dreaded interview, advising what to do or say in tough situations. Making sure students ask the right questions during the campus tour and see everything they need to see in order to make an informed decision is also discussed.

———. *Do-It Write: How to Prepare a Great College Application*, 9th ed. Alexandria, Va.: Octameron Associates, 2001. This booklet provides practical advice on one of the most dreaded tasks: writing the college essay. Advising to closely analyze what the admissions officers are looking for, and constructing the essay accordingly, this book helps students break their writer's block and begin writing. Sample essays are included, with comments on why they are or are not effective.

Robinson, Adam, and Jeff Rubenstein. *Cracking the New PSAT/NMSQT,* 2005 ed. New York: The Princeton Review, 2004. This book focuses on the techniques that students can use to score better on the PSAT/NMSQT, no matter the level of a person's intelligence. Included in the book are two complete practice tests, with answers and explanations.

Rye, David E. *Complete Idiot's Guide to Financial Aid for College.* New York: Alpha, 2000. This practical publication outlines the steps to applying for financial aid, finding the best loans, avoiding tax mistakes, and negotiating the best deals. It also tells readers where and how to request additional information on specific topics of interest.

Schlachter, Gail Ann, and David R. Weber. *College Student's Guide to Merit and Other No-Need Funding, 2005-2007.* El Dorado Hills, Calif.: Reference Service Press, 2005. This directory, for students who are currently enrolled in college, references over 1,200 sources of available funding for those who might believe they are not eligible for financial aid. No set income level is required for any of the listings in this book—they are based solely on a student's ability in a subject matter, athletic success, religious or ethnic background, and much more.

———. *Directory of Financial Aids for Women, 2005-2007.* El Dorado Hills, Calif.: Reference Service Press, 2005. This directory lists numerous funding sources for females at all educational levels—high school through postdoctoral. Sections are divided into categories such as athletics, college major, undergraduate study, graduate study, ethnic background, and more.

———. *Financial Aid for African Americans, 2003-2005.* El Dorado Hills, Calif.: Reference Service Press, 2003. This directory of funding sources for African Americans covers grants, loans, scholarships, and more. With more than 1,400 listings specifically available only to African Americans, this book uncovers financial aid resources from both private and public sources.

———. *Financial Aid for Asian Americans, 2003-2005.* El Dorado Hills, Calif.: Reference Service Press, 2003. This directory of funding sources for Asian Americans covers

grants, loans, scholarships, and more. With more than 1,000 listings specifically available only to Asian Americans, this book uncovers financial aid resources from both private and public sources.

———. *Financial Aid for Hispanic Americans, 2003-2005.* El Dorado Hills, Calif.: Reference Service Press, 2003. This directory of funding sources for Hispanic Americans covers grants, loans, scholarships, and more. With more than 1,300 listings specifically available only to Hispanic Americans, this book uncovers financial aid resources from both private and public sources.

———. *Financial Aid for Native Americans, 2003-2005.* El Dorado Hills, Calif.: Reference Service Press, 2003. This directory of funding sources for Native Americans covers grants, loans, scholarships, and more. With more than 1,500 listings specifically available only to Native Americans, this book uncovers financial aid resources from both private and public sources.

———. *Financial Aid for Research and Creative Activities Abroad, 2006-2008.* El Dorado Hills, Calif.: Reference Service Press, 2006. Researching and participating in creative activities abroad does not have to be out of your reach. This resource book shows everyone, from high school students through postdoctoral graduates, more than 1,100 public and private funding sources to make a desire to write, research, or attend conferences abroad a reality. This book does not cover studying for college credit abroad.

———. *Financial Aid for Study and Training Abroad, 2006-2008.* El Dorado Hills, Calif.: Reference Service Press, 2006. This resource book shows Americans where to find 1,000 of the top public and private funding sources to turn the desire to take college courses, intern , or attend training seminars abroad into a reality.

———. *Financial Aid for the Disabled and Their Families, 2004-2006.* El Dorado Hills, Calif.: Reference Service Press, 2004. Claiming to be the only publication dedicated solely to financial aid for disabled Americans, this book highlights almost 1,200 public and private funding sources for high school students through postdoctoral graduates who possess a disability of some kind. Money is available for a variety of purposes—college education, assistive technology, travel, and more.

———. *Financial Aid for Veterans, Military Personnel, & Their Dependents, 2004-2006.* El Dorado Hills, Calif.: Reference Service Press, 2004. Anyone with ties to the military, whether you've served yourself or have a parent or grandparent who has served, can find more than 1,200 listings of public and private funding that can be used to attend college, travel, research, and more.

———. *Funding for Persons with Visual Impairments, 2005.* El Dorado Hills, Calif.: Reference Service Press, 2005. This large-print resource book details about 270 public and private funding sources to help finance higher education for the visually impaired. High school seniors and above can expect to find only the best sources here—no award that entails less than $500 is listed.

———. *High School Senior's Guide to Merit and Other No-Need Funding, 2005-2007.* El Dorado Hills, Calif.: Reference Service Press, 2005. This directory for high school seniors who are planning to attend college references more than 1,100 sources of available funding for those who might believe they are not eligible for financial aid. No set income level is required for any of the listings in this book—they are based solely on a student's ability in a subject matter, athletic success, religious or ethnic background, and much more.

Schlachter, Gail Ann. *How to Find Out About Financial Aid and Funding, 2003-2005.* El Dorado Hills, Calif.: Reference Service Press, 2003. This publication is a directory of mostly free and inexpensive print and electronic resources available to help individuals weed out the good from the bad resources. Contact and ordering information and e-mail and web addresses are included.

Schlachter, Gail Ann, and David R. Weber. *How to Pay for Your Degree in Agriculture & Related Fields, 2004-2006.* El Dorado Hills, Calif.: Reference Service Press, 2004. College students pursuing two-year degrees through doctoral students in all agricultural fields will find out how to access and apply for more than 500 sources of public and private funding in this directory. With a minimum standard of at least $500 to qualify for a listing, the authors of this book make sure that students don't waste their time, but rather gain access to top awards only.

———. *How to Pay for Your Degree in Business and Related Fields, 2004-2006.* El Dorado Hills, Calif.: Reference Service Press, 2004. College students pursuing two-year degrees through doctoral students in all business fields will find out how to access and apply for more than 675 sources of public and private funding in this directory. With a minimum standard of at least $500 to qualify for a listing, the authors of this book make sure that students don't waste their time, but rather gain access to top awards only.

———. *How to Pay for Your Degree in Education and Related Fields, 2004-2006.* El Dorado Hills, Calif.: Reference Service Press, 2004. College students pursuing undergraduate and graduate degrees in education will find out how to access and apply for more than 600 sources of public and private funding in this directory. With a minimum standard of at least $500 to qualify for a listing, the authors of this book make sure that students don't waste their time, but rather gain access to top awards only.

———. *How to Pay for Your Degree in Engineering, 2004-2006.* El Dorado Hills, Calif.: Reference Service Press, 2004. College students pursuing undergraduate and graduate degrees in engineering will find out how to access and apply for more 800 sources of public and private funding in this directory. With a minimum standard of at least $1,000 to qualify for a listing, the authors of this book make sure that students don't waste their time, but rather gain access to top awards only.

———. *How to Pay for Your Degree in Journalism and Related Fields, 2004-2006.* El Dorado Hills, Calif.: Reference Service Press, 2004. College students pursuing two-year degrees through doctoral students in all journalism and communication fields will find out how to access and apply for more than 600 sources of public and private funding in this directory. With a minimum standard of at least $500 to qualify for a listing, the authors of this book make sure that students don't waste their time, but rather gain access to top awards only.

———. *How to Pay for Your Law Degree, 2004-2006.* El Dorado Hills, Calif.: Reference Service Press, 2004. Law students can learn how to access and apply for more than 550 sources of public and private funding for law school in this directory. Students will find funding for individual legal specialties to those requiring specific residency in a state to competitions and loan forgiveness programs.

———. *Kaplan Scholarships.* El Dorado Hills, Calif.: Reference Service Press, 2006. Anyone pursuing or considering pursuing a college degree will find this comprehensive directory of more than 3,000 sources of public and private scholarship aid a must-have resource. With a minimum standard of at least $1,000 to qualify for a listing, the authors of this book make sure that students don't waste their time, but rather gain access to top awards only. No loans are listed—only free money!

———. *Money for Christian College Students, 2005-2007.* El Dorado Hills, Calif.: Reference Service Press, 2004. Christian college students pursuing two-year degrees through doctoral students in any discipline, at any type of school, will find out how to access and apply for more than 800 sources of funding, specifically for Christians, in this directory. The directory is organized in such a way that funding that requires a specific field of study, religious affiliation, residency requirement, etc. is easy to locate and apply for.

———. *Money for Graduate Students in the Arts and Humanities, 2005-2007.* El Dorado Hills, Calif.: Reference Service Press, 2005. This comprehensive directory of more than 1,000 sources of public and private scholarship aid for graduate students pursuing degrees in any area of the arts and humanities details sources of "free" aid only—no loans are included. Scholarships of interest are easy to locate as they are organized by field of study, state of required residency, deadlines, and more.

———. *Money for Graduate Students in the Biological and Health Sciences, 2005-2007.* El Dorado Hills, Calif.: Reference Service Press, 2005. Graduate students pursuing advanced degrees in biological and health sciences will find out how to access and apply for public and private scholarship funding in this directory. With a minimum standard of at least $1,000 to qualify for a listing, the authors of this book make sure that students don't waste their time, but rather gain access to top awards only. No loans are included, and none of the listings in this book are tied to a single school where the money must be used.

———. *Money for Graduate Students in the Physical and Earth Sciences, 2005-2007.* El Dorado Hills, Calif.: Reference Service Press, 2005. Graduate students pursuing advanced degrees in physical and earth sciences will find

out how to access and apply for nearly 900 public and private scholarship opportunities in this directory. The authors of this book make sure that students don't waste their time, but rather gain access to top awards only—awards that don't require repayment. No loans are included.

———. *Money for Graduate Students in the Social and Behavioral Sciences, 2005-2007.* El Dorado Hills, Calif.: Reference Service Press, 2005. Graduate students pursuing advanced degrees in the social and behavioral sciences will find out how to access and apply for nearly 1,100 public and private scholarship opportunities in this directory. The authors of this book make sure that students don't waste their time, but rather gain access to top awards only—awards that don't require repayment. No loans are included.

Speck, David G. *College Savings Rx: Investment Prescriptions for a Healthy College Fund,* 3rd ed. Alexandria, Va.: Octameron Associates, 2002. This book, written by a well-respected financial adviser, helps parents decipher their investment options for a child's college education. Detailing varying levels of risk and including many worksheets and graphs, this book explores all avenues in college savings investing today.

Thacker, Lloyd. *College Unranked: Ending the College Admissions Frenzy.* Cambridge, Mass.: Harvard University Press, 2005. This series of essays by administrators at many of the nation's top colleges and universities does not attempt to advise students on the topics you might imagine (i.e., early college admissions or writing a great admissions essay). Instead, it encourages students and parents to avoid the trap of commercialism—the "frenzy" that college admissions has become, and to relax, avoid the hype, and really put your energy into finding the best educational institution to meet your needs .

Yank, Michael. *Find Your Passion in College.* New York: Natavi Guides, 2003. This publication focuses on encouraging students to spend their college years exploring their passions. Students are encouraged by other students to not settle into what they think they are supposed to do, but instead to get out there and meet new people, try new things, and become involved in everything that interests them.

FINANCIAL AID NEWSLETTERS AND MAGAZINES

The Black Collegian. Published monthly by IMDiversity, Inc. (Subscriptions Department, 140 Carondelet Street, New Orleans, LA 70130, 832-615-8871, http://www.black-collegian.com), this hardcopy and online magazine serves the professional and collegiate African-American community, providing searchable job banks and links to graduate schools and other advanced education sites. General African-American–related issues, global studies, and arts and entertainment topics are also covered.

CollegeBound Teen Magazine. This bimonthly magazine, published by The CollegeBound Network (1200 South Avenue, Suite 202, Staten Island, NY 10314, 718-761-4800, information@collegebound.net, http://www.collegebound.net), has a glossy teen magazine look, but it's full of meaty articles on topics like financial aid, college majors, and college life (i.e., dealing with stress, juggling priorities, dorm life, and more).

College News. Published monthly by DTC Publishing Inc. (2210 Midwest Road, Suite 104, Oak Brook, IL 60523, 630-571-5330, Doug@dtcpublishing.com, http://www.collegenews.com), this print and online publication offers insightful features on topics of relevance to college students, classified job ads, a complete database of campus newspapers from across the country, spring break advertisements and information, and much more.

College Parent Magazine. This publication (PO Box 888, Liberty Corner, NJ 07938, info@collegeparenting.com, http://www.collegeparenting.com/pn) "for the adults who pay the bills to send their child to a college or university," covers issues of importance to parents, such as financial aid, academics, admissions, news, and more. Subscriptions are available free of charge by filling out an online form.

College Spotlight. This bimonthly newsletter published by College & Career Press (PO Box 300484, Chicago, IL 60630, 773-248-6590, amorkes@chicagopa.com, http://www.collegeandcareerpress.com/pages/2/index.htm) is targeted towards high school guidance professionals and students who are preparing for college. Each issue contains feature stories as well as information on free and low-cost guidance materials, diversity issues, interesting college programs and classes, book reviews, and financial aid.

Community College Week. Published biweekly (PO Box 1305, Fairfax, VA 22038, 703-978-3535, http://www.ccweek.com), this independent publication is targeted towards administrators and faculty at the nation's two-year colleges. In-depth articles feature analysis of trends in two-year education and keep professionals on top of current news and issues of importance. A job database is also included. Sample issues are available online or by mail.

Kiplinger's. This monthly financial magazine, which is published by Kiplinger Washington Editors Inc. (1729 H Street, NW, Washington, DC 20006, 800-544-0155, http://www.kiplinger.com/personalfinance/magazine), is an excellent resource for parents who are seeking investment advice on planning for their child's college education. Articles cover topics such as financial aid in divorced and blended families, 529 plans, financial aid solutions for large households, and more.

Money. This online magazine, published by CNN (1 Chase Manhattan Plaza, New York, NY 10005, 800-633-9970, cnnmoney@money.com, http://money.cnn.com/magazines/moneymag/), offers the latest in personal investment commentary. Parents will find the college section, with articles on investing and financial aid, particularly informative. Additional features cover such topics such as lucrative college majors and maximizing your financial aid. Calculators for savings and college costs are also useful.

The Rising Star. This quarterly newsletter of the Hispanic Scholarship Fund (55 Second Street, Suite 1500, San Francisco, CA 94105, 877-473-4636, info@hsf.net, http://www.hsf.net) features articles on all areas of higher education for Hispanics. Financial aid and scholarship opportunities are highlighted.

SmartMoney. This monthly financial magazine, published by Dow Jones & Company Inc. and Hearst SM Partnership, contains a personal finance section with articles on college planning. Topics covered include investing for college, choosing a 529 plan, comparing financial aid offers, and more. Available by subscription (Customer Service Department, PO Box 7538, Red Oak, IA 51591, 800-444-4204, http://www.smartmoney.com/college). Articles can be viewed online for free, and you may also register for a free e-newsletter.

Steps to College. This bimonthly online newsletter of the National Association for College Admission Counseling (1631 Prince Street, Alexandria, VA 22314-2818, 703-836-2222, bulletin@nacac.com, http://www.nacac.com/p&s_steps.html) contains articles of relevance to students who are transitioning from high school to college. Admissions, financial aid, and scholarships are covered in depth.

Student Leader. This quarterly magazine of the American Student Government Association (412 NW 16th Avenue, Gainesville, FL 32601-4203, 352-373-6907, info@studentleader.com, http://www.asgaonline.com/ME2/Audiences/dirsect.asp?sid=7F31AE8077DB44A5A60AF114B68E9153&nm=Home&AudID=B7353D3A67F945B58C57DBC83B9C459E) primarily addresses students and student affairs professionals who are involved in student leadership activities. Areas covered include leadership techniques, elections and voting, issues and advocacy, and campus and community service.

U.S. News & World Report. This weekly magazine (Subscription Department, PO Box 420234, Palm Coast, FL, 32142-0234, 800-436-6520, http://www.usnews.comusnews/home.htm) provides coverage of national and international news, including issues related to education. A "Best College" issue is published annually, and subscribers will also find rankings and guides covering a myriad of other topics and their related products (i.e., money and business, health, science and technology, etc).

Young Money Magazine. Published bimonthly by InCharge® Institute of America Inc. (2101 Park Center Drive, Suite 300, Orlando, FL 32835, 888-436-8714, http://www.youngmoney.com), this magazine, written primarily by journalism students, targets a student audience that is interested in reading and learning about money management, entrepreneurship, investing, and more.

FINANCIAL AID WEB SITES

Academics: You Can Do It!

http://www.nasfaa.org/subhomes/doitaffordit/
    afforditcover.html

This Web site for high school students and their parents addresses the initial questions that arise about financial aid. Students will learn about what financial aid really is, what kinds of financial aid are available, how financial aid is calculated, and how to begin the application process. Everything from the basics about need and non-need based financial aid to more in-depth definitions of federal aid programs are covered.

BabyMint

http://www.babymint.com

Parents can begin saving for their child's college education through this credit card rebate program. Credit card users accrue rebate amounts when they make purchases from member merchants. College students can also apply and have rebates transferred into the account of their choice. Applicants apply online for a credit card and are able to choose where they would like their 1-percent rebate applied—a savings plan or even a student loan account.

Cash For College

http://www.nasfaa.org/annualpubs/cashforcollege.pdf

This downloadable, 12-page publication from the National Association of Student Financial Aid Administrators covers the basics of financial aid for students or family just beginning their research. Defining financial aid, and differentiating between need-based aid and merit-based aid, is the focus of the publication. Federal aid and the Free Application for Federal Student Aid is covered, as is the pursuit of merit-based aid. The topic of financial aid consultants, which some families choose to hire, is also covered.

College Answer: The Planning for College Destination

http://www.collegeanswer.com/paying/scholarship_
    search/pay_scholarship_search.jsp

Voted "the best scholarship search engine" on the Internet by Forbes.com, this free college scholarship search engine allows registered users to submit an in-depth, detailed profile of themselves and receive scholarship and grant matches. Each time registered users log on, new scholarships that have been added to the database will appear in their matches. Students can also find information about loans, savings plans, and financial aid tax benefits by clicking on appropriate links.

CollegeBoard.com

http://apps.collegeboard.com/cbsearch_ss/welcome.jsp

This testing service (PSAT, SAT, etc.) offers a scholarship search engine that features scholarships worth nearly $3 billion. You can search by specific major and a variety of other criteria.

CollegeNET

http://mach25.collegenet.com/cgi-bin/M25/index

CollegeNET features 650,000 scholarships worth more than $1.6 billion. You can search by keyword or by creating a personality profile of your interests.

College Savings Plans Network

http://www.collegesavings.org

Parents interested in learning more about Section 529 state college savings plans will find this Web site a helpful resource. The Web site lets users choose their state from a drop-down list and gives state-specific savings plan options. It also explains the difference between a prepaid tuition plan and a savings/investment plan. Families that cannot (or do not want to) rely on federal financial aid would benefit from visiting this Web site.

e-Scholar

http://www.studentjobs.gov/e-scholar.asp

The United States Office of Personnel Management maintains this Web site, which features opportunities for students to earn money or experience from federal government agencies or organizations. Separate links are devoted to apprenticeships, cooperatives, fellowships, grants, internships, and scholarships. High school students through graduate students will find opportunities of relevance on this Web site.

FastWeb

http://www.fastweb.com

Providing individualized, custom scholarship searches for local, national, and college-specific scholarships, this search engine, run by the popular job-search Web site Monster.com, helps students locate and apply for scholarships that they might otherwise not have known about. The "Resources" section also provides links to information about federal financial aid and loans as well as tips and advice on writing scholarship essays. High school students and college freshmen will also find blogs tailored to them in this section.

Federal Student Aid

http://studentaid.ed.gov/PORTALSWebApp/students/english/index.jsp

Operated by the U.S. Department of Education, this Web site outlines everything students, parents, and guidance counselors need to know about federal student aid, including information about grants, loans, and work-study programs. Since applying for federal aid is something most students should do, this Web site is a must-visit for anyone who wants and needs to acquaint themselves with the process and terminology. Also of interest to students, parents, and counselors, the Publications section offers a variety of brochures and fact-sheets, which are downloadable free of charge.

Federal Trade Commission's Consumer Information About Scholarships, Employment, and Job Placement

http://www.ftc.gov/bcp/menu-jobs.htm

This Web site offers links to information on several scholarship and grant scams of which parents and students should be aware. With a focus on making the consumer aware of fraudulent scholarship Web sites and companies, the Federal Trade Commission helps individuals decipher between "real" financial aid and bogus schemes that seldom pay off. Every parent and student should read these articles before beginning their financial aid search.

Financial Aid.com

http://www.financialaid.com

Part of the CIT Group Inc., this lending company claims to offer "the best customer service in the business." Students and parents who are considering student loans will find information on PLUS Loans and Stafford Loans as well as links to apply online. Links for students include http://www.campusdirt.com, which provide comparisons of colleges and universities, and http://www.campusclix.com, which offers networking opportunities with students from various colleges. The Web site also offers a searchable database of 150,000 scholarship awards, accessible by registering with your e-mail address.

Free Application for Federal Student Aid

http://www.fafsa.ed.gov

Students attending postsecondary education of any kind should acquaint themselves with this very important Web site. Even if students do not believe that they will qualify for grants, and do not need student loans, an application for federal student aid is a requirement for many scholarship applications. Filling out an application in no way obligates anyone to accept any funds; students have nothing to lose. The FAQ section is a must-read for parents and students beginning the financial aid process.

FreSch!

http://www.freschinfo.com

This Web site provides a scholarship database compiled from published information from more than 5,000 foundations and organizations. By providing information about your GPA, activities, interests, state of residence, memberships, and more, students can access scholarships specific to their specifications and qualifications. A link to a student loan comparison Web site is also available as are articles on a variety of topics, from avoiding scholarship scams to advice on writing the college scholarship essay.

GoCollege

http://www.gocollege.com

This Web site, which claims to have the largest scholarship database in the country, provides parents and students with valuable scholarship searches and detailed student loan facts and figures. Parents will find a section dedicated solely to them, with information about the average cost per year of a college education and ideas on how to finance that education. The Government section explains the options of federal, state, and trio programs, with links and contact information for each kind of aid.

GrantsNet

http://sciencecareers.sciencemag.org/funding?CFID=231446&CFTOKEN=90282513

With a searchable database of grants, scholarships, and fellowships in a variety of science-specific fields, this Web site is a must-visit for students who need financial aid and are majoring in a field of science. Students should have a specific chosen major, as the listings here tend to be focused rather than general. *Funding News* is a monthly newsletter for science majors; however, most of the articles target an older audience of graduate students at the master's and doctoral levels.

GuaranteedScholarships.com

http://www.guaranteed-scholarships.com

This Web site offers lists (by college) of scholarships, grants, and financial aid that "require no interview, essay, portfolio, audition, competition, or other secondary requirement."

Hispanic College Fund
http://www.hispanicfund.org
This Web site provides a scholarship database of scholarships available to Hispanic youth who can demonstrate financial need or academic achievement. A Resources page, with further information about planning for college, financial aid, scholarships, internships, and professional development, is underway (but not yet up and running) as of the printing of this publication.

Hispanic Scholarship Fund
http://www.hsf.net
This not-for-profit organization has provided nearly $170 million to Latinos over the first 30 years of its existence, and continues to offer scholarships to Latinos pursuing higher education. High school seniors through graduate students will find scholarships of interest at this Web site. The Resources page offers many downloadable publications and links to workshops and seminars pertaining to college for Latino youth and their parents. The quarterly, online newsletter, *The Rising Star*, covers additional topics of interest to Latinos seeking higher education.

HowStuffWorks—How College Financial Aid Works
http://money.howstuffworks.com/college-financial-aid.htm
This resource page for high school students and their parents answers the basic questions about financial aid—what is it and how does one get it? Covering need-based financial aid to merit-based scholarships, each description provides generalized, bullet-pointed facts and figures that everyone beginning the financial aid search process should be familiar with. The site answers questions about how financial aid is calculated, what people should do once they determine that they qualify, and when to consider taking out loans.

Illinois Career Resource Network
http://www.ilworkinfo.com/icrn.htm
Created by the Illinois Department of Employment Security, this site offers a useful scholarship search engine, as well as detailed information on careers. You can search for scholarships based on major and keyword. Available to everyone, not just Illinois residents, you can get a password by simply visiting

the site. The Illinois Career Information System is just one example of sites created by state departments of employment security (or departments of labor) to assist students with financial- and career-related issues. After checking out this site, visit the Web site of your state's department of labor to see what it offers.

International Education Financial Aid
http://www.iefa.org
Students who hope to study abroad will find a searchable database of study-abroad scholarships on this Web site as well as databases of study-abroad loans and grants. More specific links provide information on the financial aspects of studying abroad in specific countries such as England or Australia. Additional articles cover topics on budgeting tips, where to look for aid, and employment restrictions. Students will find message boards and blogs helpful in connecting them with other students, who may also be able to offer personal advice on financing a study-abroad experience.

InternationalScholarships.com
http://www.internationalscholarships.com
This Web site for students seeking financial aid in studying abroad provides a database of scholarships, grants, and loans. The database is divided into categories, which let the researcher know what majors or fields are eligible and if the scholarship is restricted to U.S. applicants or worldwide applicants. Students can also register to receive a free monthly e-newsletter that contains up-to-date information on the latest study-abroad scholarships and opportunities available.

International Student Loan Program
http://www.internationalstudentloan.com
Undergraduate and graduate students in the United States and Canada can apply for study-abroad loans through this Web site. The loans are funded by PNC Bank and guaranteed by The Education Resources Institute Inc., a nonprofit guarantee agency. Students can apply online or over the phone, though most loans will require a co-signer (parent, guardian, or other).

Nellie Mae
http://www.nelliemae.com
This lender provides sections on managing your money, budget and repayment calculators, and a library of articles about getting ready for the college experience. Ultimately, the company wants site visitors to finance

their student loans through their organization, a subsidiary of Sallie Mae, a well-known college lender. The "Loan Center" provides in-depth information on loans available to undergraduate students, graduate students, and parents. Applicants can apply online, request additional information, or call to speak to a representative.

ParentPLUSLoan
http://www.parentplusloan.com
Many financial aid Web sites mention the PLUS loan, but none devote as much time and space to explaining it as this dedicated Web site. Parents will find the Financial Aid 101 section helpful in acquainting themselves with financial aid terminology and the PLUS Loan Info section full of details on interest rates, credit history requirements, and borrower benefits. Parents with a good credit rating can apply for the loan, which is not need based, and they can apply online or print the application from the Web site.

Peterson's Planner
http://www.petersons.com
Students and parents will find individual sections devoted to them on this Web site that serves as a planner in getting ready for college. Exploring Financial Aid is one of four sections (other sections include: Getting Started, Finding a School, and Preparing for Tests). The financial aid section covers all aspects of financial aid: scholarships, federal and state aid, college-based awards, and student loans. The most up-to-date information on the Higher Education Reconciliation Act of 2005 can be found at this Web site, as can updates on all important financial aid news. Students can register to search the database for available scholarships or be directed to the Sallie Mae Web site to apply for student loans.

SavingforCollege.com
http://www.savingforcollege.com
Teaching individuals everything they need to know about 529 savings plans is the primary objective of this independent Web site, which provides overviews and news relating to saving for college, but does not try to sell a product—other than extended use of its compiled material. For a monthly fee, users can gain access to detailed information (though this fee-based service is primarily geared for tax professionals). Parents, however, can compare 529 plans, 529 plan ratings, find a 529 professional in a directory, read the latest 529 news, and more—for free.

Scholarship America
http://www.scholarshipamerica.org
This nonprofit organization works through its local Dollars for Scholars chapters throughout the United States. In 2003, it awarded more than $29 million in scholarships to students. Visit Scholarship America's Web site for more information.

Scholarship Experts
http://www.scholarshipexperts.com
High school and college students can tailor their search for scholarships through this Web site. Once a fee-based service, this company has recently changed its structure and now offers its services free of charge. Students must register and complete an e-profile in order to obtain scholarship listings. The site also provides links to the Kaplan test prep center, financial aid links, and expert advice (tips on anything from student banking to summer jobs).

ScholarshipHelp.org
http://www.scholarshiphelp.org
This Web site provides an easy-to-navigate introduction to applying for college scholarships. With pages on college cost facts, college loans, types of scholarships, judging the scholarship application, and more, students will become acquainted with what to expect when starting the college application process. The scholarship opportunities link does not offer a unique search engine, but an overview—with links—of what it considers good search engines to try. Information on the college essay, letters of recommendation, and a complete list of four-year colleges by state can also be found at this site.

Scholarships.com
http://www.scholarships.com
Scholarships.com offers a free college scholarship search engine (although you must register to use it) and financial aid information.

SmartMoney.com: College Preparation
http://www.smartmoney.com/college
This personal finance and investment publication provides informative articles on financing a college education. Savings worksheets help calculate how much money parents need to save for future education, how much financial aid a family can expect, and more. Students will also find a link to a scholarship research center that takes them to htttp://www.collegejournal.com, a division of The

Wall Street Journal. Articles on demystifying the 529 savings plan prevail.

SRN Express
http://www.srnexpress.com
The Scholarship Research Network Web site offers a free, customized search for scholarship aid. Students can register and begin searching immediately. The Web site also sells a publication, The Care Book: College Aid Resources for Education.

Stafford Loan Resource Center
http://www.staffordloan.com
Run by the privately managed Student Loan Network, this Web site defines and explains the different types of federal Stafford Loans (subsidized and unsubsidized) and how to get them. Students and parents will benefit from the glossary of terms and online Powerpoint financial aid presentations. Students can apply online or download paper applications.

Studentawards.com
http://www.studentawards.com/english/us/default.asp
Offering scholarships from private sector business and not-for-profit organizations, this Web site allows students to register and search for scholarships it claims are not available anywhere else. Students create a personalized profile, which then links them to scholarship matches. A very organized Web site, you won't get lost in any clutter here. In addition to the scholarship search, an online forum section, with message boards on all matters relating to college, can be accessed for free.

Upromise
http://www.upromise.com
This rebate incentive program allows parents, students, family, and friends to register their credit cards online in a student's name. With every purchase made at participating retailers, a small percentage is placed in the student's college savings account or applied to student loan payments. Membership is free, and friends and families can visit the Web site at any time to add their credit cards to a student's account.

Wachovia
http://www.wachovia.com/personal/page/0,,325_496,00.html
This financial services company offers educational loans to college students. The Web site is targeted to students, parents, and financial aid professionals, with the "Just for You" section allocating appropriate content for each target segment. Students can register to receive the free College Bound e-newsletter, while college financial aid professionals can register for EdLines newsletter, which covers industry news. Parents will primarily find financial information about their loan options. Several random drawings can also be entered to receive monetary awards.

Wells Fargo Student Financial Services: Planning Your Education
https://www.wellsfargo.com/student/index.jhtml
This well-known bank is also one of the leading student loan lenders. The bank's Web site provides parents, students, and financial aid counselors with everything they need to know about financial aid (and why they should choose Wells Fargo as their lender). Students will find links to scholarship searches and an opportunity to receive free e-postcards containing college preparation tips by entering the company's CollegeSTEPS Program Sweepstakes, where they'll also be registered to win a $1,000 tuition prize. Parents and students alike will also benefit from visiting the section on money and debt management.

INDEXES

LOCATIONS INDEX

LOCATIONS INDEX

MAJORS INDEX

MAJORS INDEX

ORGANIZATIONS INDEX

ORGANIZATIONS INDEX